Social Development

Joan E. Grusec   Hugh Lytton

Social Development

History, Theory, and Research

Springer-Verlag
New York Berlin Heidelberg
London Paris Tokyo

Joan E. Grusec
Department of Psychology
University of Toronto
Toronto, Ontario
Canada M5S 1A1

Hugh Lytton
Department of Educational Psychology
The University of Calgary
Calgary, Alberta
Canada T2N 1N4

Library of Congress Cataloging-in-Publication Data
Grusec, Joan E.
   Social development.
   1. Socialization.   2. Child psychology.
I. Lytton, Hugh.   II. Title.
BF723.S62G78   1988   155.4'18   87-20550

Typeset by Asco Trade Typesetting Ltd., Hong Kong.
Printed and bound by R.R. Donnelley & Sons, Harrisonburg, Virginia.
Printed in the United States of America.

9 8 7 6 5 4 3 2 1

ISBN 0-387-96591-2   Springer-Verlag New York Berlin Heidelberg
ISBN 3-540-96591-2   Springer-Verlag Berlin Heidelberg New York

Preface

For many years students who took courses in social development had no text available for their use. Those of us who instructed them had to rely on assigning journal articles to be read and providing an overview and synthesis of the area in our lectures. In the last few years, the situation has changed markedly. There are now several very good textbooks that fill the void, reflecting an increasing interest in this area of research and theory. Here is one more.

There are many ways to tell a story. Our book, we think, tells it differently enough to have made it worth the writing. As we began to talk, some time ago, about undertaking this project, we found we had a mutual interest in trying to present the study of social development from a historical point of view. The field has changed dramatically from its inception, and we have both been in it long enough to have witnessed first-hand a number of these changes. Modifications of theoretical orientations and the development of increasingly sophisticated and rigorous methodology have brought with them the stimulation of controversy and growth, as social developmental psychologists argued about the best ways of going about their business. Certainly the same things have happened in other areas of psychology, but the arguments seem to have been particularly vigorous in our own domain. A well-educated student should understand the intellectual history of the field, and should also be sensitized to why psychologists have asked the questions they have and have attempted to answer them in the particular ways they have. That is one of the reasons we wanted to write the book.

Another reason was to show honestly the controversial nature of our domain. We wanted to present the debates between competing theories and the evidence that each can summon up, as befits a text intended for advanced undergraduate and graduate students. So as not to confuse the reader totally, we have attempted to resolve some of these differences or, at least, to discuss what conclusions existing research actually enables us to draw. The aim toward which we have striven throughout has been to be both scholarly and readable.

Another feature characterizing the book is its emphasis on the biological foundation of behavior and its interaction with social forces in the development of the child.

The two of us come to the task with very different orientations. One of us (J.E.G.) was an undergraduate at the University of Toronto and a graduate student at Stanford University during the early 1960s, the heyday of social learning theory and the use of the laboratory experiment as a research tool. Undergraduate days were particularly exciting as Richard Walters, one of the pioneers of social learning theory as we know it today, struggled to use the notions of radical behaviorism to bring order to our understanding of social behaviors such as aggression, dependency, and morality. At Stanford, Albert Bandura and Walter Mischel developed and continually refined the approach in a setting equally exciting intellectually for those of us fortunate enough to have been a part of it. Much has changed since then and other influences have been considerable. But the early debt must be acknowledged.

The other of us (H.L.) comes with a background in teaching and clinical work with children. He underwent training in clinical child and school psychology at a psychoanalytic institute (the Tavistock Clinic in London, England), but tried to keep a scientific and rational balance by doing research in the tradition of objective measurement, espoused by Philip E. Vernon at the University of London. The two of us thus span the two disciplines of scientific psychology—the experimental and the correlational—of which Cronbach has written, and we find common ground in stressing the importance of a third approach, namely that of careful observation of children's naturally occurring behavior.

This book deals with social development in children and touches on adolescence. It says nothing about development through the life span, nor about social developmental processes among other species or (except occasionally) in other cultures. This is purely because of the limitations of space. Any treatment, unless encyclopedic, must be limited in its approach.

The book is divided into four parts. Part I deals with historical, theoretical, and methodological issues. It attempts to show how theories have developed in different cultural, economic, and historico-political climates and how this has had an impact on the way questions are formulated and data interpreted, a theme that continues throughout. It also traces the development of methodological approaches from a historical perspective, and tries to capture some of the heated debate which has accompanied these developments. In Part II of the book, we look at the biological roots of social behavior and its social underpinnings, including a discussion of the early foundations of social behavior, socialization processes, and the influence of the peer group. Part III provides an overview of major content areas in the study of social development, dealing with social cognition, self-control and aggression, altruism and morality, and sex differences and sex roles. As well as presenting the research, we have tried to show how interest in a particular area has developed historically, and the influences from outside that have guided this development. Part IV is a brief attempt to show how social development research has addressed itself to pressing social problems and the implications of research findings for planning and policy decisions. We have selected two examples of this—the phenomenon of divorce, which touches the lives of so many children, and the issue of maternal separation, which has particular repercussions for the increasing need for day care in our society as more and more families find both parents, or the custodial parent, in the work force.

We have read and commented on many drafts of each other's chapters. Basically, however, half the chapters (Chapters 1, 2, 7, 8, 9, and 11) are the work of the first author, and the other six chapters the work of the second author.

H.L. was aided in writing his part of the book by being awarded a Killam Resident Fellowship for one term by the University of Calgary, for whose support he is grateful.

Many students, too numerous to name, have read and responded to our chapters. We acknowledge our debt to them for their invaluable aid in helping us to express ideas more clearly, correcting our errors, and raising new issues for us to respond to. We also acknowledge the support of our spouses, Robert Lockhart and Cornelia Lytton, for their reading of and comments on much of the manuscript, their discussion of issues, and their moral and practical support.

Joan E. Grusec
Hugh Lytton

Contents

PART II
The Foundations of Development

Part I   Historical, Theoretical, and Methodological Considerations

1
Historical and Theoretical Foundations

People change. They are altered continuously, not only in temporary and reversible fashion, but in enduring and irreversible ways. They grow larger and smarter and more adept at social interaction. Such alteration is an inevitable fact of life. Because bodies mature and environments are never static, change *must* be one of the salient characteristics of human functioning. In fact, it is stability, not change, that should puzzle us, for stability poses a far greater challenge to understanding.

Maturational and environmental events combine to produce irreversible changes in thought and behavior and these changes are revealed in the course of development. Our purpose in this book is to describe the attempts of psychologists to understand this process of development in the social domain. We will address the problem of how enduring changes in thinking, feeling, and behavior occur in living organisms as a function of their exposure to, and interaction with, the environment, and we will focus our attention on those changes occurring in situations and settings that involve other people. Simply because of the limitations of space we will confine our consideration to changes occurring between birth and adolescence.

Developmental Theories in Historical Context

The scientific study of change necessitates the gathering of facts. But researchers do not gather facts in isolation. Their preconceptions of how development proceeds determine which events they believe important to study; preconceptions that range from simple hypotheses to complex theoretical structures. Once the facts are gathered, they gain meaning only when some kind of order is imposed on them. They are fit into already existing frameworks or, if that is not possible, into modified (but not too modified) frameworks. For this reason, our discussion of social development begins with a consideration of some of the major theories that have guided the collection of data.

It should be noted that theories do not develop independently of the personal beliefs, attitudes, and values of their originators. They have to have some basis in the everyday experiences of the people who devise them. For this reason, they must be viewed in their historical context. Current social, political, and moral values impose their influence on those who wish to understand human development. To some extent the theories reflect current realities and to some extent they reflect what their authors feel reality *ought* to be. As such they are part of a larger cultural and historical system to which they are inextricably linked, and they cannot truly be appreciated outside that system.

The study of theories in historical context would be important even if it served merely to satisfy intellectual curiosity. But it has a more practical importance as well. By stepping back and looking at how and why ideas about the developmental process have been influenced by the prevailing popular beliefs and attitudes at the time they were formulated, we are helped to see how our current conceptions are conditioned by the social climate in which we presently operate. This insight provides scientists with greater flexibility in their approach to the acquisition of knowledge and a better appreciation of the degree to which their perception and ordering of data are influenced by their own value systems.

The Concept of Childhood and Its Nature

It is difficult not to think of the child as an independently existing entity, with characteristics waiting to be discovered by a perceptive scientist. Recently, however, a number of people have argued that the very concept of childhood, as well as of its nature, is to a degree an invention imposed by society for a variety of social and economic reasons. One of the first to take this position was Philip Aries (1962). In his book, *Centuries of Childhood*, Aries maintained that the elaborate ideas we now have about the nature of childhood did not emerge until just after the Middle Ages and, for the lower classes, appeared even later than that. Thus, once children were thought to be able to function without mothers or nannies—about the age of 7 years—they moved immediately into the adult world of work and play.

This lack of awareness of childhood as a special stage is reflected in a number of ways. Kett (1971) notes that biographers writing before 1800 simply ignored the childhood of their subjects, or noted only remarkable events such as narrow escapes from death or the experience of unusually good fortune. The idea that unexceptional childhood events might be of interest in elucidating adult life did not appear until the 19th century.

Aries demonstrates how attitudes about childhood are reflected in the productions of artists. A miniaturist depicts the gospel scene in which Christ bids little children to come unto Him by grouping 8 small men around Jesus. The child Ishmael, in a Psalter dating from the late 12th or early 13th century, is shown with the abdominal and pectoral muscles of a grown man. In another painting, Isaac sits between his two wives and is surrounded by 15 little men, their children.

According to Aries, it was a revival of interest in education, dating from the 16th and 17th centuries, that finally led to the separation of child and adult worlds. Reformers and moralists propagated the notion that children were innocent and corruptible and must be quarantined from society and trained before they could join the world of adults. The traditional apprenticeship—learning in the real world—was replaced by a special school with strict discipline. The child was removed from adult society and thereby assumed a separate identity.

Kessen (1979) discusses events in the 19th century that led to our current conceptions of the nature of childhood. In "The American Child and Other Cultural Inventions," he argues that how we see children, once we have decided that they are there to be seen, is determined by political, economic, and ideological forces in a way that we frequently fail to appreciate. Take our modern view of childhood as a time of relative innocence and our belief that early experience with a loving mother is crucial for healthy growth. The seeds of these ideas lie in events of the early 1800s. With the advent of the Industrial Revolution, work and home, which had once coexisted, became separate domains. Women now were excluded from the labor force so that home became the place where men did not work. To discourage women from an interest in the working world, it was characterized as ugly, aggressive, sinful, and corrupting, whereas home was seen as chaste, calm, cultured, loving, and the source of godliness and moral training. Children, whose care continued to be assigned to women, took on through association the characteristics of home. They were sentimentalized and viewed as innocent. While the Puritans "viewed childhood as a condition to be worked off with all due speed" and "applauded children who acted like adults" (Kett, 1971), 19th-century thought celebrated juvenile innocence.

The age of adolescence, a period we take for granted, also can be seen as a product of social and historical conditions. Why is there any need for such a state? Again, the roots lie in the 19th-century sentimentalization of the child. If childhood is pure and adulthood evil, then the point of departure from one place to the other is bound to be a traumatic and potentially dangerous one. Therefore the admiration of youth's idealism had to be accompanied by societal concern for the dangers of bad judgment and unresisted temptation, a concern that brought this time of transition into prominence. For girls, passage into the world of work was not a problem because they merely moved from one domestic setting to another. But the onset of sexual maturity did pose a threat to feminine virtue, thereby making postchildhood years a danger for females as well as males (Kett, 1971).

Cultural inventions do have an impact. When young people are treated as qualitatively different from older ones, or when they are seen as innocent rather than depraved, they tend to take on the characteristics attributed to them. Modern theories of development do not deal with fictions but with real events. They are events, however, that are affected very much by the beliefs of the time in which they exist. The child of the 1980s is not the same as the child of the 1880s or 2080s or even the 1940s. It also should be noted, however, that there are characteristics of human development that remain unchanged despite changing cultural conditions. One of the biggest challenges to any developmental theory is to tease out the invariances by trying to discover what is most easily and what is least easily modified by sociocultural events.

From within our present historical perspective there have been three major theories of human development: the psychoanalytic, social learning, and cognitive developmental. In addition, evolutionary approaches have come to play an increasingly major role in formulations of social development. We will describe these four orientations in some detail. Sears (1975) has noted that history has to be rewritten depending on what problems or theories are currently extant. We are writing the history of social developmental psychology in the 1980s. As human genetics and endocrinology come to play a large role in developmental formulations, the history will have a more medical and biological cast.

Theories of Social Development

PSYCHOANALYTIC THEORY

The first important modern theory of human development was proposed by a neurologist, Sigmund Freud. The influence of psychoanalytic theory on current developmental thinking is substantially less than it once was. It has, however, had such a major impact on the course of developmental psychology that any historically oriented discussion would be incomplete without its inclusion.

The developmental aspect of psychoanalytic theory was based on Freud's interpretation of the free associations of adult neurotics during treatment. Thus the data are far removed from our object of interest, that is, the normal child. Freud, however, found that his patients inevitably dwelled on incidents from their early childhood, and he came to believe that these childhood events, whether real or imagined, had played a primary role in the development of their adult personalities. He also believed that the study of his patient's abnormal behaviors could shed light on the understanding of normal behavior. Direct observations of the free play of young children by psychoanalytic theorists such as Melanie Klein, Anna Freud, and Erik Erikson have extended the theory's data base and led to its modification. Although the theory has seen substantial modifications by many other of Freud's successors, it is the work of these individuals that has had the strongest impact on the mainstream of developmental psychology.

Psychoanalytic theorists have speculated about the origins of most of the social behavior we consider in this book. How do babies become attached to their caretakers? How do they learn to trust others? What is the source of aggressive behavior? Why do boys and girls come to behave in "masculine" and "feminine" ways? How do apparently impulsive, self-centered beings learn to behave morally? Current views have moved some distance from those of psychoanalytic thinkers, but the roots of modern beliefs frequently reside in pioneering efforts to understand social and personality development. Knowledge of these roots provides insight into current conceptualizations.

Thoughts and feelings, rather than behavior, are the major focus for psychoanalytic theory. Because a given behavior can be explained by any of several different mechanisms, it is necessary to analyze underlying motives and thoughts in order to understand human functioning. We will begin with the psychoanalytic theory of emotional and motivational development and then turn to its account of cognitive development.

Emotional and Motivational Development

In 1905, Freud first formalized his ideas about emotional and motivational development in *Three Contributions to the Theory of Sex*. According to the theory, the roots of adult personality lie in the first 5 years of life. This is an important contention because it implies that the effects of early experiences are difficult to reverse and that adult functioning has been largely determined in the first few years of existence. If this is correct, personality characteristics should remain stable through the life span. The issues of stability and reversibility of personality are central ones for social developmentalists, and we will refer to them frequently.

Freud maintained that the child passes through stages of psychosexual development; stages which are determined by the fact that different parts of the body provide a source of sexual, or libidinal, gratification at different points in development. In each stage, the child is faced with a problem caused by the conflict between wanting to satisfy bodily desires and needing to comply with the demands of society. When society allows adequate bodily gratification, the conflict can be resolved satisfactorily, but under- or overgratification is reflected in remnants of behavior from that stage in adult life. Thus adult personality or behavior is determined by early experience. It is also suggested that a given individual may have a constitutional tendency to develop personality characteristics associated with a certain stage of development.

Freud felt that the stages of psychosexual development reflected a maturational process but others, such as Erikson (1950), have suggested they result from the way in which children are socialized. Regardless of their source, the behavior of the child's caretaker determines whether each stage has a positive or negative impact on subsequent psychological functioning and interpersonal relationships. Thus the model of functioning or adjustment to the environment that a child develops during any stage becomes the prototype, or model, for later behavior. Presented are some examples of this from the first three stages through which the child is said to pass.

In the oral stage, which extends through the first year of life, unsatisfactory experiences or excessive gratification leads to adult oral characteristics. For example, tenacity and determination may characterize one who was weaned severely and still wishes only to hold on to the bottle or breast, or an insatiable hunger for knowledge and power may characterize one who never had enough to eat. Toilet training leaves its mark on the developing personality during the second year of life—the anal stage. Because bowel movements are so important to parents, the child may be convinced that elimination is a creative act and may reveal this in later creative pursuits such as art or music or, at least, may become charitable and generous. If parents overemphasize the value of feces, the child may feel he has lost something worth keeping and thus become obstinate as an adult. Concern for cleanliness and orderliness also originate in this stage.

During the phallic stage, which commences about the age of 3 years, children become curious about sex. For boys, the mother becomes desirable as a sexual object (she was previously viewed only as a loved object because she was the provider of food and security.) As a result the Oedipus complex emerges and the young child sees himself as a rival with his father for his mother's love. The whole situation is defused, however, by the young boy's fear that he will be castrated by his father. The anxiety produced by this fear is reduced by identifying with, or becoming like, the father or, more correctly, with the boy's conception of what the father is like. Through the process of identification with the aggressor, boys assume their appropriate sex role as well as adopt, or internalize, the moral values of society as they are manifested in the father. Thus the superego is said to arise from the boy's introjection, or internalization, of parental prohibitions, commands, and standards at the time of the resolution of the Oedipal conflict.

The process cannot be so clear-cut for girls. Indeed, the theory is vague at this point. Although girls also are supposed to have sexual feelings for their opposite-sex parent and view their mother as a rival (the Electra complex), they cannot fear castration because they believe they have already lost a penis. The loving attachment to the mother, based on the latter's provision of food and security, is there; the girl continues to want to be like her because of this attachment. But this mechanism for introjection is not so powerful as the mechanism of identification with the aggressor. So the theory tells us that girls will never be as highly developed morally as boys.

This is because their identification, based as it is on love for the mother, is less independent of its emotional origins and therefore more inclined to be guided by feeling than is that of boys who, therefore, have a greater sense of justice and approach decisions in a more impersonal way. For the same reason, girls are supposed to be less strongly sex-typed than boys are. These are hypotheses that will be scrutinized closely in Chapters 9 and 10.

According to Freud's formulation, two more stages follow. During the latency period, which encompasses the elementary school years, sexually oriented activity and, therefore, conflict subsides to a great extent. This is the time when many new skills, values, and roles are learned. The final period of development, the genital stage, is reached during adolescence where the beginnings of socially appropriate heterosexual relationships emerge. Love now takes on an altruistic and tender character rather than an egocentric and exploitative one as in earlier stages of development.

Freud's stages end at this point because of the singular importance he attached to the early years of the life cycle. The impact of his thinking is reflected in the almost exclusive concentration of developmental researchers on childhood events until very recent years.

Erikson, on the other hand, did appreciate that development continues throughout the life cycle. Because he was not tied to biological changes in his conceptualization of the developmental process, he could deal with social changes in later life. Erikson recognized the importance of friendships and intimate relationships in adulthood, discussed the task of parenting and the subsequent feelings that emerge from having or not having an impact on the next generation, and lastly, dealt with the emotions of pleasure or despair that result from a final evaluation of the quality of one's life and that permit either equanimity or depression in the face of impending death.

In addition, Erikson elaborated and modified Freud's views of the psychosexual stages by focusing on specific social conflicts experienced by the child in each stage; conflicts that lead to psychosocial crises. In the first stage, for example, the important event for the child is the learning of trust. Either the world is seen as a benevolent place where people can be relied on for adequate care or it is viewed as an unreliable place. Regardless of whether a sense of trust or mistrust develops, infants are forced to be passive. They cannot have any impact on their environment, so there is no active protest when life goes badly. Thus passive emotions of optimism (trust that all will go well) and pessimism (mistrust) originate in this stage.

In the second stage, the conflict is between autonomy and shame. The young child is becoming independent but is being socialized by his parents for obedience and self-control. Shame and doubt arise in response to parental disapproval for lack of self-control. In the third stage, the child is at a point in life where he is encouraged to take initiative for his actions while respecting the rights of others. In Erikson's analysis attraction to the

TABLE 1.1. A comparison of Erikson's and Freud's stages of social and personality development.

Chronological age	Psychosocial crisis (stage)	Significant persons	Corresponding psychosexual stage
Infancy (0–1 yrs)	Trust vs. mistrust	Mother	Oral
1–3 yrs	Autonomy vs. shame and doubt	Parents	Anal
3–6 yrs	Initiative vs. guilt	Family	Phallic
6–12 yrs	Industry vs. inferiority	Neighborhood, teacher, school	Latency
12–17 yrs (adolescence)	Identity vs. role confusion	Peer groups, out-groups, idealized "heroes"	Adolescence (early genital stage)
Young adulthood	Intimacy vs. isolation	Friends, heterosexual partners	Genital
Adulthood	Generativity vs. stagnation	Spouse, children	Genital
Old age	Ego integrity vs. despair	Self in relation to others	Genital

Note. From "Social Psychology from a Social-Developmental Perspective," by D.R. Shaffer, in C. Hendrick (Ed.), *Perspectives on Social Psychology.* Copyright 1977 by Lawrence Earlbaum Associates. Reprinted by permission.

opposite-sex parent also takes place, but it is seen merely as an attempt to win that parent's affection. Such attraction, however, may produce guilt because it interferes with the rights of the same-sex parent.

During the stage that corresponds to Freud's latency period, children are working to acquire skills and, when they compare themselves with others, may come to feel inferior. Finally, in what corresponds to the genital stage, we see adolescents playing a variety of roles in an attempt to understand who they are. Thus we have the psychosocial crisis of identity versus role confusion. Freud's stages of psychosexual development and Erikson's stages of psychosocial development are outlined in Table 1.1.

Cognitive Development

Changes in the motivational and emotional life of children parallel changes in their cognitive life, that is, in how they think about events in the world surrounding them and thereby come to manage the social problems they encounter. An excellent summary of the psychoanalytic theory of cognitive development is provided by Rapaport (1959). According to the theory, when cognitive processes occur often enough they become habitual and are called structures. Personality is divided into three such structures: id, ego, and superego.

Newborns are impulsive, self-centered, and unable to delay gratification; they are completely governed by primary-process thinking which is archaic, prelogical, and quite unaffected by reality. The only structure contained in their personality is the id, which is controlled by the pleasure principle whose main purpose is to avoid pain or discomfort. Young infants, of course, are doomed to frustration. They do not have all their needs satisfied immediately. Therefore, when they are unsuccessful in achieving drive reduction, they hallucinate the object of their drive, such as the mother's breast. This hallucination results from the memory of times when wishes were actually gratified and is the beginning of conscious experience. It is not successful, obviously, in producing drive reduction.

As infants mature a second structure, the ego, develops out of the id. This second structure operates in a realistic way and can control drives by inhibiting and restraining them until the appropriate occasion for gratification presents itself. The ego is guided by the reality principle and secondary-process thinking, and is thereby capable of logical thinking. The child can now distinguish between mental ideas and real objects, can use thoughts to solve the problems of reducing need states, and can even think about painful events if this is necessary for the achievement of satisfaction. The ego also controls the access of ideas to conscious awareness so that, by preventing an idea from becoming conscious, it prevents instinctual drives from manifesting themselves in overt behavior. Defense mechanisms such as repression and denial are part of the ego and prevent anxiety-provoking ideas from coming into consciousness. Thus repression involves the raising of the threshold of conscious awareness so that a dangerous idea stays in the unconscious, and denial involves perceiving the world as one wishes it were rather than as it really is. The latter is a primitive defense mechanism that serves as long as the ego is not well developed and can allow consciousness to be distorted. These are the ways, then, in which young children are supposed to cope with the frustrations of daily life. We shall discuss approaches to coping with frustration further in Chapter 8.

The third structure of personality is the superego. While both the id and the ego exist to serve the needs of the individual, the superego represents the demands of society. For the social order to be maintained, individuals must give up some gratification. Thus the rules of society become part of, or are incorporated into, the personality through the superego. The ego, then, is responsible for finding ways to satisfy id impulses within the constraints of the superego (which often can be irrational in its striving for perfection) as well as the restrictions of reality.

Appraisal

Psychoanalytic theory originated in Europe but soon fell on fertile soil in North America. Freud's official introduction to the American scene came in 1909 when he was invited to Clark University by G. Stanley Hall, the founder of developmental psychology in the United States, to assist in celebrations of the 20th anniversary of the university's establishment.

Although Freud's ideas about infantile sexuality met with some resistance in America, he did provide a conception of human behavior much richer and more comprehensive than that of any then extant. He was willing to speculate about *why* people behave as they do. For these reasons, his theory appealed to professionals who were working in child guidance clinics and other applied settings, although his reception in academic settings was mixed (Sears, 1975). During the 1930s many analysts fled from Germany, and their arrival in the United States made psychoanalysis an American specialty. Indeed, the theory struck such a responsive chord that its influence spread beyond psychological circles into literature and everyday thinking.

The impact of psychoanalytic theory on child-rearing advice (and presumably on child-rearing practices) was also marked, to a large extent because of the popular writings of Benjamin Spock. This impact will be described in detail in Chapter 5, but for the present we note that advice moved from an emphasis on strictness and regimentation in feeding and toilet training and abhorrence of any sexual interest (conditions hardly likely to assure satsifactory passage through the psychosexual stages) to one of permissiveness in these areas.

Given enthusiastic reception of the theory, why then has its influence on developmental psychology waned? Part of the problem lies in the difficulty of applying accepted scientific criteria to the assessment of psychoanalytic hypotheses. The theory is rich, detailed, and differentiated in its content. But too much of that content is hard to define operationally and thus submit to scientific evaluation. Predictions are difficult to pin down. For example, given events in childhood can lead to any variety of outcomes; children weaned severely should exhibit oral traits as adults, but if they do not, this can be attributed to the operation of defense mechanisms that block the expression of oral needs from conscious awareness and hence from expression. A compulsive adult who experienced a quite normal toilet training has to be declared compulsive by virtue of a constitutional predisposition. To further complicate matters, proponents of the theory have usually insisted that it can be validated only by the psychoanalytic method and the actual free associations of patients undergoing analysis or, in the case of children, their behavior during play. But these free associations or play behavior are subject to interpretation by the analyst who is trained in the theory, and so the theory cannot be evaluated independently. Many researchers who are not analysts have attempted to test psychoanalytic hypotheses using more traditional methodologies (e.g., Beller, 1955; Blum & Miller, 1952; Thurston & Mussen, 1951) but the usefulness of these tests (whose outcomes have been mixed with regard to support for the theory) has been disputed by those espousing the psychoanalytic orientation.

Aside from specific issues of scientific evaluation, the popularity of an approach rests on how well it works in practice. Does psychoanalytically oriented psychotherapy lead to improvements in psychological functioning for either children or adults? The answer to this question is not a resounding "yes." The extent of its effectiveness has been questioned in recent years and a number of alternative approaches to treatment, which make very different assumptions about the course of human development, have been offered in its stead.

Freud (but not Erikson) largely ignored the role of cultural variables in personality development. This is understandable in that he was part of a European philosophical tradition that was less concerned with how individuals could be altered and improved than it was with describing their functioning at different points in time, with each point evaluated within the framework of its own standards. Such an approach does not draw a sharp contrast between biological and sociocultural events. But North Americans, for reasons that we shall discuss later, find it difficult to believe Freud's thesis that one's destiny lies in one's biology and that psychological functioning is so closely linked to bodily maturation. Feminists are hardly enamored of the notion that the lack of a penis can have such inevitable negative social consequences for women. If a highly developed sense of justice and the ability to consider events in an unemotional way are greatly valued, and if they are so intimately linked to physiology, then women must be relegated forever to an inferior position in the management of society. In his view of women, Freud reflected the prevailing beliefs of 19th-century Europeans.

It is possible to quarrel with other details of psychoanalytic theory. Freud predated the work of the ethologists on critical periods when he argued that organisms are particularly prepared at certain points in their development to benefit from specific experiences. Maternal love and oral gratification are required during the oral stage, for example, and no amount of remedial experience can alleviate the negative effects of early deprivation. The question of how permanent the effects of early experience are continues to plague psychologists, and the issue of whether or not personality development is continuous will, as we have said, reappear throughout our consideration of social development.

Despite these reservations, the tremendous historical importance of psychoanalytic theory must be acknowledged. In his belief that human development is determined by lawful and understandable events, Freud paved the way for a science of developmental psychology, a contribution that cannot be overemphasized. He made it clear that young children are not innocents, but that they have passions and emotions that give crucial importance to the experiences of early childhood. He brought to our attention the important notion that early social relationships lay down a pattern for later ones, even though the form of that pattern might be altered. The existence of unconscious motivation exemplified by mechanisms of defense is a notion that still has general appeal today. In its concern with attachment, aggression, moral development, and sex-role acquisition, psychoanalytic theory determined the content of much of the study of social development and is still the source of some hypotheses about developmental functioning. One cannot underestimate the impact of the theory on literature and on popular conceptions of human functioning.

SOCIAL LEARNING THEORY

Early Developments

Social learning theory is a truly North American invention whose historical roots lie in the ideas of John B. Watson. Watson's thesis was twofold: First, that a science of psychology must eschew mentalistic constructs since only behavior can be studied scientifically; and, second, that the ability to modify behavior through the manipulation of environmental events is virtually unlimited. Hence Watson's famous claim:

> Give me a dozen healthy infants, well-formed and my own special world to bring them up in and I'll guarantee to take any one at random and train him to become any type of specialist I might select—doctor, lawyer, artist, merchant-chief and, yes, even beggar-man and thief—regardless of his talents, penchants, tendencies, abilities, vocation, and race of his ancestors. (1925, p. 104)

The approach was eminently suitable for the place and the time and was wholeheartedly accepted in a society that had been founded on rugged individualism and pragmatic philosophy, a society more concerned with action than with thinking and reflection (Buss, 1975).

Watson was interested in the process of social development, proposing a conditioning theory of emotional development based on the three unconditioned reflexes of fear, rage, and love (Watson, 1913). He was in large part responsible for some of the stringent child-rearing practices advised before the advent of Freudian permissiveness. Specifically, he recommended that children not be allowed to dominate their parents and that all caretaking activities be carried out on a schedule determined by the parent. Parents were to be unemotional teachers, following a carefully thought-out plan of training based on the principles of conditioning. The behaviorist tradition spawned the learning theories of Guthrie, Tolman, Hull, and Spence and was the predominant theoretical force in American psychology for almost 50 years.

During the late 1930s, a strange marriage took place between learning theory, particularly in the form proposed by Clark Hull, and psychoanalytic theory. At the Institute of Human Relations at Yale University, a number of social scientists, including John Dollard, Neal Miller, O. Hobart Mowrer, and Robert Sears, attempted to translate psychoanalytic ideas into the terms of learning theory or, more precisely, to reinterpret Freudian hypotheses within the framework of stimulus-response theory. The exercise appeared to enrich the starkness of a general theory of behavior based solely on the conditioning of responses and to make a theory based on clinical observation and interpretation more rigorous and respectable.

Certainly similarities between the two theories facilitated this reinterpretation, albeit with some serious violations of their individual integrities. For example, both viewed the goal of behavior as drive reduction, and reinforcement and the pleasure principle were easily equated. Out of the alliance emerged a number of well-known works including a monograph on frustration and aggression (Dollard, Doob, Miller, Mowrer, & Sears, 1939), a treatise on psychotherapy (Dollard & Miller, 1950), and theories of identification. As an example of the latter, it was suggested that children behave in a manner similar to their parents because the reproduction of this behavior is secondarily reinforcing, having been paired originally with drive reduction (Mowrer, 1960; Sears, 1957). The reinterpretation of psychoanalytic theory in learning theory terms was christened social learning theory.

The Work of Bandura

In 1963, Bandura and Walters' book, *Social Learning and Personality Development,* broke new ground by casting off the psychoanalytic orientation of early social learning theory and analyzing social and personality development solely in terms of learning theory. Richard Walters, at that time a member of the University of Toronto faculty, had been a student of Sears at Stanford University. Albert Bandura, a graduate of the University of Iowa where Kenneth Spence had been a prominent influence, was on the faculty of Stanford University. Bandura and Walters began their fruitful collaboration with a study of adolescent delinquency which was guided by the original hybrid social learning theory. But they became influenced increasingly in the late 1950s by the radical behaviorism of B.F. Skinner, and this influence laid the groundwork for modern social learning theory. They added to the Skinnerian perspective, with its emphasis on operant conditioning and contingencies of reinforcement, the notion that one very potent determinant of behavior is the tendency of human beings to model or imitate the behavior of other human beings. Although others also have proposed forms of social learning theory (e.g., Bijou & Baer, 1961; Rotter, 1954; Staats, 1975), Bandura and Walters' has been the most influential.

It often is suggested that the focus of social learning theorists is on behavior, in contrast to the Freudian emphasis on feeling and the Piagetian emphasis on cognition. Although this distinction produces a neat categorization, it is misleading in the case of Bandura and Walters (although less so for theorists such as Bijou and Baer). In their original formulation Bandura and Walters made it clear that human functioning could not be understood independently of an understanding of mental activity; a point that has been elaborated and underlined on many occasions (e.g., Bandura, 1974, 1977a). Mischel (1973) has gone so far as to rename the approach "cognitive social learning theory" in recognition of the role played by mental constructs such as encoding strategies, expectancies, incentives, and competencies. Whereas Piaget gave primacy to thought as the major determinant of psychological functioning, the social learning position is that thought and behavior are equally important and that an adequate understanding must include knowledge of both external events and cognitive operations.

The Origins of Behavior

Bandura sees the origins of behavior in direct learning mediated by contingencies of reinforcement and in observational learning. Thus development of the ability to trust others, inhibit aggression, behave morally, and so on, all can be understood not as products of psychosexual development but as the result of learning through direct reinforcement and observation. Aggressiveness, for example, can come about because it is reinforced—in Bandura and Walters' study of adolescent aggression, the fathers of delinquent boys were much more likely to reward their sons for fighting than were fathers of nondelinquents. Furthermore, individuals become aggressive when they are exposed to examples of violence in others. Bandura considers direct learning a more rudimentary process than observational learning. In direct learning, actions have positive or negative outcomes which determine whether or not the actions are repeated. Response consequences achieve their effect in two ways: through imparting information and through serving as motivators of behavior. By observing the result of their own actions, individuals develop hypotheses about what behavior is appropriate in a given setting; hypotheses that are subsequently confirmed or disconfirmed as they continue to guide action. The anticipation of outcomes motivates people either to engage in particular behaviors or to avoid them.

Direct learning, however, is inefficient and can be hazardous. People learning to drive a car, dive into a swimming pool, or parachute from a plane, for example, could be severely injured if they were testing an incorrect hypothesis about which actions led to reinforcement. Young children learning when to assert themselves and when to give way graciously to the demands of society could be subjected to excessive amounts of punishment before they finally mastered the correct contingencies. Fortunately, however, much of human behavior is acquired through the observation of either live or symbolic models (e.g., television characters, written or verbalized instruction), and so many needless mistakes can be avoided. In all cases, information is coded and serves as a guide for later action.

In many ways observational learning is similar to the psychoanalytic process of identification. The explanation offered for it, however, is quite different. The processes Bandura hypothesizes to be involved in modeling are presented schematically in Figure 1.1. The first thing that a child or adult must do is attend to the model's behavior. Attention is determined by a variety of variables including the model's attractiveness and power and the conditions under which behavior is viewed. For example, the effects of models presented by means of television are very great because that

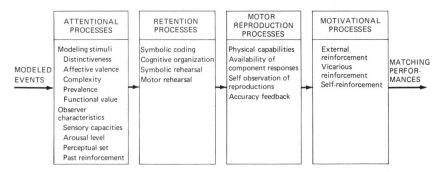

FIGURE 1.1. Component processes governing observational learning in the social learning analysis. From Albert Bandura, *Social Learning Theory*, 1977, p. 23. Reprinted by permission of Prentice-Hall, Inc., Englewood Cliffs, NJ.

medium is so effective in capturing and holding attention: that is why antisocial behavior portrayed on television is thought to be particularly effective in promoting aggressive and hostile behavior, although the relationship between aggression and television violence is a complex one, as will be discussed in Chapter 8.

The second process involved in observational learning is retention. Events that have been attended to must be remembered, with the observed behavior represented in memory either through an imaginal or a verbal representational system. In the latter case, events have to be coded into verbal symbols. Mental rehearsal also aids in the memory process. Third, symbolic representation must be converted into appropriate actions that are similar to the original modeled behavior. This is not always easy because individuals may not be able to perform some of the necessary parts of these actions, or may not reproduce them accurately the first time. Thus one cannot produce Bach's "Goldberg Variations" just by listening to them being played by Glen Gould. Some trial-and- error behavior is frequently necessary before exact motoric reproduction is achieved.

The final component process governing observational learning involves the presence of sufficient incentive to motivate the actual performance of modeled actions. A child may be quite capable of reproducing another's temper tantrum in response to frustration, but will not if such an act is likely to be punished.

Self-Regulation

Another feature of Bandura's theory is self-regulation. Much human behavior, he maintains, is controlled by self-generated consequences. People set standards of achievement for themselves, self-administering reinforcement when the standards are met and self-administering punishment when they are not. A good day's work (as perceived by the self) results in feelings of satisfaction and perhaps the luxury of a night out. A poor day's work means feelings of dissatisfaction and perhaps even self-denial. Through these self-regulatory mechanisms, then, behavior is maintained independently of external coercion. Society's standards are adopted by the individual, and externally administered consequences are less necessary. In this way, Bandura deals with the problem of how societal demands are internalized, a task that is handled in psychoanalytic theory by the concept of internalization.

Standards of achievement are originally established by modeling and direct tuition. Adults set certain standards for their children's behavior, as well as for their own, and children adopt these standards. A boy is not allowed to go out to play, for example, before he has spent a certain amount of time practicing the piano. In addition, adults instruct children to adopt specific standards and reward or punish them for following or not following these instructions. The self-denial involved in adopting standards for self-reinforcement must, in the end, be maintained by external contingencies or the behavior will eventually extinguish. Thus unmerited self-reward may produce criticism from others, while self-punishment may be approved of by others. Self-regulation may produce personal benefits that also maintain the behavior. As an example, by practicing self-denial fat people grow thinner, students pass examinations, and writers produce books. Finally, the modeling of self-control by others plays a role in the maintenance, as well as the origin, of self-regulation.

Self-Efficacy

Recently, Bandura has focused his attention on the concept of personal efficacy (Bandura, 1977a, 1981). People develop beliefs about their own abilities, characteristics, and vulnerabilities, and these beliefs, or self-percepts, guide their behavior by determining what actions they attempt to perform and how much effort they put into this performance. When individuals believe they are inefficacious, or do not possess the ability to perform well, they become preoccupied with themselves and emotionally aroused, conditions that distract them from effective performance. Thus an individual who believes he cannot do well at mathematics will perform much more poorly than another individual with the same mathematical ability but greater feelings of self-efficacy.

Beliefs about the self come from a variety of sources, the major one being one's own achievements to date. Even young infants develop a sense of personal agency if they are successful at controlling their environment. Such success makes them pay closer attention to their own behavior, and therefore they become even better at learning that their actions are effective. Overprotective parents, of course, undermine the development of self-efficacy because they deny children the opportunity to achieve and therefore experience success.

A second source of self-efficacy is observation of what others are able to accomplish. Peer comparison is an important vehicle here. In addition, the attempts of others to mold self-efficacy by persuasion, as well as conclusions emerging from considering one's own physiological state as being a reflection of one's personal capabilities and limitations ("I have butterflies in my stomach. Therefore I can't be very good at this."), play a role in its development. In his discussions of self-efficacy, then, Bandura emphasizes once again the role of thought and judgment in determining behavior. Indeed, self-percepts provide a framework or structure against which information is judged, a concept very much in keeping with current cognitive and information-processing approaches to the understanding of human behavior.

The Developmental Aspects

So far we have said nothing about the developmental aspects of social learning theory. This part of the theory is less well formalized. The qualitatively different stages of functioning, which are a prominent part of psychoanalytic and cognitive developmental theory, do not figure in social learning theory. Development is seen primarily as a quantitative phenomenon, a result of increasing experience. To be sure, the influence of biology is not discounted. Physical development affects behavior potentialities, and experience and biology are believed to interact in subtle and inseparable ways to influence behavior. In the case of modeling, for example, deficits in attentional processes, memory limitations, physical inability to perform complex motoric behavior, and inability to see the possible consequences of matching another person's behavior all would contribute to poor performance in the course of development. Early in life children's modeling is confined to immediate imitation. As their symbolic skills improve, as well as their ability to translate symbolized experience into motor performance, they become increasingly capable of delayed imitation. The emphasis, however, is on changing cognitive and physical skills rather than on qualitative changes in the organization of behavior. Thus the legacy of Watsonian environmentalism (although not Watsonian behaviorism) looms large in the theory, which is supremely optimistic about the possibilites of modifying behavior through the judicious manipulation of environmental events.

Appraisal

During the 1960s and early 1970s, the influence of Bandura's social learning theory was great. Studies inspired by it filled the psychological journals, and the power of a concept such as observational learning quickly became evident. Unlike psychoanalytic theory, social learning theory was supported by hundreds of well-designed studies that met the generally accepted criteria for scientific rigor. Thus there was ample evidence that children imitate, that their behavior is controlled by reinforcement contingencies, and that self-regulating mechanisms exist and seem to function as the theory suggests (see Bandura, 1977a, for reference to many of these studies).

Despite this success, the influence of social learning theory began to wane in the 1970s as mental events became an increasingly popular object of inquiry. Although there had been attempts to formulate cognitive theories of learning, it was the more behaviorally oriented ones that had won out in the final analysis, and they dominated North American psychology for 30 years. In the 1960s, however, cognition was rediscovered. Studies of information processing, attention, and memory proliferated. Piagetian theory became better known and more popular, and children's thinking grew in importance as an object of psychological investigation. The tremendous interest in cognitive activity eclipsed the greater interest shown by social learning theorists in the behavioral outcomes of both cognitive and environmental events. Certainly, social learning theorists had not given the kind of detailed attention to thinking that it was now receiving.

Social learning theory also suffered from its association with a particular scientific methodology. One of Bandura and Walters' most intriguing contributions had been their way of testing hypotheses. They were able to answer questions about social behaviour by devising laboratory analogues of real-life situations, manipulating variables, and observing their effects under laboratory conditions. In this way, they could achieve a high degree of control over the experiences of their subjects and could also make direct inferences about causal relationships. This was an approach inspired both by the experimental laboratory methodology of learning theory and by the work of the social psychologist Kurt Lewin who had studied such problems as the effects of frustration on children's play and their reactions to different forms of leadership in an experimental setting. However, serious questions began to arise regarding the representativeness of laboratory behavior of real-life behavior and experimental methodology in general. The resolution of methodological problems in psychology has certainly not yet been accomplished, as will be discussed at length in Chapter 2. For the present we note that concern has been expressed about the meaning of many findings that have formed the evidence for social learning theory. Thus the data base is not so strong as was once supposed. This is not to say the theory has no support, but that some of the support to date may be of limited usefulness.

Finally, the influence of Piaget sensitized psychologists to the importance of age as a variable. Developmental changes were not a major consideration in many of the early studies carried out in the social learning tradition and the age of subjects studied was often determined simply by whether or not they were available to participate in the research. This is no longer the case. It is true, however, that more attention needs to be paid to specific developmental changes in such abilities as attention, memory, and comprehension of observed material. A good example of interest in the latter is the work of Collins on children's developing understanding of the relationship between a model's behavior and its consequences (Collins, 1973).

No theory is complete, and social learning theory will have to respond to current challenges. Few psychologists, however, would deny the importance of processes highlighted by social learning theorists in their attempts to understand social development.

COGNITIVE DEVELOPMENTAL THEORY

Genetic Epistemology

Jean Piaget was born in 1896 and spent most of his professional life at the Institut J.J. Rousseau in Geneva, Switzerland. Throughout his career he was immensely prolific, although his research and theorizing only began to have a substantial impact on North American psychology in the late 1960s. Piaget developed a theory of genetic epistemology: Epistemology is that branch of philosophy concerned with the human conception of the real world, whereas genetic psychology addresses itself to the beginnings, or genesis, of psychological functioning either within the individual or in the human species as a whole. The latter is referred to as phylogenesis, the former, which was Piaget's interest, as ontogenesis. Thus Piaget was concerned with how the individual comes to acquire knowledge about, or an understanding of, the real world, including both its social and physical aspects.

According to Piaget, the problem of knowledge cannot be considered separately from that of the development of intelligence. To know what knowledge is one must ask how it grows, establishing the process whereby the individual progresses from insufficient knowledge to better knowledge. The epistemological problem, then, reduces to analyzing how individuals are progressively better able to know the external world.

Mechanistic theories of learning such as those of Watson, Hull, and Spence, characterized human beings as passive individuals acted on by their environments. The influence of Piaget's training in biology was clear in his contention that human beings are not passive organisms, but are spontaneously active in dealing with their environments. They interact with these environments, constantly constructing their own experience as well as formulating and correcting their own knowledge. Objective knowledge is not acquired by a mere recording of external information, but by interaction between the individual and the external world and that individual's construction of reality during the course of development. In this way both environmental events and spontaneous organismic growth are integrated in the ontogeny of knowledge.

James Mark Baldwin's Contribution to Piaget's Theory

The discipline of genetic psychology had been established at the beginning of the 20th century by an American psychologist, James Mark Baldwin, and we digress briefly to a discussion of his work for reasons that will soon become apparent. Much of Baldwin's theorizing appears to predate Piaget's, and many of his concepts bear a striking resemblance to those of Piaget. Baldwin used terms such as "accommodation," "assimilation," "scheme," and "circular reaction," all of which play a prominent role in Piaget's theory. For Baldwin, as for Piaget, development proceeds in a series of stages appearing in an irreversible order, which involve a qualitatively new way of construing reality. In the social realm, according to both Baldwin and Piaget, the child proceeds from a stage of self-centered egocentrism, where the only reality is that which is experienced by the self, to a stage where the point of view of others can be appreciated. (Baldwin also suggested that the self- concept derives from the evaluative and descriptive input of others, an idea which predates George Herbert Mead's views on personality development.)

Baldwin was an extremely influential figure in American psychology at the turn of the century. He was president of the American Psychological Association in 1897, helped to establish several major psychological journals, and founded psychological laboratories at Toronto, Princeton, and Johns Hopkins Universities. Yet for many years his contributions to developmental psychology were largely ignored until a recent upsurge of interest in his work (e.g., Broughton, 1981; Cairns, 1980; Mueller, 1976). Much of this interest has focused on the uncertain extent of his influence on Piagetian formulations. Mueller (1976) reports that Piaget felt that Baldwin had a great impact on him. Broughton (1981) states that Piaget believed Baldwin had no specific effect on his work and that apparent influences were nothing more than "simple convergences." Moreover, he suggests that Baldwin was aware of and impressed by Piaget's work but did not feel it was in a direct line of descent from his own.

The problem of influence aside, the interesting question is why Baldwin disappeared from view and why Piaget became so prominent some half-century later. Part of the answer lies in Baldwin's alienation from the emerging ethos of psychology as a science of behavior. His ideas did not fit into the behavioral zeitgeist and he seemed more interested in philosophical inquiry than in empirical investigation. Piaget, on the other hand, provided empirical evidence for his views. That empirical evidence helped to promote recognition of his importance when Americans renewed their interest in cognition in the 1960s.

Adaptation, Equilibration, and Stages

Piaget's theory centers on thinking. It is cognition that is basic for an understanding of all psychological processes. Although Piaget devoted greater attention to thinking about the physical world, his observations were just as relevant to knowledge of the social world. How children think about the nature of morality, for example, determines the sophistication of their moral behavior. Indeed, Piaget addressed himself quite specifically to issues of morality. His ideas about the subject, and their extension in Kohlberg's work, will be discussed in Chapter 9. In recent years increasing attention has been paid by social developmentalists to thinking about the social world and, accordingly, Piaget has assumed even greater prominence in the area of social development. This is particularly evident in Chapter 7, which is concerned with social cognition.

Like Freud, Piaget proposed a stage theory of development. The focus, however, was on cognitive rather than emotional events. In each stage he believed that children have qualitatively different ways of viewing reality. Stages occur in invariant order, with each one representing a different underlying way of thinking about the world, and each a better way of thinking because it accounts for even more than its predecessor did.

One of the characteristics of developing mental functioning, which has been particularly crucial for the understanding of social development, is the inability to see that events can be manipulated mentally, a characteristic of thinking in the preoperational stage (which occurs between 3 and 7 years of age). Because preschoolers cannot manipulate events mentally, they cannot comprehend any perspective but their own. They are egocentric. To them reality is as they perceive it and they are unable to understand that anyone could have a point of view different from their own. Egocentrism makes social interaction difficult because it means that young children have problems understanding the needs, feelings, and thoughts of others. They may, therefore, have difficulty behaving in socially acceptable ways because of deficiencies in their thinking rather than because of an underdeveloped superego as psychoanalytic theory would have it, or a failure to employ self-regulatory mechanisms as social learning theory maintains.

Two important mechanisms in cognitive developmental theory are assimilation and accommodation. The former is the process of dealing with environmental events using already existing mental structures or habitual ways of organizing and responding to objects. The latter refers to changes in mental structures that must occur if situations and problems are too difficult to be dealt with by currently existing structures. Although individuals are generally motivated to maintain equilibrium between assimilation and accommodation, there are two kinds of cognition for which the two are decidedly not in equilibrium. One is play, where the goal is assimilation of reality to the world of the child. The other is imitation. Here accommodation reigns supreme, and the primary object is to adapt the self to reality. Thus disequilibrium is a motivating influence. Those behaviors that are moderately incongruent with existing mental structures will be imitated because they provide an impetus for accommodation that behaviors too easy or too difficult to reproduce do not. Contrasting this view with the social learning approach to imitation provides a good example of how differently the two theories view motivation. In the former case the impetus to behavior comes from internal sources, the active desire to understand or master the world, whereas in the latter case it derives from external contingencies for which the individual may or may not choose to perform. In the cognitive developmental perspective aggressive models are imitated because their behavior is interesting and challenging to perform. In the social learning perspective it is because aggressive behavior is likely to be admired by others or rewarded by the attainment of a desired object.

Appraisal

As noted, Piagetian theory made particularly strong inroads into North American psychology during the 1960s and 1970s. Dissemination of Piaget's views, many of which had not been translated into English, was helped by scholarly and comprehensible summaries of the theory that appeared in English early in the 1960s (Flavell, 1963; Hunt, 1961) as well as by the intensification of interest in cognition. Piaget provided a great deal of empirical data to support his position. These data were obtained primarily by observation and by the clinical interview method where formulations were tested by assessing children's reactions to disrupted or altered environmental conditions. Researchers were frustrated to some extent by Piaget's selective reporting of evidence. Frequently, rather than analyzing data in the orthodox fashion, he would present representative protocols as evidence for generalizations. For this reason many of his studies have had to be "redone." Nevertheless, many of his formulations had great popular appeal.

The theory was not, however, adopted in a totally wholehearted way. Many basic assumptions were not easily accepted by researchers who repeatedly asked what has been referred to by Piaget as "the American question." Not content with a theory that was essentially descriptive, Americans wanted to know how the process of development could be sped up. This question had little meaning within the context of cognitive developmental theory.

The American Question

To understand the American question, and European perplexity when faced with that question, we need to look briefly at the philosophical roots of the two systems of psychological thought. American psychology generally has been more oriented toward helping and changing people, a reflection of North America's frontier history. The Lockeian notion of the tabula rasa with its emphasis on the accretion of experience on a blank slate fits with this tradition. Continental European psychology, on the other hand, has been more concerned with the understanding of human functioning. Blank slates mean much less in the Leibnitzian approach, for example, which views the mind as having a potentially active core of its own. In the first case, then, concern would be with change and control, whereas in the second it would be with description and understanding.

Riegel (1972) and Buss (1975) have attempted to show how economic and political ideologies in Europe and America gave rise to these distinctively different approaches. Both Piaget and Freud can be seen as participants in a world view that emerged from a continental European society that had a highly defined class structure for hundreds of years. Power and prestige accrued to nobles and clerics who exploited peasants and workers. Merchants were necessary for such aristocratic pursuits as fighting wars and maintaining impressive courts, but they were never allowed to achieve the same level of wealth as the aristocracy. It was an awareness of the inequalities of this system that eventually resulted in the French Revolution. However, the system also produced approaches to philosophical thought that attempted to justify existing social orders in order to prevent further political upheavals. Examples of these approaches can be seen in the philosophies of Leibnitz and Hegel. What these approaches did in the process of attempting to preserve the status quo was to strengthen awareness of and sensitivity to group differences. Any group in society was to be considered in terms of that group's own standards and accepted as such. This was the background that produced Piaget and Freud, men interested in and appreciative of each stage of development and not inclined to hurry the child through any one of them.

This appreciation of individual differences did not, however, exist in North America. Successful people were those whose activities fit into the society of which they were a member. Those who did not were considered substandard. Children were regarded as incomplete adults, old persons as deficient, members of the lower classes as less desirable than those of the middle classes. The source of differences was seen to be in the presence or absence of environmental opportunity. It was to America that the poor and oppressed fled so that they could be raised from a substandard state to one that was optimal. There was nothing admirable about children unable to understand the perspective of others or to think abstractly and no reason for them to stay in that state for any longer than minimally necessary. Thus we see the American desire to speed the process of development as much as possible.

It was this atmosphere, then, that prompted investigators to demonstrate how the acquisition of knowledge could be accelerated, or how Piaget had seriously underestimated the cognitive capacities of the child by using tasks so difficult that underlying capacities were masked. Bandura and McDonald (1963), for example, attempted to demonstrate that children could be induced to engage in either more or less sophisticated moral thinking by observing the moral judgments of others. Shatz and Gelman (1973) argued that even children as young as 4 years of age could understand the perspective of others and that the case for egocentrism had been overstated.

The Current Perspective

No doubt many details of Piagetian theory are incorrect. He clearly underestimated many of the developing organism's capacities. He no doubt underestimated the importance of experience. He may have incorrectly identified the specific nature of limitations at different points in development. The course of cognitive development may be marked, not by qualitative changes in thinking at different times, but by quantitative changes in the ability to attend, to remember, and to learn. Piaget maintained, for example, that children in the concrete operational period (between the ages of 7 and 11 years) are unable to think and reason about abstract concepts because their mental operations can be applied only to objects and events that are familiar or easily imagined, that is, that are concrete. Bryant and Trabasso (1971), however, argue that children are limited in the amount of information they can remember and that the presence of concrete objects makes problem-solving easier simply because the objects serve as an aid to memory. The specific deficit lies with memory, *not* with a qualitatively distinct way of viewing the world.

These considerations do not detract, however, from the singular contributions made by Piaget. He did orient psychologists to the important changes that occur as children grow older and to the fact that they should study children at different points in the developmental process. He also emphasized the basic role of thought in action and underlined the active role of individuals in organizing their world and in accepting, rejecting, or reformulating experience. These are two contributions that have altered the character of research in social development considerably in the last few years.

EVOLUTIONARY APPROACHES

The Limitations of Learning Theory

In 1961 Marian and Keller Breland puhlished an article in *American Psychologist* in which they described their failures as behavioral engineers. Well versed in the techniques of operant conditioning, they had for some years been using their expertise to train animals to engage in entertaining acts for zoos, museums, fairs, and television commercials. Although they began with limitless faith in the utility of principles of operant conditioning for modifying animal behavior quickly and efficiently, their enthusiasm was somewhat dampened over time.

The Brelands described several instances in which animals seemed incapable of learning relatively simple responses for food reinforcement even though they came quite close to starving themselves to death. In one case, for example, a pig was supposed to put wooden discs into a piggy bank. Although the pig was intelligent, friendly, loved to eat, and initially learned quite well, its behavior soon deteriorated and, instead of inserting the discs into the bank, it insisted on repeatedly dropping them onto the ground, tossing them into the air, and rooting. Nor were the Brelands any more successful with a racoon who was also dextrous, intelligent, and cute.

Although the racoon performed properly on a schedule of continuous reinforcement, as soon as reinforcement was not administered for every response it began to misbehave, slipping two coins in and out of the container and clutching and rubbing them together. The Brelands concluded that their problem in all cases was that the animal's species-specific behaviors for obtaining food were interfering with the responses they were trying to teach. Thus the learned response gradually drifted into food-related behaviors. Pigs root when they are looking for food and racoons wash food as, for example, when they remove the exoskeleton of a crayfish, and neither of these behaviors is compatible with slipping coins into a slot. The Brelands concluded that the behavior of any animal cannot be adequately understood, predicted, or controlled without some knowledge of its instinctive patterns, evolutionary history, and ecological niche.

The Ethological Tradition

Although the Breland's observations were not ignored, psychologists did not know what to make of them at the time. Behavioral scientists in the early 1960s were still strongly committed to the idea that the same principles of learning hold across all species and that all responses are equally conditionable. If cats were difficult to train it was because the food they were offered as reinforcement was not sufficiently delectable, and octopi posed a problem only because their tentacles kept getting wound up in the manipulandum. It took repeated reports of different capacities in different species for acquiring the same skills (e.g., Garcia & Koelling, 1966) before researchers responded to the idea that different species have evolved so that they are adapted to specific environments, and that they may therefore be more sensitive or attuned to some environmental events than others. European ethologists (e.g., Lorenz, 1953; Tinbergen, 1951) had been making this point for some time, but they found a more receptive audience on their own continent than in America. With the weakening of learning theory as a force in American psychology, however, ethology began to make an inroad into conceptualizations of the developmental process. Ethologists argued that the manner in which different species have adapted to their environment during the course of evolution has determined the nature of their behavior and motivation. Closely linked to this theoretical orientation was a particular methodology for studying behavior, that is, the use of observational techniques to gain information about the behavior of different species in their natural environment.

Ethology's greatest impact on the study of human social behavior has been by way of this methodology, with the observation of children in their natural settings becoming particularly popular in recent years. Natural observation itself is not a new approach in developmental psychology. Many observational studies of children were carried out in the 1930s. The modern ethological approach, however, was borrowed from the methodological procedures of individuals who studied animals. Thus the observational work of Blurton Jones (a student of Tinbergen's) with fish, of Hinde with mother-infant relations in monkeys, and of Strayer with dominance hierarchies in monkeys formed a procedural prototype for observational studies of children.

Strayer (1980) has described properties of the ethological appoach that distinguish it from other attempts at natural observation. Child ethologists are committed to making detailed descriptions of behavioral patterns that are common to all young members of the human species. As an example, they might observe and describe specific gestures that are made by children such as hitting, frowning, and threatening arm movements. These behavioral patterns are then organized into a more meaningful descriptive system, "aggressive exchange." In this way the ethologist is able to identify events that cause particular behaviors as well as to assess the function of these behaviors. The outcome of aggressive encounters, for example, determines the place of an individual in a dominance hierarchy. Once a stable dominance hierarchy has been established in a group of children, aggressive encounters are less frequent because access to resources is determined by position in the hierarchy. In this way group cohesion is promoted by minimizing aggression.

That groups which have efficient ways of minimizing aggression are the ones to survive demonstrates the concern of ethologists with distal as well as proximal causes of behavior. In fact, the main aim and distinguishing mark of ethology is its concern with viewing behavior from an evolutionary perspective. The ability to analyze the immediate causes and functions of behavior in a specific setting follows from this and is a way of answering evolutionary questions.

Ethological analyses of human social behavior have been plentiful in the last decade, with much of the work focused on the social structure of preschool groups and the cross-cultural study of emotional expression. John Bowlby (1969, 1973) has speculated about the formation of affectional bonds between caretaker and child from an ethological perspective, and we shall consider his ideas in Chapter 4.

Sociobiology

It is not only ethologists who have concerned themselves with the relationship between behavior and evolution. The new discipline of sociobiology also deals with issues of biology, evolution, and survival as they relate to social behavior. At the moment sociobiology is not a theory about ontogenetic development and so we will consider it only briefly. The popular appeal of sociobiological ideas (despite a rather sparse empirical base) attests, however, to increasing sensitivity in the last decade to the evolutionary significance of behavior.

Sociobiology is "the study of the biological bases for all behavior" (Wilson, 1975). It attempts to show how social behaviors evolve in order to satisfy one goal; continued existence of the individual's genes in a population's pool of genes. The focus, therefore, is not on individual organisms but on indiviual genes and their reproduction. The gene is the ultimate unit of life. Altruism, or self-sacrifice, is a central issue for sociobiologists (e.g., Dawkins, 1976) because it is not immediately obvious why individuals should endanger their own existence in order to aid others. Sociobiological attempts to explain altruism provide an example of how this theory works. Their proposed explanation for the existence of altruism lies in continued existence of the gene. If loss of one's life or reduced reproductive potential for oneself enables offspring and other relatives to live and reproduce, then the goal of gene survival has been achieved. Another mechanism the sociobiologists call on is reciprocal altruism (Trivers, 1971). They suggest that there has been a strong evolutionary tendency to select individuals who reciprocate altruism, even to those to whom they are not related. Such a tendency requires a high probability of future interaction for the altruistic dyad, and a predisposition not to extend continued altruism to those who fail to reciprocate.

One of the difficulties with current approaches to sociobiology lies in the issue of definition (e.g., Cairns, 1979a). Terms such as altruism, selfishness, and cooperation are borrowed from descriptions of human social behavior and redefined so they fit into the concepts of population genetics. When they are translated back into the domain of human social functioning, however, they have lost much of the complexity and richness of their original meaning. Although an "altruistic gene" may be involved in some instances of apparently selfless behavior, it cannot account for the whole variety of causes of altruism in human beings or the many behaviors that make up the concept. Sociobiological theory also suffers, thus far, from having little good evidence for its tenets. It is an attempt, which many find intriguing, to explain difficult facts. Whether or not these explanations will be supported by empirical evidence remains to be seen.

Developmental Psychobiology

This is an orientation that, to date, has had less impact on the study of human development than any of those we have discussed so far. Although there is a long history of research in the psychobiological tradition, most of it has been conducted with nonhuman subjects. Generalization from animal to human social behavior must be done with great care and always bearing in mind that two superficially similar behaviors may have different developmental origins, be maintained by different environmental events, and serve different functions in social organization. Recently, however, Cairns (1979b) has provided a fine example of how concepts derived from animal studies can begin to elucidate processes of human social development.

The basic assumption of developmental psychobiology is that a complete understanding of behavioral development is possible only with knowledge of the functional and structural aspects of the organism's physiology. Therefore the psychobiologist studies both experiential and biological processes as they interact to produce behavior. Cairns suggests that "holistic theory" would be a suitable label for the approach because it emphasizes the need to consider the organism and its behavior as a whole.

Some of developmental psychobiology's major guiding principles are: (1) Behavior is an organized system in which maturation and experience must be viewed as fused. As an example, the vocalizations embryonic birds make affect the species preferences they display immediately after hatching. (2) In social development maturational factors elicit and maintain experiential changes while, at the same time, experiential changes modify biological states and behavior potentials. Castrated cats and dogs, for example, continue to perform sexually if they have had mating experience before gonad removal, but they never establish the activity if they have had no such prior experience; (3) Comparisons between species and developmental stages must be made on the basis of the organization of which the activity is a part. For example, it is inappropriate to generalize from the social behavior of army ants to the social behavior of human beings because the former has a much greater dependence on biological controls than the latter; and (4) Organisms are adaptive and active throughout their life span. Thus development is bidirectional (between biology and experience) from birth to death. Cairns provides an example of this bidirectionality between structure and function in the area of cultural attitudes and sex-role typing. There are few differences in the actual capabilities of girls and boys between the ages of 3 and 10 years. Yet marked differences in their play occur during these early years—differences dictated by cultural expectation. The different opportunities provided anticipate future biological differences in size and strength and produce different levels of ability which simply augment those biologically produced differences that occur at adolescence. Thus different play patterns are neither biologically nor culturally determined.

These guiding principles provide an excellent orientation for any theory of social development. At the present stage of the field's development they are more easily appreciated and incorporated into thinking than they would have been 10 or 20 years ago.

Current Themes and Issues

The days of stringent adherence to one theoretical position are past. Social developmentalists have become less rigid in the ways in which they organize their data. This is a healthier, although possibly less exciting, approach to the understanding of human social development than one in which strongly held opposing viewpoints are pitted against each other. The goal is no longer one of achieving a state of final knowledge with one all-encompassing theory. Theoretical structures must be seen within the context of the present. The conceptual framework imposed on data is altered by current belief systems.

The organisms we study also are affected by contemporary cultural attitudes and values. The very object of our study, then, is modified by its historical context. This is not to argue, as has Gergen (1973) with respect to social psychology, that social developmental psychology is a historical inquiry dealing largely with unrepeatable events. To some extent our understanding of social development can transcend its historical boundaries because human biology changes much more slowly than does the cultural surround. The challenge for the developmentalist is to see how biology and cultural experience are intertwined and fused.

A recurrent theme runs through much of contemporary social developmental psychology. It says that nothing can be studied or understood in isolation from its context. We already have seen one manifestation of this theme in the argument that the history of the science cannot be understood in isolation from its cultural context. Systems interact, and adequate knowledge of any one system is not possible unless it is viewed as part of a larger set of systems, with each system influencing and being influenced by the other. This point is elaborated by Sameroff (1983) who discusses the applicability of general systems theory (Bertalanffy, 1968) to the study of social development.

This viewpoint highlights the complexity of human behavior and the difficult task facing a science of psychology. It is not a particularly novel or revolutionary one, and any sensitive researcher always realized at some level that the determinants of human behavior were multifaceted. However, it is also true that much of psychology has been characterized by an attempt to isolate a phenomenon of interest from the context in which it normally occurs and subject it to analysis in a relative vacuum. This procedure has provided limited information. What makes the current concern with context particularly exciting is its coupling with increased methodological sophistication and specific suggestions for how interacting systems can be studied in a scientifically meaningful fashion. Some of these methodological advances will be described in Chapter 2.

The concern with systems in interaction manifests itself in several ways. Thus we must consider the interaction among thinking, feeling, and behaving in a given organism, between the organism and its environment, between the person and the situation, between two or more individuals in a social interaction, and between individuals and the social systems directly and indirectly affecting them.

THOUGHT, AFFECT, AND BEHAVIOR

Thought and feeling ultimately manifest themselves in behavior. How they do this, and the manner of their interconnection, is a question that has begun only lately to receive much attention. Different theoretical approaches considered different aspects of this psychological triumvirate to be primary. Because of this, researchers tended for a long time to focus their efforts on only one process.

Behavior was the dominant interest of social developmentalists for many years. Then Piagetian theory stimulated an interest in the development of thinking about the social as well as the physical world. Augmenting this interest was the influence of social psychology which, beginning in the 1960s, was focusing much of its attention on how individuals come to attribute emotions, attitudes, and dispositions to themselves and others.

The Study of Attributions

The study of attributions has had a long history in social psychology. William James maintained that we gain knowledge of our own characteristics by comparing ourselves with others. During the early 1900s George Herbert Mead proposed a "social looking glass" theory about the development of self-knowledge (the self-concept) in which he maintained that we learn about ourselves by observing the responses we evoke in others. If they laugh at our jokes, for example, then we must have the ability to amuse. In the early 1970s Daryl Bem argued that we learn about ourselves by observing our own behavior just as we learn about others by observing theirs. If we find ourselves listening to classical music then we assume that we in fact enjoy classical music.

Recent research on attributions about others has its roots in Fritz Heider's theory of naive psychology. Heider wrote about the conditions under which people attribute responsibility to others for their acts, arguing that this happens to the extent that an act causes an effect that was foreseen and that was the intention of the act. A girl who intentionally sticks out her foot to trip her brother, hoping he will fall, is more responsible for harm that occurs to him than is one who unintentionally trips her brother, or trips him in a playful way. As well, when environmental influences are such that most people would act in a particular way, individuals are held to be less responsible than if they act in a way most people would not. Social psychologists (e.g., Jones & Davis, 1965; Kelley, 1967) have expanded these basic notions to show how people try to comprehend and explain the actions of others. The areas of concern identified by attribution theorists, then, provided additional grist for the mill of social developmentalists as they studied the growth of thinking about social events (see Chapter 7).

Missing from all this activity, however, was an attempt to relate thinking to behavior. Only lately have psychologists begun to study thoughts as mediators of behavior and to demonstrate how modification of these thoughts can produce changes in action (e.g., Meichenbaum, 1977). In the moral domain many have addressed themselves to the relationship between thought and behavior. The nature of the relationship has not been easy to establish, in part because the same act may be the manifestation of different underlying principles (a child may tell the truth to avoid punishment or because he knows his mother would be disappointed in him for his dishonesty) or because the same underlying principle may produce opposite behaviors (those who value human life and dignity above all else may go to war to defend these principles or refuse to go to war because they are pacifists).

Affect

Behavior is also mediated by affect, as Freud so clearly demonstrated. Attempts to study empirically the relationship between the two are of recent vintage, however. Those who believe they have no control over what happens to them feel helpless, become depressed, and manifest this depression in a severely reduced activity level (Seligman, 1975). Happy children share more than unhappy ones (Moore, Underwood, & Rosenhan, 1973). People who attribute achievement on a difficult task to personal ability feel good and are motivated to attempt additional difficult tasks. Again, their thoughts about or attributions for success affect subsequent emotional states (e.g., Weiner, 1980), and so the process continues. The role of empathy or feelings of distress at the suffering of others has received a great deal of attention from investigators interested in the development of altruism as well as the control of aggression. Much of this work will be reviewed in Chapters 8 and 9.

BIOLOGY AND ENVIRONMENT

The question of the relative contribution of biology and environment to development has been a source of considerable and heated debate over the years. Are differences in intelligence inherited? Are gender differences biologically or culturally determined? For a long time the issue was viewed as a dichotomous one, with investigators aligning themselves in either the environmentalist or biological camp. The British tradition, exemplified in the work of Francis Galton, viewed individual differences as genetically determined. The North American position obviously has been more environmentalist, with certain notable exceptions. Early in the century, G. Stanley Hall adopted a compromise position, believing that development was biologically determined until adolescence, but that the effects of experience manifested themselves thereafter. Two of his students, Arnold Gesell and Lewis Terman, moved against the American mainstream by adopting an extreme biological position. Thus Gesell saw growth and development as governed totally by maturational factors and Terman argued for the prominence of genetic variables as determinants of intelligence. In opposition were the majority of psychologists who advocated the importance of experience, maintaining that the assignment of change to maturation and growth was not an adequate explanation of change, and that psychologists must identify those environmental conditions that produce development.

This dichotomous approach was certainly too simplistic. Clearly, biology establishes a great many limitations on the effects of experience, and the problem is to establish how strong these biological limits are and/or how easily they can be overridden. Some things no one will ever be able to do, no matter how skillfully the environment is engineered. These include running a mile in one minute and committing to memory overnight the complete works of Shakespeare.

Other activities may be mastered more easily by some individuals than others. It is impossible, however, to disentangle fully the effects of biology and experience, and more accurate to depict the developmental interaction as between the organism and its environment rather than between heredity and environment. The psychobiological approach, which we described earlier, is an example of how some investigators have begun to handle the complexity of this interaction. In recent years, the organism-environment problem has revealed itself in forms other than that of the source of differences between individuals or groups of individuals. Ethologists and many learning theorists have argued that there are differences among species in how easily they benefit from the same experience. And stage theorists, although not particularly interested in individual differences in development, have oriented developmentalists to the interplay between developmental level (determined both by biological maturation and experience) and responsiveness to environmental events.

We want to sound a note of caution in the attempt to assess the roles of organism and environment in any behavioral outcome. There are at least two issues here. First, apparently universal phenomena, attributable at first glance to organismic factors, may actually be a result of experiences that are common to all human beings. These experiences may be determined by common biological properties, but it is the experiences, rather than the biology, that directly affect psychological functioning. The effect of biology is indirect. Consider, for example, maternal behavior and childhood dependency. It will be argued in Chapter 4 that biological events play an important role here. But there are alternative explanations. Females, for example, may not be inclined innately to greater nurturance of and affection for the young. But the fact that they are the ones who must carry, give birth to, and (in the absence of artificial means) feed offspring means that they have greater exposure to the young. And it may be that the experience of exposure makes them more attached. The desire for human contact may not be innate, but a result of immaturity at birth which forces the young into a period of prolonged dependency and reinforcing interactions with adults. The experience of dependency and reinforcement, then, is what promotes the need for social contact. Or, as another example, children who are physically attractive may be more socially competent not because these two characteristics tend to covary genetically, but because attractive children are more often the target of positive social overtures from both other children and adults, and so they have more opportunities to acquire social skills.

A second precaution is that society's own timetable may limit the experiences to which a child is exposed. Certainly these timetables can reflect genuine maturationally determined limitations in the young organism. But they may reflect other variables as well, such as the value and importance given to a particular accomplishment. When cleanliness is seen as a virtue children are toilet trained much earlier than when cleanliness is emphasized less. Similarly, a society that values politeness may demand politeness from young children earlier than one that is more permissive in this sphere.

Recent work (e.g., Goodnow, 1984; Hess, Kashigawi, Azuma, Price, & Dickson, 1980) indicates that parents in different cultures do indeed have different beliefs about age-related abilities of their children that seem to reflect something other than genetically determined differences in their offspring. Hess et al. found that Japanese mothers, for example, think their children are capable of emotional maturity, courtesy, and obedience earlier than do American mothers. American mothers, on the other hand, believe their children are capable of verbal assertiveness and social skills (such as resolving disagreements without fighting) and taking the initiative in playing with others earlier than do Japanese mothers. These different beliefs may well reflect the relative importance placed by the two cultures on these various skills.

THE PERSON AND THE SITUATION

Is personality continuous or discontinuous? Are behavioral patterns laid down early in the course of development and do they reveal themselves in the organism's subsequent functioning? Was Freud correct in arguing that the substrates of psychical organization develop very early, and that these substrates will continue to manifest themselves in adult behavior, proving themselves very resistant to any attempts at change? Perhaps it is more correct to think of behavior as influenced by the situation in which people find themselves. Should we really expect to find that later behavior can be easily predicted from earlier behavior, or that similar behavior should be exhibited in two different situations? The first part of this last question pertains to the issue of longitudinal stability of behavior, the second to cross-situational consistency of behavior.

For a long time it was popular to think of behavior as being directed by personality traits. An aggressive individual was expected to behave aggressively in all situations. The aggressiveness could be seen early and would continue to manifest itself throughout life. It could be modified, but not without considerable effort. Certainly the effects of situational context on behavior could be detected, with circumstances dictating the extent to which a trait would be revealed. But the rank ordering of individuals would remain unchanged across situations, so that the individual with the most aggressive personality would always reveal the most aggression in a given context. Personality, then, was determined by temperamental characteristics with a major genetic component or by previously learned characteristics that were relatively resistant to change.

The trait model of personality was strongly attacked in the late 1960s. The new argument held that behavior is largely determined by stimuli in a situation, along with associated reinforcement contingencies, and not by some underlying, enduring dispositional characteristic. The foremost proponent of this position was Walter Mischel who argued convincingly that consistencies between similar behaviors in different situations were small indeed, yielding correlations between acts of approximately .30. Although Mischel did not argue that there was absolutely no consistency in behavior, he certainly attracted attention to the overriding importance of situational factors. Indeed, the whole concept of personality fell out of favor in many circles. It was the heyday of social learning theory and situational specificity was a guiding theme.

Recently we have come to believe that behavior is determined both by enduring behavioral propensities as well as by specific characteristics of situations. The interaction between personality characteristic and situation has been found to account for a greater amount of variance in behavioral measures than either personality factors or situation factors alone (Bowers, 1973; Endler & Magnusson, 1976). We know, for example, that the same situation can be seen differently by different individuals, and that this differential perception is determined by more or less enduring characteristics of the observer (e.g., Dodge, 1986). Thus, although a situation might call out a fairly specific set of behaviors in a given individual, the interpretation of the situation is determined by characterological predispositions of the individual. Whereas John, who is timid, may see a sheep dog as a terrifying animal, Harold, who is bolder, may see it as a potential fuzzy playmate despite the fact that neither has had any previous experience with either friendly or unfriendly canines. People also appear to differ in those behaviors in which they are consistent and those in which they are not (Bem & Allen, 1974), a result of their placing different value and importance on different domains of behavior.

Failures to find temporal and situational consistency in behavior have been attributed to a variety of causes. If continuity is defined as behavioral identity, then behavior may not appear to be very continuous. But if qualitative similarity in behaviors is the criterion of continuity then the picture may be much more impressive. Those who study attachment, for example, argue that the quality of mother-infant attachment reveals itself in later instances of social competence, such as the ability to relate well to one's peers. Thus we would not expect to find a relationship between how securely children are attached to their mothers at the age of 12 months and at 4 years. What we should find is a relationship between security of attachment at 12 months and popularity with peers at the age of 4 years. Some underlying propensity is hypothesized to manifest itself in these two qualitatively different behaviors. The challenge, of course, is to establish criteria for determining which behaviors should, in fact, be considered equivalent at different developmental points.

Another reason why behavioral consistency was hard to establish was the tendency of researchers to rely on only one assessment of the behavior of interest. Lately, however, investigators have begun to realize the importance of measuring a given event several times and/or in several ways. Because there is always error associated with the measurement of any event, it becomes important to make multiple measures in order to obtain a stable estimate of the variable of interest. With multiple measures, errors tend to average out. Rushton, Brainerd, and Pressley (1983) have described a number of areas of research in which single measures of behaviors lead one to assume that there is little behavioral consistency, whereas multiple measures lead to the opposite conclusion. In the domain of attachment between a mother and her infant, for example, consistency of behavior between 12 and 18 months of age is low when individual measures of attachment are correlated ($r = .12$, on average). When individual measures—seeking proximity and contact, maintaining contact, resisting, avoiding mother, etc.—are considered together as a measure of attachment the correlation rises to .44. In the first case the conclusion has to be that there is not continuity in the quality of the infant's attachment to his mother. In the second case the conclusion has to be that there is continuity.

SOCIAL INTERACTIONS

For Watson infancy and childhood were a formative period during which society's training was done. He urged parents to be unemotional and rational in their dealings with children, picturing them as blacksmiths shaping metal at a forge. This was an image that dominated research for many years. Parents affected children, and no one was very interested in the possibility that children might affect parents. On reflection and with the wisdom of hindsight, it is naive to think that children are reactive to events around them while socializing agents are not. But investigators continued to concentrate their energies on the single organism, ignoring the human responsive qualities of those in the child's environment. In part this was due to the complexity of analyzing exchanges in a social situation as well as to the view of the child as a relatively powerless and passive organism.

A social interaction involves, by definition, at least two people. Sears, as early as 1951, urged that students of social behavior develop methods for studying the dyad, that is, the two people involved in any social exchange. He pointed out that the participants in a social situation influence each other, and that an adequate analysis must deal with their mutual effects. The idea of the dyad was easier to understand when psychologists began to view the child as spontaneously active, an image promoted by Piagetian theory as well as by modifications of psychoanalytic theory depicting the ego as developing autonomously rather than emerging from the id. Rheingold (1969), in an influential paper, reminded psychologists of the impressive power of the young infant to manipulate its caretaker by the simple but incredibly effective device of crying. No one exposed to the piercing cries of an unhappy baby could fail to note that even very young organisms wield great influence in the process of socialization—so aversive is that cry that parents will do almost anything to stop it.

Sensitivity to children's contribution to their own development was further enhanced by Richard Bell's argument that congenital temperamental differences in children affect how they react to parent discipline, and that parents adjust their behavior accordingly (Bell, 1968). Difficult children require punitive behavior from their parents in order to comply. Thus it is not that punitive parents produce difficult children, as is frequently believed, but that difficult children produce punitive parents.

More and more, attention has been shifting to the mutually interactive process that goes on in the course of social exchange. When peers fight, for example, this social interaction is comprehended better by studying events that precede and follow a hostile act, rather than focusing only on the hostile act. The former dyadic analysis suggests which social events are likely to elicit aggression, which reactions this aggression elicits from others, and how these reactions suppress, maintain, or promote even more aggression. By making detailed observations of interactions among family members, Patterson and Cobb (1971) demonstrated that young children often bring punishment on themselves and that some even train their mothers to be physically assaultive by responding only to highly coercive forms of persuasion. Rather than looking at the products or outcomes of socialization, then, these investigators have concerned themselves with processes of interaction. Positive social behavior must also be understood in the context of social interaction. Babies engage in lovable behavior. They coo and smile and cuddle, thereby eliciting and rewarding adult attention. In many situations both children and adults enjoy being imitated and so they react positively to and encourage this social act (Grusec & Abramovitch, 1982).

So great has been the recent emphasis on the child's contribution to adult- child interactions that we now run the risk of underemphasizing the important role played by adults. When new ideas assert themselves the pendulum often swings too far too fast. Intrigued by the notion that abused children contribute to their own fate, for example, researchers have probably attributed too much responsibilty for their plight to these children themselves. Adults are older, more experienced, and more powerful. One must be careful to assign them their due. Some of the ways in which the relative contributions of adult and child to a given social situation can be assessed will be discussed in Chapter 2.

INDIVIDUALS AND THE SOCIAL SYSTEM

The social behavior of children cannot be understood adequately unless one takes into account how that behavior affects the reactions of others. Nor can it be understood except as part of the even larger social context that goes far beyond the immediate situation. The social system in which the acts of individuals are embedded must be considered. The growing child is subjected to a variety of influences—parents, peer groups, relatives, school, media, clubs—all of which leave their imprint. Most important, these influences interact with and modify each other's impact. Thus a child who is part of a loving relationship with parents he respects may be unaffected by the antisocial acts of a peer or even actively oppositional to them. A rebellious child whose family relationships are troubled may be much more easily swayed by the same antisocial acts. For some children, then, deviant peers could increase antisocial behavior through modeling and reinforcement, have no effect because parents were more potent models and sources of reinforcement, or decrease antisocial behavior by making the prosocial teachings of parents more salient.

The importance of the complex environment in which individuals find themselves was emphasized by Kurt Lewin. Lewin talked about the "life space": all those factors determining an individual's behavior at a given point in time. He refused to reduce behavior to its molecular components, or to seek explanations in terms of past history or conditioning experiences. For Lewin, interest was to be focused on the entire psychological impact of a situation on the individual who was in it.

A concern with the total environment also characterized the work of Roger Barker, one of Lewin's students. Barker was an "ecological psychologist" who studied the mutual accommodation between the developing organism and its entire changing environment. He felt that any science of behavior must be aware of the full extent of events having an impact on the individual. Therefore, he set out to describe the child's total environment, making a complete and detailed record of children's behavior and experience over the course of entire days (Barker & Wright, 1955).

Barker and Wright's work did not redirect the thrust of research in social development. Although acknowledged as an interesting idea, the problem of how to summarize or relate the totality of events in the child's environment to psychological outcomes remained a serious one. It was much more manageable with the then current conceptual and methodological techniques to look at the operation of only a few variables at a time. Modern methodological and statistical advances have, however, made it easier to put the tenets of ecological psychology into operation.

Although Barker emphasized the importance of knowing about the environment of the child, he concerned himself only with those events that were occurring in the child's immediate surroundings. For Urie Bronfen-brenner (1977), who has recently urged consideration of the complex and changing environment in which developing organisms find themselves, that environment includes not only immediate temporal and physical events but the much wider social world. Thus a child's environment contains the immediate setting (e.g., nursery school), other major settings in which he or she is a participant at one time or another (e.g., home, friend's house), major institutions of society (e.g., the world of work, agencies of government, communication facilities), and the ideology of society (e.g., formal and informal rules about how life should be conducted). Many research findings show how these nested structures have an impact on the child. Divorce is frequently followed by less effective maternal discipline and disturbed behavior on the part of the child, but not when the father provides psychological support for the mother's parental role (Hetherington, Cox, & Cox, 1978). Child abuse is more frequent among mothers who have little external physical or psychological help for child care and are economically deprived (Garbarino, 1976; Steinberg, Catalano, & Dooley, 1981).

A good historical example of how the impact of given events on a young child can be altered dramatically, depending on the social context in which they occur, is offered by Burns and Goodnow (1979). The first generation of Australian settlers were mainly convicts. Although the crimes for which they were deported were often minor, the conditions under which they lived in Australia were not likely to induce a strong interest in family life, nor regular and moral habits. They did, however, reproduce prolifically, and there was little confidence that the next generation was likely to fare any better than the first. Even in the 1790s it was known that cultures of poverty perpetuate themselves. But life was different in a new land. Inspired by the current philosophy that even offspring of the most degraded parents could be educated into virtue, the authorities established schools. Moreover, an alternative to the lifestyle of their parents was genuinely open to the second generation in a colony where the need for labor was very great and jobs were readily available. Finally, adolescent rebellion took as its form a rejection of parental licentiousness and criminality in favor of temperance, industry, and honesty. The second generation thus became sober, steady, self-respecting citizens. Familial conditions that ought to have produced deviant behavior did not when the cultural context was altered.

KNOWLEDGE AND APPLICATION

Although not at the level of the individual organism, one other kind of interaction deserves our attention, that between science and practical problems. Developmental psychology differs from most other subareas of psychology in its origins. Rather than emerging from an academic setting, the field grew out of a need for practical information (Sears, 1975). Children had to be educated, delinquents had to be reformed, and the emotionally disturbed had to be helped. With pressing problems to be solved and an optimistic faith in the value of science that characterized the times, it was natural that scientific input should be welcomed. World War I, for example, produced an upsurge of interest in educational research because large-scale testing of recruits revealed for the first time that a great many American males were illiterate. In 1917 the Iowa Child Welfare Research Station was established, based on the premise that if research could improve cows and hogs it could improve children. (Sears notes the lack of universal agreement with this sentiment. The forces of science, however, did prevail.) Money to fund several institutions of child study in both the United States and Canada was made available by the Laura Spelman Rockefeller Memorial Fund and provided a major impetus to developmental research.

At the same time developmental psychology was making inroads into academic settings. James Mark Baldwin, G. Stanley Hall, John B. Watson, as well as other eminent figures in the area such as John Dewey and Edward Thorndike, were academics. The Institutes of Child Study established by Rockefeller funding were attached to universities. The opportunities for cross-fertilization between practical problems and scientific methodology and knowledge were extensive.

To a certain extent these opportunities are being realized, and developmental psychologists are involved currently in much research relevant to pressing social developmental problems. To highlight the close link between academic psychology and social issues we have chosen, in the last section of this book, to discuss some of this applied research.

Summary

The purpose of this book is to describe the process of development in the social domain and to try and understand how the human organism changes as it interacts with its environment. Several theories have been advanced to organize this understanding, but these theories must be seen as heavily influenced by the political and historical context in which they developed. Even the concept of childhood is one that has changed over time, depending on economic and philosophical considerations.

The first important modern theory of development was psychoanalytic theory. Its major focus was thought and feeling. Freud argued that early experience as the child passes through various biologically determined psychosexual stages leaves irreversible effects on the developing personality. Erikson characterized stages in terms of psychosocial conflicts, focusing less on maturational events and more on the effects of socialization. He also proposed many more stages than Freud, extending them into old age.

The cognitive aspect of psychoanalytic theory is concerned with the development of the ego which helps the organism adjust to the demands of reality. Freud's emphasis on biology can be seen in terms of the time and place in which he formulated his theory: It emerges from a European philosophical tradition that describes events as they are, rather than focusing on how they can be changed. Social learning theory, on the other hand, flourished in North America where the dominant theme was the ability of the individual to be altered and improved. Experience plays a central role. The emphasis is on behavior although the theory's major proponent, Bandura, has emphasized that behavior cannot be understood in the absence of an understanding of mental activity. Learning through observation of others is an important feature of the approach, as are the concepts of self-regulation of behavior and personal efficacy.

Cognitive developmental theory oriented American psychologists to the importance of developmental stages and to the fact that organisms actively respond to or ignore experience depending on their readiness to accept it. Although Piaget focused on the child's developing knowledge about the physical world, characteristics of children's thinking at different stages also have an impact on their dealings with the social world.

A recent focus in North American developmental psychology has come from the ethological tradition whose distinguishing mark is the viewing of behavior from an evolutionary perspective. Its greatest impact has been methodological, promoting an interest in the observation of children in their natural settings. Finally, developmental psychobiology orients researchers to the interplay between the organism—an accumulation of biology and experience—and its environment. Maturation and experience are fused.

No one theoretical position currently dominates the field. But one theme does seem to emerge, and that is that nothing can be studied or understood in isolation from its context. The theme reveals itself in several areas. Behavior must be understood in the context of accompanying thought and affect. The effects of biology and environment are closely interconnected in the developing organism. Behavior has to be seen as a function of some core of relatively continuous personality and the situation in which individuals find themselves. The social behavior of children cannot be understood unless one takes into account the effects of their behavior on others. Finally, behavior must be understood not only in terms of the immediate setting in which it occurs, but also in response to other settings in which the child participates, that is, major institutions of society and the ideology of society.

2
Methodology: History and Issues

There are many legitimate ways of understanding human experience and behavior. Poets, novelists, historians, philosophers, and psychologists all have a contribution to make to the task of comprehending the human condition. Each, of course, has a distinctive way of going about the task of studying people. What is special about the psychological approach is a belief that experience can be understood through the use of scientific methodology. One of the hallmarks of the psychologist's approach, then, is a concern with the collection and analysis of data carried out according to the tenets of scientific methodology. Its essence is that it is based in methods of science developed within the last 100 years. These methods require that events being studied can be observed publicly, that objective rules of evidence are established, and that a common terminology is employed to aid communication. So important is methodology that the development of methodological approaches is nearly as important in the history of the discipline as is the development of substantive knowledge. Without advances in methodology, many advances in knowledge would be impossible.

Because methodology is so central to the psychological pursuit, it is hardly surprising to find that much energy has been expended in trying to decide on the best method for providing scientific answers to psychological questions. In fact, debates about the best way of going about the psychological enterprise have, at times, become quite heated. For a variety of reasons some of the most intense questioning has occurred in the area of social development. Thus a historical survey of approaches to the scientific study of social development comprises a large part of the history of the field in general. Such a survey, which is the subject of this chapter, parallels and intertwines with the historical material described in Chapter 1. We do not attempt to offer a comprehensive overview of methodological, design, or statistical issues in social developmental psychology. We will focus on those controversies we consider among the more important in shaping the direction in which the field has headed.

How Methodology Determines the Questions Asked

It is interesting to note that certain psychological questions cannot be addressed adequately until methodological tools for dealing with them have been developed. When they cannot be addressed, they are most frequently ignored. The area of social interaction is a case in point. Influences in social relationships are bidirectional. This point was made in Chapter 1. However, until the advent of methodological techniques enabling researchers to determine what was going on in a sequence of interactions, and to determine the nature of the effect of one person's behavior on another in this sequence, the issue could not be studied satisfactorily. As a result, notions of reciprocal influence never played a prominent role in developmental theories. In this sense, then, methodological deficiencies were responsible for a somewhat narrowed view of the world.

The contribution of technological advances in furthering scientific analysis also should be noted here. One difficulty for investigators studying social interaction is the sheer volume of what they must observe. Limitations on the human capacity for information processing have sharply curtailed the kinds of questions that could be asked. The development of automated recording devices in the last few years, however, has changed the situation dramatically. Videorecording equipment, which can be carried easily and is relatively inexpensive, enables scientists to obtain a permanent record of interactions that can be viewed repeatedly in order to analyze all it contains. Equipment that allows events to be recorded by observers as they occur, and simultaneously analyzed statistically, also has led to major changes in the kind of knowledge that can be acquired. The amazing development of computer technology in the last few years now permits statistical analysis of prodigious amounts of material that would not have been possible only a short while ago.

Changing Fashions in Methodology

In our historical survey we will discuss how certain methodological approaches are widely utilized, abandoned, and then reappear among the research techniques of psychologists. This does not mean that psychologists are not making progress in their approach to methodology. Observational studies of children, for example, were very popular in the 1930s: They have reappeared in the 1970s and 1980s. What makes contemporary observational studies different, however, is a breakthrough in the ease with which recording can be done and hence the detail in which observations can be analyzed. Also, the level of statistical sophistication that is possible has increased dramatically in terms of the advent of new statistical techniques and the development of computer facilities alluded to earlier. Because of this increased sophistication more inferences can be drawn from the collected data.

Sometimes methodological approaches fall out of favor because their inadequacies become glaring and their usefulness is, as a result, seen to be limited. When new developments offer a way to correct these serious limitations their use is revitalized. A case in point is the correlational approach, which was the predominant methodolgy used during the 1950s in the area of social development. It offered an apparently insoluble source of frustration because it did not enable investigators to make causal inferences about the relationships they were studying. If aggression in the child and harsh punishment in the parent were correlated, for example, was it because parents made children aggressive by the kind of behavioral example they provided, was it that the child's recalcitrant behavior forced the parent to extremes in the discipline encounter, or was it because parent and child shared some genetic tendency toward aggressive behavior? In the absence of any method for untangling the confusion, researchers gave up the approach in favor of an experimental methodology which allowed them to make inferences about the direction of causal relationships. In recent years, however, statisticians have developed such techniques as time-lagged correlational analysis and causal modeling (approaches described later in the chapter), which allow investigators, using correlational data, to choose between competing models of causal relationships and eliminate those that are shown to be implausible by the data. With a serious limitation lessened, the correlational method has returned to favor, particularly in situations where the manipulation of variables is impossible or undesirable.

Early Studies of Social Development

THE 1930S: OBSERVATIONAL STUDIES

One of the major journals in the area of developmental psychology, *Child Development*, began publication in 1930. Perusal of its early issues provides a good sampling of the nature of research activity in social development during the late 1920s and the 1930s. The largest proportion of studies was devoted to cognitive development. But social development received attention as well. By and large, studies were of children in nursery school settings with data consisting primarily of observations made of the children in situations where no variables were manipulated. Thus researchers were describing events as they occurred in the natural world of the child. In these early studies data analysis was generally descriptive and confined to numerical summaries of the material observed.

In a representative study, Smith (1932) reported on the preschool child's use of criticism. From a previous investigation in which 20,000 sentences spoken by children between the ages of 2 and 6 years had been collected, Smith selected all those that expressed criticism of another adult or child. Altogether, 325 instances of criticism were identified. In the early preschool years, Smith reported, criticisms are initially directed to someone other than the source of the child's problem. They are apparently intended to solicit help, and are generally of a tattling nature. Increasingly, as children grow older, they direct their criticism to the person who is the object of that criticism. The most frequent complaints, Smith observed, were of interference, lack of knowledge, failure to conform, and undesirable personal traits.

1940s TO 1960s: CORRELATIONAL STUDIES OF PARENT EFFECTS

In the 1940s attention turned more to the home and the role of parents in the social development of their children. With this increased emphasis on parenting, studies began to be guided by hypotheses derived from theory—primarily psychoanalytic theory and, later, learning theory—rather than being relatively atheoretical in their nature as had been the case in the 1930s. During the 1940s, then, we begin to see some of the classic studies of the forces directing personality development. Mothers were interviewed about their early child-rearing practices in such areas as feeding (e.g., whether or not their child was fed on a strict schedule and the severity with which the child was weaned) and toilet training. These practices were correlated with the child's subsequent personality characteristics, with personality characteristics often measured using projective techniques. In 1957 Sears, Maccoby, and Levin published a book describing the results of a large-scale study of the child-rearing practices of 379 mothers living in the Boston area. Each mother in their sample was asked 72 open-ended questions about her practices in the areas of feeding, toilet training, sex, dependency, and aggression, as well as how restrictive and demanding she was of her child. In addition she was asked to describe her child's behavior in these domains. Sears et al. were thus able to learn how it is that mothers raise their children and, by correlating maternal techniques with maternal reports of child behavior, gained some idea of what approaches might be most effective.

Methods of Data Collection and Analysis

In these various studies of social and personality development the main tool of research was the interview. The informant was usually the mother, and the results of her reports were usually distilled into a set of ratings. Some research also elicited information on parent behavior from children. Most frequently, the mother served both as a source of information about her own child-rearing practices as well as the behavior of her child. Very

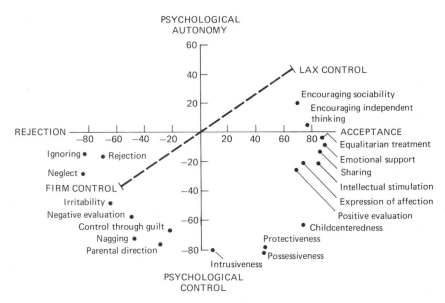

FIGURE 2.1. Children's reports of parent behavior. From "A Configurational Analysis of Children's Reports of Parent Behavior" by E.S. Schaefer, 1965, *Journal of Consulting Psychology, 29*, 552–557. Copyright 1965 by the American Psychological Association. Reprinted by permission.

occasionally investigators would actually observe the behavior of parent and child in the home, although the technique was generally avoided for reasons that are not altogether clear. When observation was actually carried out the recording was very informal and, therefore, open to distorting influences by an investigator who probably already had some preformed notions of what he or she might observe.

Raw data yielded by the interview or infrequently by observation, even when they were translated into ratings, provided a markedly complex picture of parent-child interaction. To reduce this complexity and to identify some of the underlying dimensions, raw measures often were submitted to factor or cluster analysis. Using these statistical techniques, researchers were able to identify a relatively small number of factors that could account for the pattern of intercorrelations among the much larger number of measures yielded by the various rating scales. One example of such an approach is provided in the work of Earl Schaefer (1965). Schaefer's basic data were provided from children's reports of their parent's behavior. His conceptual model of parent behavior is shown in Figure 2.1. The model consists of three dimensions: acceptance-rejection, psychological autonomy-psychological control, and firm control-lax control. When these dimensions are plotted, as in Figure 2.1, they provide a visual aid for understanding the nature of the dimensions. For the sake of simplicity only those raw variables that define the first two dimensions are shown in Figure 2.1.

Other investigators have generated models yielding dimensions similar to those of Schaefer. For Becker (1964), analysis of psychologists' ratings of parental behavior yielded three dimensions as well: warmth-hostility, anxious emotional involvement-calm detachment, and restrictiveness-permissiveness. Clearly, there is some overlap between the two sets of dimensions, although other investigators (e.g., Baumrind 1973), starting from a different set of theoretical assumptions and working within a different framework, found somewhat different dimensions of parent behavior. Indeed, it must be recognized that the dimensions that emerge from a factor analysis depend entirely on the kind of variables that are entered into the analysis in the first place. Baumrind included parental use of reasoning and responsiveness in her measures and so obtained dimensions reflecting these characteristics in her data summaries; dimensions that could not be obtained by Schaefer and Becker because they did not collect the relevant data.

Another way of trying to understand the underlying structure of parent behavior and attitudes, that is, to see which practices and attitudes tend to occur together, is to "eyeball" the correlations between individual ratings or behavior counts (in the case of observational data) and form clusters of variables accordingly. Using this approach Lytton (1980) discovered that correlations of mother's characteristics (and father's, although to a lesser extent) fell essentially into three clusters: affection (warmth, praise, responsiveness), negative control (punishment, criticism, restrictiveness), and positive control (reasoning, consistency of rule enforcement, encouragement of independence).

Limitations of the Methodology

This general methodology of questioning mothers about their own actions and that of their children had its limitations. Although some relationships did emerge with some consistency across different studies addressing the same issues, there were many inconsistencies. Moreover, the correlations reported by investigators were usually very low.

One investigator who early expressed concern with the limitations of the approach was Yarrow (1963). She pointed out that mothers talking about themselves and their children are extremely ego-involved reporters. Thus it was important for mothers in these studies to present themselves in as good a light as possible. Moreover, because their reports dealt with an area in which much expert advice was available, they were probably contaminated by the effects of this advice. Indeed, argued Yarrow, there was probably no other area in psychology in which such heavy reliance had been placed on self-report without a compensating exercise of extreme caution in interpretation of the data. As well, the research interview required mothers to make very difficult discriminations and syntheses by characterizing their general approach to child rearing rather than describing their actual behavior. By asking for modal behaviors, which is what interviewers did when they made such inquiries as "What do you do when your child asks for help?" or "What do you do when your child gets into a fight with another child?," investigators were not tapping the complexity of parent activity. They were not finding out what the effect of different situations was on how mothers behaved, or how the mother's momentary psychological state affected her actions, or how children's developmental level determined what happened to them. Ignored as well was the fact that parent practices change over time, in concert with the degree of success or failure the parent is experiencing. Thus a parent may begin with reasoning, accelerate to physical punishment, and subside to withdrawal of love as a child attempts to inhibit certain acts. To ask a mother how she typically responds to her child's anger is to lose the nuances of this changing approach.

There were other difficulties with these procedures, all of which Yarrow noted. It is evident that when parents are asked to rate their children on certain dimensions they may not have referents for the behavior, or they may have referents that vary. How, for example, can one rate the aggressiveness of one's child independent of extensive experience, which most mothers lack, with aggressiveness in other children? Another problem arose in these early studies when mothers not only provided information about themselves, but about their children as well. This served as an undesirable source of contamination because how a mother viewed her child's behavior would be very affected by the attitudes and beliefs she had about different classes of behavior. A mother who was very restrictive in her child-rearing practices, for example, would be more prone to identify anything her child did as negative, whereas the child's behavior might appear much more positive in the eyes of a less demanding observer.

A final problem we note in the use of maternal reports of parent and child behavior is the fact that maternal recall of past events involving their own and their children's behavior is notoriously poor. We see evidence of this in a study carried out by Wenar and Coulter (1962). They elicited the cooperation of mothers who had sought help from a child guidance clinic some 3 to 6 years earlier. The mothers were asked questions similar to those they had been asked at the time of their initial contact. To increase the chances that consistent information would be provided they were asked to remember information they had provided at the time of the initial interview rather than to talk about their present feelings and attitudes. Mothers were accurate in their recall only 67% of the time, hardly an encouraging figure for those interested in learning something about a child's past history. Some information was remembered more accurately than other information. The great majority of mothers remembered whether their children had been breast or bottle fed, what illnesses they had had, and whether or not they were wanted. They were not so good, however, at providing consistent information about how they themselves had felt about the problem that brought them to the child guidance center initially, about their health during pregnancy, the relationship of their child to his parents, or the discipline techniques they had initially reported using.

Refinements in Correlational Methodology

As researchers studying the developmental process became more attuned to some of the difficulties associated with interview and questionnaire studies, they began to refine their methodologies. They avoided the use of mothers as informants about all aspects of family life, asked them only about recent practices and events, and avoided asking them to make inferences about their children's behavior. In addition, they used other techniques to assess psychological functioning. A study by Hoffman and Saltzstein (1967) provides one example of increasing variation in methodology.

Hoffman and Saltzstein were interested in the relationship between children's moral development and the child-rearing practices used by their parents. In order to assess the level of moral development, they employed four approaches when interviewing children. The first was a projective measure of guilt, in which subjects were asked to complete a story about a child who had transgressed (e.g., a child who cheated in a swimming race and won, or a child whose negligence contributed to the death of another child), describing what the story protagonist felt and thought and what happened afterwards. These stories were coded for guilt—extreme guilt, for example, was coded if the protagonist underwent a personality change or committed suicide. In the second measure, children were requested to make judgments about a variety of hypothetical moral transgressions, with judgments rated as having an orientation toward control by fear ("Your parents will be angry with you") or control by internal means ("It's wrong to violate someone's trust in you"). Hoffman and Saltzstein also assessed children's overt reactions to their own misdeeds by asking teachers and mothers to describe how the child typically responded after transgression. Their final measure of moral development employed a sociometric technique, with children nominating classmates who were most likely to care about the feelings of others and to defend people who were being ridiculed.

When they assessed parent behavior these investigators also extended the techniques used by early pioneers in the field. Both parents, not just mothers, were asked to imagine four concrete situations involving a child who misbehaved, that is, who did not comply immediately with the parent's request, engaged in careless destruction, talked back, and failed academically. They then were asked to select from a list of discipline techniques how they would respond at present and how they would have responded several years earlier. In another measure of parental behavior the children themselves were asked to say what their parents would do in each of these situations (although they were not asked to describe their early behavior).

Although these various approaches led to great improvements in the quality of research being conducted by social developmentalists, all was not well. The major problem was that correlational studies do not allow for causal inferences. The time was ripe for a new approach, and such an approach arrived with a vengeance in the 1960s.

Experimental Studies of Social Development

Experimentation was not new to psychology. For many years it had been employed in the study of learning, physiological psychology, comparative psychology, and even social psychology. This reflected the belief that the predominant model of the physical sciences was the appropriate one for psychologists to adopt. As the results of traditional studies of personality and social development became less satisfying, and the limitations of methodology more bothersome, investigators turned with enthusiasm to a model highly regarded by the majority of psychologists.

EARLY STUDIES

It is not that experimentation was unknown in the developmental area. Indeed, there had been sufficient isolated examples of the approach throughout several decades preceding the 1960s to provide substantial material for a review, in 1960, by Sidney Bijou and Donald Baer of the laboratory-experimental study of child behavior. In that review Bijou and Baer reiterated the experimentalist's belief that the complexities of the child's real world are merely combinations of simple processes that are best studied under the controlled conditions of the laboratory. Psychologists, they declared, must first study the parts of the child. Then they could see if the whole child was more than the sum of his parts, as opponents of the experimental approach maintained.

Most of the early experiments conducted with children were designed simply to reveal that a variety of responses could be produced in this particular group of organisms using techniques of instrumental and classical conditioning. Kantrow (1937) showed that a buzzer paired with a nursing bottle could come to elicit sucking in the absence of the bottle even in very young infants. More recent studies revealed that smiling and vocalizing could be instrumentally conditioned in babies using social reinforcers such as smiling and touching (Brackbill, 1958; Rheingold, Gewirtz, & Ross, 1959), and that cooperative behavior could be established in 7- to 12-year-olds by using candy as the reinforcer (Azrin & Lindsley, 1956).

In a somewhat different domain, Davis, Sears, Miller, and Brodbeck

(1948) found that breast-fed infants engaged in more nonnutritive sucking than cup-fed infants. They concluded that this supported the hypothesis from learning theory that sucking would increase when reinforced, rather than support the psychoanalytic hypothesis that sucking is a biologically based drive demanding certain amounts of gratification. In an elaborate and important study, Harriet Rheingold (1956) served as the sole caretaker of some institutionalized infants for $7\frac{1}{2}$ hours a day, 5 days a week, for 2 months: She found that these children were more socially responsive than those cared for under the more typical regime of multiple caretaking. These last two studies represent attempts to make experimental conditions more natural, or closer to the events of the child's everyday existence. Thus they were conducted in the child's natural environment ("the field") instead of in experimental laboratories. In addition, the Sears et al. study was a "natural" experiment, that is, it depended on a phenomenon that happened to occur naturally (the decision of some mothers, on the recommendation of their doctor, to cup feed rather than breast feed very young babies) rather than being manipulated by an experimenter.

LABORATORY ANALOGUES OF REALITY

The use of laboratory experimental methodology, however, became the technique of choice during the 1960s. It was during that decade, and the early 1970s, that journals devoted to issues of social development were filled with descriptions of studies designed as laboratory analogues of reality. One of the leaders in the area was Albert Bandura, whose work was influenced by the pioneering efforts of Kurt Lewin in social psychology. Bandura devised elaborate procedures to mimic some of the processes which he believed to go on during childhood socialization.

Most of Bandura's experimental attention during the 1960s was focused on the phenomenon of imitation. A study by Bandura, Ross, and Ross (1963a) is typical of the way he proceeded to investigate the imitative process. In this particular study, Bandura et al. wished to compare three theories of why imitation, or identification, occurs. The three theories are known as the status envy, social power, and secondary reinforcement theories. The first says that children become like individuals who consume desirable resources, the second that they become like individuals who control desirable resources, and the third that they become like individuals who give them desirable resources. In the first two cases, young people are said, through identification, to vicariously enjoy valuable resources whereas, in the third case, they become like those who dispense rewards because the characteristics of the dispenser are secondarily reinforcing. To assess the three theories, the researchers invited nursery children to a "surprise room" in the school where they met two adults: an adult who either had candy, interesting toys, and other attractive objects (in the social power and secondary reinforcement conditions) or who was given these objects (in the status envy condition). In the secondary reinforcement condition the adult, in addition, gave these items to the child. The adult then engaged in a series of distinctive behaviors and the child was observed to see the extent to which these behaviors were imitated. In fact, there was less imitation in the status envy than in the other two conditions.

Many others, besides Bandura, studied social development experimentally. One specific paradigm was borrowed directly from the animal laboratory. In the late 1950s, Richard Solomon studied the development of resistance to temptation and guilt in puppies (Solomon, Turner, & Lessac, 1968). He swatted these puppies with a rolled-up newspaper either just as they approached a bowl of horse meat or several seconds after they had begun to eat it. Solomon found no difference in the speed with which the animals learned not to eat the horse meat when the trainer was in the same room. How they behaved when they were alone, however, was of greater interest for anyone interested in conscience, or the suppression of prohibited behavior in the absence of surveillance. Solomon found that animals punished early showed greater resistance to temptation, when alone, than those punished after they were well embarked on the forbidden response. The latter group of puppies was also influenced by their training, however, showing much agitation and anxiety (guilt?) when they had finished eating the forbidden horse meat. This paradigm was adapted for the study of conscience development in children, with the substitution of attractive toys for horse meat and a loud buzzer for the rolled-up newspaper (Aronfreed & Reber, 1965; Parke, 1974). In a number of studies, for example, Parke and his collaborators manipulated such variables as the loudness of the punishing buzzer, its time of onset, the consistency of its application, and whether or not rationales for not deviating were provided to subjects. From the results of these studies they drew a number of conclusions about the effectiveness of punishment on the inhibition of response in young children. Some of these studies are described in Chapter 5.

THE ONSET OF DISCONTENT

The laboratory experiment, as we have noted, dominated social developmental psychology in the 1960s and early 1970s. In most of the rest of psychology it had been the method of choice for many years. Now developmental psychology, and the study of social developmental processes, was put on the same scientific footing as "rigorous areas" such as learning and physiological psychology, not to mention physics and chemistry. Control over variables had been achieved, causality could be inferred, and people's ingenuity in devising experimental situations which appeared to tap into real-life psychological processes was marked. The scientific study of social development was well on its way.

Rumblings of discontent began to be heard, however, early in the 1970s. Indeed, experimental social psychologists were already engaged in a period of intensive self-doubt and self-examination (e.g., Gergen, 1973), and their concerns naturally spread to the domain of children's developing social behaviors. Criticisms of existing approaches in social development focused on two areas. First, it was argued that the experimental paradigm was an inappropriate one for gaining an understanding of human social behavior because of the virtual impossibility of mimicking the complexities of real life in an artificial setting. Second, the view was expressed that psychology had tried to move too quickly by leaving out the crucial stage of scientific description. Instead of finding out what phenomena needed explanation by cataloging the range of children's behavior, psychologists had behaved as though this was already known and had jumped immediately to the stage of explanation. In their laboratories, then, they were not discovering how children behave in natural settings or which real world phenomena needed investigation. They had already moved to the stage of trying to explain why children behave as they do under contrived, and possibly unrealistic, conditions.

Another development that cast a shadow over the initial popularity of the laboratory experiment was an increasing concern with the ethics of research and a growing opinion that it was unacceptable to subject children to manipulations designed, for example, to make them more aggressive or less self-controlled. It became more difficult to justify the use of punishment, such as a loud buzzer, to investigate social developmental processes. These ethical concerns began to limit the kinds of issues that could be addressed experimentally.

Criticism of the Laboratory Experimental Approach

A number of critics began to argue strongly that the logical positivist approach, although successful in the physical sciences, was not appropriate for the study of social behavior. They expressed strong misgivings about the belief that knowledge of cause and effect relationships in the real world could be gained by manipulating events in an artifical situation (e.g., an empty room in the nursery school, or a trailer specially designed for research parked in the school yard, and then looking at the consequence of this manipulation on some dependent measure reflecting an operational definition of the psychological construct of interest. Laboratory experiments, they claimed, lack ecological validity, that is, the relationships between two variables observed in this artifical setting bear little or no relationship to the events of a real-life setting they are supposed to mimic. Indeed, Bronfenbrenner (1977), in an oft-quoted remark, noted that much of contemporary developmental psychology was "the science of the strange behavior of children in strange situations with strange adults for the briefest possible periods of time" (p. 513).

Because of the lack of ecological validity, little was to be gained in understanding many typical social interactions. The frequently highly emotionally charged discipline situation, for example, was not well studied by looking at how children react when a strange experimenter forbids them to play with an arbitrarily designated toy and sounds a loud buzzer when they fail to heed this instruction. Although the study of physical objects or of simple perceptual or cognitive processes in human beings might well be appropriately carried out in a laboratory setting without undue interference with natural reactions, such was not the case—the argument went—with the study of human social behavior. In the latter case, individuals who were objects of study could not fail to be influenced by their involvement with an experimenter and an experiment, and their perceptions, expectations, and beliefs about what was happening to them would interfere with their more natural reactions. It was these natural reactions, however, that laboratory investigators were trying to study but whose comprehension was denied to them because of the tendency of human beings to try and find meaning in whatever situation they find themselves in. Furthermore, the experimental situation was not adequate for studying social interactions because it lacked the reciprocity that exists in real-life situations where adults are affected by children rather than having complete control over the situation. Finally, children do not have the history of a complex emotional relationship with an experimenter that they do with parents or teachers. Thus their laboratory behavior will be modified accordingly.

It should be noted that these arguments were not new. Indeed, Kroger (1982) has recently pointed out that the father of experimental psychology, Wilhelm Wundt, had never intended that the experimental method be extended to the investigation of social behavior. Wundt argued for two kinds of psychology. Experimental methodology, he felt, was useful only for the study of mental processes on the most basic sensory level. Aspects of human experience reflecting the impact of social and cultural factors, on the other hand, were more appropriately the subject matter of an interpretive and historical Voelkerpsychologie (psychology of peoples). The presence of others, Wundt maintained, could in no way be considered the mere equivalent of any physical stimulus. And yet this is how it was being construed by those who chose to study social behavior in the laboratory.

The issue of amenability of their subject matter to experimental manipulation is an interesting one for psychologists. After decades of strong identification with the experimental sciences it was difficult for many to believe that their lot might lie, in whole or in part, with those sciences that were nonexperimental. Yet many highly respectable scientific endeavors are carried out in the absence of experimental manipulation. Astronomy, paleontology, and geology are successful sciences, but they do not employ the experimental method. McCall (1977) notes that the science of epidemiology is not in a state of distress, even though it has not deified the experimental method. Epidemiologists rely on a variety of methodological approaches none of which is, in isolation, completely satisfactory but all of which, in concert, provide valuable insights into understanding the spread of disease. And epidemiologists are quite happy to live with this state of affairs. If an epidemiologist finds that X produces Y in the laboratory, that X and Y are related in a natural setting, and that the introduction of X into a natural setting leads to Y, then he or she is reasonably content that, through the use of converging operations, some understanding of the relationship between X and Y has been obtained.

Is Explanation in Psychology Premature?

In its eagerness to be scientific and achieve the same status as the physical sciences, some argued that psychology had omitted an essential step in the scientific process. Before trying to explain phenomena, it is first necessary to identify the phenomena that need explanation. Any science must go through a descriptive phase in its initial stages before moving to the stage of explanation. This position was argued by McCall (1977), for example, who lamented that after two decades of rapid expansion, made possible by extensive utilization of experimental methodology, developmental psychology still lacked a substantial science of naturalistic developmental processes. Knowledge was of no value, he argued, if it was not relevant to real children growing up in real families in real neighborhoods—a complaint echoed by Bronfenbrenner (1977). The basic issue, according to McCall, was one of "can" versus "does." The laboratory experiment had yielded much information about the conditions that *could* produce certain outcomes. The important question, however, was whether or not, in real life, these conditions *did* produce the specified outcomes. It is true that children will imitate the actions of an adult who is powerful and controls attractive resources. But is this really a major mechanism in the development of personality? Are there other, more important, determinants of the process of personality formation? If a developmental science was to provide answers about real children in real life, then it had to address itself to what happens to those children in real life. After these happenings had been documented it could *then* turn to trying to explain them, using a variety of methodological techniques including, but not confined to, the laboratory experiment.

Naturalistic description, McCall maintained, was not a great delight to many psychologists. Explanation no doubt provides greater intellectual challenge than does simple description. Nevertheless, McCall and others argued that psychologists must become more empirical in their selection of behaviors to investigate, their measurement variables, the age of the subjects studied, and the ecological context in which they were studied: ". . . much of our recent research represents a nearly blind run into a forest of behavior to study the growth of a single tree" (McCall, 1977, p. 337). It was argued that by observing natural development one could establish when behavior was more plastic (by establishing the point in the developmental process at which individuals showed the greatest variability in the behavior of interest), and that observed relationships between variables could suggest causal relationships that might eventually be amenable to experimental investigation, although this might not always be the case.

Some Conclusions

It must not be thought that social developmentalists have moved as one to reject experimentation or to a single-minded concern with description rather than explanation. Bronfenbrenner (1977), for example, denies what many critics were setting up as an explicit dichotomy between relevance and rigor. He points out that, in the final analysis, it is not possible to understand a phenomenon completely unless one can manipulate or control it. For this reason the experiment must always be part of the set of research techniques used by psychologists. He also argues that structured experiments are appropriate at an early stage in science. For instance, had 19th-century biology had our modern knowledge of research strategies, it would have been able to bypass years of painstaking description in arriving at a formulation of laws and principles. Bronfenbrenner suggests that experimentation early in the development of a science may facilitate the identification of more appropriate taxonomies for description of the science's subject matter. Thus phenomena that are assumed to be related may, in fact, be viewed as distinct by virtue of the fact that they react differently to the same experimental manipulation.

The controversy of experiment versus observation and description is by no means resolved. There are still many who argue that psychology will advance best in a laboratory situation where extraneous variables can be excluded and control can be achieved. As Bronfenbrenner points out, the problem is that although one can study physical objects in a vacuum, it is much more difficult to study people in a social vacuum because they have a nasty habit of immediately filling vacuums with meaning. Indeed, the tendency to try to understand strange situations (a tendency revealed by most people who find themselves in psychological experiments) may well be a mechanism that has helped the human race to survive.

The solutions to these problems are not clear. What has happened in psychology, and to a particularly great extent in the area of social developmental psychology, is that in the past few years a whole collection of new methodological approaches has been devised in response to these methodological issues and disputes. These new approaches have allowed investigators to assess the validity of relationships suggested by the older approaches—correlational as well as experimental. They also have enabled researchers to ask new questions that were previously not amenable to scientific investigation and to address old questions in a more adequate way.

New Methods

THE FIELD EXPERIMENT

Despite the example of nonexperimental sciences, some researchers who rejected laboratory experimentation were loathe to forsake entirely the experimental method. One compromise between laboratory control and ecological validity has been the field experiment. Here independent variables can be manipulated and their effects assessed, not in the laboratory, but in the child's everyday world—nursery school, home, or school playground.

A good example of the field experiment is provided in a study by Yarrow, Scott, and Waxler (1973). They were concerned with the extent to which children will imitate concern for others, or altruism, that is displayed by adults they observe. In addition, Yarrow et al. wanted to know whether a warm and nurturant relationship between the adult and the child observing that adult would facilitate imitation. As we have seen, both psychoanalytic and social learning theories of identification suggest this should be the case. Experimental studies of these questions, however, have produced somewhat equivocal answers. Although children certainly imitate altruistic models to whom they are exposed in a laboratory context, nurturance (presented in the form of a 10- or 15-minute pleasant play session between child and model) does not always increase the amount of that imitation (Grusec, 1971; Weissbrod, 1976). Is this because the theories are wrong in the way they construe the socialization of altruism, or is it that there is some characteristic of this particular laboratory situation that does not allow it to provide an adequate test of the hypothesis? Although we note that a short positive interaction between model and child does facilitate the imitation of neutral behaviors (Bandura, Ross, & Ross, 1963a), it might be that the effects of the interaction are different depending on the behavior being modeled. Perhaps, for example, children who see a friendly adult behave altruistically feel less constrained to be generous to others because they are more relaxed. This explanation would mean, however, that the specific experimental situation, by virtue of its properties, is not providing a test of the particular hypothesis intended by the experimenter. Indeed, it may be very difficult to mimic the kind of long-standing and intense relationship that develops between children and significant people in their natural social environment in the laboratory.

In the Yarrow et al. field experiment, nursery school children were assigned to a female teacher who was instructed to be either warm and rewarding or reserved and aloof for a 2-week period of time. (Contrast this treatment with the laboratory manipulation of warmth and nurturance lasting approximately 15 minutes.) The teachers then modeled altruism for the children either by play-acting concern with miniatures of animals and people in distress, or by combining this play training with modeling of help-giving in real situations. Children's altruism to real victims of distress increased primarily when play training and real life help-giving were combined, and primarily when the teacher was warm and rewarding. The conclusion to be drawn is that Yarrow et al., in their field experiment, may have provided a more adequate test of the hypothesis that the modeling of altruism by nurturant caretakers increases children's concern for others. Fifteen-minute friendly interactions between subjects and experimenters may be an inadequate simulation of the kind of relationship that develops between parent and child, or even nursery teacher and child, over a much longer period of time.

In another well-known field experiment Friedrich and Stein (1973) tested the hypothesis that watching television has a marked effect on the behavior of children because of their strong tendency to mimic events observed in that compelling medium. They were particulary interested in finding out whether aggression and violence are modeled and, contrarily, whether prosocial television content could have a positive influence on young viewers. Many laboratory experiments had demonstrated that the observation of aggressive models in carefully controlled settings leads to dramatic increases in the amount of aggression children subsequently display in these settings, with young children emulating the punching and hitting of inflated plastic dolls and reproducing hostile verbalizations. But would these same effects occur as a result of viewing televised material akin to that seen in the home on a television set, and would the behavior actually occur beyond the confines of a laboratory enclosure?

Friedrich and Stein divided children who were attending a nursery school into two groups, one of which watched television programs at school that had highly aggressive content—specifically, "Batman," a television show that was popular at the time. The other group of preschoolers watched, again in the nursery school, the program "Misterogers' Neighborhood," a production intended to foster sensitivity, concern, and good behavior in its young viewers. The children watched their assigned television fare three times a week for 4 weeks. Prior to the experimental manipulation their play behavior in the nursery school had been observed, and after the manipulation it was observed again. Friedrich and Stein found that the children imitated both the antisocial behavior they had observed while watching "Batman," as well as the prosocial behavior observed when watching "Misterogers' Neighborhood." Thus aggressive acts during play periods increased between the premanipulation and postmanipulation observations for the one group, whereas concern for others and responsibility increased for the other groups. Not all children demonstrated these changes in bahavior. Interpersonal aggression increased in frequency only for children who were above average in aggression in the first place and prosocial behavior occurred more frequently only for those children who came from families of lower socioeconomic status. The results, nevertheless, suggest that findings obtained under the controlled conditions of the experimental laboratory also can occur in a less artificial environment.

Field experiments are not the final answer to the dilemma of control versus ecological validity. They do not allow the same amount of control as laboratory experiments. Nor do they, on the other hand, completely preserve naturalness. With reference to the problem of control, it is evident that although an experimenter can, in the laboratory, assure that conditions are identical for all groups except for the variable being manipulated, such rigid control is not possible in the field. Suppose, for example, that a child in Friedrich and Stein's Batman group was hit by another child while being observed during the postmanipulation period. A retaliatory hit might well be observed. But the only way in which the cause of the retaliatory hit could be inferred as resulting from television diet would be if a similar hostile attack were made on a child in the control group and he did not retaliate. Nature does not arrange herself so conveniently, however. As for the issue of ecological validity, field experiments cannot always be completely natural. Although watching television shows in the nursery school may be more akin to real life than observing a grown-up hitting a plastic doll with a hammer in an empty nursery school room, it is still not identical to the child's daily experience. For example, children usually select their own television programs—perhaps within the limits of parent supervision and permission—but they are not generally lined up in front of a television set to avail themselves of a preselected diet of entertainment. The problems this can engender are revealed in a study conducted by Feshbach and Singer (1971). In their study a control group of male adolescents was prohibited from watching any television shows depicting violence and aggression. The subjects rebelled against the manipulation, however, and were eventually allowed to watch one of their favorite programs, "Batman." It is obvious that this change of plan seriously limited any conclusions that could be drawn from the study.

A sharp dichotomy between field and laboratory is, in fact, unnecessary. The two approaches to the acquisition of information can go hand in hand. Yarrow et al., for example, did not confine their experimental activities to the field. Although they manipulated the variable of nurturance in the more natural context of a children's nursery school, they did, in fact, assess the effects of that manipulation in a highly structured and elaborately contrived context. Thus they measured children's altruism by observing their willingness to retrieve some toys that had fallen out of a baby's playpen as well as their willingness to pick up a basket of sewing materials that had fallen off a table. In all cases the test situation was identical for each child, reflecting a degree of control impossible had they waited to observe opportunities for altruism seized or rejected by the children in their everyday interactions in the real world. Indeed, the measurement of a dependent variable in a highly controlled context helps to solve the problem of dealing with behaviors that have a low base rate of occurrence. It may take many hours for the spontaneous occurrence of conditions that could elicit acts of interest. If the experimenter can speed up the frequency of their happening, without distorting the process being studied, so much the better for efficient science.

PASSIVE OBSERVATION: DESCRIPTION AND THE RETURN TO CORRELATIONAL ASSESSMENT

Another response to the increasing unhappiness with virtually exclusive reliance on experimentation was to substitute the use of naturalistic observational techniques. This approach had several advantages. It answered the criticism that psychology was not descriptive enough, for it provided descriptions of what children were actually doing in their everyday worlds. It overcame the objection that psychological research was lacking in ecological validity because it made no attempt to simulate real-life events. In addition, it addressed the ethical problem produced when behavior was manipulated. Although passive observation must be carried out responsibly because it requires intrusion into the private lives of those being observed, at least it does not involve active attempts to change those lives.

A return to observation in the form of more sophisticated questionnaire and interview approaches was one alternative. Increasing awareness of the activities of ethologists, however, provided social developmentalists with a new direction, and the methodology of ethology began to be adopted in the area of developmental psychology (e.g., Blurton Jones, 1972). Just as careful observation of the activities of three-spined sticklebacks, herring gulls, and monkeys in their natural habitats had enabled investigators to gain knowledge about the naturally occurring behavior of these animals, as well as to understand the mechanisms governing it, so too it seemed that careful observation of children in their natural habitats could shed light on their functioning.

Other developments accelerated acceptance of ethological methodology. Portable videotape cameras meant that children's behavior could be recorded as they went about their daily activities without constraining them to one setting. Although the occurrence of a given behavior could be noted on a checklist, the task was made even easier by the invention of automated recording devices. Now the observer could press a key on a box whenever a designated behavior occurred and a computer-readable output would allow immediate summary of the data. Small cassette recorders enabled observers to follow their subjects about, and to record whispered descriptions of behavior in an unobtrusive way. With these sophisticated data-recording techniques, and with the opportunity to review material repeatedly, the level of analysis possible was greatly increased. By the 1970s researchers had become very aware of the fact that the study of social activity must include all members of the group and they were generally eager to study the reciprocal nature of social interactions. Observational methodology made this task easier. Passive observation—a term used by Cook and Campbell (1979) to distinguish this methodology from observation that occurs in all research, including experimentation—still did not allow the researcher to formulate causal inferences. New statistical developments began to make such inferences possible. Some of these statistical developments will be discussed toward the end of this chapter.

The observation of children has a long history. In 1877, for example, Charles Darwin published a report of his son Doddy's behavior and development, focusing on early evidence of fear and anger, and the development of reasoning and morality. Piaget was another famous observer of the behavior of his own children. We have already noted that psychologists during the 1930s routinely observed children's behavior, primarily in nursery school settings. We have noted as well, in Chapter 1, the attempt of Barker and Wright (1955) to record everything that occurred in the child's day from time of waking to falling asleep. Observational studies of the 1970s and 1980s, however, had a new look. They allowed a molecular analysis of behavior. With the help of videotapes, which not only allow repeated viewing but allow the viewing of behavior in slow motion, investigators could describe the behavior and expression of their subjects in extensive and careful detail. Direction of gaze, eyebrow movement, body posture, and position of the mouth all could be considered in ways not previously possible. However, the ability to analyze in such detail has its difficulties. If molecular descriptions of behavior are unguided by theory, the tendency is often to try and describe everything in the data record. Investigators can become mired in the sheer weight of the data they have available to analyze. One is reminded, for example, of the problems experienced by Barker and Wright who had some difficulty in understanding and reducing to manageable proportion the masses of data they collected. For this reason their work had less impact than had they been able to summarize it efficiently. As long as the temptation to observe everything and analyze all possible relationships is avoided, however, the microanalysis of behavior has proved to be a major advance in methodological approaches. The challenge, then, is the collection of manageable amounts of data, something most successfully accomplished when research is guided by specific questions rather than by a general desire to see how people behave in different situations.

Just as the complexity of data collected from parent interviews or questionnaires can be reduced by subjecting it to factor analytic techniques, microdescriptive units of observed behavior also can be combined into macrounits. (Note that if observations are collected in macrounits, for example, "positive response" rather than "smiles," they cannot be broken down into finer microunits—hence there is a further source of temptation to collect data in as specific a form as possible.) Thus whining, teasing, crying, and yelling all could be subsumed under the label of negative or aversive behavior. The important thing here is to make sure that those behaviors described by one label are functionally equivalent for participants in the social relationship. This is not easy to accomplish, although it is attempted by submitting lists of behaviors to judges to see if they consider them equivalent, or by seeing if the various behaviors are facilitated by the same stimuli (e.g., Patterson, 1974).

Another potential source of distortion in data interpretation involves the way in which observations are recorded. Here the problem is one of recording an event each time it occurs—event sampling—or recording what is happening whenever a unit of time, for example, 5 seconds, has passed—time sampling. The first approach provides information about how many times a behavior occurs but not the duration of that behavior. One could ask, for example, whether the effect of one word is the same as that of a string of sentences: Using event sampling techniques, both would be recorded as a single act of vocalization. A measure of duration might present a truer picture of the psychological impact of the event on the recipient. On the other hand, if the event of interest is of short duration, a time sampling measure might miss it if that event fell between the designated points of observation. Yet each instance of the short event might be of major psychological import for the recipient. One way around these problems is, where possible, to make continuous records of the behavior of interest.

The Biasing Effects of an Observer's Presence

No research methodology is perfect, and naturalistic observation is no exception. One difficulty researchers encounter, for example, is that the presence of an observer may have an inhibitory effect on the behavior of those individuals being observed. If children are observed through a one-way mirror in a classroom such inhibitory effects do not occur. Observers in the nursery school using behavioral check lists or speaking quietly into a tape recorder may quickly be accepted as part of the ever changing landscape by preschoolers accustomed to the coming and going of strange adults. Adults making movies in the classroom or nursery school may distract curious children, however. Parents interacting with their children in structured or unstructured laboratory situations, even if observers are concealed, may be inhibited both because of the knowledge that they are being observed and because the laboratory is not familiar territory for them.

Most intrusive is the presence of observers stationed in people's homes, observing their every action under such trying conditions as mealtime and bedtime. We all try to behave in socially desirable ways when others are present and thus observers in the home may not see the true extremes of behavior that occur in settings of complete privacy, although behavior becomes more normal once habituation to the observer's presence occurs. Certainly the desire to present one's self in as flattering a light as possible is a difficulty encountered in *any* kind of research, whether it involves telling those perceived as experts how one deals with children's misbehavior, attempting to behave in an appropriate way in a laboratory experiment, or eating dinner in a civilized fashion while a stranger located in the corner of the dining room watches one's every move.

Some attempts have been made to assess the extent to which behavior is actually influenced by an observer's presence. In one, Patterson and Reid (1970) asked a mother to observe her family without their knowledge. Her data were compared with those collected by an official observer at a different time. Patterson and Reid reported that in the latter case the father made more than twice as many positive reactions than when he believed no one was watching him. In another study Lobitz and Johnson (1975) observed the families of aggressive boys and normal control boys in their homes. Before the observations began parents were sometimes asked either to make their children appear "good," that is, to present the most positive picture of family interaction they could, or to make their children appear "bad," that is, to make them misbehave. These instructions were not made known to the observers so that their observations would not be influenced by expectations of the effects the instructions would have. Lobitz and Johnson found that parents could quite easily induce their children to misbehave by acting in a critical and unkind way. On the other hand, neither the parents of the aggressive nor the control boys were successful in making their children act in a more positive way than they did under normal conditions. One infers, then, that it is not always that easy to present one's self and one's family in a particularly favorable light.

Lytton (1980) attempted to reduce problems of observer influence by using a videotape camera with the families he was observing, hoping that this would be less embarrassing for them than the intrusion of a live observer. The contrary occurred, however. Mothers reported they were more conscious of, and felt more constrained by, the presence of the camera than they were by the presence of human observers. In addition, Lytton notes that the presence of a fixed camera meant that some of the parent-child interactions he hoped to observe were lost as subjects moved out of camera range.

Mothers as Observers and Recorders of Their Own Behavior

Stationing observers in the home has some problems, although they are certainly not sufficient to reduce substantially the value of passive observational procedures. Another approach to observation, which overcomes the problem of intrusiveness (but has its own set of limitations), is to use mothers themselves as observers. Mothers have the advantage of being present in the home for long periods of time, and they are not likely to make their families self-conscious. Such a technique was first used by Florence Goodenough (1931), who was interested in studying the causes, frequency, and duration of outbursts of anger in young children, as well as discovering the methods parents used to handle such outbursts. She provided mothers with data sheets on which they were to record each time their child displayed anger, noting the cause, the duration of the angry episode, a description of behavioral manifestations of the anger (e.g., kicking, stamping, holding the breath, making the body go limp, arguing), and the technique used to deal with it. Mothers were, in fact, provided with a list of possible techniques so as to make their task easier.

An interesting aside here is that, before her mothers began to make daily records, Goodenough asked them to respond to a questionnaire about the techniques they used to control their children's behavior. Thus she was able to compare their global answers to the questionnaire with information obtained from the recording sheets. Goodenough found little relation between the two reports of frequency of usage of different control techniques: Of the 43 mothers who took part in her study, only nine never recorded the use of techniques that they denied using in their answers to the questionnaire.

The disadvantages of this method of data collection are as follows. As mothers are made conscious of their specific behaviors—a necessity if they are to make records—their behavior may change. Because they are giving serious thought to what they are doing and may even consciously attempt to modify their responses natural behavior is altered by the self-monitoring process. It is likely too that people who are involved in situations, particularly those that are emotionally charged (e.g., child misbehavior and discipline), may misperceive what is happening both to themselves and to others. Thus it is not clear that they will be able to make a reliable report of what has actually transpired. The measurement of observer reliability is another problem. In any observational study an index of observer agreement is mandatory to assure the recording is not done in a private or idiosyncratic way. However, as soon as a new observer is introduced into the home, behavior becomes constrained unless, of course, the observer is the father.

Because of these kinds of difficulties and because observation in general fell out of favor, Goodenough's approach lay dormant for 40 or 50 years, when it was borrowed by Radke-Yarrow and Zahn-Waxler (e.g., Zahn-Waxler & Radke-Yarrow, 1982). They used it to study the development of young children's reactions to distress in others. Mothers were hired as research assistants and trained for 8 hours in two group sessions and one individual session. They were asked to taperecord all their observations, including the antecedents of each distress situation, and the reaction of both their child and themselves. Observer reliability was assessed by an investigator who visited the home every third week and who recorded what happened when the mother simulated distress such as crying or choking. Thus both the visiting investigator and the mother were able to report on the same incident and their observations could be compared. Reliability was reasonably high. Moreover, the observations made by mothers at the beginning of the period of investigation were not dissimilar from those made later on, an indication that they were not, in fact, modifying their behavior or changing their recording in some way.

This same technique has been used by one of us (Grusec, 1982, 1985). Mothers have been trained to report on their children's manifestations of prosocial behavior, including helping, sharing, comforting, defending, and showing concern, and on the reactions these behaviors received. Rather than tape-record their observations, they made written notes of them. Observer reliability was measured in two ways. First, mothers viewed a videotape of family interaction and were asked to identify instances of altruism in that tape. In this way it was possible to determine that they were labeling as prosocial those same behaviors so labeled by the investigator. Second, mothers were visited by a research assistant who asked them to make two requests for prosocial behavior from their child. Responses to these incidents were recorded by both observers. In both cases observer agreement was high. Mothers' reports for the first and second halves of the observation period (1 month) were compared and no difference was found in the nature or frequency of the items they reported. Thus they did not appear to change their behavior as a result of becoming conscious of it.

Some Comments on Observer Reliability

We have commented on the importance of a measure that indicates whether or not events are being observed in an idiosyncratic way and that more than one person is seeing them in the same way. Machines generally measure reliably (although this certainly must be assessed), whereas human beings are not as rigidly calibrated and can be inconsistent and unreliable when complex events are the object of their attention. On the other hand, they are more flexible and sensitive than machines. Radke-Yarrow and Zahn-Waxler (1979) note that there are individual differences in how reliable observers are; differences not always eradicated by efficient training procedures. Good observers are individuals who can sustain attention to observed events without becoming habituated to them, can take in a high load of environmental stimulation without confusion, are compulsive, intense, analytic, and introspective, and have insight into biases and theoretical commitments that might distort their perception in a particular way. In other words, a good observer does not "tune out" or grow bored easily and does not allow hypotheses or preconceptions to distort reality. Radke-Yarrow and Zahn-Waxler also observe that some individuals are simply easier to observe reliably than others because their behavior is more predictable. It might be misleading, then, to base one's measures of reliability on observations of a small number of individuals, for the measure might be too high or too low depending on the behavioral predictability of individuals chosen for observation. Observer reliability is a complex subject and the interested reader should refer to more extensive discussion than can be undertaken here.

The Use of Ratings

One of the distinctive features of observational methodology is the use of objective behavior counts to describe behavioral attributes. The most aggressive child is the one who is responsible for producing the highest number of observations of hitting, kicking, pinching, and so on. Some measure of the intensity of these acts might also be included. This is in marked contrast to the older approach in which judges, on the basis of their observations, made ratings of individuals on various dimensions. Although the use of subjective ratings has been criticized (e.g., Mischel, 1973) it recently has attracted renewed interest as a methodological tool. Cairns and Green (1979) note that ratings indicate, for example, greater consistency and continuity in behavior than does precise assessment of actual behavior. They suggest this mirrors a true state of affairs rather than a reflection of the needs of an observer to impose consistency on the diversity he observes. Thus judges, when making ratings, are able to take into account the context in which behavior occurs and make adjustments for the effects of that context. In contrast, were events to be assessed merely on the basis of numbers of actual acts, situational effects would add so much variability that consistent behavioral tendencies would be submerged. There is no doubt that human judges cause distortion of what they see. Their preconceptions and their desire to bring order into a confusing world may bias their conclusions. On the other hand, they also bring a sensitivity to the task of describing behavior that piecemeal observation cannot.

VARIETIES OF SETTING AND CONTROL

There are other approaches to data collection in addition to field experiments and passive observation in the nursery school and home. Individuals can be observed, not in their everyday settings, but in an unstructured laboratory situation. In this way the researcher can gain some control over what happens, even if he does not actually manipulate events in a differential way for different groups of subjects. It is possible to learn about mother-child attachment, for example, by watching the behavior of young children when their mother leaves the room. This can be done under more ordered conditions if it occurs in a laboratory setting than if it occurs in a home where all kinds of distractions and variations can occur. Researchers also take advantage of "natural" experiments, such as comparing the development of children who are in day-care with those who are not. Day-care experience, of course, is a variable not easily manipulated, but something about the effects of early experience can be learned from observation of the results of events that occur naturally in the real world. The inability of investigators to assign subjects randomly to experimental and control groups and the problems of comparison this imposes can be offset to some extent by attempts to match groups as closely as possible on what are con-

TABLE 2.1. Degrees of control possible along a dimension of naturalness.

Type of investigation	Setting	Independent variable	Dependent variable
Passive observation	Field	Low	Low
Passive observation	Laboratory	Low	Low
Natural experiment	Field	Low	Low
Field experiment	Field	High	Low
Controlled field experiment	Field	High	High
Laboratory experiment	Laboratory	High	High

Note. From *Parent-Child Interaction: The Socialization Process Observed in Twin and Singleton Families* by H. Lytton, 1980, New York: Plenum. Copyright 1980 by Plenum. Adapted by permission.

sidered to be relevant variables. Matching, however, brings problems of its own (Cook & Campbell, 1979). Among other things it assumes that the researcher knows what those relevant variables are; such knowledge, however, may require a great deal more understanding of the phenomenon being studied than actually exists.

The primary concern of researchers, of course, is to study behavior in such a way that results of observations can be generalized to the child's everyday world. Lytton (1980) has argued that the main dimensions of naturalness are setting and control. In Table 2.1 we see an array of methodologies arranged along a continuum of naturalness. Although naturalistic home observation and controlled laboratory experimentation clearly mark the ends of the continuum, the intermediate positions are more arbitrarily ordered. Table 2.1, nevertheless, provides a good summary of the range of techniques that can be used to answer questions about social development.

The Problem of Causal Inference

Disenchantment with experimental methodology and renewed interest in observing ongoing interactions in natural environments leaves one major problem unsolved. Observation of any naturally occurring relationship does not allow the inference of causality. Which of the related variables is responsible for changes in the other one? Are the two related variables in fact both caused by yet another variable not even measured? Whatever its deficiencies, one great virtue of experimental methodology is that it gives the researcher the opportunity to draw conclusions about causality and hence extend knowledge to a much greater extent than would be otherwise possible.

One can, however, make at least some inferences about causality from data that have not been generated as a result of experimental manipulation. We now will discuss a variety of procedures recently developed to achieve this end. The development of these procedures has been viewed as especially important as psychologists have begun to emphasize that the relationship between individuals in any social interaction is a two-way process, with both individuals contributing to that interaction. Even in the case of parents and children, where one member of the dyad (or triad) is less powerful, causality is bidirectional—a point that has been emphasized in the preceding pages and will continue to be emphasized throughout this book. To acknowledge that influence is bidirectional is one thing. To be able to make statements about the probable impact of each contributor on the interaction is a vastly more complicated undertaking, but one which is becoming progressively more possible.

Short-Term Cause-Effect Relationships

When individuals are observed in social interaction, one question researchers ask is how the behavior displayed by one triggers or produces an immediate behavior in the second. Thus there is interest in the moment-by-moment pressures that individuals exert on each other. The most common way of determining this involves the computation of conditional probabilities. If a particular response is followed by another response more frequently than would be expected, given the baseline probability of the latter response, then it is possible that the former response sets off, or facilitates, the latter (although a third variable could trigger these two variables, as will be pointed out later). Suppose, for example, that over the course of hours of observation in a home setting, aggressive behavior comprised less than 1% of the total number of acts observers recorded. Suppose, however, that every time the observed child was the recipient of an aggressive act from some member of his family, the probability of an aggressive act from the observed child increased to .05. Here we would have evidence that aggression produces aggression, and that hitting, yelling, and other acts of hostility are likely to be reacted to in a reciprocal manner. The opposite possibility, that aggression decreases aggression because it has a generally inhibiting effect, would be revealed by a decrease in the probability of aggressive responding, from the baseline figure of less than .01 to a figure substantially below that.

The application of this procedure for making inferences about the characteristics of social interaction allows the consideration of actual sequences of actions along a time line. Thus parent action A—child action B—parent action C—child action D, and so on, can be described. One kind of action is arbitrarily designated as the criterion response (R) and a preceding action thereby becomes the antecedent (A): Their roles can, of course, be reversed in subsequent analysis. By comparing the actual occurrence of R after A with R's baseline rate of occurrence, one can assess whether or not A facilitates, or is possibly one of the causes of, R. In this way the effects of A can be detected above the noise of all other behaviors going on at the same time by statistically controlling for these other variables. Employing this approach, Lytton (1980) was able to understand the immediate effects of parents' actions on children's actions, and vice versa, in the areas of compliance and attachment. He concluded that parents' control (commands, prohibitions, suggestions, reasoning) had a marked effect on their children's compliance and noncompliance but that the effects of children's compliance or noncompliance had a much smaller effect on parents' subsequent behavior. Whereas noncompliance increased the likelihood of some modes of control, after compliance the different parental behaviors maintained the rank order of their base rates. Attachment presented a quite different picture, however, with child behavior appearing to drive the interaction to an equal or even greater extent than parent behavior. Thus mothers responded to their children's needs and wishes. Children, on the other hand, were less affected by maternal actions, unless they were negative in character.

The use of conditional probabilities only enables the investigator to identify immediately triggering causes of the criterion response. Suppose, for example, that a child's immediate response to a command paired with threat of punishment is to comply with that command. The long-term effects of threatened punishment may well be just the opposite, and are determined by other means than the use of conditional probabilities. Another problem in establishing relationships derives from perseveration, that is, a behavior that occurred before a response may occur after the response because it is simply a continuation. A child cries, is comforted, and continues to cry. To say that crying is a response to comforting would be misleading—it is just that crying tends to produce more crying before the effects of comfort take over. There are ways of coping with this difficulty by, for example, counting only initial instances of the behavior of interest, but not subsequent parts of sequences.

Although sequential analysis as just described does make it possible to draw causal inferences, such inferences must be qualified. Thus the criterion variable may covary with the antecedent not because it is being caused by the antecedent but because it is caused by another event which covaries with the antecedent. Lightning regularly precedes thunder but does not cause it. Something else causes both. At least we can say, however, that thunder does not cause lightning.

Longer Term Cause-Effect Relationships

When interest focuses on the effects of a given variable on a more distant outcome, researchers have turned to the use of cross-lagged panel analysis (CLPA) and, more recently, causal modeling. We shall consider these two methods in turn.

Cross-Lagged Panel Analysis

In CLPA, observations are made on two or more variables at two or more points in time. Suppose, in the simplest case, that an investigator wishes to

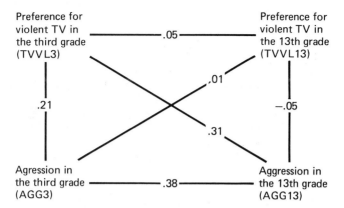

FIGURE 2.2. The correlations between a preference for violent television and peer-rated aggression for 211 boys over a 10-year lag. From "Does Television Violence Cause Aggression?" by L.D. Eron, L.R. Huesmann, M.M. Lefkowitz, and L.O. Walder, 1972, *American Psychologist, 27*, 253–263. Copyright 1972 by the American Psychological Association. Reprinted by permission.

determine whether a parent's use of physical punishment when the child is a preschooler is responsible for aggressive behavior when the child reaches adolescence, or whether aggressive behavior in the child forces the parent to use strong forms of discipline such as physical punishment to gain compliance. To try and answer the question, parent discipline and child aggression would be measured, simultaneously, at two points in time, during the preschool years (T1) and during adolescence (T2). If parent discipline produces child aggression, the correlation between discipline at T1 and aggression at T2 should be greater than the correlation between aggression at T1 and discipline at T2.

Many researchers have used CLPA in their attempts to infer causal patterns in nonexperimental data. A well-known example is that of Eron, Huesmann, Lefkowitz, and Walder (1972) who were concerned with the causal connection between early preferences for the viewing of violent television material and later aggression. The results of their analysis are pictured in Figure 2.2. Here we see that the correlation between preference for violent programming in the third grade and aggression in the 13th grade is a significant one, whereas that between aggression in the third grade and preference for violent programming in the 13th grade is not. Such a pattern provides some support for the hypothesis that preferring to watch violent television is a cause of aggressive behavior, as opposed to a hypothesis which places causal responsibility on the aggressive behavior.

This method is limited in its usefulness, however, as Rogosa (1980) has recently demonstrated. He notes that CLPA does not provide sound information about causal effects and may indicate their presence or absence when just the opposite it true. The use of CLPA, for example, rests on the assumption that the variables being measured are equally stable over time.

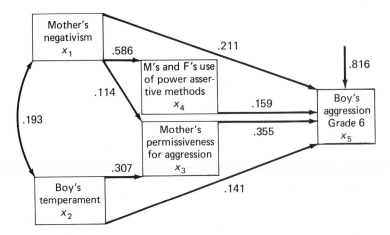

FIGURE 2.3. Path diagram for trimmed causal model. (Sample 1 in Grade 6, $n = 76$. $R = .579$, $R^2 = .335$. M's = mother's; F's = father's. A path coefficient—a standardized partial regression coefficient, beta—above or below a unidirectional straight arrow indicates the direct causal effect of one variable on another while all other causal variables are held constant.) From "Familial and Temperamental Determinants of Aggressive Behavior in Adolescent Boys: A Causal Analysis" by D. Olweus, 1980, *Developmental Psychology, 16*, 644–666. Copyright 1980 by the American Psychological Association. Reprinted by permission.

If this is not true—as frequently may be the case—then CLPA favors the assignment of causal predominance to the variable that has increasing variance over time. Rogosa also criticizes the emphasis in CLPA on a "causal winner." We know, of course, that many social and developmental processes are reciprocal and to assign victory to one over the other is an oversimplification of the researcher's task.

Causal Modeling

Causal modeling is a second attempt to deal with the task of understanding the nature and direction of long-term relationships between variables, requiring the investigator to set up a theoretical model of these relationships. If the model does not fit the data acceptably then it is rejected as a reasonable representation of the possible causal relationships between variables.

One kind of causal modeling is known as path analysis and we will describe it as one example of the procedure. It involves formulation by the investigator of a hypothetical model of causal relationships among a set of variables. These relationships are determined by previous research as well as theoretical considerations. The model is written as a set of structural equations and is depicted in a path diagram like the one presented in Figure 2.3. Arrows in the path diagram indicate the direction of causal influence of one variable on another. The parameters of the structural equations are then estimated, using multiple regression techniques. In this way, the usefulness of the causal model can be determined.

An example of the use of path analysis is provided by Olweus (1980). Figure 2.3 is, in fact, taken from Olweus and depicts a causal model relating mother's negativism during her boy's first 4 to 5 years of life, her boy's temperament in his early years, mother's permissiveness for aggression, parental usage of power assertion (punishment), and the outcome variable, that is, aggression in Grade 6. Olweus found no reason to assume that temperament and maternal negativism bore any specific causal relationship to each other. Therefore, their relationship was left unanalyzed and was represented in Figure 2.3 by a curved bidirectional arrow. This model was recursive, that is, it involved no suggestion of reciprocal causation though there are nonrecursive procedures that do allow the specification of reciprocity. The partial regression coefficients in the path analysis were based on data collected from Grade 6 boys. Figure 2.3 is actually a trimmed model in which two causal paths (boy's temperament to parent usage of power assertion, and mother's permissiveness for aggression to parent usage of power assertion) that were originally hypothesized have been removed. Olweus then applied the causal model to data obtained from Grade 9 boys to assess its accuracy: The marked similarity between the estimated correlation coefficients of Figure 2.3 and those of the Grade 9 sample attest to its usefulness in understanding some of the antecedents of aggressive behavior. Thus Olweus concluded that maternal negativism and permissiveness for aggression have the greatest causal effects. In addition, he concluded that temperament has an indirect effect on aggression by way of its effect on mother's permissiveness for aggression, as revealed by the stronger relationship between temperament and maternal permissiveness and the much weaker relationship between temperament and aggression.

Another, and more sophisticated, form of causal modeling involves the estimation of latent variables in determining relationships, using the LISREL* computer program (Jöreskog & Sorbom, 1978). It is typically used on survey data based on large samples. When a number of measures (called manifest variables) of a particular phenomenon are obtained they are clustered together to form what is designated as a latent variable. The latent variable, based on many measures, is a more reliable measure of the variable of interest than just one measure. The researcher has to specify a model of the relationships which, on theoretical grounds, he expects will hold among the latent variables (the "structural model"). This model would include the researcher's hypothesis about the direction in which influence will flow. The program then estimates the parameters, or values, of the causal model from the measures collected and the chi-square test

---

*Copyright K.G. Jöreskog, University of Uppsala, Department of Statistics, P.O. Box 513, S-751 20, Uppsala, Sweden.

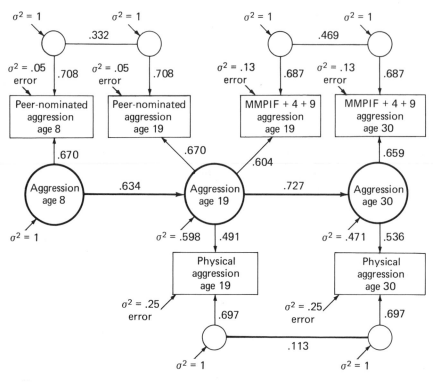

FIGURE 2.4. A structural model showing the stability of an hypothesized latent trait of aggression within all subjects over 22 years. For all subjects, stability (Agg 8 → Agg 30) = .461, chi-square = 2.67, df = 8, p = .95. From "Stability of Aggression Over Time and Generations" by L.R. Huesmann, L.D. Eron, M.M. Lefkowitz, and L.O. Walder, 1984, *Developmental Psychology*, *20*, 1120–1134. Copyright 1984 by the American Psychological Association. Reprinted by permission.

is used to assess the overall fit of the model to the observed data. The LISREL program enables the investigator to estimate the model parameters. Detailed discussions of LISREL are provided, among others, by Bynner and Romney (1985) and Maruyama and McGarvey (1980).

   An example of the application of LISREL is provided by Huesmann, Eron, Lefkowitz, and Walder (1984) in their attempt to assess the stability of aggression between the ages of 8 and 30 years. Their measures of aggression were not perfectly reliable and they had taken different measures of aggression at different points in time. For these reasons it made sense to estimate the coefficients of a structural model involving a latent variable representing the "trait" of aggression. In this estimation, LISREL was used, and Figure 2.4 shows their model which depicts aggression as a good predictor of later aggression, that is, maintains that aggression is stable. The large circles in Figure 2.4 represent the latent variable of aggression and the rectangles are the measures of aggression (e.g., peer nominations of aggression, ratings by spouse of subject's aggression, severity of punishment by subjects of their children, number of moving traffic violations), which are clustered together to form the trait measure of aggression. Smaller, blank circles represent all determinants of the manifest variables other than the latent trait aggression and random error (the latter being based on previous analyses of reliability). Actual data were compared with the parameter values estimated by LISREL, using chi-square, and yielded a close fit ($\chi^2 = 2.67$, $df = 8$, $p = .95$). Thus Huesmann et al. concluded that aggression remains remarkably stable from the age of 8 years.

The use of causal modeling provides a substantial step forward in the understanding of correlational data. It must be emphasized, however, that its usage does not permit the investigator to determine causality. Although it tests the plausibility of competing theoretical relationships, it cannot do what is impossible, that is, deduce causal relations from correlational data.

Conclusion

Heated debates about appropriate methodologies for studying social development, waged in the 1970s, have abated to a large extent in the 1980s. It is evident that each methodology has its advantages as well as its disadvantages. Psychologists will continue to refine and develop each of these approaches to understanding human behavior and, in this way, our knowledge will continue to advance. No doubt debate will continue about the relative importance of description of behavior as opposed to its explanation. Such debate is healthy because it sensitizes investigators to the assumptions they automatically make when they set out to study a particular area. Different people will take different approaches to the study of the same problem, and in this diversity lies strength. For if the picture that emerges about a given phenomenon is consistent, no matter what methodological technique has been employed, then our faith in the reliability and validity of findings becomes stronger. When different approaches produce different results, then attempts to explain the differences open up new avenues of thought and hypothesis that may not have occurred to the investigator.

The importance of using a variety of methodologies cannot be overestimated. In this way the investigator is provided with a comparative viewpoint that would not be possible otherwise. Two strategies often can lead to different interpretations of data than a strategy used alone. We provide two examples of this point. In a sequence analysis of the behavior of young children and adults in a nursery school, Yarrow, Waxler, and Scott (1971) found that adults most frequently responded to children's clowning with positive attention. Whereas this process analysis suggested that adults are accepting of clowning, a trait analysis yielded quite a different story. Children who clowned more were more likely to be given negative attention when they were *not* clowning. Taken together the data suggest what could not have been detected individually, that is, although clowning might be accepted immediately upon its occurrence, in adults it generates dislike, which reveals itself under other circumstances.

In a second example Paris and Cairns (1972) combined naturalistic and laboratory methods to learn about the relative effectiveness of positive and negative comments. Initially they noted, in a laboratory experiment, that negative comments after incorrect responding were much more effective in inducing learning in young children than were positive comments after correct responding. The reason for this difference became apparent after they conducted a second study in a naturalistic setting of classrooms where they observed that positive comments often were used indiscriminately in that they were not always contingent on something that the recipient had done. Negative comments, on the other hand, were much more likely to be used contingently. This new understanding of how positive and negative consequences are used in the child's everyday world, then, made laboratory findings more comprehensible.

Summary

We began this chapter by noting that advances in knowledge are determined to a considerable extent by the development of appropriate methodological tools, as well as by technological improvements that enable researchers to collect and analyze data in a way not previously possible. We also noted that different methodological approaches have characterized the field of social developmental psychology at different points in its history, but that these approaches have become increasingly sophisticated over time, thus ensuring progress in the acquisition of knowledge.

Early studies of social development were observational in nature, generally of children in nursery school settings. Data analysis was descriptive, involving only numerical summaries of those events observed. In the 1940s interest shifted to the role of parents in their children's social development, and research was driven by psychoanalytic and learning theories. Now the approach was correlational, with much data gathered through the use of questionnaires and interviews. Raw data were subjected to statistical analysis and evaluation, including factor or cluster analysis: Such analyses enabled investigators to identify, among other things, dimenions of parent behavior that were deemed important in the socialization process. Although this approach yielded much useful information, it had its limitations. Extensive reliance on self-report (by mothers of their own behavior) and on mothers' reports of the behavior of their own children presumably produced biased conclusions. Typical interviews failed to get at the complexity of parent-child interactions or consider difficulties mothers might have in knowing how their child behaved relative to others, as well as difficulties they might experience in remembering events that had occurred in the past. Although later research overcame some of these problems, there was no escape from the fact that correlational studies do not allow the making of causal inferences.

The experimental laboratory study was a major step forward in the acquisition of information about social development, and its use mushroomed in the 1960s. Early in the 1970s, however, a number of concerns about this technique were expressed. It was argued that the laboratory experiment lacks ecological validity because the complexities of reality cannot be captured adequately in an artificial setting. Additionally, critics maintained that psychologists had moved too quickly by testing hypotheses about the development of behavior before they had simply observed and described the behavior to be understood. As investigators became more sensitized to issues of research ethics, it became increasingly difficult to manipulate a number of behaviors in the experimental laboratory.

In response to these various criticisms, a number of changes took place. Although laboratory experimentation is still used, it has been augmented by a number of other approaches. Increasingly the field experiment has been employed, often in conjunction with manipulation in a more contrived context. Observation of individuals in their natural settings has become an increasingly popular technique, helped by the development of more sophisticated techniques for data collection and analysis than existed in the 1930s. The presence of observers does affect the behavior of those observed—the use of mothers as recorders of their own behavior and that of their children overcomes this problem, although it poses problems of its own. A number of factors influence the reliability of observers, including their ability to sustain attention as well as the predictability of the behavior of those individuals being observed.

Renewed interest in naturalistic observation has made the problem of causal inference salient once again. A number of techniques have been developed to aid investigators to make better guesses about the direction of causal relationship between variables.

Part II   The Foundations of Development

3
Genetic and Biological Bases of Social Behavior

That humanity's destiny is shaped not only by external influences, but also by biological forces operating from within, is one of those blindingly obvious truths that has been rediscovered in recent years. The purpose of this chapter is to show how human behavior, including social behavior, has its roots in millenia of evolutionary history and also how culture and learning go hand in hand with evolutionary and biological forces. Ethology, psychobiology and behavior genetics, as well as sociobiology, discussed in Chapter 1, are the main disciplines that have adopted a biological perspective in viewing and explaining social behavior. Their viewpoints have gained a wide hearing and acceptance in more recent times (cf. Hinde, 1983; Scarr & Kidd, 1983), although the more far-reaching claims of sociobiology remain contentious. Developmental psychologists have come to utilize the concepts of these disciplines in the service of explaining the development of behavior, and social behavior in particular.

A biological viewpoint accepts that there are biological constraints, differing from one individual to another, which set limits on one's power to adapt. In other words, it implies that human beings differ from birth, and that human malleability is limited. However, we should stress that if no two human beings are, for biological *and* environmental reasons, ever identical, this does not mean that they should not be accorded equality—equality before the law and equality of opportunity. Equality is, in fact, a social and ethical, not a biological, concept.

This chapter will explore the biological aspects of social behavior (e.g., smiling, protest on separation from mother, fear of strangers, inhibition, sociablity) and the interrelations between biological and cultural and situational influences. The chapter is divided into three sections: the first one will deal with the evolution and biological adaptedness of universal human characteristics; the second will discuss genetic influences on behavior in which individuals differ; the third will explore the effects of the biological environment, that is, prenatal, physiological, and chemical influences.

Evolution and Biological Adaptedness

EVOLUTION

To help the reader understand the discussion of evolutionary processes, we will first explain a few terms of evolutionary science.

We must distinguish between *genotype*—the genetic basis of an organism—and *phenotype*—the observable or measurable characteristics of an organism. Charles Darwin discovered and gave names to the evolutionary forces that have shaped the course of the development of species. Foremost among these forces is the mechanism of *natural selection*, which favors those variations of genotypes that are manifested in phenotypes and that have the greatest chance of surviving and reproducing offspring, that is, it operates to increase *fitness*. Any behavior that serves to increase fitness is called *adaptive*, although some characteristics that were adaptive in an earlier evolutionary age may no longer be so.

Evolutionary changes and adaptations are, of course, not subject to experimental test. The notion that certain kinds of behavior were adaptive and served fitness in the course of man's evolution is based on the theory of natural selection and is inferred from what we know of the history of the species; however, this notion is widely accepted. The fossil record, which documents the evolution of the hominid line and the development of larger brain size (see below), provides convincing evidence that evolution has contributed to the development of present-day human behavior (Scarr & Kidd, 1983).

Often we find behavior analogous to human behavior patterns among nonhuman species. The existence of analogous behavior patterns by itself, however, does not imply that they necessarily serve the same purposes since crucial species differences also exist (Cairns, 1979b; Hinde, 1983). The existence of language and cultural transmission, for instance, adds a whole new dimension to human behavior. Further, it is obvious that any behavior pattern is much less rigidly fixed in humans than in animals, and much more subject to individual learning experiences and to change by cultural and technological forces, as will be discussed later. However, the evolutionary appproach provides a perspective for viewing human behavior that complements the perspective given by a cultural approach, and analyses at both levels are always appropriate. Often species differences are more illuminating than species similarities as, for instance, in the study of milk composition and suckling frequency.

Evolutionary Adaptations

What adaptations did *Homo sapiens* and his hominid ancestors undergo in the course of evolution to give us our characteristic human social and intellectual qualities?

It is salutary to remind ourselves that the ancestors of each of us only

100,000 years or 4,000 generations ago were probably hairy, half-human creatures, and 40,000 generations ago were certainly that. And these creatures in turn evolved, through millions of years of development, from mammals and much earlier forms of life, life that probably began in a "probiotic soup of amino-acids" some 3 billion years ago.

In the course of these millenia many human characteristics evolved that were adaptive in that they favored the survival of the individual and the species. The constant availability of the mother, for instance, may have evolved as an adaptive arrangement. Comparative studies show that suckling frequency is inversely related to the protein content of the milk. Human milk has relatively low protein content, suggesting that frequent feeding, when the infant's hunger demands it, is adaptive (Blurton Jones, 1972). This required constant availability of the mother, at least in earlier millenia, although it is impossible to say which came first: low protein content of human milk or mother availability.

Natural selection acts on genes, not individuals. Hence, recent evidence and theory (Hamilton, 1964) suggest that selection may favor acts by an individual that decrease his own chances of survival or reproductive success but increase those in several other related individuals who possess a large proportion of the same genes. This is referred to as maximizing *inclusive fitness*, and modern revisions of Darwinian theory have considered that in this way natural selection operates by *kin selection*, rather than by individual selection.

From the point of view of inclusive fitness, it is in a female's interest to care for her own offspring or that of relatives who carry her own genes. But it is not in her interest to devote care to the young of other females. Leaving aside the possible, but uncertain occurrence of altruistic behavior, it may be better for her to avoid or even harm unrelated young. It follows that fear of strangers aids survival and is adaptive, and, indeed, there is evidence of fear of strangers in many species (Hinde, 1983). It also follows that it is in the young's interest to seek nurturance and protection primarily from the mother, that is, to display attachment behavior.

Since natural selection operates at the level of the kin group, evolution has favored the cohesion of individuals into small family groups. In this way related individuals will be better able to aid each other, both in nurturing the young and in defending themselves. Archaeological evidence, in fact, suggests that early human groups consisted of 12 to 50 individuals, most of whom were related (Hinde, 1983).

Some of the adaptations brought about by evolutionary forces were adaptive for the living conditions of hunter/gatherers 1 million or half a million years ago, but are maladaptive now. For example, human obsession with sexuality is no longer necessary for the survival of the species, although it may have been adaptive for keeping the species alive in the Pleistocene when there were far fewer humans on earth. Adaptations to changed circumstances of living nowadays come much more through social and technological innovations, for example, contraception, than through mutations of genetic material. Dissociation of sexuality from reproduction, for instance, may bring about changes in the sexual roles and the social status of women and hence in family structure, which will have repercussions also on the child's experiences and development (Bruner, 1972).

Some of the major and crucial adaptations in the evolution of the human species over the last 2 million years or so have been: (1) the change from walking on all fours to walking erect (bipedalism); (2) the doubling of the brain size and with it the emergence of a social-technical way of life, marked by tool use (present also in nonhuman primates) and by symbol use; (3) the prolongation of parental care. We will now discuss what are, from our point of view, the most salient adaptations, namely, brain size and parental care.

Brain Size

Species below primates depend on fixed systems of behavior and communication, or on "closed programs" in the brain (Mayr, 1982). Thus, mechanisms for sharing habitats and defending territory, systems for signaling that are effective against predators, and mating systems that depend on recognizable stereotypical features in the mate (Tinbergen, 1951) have been locked into the genes of those species. By comparison, primates have developed "open programs," that is, more flexible systems of responses. Primates, in contrast to other mammals, develop more through learning than through maturation, and this requires a larger brain size in both infants and parents. Human development is but a further extension and intensification of the nonhuman primate pattern.

The increased size of the brain, however, meant that if it was of full adult size it could not pass through a birth canal that was at the same time being narrowed because of the pressures of erect posture. The adaptation necessitated by these opposing tendencies was that the infant came to be born at a more immature stage of development in order to assure a safe passage into the world. This meant that the greater part of development had to take place outside the womb, thereby lengthening the dependency period of the infant on its parents. However, at this point our knowledge allows us only to say that greater primate brain size and intelligence, greater immaturity at birth, and longer parental care are interdependent and coadapted. It is impossible to decide which came first (Scarr & Kidd, 1983).

The spectacular doubling of brain size between about 1.3 and 0.3 million years ago, however, met the needs of big game hunting. This, we may speculate, provided the stimulus for cooperation among our hominid forefathers, and it also facilitated the emergence of social life and, above all, language. Although there is little evidence, it is likely that the populations that survived had genes ensuring cooperation among individuals, which meant effective use of speech as a symbol system, as well as the efficient use and making of tools (Young, 1971).

There has been no increase in brain size over the last 30,000 years or so.

Presumably the increase halted because the social structure of society abolished the necessity for it. Technological advances, produced by the culture, that is, by the combined efforts of many individuals, have become available to all. Now that most members of the species can learn language and the rules of the culture effectively, and thereby gain its benefits, selection pressure for a larger brain will be much reduced.

Parental Care

The evolution of prolonged infancy and childhood, characteristic of humans, that was necessary for developing behavioral skills by means of learning, has meant a lengthened period of parental care and of dependence by the young on this care. As a result, the most adaptive strategy for parents has been to concentrate investment in a smaller and smaller number of offspring. Cultural pressures also have contributed to smaller family size in developed countries, but such pressures are a more recent phenomenon.

The principle of fitness imposes competing biological interests on parents and offspring. Parents use up resources in caring for their young, which reduces the chance of their rearing further offspring, and thereby their fitness. To some extent, of course, the lessened chance of propagating their genes is offset by the increased survival chances of the offspring they have already produced. Improved chances of survival come about through the infant's better adaptation to more flexible living conditions in variable environments, for which learning rather than maturational processes are necessary.

This cost-benefit balance, however, changes with time. At first, the young infant is entirely dependent on parental care and nourishment for survival, and it pays parents to provide these in order to ensure the survival of their kind. At a later age it is in the interests of parents' inclusive fitness to reduce the care and attention to the older child in order to devote resources to later offspring. But the (older) child's goals are better served by the maximum amount of parental investment and more investment than it is in the parents' interest to provide. Thus a biological conflict of interests arises (Trivers, 1974). Such divergence of interests is consonant with the finding that in monkeys it is the mother's rather than the infant's actions that are responsible for the infant's gradual moving away from the mother and thus gaining independence. Similar principles will apply in the human case, too, with mothers often, for instance, weaning the infant from the breast to solid food at a faster pace than the child, given the choice, would adopt. Cultural and personal factors will, of course, come into play here too, but the point is that such parental action also can be explained at a biological level (Hinde, 1983).

Adaptiveness of Differing Parental Behavior

As Hinde (1983) points out, it is inappropriate to label one type of parental or child behavior as universally best or universally adaptive. Under the evolutionary perspective, it is the "ecological niche" in which the individual finds himself that will dictate which behavior is adaptive. Altmann (1980, cited in Hinde, 1983) divided baboon mothers into "restrictive" and "laissez-faire" types. Restrictive mothering guarded the infants better against kidnapping, predation, etc., but infants of low-status mothers were more in danger of this than infants of high-status mothers. Laissez-faire mothering, however, probably allowed the infants to grow independent more quickly, which would better enable them to survive if orphaned. Hence restrictiveness is likely to be more adaptive for low-status mothers, and laissez-faire mothering for high-status mothers. In the case of humans, too, it has been found that lower class parents are more restrictive and expect immediate obedience more than do middle-class parents (cf. Clarke-Stewart & Apfel, 1978), and such differences also may be explained by the ecological niche in society that each group occupies.

The child's sex also will influence the amount of parental investment in care. In humans it is generally greater for boys. From the evolutionary perspective this is usually explained by the greater reproductive potential of boys (Hinde, 1983), but a cultural perspective also could explain it by the greater social value conventionally placed on them.

Behavioral styles conducive to reproductive success in males differ from those in females (see Chapter 10 for a longer discussion). Natural selection, therefore, would be expected to favor mothers who enhance sex-appropriate behavior in their offspring. Hinde, Easton, Meller, and Tamplin (1983) found that 4-year-old shy girls had a more positive relationship with their mothers than nonshy girls, whereas shy boys had a more negative one than nonshy boys. Mothers evidently found shyness in girls more acceptable than shyness in boys, and this may be explained as enhancing adaptiveness if we assume that shyness favors greater reproductive success in females, and lack of shyness does so in males. We should note, however, that such sex-differentiated dispositions are also in accord with social expectations, and it is not certain how far they are related to reproductive success.

Cultural Evolution

Culture does not act in opposition to evolution, but acts with it. Culture has, in fact, played an essential part in furthering selection in human societies. Those who were better adapted to absorb new means of communication, and new uses of tools and amplifiers of human capacities were at a selective advantage compared with those less well adapted. Evolution has imposed requirements on individuals to adapt to the demands of group living and has conferred advantages on those best able to do so (Scarr & Kidd, 1983).

Cultural norms, expectations, and skills are transmitted from one generation to the next by example and verbal communication. This transmission begins in infancy, through the process of socialization, but continues throughout life. Bruner (1972) suggests that both nonhuman primate and human infants are preadapted to profit from the prolonged infancy period that marks these species, by being able and ready to learn through observation, instruction, and play. Human infants are particulary "tutor-prone," and they use play as an opportunity to try out new skills and knowledge in a context of safety, where no serious consequences attach to failure.

Not only environmentalists, but evolutionists, too, have acknowledged the essential role of culture in the evolution of human development. However, culture and biology work in different ways. As Wilson has stated: "Cultural evolution is Lamarckian and very fast, whereas biological evolution is Darwinian and usually very slow" (Wilson, 1978, p. 78). Further, Dobzhansky, the well-known geneticist, has pointed out: "Human genes have surrendered their primacy in human evolution to . . . a nonbiological agent, culture. However, it should not be forgotten that this agent is entirely dependent on the human genotype" (quoted by Wilson, 1978, p. 21).

Brain and Behavior

The previous section has discussed how we, as living organisms, are rooted in evolutionary processes. It has dealt with the question: Why have human beings developed certain responses? For example, what are the advantages of becoming attached to a caregiver? The question typically is asked for behavior about which we are not quite sure, like attachment behavior. It hardly ever is asked for behavior like eating or sexual behavior. Yet the answer would be the same for both categories: these behavior tendencies are adaptive, in that they ensure survival and fitness. In the ecological circumstances in which humans have lived out their lives over hundreds of thousands of years, these propensities have become locked into our genes and we are naturally predisposed to act them out. (The fact that there is a biological basis for many behaviors does not invalidate the well-documented fact that the expression of these behaviors is subject to the influences of learning and the environment.)

But another question has to be answered: What causes this behavior at this moment? That is, we are seeking a more proximal cause in the individual and here internal and external causes are enmeshed with one another. Physiological mechanisms in the brain and glands are involved, but they interact in complex ways with environmental stimuli. Thus, causal networks are operating, with internal mechanisms being triggered by external stimuli, for example, attacking behavior is stimulated in the male stickleback by the approach of another male to his territory, and in humans aggressive behavior may be elicited when a person's goal is blocked.

What are the physiological mechanisms that underlie social and emotional behavior? One area of the brain that plays an important role in this is the hypothalamus, which lies at the base of the brain beneath the cortex.

It plays a central part in ensuring self-preservation and the activation of the individual's genetic program. Hence it controls eating and drinking, sexual development and copulation, and it governs the action of the pituitary gland. The hypothalamus prepares us for defence when we are attacked, that is, it controls aggressive behavior. Instigation and inhibition of aggressive acts are, in part, controlled by different sections of the hypothalamus, so it can be seen that the physiological control of aggression (not to speak of its psychological control) is quite complex (Young, 1978).

Another example of physiological mechanisms are the hormonal systems that prepare any animal, including the human, to react to signs of danger by either fight or flight. Such signals of danger activate a stress-reaction program in the body. It has long been known that in response to alarm and stress, the adrenal gland releases adrenaline into the blood stream, a hormone that prepares the body for vigorous action, such as fight or flight. More recently it has been found that aminergic nerve cells in the brain, which transmit substances (monoamines) similar to adrenaline, also are involved in aggressive and defensive actions (Young, 1978). We can see connections between programs of fear and anxiety, which are activated through fear-arousing stimuli, and programs of defence and attack.

BIOLOGICALLY ADAPTED BEHAVIOR AND ITS MODIFICATION

For which social behaviors have humans been preadapted by their evolutionary history, that is, which behaviors have a biological base? Rossi (1984) suggests four criteria for deciding whether biology is involved in a sex difference in social behavior, and these criteria can be extended to behavior apart from sex differences. Following Parsons (1982) she proposes that if two of them are met there is presumptive evidence for a biological influence on the behavior. The criteria, slightly modified, are: (1) consistent correlations between social behavior and circulation of certain hormones; (2) the pattern is found in infants and young children prior to major socialization influences; (3) the pattern is stable across cultures; (4) similar behavior is noted across species, particularly the higher primates most genetically similar to the human species. We now will turn to some behaviors whose development seems to follow a genetic program, although learning also will be involved in their precise expression.

Much of the newborn infant's repertoire of behavior is preprogrammed. However, a realistic appreciation of the nature and extent of the preprogramming makes us sharply aware of the importance of the environment in molding the infant's behavior. Bowlby (1971, p. 336), for instance, has stressed the crucial role played by an "environment of evolutionary adaptedness," that is, the environment that existed in the hunting-gathering era of man's history, for guiding behavior in given directions. If genetic predispositions push the organism along a certain path of development, it may encounter environmental "mountains" and "valleys" that may tend to deflect it from its course. Waddington (1957) has argued that the organism is endowed with compensatory tendencies that will ensure the eventual return to its normal developmental course, or not too far from it—a process he has called "canalization." The tendency of the body to return to its normal weight after a period of malnutrition is an example of this process.

The infant's responses are preadapted so that they will occur in the appropriate context. This context is of great significance, however, in eliciting and shaping them. For example, the infant learns quickly to adapt her posture for feeding from the breast when the mother gives the signal that feeding is imminent. When the infant is in the nursing position, there is a rough side-to-side movement of the head, which causes the nipple to brush against the cheek. When the nipple touches the cheek, the head turns so that the lips are against the nipple, which is then taken into the mouth. All these movements are integrated into a rapid, smooth adaptation. Moreover, the infant's eyes are also adapted to the nursing position: they have a relatively fixed focus at 19 cm which is approximately the distance to the mother's eyes when the baby is breast-feeding (Stratton, 1982).

Social Releasers

A good example of behavior that is thought to be biologically preadapted are "social releasers." These are species-specific stimuli that elicit a specific social response in an animal exposed to them (under given conditions). This has been demonstrated among animals very clearly, for instance, in Tinbergen's (1951) classical study of the male three-spined stickleback. This fish will attack an intruder into his territory where he has built a nest. Tinbergen introduced wooden models of different shapes, more or less resembling sticklebacks, near the nest and found that a red belly would elicit attacking behavior, even if the shape was remote from that of a stickleback, whereas stickleback-like shapes without the red belly would not elicit an attack. Clearly, here the red belly acts as a social releaser of stickleback fighting behavior.

Lorenz (Lorenz, 1943, cited in Nash, 1978) has hypothesized that in humans, the "cute baby" look, produced by a short face and large forehead, together with chubby cheeks makes the baby lovable and attractive to adults in general, and may act as a social releaser for a parenting response. Lorenz points out that Walt Disney has capitalized on features of this sort in creating his cuter animal characters. Other social releaser-like behaviors in man include the baby's cry, which adults find very difficult to ignore, as well as the smile (see below). The concept of social releaser does not imply, however, that learning is absent or that experience plays no part in shaping a given behavior (Hinde, 1983).

The baby's smile has been studied a great deal as a universal sign of friendly greeting and it appears in identical form in all cultures. Something akin to the smile also appears in social play in chimpanzees, though it may not have the same feeling tone attached to it as in humans. The human face is the most reliable releaser of the baby's smile. At first, a schematic partial representation of the face is sufficient for eliciting smiling, though later the child becomes more discriminating. The smile itself, like the "cute baby" look, may have been adapted to act as a social releaser for parenting responses; it is instrumental in establishing ties of affection between the infant and those around her (who can resist a baby's smile?), and it will thus help in the formation of attachment bonds between parents and child, in particular.

Smiling in the early weeks is often thought to be due to digestive processes, though some of it may be social even then. At any rate, by 3 months of age smiling in social situations is a reliable event in most infants. At this age it has been noted in !Kung San infants in Botswana (Konner, 1979), in Israeli town and kibbutz children (Gewirtz, 1963), and, of course, in many Western countries. In blind infants smiling is delayed somewhat, but it is elicited by the same social events as in normal children (Freedman, 1974).

The regularity and uniform timing of the emergence of smiling in all societies studied suggests that its onset is under maturational-biological control. Konner (1979) suggests that the maturation of certain brain structures, for example, the formation of myelin sheaths (myelination) around visual and motor nerve fibers at 3 months (which makes finer muscle control possible) and increased attentional capacity may be responsible for the emergence of social smiling. Its further development, however, will be subject to environmental events, particularly social reinforcement. So we see here, too, the interweaving of maturational and environmental forces.

Emotion Expression

Darwin (1872) was the first to interpret nonverbal communication, particularly the expression of emotions, in animals as adaptive behavior that served to increase fitness. He also noted that a comparable system exists among humans. In more recent years the facial expression of emotions in humans, as a form of nonverbal communication, has received a great deal of study as one of those human behaviors that may have universal application and interpretation. A recent review (Ekman & Oster, 1979) has presented a summary of these studies.

Cross-cultural research has shown that observers label certain facial expressions of emotion (e.g., of surprise or sadness) in the same way, regardless of culture. Even people from preliterate cultures agree on the interpretation of expressions of, say, anger or disgust, as produced by Westerners. Members of different cultures show the same facial expressions when experiencing the same emotion, unless culture-specific display rules interfere. It was found, for instance, that when a person in authority

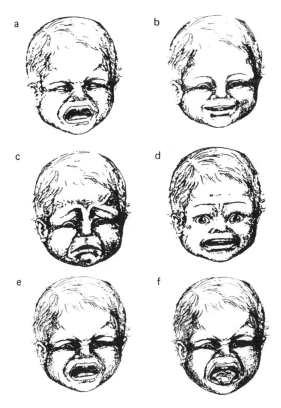

FIGURE 3.1. Facial expressions of basic emotions in infants: (a) anger-rage; (b) enjoyment-joy; (c) sadness-dejection; (d) fear-terror; (e) discomfort-pain; (f) disgust. From *Maximally Discriminative Facial Movement Scoring System* by C.E. Izard, 1979, unpublished manuscript, University of Delaware. Reprinted by permission.

was present, Japanese subjects smiled more and showed more control of facial expression than did American subjects—something that could be predicted from the different display rules in the two cultures (Ekman, 1972).

Distinctive facial expressions resembling certain adult ones are present in early infancy. Crying, as an expression of distress, is present from birth, but both Darwin (1872) and others observed that young infants, as distinct from adults, lower their brows and close their eyes tightly in discomfort and pain. The classical expressions of fear and anger, however, do not seem to emerge in children under 6 months of age (Izard, 1979, cited in Buck, 1981). (Typical infant expressions of certain emotions, as put into schematic form by Izard [1979], are shown in Figure 3.1.) Such infant facial expressions, moreover, elicit adaptive responses from adolescent and young adult observers, that is, more "find out" reactions to distress/pain expressions, and more "cuddle/hug" responses to sadness expressions (Stettner & Loigman, 1983).

While infants, no doubt are, genetically predisposed to emit certain affect signals in rigid form, the expression of affect is also partly socialized by learning from parents and peers. Zivin (1983) has studied what she has called the "plus face"; a facial expression that conveys a sense of confidence and openness to challenge. She concluded that this expression starts out as an involuntary manifestation of an internal state, but that in later childhood it becomes transformed through learning processes into a flexible signal, emitted deliberately.

Thus recent research has reaffirmed the generality and universal similarity of emotion expression. Expressive behaviors serve both biological and social functions. They serve a biological function by providing sensory feedback for the conscious experience of emotion, and they serve a social function by providing nonverbal signals that communicate the actor's emotion to others and thereby influence others' behavior.

Wariness of Strangers

The onset of fear (or wariness) of strangers may well be another biologically adaptive kind of behavior. Its onset has a very similar timing—peaking between 9 and 13 months—in the !Kung San, two Guatemalan societies, the Israeli kibbutz, and in Boston, Massachusetts, for both home-reared and day-care children (Konner, 1979). Such regularity of development can, no doubt, best be explained by maturational forces, for example, by the myelination of certain parts of the "old brain" (that is, the brain below the cortex) toward the end of the first year of life (Konner, 1982). The onset of fear of strangers can, however, also be explained through certain cognitive advances at that age, plus the establishment of affectional ties with a mother figure, something which we will discuss in Chapter 4. The course of development that fear takes later will in any case be more dependent on the child's experiences, for example, her relationship with her mother and others in her environment.

Other Early Social Behaviors

Evidence for the hypothesis that many social behaviors may have a genetic component, and be rooted in biological predispositions, also comes from cross-racial comparisons of very young children. Kagan, Kearsley, and Zelazo (1978) studied the development and reactions of Chinese-American and European-American children from $3\frac{1}{2}$ months to 2 years in age, in day-care and home settings. They found that the Chinese-American children, as compared with the European-American children, were quieter, stayed closer to mother, played less when they were with unfamiliar children or adults, and cried more often upon maternal departure. They also had more stable heart rates. The authors concluded that "this cluster of qualities implies a disposition toward inhibition among Chinese children, a disposition that may have a partially biological basis" (p. 268).

If the objection is raised that the parents' socialization practices may have had ample time and scope to produce these differences, one can point to an investigation of European- and Chinese-American newborns (Freedman, 1974), which also showed the Chinese newborns to be calmer and less perturbable, although the two groups were essentially equal in sensory and motor development and in social responsivity. Although the parents may have reinforced and strengthened these differing behavioral tendencies in their children at a later age, it does seem that some of these so-called temperamental characteristics were built into the children's nervous system from the start. (The nature of temperament will be discussed in greater detail in Chapter 4.) It is not easy to see, however, why it should be "adaptive" for the Chinese children to be calmer and for the European children to be more excitable.

Apart from the head-turning for feeding at the breast, none of the preadapted behaviors that we have reviewed displays the characteristics of a completely "fixed action pattern," as it manifest itself in many animals. In view of the great variability of human experience, and the notable capability of humans to shape and modify their behavior through learning, fixed action patterns are, indeed, not to be expected in humans in later life.

Genetic Influences

BEHAVIOR GENETICS

The theme of the last section has been that many human behavioral characteristics are biologically adaptive and preprogrammed in the individual, and that these are present roughly to the same extent among humans the world over. This implies that these dispositions are transmitted genetically. Ethologists and sociobiologists differ from geneticists in that the former typically infer genetic transmission from the history and universal presence of the behavior. Geneticists, on the other had, actually investigate the genetic (and environmental) mechanisms that influence behaviors on which individuals differ. In this section we will discuss by what methods genetic and environmental influences on individual differences are detected, and also explore the important question of how far such attempts have helped us to an understanding of the origins of social characteristics.

Behavior genetics attempts to assess the degree of genetic influences on various characteristics in animals and humans. This science has been called a hybrid discipline, because it stands at the intersection of genetics and the behavioral sciences. The discipline applies the various techniques of genetics to behavioral characteristics in animals and man in order to trace the pathways of genetic influence. This involves physiological, molecular and cytological investigations (cytology is the study of cells) and, above all, quantitative-statistical analyses, which we will discuss below.

GENETIC AND ENVIRONMENTAL MECHANISMS

The science of genetics originated with Mendel, whose pioneering experiments in the 1860s lay long forgotten and were rediscovered about the year 1900. He was preoccupied with how simple, discrete characters, such as the color of garden peas, were transmitted to succeeding generations, and his seminal discovery was that a given character, such as the yellow color of peas, was transmitted in certain regular proportions to the offspring. Although this is not the place for a detailed account of Mendelian genetics (for further details see, for instance, Plomin, DeFries, & McClearn, 1980), we should note that Mendel deduced from his findings the fundamental theory that each parent possesses two elements—later to be called *genes*—that, acting in one locus, determine each trait. Mendel recognized two types of genes: dominant and recessive. If a dominant gene from one parent joined up with a recessive gene from the other parent the dominant gene won out, for example, a yellow color would prevail in peas. But a recessive trait, such as green color, would be expressed only if two recessive genes were paired.

Over the last 100 years or so, our knowledge of the physical properties of the genetic material has increased enormously, for example, it is known that genes are collected together on *chromosomes*. Since Mendel's time a number of complications have been introduced into his simple picture, but basically it is still the foundation for explaining the transmission of discrete, "single-gene characters." For humans this approach is useful mainly for explaining certain defects, for example, phenylketonuria (PKU), which is a recessive single-gene character, which we will discuss later.

Most human traits, however, are not all-or-none, but continuously graded characteristics and, so far as they are genetically determined at all, are not determined by a single set of genes but by many genes acting together, that is, they are subject to *polygenic* effects. To study the transmission of such traits quantitative statistical methods are employed, which are an extension of Mendelian theory in that they still assume that genes are transmitted independently of each other, and that the integrity of each gene is preserved so that it does not blend with any other gene. The continuous distribution of a trait, where interindividual differences are marked by small gradations, is brought about by the additive effects of many genes bearing on the same trait. Our discussion will be almost entirely concerned with quanitative genetics.

The question of how far one can assess the relative impact of heredity and environment has often been misunderstood. We cannot say how much of a behavioral trait per se, for example, aggression, is due to genetic and how much to environmental factors, as genes do not operate in a vacuum. The development of the organism and of behavior is always guided into certain channels by the joint action of genetic information and environmental factors. On the other hand, the relative importance of genetic differences or of variations in environments can be assessed for behavioral *differences among individuals*. Behavior genetics does not deal with the question of the causes of behavior in an individual, but rather with the causes of differences among individuals, that is, it assesses the relative contributions of heredity and environment to *individual differences* in a given trait.

Strictly speaking, behavior can never be inherited. What is transmitted are genes which carry genetic information. This information directs the production of specific enzymes or other proteins that control the metabolism of the cell which, in turn, affects behavior (Plomin et al., 1980).

The phenomenon of PKU illustrates the pathway whereby a gene affects behavior and it also provides a clear example of how a phenotype depends on both a genotype and environmental factors for its manifestation. The genetic defect in this case arises from the fact that the PKU gene inhibits the production of phenylalanine hydroxylase. This is an enzyme that normally metabolizes the amino acid phenylalanine into tyrosine. If this conversion is blocked, phenylalanine levels increase and phenylalanine-derived toxins accumulate in the body, thereby causing mental retardation. However, if the infant is given a phenylalanine-free diet in the early years the brain appears to develop normally. The genetic defect is still present, but its effects are mitigated by means of environmental action. Adults do not have to adhere to a phenylalanine-free diet, as their brain is not affected by the toxic substances.

It also is useful to think of the genotype of a trait not as a fixed value, but as possessing a reaction range, with the phenotype occupying a position within this range that depends on environmental factors. For instance, the height of children born to ethnic Japanese parents in North America is greater than that of Japanese children born in Japan. Assuming that there is no selective migration, this is a good example of a phenotypic variation that occurs within the reaction range of a given genotype as a result of environmental factors—presumably an improved pre- and postnatal environment for Japanese Americans. Figure 3.2 illustrates the concept of the reaction range by applying it to data on adolescent height (Gottesman, 1974). Each curve represents in schematic form the variation in height of a particular genotype, that is, its reaction range under different environmental conditions, crudely categorized as "restricted," "natural habitat," and "enriched." This example illustrates how environmental factors can interact with the genotype, that is, how some genotypes are more responsive to environmental changes than are others. Thus Genotype D appears to be more affected by environmental factors than does Genotype A.

Overall we must think, then, of a maturational program that controls the

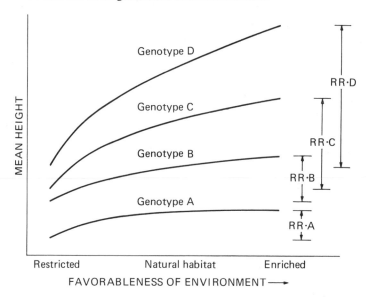

FIGURE 3.2. The reaction range concept applied to adolescent height (units for both X and Y axes are only ordinal and are not to scale). From "Developmental Genetics and Ontogenetic Psychology: Overdue Detente and Propositions From a Matchmaker" by I.I. Gottesman, 1974, in A.D. Pick (Ed.), *Minnesota Symposia on Child Psychology*, Vol. 8 (pp. 55–80), Minneapolis: University of Minnesota Press. Copyright 1974 University of Minnesota Press. Reprinted by permission.

development of the individual from conception to death. It constrains development within a certain range and, at the same time, the existence of genetic variability ensures the development of individual differences at the phenotypic level. In addition, the genotype is susceptible to environmental influences and this great flexibility is itself a part of the genetic program: human genes predispose us to learn.

Methods of Human Behavior Genetics

If we are dealing with animals we can study the inheritance of individual differences very conveniently by breeding studies. One approach is to use inbred strains, which after several generations of inbreeding are genetically uniform. Such genetically identical animals can than be exposed to differing environments to investigate the effects of variation in the environment. In this type of study genetic variation is kept at zero and environments are allowed to vary, so that any resultant variation in behavior is bound to be attributed to environmental sources.

A diametrically opposite kind of experiment is to select animals according to some characteristic and then arrange for mating within the selected groups, possessing opposite tendencies. Tryon (1940), for instance, started with an unselected population of rats, tested them for maze-running ability and then mated the "bright" males (those good at running mazes) with the bright females and the dull males with the dull females. He continued to mate the brightest offspring with each other and the dullest offspring with each other, until after eight generations the bright and dull rats formed two nonoverlapping populations (the dullest of the bright rats was brighter than the brightest of the dull rats). In this way he demonstrated the paramount importance of genetic factors in maze-brightness in rats. Note, however, that he carefully kept the environment for both groups the same—they were all reared in bare cages. Since the environmental variation was zero, and only genetic factors varied, the situation was a mirror image of that in the inbreeding studies, so that genetic factors were bound to appear as the sole reason for variation in brightness. Neither type of experiment permits the normal coaction of genes and environment to show its effects.

For humans, breeding experiments have generally been considered unethical, although recently established sperm banks are a kind of breeding experiment, which may, however, be questionable on social and other grounds. Other methods of detecting genetic effects have therefore been employed. Pedigree studies, for instance, were carried out by Sir Francis Galton in Britain at the end of the 19th century for the purpose of investigating the inheritance of genius or other, more normal, human characteristics. Pedigree studies can distinguish different modes of inheritance, for example, sex-linked versus non-sex-linked effects. Such investigations have also been done on characteristics such as mental retardation, reading disability, and schizophrenia.

The most widely used method of human behavior genetics has been the comparison of identical (monozygous [MZ]) with fraternal (dizygous [DZ]) twins. Since MZ twins arise from a split in the same fertilized ovum after conception, they are deemed to be genetically identical. Fraternal twins, on the other hand, arise from the fertilization of two different ova by two different sperm. They therefore share, on average, 50% of their genes, as do any sibs, and their genetic correlation is expected to be .5. Given certain assumptions, statistical comparisons of the average within-pair similarity of MZ twins with the average within-pair similarity of DZ twins can reveal the existence of a genetic component in a trait, and with a lesser degree of confidence, its magnitude. Environmental influences can be detected in parallel ways (see details below). Monozygous twins reared apart provide a special opportunity of assessing the influence of the environment on development, since all differences between such twin partners must, by definition, be of enviromental origin. However, such twins are rare and difficult to find.

Their relative simplicity, and the fact that age is automatically controlled, makes twin studies a very attractive method of investigating traits presumed to carry polygenic effects. An important assumption of the twin method is the "equal environments assumption," that is, that MZ twins are not treated more alike than DZ twins. If they are, the greater resemblance of MZ twins may result from more similar treatment rather than from genetic factors. In fact, there is evidence that parents do treat MZ twins more similarly than DZ twins in several respects (Jones, 1955; Lytton, 1980; Scarr, 1968). However, Scarr (1968) and Lytton (1980) showed, partly from data on twins whose zygosity had been misdiagnosed, that it is the twins' actual zygosity, not their parents' belief about this, that determines the degree of differential treatment. In other words, parents' treatment reflects the degree of genetic similarity in the twins, and parents respond to, rather than create, existing differences between the twins. The more similar treatment of MZ than of DZ twin partners therefore appears to be a genetically induced effect. This conclusion is consonant with the evidence that parents' treatment is itself in part molded by the children they are rearing (Bell, 1977). All this means that differential treatment does not erroneously inflate the estimate of genetic influence and hence this particular objection to the twin method is not well founded.

More recently, adoption studies have come into vogue as potentially powerful means of disentangling genetic and environmental influences. Here two questions can be asked: (1) To what extent do children resemble their biological parents and biological siblings?—a measure of hereditary influence, since the children were not reared by their biological parents—(2) To what extent do they resemble their adoptive parents and adoptive siblings?—a measure of environmental influence. A drawback of adoption studies is that adoptive children and their parents and siblings are not the same age and therefore parents and children have to be given different tests. But tests of the same personality trait for different ages (for example, Eysenck's adult and junior personality inventories) are not identical and may be only roughly equivalent. Differences in tests and age are therefore potentially confounding sources of variation, that may depress the correlations of interest.

Heritability

Heritability is a term widely bandied about and it is therefore important to understand its meaning clearly. Following genetic theory, we can decompose the phenotypic variance of a trait into genetic and environmental components. Heritability is defined as the proportion of phenotypic variance $[V(P)]$ of a trait in the population due to genetic variance $[V(G)]$, that is, heritability $= V(G)/V(P)$. Its possible range is from zero to one. In more common parlance, the calculated value indicates the degree to which actual *individual differences* in a trait are attributable to genetic differences.

If we assume that a trait is inherited, then MZ twin partners are expected to be more similar in it than DZ twin partners. Hence, if on average we find greater similarity in MZ twin partners, then we know that individual differences in this trait are to some extent due to a genetic component. One method of assessing heritability therefore involves comparing the intraclass (or within-pair) correlations of MZ and DZ twins for a given trait, since the intraclass correlation indicates the degree of similarity between the partners.

The meaning and limitations of heritability figures must be understood. First, heritability estimates are population statistics and not individual statistics. If, for instance, sociability has a heritability of .40, this does not mean that 40% of a child's sociability is due to heredity, but only that 40% of the variation in sociability in a population is determined by genetic differences among members of that population.

Further, it must be realized that estimates of heritability refer only to a specifically defined trait in a particular population at a given time and in given environmental conditions. Such estimates may change in different populations and under different circumstances. As discussed above, the range of relevant environmental variation in the population studied will affect the heritability. Donald Hebb has invented an extreme fictitious example to illustrate this point: he imagined a heterogeneous collection of children, all being reared in uniform barrels and not being allowed out of them. Though their intelligence, tested after some years, would vary, it can be expected to be generally very low, and we would sensibly ascribe this to their depriving experience. Yet, since the environmental variation was zero, the calculated heritability would be 1.0, that is, 100%. (See Scarr & Kidd, 1983, for a longer discussion of these points.)

Hebb's example is, of course, an unrealistic one, and for continuously distributed traits, such as intelligence or extraversion, heritability may be a useful statistic about a defined population, so long as its limitations are recognized. To assess genetic determination in discontinuous or all-or-none characteristics, such as schizophrenia, it is more usual to calculate concordance rates, that is, the number of twin partners of affected twins who also show the disease.

GENETIC STUDIES OF PERSONALITY AND TEMPERAMENT

Twin Studies

What degree of genetic influence on personality and temperament has actually been detected in empirical investigations? Nichols (1979) has integrated a vast mass of data from the twin literature on ability, personality and interests, published up to 1971. He concluded that the mean difference between MZ and DZ intraclass correlations is about .20 (which works out to an average heritability estimate of .40), whether one measures abilities, personality, or interests; in other words, the degree of genetic influence is about the same for all three domains. However, not all the heritability estimates are of such a magnitude that they reach statistical significance. If one looks at the areas that show a significant genetic component, one finds that the genetic influence varies between the different realms. Using this more rigorous approach we find that genetic influence is weaker, or is less easily detected, in personality variables than it is in cognitive abilities, as measured, for instance, by intelligence or language achievement tests.

That temperament and social behavior appear to be less genetically influenced than physical development and intelligence also has been demonstrated in two more recent investigations that included these different domains. Goldsmith and Gottesman (1981) studied about 300 pairs of twins from the Collaborative Perinatal Project and found that physical development (at 8 months) and IQ (at 4 years) showed evidence of greater genetic determination than did their temperament measures. Lytton, Watts, and Dunn (1988), in a follow-up of 35 sets of male twins, aged about 9 years, were able to detect a significant heritable component by at least one method in 50% of physical and cognitive variables, but in only 36% of social characteristics.

Recent genetic investigations of personality characteristics in children have been well summarized by Goldsmith (1983). What emerged was a picture of only patchily significant results, though moderate consistency across studies was apparent for certain selected variables (see below). Most of the samples were small, but larger samples, for example, those of Goldsmith and Gottesman (1981), or of Loehlin and Nichols (1976) did not produce more consistent results.

A demonstration of a genetic component in a trait at different ages, if it can be achieved, would provide a convincing argument for concluding that the trait is, indeed, partly under genetic control. Hence longitudinal twin studies that examine genetic variance in the same sample and the same social traits (at least traits that have equivalent labels) at different ages are important. A number of such studies have been carried out and their results are summarized in Table 3.1. Clearly, relatively few social-personality variables show consistent genetic determination over age, especially since Torgersen's (1981) data, because of some technical problems, are somewhat doubtful. Matheny (1980) has demonstrated some of the most consistent genetic variance over age in the Louisville twin sample. In this study individual behavioral variables at ages 3 to 24 months were reduced by factor analyses to factors, and those with the greatest genetic variance are shown in the Table 3.1. The profile of factors represents the pattern of mean levels of scores across all the derived factors. The fact that this profile had a consistent genetic component suggests that the organization of these temperament variables within the individual partly followed a genetic blueprint.

In summary, what are we to make of this evidence? As far back as 1939, Portenier noted that twins were less alike on personality traits than on intellectual or physical traits. It is clear that it is more difficult to demonstrate significant genetic variance in personality than in cognitive variables

TABLE 3.1. Longitudinal twin studies of personality attributes (including temperament).

Matheny (1980): 72–91 MZ, 35–50 DZ pairs; factors derived from Bayley's Infant Behavior Record.

	Significant differences between MZ and DZ intraclass correlations					
	3 months	6 months	9 months	12 months	18 months	24 months
Task orientation	yes	yes	no	yes	yes	yes
Test affect-extraversion	no	yes	no	yes	no	yes
Activity	no	no	no	no	yes	yes
Profile of factors	yes	yes	yes	yes	yes	yes

Goldsmith & Gottesman (1981): 110–116 MZ, 206–213 DZ pairs; factors derived from psychologists' ratings.

	Significant differences between MZ and DZ intraclass correlations	
	4 years	7 years
Spontaneity/activity	no	yes
Task persistence	yes	no
Irritability	yes	not a factor
Fearfulness	not a factor	no
Agreeableness	not a factor	no

Torgersen & Kringlen (1978), Torgersen (1981): 34 MZ, 16 DZ pairs; temperament categories, based on NYLS, derived from mother interviews.

	Significant F ratios: $\dfrac{\text{DZ intrapair variance}}{\text{MZ intrapair variance}}$	
	9 months	6 years
Regularity	yes	yes
Threshold	yes	yes
Approach	yes	yes
Intensity	yes	yes
Activity	yes	yes
Persistence	yes	yes
Distractibility	yes	not measured
Mood	yes	yes
Adaptability	yes	yes

Lytton (1980), Lytton, Watts, & Dunn (1988): 13–17 MZ, 22–29 DZ male pairs; behavior categories derived from mother interviews (and behavior count, age 2).

	Significant F ratios	
	2 years	9 years
Attachment	no	no
Compliance[a]	no	no
Conscience	no	no
Independence	yes	no

TABLE 3.1. *Continued*

| | Significant *F* ratios | |
	2 years	9 years
Speech[b]	yes	yes
Verbal IQ	no	no
Nonverbal IQ	not obtained	yes

Dworkin, Burke, Maher, & Gottesman (1976, 1977): 25–79 MZ, 17–68 DZ pairs; MMPI and CPI scores at adolescence and adulthood.

Significant MZ vs. DZ intraclass correlation differences or significant *F* ratios

MMPI

Anxiety and dependency significant in adolescence and adulthood.

7 scales significant in adolescence only.

3 scales significant in adulthood only.

3 scales not significant at either age.

Profile contour not significant at either age, nor in change over age.

Mean level of scales significant in adolescence and in change over age, not in adulthood.

CPI

Dominance and good impression significant in adolescence and adulthood.

7 scales significant in adolescence only.

3 scales significant in adulthood only.

6 scales not significant at either age.

Profile contour significant at both ages and in change over age.

Mean level of scales significant in adulthood and in change over age, not in adolescence.

Note. MZ = monozygous; DZ = dizygous; NYLS = New York Longitudinal Study; MMPI = Minnesota Multiphasic Personality Inventory; CPI = California Personality Inventory.
[a] Compliance rating by teacher had significant *F* ratio, but not those by mother or father.
[b] Count at age 2, rating for quality at age 9.

and that such variance tends to be found less consistently from study to study.

However, there are also some convergent findings from a number of studies that confirm the existence of a genetic component in certain social characteristics. Genetic factors have been found to make a contribution to social orientation or sociability (cf. Buss & Plomin, 1975; Matheny & Dolan, 1980; and others), extraversion (cf. Eaves & Eysenck, 1975), activity level (cf. Goldsmith & Campos, 1982) and to social maladjustment—both when it takes the form of antisocial conduct (Lytton et al., 1988) and of neurotic anxiety (Shields, 1976).

Further, there is an intriguing convergence of evidence from several samples of different ages for a genetic contribution for dominance, that is, assertive behavior, in males but not females (Dworkin, 1977; Loehlin & Nichols, 1976). Such a finding of genetic determination for males, but not females, throws an interesting sidelight on the fact that dominant behavior usually has been found to be more marked in males than in females (Jacklin & Maccoby, 1978).

Adoption Studies

The rationale for studying adopted children in genetic research has been explained above. Three large-scale adoption studies have been undertaken recently to assess genetic and environmental variance in ability and personality variables: the Minnesota, the Texas, and the Colorado Adoption Projects. What do these adoption studies have to tell us about genetic influence on personality variables?

Both the biological parent-child and the adoptive parent-child correlations for personality variables tend to be rather low, thus suggesting neither a strong genetic nor strong environmental influence. The difference between biological parent-child and adoptive parent-child correlations in the Minnesota project (indicating genetic influence) are significant for extraversion and for neuroticism, but the estimate of genetic variance is lower than that generated by twin studies in general (Scarr, Webber, Weinberg, & Wittig, 1981). In the Texas project no genetic influence on personality traits, measured by the Cattell personality scales and parental ratings, was discernible (Loehlin, Horn, & Willerman, 1981), nor could any be detected in the Colorado project (Plomin, 1982).

On the other hand, these studies do report a small degree of resemblance between adoptive family members in a number of personality areas, for example, Scarr et al. (1981) found a median correlation of .06 for adoptive parents and children and Loehlin et al. (1981) a median correlation of .17 for same-sex adoptive siblings on traits such as extraversion and neuroticism. This suggests that living together in the same family does tend to lead to some personality resemblance.

The adoption studies, therefore, provide even less support than the twin studies for the proposition that variations in normal personality traits can be explained by genetic factors, except in the case of extraversion. By analyzing data from twin and adoption studies together, Loehlin (1986) also found genetic effects in extraversion and activity level. The adoption studies manifest a small degree of common environmental influence, as well.

Juvenile delinquency and later adult criminality are worth a special mention. As for juvenile delinquency, twin studies show little difference in concordance rate (a term explained above) between MZ and DZ twins, and adoption studies also provide only doubtful evidence of a genetic component in this disposition (Cloninger & Reich, 1983). This, however, applies to delinquents in general, a group which includes a large proportion of one-time offenders for whom delinquency is only a transient phenomenon of adolescence. There is good evidence, on the other hand, for the importance of genetic influences in criminality in adults. This evidence comes chiefly from adoption studies which demonstrate that the sons of biological fathers with a criminal record, who had been adopted by other families, are considerably more likely to become criminals than sons of noncriminal biological fathers. On the other hand, criminality in adoptive fathers has little effect on adopted sons in the absence of criminality in the biological fathers. Thus gene-environment interactions are evident. As well, the probability of criminality in sons, adopted by other families, increases in line with the number of convictions that their biological fathers had, that is, the genetic influence—though it is not the only influence— seems particularly striking in the case of repeat offenders (Mednick et al., 1983). Persistent antisocial disorder in adults, it should be noted, often will have begun in childhood (Rutter & Giller, 1983).

COMMENTS ON GENETIC AND ENVIRONMENTAL INFLUENCES ON PERSONALITY TRAITS

It clearly is more difficult to detect significant genetic contributions to normal personality traits than to cognitive characteristics using the statistical methods of behavior genetics. Genetic variance can, however, be shown to play a part in certain personality variables, and for some this can be demonstrated repeatedly at different ages (cf. Table 3.1). On the other hand, investigations that have sought to show consistent genetic determination across samples or over age have not always been successful. For example, in summarizing three studies with separate samples, Vandenberg (1967) showed that no variable in the Minnesota Multiphasic Personality Inventory (MMPI) or Cattell's High School Personality Questionnaire scales had significant F ratios across all three studies.

Lack of consistency of genetic components over age in the same sample can be seen in several studies summarized in Table 3.1. It may be argued that despite this inconsistency genetic components still are present. For example, in infancy and early childhood characteristics may not have attained stability, so that inconsistency in genetic control at those ages would not damage the genetic hypothesis. In adolescence and adulthood, however, this argument is hardly tenable. It can plausibly be argued, though, that a trait may manifest diminished heritability at a later than at an earlier age, because differing environmental experiences of twin partners tend to accumulate. Therefore, environmental effects may become more pronounced with age.

However, in some cases genetic variance emerges only in adulthood. That genes switch themselves on and off over time has sometimes been advanced as an explanation of the later emergence of genetic components. But this phenomenon has actually been shown only for bacteria (cf. Gottesman, 1974) or embryonic development from an undifferentiated to a differentiated cell structure (Davidson, 1976). It is not at all clear how far such explanations are applicable to human personality traits with a presumed polygenic basis. Still, it is possible that genes switch themselves on and off for behaviors that are more maturationally appropriate at certain stages in life than at others—sexual behavior would be a case in point.

We have discussed that many human behavioral characteristics are directed by brain mechanisms and are biologically adaptive. This argument implies that these behavioral characteristics are genetically transmitted. It is paradoxical that such a genetic base is very difficult to pin down for most personality patterns by behavior genetic methods, and hence for many personality characteristics genetic determination cannot be claimed with certainty.

Possible environmental influences, on the other hand, do not easily bear the burden of explaining the development of personality characteristics either: environmental effects shared among members of a family appear to carry relatively little weight and environmental influences that differentiate between family members seem to act almost in random fashion within families, as shown in Loehlin and Nichols' (1976) study, discussed above. The fact that environmental factors operate in such complex ways in itself points to the importance of person-situation interaction in explaining the variance of personality traits (cf. Endler & Magnusson, 1976). The finding of significant genetic determination in the person-situation interaction for at least one such trait—anxiety (Dworkin, 1977)—suggests that genotype-environment interaction may play a role in some personality variables.

Environmental forces need not only be thought of as factors that influence development independently, jointly, or in interaction with the genotype. We may also consider environments as being genotype-induced. Thus, Scarr and McCartney (1983) note that ". . . the genotype is the driving force behind development, because . . . it is the discriminator of what environments are actually experienced" (p. 425). In a provocative, speculative analysis Scarr and McCartney distinguish three types of genotype → environment effects: (1) the passive type, in which genetically related parents provide a rearing environment that is correlated with the child's genotype; (2) an evocative type, in which the child evokes responses from others that are influenced by her genotype; (3) the active type, in which the child selects and attends to those aspects of her environment that are correlated with her genotype, that is, the child seeks her own niche. The passive type is more salient for younger children, and the active type more relevant for older children, since the latter are more able to create their own environment as they transcend the family circle.

Complex systems of reciprocal effects and coaction between genetic program and environment thus exist. The inconsistency of genetic findings in many personality areas may be due to the very complexity of the relationships, or the fault may lie with the unreliable instruments with which we measure the traits. The small sample sizes of many studies are less likely to be a valid explanation, since the large-sample investigations also often fail to generate consistent results.

In any case, it seems advisable to require replication across studies or across ages, before accepting a genetic component as real. Since some personality characteristics showing consistent genetic components have been identified, a research strategy that is more selective and chooses to study traits which, judging from theory and past evidence, are more likely to demonstrate replicable genetic variance, may be more productive. When advances in neurophysiology and molecular genetics are combined with findings from quantitative behavior genetics, we can expect great strides to be made towards a fuller understanding of the relationships between genetic substrate and enviornmental factors.

The Biological Environment

Environment often is mistakenly equated with purely social forces that have their impact on the developing child postnatally. Yet some physio-logical-biological factors, distinct from hereditary-genetic ones, also form part of the environment that influences development. Biological forces act in the womb, which is the child's most important physiological environment, and also during her birth which is the most important physiological event in her life. But physiological forces also act postnatally, through the air, food, and water that the child absorbs, which all will contain both beneficial and deleterious agents (e.g., lead or hydrogen sulphide). Our discussion will now turn to the effects of such physiological factors emanating from the child's environment, and particularly the prenatal environment. The chief purpose of the discussion is to illustrate the powerful role that biological and chemical factors in the environment can play in shaping development.

RISK FACTORS IN PREGNANCY AND BIRTH

Biological Risks

Preterm birth and various complications of pregnancy (to be discussed below) have been found to be associated with a variety of disorders, ranging from miscarriage and perinatal death through cerebral palsy, epilepsy, mental deficiency, behavior and emotional disorders, to milder disorders such as reading disabilities. Pasamanick and Knobloch (1966) have referred to these disorders as the "continuum of reproductive casualty." The direct effects of biological adverse events will be modified by other factors, particularly the environment in which the child is reared, something that Sameroff and Chandler (1975) have called the "continuum of caretaking casualty." Optimal environments may mitigate the effects of adverse biological events, as will be demonstrated. Yet these biological effects are still real for at least a portion of the population. We will give greater emphasis in this chapter to the adverse outcomes affecting social-emotional development and malfunctioning than to the effects on physical and intellectual development, which receive more extensive coverage in general child development texts.

Nonhereditary Chromosome Anomalies

Chromosomes can be subject to many anomalies that are not hereditary and do not run in families. Irregularities may, in particular, occur during meiosis (cell division for reproduction), so that two chromosomes instead of the usual one go to a daughter cell (egg or sperm). With the chromosome coming from the other partner this makes three chromosomes per cell, a condition called *trisomy*. This defect is not necessarily hereditary, but occurs before conception and is genetic only in the sense that the genes are obviously involved.

It is usually excess or deletion of genetic material that causes damage. Down's syndrome, formerly called mongolism is the most common anomaly of autosomal chromosomes (chromosomes not involved in the determination of sex). It is caused by the addition of an extra chromosome to a certain pair (trisomy), so that there is an excess of genetic material. The physical features and mental retardation of Down's syndrome children are well known. They are usually held to be friendly, amiable, and of an easygoing disposition, although epidemiological studies have not always given support to this characterization. The most severely retarded, institutionalized, Down's syndrome children tend to show more hyperactivity and aggressiveness than those in the community (Corbett, 1977). Nevertheless, overall they exhibit less conduct disorders and are more cheerful and friendly than other retarded children.

Problems also may arise from an abnormal number of sex chromosomes. Thus individuals may have only one X chromosome (XO), three X chromosomes (XXX), or two X chromosomes and a Y chomosome (XXY). The general finding is that the larger the excess of X chromosomes beyond the normal complement of two (in females), the greater the degree of mental retardation.

Men carrying an XYY chromosome set were at one time thought to be prone to violence and aggression. More recent studies have cast some doubt on this particular assertion, but have confirmed that XYY men are more given to crime than men in general (Witkin et al., 1976). Thus, XYY men form a much larger proportion of inmates of correctional institutions (about 2%) than they do of the general population (about .1%) (Jarvik, Klodin, & Matsuyama, 1973). They also are characteristically taller than average. All these abnormalities demonstrated that the excess and change in organization of genetic material produces widespread consequences in the individual, that go beyond the contribution each chromsome may make individually.

Pregnancy Complications

Certain physiological conditions in a pregnant woman, and certain chemical substances ingested by her, are known to cause physical defects or mental retardation in the infant. Such *teratogenic agents*, as they are called, include virus infections (e.g., rubella), toxemia (or high blood pressure), certain drugs (of which thalidomide is the outstanding example), alcohol, and malnutrition. Some of these factors (e.g., rubella, thalidomide) cause adverse effects only during the early part of pregnancy, when they affect the organ systems that are in the stage of most rapid development. Because the deleterious effects produced by these teratogenic agents have been noted and studied mainly in physical structures and cognitive abilities, and little is known about their effects on social-emotional development, we will pass them over in this discussion.

Emotional Stress

Imposing stress experimentally can, of course, only be done with animals. But studies in which this has been done do provide us with some useful hypotheses about the effects of prenatal stress on human functioning. It has been found, for example, that when pregnant rats are subjected to stressful experiences (e.g., when they are exposed to the sounding of a bell or buzzer which had previously been paired with electric shock), their offspring are slower in maze learning and defecate more frequently, that is, they show disturbed emotionality. The possibility of the stressed mothers handling their young differently postnatally, and thereby affecting their behavior, was excluded by having some of the young reared by different mothers (Thompson, 1957, cited in Joffe, 1969).

Studies of emotional stress in humans have defined it by criteria such as trauma or shock, for example, husband's death or desertion, extramarital conception, or cramped accommodation that involve stressful human relationships. However, anxiety, poor emotional control, and emotional immaturity have also been implicated in pregnancy conditions, and hence in summarizing a number of studies it is more appropriate to speak of the findings as having demonstrated effects arising from "emotionality," an indicator of anxiety.

Carlson and Labarba (1979) have reviewed the literature on emotionality in human expectant mothers and the effect this has on their infants. They found many methodological weaknesses in studies searching for a possible link between emotionality in pregnancy and reproductive outcome. Nevertheless, the better designed studies support the conclusion that emotionality and reproductive outcome are related, and such a conclusion is strengthened by the animal research cited above. A link between emotionality in the mother and habitual abortion, pronounced vomiting, toxemia, and excessive crying in the infants has received support in these better studies (e.g., Ottinger & Simmons, 1964). The clearest results emerged when anxiety in the mother was related to a composite score for delivery and pregnancy complications.

Stott (1969) found, with a retarded group, that emotional stress (e.g., death of husband) during mother's pregnancy was closely associated with timidity in the child. Two of Stott's students also found a relationship be-

tween physical and emotional stresses in pregnancy and behavior disturbance in elementary school children and lack of effectiveness in 4-year-old
nursery school children.

Emotional stress, of course, does not act uniformly. Its timing during the
pregnancy, its intensity, and duration will be critical modulating factors.
Various mechansims by means of which detrimental effects are transmitted
to the fetus may be postulated: stress may act through adverse behavioral
factors in the mother (e.g., greater accident-proneness, lesser attention to
necessary diet and health care, or excessive smoking), or it may act via
stress-generated hormones that are transmitted to the infant. Moreover, a
constitutional factor may also be responsible for both the mother's emotionality and the reproductive complications, that is, the mother may transmit a certain lability by her genes, although the lability may express itself in
different forms in her child (Joffe, 1969).

Furthermore, prenatal states are also related to postnatal attitudes to the
child, as we will discuss further in Chapter 5. Maternal prenatal emotionality may continue postnatally and thereby influence the social and caretaking environment in which the child will be raised. In humans it is difficult
to separate out the effects on the child of the prenatal state from those of
postnatal treatment. The animal studies cited above, however, were specifically designed to keep these two sets of factors distinct and have found
an effect arising from the mother's prenatal state, separate from the effect
of her treatment of the young. (We will return to this point in discussing
the antecedents of "difficult" temperament in Chapter 4.) Although the
evidence linking emotionality during pregnancy to adverse behavioral
characteristics in human offspring is not conclusive, it is persuasive, especially since it emerges repeatedly in so many studies.

Overall, we may conclude that any maternal condition that impairs fetal
oxygen and nutrient transport or exchange of metabolic waste products,
or that releases an excess of particular hormones across the placenta is a
teratogenic influence that has the potential of deleteriously affecting the
ongoing development of the fetus. The kind of outcome in the child will
depend on the timing (as well as the nature) of the injurious influence,
since the developmental status of the organism is of importance. Thus, a
teratogenic agent that acts during early pregnancy may result in gross
structural defects, such as loss of limb or blindness, whereas a teratogenic
process in later pregnancy is more likely to produce growth retardation or
disturbance of psychological functions, such as mood (Kopp, 1983).

Perinatal Complications

Foremost among these complications is birth before the 40th week of
gestation, or preterm birth. Infants born preterm can be subdivided into
those who are small for gestational age versus those who are of appropriate
weight for gestational age, with the risks being higher for the former group.
Birth before the full term may arise from untoward conditions in the

mother, for example, adverse physiological, health, or nutritional state, from emotional stress, or from prenatal stresses in the infant. The incidence is much higher in poorer social classes and nonwhite populations, a fact which demonstrates the importance of environmental conditions.

Mortality and morbidity rates for neonates, and particularly for early births, have decreased sharply over the last 30 years or so, thanks to advances in prenatal care, perinatal medicine, and the intensive use of technology in caring for high-risk infants. However, pre- and perinatal events making for risk still occur; what has changed is mainly methods for dealing with the outcomes (Kopp, 1983).

Whereas Drillien (1964) reported that 40% of her total sample later showed intellectual or neurological sequelae, this percentage nowadays would be much lower. Kopp (1983) has summarized a number of more recent investigations of preterm infants and drawn the following conclusions: (1) As a group, with all weights averaged together, preterm infants of today show less serious consequences and higher intelligence test scores than those of a generation ago; (2) Healthy, heavier infants show less serious adverse consequences than lighter and sicker infants; (3) School problems continue to be noted in a proportion of preterm infants, but postnatal environmental conditions are likely to play a contributory role in these; (4) Investigations that have distinguished between advantaged and disadvantaged children have found a substantial performance difference between them—as did Drillien as early as 1964.

Although these conclusions relate to cognitive performance, they parallel findings concerning the later social behavior or behavior disorders of preterm infants. More disturbed behavior has been found in preterm infants than in sibling controls at age 5, with the most marked difference being seen in an excess of restless overactivity. A combination of low birth weight, complications of pregnancy and delivery, and severe family stresses (e.g., poverty) exert an even greater, cumulative effect on behavior disturbance (Drillien, 1964). Middle-class mothers of preterm infants have also reported more behavior problems at age 2 (e.g., hyperactivity, irritability, and short attention span), and less social maturity than have the mothers of full-term infants (Field, Dempsey, & Shuman, 1981).

The authors of a prospective large-scale study of all children born on the island of Kauai during 1955 and 1956 reported that preterm infants as a whole seemed to have made up their initial IQ deficit by age 10 (Werner, Bierman, & French, 1971). However, a later follow-up of the same sample reported that at age 18 three times as many mental health problems and twice as much mental retardation was found in a group who had experienced even moderate perinatal stress than in the cohort as a whole (Werner & Smith, 1982).

One study (Taub, Goldstein, & Caputo, 1977), found no difference between preterm and full-term infants in social behavior in middle childhood.

However, the difference in findings between this study and that of Field and her colleagues may be explained by the higher mean birth weight of the preterm infants in the Taub as compared with the Field investigation (1,600 vs. 2,100 gm).

Overall, the evidence suggests that in the more severely affected children, preterm birth may be a contributing factor to behavior disturbances and, particularly, hyperactivity, as well as to mental health problems. This may be connected to the deprivation of oxygen often suffered by preterm infants.

Anoxia refers to an insufficiency of oxygen in body tissues during, or immediately after, birth. It is a major hazard in preterm birth, but also occurs in infants born at term. Although it is connected to neurological impairment in the neonate, most studies show that intellectual deficits diminish over the years and all but vanish by middle childhood (e.g., Corah, Anthony, Painter, Stern, & Thurston, 1965). However, anoxic children and neonates of generally poor physical condition do seem to exhibit heightened maladjustment, distractibility, and lowered social competence, as compared with control children even in middle childhood (Corah et al., 1965; Stevenson, 1948).

Social Environmental Interacting with Biological Risk

Whenever socioeconomic status has been taken into account in an analysis of the effects of prenatal and perinatal complications, it has been found that these effects are compounded by poor socioeconomic conditions. Only cognitive functioning has been examined from this point of view and we will therefore summarize the findings briefly. Various investigations (e.g., Drillien, 1964; Werner et al., 1971) show that perinatal complications result in physical and psychological deficiencies in later childhood to a much larger extent when they are combined with persistently poor environmental circumstances, for example, in lower social class populations. On the other hand, a good, stimulating environment, as is provided in higher social classes, or educational intervention with disadvantaged children (Breitmayer & Ramey, 1986), largely compensates for the initial cognitive deficits that beset children who suffered nonoptimal birth conditions. Broman, Nichols, and Kennedy (1975) have also shown that mother's education and social class factors contribute considerably more to variation in IQ at age 4 than do pre- and perinatal adversities. We may conclude, as Kopp (1983) does from some additional investigations, that social class factors are much more important than are perinatal events for child outcome.

The importance of social class influence is no doubt due to the fact that they are translated into concrete experiences that surround the child daily: they are seen in the physical conditions of the household and its crowdedness, in nutrition, the availability of stimulating toys, and the amount of attention and responsiveness, especially verbal responsiveness, that the mother devotes to the child. Perinatal factors, on the other hand, are one-time events, the consequences of which, though they may be serious, also may be overcome with the help of good rearing conditions. Moreover, perinatal complications affect a far smaller percentage of the population than do poor economic conditions, and therefore they will explain a much smaller proportion of the variance for the population as a whole.

Because the summary variable of social class will express itself, as we have just noted, by some concrete parental behavior, a number of researchers have examined the degree and nature of maternal interactions with preterm and full-term infants and have looked for effects that may arise from these. Observation of mother-child dyads at different ages during the first 2 years of life indicate that preterm infants, irrespective of class, are relatively inactive and unresponsive. Parents respond to this by trying to stimulate and engage them in activity more than they would full-term infants—an approach, however, that leaves the infants as inactive and unresponsive as before. Parents' attempts in this respect seem to be unproductive (Bakeman & Brown, 1980; Beckwith & Cohen, 1980; Field, 1980; Goldberg, Brachfeld, & DiVitto, 1980; Greenberg, Crnik, Ragozin, & Robinson, 1983).

While parents of preterm infants try to be particularly stimulating, the quality of the interactions suffers. Mothers of such infants appear to be less contingently responsive and engage in less game-playing and childlike behavior, and there seems to be less overt enjoyment of the interaction by both mother and child (Field, 1980; Greenberg et al., 1983). Moreover, when a group of preterm infants were matched for age from conception (to allow for their premature birth) with full-term infants, the preterm infants still evinced more negative and less positive affect, and their parents were more active (Goldberg et al., 1980). Thus, the difficulties of the preterms cannot be attributed to simple developmental lag.

Does the kind of interactions preterm infants have with their mothers in the first months of life affect their later development? Bakeman and Brown (1980) report that simple amount of interaction between mother and infant, summarized across a number of behavior categories observed during the first 3 months, did not predict cognitive or social competence at age 3. Beckwith and Cohen, however, classified interactions into different kinds and found that certain types of maternal behavior observed during the first few months, particularly smiling during mutual gazing and talking, that is, mother-child social interactions, predicted mental test performance at age 2, and child-caregiver interaction at 2 years predicted test performance at age 5, over and above the prediction provided by social class alone (Beckwith & Cohen, 1980, 1984). Although the amount of variance accounted for was small and only limited predictability of mental development seemed possible, the study offers some hope that certain types of interactional experiences during the first few months may be helpful to the development of preterm infants. We may speculate that such good experiences are also likely to have a beneficial effect on the child's social adjustment.

Some social class differences in the expected direction also have been found: Higher social class mothers are more active, talk more, and engage in more social interchanges with their infants than do lower social class mothers (Beckwith & Cohen, 1980; Field, 1980). Since such verbal stimulation has not been found productive with young preterm infants in general, why does middle-class rearing, that emphasizes verbal interchanges, compensate for the vulnerabilities of preterm birth, as noted in other studies cited above? We do not know for sure, but it is possible that the compensatory effect is due to the generally more cognitively oriented climate of middle-class homes, to more sensitive responding by middle-class mothers, and to verbal stimulation becoming a more effective facilitator of cognitive development at lager ages.

Training parents of preterm infants in order to improve their sensitivity and responsivity to their child's signals and thus increase their interactional skills can pay off, particularly if the intervention program extends over the baby's first year. One intervention program of this kind, for example, produced behavioral changes in mother-infant interaction, improved the quality of the home environment, and also had some positive effect on the child's cognitive development (Barrera, Rosenbaum, & Cunningham, 1986).

There are two types of forces that make for deviant outcome: biological insult and malfunction on the one hand, and detrimental environmental conditions on the other. How can we sum up their respective roles in the child's development? As Sameroff and Chandler (1975) point out, in view of the range and variety of biological and environmental influences impinging on the fetus and neonate, the range of outcomes is surprisingly narrow. Evolution seems to have equipped the human organism with self-righting tendencies that will ensure a normal outcome, except under the most adverse circumstances.

If the adverse impact of either of these two forces is sufficiently severe, it may produce deleterious consequences by itself, for example, a brain severely damaged by rubella, or a seriously depriving environment such as being raised in total isolation, will separately produce developmental defects. The two forces are, however, strongly interrelated. Sameroff and Chandler (1975) argue convincingly that, where they occur at a less intense level, perinatal and prenatal complications will produce deviant outcomes only if they are compounded by environmental deficiencies. An impoverished environment may, however, produce adverse outcomes by itself.

PHARMACOLOGICAL INFLUENCES ON BEHAVIOR

In an earlier section we discussed the physiological structures in the brain that underlie social-emotional behavior, and the function of adrenaline in stress situations. In this section we will explain how certain chemical substances, particularly the sex hormones, that we have not classed among the risk factors in pregnancy (although some could well have been) are also biological-environmental forces that have an impact on enduring behavioral characteristics. This will underline the point of how much our social and emotional behavior is under the influence of the biochemistry of the body, as well as artificial substances manufactured to mimic bodily products (e.g., progestins which are similar to natural progesterone).

Newborn State

By way of introduction, let us first discuss pharmacological influences on the newborn state. The state of newborn infants is affected adversely by obstetrical medication administered to the mother. Both analgesics, which relieve pain, and anaesthetic substances, which render a person unconscious, have been shown to be related to lowered muscle tension, decreased responses to visual and auditory stimuli, and less efficient sucking in neonates. Anaesthetic (but not analgesic) agents, used during delivery, have even been found to affect mental and motor development at 1 year (Brackbill, 1979).

Other substances, too, affect the newborn state. For instance, there is evidence that variations in the level of serotonin (a neurotransmitter involved in sleep) in newborns' brains may modulate their arousal behavior. Healthy, full-term neonates in one investigation were fed a diet containing tryptophan (a precursor of serotonin) and they entered sleep sooner and tended to spend more time asleep and less time in an alert state than a control group of infants who were fed a different diet (Yogman & Zeisel, 1983). Elevated levels of bilirubin (jaundice) have been found to have similar effects on sleep and wakefulness in neonates (Freedman, Werthmann, & Waxler, 1983).

Androgens

Progestin

Money and Ehrhardt (1968) have studied the effects of prenatal exposure to an excess of androgenic (i.e., male) hormones on genetically female fetuses. The mothers of one group of children had been given synthetic progestins during pregnancy in order to avoid a threatened miscarriage. Synthetic progestins are similar to progesterone that is naturally produced by the body during pregnancy, but female sex hormones like progestins, when present in excess, also have androgenic qualities—a fact not known at the time (Daly & Wilson, 1983). A second group of girls studied suffered from the congenital adreno-genital syndrome, or female hyperadrenocortical hermaphroditism, which is a recessive genetic trait. In each case the female fetus is exposed to an excess of either exogenous (progestin) or endogenous (adreno-cortical) androgen. The timing is such that internal sexual organs remain unchanged, but external genitalia become masculinized to varying degrees under both conditions.

What is of greatest interest to us is the fact that behavior not linked to reproduction was also affected. The girls were between 4 and 16 years of age when they were assessed, and the two groups were very similar in interests and preferences but displayed sharp contrasts with a third group of girls suffering from Turner's syndrome (XO chromosomes). The reason for choosing Turner's syndrome individuals as a control group was that individuals with this syndrome have no fetal sex hormones to influence sexual differentiation and yet become girls. This syndrome therefore illustrates the principle that in the absence of either male or female sex hormones, differentiation occurs in the female direction.

Of the androgenized girls, 90 to 100% showed intense interests in outdoor physical and athletic activities, 75 to 90% were known to themselves or others as tomboys and showed more interest in boys' toys and less in dolls, something that the authors interpret as reduced maternal tendencies, and most of them preferred slacks, shirts, and shorts to dresses. All these are stereotypical masculine preferences. Hence it seems that fetal androgens may affect psychosexual differentiation in genetic females, although this in no way amounts to a complete psychosexual reversal. It has been argued that the masculine tendencies of these girls may be explained by parents' expectations evoked by the masculinized appearance of the girls, that is, the label "tomboy" may have preceded tomboyish behavior. However, at least in some cases surgical intervention was undertaken to correct the external genitalia. Parental attitudes towards their masculinized daughters did, in fact, not differ consistently from parental attitudes to a control group of girls (Ehrhardt, 1973). One would, in any case, expect parents to exert their influence, if at all, in the direction of trying to counteract the unfortunate consequences of the hormonal exposure and to encourage feminine interests and activities in accordance with the assigned gender.

Testosterone

The administration of testosterone prenatally has no therapeutic purpose and therefore is, fortunately, not practiced with humans. Hence what we know about the effects on female fetuses of administering testosterone prenatally comes from animal studies. Such studies (e.g., Goy & Kemnitz, 1983; Phoenix, Goy, & Resko, 1969) show that when pregnant rhesus monkeys are injected with testosterone propionate for a considerable part of the pregnancy, female offspring become "long-term pseudohermaphrodites." External genitalia are masculinized and other behavior identified with the juvenile male (in monkeys) is increased: rough-and-tumble play, or high energy expenditure, and mounting behavior are raised above the levels for untreated females; the latter behavior has been found to occur at an increased level even in the fourth year of life. In other words, some effects are persistent and some may not become manifest for many years. The similarities between the effects of prenatal testosterone in rhesus monkeys and those of prenatal progestin in humans are very striking.

It generally has been thought that for any long-term effects to materialize, the androgenic influence must occur prenatally at the time of sexual differentiation (Money & Ehrhardt, 1968; Phoenix et al., 1969). However, there is some evidence (Joslyn, 1973) that when androgen is injected into infant female rhesus monkeys, who have not been sensitized prenatally, their aggressive behavior is increased, at least for a time. Their playful and sexual behavior, however, remains feminine.

Goy and Kemnitz (1983) conclude that there is no reason to think that behavioral effects from chemicals are unique to androgens or to other hormones. All kinds of chemical substances introduced into the fetal circulation can produce effects. They may affect very specific behavioral systems and they may affect different systems in differential ways.

Pharmacological Influences on Mental Disorders

It is appropriate here to include a brief discussion of the involvement of biochemical substances in some of the major mental and emotional disorders to illustrate the important role that these substances play in psychological well-being or disorder. It should be stressed that the evidence in this area is not completely conclusive, in that much of it derives from animal studies, or from the effects that certain drugs with known chemical constituents have in humans in relieving or exacerbating a given disorder. Nevertheless, the evidence for the involvement of some biochemical agents in the major mental disorders is quite strong.

Studies of the mechanisms whereby antidepressants achieve their effects have produced much suggestive evidence that some amine neurotransmitter systems, such as serotonin, dopamine, and norepinephrine, are involved in the development of depression, that is, depressive patients may suffer from a deficiency of norepinephrine or serotonin. Moreover, several of these neurotransmitter systems may act in combination with each other. However, studies of different receptor sites and different antidepressants sometimes yield conflicting findings and therefore it is likely that multiple biochemical pathways, rather than one single pathway, for depression exist (McNeal & Cimbolic, 1986).

Biochemical pathways involved in schizophrenia are imperfectly understood. There is only indirect evidence that hyperactivity of the central dopaminergic system plays an important role in the genesis of schizophrenia. Drugs which increase the activity of this system, particularly amphetamines and L-dopa, are known to aggravate schizophrenic symptoms. Amphetamine, in higher doses, causes stereotyped behaviors symptomatic of schizophrenia, and prolonged administration of amphetamine leads to a behavior syndrome that mimics, and is clinically difficult to distinguish from, paranoid schizophrenia (Groves & Rebec, 1976). But there is no direct evidence that increased dopamine turnover is a cause of schizophrenic episodes.

The present state of knowledge indicates that psychiatric syndromes are probably not determined by one well-defined biochemical lesion; more probably several biochemical functional disorders (plus social environmental events) underlie these disorders (Van Praag, 1977).

Summary

Human development is shaped by biological as well as environmental forces, and this chapter has examined the evidence for the belief that any individual is the product of the joint action of both these factors. Many existing human features have arisen in the course of evolution, because they were adaptive for man's survival and reproduction in his ecological niche. Larger brain size and longer parental care for the infant are two such features that are interdependent and that have evolved because they are adaptive for the kind of flexibility in behavior that has enabled man to become the dominant species on earth.

Cultural evolution is nowadays more important than biological evolution, but the ability to profit and learn from the environment the way we do itself depends on human genes. We have reason to believe that infants are preprogrammed to manifest many behaviors typical of humans across all cultures, such as smiling, distress on separation from mother, or the characteristic expression of different emotions. Yet, these behaviors, too, are modified in some ways by learning and thus illustrate the constant intermeshing of genetic and environmental forces.

All social-emotional traits, such as extraversion or independence, are continuously distributed, and such traits are influenced by many genes, acting together. Behavior genetics attempts to disentangle the genetic and environmental variance in these traits by statistical methods. We cannot assess the contribution of heredity to the development of a trait as such. We can only evaluate the relative impact of heredity and environment on individual differences, or on the variance of the trait in the population. Twin studies do this by comparing the relative similarity of identical and fraternal twin pairs. Adoption studies do it by comparing the similarity of adopted children with their biological versus their adopted parents or siblings. In the personality area consistent genetic components have been found for sociability, extraversion, activity level, and some behavior disturbances. However, the genetic influence on personality and temperament is, on the whole, less strong and consistent than that on physical and intellectual characteristics. The inconsistency of findings in this area may be due to the very complexity of the transactions between the genetic program and environmental forces, or to the generally lower reliability of measures of social-emotional characteristics.

Conditions that affect the unborn child in the womb are part of her environment—they are the biological environment. In general, adverse conditions in pregnancy may affect the child physically, intellectually, and emotionally. Specifically, emotional stress and a high degree of emotionality in the mother, as well as birth before the full term, may put the child at risk for temperamental and adjustment problems, and preterm birth also may affect her cognitive development. However, the social conditions in which the child is reared interact with biological risk: Poor social conditions exacerbate the effects of biological trauma, whereas good conditions compensate for them. Thus the continuum of caretaking casualty is at least as important as the continuum of reproductive casualty.

Exposure to certain hormones in the womb may have long-lasting effects on the child and hormonal changes throughout life similarly affect behavior. Such facts demonstrate that social-emotional behavior is to a large extent under the influence of the biochemistry of the body.

4
The Origins of Social Behavior

Now that we have discussed the biological underpinnings of behavior, including those of emotions, we will move on to the beginnings of emotional behavior and of social interactions as they evolve over the first months of life.

The newborn, far from being a bundle of disorganized behavior and bodily functions, as is sometimes thought, actually arrives with many sensory and motor capabilities ready formed. The infant, from very early on, also displays temperamental qualities, such as mood or soothability, that are intimately related to the way she interacts with others. The beginnings of such social relationships lie in the interactions between parents and child, and these have been of considerable interest to child psychologists because they are thought to lay the foundation for later relationships throughout life, and this is particularly so for the development of attachment.

In this chapter we will therefore explore the topics of the infant's temperament, her attachment and relations to her parents, as well as other early social behaviors.

Temperament

DEFINITION

There are as many definitions of temperament as there are investigators of it, although there is convergence among them on some basic features that distinguish it. To make the theoretical discussion more concrete it is perhaps best to start with some instances of what has generally been regarded as temperament: activity level (included by all researchers), fearfulness, distractibility, irritability, mood, and soothability.

How can we subsume these disparate characteristics (and others) under a conceptual umbrella? Thomas and Chess (1977) consider temperament to be the *how* of behavior, that is, behavioral style. However, this is too simple because the content of behavior is involved, too; for instance, irritability, one of the temperament qualities, is a characteristic in which the how and the what of behavior are difficult to distinguish.

If we consider some features that most investigators would regard as pertaining to temperament, this will lead us to our definition of the concept. To include a behavior in the category of temperament it should appear early in infancy, be emotional in nature, affect interpersonal processes, and (less certainly) be presumed to have a constitutional basis. Some temperamental qualities also indicate the degree of ease with which behavioral and physiological systems are aroused.

Our definition of temperament (partly based on Campos, Barrett, Lamb, Goldsmith, & Stenberg, 1983) is: *Temperament refers to individual differences in the strength, timing, and regularity of arousal and emotions.*

This definition excludes cognitive and perceptual processes, although temperament may be related to them and affect them, and it excludes affective states (e.g., anxiety) themselves, although the degree of expression of affective states may depend on temperament (cf. Goldsmith & Campos, 1982).

Temperamental qualities form the basic components of personality, but there is no clear-cut distinction between temperament and personality. Perhaps personality can be distinguished from temperament in degree by the increasing salience, in personality constructs, of social relations with others, and an emerging self-concept (Goldsmith & Campos, 1982). Moreover, personality constructs imply a "higher-level" integration of behavior than do temperament constructs (e.g., we think of independence, aggressiveness, or morality as personality, but not as temperament variables).

HISTORY

The term "temperament" can be traced back to antiquity. Then it was thought to be determined by a combination of Galen's (129–70 B.C.) four humors (blood, phlegm, black bile, yellow bile). In more modern times, Allport (1937) incorporated temperament in his theory of personality, and his definition of temperament has a decidedly contemporary ring to it. He thought of temperament as characteristic phenomena of the individual's emotional nature, which include the customary strength and speed of response, the quality of the prevailing mood and its intensity, and he considered them as constitutional components of personality.

The scientific study of temperament, however, originated with the New York Longitudinal Study (NYLS) by Thomas, Chess, Birch, Hertzig, and Korn (1963). These authors' focus on temperament was prompted by a reaction to the environmental emphasis of the theories of the 1950s and 1960s. "In these theories, a loving and accepting mother should have a happy and contented child, from which it follows that an unconscious maternal attitude of rejection could be the only explanation for a difficult screaming child. As a result of reliance on these theories it was not unusual for the mother of a difficult infant . . . to develop self-doubts and feelings of guilt, anxiety, and helplessness . . ." (Thomas, Chess, & Birch, 1968, p. 79).

Interest in temperament, which has kept the study of this topic a thriving industry ever since the 1960s, stemmed from several sources. Psychiatrists, such as Thomas and Chess, had a strong interest in it as a way of shedding light on the clinical phenomena that they encountered. Rutter (1979), for instance, found that in homes marked by contention and discord, temperamentally "difficult" children suffered most, whereas temperamentally "easy" children escaped relatively unscathed. Interest in temperament was also fueled by concerns with educational problems, since it became apparent that hyperactivity, or disturbances of attention, affect school performance (e.g., Halverson & Waldrop, 1976; Thomas & Chess, 1977). Such findings support the view that temperament mediates cognitive learning, and that it is related to the child's social functioning, both at school and at home.

A significant impetus for the study of temperament also came from the fields of behavior genetics and developmental psychology, which saw in its investigation an avenue of exploration of the genesis of personality, and of the interplay of genetic and environmental factors that shape its development. A distillation of this interest can be seen in the review chapter by Campos et al. (1983).

Temperamental attributes characterize individuals throughout their life span. Our discussion, however, will focus on infancy, since the study of temperament at this age has provided the main body of literature in the area. The reasons why temperament has been studied almost exclusively in infancy are: (1) that it is thought that at this period of life socialization processes have not had sufficient time to exert influences which may, at later ages, mask underlying temperament; (2) that behavioral expressions of emotions are likely to be less influenced by cognitive self-regulation in infancy than later on (cf. Goldsmith & Campos, 1982).

MEASUREMENT

The NYLS (Thomas et al., 1963) derived its infant temperament ratings from detailed interviews with parents. Temperament categories were developed through an inductive analysis of the interview protocols, and ratings were allotted on the basis of mothers' descriptions of concrete behavior in varying situations; the researchers thus avoided more inferential interpretations. Nine categories were identified: activity level, rhythmicity, approach-withdrawal, adaptability, threshold of responsiveness, intensity of reaction, quality of mood, distractibility, and attention span. Other researchers have constructed questionnaires, often based on the NYLS dimensions (e.g., Carey, 1972), as a less time-consuming instrument. More recently, home and laboratory observations have also been pressed into service to provide assessments of temperament or temperament-like qualities (e.g., Lytton, 1980; Plomin & Rowe, 1979). However, parental report still constitutes by far the most popular method of assessing temperament. The review by Campos et al. (1983) mentions 22 temperament-related interview schedules, questionnaires, and so forth.

The measurement of temperament has been beset by a variety of problems. The nine dimensions of the NYLS—arrived at by clinical intuition— often do not emerge as factors in factor-analytic studies and hence cannot be regarded as reliable clusters of behavior. Thomas, Chess, and Birch (1968), however, found a factor representing "difficult" temperament, with loadings on approach-withdrawal, adaptability, mood, and intensity, and such a factor has been confirmed by Bates (1980).

Can temperamental qualities be rated reliably? The inter-judge reliability of ratings tends to be quite high and parents' reports of their children's temperament agree moderately with one another, but the test-retest reliability varies from category to category (Hubert, Wachs, Peters-Martin, & Gandour, 1982).

Do temperament ratings represent real behavior tendencies within the child; that is, to what extent are they valid? The ratings' validity has sometimes been tested by comparing them with observations of child behavior, and the outcome has been mixed. Agreement between mothers' reports and observed behavior reached 80% or more when children who scored extremely high on a given category were contrasted with the rest of the sample (Dunn & Kendrick, 1980). However, most studies have found only moderate convergence (e.g., Bates, 1980; Thomas et al., 1963). But then, as Rothbart and Goldsmith (1985) discuss in detail, high correlations between reports and observational measures are not to be expected in view of the different biases inherent in the different methods. Outside observers, for instance, see only a small slice of the children's behavior, whereas mothers can base their judgment on life-long acquaintance with their offspring. On the other hand, mothers' own characteristics may influence their perceptions of their children to some extent (Bates & Bayles, 1984), and this implies also that the standards that parents apply in their reports are relative; a mother who is more bothered by crying in her infant than other mothers may for this reason overstate the frequency of negative mood. Indeed, a lively debate has arisen around the question of whether a temperament quality can be regarded as an attribute residing entirely within the child, as Thomas, Chess, and Korn (1982) continue to claim, or whether it is better conceived as an attribute-as-perceived-by-a-parent, that contains both objective and subjective components, as Bates (1980) maintains.

The psychometric qualities of temperament measures obviously leave something to be desired. Yet, even though no completely satisfactory instrument exists and measurement is shaky, some aspects of temperament have considerable predictive power in the clinical area, as we shall see below, and the construct therefore has usefulness.

CONTINUITY OF TEMPERAMENT

Most researchers explicitly or implicitly assume a certain degree of stability in temperamental qualities in early childhood. Moderate, but not overwhelming, stability during infancy has, indeed, been the general tenor of findings of a number of studies that measured temperament by parental reports (e.g., Rothbart, 1981; Thomas & Chess, 1977). Stability in temperament has also been found in studies that relied on observation, although it was weaker in these, perhaps partly because the observational measures tend to be less reliable (e.g., Matheny, Riese, & Wilson, 1985; Rothbart, 1981). Among the dimensions of temperament, activity level and the quality of inhibition, or fearfulness, have emerged as salient and relatively stable characteristics of children (Thomas & Chess, 1977; Kagan, 1982a).

As Thomas and Chess (1977) stress, linear continuity in temperament dimensions is not to be expected, if we take the transactional view of development seriously. According to the transactional view (Sameroff, 1975), psychological development proceeds through constant processes of interaction between the organism and the environment, each modifying the other at every step. Relations between the organism and the environment (e.g., infant and parents) are thus constantly being restructured, and infant temperament is intimately connected with these relations.

TEMPERAMENT AND ITS CORRELATES

The reason for discussing temperament, as we noted earlier, is the fact that it is related to, and regulates, other child behaviors, social interactions with others as well as cognitive performance.

In the cognitive area persistence and attentiveness in infancy and at toddler age have been shown to predict cognitive competence at school age, 3 or 4 years later (Goldsmith & Gottesman, 1981; McCall, Eichorn, & Hogarty, 1977). Infants who smile and vocalize more to an unfamiliar observer, that is, who display positive affect, also perform more competently on mental tests at 2 and 5 years (Beckwith & Cohen, 1984). But the influence does not necessarily run in one direction only, from temperament to cognitive performance. There may be an underlying factor influencing both, as has been shown by Crano (1977), who demonstrated that earlier cognitive competence was related to later sociability. This author considered the underlying factor, tapped by the mental scales, to be "psychological integrity," in other words, psychological health.

In 8-month-old infants activity level has been shown to be related to mental and motor developmental scores (Goldsmith & Gottesman, 1981). However, at later ages we must distinguish between different types of activity: vigorous behavior that is directed to tasks or expressed in social participation predicts higher cognitive development, whereas high physical activity of an impulsive, uncoordinated kind, is related to lowered cognitive development (Halverson & Waldrop, 1976).

Temperamental qualities are not identical with the infant's social interactions with others (e.g., attachment relationships), but they help to determine them and are determined by them. Cuddliness is such a quality that may affect the infant's interactions with her caregiver (Schaffer & Emerson, 1964b), and a predominance of smiling or, alternatively, crying may do so, too. Differences in temperament shown at birth may also be factors in determining the quality of the infant's attachment to her mother (see below). Many temperament dimensions, such as soothability or irritability, are, in fact, inevitably confounded with interactional processes.

DIFFICULT TEMPERAMENT

The aspect of temperament theory that has been of greatest concern and practical utility in clinical practice is the concept of *difficult temperament*. Thomas, Chess, and Birch (1968), whose work first gave rise to this concept, identified its defining characteristics as irregularity of functioning (e.g., of sleep), withdrawal from and low adaptability to novel stimuli, high intensity of affect expression, and a preponderance of negative mood. The cohesion of this category or type, first arrived at by intuitive methods, was confirmed by factor analysis. When Bates (1980) asked mothers to define "difficultness" he found that they perceived fussiness and crying (negative mood) to be its outstanding features. Difficult children constituted 10% of Thomas and Chess' sample, whereas "easy" children—who displayed the opposite characteristics—made up 40%.

A Search for Origins

When we discussed the genetic determination of temperament in the last chapter we noted that temperament—and personality—variables showed less genetic variance than did physical or intellectual facets of the individual. However, some attributes, usually subsumed under the temperament label, namely sociability and activity level, have been shown in several studies to have a significant and reliable genetic component. Lack of sociability (via withdrawal and negative mood) may be thought to be implicated in difficult temperament.

An interesting light has been thrown on the possible biological origin of difficultness by the discovery that certain minor physical anomalies, present at birth (e.g., misshapen ears and toes, curved fifth finger, wide gap between first and second toe), are associated with temperament-related behaviors. Having a large number of such slight physical anomalies has been found to be associated with short attention span in boys and girls, as well as with poor self-control in boys, and with withdrawn behavior and inhibition in girls (Bell & Waldrop, 1982). Whether these physical anomalies are due to genetic defects or to teratogenic influences in early pregnancy is as yet uncertain. However, it is clear that they date back to physiological-biological agents in early pregnancy and that these same factors also affect behavioral systems, particularly arousal and self-regulation.

Antecedents of difficult temperament have also been sought in maternal personality characteristics. Bates (1980) has shown that less extroverted mothers see their children as more difficult than do more extroverted mothers. A number of studies have found that a greater degree of maternal anxiety during pregnancy distinguishes difficult from nondifficult children at about 6 months of age (Vaughn, Bradley, Joffe, Seifer, & Barglow, 1987). As already pointed out in Chapter 3, several interpretations of such findings are possible: (1) the connection between anxiety and difficultness could be genetic; (2) there may be an indirect pathway from anxiety via hormonal influences to the child's difficultness; (3) the anxiety may carry over to postnatal life and express itself in mother's possibly nonadaptive treatment of the child; (4) difficultness, when rated by mother, may be more a reflection of her own characteristics than of those of the child.

Carey, Lipton, and Myers (1974) carried out an interesting investigation of 6-month-old adopted children's temperament. The biological mothers' prenatal anxiety was assessed retrospectively from case records. Difficult temperament was noted somewhat more frequently among children whose biological mothers were highly anxious during pregnancy than in children of low-anxious mothers. Since any postnatal anxiety of the biological mothers would have no effect on these adopted children (and adoptive mothers' anxiety is assumed to have been average across infants), the finding indicates that biological factors play a role in the anxiety-difficultness link. However, as the difference fell just short of significance, the evidence is only suggestive and other factors are likely to be operating also.

Mothers' perceptions may also play a part in their reports of difficultness in their children. Bates has produced evidence for his thesis that difficultness lies partly in the eye of the beholder, by showing that mothers of difficult children are more willing to describe *themselves and* their infants in negative terms, that is, are less subject to a social desirability set, than are other mothers (Bates & Bayles, 1984). Nevertheless, maternal perceptions also contain an objective component; thus, an overlap exists between observers' and mothers' perceptions (Lee & Bates, 1985), as well as between fathers' and mothers' perceptions of difficultness (Bates & Bayles, 1984).

Difficult Temperament and Mother-Infant Interaction

As noted earlier, temperament is intimately related to mother-infant interaction, and this will apply equally to difficult temperament. Some investigators have reported that mothers are less responsive, or respond more negatively, to infant cries in difficult children than in controls (e.g., Campbell, 1979; Kelly, 1976). In the NYLS, too, maternal rejection-disapproval was greater for difficult than for easy children at 3 years (Thomas et al., 1982). The authors state that a search of the records of earlier interactions suggests that maternal disapproval was a consequence, and not a cause, of the child's difficultness. On the other hand, several studies have found no relationship between perceptions of difficult temperament and mother-infant interaction (e.g., Vaughn, Taraldson, Crichton, & Egeland, 1981), and Dunn and Kendrick (1980) report that difficult children were no more likely to be punished than other children. The latter authors also found that difficultness was not the outcome of the birth of a younger sibling, although the strained relationships between the mother and the older child, the negative mood and intensity that marked their extreme group of difficult children were noted before the sibling's birth, and remained the same afterwards (Dunn & Kendrick, 1982a). Nevertheless, difficultness often seems linked to mother-infant interactions (see above), and the evidence on the whole suggests that the causal arrow points from child's difficultness to altered relations.

The effects of difficult temperament may also vary with the sociocultural context in which it is embedded. Thus, Super and Harkness (1982) found a more relaxed response to children's night-waking in a farming community in Kenya than in upper-middle-class families in Boston. In different cultures, with differing demands and expectations of the child, difficult temperament may therefore not impose the same stresses on the parents.

Relation to Behavior Disorders

If it can be shown that children who show difficult behavior early in life are at risk for developing behavior disorders at a later stage, we have evidence for the predictive validity—and the usefulness—of the "difficult temperament" typology.

A number of studies have in fact shown significant associations between early difficult temperament and the incidence of later behavior disorders. Children in the NYLS who were assessed as difficult at ages 2, 3, and 4 showed greater behavior disturbance in the home at age 5 than other children (Thomas et al., 1982). The temperamental differences were present, it will be noted, before the onset of overt symptoms. Similar findings have been reported by Bates, Maslin, and Frankel (1985). Studies in Britain, using different populations and slightly different definitions of difficultness, also found that difficult children were at high risk (three times the risk of other children, in one study) of developing behavior disturbances in middle childhood (Graham, Rutter, & George, 1973; Rutter, Quinton, & Yule, 1977).

Thus several studies of children in different kinds of families have shown that difficult temperament is a powerful predictor of behavior disorder. Conversely, children with an easy, adaptable temperament and positive mood are much less likely to develop such disorders.

However, difficult temperament need not by itself lead straight to later pathology. Rather the "fit" between parent and child behavior may be the deciding factor. An important aspect of Thomas and Chess' temperament theory is the concept of *goodness of fit*. If environmental demands and expectations match the infant's abilities, motivations, and temperament at a given time, goodness of fit exists and favorable psychological development will be promoted. If, on the other hand, such expectations are dissonant with the infant's capacities or temperament, the fit is poor and unfavorable outcomes are likely to ensue.

Thomas and his colleagues write: "A given pattern of temperament did not, as such, result in a behavioral disturbance. Deviant, as well as normal, development was the result of the interaction between the child with given characteristics of temperament and significant features of his intrafamilial and extrafamilial environment" (Thomas et al., 1968, p. 79). This statement finds support in the fact that the association between difficult temperament and behavior disorders, which was clearly present for the middle-class children of the NYLS, was not found for Puerto Rican working-class children, also studied by the New York group. The most likely explanation, Thomas et al. (1982) suggest, is that middle-class mothers make more demands on their children for regularity and conformity of behavior than working class mothers do, demands which are particularly stressful for difficult children. The behavior disorders then result from the transactional processes occurring between difficult children and their mothers, when the latter are unable to adapt to their children's "difficult behavior." Lee and Bates (1985) have observed the operation of such a process: mothers of children, rated "difficult" at 6 months, used more intrusive control strategies than other mothers when the children were 2, and had more conflictful interactions with them. Thus, the quality of early mother-child interaction may form the link between difficult temperament and later behavior disorders.

Interest and research in children's temperament has grown by leaps and bounds in recent years, as psychologists have sought to trace children's characteristics and behavior problems back to biological roots, or to children's earliest behavior tendencies. Whether difficult temperament, in particular, resides only in the child or is an amalgam of child behavior and maternal interactions and perceptions, it is recognized more and more as a significant precursor and predictor of later behavior problems and hence represents an important potential source of knowledge and area of research.

Attachment

The beginnings of social responsiveness date from the earliest months of life. Looking, crying, and smiling are such social responses that depend on interactions; for instance, infants smile more when caregivers respond (Gewirtz, 1965), and crying brings about an interaction between mother and child. It is through such constant interactions and commerce between a particular adult (usually the mother) and the child that mutual links are woven and strengthened over the first few months. As these links become enduring and permanent we call them "attachment." In keeping with the literature, we will use this term to refer to the child's tie to a caregiver, and will reserve the term "early bonding" to its converse, that is, the mother's tie to the child—a topic to be explored at the end of the section.

In the first few months the baby has no social preferences—her smile is directed to any person and she accepts anyone's ministrations with equal contentment. Around 7 to 12 months, however, the infant begins to show a preference for one or two persons. She selects that one person because she has had many intimate contacts with her over the months, and she shows her preference by wanting to be cared for by that person and by manifesting unhappiness in her absence. (Since this is usually the mother, we will, for convenience, refer only to her, though it could also be the father or another caregiver.) The development of attachment is also facilitated by the recognition in the infant that an object—and a person—continue to exist, even though they are out of sight. The child develops this notion of "object permanence" around the third quarter of the first year of life. At the same time the infant generally begins to protest if a stranger picks her up and holds her, that is, she develops a wariness of strangers.

The infant's protests at separation from mother, and the urge to be near her, grow apace from about 7 months on and are strongest between the ages of 13 and 20 months. Thereafter, the intensity of attachment *behaviors* (but, we presume, not of the inferred attachment bond) wanes, and a decrease in distress at separation is particularly noticeable from about 2½ years on. Between the ages of 1½ and 5 years the child is, in fact, able to play at greater and greater distances from her mother, as Rheingold and Eckerman (1970) found.

Just as the growth of the infant's cognitive capabilities made the development of attachment possible in the first place, so further developments in their capabilities also make for the decrease in the intensity and frequency of attachment behaviors. The child no longer depends on mother for all her satisfactions, but can accomplish more things independently. She also develops language, which enables her to communicate with other partners and with her mother from a distance. Further, with the development of language comes greater cognitive foresight which enables the child to build a mental bridge between herself and an absent mother, that is, the child can bridge time.

Slowly attachment becomes transformed into a bond that no longer requires immediate and continuous proximity between the partners. Rather, what keeps it going is the child's and mother's mutual trust in each other's affection and the personal characteristics and attitudes that they share, as well as contacts that may become more and more intermittent as the years go by. In later life attachments are formed to friends, sex partners, and one's children; even though the bond will be apparent mainly in verbal expressions, only intermittently, or in private through physical closeness, such attachments are at the root of everybody's psychological adjustment throughout life.

HISTORY OF INVESTIGATION

The history of the attachment concept starts with psychoanalytic theory that placed great importance on the effects of early mother-child relations on the child's psychological development—for good or ill. The child's tie to her mother was usually called "dependence," and Freud was at one with social learning theorists in explaining it by a "secondary drive theory," which posited that attachment was the secondary outcome of the fact that the mother gratifies the child's physiological need for food.

Harry Harlow (1958) in a classic series of experiments showed that this last explanation did not hold true for rhesus monkeys. He asked the question whether infant rhesus monkeys would seek closeness more with artificial surrogate mothers made of wire, who provided milk for them, or with artificial mothers made of terry-cloth who did not feed them. In fact, the infant monkeys displayed greater attachment to the terry-cloth mothers, whose cuddly bodies provided contact comfort, though they did not feed the infants. Consequently the "secondary drive theory," based, as it was, on the feeding relationship between mother and child and therefore sometimes called the "cupboard love theory," was also questioned as a viable explanation of attachment for human infants.

John Bowlby's interest in the subject, like that of other psychoanalysts, stemmed from being confronted with the ill effects of lack of attachment, as described in his early work (Bowlby, 1946) on "44 juvenile thieves," a subject which we will examine in greater detail in Chapter 12. About the time that Harlow carried out his studies on attachment in monkeys, Bowlby (1958) made his first attempt at formulating his attachment theory. Although his starting point was psychoanalytic theory, ethological and control systems notions (see below) already played a greater part in it. Bowlby's concepts, which are generally grouped under the ethological theory of attachment, gave rise to many investigations (which we will discuss below) that illustrated, developed, and refined his ideas.

ETHOLOGICAL THEORY OF ATTACHMENT

Bowlby's Work

The ethological influence on Bowlby can be seen firstly, in that he viewed attachment in humans from an evolutionary perspective, that is, in relation to similar behavior systems in animals, and secondly, in his emphasis on observations of behavior in normal young children as the royal road to secure knowledge about the child's development and relationships. For Bowlby (1971) attachment in humans is the result of the operation of several behavior systems that have proximity to mother as their predictable outcome. He draws parallels with similar phenomena in animals. Thus, separation of young sheep from their mother causes extreme agitation and disorganized behavior in the lamb. The development of this attachment does not depend on physical contact—it is just as strong when the lamb is separated from the ewe by a wire fence (Cairns, 1979b). Harlow in his "wire mother" experiments, mentioned above, also demonstrated that separation from the real mothers produced adverse effects on young monkeys, and we will discuss these effects in a later chapter.

Bowlby (1971) specifies two kinds of mediating behavior for attachment in humans: (1) signaling behavior, which brings the mother to the infant—crying, smiling, babbling, and calling; (2) approach behavior, which takes the infant to the mother—following, clinging, and sucking. Bowlby calls his theory a "control systems theory of attachment." This asserts that attachment after the first year of life is mainly a "goal-corrected" behavior system. This means that the system is constructed so as to take account of discrepancies between the system's set goal (proximity) and the present state (e.g, distance from mother), and activates behavior designed to reduce the discrepancy. The system does not act automatically, however, and experience will modify the actual behavior.

Under the evolutionary perspective, which Bowlby adopts, social behavior systems, such as attachment, evolved because they were adaptive in the "environment of evolutionary adaptedness," by which he means the period of primeval living. During the lengthy period of immaturity, biological safeguards had to exist to ensure parental care of the young. The biological function of attachment, in his view, was the protection of the young against predators, a protection that increased the survival chances of cave-dwelling hunters. In psychological terms, its function was, and is, to bestow "felt security." Security for the child arises, in Bowlby's view, when she can depend on a prompt and appropriate response from the caregiver when the child is in need of comfort and support. Such dependable expectancies enable the child to explore the world around her and to interact confidently with others.

Bowlby coined the term "monotropy" to indicate that the infant has a predisposition to form a primary attachment relationship, usually to the primary caregiver, which remains more important than other attachment relationships. The primary attachment object will be a single, available, and responsive person. But this does not imply that the attachment object must be the mother and Bowlby acknowledges that having a caregiver other than the natural mother does not necessarily lead to abnormal personality development.

Definitions

We should clarify the relation of the terms attachment and dependence, as readers will often meet this latter term. In earlier decades the infant's close link with her mother was generally called "dependence" and psychoanalysts regarded this as a crucial process in personality development. Historically the investigation of dependence preceded that of attachment, and operationally they are defined partly by the same measures, namely proximity-seeking, but dependence also subsumed help-, comfort- and attention-seeking. The question of whether or not dependence was a "drive," parallel to the physiologically based drives, was also hotly debated, and we will discuss the same question in relation to attachment.

Bowlby has two objections to the term dependence: (1) he considers that the term has its roots in secondary-drive theory—psychological dependence derives from physical dependence; (2) though psychoanalysts have viewed it as a natural and necessary process in young children, dependence has often carried with it pejorative connotations of immaturity—it is disparaging to say of someone that he is "dependent." On the other hand, attachment (when "secure") carries with it positive implications for future healthy personality development, and this is the crux of Bowlby's theory.

Social learning theorists (e.g., Gewirtz, 1972) make a value-free distinction between the two terms. For them attachment denotes behavior addressed to one or two individuals. Although dependence denotes the same behavior, the term indicates that a person characteristically directs this behavior at many persons, that is, not only at parents but also, for instance, at teachers and friends.

Mary Ainsworth, who worked with Bowlby at the Tavistock Clinic in London in the 1950s, shares his views. Attachments, she points out, are characteristic of all ages, but dependence is the antonym of independence, and is expected gradually to give way to it. She further adds the important component of affect and defines attachment as ". . . an affectional tie that one person forms to another specific person. . . One may be attached to more than one person, but one cannot be attached to many people" (Ainsworth, 1973, p. 1).

Overall, then, the concept of attachment offers a different perspective on some of the same behaviors that are subsumed under the term dependence, and it is particularly applicable in early infancy. Nevertheless, that there is some overlap between the terms is acknowledged, also by workers in the ethological fold. Thus, Sroufe, Fox, and Pancake (1983) equate "secure attachment" with "effective dependency" in infancy (p. 1617). Insecure attachment (presumably ineffective dependence), they show, leads to later overdependence in the preschool-age child.

Attachment implies an enduring feeling or bond with a person. This can be distinguished conceptually from its manifestation: *attachment behavior.* Institution-reared infants, for example, tend to show a great deal of clinging and following behavior (i.e., attachment behavior), but are less likely than home-reared children to form lasting selective bonds and deep relationships (Tizard & Rees, 1975).

Attachment behavior, when expressed with great intensity and frequency, cannot escape some negative implications of insecurity, since the strongest attachment behavior occurs when the infant is intensely alarmed and apprehensive, as Ainsworth (1972) also notes. Indeed, if its biological function is to elicit protection, it follows that attachment behavior is emitted relatively more by immature organisms in a situation of insecurity.

One of us (Lytton, 1980) has conducted a study in which the interactive behaviors of 2-year-old twin and singleton boys and their parents were observed in the home and recorded in detail, a procedure which provided an opportunity to note the children's attachment behaviors (e.g., proximity- or attention-seeking). It should be noted that this research was concerned with the frequency, not the quality, of attachment behavior.

Frequency counts of attachment behavior, although they do not index the quality of attachment, have their use in establishing normative trends and in allowing the investigator to study the interrelationships of the separate attachment behaviors. In this study attachment behavior fell into two categories: (1) nonverbal attachment behavior, consisting of approaching, touching, and sitting on knee; (2) verbal attachment behavior, which comprised seeking attention, help, and permission. In the study, frequency of nonverbal attachment, particularly, was a sign of immaturity, as might be expected on theoretical grounds (see discussion above): a greater degree of nonverbal attachment went with lower age, even within the restricted age range of this sample (2 to 3 years old), as well as with lower vocabulary IQ. Verbal attachment behavior, on the other hand, occurred as frequently among the older as among the younger children in the study.

Is attachment a "drive"? Bowlby and Ainsworth prefer to avoid this term. In Ainsworth's view (1972) attachment manifests itself by a stable propensity to seek proximity and contact with a specific figure, and she further assumes that there must be a stable basis within the individual organism that controls this propensity. She calls this a "hypothetical construct" or "mediating process." One cannot help feeling that the distinction between this "construct" and the term "drive" is a purely semantic one. The propensity to seek proximity is universal and does not have to be learned (Bowlby writes of "fixed action patterns" in the early months). Moreover, the propensity is strengthened when it is not gratified; for example, when parents deprive the child of attention and reinforcement by being unavailable or ignoring her, this increases the child's tendency to seek their proximity and attention (Gewirtz, 1954; Lytton, 1980). Thus it seems that attachment operates under the same laws as the primary appetitive drives, such as hunger and thirst.

There is therefore no reason to avoid the term "drive" as a descriptive term. Indeed, by its economy, it aids conceptualization, though we must remember, as Hinde (1974) points out, that it does not explain *why* certain behavior occurs.

AINSWORTH'S TYPOLOGY

Ainsworth (1973) has pointed out that approaches that simply measure the frequency of attachment behavior do not adequately reflect the quality of the attachment bond, which is important to the child's future development. She made her distinctive contribution by formulating a typology of the quality of attachment and by devising an experimental situation—the "strange situation"—to assess this quality. However, she does not query the validity of the frequency approach to assess normative factors, for example, relative attachment to mother or father. Quality of attachment, however, she contends, has to be assessed by a constellation of child behaviors in certain attachment situations.

Ainsworth's "strange situation" laboratory paradigm (cf. Ainsworth, Blehar, Waters, & Wall, 1978) has now been used in hundreds of studies with infants and toddlers. This experimental procedure consists of eight episodes, in some of which the mother (or other attachment figure) leaves the child with a stranger or alone. Mother's departure typically causes stress and crying in a 12- or 18-month-old infant. The child's behavior is noted and assessed, and particular importance is attached to the child's reaction when mother returns in the so-called "reunion episodes." The child is then classified as "avoidant" (category A), "secure" (B), or "ambivalent" or "resistant" (C), based on the configuration of behaviors, as shown in Table 4.1. Children in the secure category are distressed by mother's absence and seek her proximity when she returns; children in the avoidant category ostensibly avoid rather than seek her proximity on reunion, and children in the ambivalent category both seek her proximity and at the same time resist contact with her when it is offered. Children in the avoidant and ambivalent categories combined are often called "insecurely attached."

Stability

How stable are attachment classifications over time? Campos et al. (1983) summarize several studies that show results varying from near perfect stability to stability at chance level. Waters (1978), for instance, found excellent stability over 6 months in a middle-class sample. When major changes

TABLE 4.1. Summary of strange situation classifications.

Classification	Descriptor	Classification criteria (from reunion episodes 5 and 8)[a]				
		Proximity seeking	Contact maintaining	Proximity avoiding	Contact resisting	Crying
A (2 subgroups)	Avoidant	Low	Low	High	Low	Low (preseparation), high or low (separation), low (reunion)
B (4 subgroups)	Secure	High	High (if distressed)	Low	Low	Low (preseparation), high or low (separation), low (reunion)
C (2 subgroups)	Ambivalent	High	High (often preseparation)	Low	High	Occasionally (preseparation), high (separation), moderate to high (reunion)

Note. From "The Reliability and Stability of Individual Differences in Infant-Mother Attachment" by E. Waters, 1978, *Child Development, 49,* 483–494. Reprinted by permission. See Ainsworth et al. (1978) for detailed classification instructions.
[a] Typical of the group as a whole; subgroups differ in nonreunion episodes and to some extent in reunion behavior.

in attachment status have been found, they usually have been attributed to the intervention of stressful life events, either in lower class (e.g., Egeland & Farber, 1984), or in middle-class samples (e.g., Thompson & Lamb, 1984). In Egeland and Farber's (1984) study, for instance, 70% of infants who changed from the B group at 12 months to the C group at 18 months had single mothers who were not living with boyfriends and who presumably, therefore, may have been subject to greater stress.

In socially disadvantaged families, changing family circumstances, are thought usually to be accompanied by more severe levels of stress because of economic circumstances. Parents in such families are also typically socially isolated and hence lack extrafamilial sources of support. Changes in family circumstances are therefore more likely to produce negative effects on the quality of mother-child interaction and on the security of the child's attachment, as in Egeland and Farber's sample. In middle-class families, on the other hand, changing circumstances and stresses tend to be less overwhelming and parents are better able to modulate potentially deleterious effects. This may explain the fact that changes in the child's quality of attachment have been found not only in the direction of secure to insecure, but also in the opposite direction of insecure to secure (Thompson & Lamb, 1984).

It may be that changes in attachment status can meaningfully be attributed to changes in real-life experiences and patterns of care. Attachment relationships are dynamic and do develop. However, as Campos et al. (1983) point out, instability in attachment status may also be due to methodological factors. Classification by complex criteria cannot always be accomplished with certainty and there is an unknown error rate in this procedure. Moreover, since in American samples about 65% of children have generally been classified as secure, there is a bias towards classifying children as B, and this means that earlier A and C classifications can easily change to B on a later occasion. If this is the case, a "secure" and "insecure" attachment label cannot always be taken at face value.

Validity

Since the attachment classifications are derived from laboratory experiments, one has to ask how far behavior displayed in the "strange situation" reflects real-life behavior. Ainsworth et al. (1978) present evidence to show that children classified as securely attached (B) in the "strange situation" differ from children in the other two categories regarding their behavior with their mothers in the home (e.g., B children cry less, show more positive responses to being held, and fewer negative responses to being put down than do either A or C children). The authors conclude therefore that the "strange situation" assesses general aspects of the infant's relationship with her mother, that is, security versus anxiety, that are also observable in natural behavior in the home. However, the conclusions are not as solidly founded as might appear. They are based on a small group of 23 infants; moreover, the "strange situation" classifications were established by the same persons who had already noted the children's home behavior, and therefore the second classification may have suffered from some unwitting bias. Conflicting findings have, in fact, been reported by Ragozin (1978). She observed children's behavior on separation from and reunion with mother in day care, as well as in the "strange situation," and found virtually no consistency in attachment behaviors from the laboratory to real-life separation.

In summary, the question whether "strange situation" behavior reflects children's normal behavior with their mothers is still an open one. The ease and seeming objectivity (we will discuss below some problems of classification) of a short and highly structured set of interactions in the laboratory should not blind one to the fact that this provides only limited evidence on the nature of mother-child interactions and child personality in general.

There is some validity to the A, B, and C groupings within the laboratory paradigm, but Gardner and Thompson (1983) suggest the groups may not represent distinct types of children, but rather reflect underlying dimensions that have been artificially trichotomized. Other groupings may, indeed, be found in the future.

Maternal Behavior and Secure Attachment

Sensitivity

Ainsworth's attachment theory claims that secure attachment develops in children if their mothers are responsive and sensitive in their handling of them. From her longitudinal study she and her colleagues conclude that mothers of B babies are more affectionate, more effective in soothing, and in general less intrusive and more sensitive to their children's needs than mothers of A and C infants (Ainsworth et al., 1978). However, these conclusions have been criticized (cf. Campos et al., 1983) because: (1) contamination was possible, since the home measures were developed by persons who often knew the infants' "strange situation" classification, as mentioned earlier, (2) mothers' behavioral differences may have been due to the infants' characteristics, rather than the other way around. This latter alternative cannot be excluded because the relevant statistical test that would have tested this possibility was not carried out. Whichever way the influence may flow, there is support from other studies showing that sensitivity marks out mothers of B infants more than mothers of other children (Egeland & Farber, 1984; Grossmann, Grossmann, Spangler, Suess, & Unzner, 1985; Smith & Pedersen, 1983).

This support is not unequivocal. Grossmann et al. (1985), for instance, found that maternal sensitivity was not related to the "strange situation" classifications when the infants were 10 months old (although it was related for several assessments overall). It would appear from this study that the "strange situation" classifications and the associated relationships are more culture-bound than "security of attachment" per se would imply. Thus in the Grossmann's North German sample, 33% of children fell into the B category and 49% into the A category, compared with 65 and 25%, respectively, in U.S. studies generally. Moreover, they noted that mothers of A infants were not particularly insensitive. The authors comment that in the North German culture there is pressure to foster independence and self-reliance early and with this goes a certain amount of deliberate maternal unresponsiveness which is, however, not tantamount to rejection. Some children react to these cultural demands by not seeking mother's proximity too much and by decreasing social interactions and, instead, turning their attention to objects, that is, they become A children. This reaction was, however, not predictive of later maladjustment, since the A children showed no signs of disturbance when they were observed in interactions with their parents at 24 and 36 months (Grossmann & Grossmann, 1983).

It is questionable whether or not a single style of parenting is optimal under all circumstances, as Hinde (1983) points out. Although the protection of infants is necessary for their survival, it is also in the mother's biological interest to promote their independence as soon as possible so that she can care for later offspring. Natural selection will therefore also favor mothers who adopt this strategy and infants must be adapted to cope with this. Indeed, different styles of mothering may be adaptive according to circumstances. (See Chapter 5 for a further discussion of this point.)

Hence it is not surprising that a positive association between maternal sensitivity and secure attachment has not always been found and that this relationship is weaker than has sometimes been claimed (cf. Lamb, Thompson, Gardner, Charnov, & Estes, 1984).

External Factors

The child's security of attachment will also be influenced by external factors that affect mother's interactive style. Thus, in Egeland and Farber's (1984) study, mothers who lived with husbands or boyfriends during the first 12 months of the child's life had infants who were more likely to be securely attached. Crockenberg (1981) found that father's social support for the mother was particularly important for irritable babies—only if this was present did irritable babies develop a secure attachment relationship. This is a good example of the role played by the interactions between different ecological systems in which children live—in this case between parents' behavior and the social environment in which they find themselves (cf. Bronfenbrenner, 1977).

Attachment and Maltreatment

In animal studies it has often been found that punishment does not eliminate attachment behavior towards the punisher; paradoxically, it may even increase it, as in puppies (Scott, 1962) or monkeys (Cairns, 1979b). Young animals learn to avoid the mother's attacks by seeking her proximity and thus they learn in effect to adapt to the exigencies of a bad situation. It should be noted that these findings in animals relate to the frequency and intensity of attachment behavior.

How secure is infants' attachment to their abusive parents? Schneider-Rosen and Cicchetti (1984) report that there were more insecurely attached children among maltreated than among nonmaltreated 18-month-olds, and Lamb et al. (1984) review several reports showing similar findings. It is not clear whether or not the insecurity of attachment in these cases was manifested by a high frequency of attachment behaviors, as one might expect on the basis of the studies quoted above. It is surprising that any maltreated children at all should be "secure" in their attachment. Egeland and Sroufe (1981) explain the fact that they found some securely attached infants among a group of maltreated children by the presence of a supportive family member (e.g., a grandmother), a less chaotic life-style than in some other families, and, in some cases, by the inner robustness of the infant.

There may be several more general explanations for the fact that some maltreated children are still attached to their abusers, even if often "insecurely" so. Cairns (1979b) suggests that young animals may seek the proximity of punitive caregivers because their attachments center on those animals around whom their activities and emotions are organized, even if this came about through punitive means. Another reason may be that abuse, by engendering insecurity, ensures that the child clings to her mother all the more closely to reduce this insecurity and thus a vicious circle is established. (Note that increased proximity-seeking by the child has been shown to follow mother's unresponsiveness [Lytton, 1980].) Finally, the child cannot imagine any object of attachment or source of support other than her parents and so feels she has nowhere else to go.

Temperament and Attachment

Could security/insecurity of attachment arise from temperamental dispositions, rather than from maternal attitudes? Kagan (1982b) has suggested that differences among avoidant, ambivalent, and securely attached infants may not reflect a history of mother-infant interaction, but rather individual differences in susceptibility to any stress, not just temporary loss of mother. Avoidant infants may be those who are not very distressed at being separated from their mothers, ambivalent infants those who are very distressed, and securely attached infants are intermediate between these two categories. Is attachment status then a matter of temperament and constitution?

There is some evidence that security/insecurity of attachment is related to factors in the child present at birth, for instance far more infants in the

Grossmans' (1985) sample, assessed as B at 12 months, showed good orientation on the Neonatal Behavioral Assessment Scale as newborns than did other children. Infants of the C classification, in particular, have been singled out as being different from other children already in the first months of life, for example, they have been reported as showing greater irritability (Miyake, 1983), being less alert and active, and developing more slowly than other infants, when assessed on the Bayley Scales (Egeland & Farber, 1984).

There are several strands of evidence that support Kagan's (1982b) contention that the infant's attachment category indicates basic reaction to stress and that this reaction forms a continuum. First, there is evidence from Ainsworth's own study which shows that crying increased and exploration decreased regularly from A to B to C children in all episodes of the "strange situation," that is, not only when the mother was absent (Ainsworth et al., 1978, p. 99). This suggests that degree of crying or exploration is a characteristic of the child in all situations. Gaensbauer, Shultz, & Connell (1983) report that infants who are not upset by separation from mother in the "strange situation" show most avoidance on reunion, but for infants who are very upset the reverse is the case. This would suggest that avoidant infants may appear so on reunion simply because they are not distressed by separation.

Another strand of evidence comes from research on hormonal effects. The excretion of the hormone cortisol is an indication of stress. Tennes (1982) measured cortisol level in 1-year-old children and found a linear relationship between the level of cortisol and the degree of distress children displayed on separation from mother. Children who showed no distress had the lowest level, as did children who were classified as "avoidant" by Ainsworth's system. The author comments: "The avoidant infants with low levels of adrenocortical activity were neither distressed by the mother's absence nor delighted with her return. Our data do not imply that these were poor or impoverished mother-child relationships. They indicate only that the emotional expression was low-keyed as compared with the distress and excitement of infants in the responsive category with high levels of corticosteroids" (p. 79).

The meaning of avoidance in this categorization scheme therefore raises some questions. Are these children insecure in their attachment, or do they simply have an easy, not readily distressed temperament? The hormone study and the Gaensbauer et al. (1983) research support the latter interpretation. Group A children have been shown to be self-reliant and object-centered, though less communicative, but not disturbed in later toddlerhood (Grossmann et al., 1985), and they have been found to be more competent in mastery tasks than children in other groups (Spieker & Booth, 1985). These findings suggest that the pure avoidance syndrome will not always predict dire outcomes. Consequently in the last-mentioned study, a new group of "AC" children was identified, who clearly combined avoidance with resistance to mother, and it was these children who were the most insecure in their behavior and whose mothers had suffered the most adverse life experiences.

The Ainsworth group, however, maintains that avoidance is the result of maternal interaction style. When the mother is aversive to cuddling or a great deal of physical contact, the child learns to avoid her. This avoidance does not come about by choice, but the child is forced into it by being faced with an unavailable and rejecting mother, so that eventually, following this theory, accumulating anger and distress make avoidance seem the lesser evil (cf. Main & Weston, 1982). This behavior is, in fact, adaptive for the child. Nevertheless, since the mother is the child's attachment object, the child is wracked by conflicting emotions and feels insecure in her attachment. Advocates of this position also can call on some evidence in that A-group children, like C-group children, have shown maladaptive behavior later, at least in some studies, such as overdependence on the teacher (e.g., Sroufe et al., 1983).

The Ainsworth group strongly contends that attachment classifications measure a *relationship* (Sroufe, 1985). Nevertheless, it is admitted by these theorists that characteristics of the child, such as her temperament or rate of general development, also may affect the attachment relationship (Sroufe, 1985). A good case can, in fact, be made for temperament and maternal sensitivity acting in concert to produce transactional effects. Thus, children who as neonates showed good orientation (attended to stimuli in the environment) *and* who had tender-talking, sensitive mothers all were classified as securely attached at 12 months. For poor orienters with less sensitive mothers, however, the chances of becoming securely attached were very slim, with the children who had *either* a good orientation *or* a sensitive mother occupying an intermediate position (see Figure 4.1; Grossmann et al., 1985).

What Follows Secure Attachment?

The advantage of considering the quality of attachment, rather than the frequency of attachment behavior, is that this quality represents the child's adaptation to the developmental task of infancy. There is evidence that good adaptation in this early task predicts good adaptation to other developmental tasks that lie ahead. A number of studies categorized children on the basis of the "strange situation" at 12 or 18 months and then observed these children later in the laboratory or nursery school. There have been repeated findings that B children, more than A or C children, are more enthusiastic and competent at problem-solving, more ingenious in play, show more positive affect, and are more ego resilient, that is, are adaptable and flexible in changing circumstances (Arend, Gove, & Sroufe, 1979; Matas, Arend, & Sroufe, 1978; Waters, Wippman, & Sroufe, 1979). Most studies investigating this topic also found that secure attachment pre-

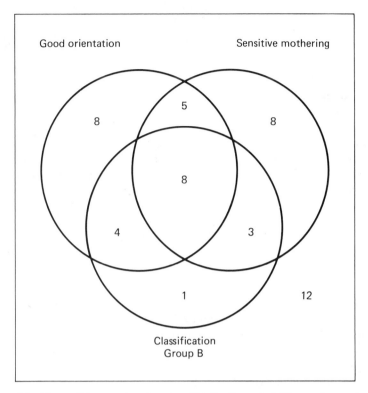

FIGURE 4.1. Venn diagram showing the distribution of children who were good orienters (above the median) as newborns, whose mothers were rated sensitive during the first half year, and who were classified as group B (secure) in the "strange situation" with their mothers at 12 months. From "Maternal Sensitivity and Newborns' Orientation Responses as Related to Quality of Attachment in Northern Germany" by K. Grossman et al., 1985, in I. Bretherton and E. Waters (Eds.) "Growing Points of Attachment Theory and Research," *Monographs of the Society for Research in Child Development, 50*, 1–2. Reprinted by permission.

dicts compliance and cooperativeness in preschool (Joffe, 1981; Londerville & Main, 1981; Matas et al., 1978), and is the forerunner of sociability and skill in interaction with peers (Main & Weston, 1981; Pastor, 1981; Waters et al., 1979). Insecurely attached children, on the other hand, seem to show overdependence on the teacher in preschool (Sroufe et al., 1983). In almost all of these analyses, it should be noted, A and C children were grouped together as insecurely attached.

Thus, certain meaningful relationships between behavior in the "strange situation" and later adaptation in competence- and peer-related contexts are well documented. Secure early attachments may form a secure base for exploration contemporaneously, as Bowlby already stated, and they clearly predict later positive social relations, ego resiliency, competence, and self-confidence. However, one should not deduce from this that sensitive mothering in the first year of life immunizes the child against all psychological disorders in later life. The evidence suggests rather that continuity in social adaptation can be explained by a combination of two factors: (1) a parallel continuity in the quality of parental practices that affects the child continuously (cf. Lamb et al., 1984), (2) by temperamental factors that make for stability in cognitive and social functioning, regardless of later experiences and minor changes in relationships (e.g., Tennes, 1982). Secure attachment, in the final analysis, is an indicator of good adjustment all around, and it is such inherent resiliency—whatever its source—that will buffer the child against many environmental adversities.

ATTACHMENT TO FATHER AND OTHERS

Fathers and Mothers

Considerable evidence exists that there is a hierarchy to children's attachment figures, in that children form a primary attachment to one (or two) persons that is stronger than other attachments. Although the primary caregiver tends to be thought of as the principal object of the child's attachment, the trend in the modern family towards greater sharing of child-rearing roles has given rise to the question whether father (even when he is not the primary caregiver) could not also be an attachment figure, and some recent research has been devoted to exploring attachment to father.

In the study of 2-year-old boys, mentioned earlier (Lytton, 1980), the frequency of attachment behaviors directed towards fathers, as well as towards mothers, was noted. It was quite clear that the average frequency of attachment behavior (equalized to allow for differences in mother's or father's presence) was much greater for mother than for father. Individually, about 70% of the children displayed more attachment behavior to mother and 30% to father. But it must be stressed that almost all children showed some attachment behavior to both parents. Schaffer and Emerson (1964a) report very similar figures. They also note that children do form attachments to both parents, as attested by the fact that 85% of the children in that study protested separation from both mother and father.

What distinguishes a *father-attached* group (those who show preferential attachment to father) from a *mother-attached* group? In the Lytton study the father-attached children themselves were less mature in speech and vocabulary, though this may be explained by the fact that there were relatively more twins among them, who generally were more immature than singletons. Father characteristics did not distinguish the groups from each other, but mother characteristics did. The father-attached group had mothers who displayed less attractive qualities, for example, fewer positive interactions and more physical punishment. It seems it is not so much father's attractive qualities, but less harmonious relationships with mother that induce the child to search for another attachment object.

In the "strange situation" the child's reactions to a stranger's departure differ from those to either mother's or father's departure. Kotelchuck (1976) has shown that when either mother or father depart, children play much less after the departure, and this effect is strongest with mother; however, when a stranger leaves, the child's play increases. This finding demonstrates the child's special relationship with mother and father ("attachment"), which does not exist with a stranger.

The majority of studies have, in fact, found greater attachment behavior to mother than to father both during the first year (Ban & Lewis, 1974; Lamb 1976) and the second year (Cohen & Campos, 1974; Kotelchuck, 1976). Some have found equal amounts of attachment behavior addressed to mother and father for 1- and 2-year-olds (Lamb, 1977; Lewis, Weinraub, & Ban, 1973). Children under stress certainly tend to seek out mother more, but the tendency seems to go beyond this. No study has found, on average, greater preferential attachment to father than to mother, if we define attachment behavior as proximity- or comfort-seeking. Nevertheless, in all these studies fathers, too, were generally the object of the child's attachment and were treated differently from strangers.

When father takes over the role of primary caregiver—something that is still a relatively rare occurrence—he more frequently may become the primary attachment figure. An instance of strong attachment to a primary caregiver father is known to us: when the father was absent for 2 weeks, while on vacation, his 2½-year-old daughter fretted, would not eat properly, and was generally sad. When she was reunited with her father she cried because she was "so happy."

The observations in Lytton's (1980) study were carried out during the early evening, time that was typically father's playtime, and these boys engaged in considerably more play, and particularly rough-and-tumble play, with father than with mother. Indeed, affiliative behavior (i.e., vocalizing, smiling, showing or offering objects, and play or romping), which involves less emotional intensity than attachment behavior proper, has repeatedly been observed to be addressed more frequently to father than to mother (Belsky, 1979a; Lamb, 1976, 1977). It appears that children usually consider father the most appropriate person for play and general activities, and mother the appropriate person for comfort and attention, that is, father is seen as the playmate and mother as the caregiver. The different kinds of experiences that children derive from their interactions with father (e.g., play) will have a significant influence on their development.

In Schaffer and Emerson's (1964a) study a person's amount of interaction with the child, or availability, by itself was not the main determinant of whether the child attached herself to that person. What was important was willingness to interact intensely and appropriately with the child, even though for a shorter period. Mother, as the primary caregiver, has more opportunity to be responsive to the child and to become a salient object in her world, and hence one would expect mother generally to become the prime object of attachment, as has, indeed, usually been found.

When researchers assessed the quality of attachment to both mother and father, using Ainsworth's "strange situation," the classifications for the two sets of interactions tended to overlap, although they were by no means identical (Lamb, 1978b; Main & Weston, 1981). Such findings illustrate the differing kinds of interactive relationships that children can have with each parent.

Siblings and Other Persons

Although in the majority of families, mothers and fathers are by far the most common attachment figures, siblings (even preschool siblings) also can fill this role, particularly in combination with others (Schaffer & Emerson, 1964a). Preschool children have also been seen to provide reassurance and comfort to their younger siblings in mother's absence (Stewart, 1981).

A famous study describes the rescue of a group of young children whose parents had been killed by the Nazis in Europe (Freud & Dann, 1951). While these children were living in camps they had frequent changes of caretakers, but were always kept together, so that they were the only constant element in each other's lives. In this way they formed very strong mutual attachments. When they were brought to England after World War II they clung desperately to one another and were as upset, if one was separated from the others, as other children would be by separation from mother.

Even a relative stranger who becomes a child's friend by playing with her for a few hours over several days can become an attachment figure. In one such study (Cairns, 1979b) a child reacted to the friend's departure much as he would to mother's, that is, he protested by crying and joyfully approached the friend on her return, whereas he did not do this with a noninteracting adult. Attachment to the main attachment figure does not, it seems, differ in kind from attachment to other figures, but the intensity of attachment to the primary figure is much greater than that to secondary, or minor temporary attachment objects.

MOTHER-INFANT BONDING

The term "bonding" has commonly been used to mean the establishment of a long-lasting attachment of a mother to her child as the result of skin-to-skin contact during a few hours or days after birth when, because of hormonal action, such contacts are assumed to have special effects on the mother. Our discussion will be concerned with the evidence for this proposition, although the pioneers in this field have more recently broadened the definition of bonding somewhat to include other, later processes lead-ing to the attachment of mother to child (Klaus & Kennell, 1982). This has been a burgeoning area of research since the 1970s and readers interested in greater detail can turn to several good reviews (e.g., Goldberg, 1983; Lamb, 1983).

Klaus and Kennell (1982) and others have proposed that there exists a sensitive period immediately after delivery when a mother is particularly open to forming an affectionate attachment to her newborn, and that this bonding process is facilitated if she has extended contacts with her nude baby during the first few hours after birth, as well as over the next few days. The usual obstetrical practices in hospitals, they felt, introduced separation of child from mother at the crucial time, something which might hinder the bonding process.

The model of the importance of early contact stemmed from work with animals. It has been shown, for instance, that separation of the young from the mother sheep or goat immediately after birth caused the mother to reject her offspring when the latter was returned to her some hours later. Mothers who had continuous contact with their young after birth, or who were separated only after establishing initial contact with them, on the other hand, engaged in normal maternal behavior (Lamb, 1983). For these ungulates, therefore, it appears there is a sensitive period after birth when the mother is ready to establish maternal behavior and to recognize her young, but that this period is of very limited duration. Such a biologically sensitive period, however, has been demonstrated only in a few species. Whether a similar sensitive period exists in humans has to be established by research on humans.

What has this research shown? The prototype study in this area was the one by Klaus, Jerauld, Kreger, McAlpine, Steffa, and Kennell (1972). In that study primiparous mothers from a disadvantaged background who had given birth to full-term infants were divided into two groups: (1) the routine care group who received the usual hospital treatment, that is, a glimpse of the baby, then separation for 6 to 12 hours, and thereafter about 30-minute contacts for feeding every 4 hours, (2) the extended contact mothers who were given their nude babies for 1 hour during the first 3 hours postpartum, and for an additional 5 hours each day for the first 3 days after delivery.

At 1 month the extended contact mothers showed more soothing be-havior, fondled the infants more, took up an *en face* position with them more and were more reluctant to leave them in the care of another person. The inference is that the extended contact mothers were more attached to their infants than the routine care mothers were. At a follow-up at 1 year, the extended contact mothers soothed their babies more and helped the doctors more with the physical examination. The signs of greater attach-ment were obviously much reduced by then, and the fact that the extended contact mothers helped the doctors more with the examination may be due to the fact that they had been given greater attention by the doctors and hence were more familiar with them. At 2 years (as well as at 1 year) mothers' speech to the children was examined and although it was found that at 2 years the extended contact mothers used more complex language than the routine care mothers did, this exactly reversed the relationship found at the 1-year follow-up (Ringler et al., 1975). In order to conclude that the more optimal speech at 2 years was the result of the extended contact after delivery, we have to assume that this effect lay dormant for 1 year or more, only to emerge at 2, something which requires considerable suspension of disbelief. With a sample size of five in each group, it is much more likely that these are fluctuating, chance findings. So we see that the evidence for long-term effects is weak, even when it comes from the Klaus and Kennell group.

Several other researchers have also reported positive short-term effects arising from extended contact (e.g., Anisfeld & Lipper, 1983; de Chateau, 1980; Grossmann, Thane, & Grossmann, 1981). But others, for example, Svejda, Campos, and Emde (1980), in a carefully conducted study could find no demonstrable effects even in the short term. Long-term effects have in general been more difficult to detect; for example, de Chateau (1980) found some positive effects at 1 year, but these disappeared by age 3, and many others could discover no long-term effects at all. The effects in the study by Grossmann et al. (1981) did not even last to the ninth day after birth.

As Lamb (1983) and others have pointed out, even where positive effects from early and extended contact have been claimed, the many methodological flaws as well as problems of interpretation in the research make it difficult to place great reliance on the findings. For instance, in some studies the effects were seen at one age, but disappeared at another (see the above discussion of the study by Ringler, Kennell, Jarvella, Navojosky, & Klaus, 1975), or the behaviors that distinguished extended contact mothers from others were sometimes of very doubtful relevance to the maternal attachment that was supposed to be enhanced (e.g., mother sits up versus leans on elbow); moreover, significant group differences in a few measures out of many could easily have arisen by chance.

Further, in the design of many of the studies factors existed that would compromise any conclusion that the observed effects actually arose from the treatment of extended contact, for example, mothers were made aware that they were receiving special treatment, as part of an experiment, and may have known the hypotheses the experimenters wished to prove, and this may well have spurred them on to make extra efforts to be affectionate to their infants (e.g., Anisfeld & Lipper, 1983). Thus, a "Hawthorne effect" may have operated. Svejda et al. (1980) took precautions to exclude this possibility and then found no positive effects. Finally, preexisting characteristics in mother or child may affect maternal behavior as much as extended contact, for example, de Chateau and Wiberg (1977) found that extended contact made primiparous mothers resemble multiparous mothers given routine care. In other words, extended contact helped primiparous mothers to reach the level of involvement with their infants that multiparous mothers showed without extra contact. In some investigations, too, (e.g., Anisfeld & Lipper, 1983) extended contact affected mothers' behavior toward one sex only. Such sex differences undermine the argument that early contact is necessary for the biological unfolding of maternal behavior.

Where social class differences in the effects of extended contact have been found, they have sometimes favored lower class, and sometimes middle-class mothers (Lamb, 1983). It cannot be claimed, therefore, that extended contact is beneficial mainly for disadvantaged lower class mothers whose adaptation to their infants is marginal.

The best conclusion we can draw is that early or extended contact may have some short-term effects on some mothers, but that any long-term effects are much more dubious. The attachment relationship between mother and child (and we must not forget that the child also plays an important part in this) is a complex process that does not depend on brief events limited to a few hours or days. The relationship will be shaped and influenced by many ongoing, continuous interactions and by a multitude of other factors. It is likely that the attachment of the mother to her infant is adaptive and has an evolutionary-biological basis, but the central importance of the first few hours after birth for its development has not been demonstrated.

There is a danger that the notion of bonding may become oversimplified and mechanized, as if it was a simple act, like inoculation. This is illustrated by the hospital nursing notice, cited by Svejda et al. (1980), which read: "Do not remove the baby to the nursery until bonding has taken place." In truth, we do not know when bonding takes place—and the process is probably never completed—nor is there general agreement on the kind of maternal behavior that clearly indicates the presence of attachment.

It may be harmful to insist that certain experiences with a given time frame are important, at the least when their importance remains unproved. The thousands of adoptive mothers, those who had Caesarean sections, or whose infants were born prematurely and who therefore were unable to have the experience of early contact with their infants, may be made to feel inadequate or guilty by such insistence. Yet it is unlikely—and there is no evidence—that these mothers, or the millions of mothers who went through hospital deliveries in earlier decades, are unable to develop normal affectionate relations with their infants.

On the other hand, we should not minimize the beneficial and important effects that the work of Klaus and Kennell and their followers has had on hospital practices in Western countries. For, as the theory became popular, it provided the impetus for humanizing the birth process which, in hospitals, had become simply a sterilized, surgical procedure—a move that meets most parents' wishes.

Other Early Social Behaviors

Attachment of child to mother and of mother to child is, no doubt, the most important social process in the first 2 years of life. As we noted earlier, it is built on close early interactions between the child and her caregiver and we will now retrace our steps to describe the nature of these interactions. Furthermore, there are other aspects of social development in infancy, such as "social referencing," play, and fears, that research studies have explored and that help us to understand the growth of the child as a person. We will now turn to these topics.

MOTHER-INFANT SOCIAL INTERACTIONS

Psychological development always occurs in the context of social interactions and the way that mother and infant establish such interactions between them has been referred to as a "dialogue" that can be expressed both verbally and nonverbally. The following description of the establishment and of the prerequisites of this dialogue is largely based on Schaffer's (1979) account of its acquisition.

Certain biological prerequisites in the child make the development of the mother-infant dialogue possible. The biological functions that the child comes equipped with are the temporal patterning of her behavior, apparent, for instance, in the burst-pause rhythm of her sucking. Mothers adapt their behavior to this rhythm: during a burst of sucking they are quiet, but during the pauses they become active and jiggle or talk to the baby. Such rhythmic activity is visible also in the infant's play with objects, which is marked by an act-watch temporal pattern. Thus the child will first strike or roll an object and then sit back to watch the effect, only to start the action all over again. Later social interactions can thus build on the baby's biological rhythms.

However, such simple rhythms have to be transformed into much more complex and flexible structures over time. It is the parents' actions that provide the stimuli and context within which such transformations can grow. A certain synchrony of timing of actions exists between mother and infant from very early on. Thus they often attend to the same object, in view for both of them at the same time, with the infant leading the way and mother following appropriately (Collis & Schaffer, 1975). In this way a sharing of experience between infant and mother is brought about.

The prime example of sequential integration of behavior is the turn-taking, characteristic of adult conversation. Such turn-taking occurs also in the vocal interchanges of 1-year-olds with their mothers, even before the appearance of words; overlap episodes, indeed, tend to be infrequent and brief. Most of the fine synchronization depends on the mother, and the timing of her responses and actions is therefore of great importance.

Mostly, when mother and child share the same focus of attention, the regulation of these joint interchanges proceeds smoothly. However, if the direction of attention is not shared, or if obstacles intervene, asynchrony results and this leads to maladaptive experiences and to negative affect for the infant. The mother, therefore, has an important role to play in providing the social prerequisites for the establishment of interactive capabilities in her child.

The child's social interactions will be limited by the cognitive processing capacities that she has attained; social affect and cognition are linked. Reciprocity and intentionality are the cognitive achievements necessary for the child to be a full partner in interactive exchanges and these are attained in play.

The give-and-take games, so common in the first year, are very one-sided affairs up to about 7 or 8 months (Bruner, 1977). Mother gives a toy to the infant, but the episode usually ends by the infant just dropping it, only for the mother to pick it up again. Their behavior is complementary rather than reciprocal. By about 10 months, however, the infant often offers the toy to her mother who then returns it, and the game has become give-and-take in the full sense. However, the child seems to take part only hesitantly, and is not sure of the procedure. By the time the infant is 12 months old, the play has become ritualized and a diversity of procedures is introduced. Reciprocity is manifested as the child gives, as well as takes, toys deliberately and confidently. The drop-and-retrieve games of the end of the first year, like the give-and-take games, also arise when the child discovers that mother will respond in a predictable way to the infant's actions—the infant drops, the mother picks up. Although in this case there is never any role reversal, the infant nevertheless learns some simple notions about reciprocal behavior through taking turns and through being involved in joint action with another person (Bruner, 1977). Also, as the child learns that she can elicit a predictable response, and as she uses a means to achieve a given end, her actions may be considered intentional in the conventional sense. The infant thereby also gains a sense of effectance and, we may infer, becomes aware of herself as a person, at least in a rudimentary way.

It is through such social interactions that the infant is enabled to attain higher cognitive achievements. When the child fully participates in interactive sequences she demonstrates that she has acquired what Schaffer (1979) calls the concept of the dialogue.

"Peekaboo" is a game that perhaps comes closest to a true dialogue and, no doubt, one of its functions is to enable the child to learn the rules and conventions of play (Bruner & Sherwood, 1976). But the game may serve another function, too. Through it the child may also learn that in "make-believe" she can mimic reality and thus come to terms with her own emotions about this: she learns to cope with her fear of mother disappearing in earnest by making it happen repeatedly in make-believe, and by being reassured through her invariable reappearance.

PLAY AND PEER RELATIONS

Over the second year of life, play undergoes a number of changes in its directedness, complexity, symbolism, and duration (Kagan, 1981). From being outer-directed, play becomes inner-directed: At 17 months the infant plays with toys that happen to be in front of her and is easily distracted by a new toy or the sound of a car outside, but at 2 years she selects the objects that she will play with and makes the object conform to her own ideas. A cup becomes a hat, or blocks become a train, that is, the object becomes a symbol (Piaget's process of assimilation). The 2-year-old is able to hold ideas in mind, does not forget them, and purposefully seeks the appropriate object to carry them out.

Infants also express affect (e.g., smiles or gleeful squeals) when they are occupied with shared objects in play with their mothers, and around 18 months they make this affect part of their referential communication system (Adamson & Bakeman, 1985).

Further, the duration of play increases during the second year. At 17 months bouts of play last 10 to 15 seconds, and acts are independent of preceding ones. At 27 months, however, the child picks up a doll and plays with it for 10 or more minutes. She would then go through a whole interconnected routine of getting up, changing diapers, reading a story to the baby, etc. In other words, she has plans and goals and can execute them (Kagan, 1981).

Play with peers, like play with mother, also shows a progression from a kind of object-centered monologue to a dialogue, as described in Mueller and Lucas' (1975) account of peer interactions around the beginning of the second year. Mueller and Lucas see three stages in this progression. In the first stage an act-watch rhythm (see above) is evident. Each infant watches as the other performs, then performs as the other stops, and the acts are often imitative. In the second stage children begin actively to provide and seek contingencies. For instance, one child vocalizes, then a second child laughs at this and thereby induces the first child to repeat her vocalization, thus instituting a kind of child-child circular reaction. However, the children do not yet know how to generate a whole series of socially directed behaviors. This skill develops in the third stage at around 18 months, when the children begin to engage in intercoordinated and complementary actions. Then they try to elicit a reponse that is both complementary to, and different from, their own action. Thus, they offer and receive a toy or throw and catch a ball. Each child's action is related to the other child's action and both reciprocity and timing of actions become important.

Notice that such complementary interchanges occur earlier in mother-infant play, probably because mother is a more skilled cooperative partner than a peer is. But Mueller and Lucas' (1975) account also outlines a definite progression towards interpersonal coordination and reciprocity in the development of peer interactions.

SOCIAL REFERENCING

Infants often regulate their own behavior, particularly in uncertain situations, by means of information derived from emotional cues that adults provide. This strategy has been called "social referencing" and it is an illustration of how emotions—the infant's own and those of others around her—organize behavior. How does this ability develop?

Certain patterns of facial expressions, tone of voice, and gesture convey information about affect in adults and some of these also can be seen in quite young infants (see Chapter 3). Some major changes in the human infant's perceptual abilities, which occur mainly between 5 and 9 months of age, eventually enable her to detect the signals that specify positive and negative affect. The first advance occurs at about 5 months, when experiments have shown that infants begin to discriminate distortions of the mouth and become sensitive to inversions of features in the face; we conclude, they then become aware of the face configuration as a whole (Campos & Stenberg, 1981).

As the first year goes by, the infant becomes increasingly sensitive to affective information and uses this more and more in regulating her behavior. Between 3 and 7 months the infant can discriminate some expressions from others, but does not necessarily respond to their affective meaning. At a later stage there is evidence that the infant reacts with different emotions to different facial expressions. Six-month-old infants, but not younger ones, for instance, respond with more negative emotion to angry and sad faces than to happy and neutral ones. It seems then that the period between 5 and 9 months is the time when infants first recognize affective information in social settings. It is not clear whether this process comes about through social learning or through maturation. However, there is some evidence from studies with monkeys (Sackett, 1966, discussed below) that the ability to interpret certain emotional (threatening) gestures may be a biological predisposition. Whatever the explanation, infants, by 9 months, notice these stimulus differences and a systematic correspondence is established between the stimulus pattern and the affect it elicits.

It is the mother who becomes the main target for social referencing. When the infant is uncertain or somewhat apprehensive about a situation, she will turn to the mother to seek facial or vocal cues signaling her emotional reaction. We see the importance of this opportunity for the infant in the observation that in a strange playroom many infants will not explore attractive toys in the mother's presence if they cannot see her face. Even 2-year-olds position themselves half the time so that they are in front of their mother and within her visual field, even at the price of not playing with attractive toys stacked in the opposite corner (Carr, Dabbs, & Carr, 1975). When a stranger is in the room, infants 6 months and older tend to scan alternately the stranger's and the mother's face. The infant's reaction to the stranger is then influenced both in a positive and negative direction by the emotion shown in the mother's face (Schaffer, 1974a). Infants are also more friendly to a stranger when their mother has spoken to them in a positive way about the stranger than when she has spoken in a neutral way about him (Feinman & Lewis, 1983).

Infants cannot learn about the many important aversive consequences they might meet by first-hand experience alone. Verbal communication is limited in the first year, but social referencing can take its place and make possible some types of vicarious learning. This has been shown vividly in an experiment with the "visual cliff." When the drop-off was set at a level that produced no clear avoidance, but some fear, 1-year-old infants looked at their mothers repeatedly to resolve the ambiguity (social referencing). The vast majority of infants then crossed the "deep" section when mother showed a happy face, but no infant crossed when mother showed a fearful face and only a few crossed when she showed an angry expression. The infants thus used specific affective information gleaned from mother's face to regulate their own behavior (Sorce, Emde, Campos, & Klinnert, 1985).

Infants seek and use such affective information not only from their mothers, but also from adults with whom they are only slightly familiar and who can then serve as a source of social reference in an ambiguous situation (Klinnert, Emde, & Butterfield, 1983). The mother, however, is still a greater source of reassurance than a stranger (Zarbatny & Lamb, 1983).

As the infant learns from repeated experiences that she can rely on the mother for appraisal of possible threatening situations and uncertain events, she learns to value the mother as a resource person. When the mother is emotionally inaccessible, either through absence or inattention, this will elicit distress, and thus the infant's dependence on the mother as a source of social reference may in part explain separation anxiety.

With increasing age, infants develop their own internal strategies of appraisal and therefore social referencing will become less necessary over time. But the process probably continues throughout life, particularly in ambiguous settings, or when the need for evaluation of a situation is high.

FEARS

The best known experiment about young infants' fears we owe to the behaviorist J.B. Watson. He hypothesized that the only innate fear reactions are those to loud noises and sudden loss of support and that all other fears arise by association with these innate fears, or, in other words, by conditioning. His experiments with "Little Albert"—perhaps the best known child in psychological literature—sought to demonstrate this process. He showed that the 11-month-old Little Albert reacted with fear to a white rat only after a loud noise had been repeatedly associated with the sight of the rat (Watson & Rayner, 1920). Watson hypothesized that the fear would generalize to other furry creatures, but the extent to which the fear extended to a rabbit and a dog was, in fact, severely limited, and the fear reaction waned considerably after a month without conditioning trials. At that time the rat was allowed to crawl on Albert's chest, but the infant only "began to fret and then covered his eyes with both hands" (p. 11). After a minute's contact with the rabbit, Little Albert even manipulated its ear. The strongest fear reaction occurred to the dog, when it barked loudly within 6 inches of the infant's face!

As Harris (1979) and others have shown, Watson's own later accounts, and the innumerable textbooks that cited the experiment, embellished the evidence in the service of teaching a seemingly simple and impressive lesson about the conditioning of emotional reactions. An aspect that was mostly omitted was the following: "During the course of these experiments, especially in the final test, it was noticed that whenever Albert was on the verge of tears or emotionally upset generally he would continually thrust this thumb into his mouth. The moment the hand reached the mouth he became impervious to the stimuli producing fear. Again and again . . . we had to remove the thumb from his mouth before the conditioned response could be obtained" (Watson & Rayner, 1920, p. 13). Thus fear was elicited only when Little Albert did not have the consolation of his thumb—nor of his mother who was absent from these experiments.

Indeed, other experimenters (e.g., Bregman, 1934) were unsuccessful in replicating the effects of Watson's study and fears are evidently not as easily explained as the story of Albert suggests.

Yet young children obviously fear many different things, things that may startle them, create uncertainty, or that are unusual. The development, timing, and the strength of fears of different objects, however, are often independent of one another. Scarr and Salapatek (1970) found that the waxing and waning of fears over age differed from one fear object to another (e.g., noise, visual cliff, stranger), except that a fear of masks correlated significantly with all other fears measured.

How do such fears arise? Hebb (1946) proposed that fear in general arises in primates when they perceive a stimulus that is discrepant from something that they had become familiar with—a notion that is known as the "incongruity theory." Kagan (1974) elaborated this theory further and suggested that fearful behavior arises only once the infant is able to form hypotheses, but cannot reconcile a discrepant event to her hypothesis, that is, cannot make sense of the environment. However, many unexpected or incongruous events arouse laughter rather than overt fear in infants, for instance, when mother puts on a mask (Sroufe & Wunsch, 1972). When such incongruous events occur attention is heightened, tension is created, and the infant processes the new information. If the infant can interpret the situation in a positive light, the tension is mild and the infant will smile or laugh. If, on the other hand, the interpretation of the event is negative, because of the context or the intensity of the stimulus, the infant will cry and avoid the object. Thus, when the mother puts on a human mask within the infant's sight laughter is elicited, but when an experimenter wears a mask in mother's absence fear is produced (Sroufe & Wunsch, 1972), and particularly so when he wears a nonhuman mask (Scarr & Salapatek, 1970).

But some fears may also be unlearned responses: Thus, infant monkeys, though reared in isolation from birth, nevertheless displayed fear when they were shown pictures of threatening monkeys (Sackett, 1966).

WARINESS OF STRANGERS

The fear that is perhaps most significant for the child's development is the fear of strangers. However, to denote the whole range of negative reactions to strangers that infants display, even when they do not show frank fear, we will use the term "wariness." The topic is of importance because wariness may have biologically adaptive value and, since this behavior interacts with other behavioral systems, it also provides an organizational framework for an integrated view of the infant's emotional development.

Developmental Course of Wariness

Is wariness of strangers at all widespread? Whereas some researchers have doubted that it is very general (e.g., Rheingold & Eckerman, 1973), longitudinal studies have found that *all* infants manifest negative reactions to strangers at some stage during the first year and a half (e.g., Emde, Gaensbauer, & Harmon, 1976; Schaffer, 1966). If some cross-sectional studies have not found universal wariness, this may be because at any one point in time not all children will display it.

The course of development of emotional expression to strangers is fairly regular, although assigning certain phases of this development to typical ages will conceal a range of variation among children (Schaffer, 1966). We will follow Emde et al.'s (1976) account of this development. Up to about 5 months their infants' responses to strangers were positive and smiling was prominent. At around 4 to 5 months the infants looked alternately at mother and stranger, as if to evaluate the stranger in comparison with mother. This was followed by a sober expression towards the stranger, typical for the period between 5 and 7 months. Absolute avoidance of the stranger, whimpering or crying, set in between 7 and 9 months (see Figure 4.2). In fact, although friendly responses to the stranger lessened gradually over the months, the onset of definite stranger fear was quite sudden in

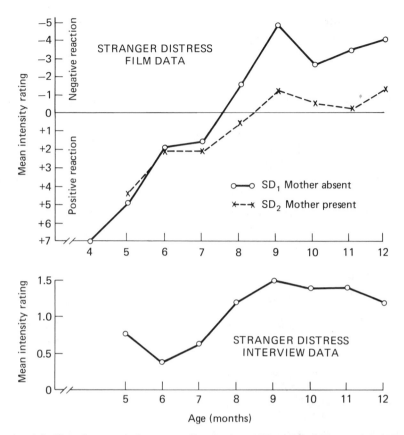

FIGURE 4.2. Development of stranger distress from "Emotional Expression in Infancy: A Biobehavioral Study" by R. Emde, T. Gaensbauer, and R. Harmon, 1976, *Psychological Issues Monographs, 10*, 1 (No. 37). Reprinted by permission.

individual infants and occurred from one visit to the next. Other accounts (Fouts & Atlas, 1979; Schaffer, 1966) describe a very similar timetable, with clear stranger fear first appearing, on average, at around 8 months, although the time of onset will vary from infant to infant. Stranger fear usually peaks between 12 and 18 months (Lewis & Brooks, 1974), and then gradually declines.

Why and How Does Wariness Arise?

As we noted above, the infant compares and evaluates the stranger against the familiar standard, that is, her mother, and wariness may result from her failure to understand the discrepant event. But it is only under certain conditions that the incongruous event (the stranger) will arouse wariness. Thus, when a strange child intrudes into the infant's space, the infant responds in a friendly and positive way (Lewis & Brooks, 1974). Hence the infant must also use herself as a standard of reference, and consider someone more like herself as less threatening. However, size is not the only critical variable that reassures the child. Childlike facial features play an even more important part in the infant's evaluation of whether another person is like her or not, as Brooks and Lewis (1976) have shown by comparing infants' reactions to a normal-sized adult, a midget, and a child. The essential fear reaction occurred both to the normal adult and the very small adult, but not to the child.

Even strange adults do not invariably evoke wariness or fear in young infants. So long as the adult is silent and inactive and keeps his distance, he hardly ever elicits a fear response, even after the onset of fear in a given child (Bretherton & Ainsworth, 1974; Schaffer, 1966). It is only when the adult becomes more intrusive (approaches the infant and touches her) that the infant displays signs of fear. Female strangers have typically been found to inspire less wariness than do male strangers, even when the approach of both sexes to the infant follows the same pattern. Perhaps this difference is due to females' greater interest in infants: One study noted that they tended to smile and play more with the infants (Smith & Sloboda, 1986).

Why, we must ask, does a strange adult who impinges on the infant become the object of such a strong negative reaction at about 8 months of age? The infant, as we have noted, has been able to compare and distinguish between different adults for several months before this age and therefore has been living with discrepant events for some time without showing acute distress. The incongruity theory fails to explain this lag. However, we know that by about 8 months the infant has built a strong selective bond with one or two persons whose ministrations she seeks, while she rejects those of others. The negative reaction to strangers occurs only after this has happened and may well represent the warding off of impending close interactions with nonselected, strange adults whom the infant experiences as threatening—possibly threatening the loss or inaccessibility of the mother (cf. Campos & Stenberg, 1981). However, the relationship between wariness of strangers and attachment is a complex one, as we shall see below.

Developments in the infant's cognitive capacities will be a necessary prerequisite, too. Before wariness of strangers emerges the infant must be able to conceive the hypothesis that a stranger may spell danger. Such a hypothesis easily springs to the mind of persons (even adults) of limited experience when they encounter anything very discrepant from usual expectations and such an encounter therefore tends to be threatening. Thus when a New Guinea primitive tribe, previously isolated from the rest of the world, met white men for the first time the experience inspired fear in them, and when the men approached some of the girls they thought the men's intention was to eat them (TV documentary)!

As for the infants, perceptual, cognitive, and emotional factors, as well as the context of the encounter (e.g., the speed with which the stranger impinges on the infant), will interact in complex ways to determine whether or not wariness of strangers is manifested in any particular encounter. Nevertheless, it has also been found that infants showed consistency in the degree to which they exhibited negative affect in encounters with eight strangers, and this consistency suggests that wariness of strangers is a characteristic of the infant (Smith & Sloboda, 1986).

Learning (for instance, of the familiar standard of reference) certainly enters into the development of stranger distress. But the fairly uniform age of onset of stranger distress argues also for maturational control of this system. The involvement of maturational factors (which would affect cognitive development) is further suggested by evidence for a contemporaneous physiological-biological shift: It is only around the age of 8 months that heart rate accelerates at the sight of a stranger, even before a fear reaction is noticeable (Emde et al., 1976). The development of stranger distress may also have an evolutionary basis, in that it was biologically adaptive for a helpless infant to be fearful of a potentially dangerous strange adult, at least in primeval times.

Although we have treated wariness of strangers as a universal phenomenon, occurring generally in the third quarter of the first year of life, children do, of course, show individual differences in the degree to which they exhibit this disposition. Such individual differences have been prominent in two recent studies which have called essentially the same behavioral tendency "inhibition" (Kagan, Reznick, Clarke, Snidman, & Garcia-Coll, 1984) and "shyness" (Daniels & Plomin, 1985), characteristics that are, of course, exhibited mainly in the presence of strangers. Children who showed such "uncertainty to the unfamiliar" at 21 months to an extreme degree, by retreating from strangers, clinging to the mother when a stranger entered, and so forth, were called "extremely inhibited" by Kagan and his colleagues. These authors showed that such children were still socially inhibited with unfamiliar peers at age 4. A certain stability thus marks this characteristics. Daniels and Plomin (1985) assessed shyness by parental reports. Their study of adopted children and biological and adoptive mothers suggests that shyness is partly of genetic origin, but that family environment is an additional important influence in its development, a conclusion consistent with the findings of Kagan et al. (1984).

Connections and Interrelations

Wariness of strangers does not occur in isolation, but rather as part of a complex of many behavioral systems. Let us now examine how different aspects of the child's emotional development are interrelated, and "put the child together again."

Infants, even during the second half year of life, display many affiliative tendencies towards strangers. They smile at them or accept toys from them and in certain circumstances they may do this more with strangers than with their mothers (Bretherton & Ainsworth, 1974). But wariness may be displayed simultaneously, or in close succession, with such affiliative behaviors. For instance, in Bretherton and Ainsworth's (1974) study 12-month-old infants looked at the stranger, and most accepted a toy when it was offered—thus displaying affiliative behavior. But vocalization decreased in the stranger's presence, most infants did not approach the stranger and averted their gaze when the stranger approached them—all signs of wariness. Those who did venture to approach the stranger quickly retreated to their mothers again and thus showed that when their affiliative tendency took them too far into uncharted territory, it immediately activated the counterbalancing systems of wariness and attachment behavior. Indeed, affiliative tendencies and the impulse to explore novel objects, on the one hand, and the fear of discrepant events and of the stranger, on the other, are systems that coexist in the same child, but they are finely counterbalanced. When one tendency gains the upper hand too much, it is checked, as in a homeostatic feedback system, and the opposing tendency takes over. Moreover, the situation will determine which tendency predominates: A securely attached infant may not be at all wary of a stranger before separation from mother, but may be very wary of the stranger on reunion with mother. As we noted earlier, fear and laughter, too, are next-door neighbors and one may imperceptibly shade into the other.

The foregoing discussion explains why the relationship between stranger wariness and the attachment system is a complex one, although one may be considered the natural corollary of the other. Emde et al. (1976) found few significant correlations between stranger distress and separation distress; however, this result may have arisen because at any one point in time the degree of intensity of these systems may not have coincided. Nevertheless, stranger distress was always more intense in mother's absence. A secure attachment bond to mother may therefore protect the child from too overwhelming a fear of strangers, as Bowlby's notion of mother-as-a-secure-base-for-exploration would lead one to expect. Indeed, sociability with strangers seems to decline most in infants who change from a secure to an insecure attachment relationship. Thus, the quality of this relationship, in addition to temperamental factors, influences sociability (Thompson & Lamb, 1984).

Different behavioral systems in the emotional and in the cognitive realm are thus engaged in constant interplay and compensatory interaction. Wariness of strangers is a prime example of the integration of the different aspects of the developing personality.

Summary

The beginnings of emotional behavior are seen in the child's temperament, examples of which are activity level, fearfulness, distractibility, mood, and soothability, among other characteristics. While the distinction between personality and temperament is ill-defined, the term "temperament" is generally applied to behavior that appears early in infancy, is emotional in nature, has to do with the arousal of behavioral systems, and may be presumed to be of constitutional origin, though we are less certain of this last point.

The modern interest in temperament stems from the work of Thomas and his colleagues. These psychiatrists focused on this topic as a way of shedding light on children's difficulties that they encountered in their clinical practice, other than attributing them simply to parental rejection or mishandling. The concept of the "difficult temperament"—as shown by irregularity of functioning, low adaptability to novel stimuli, and by the preponderance and high intensity of negative mood—has proved useful in that it identifies children who may be at risk for developing later behavior disorders. However, in the view of Thomas and his colleagues, difficult temperament does not by itself lead straight to later pathology. Rather, what does so are transactional processes set in motion by a poor fit between the child's temperament and ill-adapted parental reactions.

By about 7 to 9 months the infant forms an attachment, that is, a selective preference for, or an affectionate bond with, one or two persons in her environment. The child often becomes attached to both mother and father, but usually most strongly to mother. Like Bowlby, who first brought attachment to the forefront of attention, we look on attachment as a necessary and adaptive process which ensures nurturance, protection, and psychological security for the child, and is present in many animals as well as in humans.

Children's attachment can be secure or insecure and, according to Ainsworth who developed this typology, secure attachment follows when a mother is sensitive in responding to her infant's needs. Nevertheless, it must not be thought that any single style of parenting is necessarily optimal under all circumstances. There is evidence that the child's temperament and mental development will interact with maternal interactive style to produce security (or insecurity) of attachment. In turn, secure attachment early on is also the precursor, though not necessarily the cause, of later good social and cognitive competence. Thus, secure attachment and good functioning in the child are intimately interrelated. In the final analysis secure attachment is an indicator of good adjustment all around.

The mother also becomes attached to the infant, something that has popularly been called "bonding." It has sometimes been claimed that this can only occur when there is extended contact between mother and infant during the first few hours after birth. However, this claim has not been substantiated empirically, nor is it likely that mother-child relations are lastingly determined by the events of a few brief hours.

Among the many social behaviors that the infant manifests during the first 2 years of life, one of the most intriguing is fear, or better, "wariness" of strangers. Longitudinal studies have shown it to be present in all infants at some stage during the first 18 months. One explanation for its emergence may be that the infant detects a visual incongruity between the familiar, that is, her parents, and the stranger, and that her inability to make sense of this discrepant event and the general proclivity to attribute danger to something very strange will arouse uncertainty and fear. But since wariness of strangers invariably arises after attachment to mother has become marked, it is likely that it is also an emotional reaction to an nonselected adult, particularly when the child is in a state of alarm. We should note that throughout this period affiliative tendencies also exist side by side with wariness towards strangers. Wariness of strangers is a good example of a behavior produced by the integration of perceptual, cognitive, and emotional processes, given an evocative situation.

5
Socialization and the Family

"The process whereby the child becomes a social being" is perhaps the most comprehensive short definition of what we mean by "socialization." The word socialization implies that the individual lives in a social world, that is, within a group, and group living, by its nature, imposes its own restraints and patterns of living for animals as well as humans. It is in early childhood that the child most actively and rapidly acquires these patterns of behavior, and she does so by means and in the context of her interactions with her family. Hence the family—at least in most forms of Western society—is the primary agent of socialization.

Providing a nurturant and protective environment, a secure milieu in which the child can learn and develop, is the basis of socialization, and this topic was the subject of the previous chapter. However, socialization involves many more varieties of interaction between parent and child, subsumed under the label "child rearing," and it is to these that this chapter is devoted.

We will look at child rearing, as it has gone on for centuries, fashioned by the brute demands of living and folk wisdom, and without the benefits of prescriptions derived from empirical, "scientific" investigations. We will also survey the history and nature of the scientific study of socialization. Above all we will be concerned with parent-child *interactions*. A section will be devoted to parents' socialization practices and rearing styles, and another one to functions in the child that play a role in the socialization process. We also will address the question to what extent and in which respects children influence parents. The child is a part of a family system, hence the indirect effects that each spouse exerts through his/her relations with the other are of importance and so are the influences arising from siblings, and these will be discussed. Lastly, we will be concerned with influences on parents' practices and attitudes that emanate from sources outside the family, particularly social class membership.

Socialization has been the topic of whole books (e.g., Clausen, 1968; Goslin, 1969; and Richards, 1974), and it is difficult to condense all its different facets into one chapter, particularly as evidence from empirical investigations does not always unequivocally point to one conclusion. The child becomes part of her world also by virtue of her contacts with peers and the culture around her, be this school or the media. This aspect of socialization, which leads to her becoming more and more a person in her own right, will be dealt with in subsequent chapters.

Tasks of Human Socialization

We may summarize the tasks and goals of human socialization to be: provision of nurturance and protection; induction into the values and demands of society, including the internalization of moral norms; acquiring a concept of the self in broadening social experiences; increasing autonomy.

The inclusion of induction into society's norms and values among the chief tasks of socialization poses a problem: Is socialization merely the conservative transmission of cultural values and norms? Obviously, we must make some allowance for the evolution of new norms and expectations: The conservative force of socialization must be balanced by some evolutionary force. Such forces for change operate in the family, as, for instance, when parents react against their own upbringing, or as mothers turn more and more into "working mothers." Thus changing conditions of life (e.g., automation) and changing values in society (e.g., changing role of women) introduce new values at the level of the family, to which parents and, consequently, their children must adapt. But perhaps the forces for change are even stronger in the socialization pressures on older children and adolescents arising from peers, the school, and the culture around them.

Child Rearing in Philosophical and Historical Perspective

Child rearing, an older and more homely term for socialization, has a long history, both as to its practice and its theory. Practices have varied greatly over the centuries and people have thought and expressed views about it from Plato onward, since it has always been considered a cornerstone of society. (The history of theories about personality traits, such as attachment or aggression, by contrast, is very much shorter.) In past centuries child rearing has been largely influenced by philosophical and religious views and dogmas, and even more importantly, by the prevailing economic system and the living conditions of the time. A brief account of some of these views and the historical development of child-rearing practices in Western society will help to put present-day attitudes and methods into perspective.

PHILOSOPHICAL VIEWS

The contrasting positions of "innate sinfulness" versus "innate goodness" represented a conflict between two basic philosophies of life that has run through history. The view of innate sinfulness of human nature was long the traditional view of Judeo-Christian theology. An extreme exponent of this view was Hobbes, who thought that in a state of nature there was only war of all against all, a philosophy which he expounded in *Leviathan*, published in 1651.

The battle against this sinfulness in children was joined by the Evangelists of the 18th century. How strongly they felt about this can be seen in a letter by Susanna Wesley to her son John:

. . . the parent who studies to subdue [self-will] in his children, works together with God in the saving of a soul: the parent who indulges it does the devil's work; . . . . This, therefore, I cannot but earnestly repeat,—Break their wills betimes; begin this great work before they can run alone, before they can speak plain, or perhaps speak at all. . . . Therefore, (1) Let a child, from a year old, be taught to fear the rod and to cry softly. In order to do this, (2) Let him have nothing he cries for; absolutely nothing, great or small; else you undo your own work. (3) At all events from that age, make him do as he is bid, if you whip him ten times running to effect it. Let none persuade you it is cruelty to do this; it is cruelty not to do it. Break his will now, and his soul will live, and he will probably bless you to all eternity. (Wesley, 1872, quoted in Newson & Newson, 1974, p. 56)

We notice here a preoccuption with death, heaven, and hell that is understandable not only as an expression of Puriton theology, but also from the fact that the death of a child was a common event in earlier centuries.

The "innate goodness" theory of the child, was espoused by Froebel and by Rousseau, who gave it expression in *Emile* (1762/1974). Rousseau believed essentially that it is best to let nature take its course. His basic principle was that "everything is well when it leaves the Creator's hands, everything degenerates in the hands of man." He did not believe in complete permissiveness, but thought that lessons in conduct or restraint should arise from the nature of things and events (artifically contrived by the educator, where necessary), not from interventions by authority. He advised readers not to give the child any orders, but to let him learn from his experiences; for example, Emile would learn not to walk in the forest alone by being robbed when he did so, the robbers having been sent there on purpose by his teacher.

Modern descendants of both these positions can be found. The child's innate sinfulness was translated into secular and psychoanalytic terms by Freud. He taught that the infant's mind was dominated by the id, whose instinctul desires demanded immediate gratification, and which therefore had to be controlled.

The child has to learn to control its instincts. To grant it complete freedom, so that it obeys all its impulses without any restriction, is impossible . . . The function of education, therefore, is to inhibit, forbid and suppress, and it has at all times carried out this function to admiration . . . But we have learnt from analysis that it is this very suppression of instincts that involves the danger of neurotic illness. . . . Education has therefore to steer its way between the Scylla of giving the instincts free play and the Charybdis of frustrating them. (Freud, 1933/1937, p. 191)

(Note that Freud's German term "Erziehung," translated as "education" in the 1930s, would nowadays be rendered by "child rearing" or "socialization.")

An extreme modern follower of Rousseauan ideas is A.S. Neill, who at Summerhill School tried to put into practice the concept of letting nature take its course. On the other hand, a moderated form of the "innate goodness" theory has been adopted by Ainsworth et al. in the context of an ethological perspective: "A child is preadapted to a social world, and in this sense is social from the beginning" (Ainsworth, Bell, & Stayton, 1974, p. 99). The implications for the socialization process are spelled out in the same paper:

It seems likely to us that [the infant] will gradually acquire an acceptable repertoire of more "mature" social behaviors without heroic efforts on the part of his parents specifically to train him to adopt the rules, proscriptions, and values that they wish him to absorb. Because of these considerations we find the concept of "socialization" essentially alien to our approach.

However, the authors also introduce concepts such as maternal "responsiveness" or "sensitivity" which they found conducive to the learning or compliance. Since these constructs imply certain practices, it is evident that some practices are more effective than others. Whether one calls such actions "practices," "training," or "climate of the home" is, in the final analysis, a question of the stress one places on specific training procedures or the amount of coercion required for the process of "becoming a social being," that is, it becomes a question of relative degree. However, it may well be that children are biologically adapted to group living and therefore are born with a disposition to comply, which will unfold in an "environment of evolutionary adaptedness." If this predisposition were not there, the socialization process, indeed, would remain forever doomed to failure.

SWINGS OF THE PENDULUM IN CHILD REARING

Philosophical views are not the only factors that have influenced child-rearing practices. The conditions of life in general and, particularly, the stage of economic development a society has reached have played, and still play, perhaps an even more important part. (For part of what follows we have drawn on the Newsons' (1974) very good account of the history of child rearing in the English-speaking world.)

An overriding fact that parents in earlier centuries had to come to terms with was the likelihood of their children dying before reaching adulthood. The mortality rate of children below childbearing age in the 18th century was estimated at between 50% (France) and 75% (England). The infant mortality rate (below 1 year of age) was 154 per 1,000 live births in England in 1865; 100 years later it was 21.8 per 1,000 (Newson & Newson, 1974). In 1980 it was 13.2 per 1,000 in the United States (Kopp, 1983).

The question that preoccupied earlier generations of parents, as the Newsons (1974) suggest, was whether or not they would rear a child, not how they would rear her. When they did consider the manner of rearing, the important question was how to rear her for the longer afterlife, rather than for the "nasty, brutish and short" life on earth. Since parents had to enure themselves to the likelihood of their children dying early, they may even have been afraid of forming deep attachments or commitments to them. It takes an effort for us to realize that concerns about mental health or social and emotional adjustment are luxuries that only Western society of the 20th century could afford.

The aim of socialization throughout the 18th and 19th centuries was strict moral behavior, integrity, honesty, industriousness, orderliness, and courtesy. These ideals were the ethics of the industrial revolution, the "Protestant work ethic," and they met the needs of economic survival in early industrial society. Thus, throughout the 19th century it was the philosophy of the Puritans, rather than Rousseau or Froebel, that held sway. In fact, all classes in society adhered to it. Working-class children as young as 8 or 9 years commonly worked long hours in mines and factories during the early part of the 19th century in both Europe and North America. Child rearing then was geared to fit them for their "station in life."

In the early 20th century child rearing became dominated by medical opinion and supervision. The reduction of the mortality rate was the main aim—reflecting a new value system—not the happiness or adjustment of the child. This could only be achieved by great attention to hygiene and prevention of illness, an approach which increasing affluence made possible, and on which great hopes were pinned, based on the advances of medical knowledge. Parents therefore could ignore medical advice only at their children's peril, and they submitted to the authority of the physician as the price to be paid for the child's survival. The parallel between physical hygiene and mental hygiene was drawn without questioning—for both "regular habits" were considered all-important. Attitudes to child rearing were adjusted accordingly.

The era was called the "Truby King era" in England, after one of its leading proponents of this philosophy, who wrote:

The leading authorities of the day—English, foreign and American—all agree that the first thing to establish in life is *regularity of habits*. The mother who "can't be so cruel" as to wake her sleeping baby if he happens to be asleep at the appointed feeding-time, fails to realize that a few such wakings would be all she would have to resort to . . . . The establishment of perfect regularity of habits, initiated by "feeding and sleeping by the clock," is the ultimate foundation of all-round obedience. Granted good organic foundations, truth and honour can be built into the edifice as it grows. (Truby King, 1937, quoted in Newson & Newson, 1974, p. 60)

The changing trend of advice in the *Infant Care* bulletins of the U.S. Children's Bureau, starting in 1914, has been analyzed by Wolfenstein

(1955). The earlier editions mirrored views very similar to those illustrated above. An example would be: "It is a regrettable fact that the few minutes' play that the father has when he gets home at night . . . may result in nervous disturbance of the baby and upset his regular habits" (Children's Bureau, 1914, p. 62). The Bulletin stressed moral stance and training. It was full of the dangers of self-eroticism, to be restrained by physical means at all costs. Anything that was play or fun was bad for the child. Wanting attention or wanting play was considered a demand for indulgence, not to be granted. The child's emotions were considered as so much surplus baggage.

Building up desirable habits and avoiding undesirable ones was also the watchword of behaviorists, as exemplified by Watson (1928). In this process sentiments would only interfere: "There is a sensible way of treating children. Treat them as though they were young adults. Dress them, bathe them with care and circumspection. Let your behavior always be objective and kindly firm. Never hug and kiss them, never let them sit in your lap. If you must, kiss them once on the forehead when they say good night. Shake hands with them in the morning. Give them a pat on the head if they have made an extraordinarily good job of a difficult task. Try it out. In a week's time you will find how easy it is to be perfectly objective with your child and at the same time kindly. You will be utterly ashamed of the mawkish, sentimental way you have been handling it." (Watson, 1928, pp. 81–82).

Although this "aseptic child rearing" went against mothers' natural inclinations and instincts, they obeyed nevertheless. Mary McCarthy, a victim of the system, vividly describes in her novel *The Group*, how an educated mother of the time went through miseries of self-torture, frustration, and guilt in her obedience to the dictates of the "experts."

Once again there came a change in the value system. Opposing tendencies were growing up even as the hygienist movement was reaching its peak. Ian Suttie, a Scottish psychiatrist critical of Freudian theory, claimed that love, not sexual attraction, formed the central bond between mother and son (otherwise, where would the bond between mother and daughter come from?), and he protested against the prevailing "taboo on tenderness" (Suttie, 1935).

For the first time the child-rearing practices of the middle classes were affected by "scientific" inquiries, although these were primitive, and selective use was made of them. From inferences drawn from Freud's theories (which they misinterpreted) and from their own observations, post-Freudians came to conclusions that can be summarized as follows: If early experiences are pleasurable and if the child suffers a minimum of frustrations and is surrounded by warmth and understanding, she will grow into a well-adjusted individual. Repression was the cardinal sin (though, as we saw earlier, Freud himself did not think so), since the popularizers of Freudian theory were more afraid of creating a neurotic person than of turning out a selfish brat. Examples of such writings can be found in Josselyn (1948), Ribble (1943), and the early Spock (1946/1957).

In the eductional world Susan Isaacs (1932) carried out systematic observations of young children in nursery schools and concluded from these that curiosity, mastery, and happiness were fostered by free play. This was therefore to be encouraged as the chief, and almost exclusive, activity for young children, and the messier it was, the better for the child.

Infant Care, from its 1942 edition on, also was influenced by these tendencies. The distinction between "needs" and "whims" runs through much of child-rearing literature. Whereas in earlier editions of *Infant Care* only physical needs were considered legitimate, in later ones psychological desires—previously thought of as selfish whims and therefore sinful and to be resisted—became acceptable, too. "Babies want attention; they probably need plenty of it" (*Infant Care*, 1945). A whole new attitude pervades these later editions, an attitude that stresses that parenthood can be enjoyable. With it, however, comes a new obligation, that of "having fun," the absence of which is a cause for guilt feelings. This is in line with the general notion in post-war American society that having fun is a property of any normal adult.

The years 1940 through 1960 thus became the era of permissiveness and "fun morality" (Wolfenstein's [1955] term). This was not only because of the influence of the post-Freudians, but also because of the impact of general social forces: the poor and oppressed minorities claimed their rights, as did women somewhat later. By the same token babies were seen as having rights, too, and they were to be respected. Spock was the popular apostle of this approach. In contrast to earlier medical pundits, he did not seek to impose his views by dint of superior medical wisdom, but reassured the mother that she knew best and thus boosted her self-confidence.

But the era of permissiveness brought its own dissatisfactions: Parents became unsure of themselves when exerting demands on their children, afraid of assuming the mantle of authority. Some parents, in their retreat from imposing rules, allowed their children to impose *their* rules and demands, resulting in their becoming rather obnoxious. By 1957, the year the second edition of his *Baby and Child Care* appeared, Spock saw the danger of this and changed his emphasis. As he wrote in the Preface to his book: ". . . nowdays there seems to be more chance of a conscientious parent's getting into trouble with permissiveness than with strictness. So I have tried to give a more balanced view" (1957, p. 2).

The return to "authoritativeness" has also received some scientific underpinning from psychological investigations (see below). We should note, however, that these revolutions of thought are touched by scientific, or objective, evidence only in the most selective and superficial of fashions. Has the wheel come full circle? But the wheel, as it revolves, also advances. No revolution of the wheel of thought occurs without leaving some lasting trace and insight that will be remembered by later generations.

The Scientific Study of Socialization

The empirical, scientific approach to the study of the socialization process and its effects, as opposed to philosophical, intuitive opinions, has only a short history. Margaret Mead's anthropological observations in New Guinea and Samoa in the 1920s concentrated on socialization processes in those far-off societies, but her impressionistic methods would nowadays be frowned upon. On the other hand, empirical psychological investigations then were mainly concerned with attributes of the child—physical, intellectual, and social. Socialization did not become a major focus of psychological research until the 1930s, when institutes of child study were established in a number of places in America, under the sponsorship of the Laura Spellman Rockefeller Memorial Fund. Until then the influence of the home had been strangely neglected in empirical studies. It was not until after World War II that the longitudinal studies embarked on by the child study institutes, as well as other research such as that by the Sears group, appeared in print.

The study of parental influences has stood under the aegis of different theoretical perspectives. Bronfenbrenner (1963) distinguished three "families of hypotheses" that characterized earlier research. The first, derived mainly from psychoanalytic theory, focused largely on the affective quality of the parent-child relationship, and the research at one of the child study institutes, the Fels Institute (Baldwin, Kalhorn, & Breese, 1949), is a good example. The second formulation grafted learning theory principles onto psychoanalytic concepts and was concerned mainly with the effects of reward and punishment, as seen in the home. This approach was developed by a group at Yale, including Robert Sears and his colleagues. The third formulation of hypotheses, based on social learning theory, focused on the role of the parent as a model of behavior. These investigations in contrast to research inspired by the first two perspectives, were carried out in experimental analogue studies, particularly by Bandura and his colleagues. (Such experimental studies have also often been employed for studying the effects of reward and punishment.) In more recent times a fourth set of hypotheses, derived from ethological concepts (see Chapter 1), has joined the first three. The influence of ethology can be seen above all in the resurgence of naturalistic observations of parent-child interactions, although it also has inspired laboratory studies. The consequent research has often been concerned with the formation of the emotional bonds between parents and the infant or toddler (e.g., by Ainsworth and her group). Methods of investigation largely grew out of the theories that guided the particular research program, for example, the laboratory studies of the social learning theorists, or the naturalistic observations of the ethological school.

The different methlologies used to study socialization processes have been discussed and evaluated in Chapter 2.

Parents' Socialization Practices and Attitudes

The methods that parents use in rearing their children are embedded in a living relationship that is enduring, and also changes with the growing maturity of the child and with the changing experiences, needs, and circumstances of the parents. They will typically use a combination of several methods (e.g., punishment and the use of explanations) and will vary them according to the situation. Furthermore, the methods also are intertwined with a conglomerate of parental attitudes and feelings, not necessarily all consistent with each other. Any effects will arise from this amalgam of practices, attitudes, emotional reactions, and circumstances. Socialization research, as part of social science, however, must direct its efforts at isolating the components and identifying the combinations of ingredients that have certain effects. An analogy might be drawn with nutritional science. We eat and digest all sorts of foods at the same time, but the aim of nutritional science is to identify the need for and the effects of proteins, carbohydrates, fats, and so forth, and of their different combinations.

The enterprise of both socialization research and nutritional science is equally daunting in its complexity, and some similarities can be found also in the history of their findings: Initial claims and warnings, about cholesterol, for instance, have later been found to be premature and had to be qualified and then revised again in light of more recent and sophisticated methods of research. A parallel in socialization research would be early findings stressing the deleterious effects of punishment that were modified by later research, suggesting that such effects arise mainly from the extreme use of punishment, especially when it is a manifestation of rejection, but not necessarily from its moderate use (see section on punishment below).

We should emphasize also that any overall effects found are broad generalizations and hold only for the mythical "average expectable" child. Differences in children's dispositions will, of necessity, moderate and modify any general conclusion drawn.

To achieve data reduction of diverse ratings and observation counts and to identify underlying dimensions, researchers often used factor analysis, as shown in Chapter 2. Two dimensions recur in several factor analyses of parents' child-rearing practices: warmth-hostility and restrictiveness-permissiveness. In addition to such factor-analytic dimensions, researchers have also used a priori categorizations of parental behavior in the study of parents' socialization practices. If, in surveying the literature, we look at one of these dimensions (e.g., permissiveness-restrictiveness) in isolation, the evidence often appears very conflicting, as we shall see. However, a number of researchers have examined the combined effects of a given configuration of dimensions, something which often resulted in more coherent findings, and one that were more reflective of reality. We will discuss individually those dimensions of parents' practices that have reverberated throughout the literature—practices of restrictiveness-permissiveness, punishment, reward, induction, as well as the attitude of warmth—but will bring in important configurations of practices where highlighted by these researchers.

Children also imitate and identify with their parents, and attribute their own actions to some cause. The way these processes, which occur mainly within the child, affect the socialization outcome will be discussed under separate headings.

RESTRICTIVENESS (CONTROL)–PERMISSIVENESS

Fels Research Program

The issue of control versus permissiveness is the one on which the pendulum has swung most violently. It is also at the heart of the first large-scale empirical investigation into parent-child relations, which was carried out at the Fels Research Institute in Yellow Springs, Ohio, in the 1940s. Since the Fels program's methods and results attracted considerable attention and were influential, we will devote some space to it and compare it with a research program of the 1970s by Diana Baumrind and her colleagues that resulted in divergent conclusions.

The Fels research sprang straight from the climate of opinion that stressed permissiveness and "democracy in the home" (Baldwin, 1948, 1949; Baldwin, Kalhorn, & Breese, 1945, 1949). The Fels workers carried out home visits and based ratings on observations of family interactions, though these were informal and not clearly specified. Three main syndromes, that is, clusters of highly intercorrelated variables, were identified: acceptance (or warmth), democracy, and indulgence (Baldwin et al., 1945; Baldwin, 1949). Democracy emerged as the crucial syndrome, with the most far-reaching and pervasive effects. It was defined (Baldwin et al., 1945) by democracy of decision-making, where the child shared in decisions on regulations in the home, by noncoerciveness of suggestions, and nonrestrictiveness of regulations.

The overall outcome of the studies was clear: Democracy had beneficial effects on the whole. Baldwin (1949) showed first that children from democratic families were active and socially outgoing in both friendly and hostile ways. Second, these children were in leadership positions in the groups to which they belonged (in the experimental nursery school). Their aggression and bossing was on the whole successful. Third, these children were high on activities demanding intellectual curiosity and constructiveness. The researchers also identified a factor, labeled "control," marked by restrictiveness and readiness of parents to enforce rules. Such restrictiveness was found to generate adverse effects in the children (Baldwin et al., 1949).

Fels workers were racked by ambivalence about "control." They saw that "Democracy runs the risk of producing too little conformity to cultural demands" (Baldwin, 1948, p. 133) and that it encouraged aggressiveness and bossing. On the other hand, they feared the nonresistance and lack of curiosity, originality and playfulness in children raised in controlling homes (Baldwin, 1948). Hence Baldwin (1948) claimed, without much evidence, that democracy in the Fels families was accompanied by sufficient control to avoid the more serious consequences of the first risk. Here Baldwin seems to approach the concept of the authoritative parent, elaborated by Baumrind (see below). His values are clear: "We in child development seem at present to believe that spontaneity, even if it involves rebelliousness, is a sign of good preschool adjustment. Whether that belief is true . . . must be discovered by further research." (Baldwin, 1948, p. 136). Could it be that this ideology itself influenced the conclusions?

The research suffers from a number of problems: The classification of parental practices changes from one publication to another and is not clear; the presentation of the analysis lacks the essential details that would allow us to judge the results for ourselves. Moreover, democratic parents and their children had higher IQs and better education than did the other groups, and democratic children had more nursery school experience outside the Fels situation than did children from other homes (Baldwin, 1949). These last two factors may have affected the outcome to an unknown extent.

Baumrind's Work

A somewhat different perspective on control versus permissiveness has been adopted by Diana Baumrind whose research program (Baumrind 1971, 1973) represents the zeitgeist of the 1970s, both in method and outlook. It was begun in the 1960s when the emphasis in the clinical and educational literature was still on the negative effects of strict discipline on children, although some straws in the wind already indicated some change (cf. Spock, 1957). Baumrind's research was actuated by her philosophy and the philosophy of the times, reflecting a shift away from the influence of the post-Freudians. In turn, she has also affected and accelerated changes in child-rearing philosophy toward a more benign view of the effects of discipline within the context of an otherwise appropriate climate in the home. Baumrind and her colleagues, like the Fels workers, carried out home observations but, in contrast to the Fels research, the former made a careful record of the behavior observed. Parents were also interviewed on their practices and attitudes and ratings were anchored to specific interview responses and observed behavior. Syndromes or clusters of behavior were created by cluster analysis.

Baumrind's view of control differs from the Fels view mainly in that she makes a distinction between firm control and restrictive, punitive control: "Parental control as defined here is not a measure of restrictiveness, punitive attitudes, or intrusiveness, but is a measure of strict discipline." (Baumrind, 1973, p. 6). It is measured by parents' consistency in enforcing their rules, by their structuring the child's activities, feeling in control of the child's behavior, and by control actually being effective. From the different patterns of parents' scores on the various clusters, she generates three parenting styles: authoritarian, authoritative, and permissive.

The *authoritarian* parent values obedience as a virtue and believes in restricting the child's autonomy. This parent values the preservation of order as an end in itself; he or she does not encourage verbal give-and-take. This parent would be high on *firm enforcement* (of rules) and low on *encourages independence*.

The *authoritative* parent directs the child's activities in a rational, issue-oriented manner. She sets standards for conduct, values compliance with reasonable rules, but also respects the child's autonomy and individuality. Such parents would be high on *firm enforcement* and high on *encourages independence*.

The *permissive* parent acts in an affirmative, acceptant, and benign manner toward the child's impulses and actions. Freedom for this parent means absence of restraint, as far as is consistent with ensuring the child's physical survival. Such parents would be low on *firm enforcement*, high on *passive-acceptant*, and low on *expect participation in household chores*.

The overall outcome in the three studies of preschool children summarized in Baumrind's 1973 paper was in accordance with her implicit hypotheses. In comparison with children from both authoritarian and permissive homes, children from authoritative homes showed greater social responsibility (achievement orientation, friendliness toward peers, cooperativeness toward adults) and independence (social dominance, nonconforming behavior, purposiveness). Authoritarian control did not achieve its ostensible aim of social responsibility, and permissive noncontrol did not achieve its aim of independence. The detailed results introduce some qualifications to these generalizations. In particular, in one study (Baumrind, 1971) the sons of authoritative parents were not very independent though they were socially responsible. Since their parents were exceptionally high in *firm enforcement*, and since parental *restrictiveness* (measured separately) was also associated with low independence in boys, Baumrind herself concludes that very high control may bring with it the risk of loss of independence. Although wrinkles in the research, such as the above, show that child behavior in the two sexes is affected differentially, Baumrind (1983) concludes that the impact of the configuration of authoritative child rearing "is uniformly positive for both sexes at all ages studied, unlike any other child rearing pattern" (p. 138).

In comparing Baumrind's with the Fels research, we note that Baumrind is somewhat more rigorous in her methods and better documents her conclusions. (Some subjectivity, nevertheless, remains in the rating process, and constructs are sometimes defined inconsistently in different studies. Children of authoritative parents also have higher IQs than the other two groups, as children of democratic homes did in the Fels studies—a fact that may have affected the results.) However, ideology is, by and large, kept on the leash of the data. Her research program also demonstrates the utility of looking at patterns of behavior, rather than at one dimension alone.

The results of the Fels studies generally show adverse effects arising from control, whereas in the Baumrind research these effects are generally beneficial. This shift would seem to result from different definitions of "control," Baumrind, in following her philosophy, deliberately excluded restrictive and punitive attitudes from it. Baumrind (1983) also has suggested that the mark of authoritative parents is that they balance high control with high responsiveness and that this balance represents the critical variable. Each of these two major investigations is, in its general tenor, consistent with the spirit of its decade. Yet, examined closely, the difference is more one of emphasis than of substance. Looked at overall, both Baldwin and Baumrind concede that democracy *and* control (or respect for individuality and firm enforcement) are necessary ingredients of child rearing, but Baldwin stresses the price to be paid for too much control, Baumrind the price to be paid for too much permissiveness.

The Effects of Restrictiveness—General Comments

One of the chief difficulties in integrating rating-based research, is the variety of definitions that have been used for the traits investigated, particularly restrictiveness. The umbrella term usually covers such disparate acts as restrictions on aggression to siblings or misuse of household furniture, and restrictions on exploration and independent behavior. The former may be essential and beneficial, the latter not. Also, demands for neatness, orderliness, or good table manners often are subsumed under the label of restrictiveness, whereas many theorists would consider these actions as demands for mature behavior. These differences in definition or emphasis, no doubt, reflect the differing philosophies of the various researchers. Furthermore, effects may be produced by the varying configurations of parental practices in which restrictiveness appears, rather than by restrictiveness alone. Small wonder, then, that the results regarding child outcomes in different studies are often conflicting, as we noted in the Fels and Baumrind research programs.

That an authoritative pattern of discipline can have beneficial and adaptive consequences in social and cognitive areas is also shown by several other studies. Consistent control, reasonable restrictions with clearly defined limits, combined with latitude for individual action and reward for independence led to social responsibility and a desire to achieve (Pulkkinen, 1982), high self-esteem (Coopersmith, 1967), language facility, independence (Lytton, 1980), and cognitive competence (Lytton, Watts, & Dunn, 1986, a follow-up of part of the sample of Lytton's earlier study). There is thus considerable support for Baumrind's (1973) model. On the other hand, investigations that defined restrictivness in terms of directiveness, critical interference, or forceful physical intervention have often reported negative consequences in social behavior flowing from such an authoritarian pattern, for example, low cooperation (Merrill Bishop, 1951), low compliance (Londerville & Main, 1981), or low self-esteem (Loeb, Horst, & Horton, 1980).

Restrictiveness and encouragement of independence can go hand-in-hand, as shown particularly in Chandler et al. (1980) and Coopersmith (1967). This can occur if restrictions are imposed in a limited area (e.g., in the enforcement of well-established household rules), but the child is still encouraged to explore new situations, experiment with new ideas, and make her own decisions where appropriate.

From an extensive review of the literature we would conclude that the positive effects of restrictiveness, certainly when incorporated in the authoritative pattern, on the whole outweigh the negative ones. This is particularly the case in the area of academic achievement and achievement motivation, cooperation, and social responsibility. However, restrictiveness clearly acts negatively on originality—almost all studies agree on this. There is also some evidence that it may engender submissiveness and dependency and result in lack of altruistic behavior.

In any case, there is no doubt that extremes of restrictiveness have negative effects, especially as they are often combined with hostile punitiveness, as shown in some of the studies on delinquency and aggression (e.g., Bandura & Walters, 1959; McCord, McCord, & Howard, 1961). But the same is true of the opposite, overlax discipline—usually a sign of indifference—as demonstrated by the early studies and more recently by Olweus (1980).

As was noted earlier, restrictiveness can shade into hard demands for expected behavior. When parental actions, such as expectations of mature behavior and achievement effort, and demands for taking responsibility for certain duties are considered separately, the effects are almost all positive. Such demands and expectations—which are part of the authoritative pattern but are here considered separately—have been associated with high achievement (Rosen & D'Andrade, 1959), achievement motivation (Winterbottom, 1958), or increasing IQ (McCall, Appelbaum, & Hogarty, 1973).

Such practices also have desirable effects in the area of social behavior: they have been associated with children's independence (Hatfield, Rau, & Alpert, 1967 [but for girls only]; Radke-Yarrow, Campbell, & Burton, 1968), and with moral development and social responsibility, (e.g., Grinder, 1962; Lytton et al., 1986; Schaefer & Bayley, 1963; Sears, Rau, & Alpert, 1965). There are few exceptions to this trend. While the outcomes of restrictiveness per se are still surrounded by ambiguity and ideological controversy, the refreshing consensus among studies that have examined demands and expectations permits the conclusion that this kind of parental practice has generally desirable outcomes.

PUNISHMENT

Punishment is a common ingredient of child-rearing techniques—one that all parents would like to avoid, but only very few can. It is a motivating device, supplied by external agents, and research has been directed at the nature and effects of these contingencies on the child's development.

From the cognitive point of view sanctions can be thought of as cues to the child to enable her to evaluate her actions. Negative sanctions, in particular, also serve an affective function, namely to arouse the child emotionally, that is, to arouse anxiety. Punishment works by conditioning avoidance of certain acts; it inculcates anxiety in the child which inhibits the performance of the activity with which the punishment is associated. Learning theory suggests, however, that the effects of such motivational techniques will be limited in time and place, and we will consider later how these limitations might be overcome.

Field Studies

Studies of punishment carried out in the field (e.g., home or school) and those done in an experimental laboratory will be considered separately because the findings often differ (see below). Further, a distinction often has been made between two forms of punishment: power assertion and love withdrawal. We will now examine these two approaches.

Power Assertion

Hoffman (1970b) has defined this category to include the direct application of force, including physical punishment, deprivation of privileges, or threats of these.

From the earlier literature, summarized by Becker (1964), some interesting and replicated relationships between punishment (particularly physical punishment) and aggression and delinquency emerge. Though each of these field studies has methodological weaknesses, these differ from study to study, and the replicated findings gain credibility because the weaknesses tend to cancel out. We should note first of all that certain affectional attitudes and disciplinary practices tend to go together. Thus, it has been found repeatedly that the use of praise and reasoning is associated with parental warmth, whereas the use of physical punishment is linked to hostility (Bandura & Walters, 1959; Becker et al., 1962; Sears et al., 1957; Lytton, 1980). It is little wonder then that a number of studies have demonstrated that the configuration of high use of punishment with rejection is closely associated with aggression or delinquency in the children (Becker Peterson, Luria, Shoemaker, & Hellmer, 1962; Eron, Banta, Walder, & Laulicht, 1961; McCord, McCord, & Zola, 1959). Such a link was demonstrated once again in a more recent study that observed family interaction in structured discussions (Hetherington, Stouwie, & Ridberg, 1971), as well as in a longitudinal study of aggression (Huesmann, Eron, Lefkowitz, & Walder, 1984). Even in infancy high maternal use of physical punishment is associated with low impulse control in the infant (Power & Chapieski, 1986). We know of no study that has contradicted this kind of finding.

The earlier delinquency studies also pointed an accusing finger at erratic or inconsistent discipline, both within and between parents, as contributing to antisocial behavior (Bandura & Walters, 1959; Glueck & Glueck, 1950; McCord et al., 1959). Inconsistency, however, can mean different things. It may be one thing to vacillate between rewarding a behavior at one time and punishing it at another without good reason, constantly to issue idle threats, or for one parent to reward and the other parent to punish the same behavior. Such inconsistencies, these authors found, were conducive to delinquent behavior. It may be quite another matter for parents to take situational circumstances or the nature of the child into account, and therefore to show some variability in their reactions, even though they remain consistent with their rational goals for the child. So parents may not carry through on every threat, or they sometimes may forgive a deviant act. Parents would be inhuman if they were not inconsistent in this sense.

Eron et al. (1961) report some interesting findings on the relations between mothers' and fathers' punishment and rejection, rated from parent interviews, and their children's aggression, as assessed by classmates. It can be seen from Table 5.1 that aggression was highest when both mother and father were rejecting. However, the child's aggression was increased more by mother's than father's rejection but, conversely, more by father's than mother's punishment. Poor parental family management techniques have been found to be highly predictive of delinquency (Loeber & Dishion, 1983) and criminality in adult males (McCord, 1979). Poor management techniques included punitiveness (part of parental aggressiveness), lack of maternal supervision and affection, and marital conflict.

Overall, therefore, the evidence for an association between the punishment-rejection configuration and aggression or delinquency has been fairly well established, and intense conflict between spouses has also been shown to have a similarly detrimental effect (e.g., McCord et al., 1961; McCord, 1979). (The inconsistency in discipline matters between parents, that we discussed above, may well be a symptom of such discord.) We should stress, however, that the direction of effects is by no means unequivocal, that is, it could well be an aggressive child who elicits punishment and even rejection from his parents, rather than the other way around. That the actual direction of influence may flow in this direction is suggested by the fact that some longitudinal studies in this area have not found a significant correlation between early punishment and later aggression (Eron, Walder, Huesmann, & Lefkowitz, 1974; Johannesson, 1974; Sears, 1961).

What Western parents want to achieve through their socializing efforts is not only that children should adopt reasonable norms of behavior and re-

TABLE 5.1. Mothers' and fathers' rejection and punishment and child's aggression/delinquency.

| | Median school aggression scores | | | | Percent delinquent | | | |
| | High father[a] | | Low father[b] | | High father | | Low father | |
	High mother[a]	Low mother[b]	High mother[a]	Low mother[b]	High mother	Low mother	High mother	Low mother
Parental rejection	36	3.5	13	4.5	70	36	46	32
Punishment for aggression	21.5	34	7.5	4				

Note. The data in columns 1–4 are from Eron et al. (1961), and the data in columns 5–8 are from McCord et al. (1959). [a] Above combined median. [b] Below combined median frain from socially undesirable acts in their presence, but that they should continue to do so in their absence. This implies that children must internalize moral norms, that is, make them part of their own value system. All the field studies, summarized by Hoffman (1970b), show that power-assertive techniques by themselves tend to inhibit the internalization of moral standards and lead to low development of conscience. Maccoby and Martin (1983) state in a review of research in the area that they are not aware of any study since then that has contradicted this conclusion—nor are we. The reason power-assertive techniques produce such results—impressively documented, but certainly not intended by parents—is, Hoffman suggests, because they both elicit hostility and provide a model for expressing that hostility. However, it may be the child's defective moral internalization that drives parents to resort to power assertion, as suggested by the longitudinal studies of aggression noted above.

In contrast to the general consensus on the detrimental effects of power assertion on internalized standards for the inhibition of proscribed behavior, its effects on the internalization of prosocial behavior (e.g., helping, sharing) are not as clear-cut. Radke-Yarrow, Zahn-Waxler, and Chapman (1983) review a number of correlational studies, where positive, negative, and no associations have been found between power assertion and prosocial behavior. Power assertion may not be so clearly related to lack of prosocial behavior because parents may not consider failure to engage in prosocial actions as intolerable behavior calling for clear assertion of power and a firm stand; hence they may hesitate to use power assertion when faced with such a failure (cf. Grusec & Dix, 1982).

What are the interactive processes between parent and child that maintain a child's aggressive behavior in problem families, or reduce it in nonproblem families? This is the question that Patterson and his group addressed in a series of studies (Patterson, 1979, 1980, 1982). They observed the mutual encounters of aggressive children and nonproblem children with their parents and siblings in the home, noting the moment-to-moment interchanges during repeated visits. Aggressive children did not receive more reinforcement for their aggressive acts than did nondeviant children. What did distinguish aggressive from other children was their reaction to punishment. Whereas nondeviant children were less likely to continue with their aggressive action if punished by the parent, aggressive children were *more* likely to do so. This peculiar insensitivity of aggressive children to painful events—possibly of constitutional origin—may explain the usual punishment-aggression link found in so many field studies, but the lack of sensitivity may well produce its effects by interacting with inept parental management techniques (Patterson, 1982).

Love Withdrawal

Love withdrawal, the second of our two forms of punishment, threatens the disruption of a strong emotional bond between parent and child, something which the child will feel as a threat to her security and a cause for considerable anxiety. It is a psychological form of punishment and may take the form of an expression of disappointment or angry disapproval, of ignoring or isolating the child, of conditional withdrawal of love ("I don't love you, when you do this kind of thing,"* or of a statement implying permanent loss of love. In correlational research these forms have usually been lumped together.

Hoffman has found in his work (1970a) that heavy and indiscriminate use of love withdrawal was conducive to guilt and used most by parents of children who had internalized societal standards, but were obeying them rigidly and were convention-bound. That love withdrawal may nevertheless be a powerful method with younger children is again suggested by a recent study by Chapman and Zahn-Waxler (1982). Mothers were trained to observe and make immediate notes of their affective and disciplinary interactions with their toddler-aged children. The mother's reports revealed that love withdrawal was the single most effective technique for securing the children's compliance, although it was used infrequently and always in combination with some other technique. Although love withdrawal may thus obtain compliance on the spot, whether or not it is effective in promoting autonomous internalized standards of behavior is still a moot point.

Experimental Laboratory Research

Initially under the influence of learning theory, experimental laboratory research into various aspects of punishment with humans has abounded. An extensive review of this research, with all its ramifications, can be found in Walters and Grusec (1977). Punishment for a child in the laboratory is diluted, compared with the home, for obvious ethical reasons. It often takes the form of the sound of a buzzer, the forfeiture of candy or pennies, or just the word "wrong," when the reward is "right." (Withdrawal of nurturance by the experimenter will be discussed below.) Various parameters of punishment, such as its intensity, whether it is consistent or intermittent, its timing, and frequency and duration, have been studied.

The literature reviewed by Walters and Grusec (1977) shows that punishment is certainly effective in suppressing undersirable or proscribed behavior, as defined by the experimenter (e.g., aggressive acts against dolls or playing with forbidden toys). Some experiments provided cognitive structure for a prohibition (e.g., telling the child not to play with some toys because the experiment was afraid they might get broken and he wanted them for some other children). Although generally punishment is most

---

*Advice columns often recommend that parents should say "I don't like this action," rather than "I don't like you when you do this." While the former statement is less strong, it still implies a temporary lessening of love and the child is likely to perceive it as such.

effective when administered at the time of onset of a forbidden act, such cognitive structure overrode the detrimental effects of delay in punishment (Cheyne & Walters, 1969; Parke, 1969). In other words, the child's responses are determined not only by the visceral effects (conditioned anxiety) of punishment, but also by cognitive information and the principles contained therein.

Laboratory experiments often show that punishment has desirable consequences, whereas studies of parents and children (in the home or by interview) suggest that power-assertive punishment has undesirable consequences. The seeming contradiction can be resolved if we look at the questions that have been asked in each of these research traditions. For the experimental researchers interest has mainly centered on the suppression of behavior in the presence of an external agent, whereas the students of parent-child socialization focused their attention on internalization and more long-term response tendencies. The former was found to be facilitated by punishment, especially when it was severe, whereas the latter was found to be impeded by it. The work of one of us (Lytton, 1980), in fact, forms a bridge between the two research paradigms, since it studied immediate compliance of 2-year-olds observed in a naturalistic situation in the home, and found that this was fostered by power-assertive methods as it was in the experimental studies, although these methods did not promote compliance and conscience as long-term dispositions.

Although laboratory experiments have sometimes found that punishment increases resistance to temptation in the absence of the punishing agent (e.g., Aronfreed & Reber, 1965), such behavior in the laboratory may represent more primitive, short-lived internalization than that inferred from moral indices in real life.

Effects of Punishment—Comments

How do the effects of punishment become built into a generalized tendency towards socially acceptable, responsible, and prosocial behavior? The research that we have reviewed indicates that internalization is facilitated when parents or other educators make use of a configuration of practices that surround or moderate the act of punishment, for example, when it is part of the authoritative pattern, or if the salience of external force is reduced, e.g., by rational explanations of the reasons for the rule, as attribution theory would suggest (cf. Hoffman, 1970a; Perry & Perry, 1983—these relations will be discussed in detail below). Punishment that arises as a natural consequence of the misdemeanor and is logically related to it, rather than being arbitrarily imposed, that is accompanied by explanations which stress the requirements of the situation rather than the personal authority of the punisher, we think, will minimize the anger and hostility that might otherwise arise and generate counterproductive results. If the punishment is moderate and the relations between parents and child are generally friendly (important qualifications), there is, in fact, little evidence that punishment creates maladjustment or neurotic behavior (Walters & Grusec, 1977). It is noteworthy also that both Hoffman (1970a) and Zahn-Waxler, Radke-Yarrow, & King (1979) found that it was mothers with the most prosocial and morally advanced children who reported using physical punishment along with emotionally toned explanations. Perhaps they did so because raising a moral child was something in which their emotions were deeply involved.

Rewards

Since the use of rewards to influence children's behavior has been a less controversial issue than the use of punishment, we will confine ourselves to a short discussion. First a few words about field studies in the area. What are the effects on children's dispositions if parents tend to use rewards as a way of achieving desired behavior?

We must distinguish between parents' use of material and psychological rewards. The latter—approval and praise—are included in the authoritative parenting pattern as well as in the permissive pattern and the general conclusions that we have drawn earlier will apply: Provided these psychological rewards are not used indiscriminately and joined with clear demands for expected, mature behavior, they will tend to promote social responsibility and internalization of standards (Baumrind, 1973; Lytton, 1980).

The use of material rewards (e.g., presents or candy) is a different matter. Indeed, parents when asked about this practice in interviews, often refer to it as "bribing." Surprisingly, it seems to have rarely been studied empirically in field studies, but Lytton (1980) found it to be a negative factor, in that its use was associated with slightly lowered internalized standards. In the follow-up of this sample at age 9 (Lytton et al., 1986), the use of material rewards impeded cognitive competence and the good social functioning of the child. It should be noted that material rewards, like physical punishment, are external sanctions and, in using them, the parent does not utilize or help to build the child's own internal controls.

Experiments have generally found material rewards to be effective in producing desired learning responses. However, extrinsic rewards may have detrimental effects by undermining children's feeling of control over their own activities. Thus, in one experiment children who were promised and given a "good player" award for undertaking an intrinsically interesting activity, namely drawing pictures with Magic Markers, were less inclined to engage in this activity on a later unrewarded occasion, in comparison with children who did not expect a reward (Lepper, Greene, & Nisbett, 1973). Rewards (e.g., "Good! That's fine!") also may lose their value by being given indiscriminately, as often happens. Hence discrimination learning experiments have found that mixing in a little mild punishment for incorrect responses with the praise for correct responses (e.g., imposing forfeiture of some candy or simply saying "wrong") may help children to discriminate between correct and incorrect responses and hence lead to more efficient learning (e.g., Stevenson, Weir, & Zigler, 1959). An extended discussion of the complexities of this topic can be found in Walters and Grusec, 1977.

INDUCTION

The Work of Hoffman

Hoffman introduced the term "induction" as part of his model of discipline, to denote what is more commonly known as reasoning, or the use of explanations. Many different kinds of verbal communications are subsumed under this label, for example, factual explanations of physical constraints, moral exhortations, communications about rules, principles and values, appeals to children's pride, strivings for mastery, appeals based on their love for their mothers, attributions ("A kind boy like you helps his friend"), or explanations of the possibly hurtful implications the child's actions hold for others. The last Hoffman called "other-oriented induction."

Induction plays a central role in Hoffman's research program, covering the 1960s and 1970s, which has been concerned with the socialization antecedents of moral development, and particularly with two aspects of it, namely internal moral orientation, or conscience (e.g., Hoffman 1970a; Hoffman & Salzstein, 1967), and consideration for others, or altruism (e.g., Hoffman, 1963, 1975a).

His method in ascertaining the moral orientation of children has been to ask them to complete stories about the misdemeanors of other children in order to assess the child's feeling of guilt (the affective ingredient of moral internalization according to psychoanalytic theory) on the assumption that the child will project her own feelings onto the story's hero. In addition, he has asked for the children's judgments about behavior presented in moral dilemma stories of the Piaget and Kohlberg type. Since Hoffman has been concerned with *internalized* moral orientation, he has not obtained data on children's actual socially responsible behavior, judging this to be less directly relevant, except for mothers' reports of children confessing after wrongdoing.

Hoffman's data on parents' practices have been obtained by interviews with parents, as well as by children's reports of parents' likely behavior, based on hypothetical discipline situation, but not by observations (cf. Chapter 2).

Hoffman in one investigation (1970a) classified children on the basis of their moral judgments as displaying: a) conventional-rigid orientation, if their judgments showed rigid adherence to societal norms regardless of circumstances, or (b) humanistic-flexible orientation, if their judgments indicated concern for the human consequences of certain behavior and consideration for extenuating circumstances. He found that the discipline of parents of conventional children was characterized by the frequent use of love withdrawal and inductions highlighting the harm done to the *parent* by the child's action. On the other hand, the parents of humanistic children used more varied and discriminating discipline techniques, depending on the situation. They used other-oriented induction as well as power assertion more than did conventional mothers.

Hoffman's emphasis on the value of other-oriented induction in bringing about an internal, flexible moral orientation aligns him with cognitive-developmental theory, but in his focus on feelings of guilt he also shows affiliations with the psychoanalytic tradition.

In his overall theoretical model of parental influences on the child, Hoffman, like others whose work we are discussing, recognizes that disciplinary techniques never come alone. All discipline, he states, has power assertive, love withdrawal and inductive components, mixed in various proportions (Hoffman, 1977). The similarity between this configuration of practices and Baumrind's authoritative parenting pattern will be obvious, with a rational approach being an important ingredient in both.

The Effects of Induction—General Comments

Through the investigations that have studied induction, in all its diversity, there runs a general thread of support for the hypothesis that it facilitates the development of an internalized moral orientation, or conscience (e.g., Feshbach, 1974; Zahn-Waxler et al., 1979; earlier work reviewed by Hoffman, 1970b). But there are also a number of investigations that reported no significant association (e.g., Sears et al., 1965; Lytton 1980).

Support for the hypothesis that induction promotes prosocial behavior is more tenuous and conditional, for example, it was only partially effective in one investigation (Hoffman, 1975a) and had negative effects on altruism in an experiment (Staub, 1971). Such a mixed bag of results suggests that induction is not, in and of itself, the panacea of socialization.

What kind of induction, in which circumstances, is effective? Zahn-Waxler et al. (1979) trained mothers to observe instances of transgression or altruism, and to record their toddler-aged children's actions and their own reactions on a tape recorder. The effects were judged by the children's reparations for harm done, and by their offering sympathy, comfort, and help when they were bystanders at distressful events. The authors found that mothers' messages that proved effective were not calm, reasoned communications, but were charged with intense feeling, expressed moralizing judgments, and made statements of principle or of disappointment. These messages were "inductions," as they pointed out the effects of children's behavior, but they also contained both love withdrawal and power-assertive components. The authors concluded that the effective inductive technique is emotionally charged, sometimes harsh, and often forceful (e.g., "Look what you did! Don't you see you hurt Amy—don't ever pull hair"). On the other hand, neutral explanations ("Tom's crying because you pushed him") did not affect either reparations or prosocial behavior, although they were understood by these young children.

How does induction foster the generalization and internalization of standards? Hoffman (1977) suggests a rationale: Power assertion makes the child stop or avoid a given action, and both it and love withdrawal serve the function of arousing her (creating anxiety). Although the punishment-based avoidance of the prohibited act is likely to be short-lived, if the arousal is optimal, it will serve to render the child receptive to the cognitive structure that induction provides. The induction, it is suggested, can then supply a basis for generalizing the rule from the single prohibited act to other acts on the basis of the principle contained in it. This principle will eventually become part of the child's own cognitive structure and thinking, and as a cognitive representation will be more resistant to extinction than the effect of a few instances of punishment. Recent research on memory would suggest that the child may be expected in time to remember the content of the inductive message, but to forget its source, and therefore she may come to think of the rule as her own rather than her parents'. In this way induction can be incorporated in attribution theory (see below).

Although the evidence is not unequivocal, induction seems to be effective if our aim is to raise a child who acts autonomously and possesses internalized moral standards of conduct that are independent of external control and surveillance. This is an aim characteristic of Western society, and is held particularly strongly by the Western educated middle class; we should therefore remember that if psychologists rate induction so highly as a method of discipline, they do so in the context of this society's goals.

WARMTH

Warmth (an attitude, rather than a practice) is popularly regarded as an important ingredient in the parent-child relationship and it has been an often recurring dimension in socialization studies. Some investigations have used synonyms that are very closely related in meaning, such as acceptance (opposite: rejection), nurturance, and responsiveness, and these will be included in our discussion of nurturance as a disposition. A nurturant relationship is one that expresses caring, support, and feelings of love and acceptance (both noncontingent and contingent on the child's behavior). It is only human, and probably beneficial, even for the best of parents to make their approval contingent on the child's positive, acceptable behavior, and lack of approval inevitably implies a temporary lessening of love. Hence occasional temporarily contingent love ("I love you when you do this, but I don't love you when you do that"—essentially love withdrawal) does not negate an overall warm disposition. Although approval may be contingent, it should be accompanied by an absolute and ever-present commitment to the child's welfare, whatever the child does.

It may be questioned whether responsiveness can be equated with warmth, since the term implies that the parent reacts contingently to the child. Note, however, that the response is contingent on the child's social signals, demands, or distress, not on her acceptable behavior and hence the parent's responsiveness that is sensitive to the child's need, as a recurring behavior pattern, can be considered tantamount to warmth. Empirically, too, it has been shown (Clarke-Stewart, 1973) that mothers' warmth is highly correlated with her responsiveness to social signals or distress.

Has warmth in parents the good effects popularly expected of it? Both Hoffman's (1970b) and Radke-Yarrow et al.'s (1968) summaries of earlier research showed it to facilitate the development of conscience, or an internalized moral orientation. Indeed, in Radke-Yarrow et al.'s review it was the only parent variable to be so consistently related to any child variable. Although there are some exceptions (e.g., in Sears et al.'s 1965 study the positive effect was present only for girls), later research, which has relied more on observation than report, almost universally bears out this relationship (e.g., Londerville & Main, 1981; Zahn-Waxler et al., 1979). Lytton (1980), in an analysis of sequential behavior, found that adding positive, warm actions (e.g., a smile) to commands produced more compliance than did commands alone, whereas joining physical control or negative actions (e.g., criticisms, scolding) to commands resulted in less compliance. It also has been found repeatedly, and fairly consistently, that parental warmth is related to cognitive competence and achievement in the child (e.g., Clarke-Stewart, 1973; Lytton, 1980; Rosen & D'Andrade, 1959), as well as to good social adjustment (Daniels, Dunn, Furstenberg, & Plomin, 1985).

It is well established, moreover, that extreme lack of warmth or rejection has adverse consequences for children's social adjustment, that is, it leads to aggression or delinquency, particularly when it occurs in combination with severe punishment, as we noted earlier. Further, psychopathology of various kinds, or maladjustment, also has been shown to be related to lack of warmth (e.g., Lytton et al., 1986; Oleinick et al., 1966; Siegelman, 1966). As discussed above, rejection by mother seems to be particularly damaging. However, as with punishment, there must be some doubt whether the direction of effects runs unilaterally from parent to child.

On the other hand, the hypothesis that warmth would be related to prosocial behavior, for example, donating, helping, or empathy with distressed persons, has received more equivocal support and a number of experimental and part-experimental studies have found only patchy effects (e.g., Grusec, 1971; Hoffman, 1963; 1975a). Radke-Yarrow, Scott, and Zahn-Waxler (1973) report that a nurturant attitude on the part of caregivers initially had no effect on altruism in a nursery school, but when the caregivers trained the children in altruism over a longer period by modeling it, children with nurturant models displayed considerably more prosocial behavior when the opportunity arose, than did children with nonnurturant models.

Some of the contradictions in studies that have assessed warmth by interview may be attributed to differing standards of rating, to vagueness of definition, or insufficiency of evidence for making judgments of warmth. Where the positive effects of warmth have been in evidence, warmth has usually been part of a larger child-rearing pattern. Effective configurations of parenting practices tend to include warmth as a contextual variable, part of the background climate of the home. It may operate by making the child more receptive to parental influence, and hence it will reduce the need for the parent to resort to power-assertive techniques. Moreover, warmth has been found to be conducive to high self-esteem in the child, (e.g., Coopersmith, 1967) which, in turn, is likely to lead to good social functioning, including internalization and altruism.

SITUATIONAL INFLUENCES ON PARENTING PRACTICES

The particular pattern of practices that parents adopt will be determined in part by the specific situation that calls forth parental intervention. An interesting and important question then arises, namely, how parents discriminate between and adapt to such different situations. Hoffman's work (1970a) suggests that some parents are more discriminating than others in this. Grusec and Kuczynski (1980) addressed the question of the influence of the situation by asking middle-class mothers to describe their likely reactions to hypothetical discipline situations. They found that mothers said they would use power-assertive techniques (verbal threats, commands, or physical punishment) for short-term objectives, (e.g., lowering the noise level or stopping a ball being thrown in the living room), whereas they would use reasoning where long-term considerations were important or for behavior that is likely to recur in their absence (e.g., making fun of less fortunate others or minor theft). When children put themselves into physical danger mothers reported they would use power assertion first and follow this up with explanations.

Although such situational influences—here arising from the child—will always be at work, this does not nullify the fact that both parents' and children's dispositions also play an important part in determining patterns of parenting, an issue which we will discuss in later sections. Thus, in any given situation, some mothers may tend to react more severely than others, whatever the form of discipline used.

CONVERGING EVIDENCE ON PARENTS' PRACTICES

From the research that we have reviewed so far, what conclusions about parents' practices and their effects can we consider to be fairly well established? (Processes that may be important mediators of certain effects, but that mainly operate within the child will be discussed in the next section.)

Firstly, the findings show quite conclusively that the more parents make use of *power assertion* the less will children achieve internalized moral controls, or conscience. In particular, the punishment-rejection configuration is related to aggression and delinquency. The correlational results on which these two conclusions are based are quite compatible with the assumption that the deleterious effects of power assertion arise mainly from extreme use of it. A lesser degree of power assertion, as we have noted, is a part of all discipline techniques. It must be remembered, however, that the direction of influence in the first place, may run from child to parent, so that under this interpretation the child's initial lack of internalized control would lead to greater use of power assertion by the parents. Nevertheless, it is still true that its further use will not serve to increase internalized controls or to decrease acting-out behavior, but will tend to achieve the opposite result.

The second firm conclusion seems to be that *affectionate relations* (warmth, etc.) are positively related to the development of internalized controls, as well as to the growth of cognitive competence in the child, although acceptance of the child need not be unconditional. Affectionate relations also seem to be related to prosocial behavior, but the evidence here is weaker. In this case, too, the direction of effects need not necessarily run from parent to child. The effects of *restrictiveness* and *induction*, on the other hand, are more ambiguous.

However, parental practices do not act in isolation. What is important are the constellations of practices and attitudes that mark out a kind of parent and that constitute a "parenting pattern," such as Baumrind's authoritative pattern: "To reduce all parental control strategies to two contrasting discipline techniques (induction and power-assertion) ignores the varied repertoires of management strategies that parents use, as well as the different background contexts that may influence the meaning of specific techniques (e.g., parental anger, depression, illness)" (Zahn-Waxler, 1984).

In discussing parents' socialization practices we may have given the unintended impression that socialization consists of perpetual confrontations and a search for ways to resolve conflicts. Such occasions will inevitably arise, but their frequency will vary considerably from family to family. There are families that can function harmoniously with relatively few conflicts.

The complementary and mutual dimensions of the parent-child relationship are readily apparent in situations where parents' and child's aims coincide, but it can imbue their whole relationship in the home. This will occur in a broader context when parents and children share goals and perspectives, and when family values permeate the home and have been readily accepted by the children. Attributional approaches (discussed in Chapter 1 and again below) will increase the likelihood that children will genuinely perceive their parents' goals to be their own. Maccoby and Martin (1983) further suggest that frequent cooperative activities help towards shared goals, and that the child's increasing cognitive competence will permit greater mutuality of interests and reduce the areas of conflict. We should add that how far these interests will diverge again in adolescence will depend once more on parents' understanding of their children and also on the way earlier conflicts were resolved.

Child Processes

IDENTIFICATION AND IMITATION

We now turn to processes that facilitate socialization and occur mainly within the child, that is, identification and attributions. Taking parents as models has been presumed to be one way in which the young acquire the values and behavioral norms of their group. This process in which the child is the predominant agent comes to the aid of the parents' socializing efforts without parents having to take an active and conscious part in it; they simply are themselves.

The formal concept of "identification," loosely equivalent to this popular notion, has its roots in psychoanalytic theory. More recently, social learning theorists have operationalized identification by means of the modeling process. They have made this the cornerstone of their theory and have submitted it to extensive experimentation with the purpose of specifying more precisely how, when, and why it operates. Bandura, one of the main proponents of social learning theory, acknowledges that identification involves the acquisition of complex behaviors and motive systems, whereas imitation involves only the reproduction of discrete responses, but he considers them essentially the same process because both terms refer to the same class of behaviors (Bandura, 1969). Identification-imitation develops through observational learning, not through reinforcement, and Bandura recognizes that motivation and self-regulation, that is, cognitive processes, play a crucial role in it (see discussion in Chapter 1).

There exists much anecdotal evidence from everybody's personal experience that children, spontaneously and without reinforcement, imitate acts and words of others, particularly of those they admire. Thus, one of us once knew a 9-year-old girl who listened with impatience to her parents' remonstrances about the rough reception accorded to a newcomer in her class at school, and expressed contempt at such adult ideas. However, a few days later she was overheard repeating the exact essence of her parents' ideas to a classmate, as if they were her own and without acknowledging their source.

Experiments have demonstrated repeatedly that children imitate bizarre physical acts or aggressive actions and words that they have observed a model perform. Studies by Bandura and his colleagues (e.g., Bandura, 1965; Bandura, Ross, & Ross, 1963b) have shown that observation of a model who yields to temptation or engages in a normally prohibited (e.g., aggressive) act has a disinhibitory effect on the observer, whether the model is rewarded or not. Observing a model who resists temptation or is punished for a prohibited act also raises the observer's level of inhibition above her normal baseline, if the model's resistance is salient or obvious to the observer (Grusec, Kuczynski, Rushton, & Simutis, 1979). However, field research has produced little evidence that identification plays an important role in the development of conscience (e.g., Hoffman, 1970b, 1971; Mussen, 1967; Sears et al., 1965).

Experimental studies of prosocial behavior have generally shown that observation of a generous model enhances generous behavior in the observer immediately afterwards (e.g., Grusec, 1971; Staub, 1971—for a review see Radke-Yarrow et al., 1983). If modeling experiments are to be taken to reflect parental influences, they should also exhibit some more long-term and generalizable effects. Such lasting effects on helping and donating have, in fact, been found some weeks after the experimental modeling, and generalizations to different prosocial behaviors also have been shown (e.g., Grusec et al., 1978; Radke-Yarrow et al., 1973). Also, as demonstrated in our earlier discussion, a model whom children have experienced as nurturant over a longer period enhances the imitation of prosocial behavior in children (Radke-Yarrow et al., 1973).

Mothers are not often employed as models in modeling experiments. However, mothers who are naturally helpful, responsive, and nurturant have been found to have children who display more helpful and prosocial behavior than do other children (Bryant & Crockenberg, 1980—laboratory experiment; Zahn-Waxler et al., 1979—in the home). These instances provide empirical evidence that children do, indeed, use their parents as models for their own behavior.

That identification with parents is helpful in establishing prosocial behavior, but not internalized guilt, may be explained by the fact that children tend to imitate the prosocial behavior that they have observed in their parents, whereas they have little opportunity of observing their parents resisting temptation, or their parents' sense of guilt about wrongdoing.

ATTRIBUTIONS

Researchers in the socialization area have sought to find mediating processes within the child, in addition to identification, that would explain how the child achieves moral internalization. Attribution theory, developed in recent years, has placed such internal cognitive processes and parental supporting practices at the center of an impressive experimental research effort. It suggests that when children are induced to comply with a norm or rule, they make certain inferences about themselves and attribute their actions to certain causes. The theory asserts that when children attribute their compliance with a request to themselves, that is, make an "internal"

TABLE 5.2. Mean number of tokens donated and pencils shared in each condition.

	Internal attribution	External attribution	No attribution
Modeling			
Tokens	6.07	2.73	4.14
Pencils	4.22	4.21	4.13
Direct instruction			
Tokens	5.64	4.78	4.36
Pencils	5.79	4.36	3.99

Note. From Grusec (1982).

attribution ("I shared my candy with these children, because I like giving things to others"), internalization will be strongest and will become generalized. On the other hand, when children make an "external" attribution ("I shared my candy with these children because I was told to"), internalization will be weakest. Attribution theory also suggests that internal attributions are most likely to occur when compliance is induced in such a way that children's perception of external force being applied is minimized.

Mild threat, we can suppose, is a less salient external force than severe threat. The theory would therefore predict that children who had refrained from playing with a forbidden toy under mild threat would later show greater internalization (e.g., honesty in a game-playing situation) than children who had refrained under severe threat. This is what Lepper (1973) did, indeed, find. When the children were asked about their self-perceptions, the mild-threat children also rated themselves as more honest than the severe-threat children.

As the theory would suggest, attributing helpfulness to the child promotes later prosocial behavior, and does so more effectively than does praising the child's act (that is, social reinforcement), at least for 8-year-olds (Grusec & Redler, 1980). The kind of attributions that adults make about children's behavior will also affect their internalization, according to the theory. In one study (Grusec et al., 1978; see Table 5.2) children were induced to share their earnings either through modeling or through direct instruction. After they had shared their earnings, the experimenter provided them either with an internal (referring to their natural generosity) or an external (referring to the experimenter's expectations of sharing) attribution for their sharing behavior. For children who had been induced to share through modeling, the internal attribution enhanced and the external attribution depressed sharing in a noncontrolled situation. Thus, internal attributions joined with modeling were an effective means of enhancing prosocial behavior. Thus, in the modeling condition, when the source of their own behavior seemed ambiguous to the children, adult attributions about their generous nature influenced them. But when children's original donations were prompted by direct instructions, internal attributions did not produce more anonymous sharing later than did external attributions, presumably because the children found an adult-supplied internal attribution implausible.

Experimental studies in the attribution tradition have shown that just enough pressure to ensure compliance ("minimally sufficient discipline") will result in greater internalization than will harsher discipline (e.g., Lepper, 1973). As we noted earlier, numerous studies of parents and children have supported Baumrind's (1973) claim for the effectiveness of authoritative parenting, as opposed to authoritarian parenting, in producing social responsibility and internalization. The effectiveness of authoritative parenting can be explained by attribution theory on the assumption that parents who are classified as "authoritative" are skilled in using the minimum amount of pressure needed to ensure compliance with reasonable requests, and will reduce the salience of any external compulsion to a minimum. The child will therefore have more reason to conceive of her behavior as originating in herself. Authoritarian parenting, on the other hand, with its insensitive power assertion, can be equated with oversufficient discipline.

We should note, however, that Baumrind herself (1983) in a rejoinder to Lewis (1981) endorses social learning theory, with its emphasis on external *firm* control, as a better explanation for the success of authoritative parenting than attribution theory. This debate provides a good illustration of the weakness of socialization theory: posthoc explanations from a dozen theories can plausibly be invoked to interpret the same findings, which typically do not provide a sufficiently clear-cut basis for deciding between the different theories.

It is worth noting that attributionists state (e.g., Lepper, 1981) that if children are to attribute a compliant act to their own volition and nature, they must first have observed themselves complying with the norm. If children get away with noncompliance, they are, in fact, in danger of acquiring internal attributions relating to successful noncompliance (Grusec, 1982; Perry & Perry, 1983). Hence it is necessary for parents to apply pressure that is sufficient to ensure compliance.

Attribution research is not without its discrepant findings, however, and the theory may have overstressed the importance of cognitive factors and perceived absence of external coercion. In line with some other writers (e.g., Baumrind, 1983; Perry & Perry, 1983), we tend to think that strongly entrenched habits of prosocial, responsible behavior, even if originally acquired through external pressure in their early years, will become part of children's self-regulatory behavior pattern, that is, they will become internalized. Not only is there evidence from field studies, (cited earlier) that affectively tinged and sometimes forceful reasoning is beneficial for moral internalization (it may have been minimally sufficient discipline), but some experimental research draws the same conclusions. The investigation by Grusec et al. (1978), which we described earlier, produced results that favored internal over external attribution, but it also showed that direct instruction resulted in very high levels of donation, irrespective of attribution condition. Similar evidence comes from a study by Israel and Brown (1979). An important principle seems to be that in order for the desired behavior to be internalized, there should be absolute clarity as to which behavior is expected and which is not to be tolerated, and discipline is sufficient only if it embraces such clarity. Direct instruction may facilitate internalization particularly where the desired behavior, like sharing and donating, is not a moral imperative, since no threat for nonsharing is usually implied, and hence the external compulsion is still relatively mild.

Although younger children do make cognitive attributions about themselves or others, these do not yet represent reliably consistent and integrated concepts of, say, "helpfulness" (Dix & Grusec, 1983). There is evidence that children younger than 7 or 8 do not think of themselves as possessing enduring personality dispositions (Peevers & Secord, 1973). Basic identification and internalization processes do go on in very young children but, we may assume, they probably have a larger affective component than they do later on, though evidence on this point is lacking.

Now and again evidence comes to light that documents the tenuous nature of the relationship that exists, firstly between psychological investigations and parents' practices, and secondly between these practices and children's behavior. Grusec and Dix (1982) discovered that mothers in practice seldom use attributions of helpfulness, when the child has been helpful, although laboratory investigations have shown such an approach to be important in strengthening altruism. Mothers rely much more on social reinforcement, that is, praise, approval, or simple acknowledgement of the act ("Thanks"). Furthermore they found in their studies with parents and children—in contrast to the experimental studies cited above—no relationship between the children's level of altruism and any form of parental response to altruism or failure to be altruistic. These findings suggest that there is some other crucial variable, not included in this investigation, that contributes to the creation of altruism—perhaps emotionally charged induction (see above) or the child's own predisposition.

By the caveats that we have introduced in the preceding paragraphs, we do not want to imply that reliance on external incentive and external force is the method of choice with young children. Indeed, the use of material incentives may impede moral internalization (cf. Grusec, 1982; Lytton, 1980). It is, no doubt, better when parents consider external pressure or compulsion to be necessary, that they do all they can to attenuate the children's perception of being coerced by personal authority. To this end attributions about the child himself or about others (other-oriented induction) are likely to be helpful. For the development of prosocial behavior, training in empathy or helpfulness by modeling or verbal rationales has been found to be effective, as we discussed earlier. Yet, in practice, it is used surprisingly little.

Moreover, children cannot be fooled. Clear and firmly enforced directives will be perceived for what they are and will be seen as originating with the parents—though, after internalization, this fact may later be forgotten. On the other hand, children's belief in themselves as basically cooperative can be strengthened by appropriate attributions and, indeed, there is persuasive evidence that they are endowed with an intrinsic predisposition to cooperate and comply with society's norms (cf. Stayton et al., 1971).

Bidirectional Influences

In our discussion of parental child-rearing practices so far, we have generally assumed that it is the parents who influence the child, though we have queried this assumption in some instances. However, any relationship is a mutually regulating process in which, as in a tennis game, the actions of each partner are in part determined and modified by those of the other. Socialization, too, is such a reciprocal process. In fact, the model of the socialization process which posits that child effects on parents play as important a part in molding these ongoing encounters as parent effects on the child has by now found such widespread acceptance, following Bell's (1968) seminal paper, that it is almost the orthodox view (e.g., Belsky, 1981; Lerner & Busch-Rossnagel, 1981). The more traditional model giving pride of place to parental influences has had to fight a rearguard action (e.g., Hoffman, 1975b).

CHILD EFFECTS ON PARENTS

Considerable evidence supporting the child-effects-on-adults view exists, and has been marshaled by Bell and Chapman (1986) and Belsky (1981). Common experience tells us that the arrival of the first child brings about the most dramatic changes in the parents' life-style and that this infant, helpless as it is, with its demands and its rewards exerts the most tyrannical control over its parents. Parents' child-rearing practices respond to the age of the child and change in accordance with the child's development. The greater cognitive maturity and the more advanced perspective-taking skills of middle childhood, for instance, mean that other-oriented induction becomes increasingly effective and is adopted more frequently (Maccoby, 1984).

Evidence that implies that children influence their parents' behavior arises from research that has studied children in their ordinary life situations. Thus, Yarrow (1963) found that a foster mother adopted different attitudes to two infants of the same sex and age assigned to her at the same time. The literature on child abuse indicates that abusing parents do not abuse all their children indiscriminately. Some children, such as those who fuss and cry a great deal, or premature infants, who have less appealing characteristics, are more at risk for child abuse than other infants (Gill,

1970; Lamb, 1978a). Infants, it seems, in part contribute to their own abuse. Thomas et al. (1963) also have identified certain "primary reaction patterns" in infants, which seem to be present from birth, and which influence parental behavior.

Mothers of boys who display a difficult and strong-willed temperament in infancy, it has been reported, later become less firmly controlling and more permissive of aggression, probably because the strong pressure of the infant's temperament makes strict control difficult for the mothers (Maccoby & Martin, 1983; Olweus, 1980).

Experimental research has also demonstrated that child behavior affects adult responses. For instance, when children's behavior is experimentally manipulated to appear independent, it elicits more nondirective responses from parents, and when such behavior is contrived to be noncompliant and aggressive, it elicits more commands and aversive reactions. Conversely, when children are made to display positive behavior they evoke positive responses from adults (see Bell and Chapman, 1986, for a review of such studies).

Further, an experiment has shown that when boys with behavior problems and normal boys interact with mothers of behavior problem boys and mothers of normal boys in unrelated pairs, the problem boys evoke more control and negative reactions from both types of mother than normal boys do, but the two types of mother do not differ from each other. These results suggest that it is the child who mainly "drives" these interactions and that the child's own tendencies are the major determinant of the conduct disorder (Anderson, Lytton, & Romney, 1986).

Moreover, children's past histories will lead to certain expectations about their behavior which will, in turn, influence mothers' reactions; for instance, both Anderson et al., (1986) and Halverson and Waldrop (1970) found that mothers of impulsive, uncontrolled boys were more controlling and negative towards their own children than to others, who were equally impulsive. In this way mother's reactions may exert an exacerbating influence, contributing to the child's conduct disorder. (See our discussion of transactional effects below.)

Correlational studies of parent-child relations, based on interviews, or sometimes on observation, have traditionally been interpreted as showing parent-to-child effects. Bell (1977), however, has demonstrated how this evidence could plausibly be reinterpreted as indicating child-to-parent effects, although the data usually do not allow one to decide definitely between the two interpretations.

PARENTAL EFFECTS ON THE CHILD

As we noted earlier, correlational evidence has generally been construed as indicating a parent-to-child effect. Responsive, warm, stimulating parental behavior has been thought to influence the child's cognitive development for the better (e.g., Clarke-Stewart, 1973), and it has also been regarded as influencing the child's social-emotional characteristics, for example, the child's attachment (Ainsworth et al., 1978), or conscience, as reviewed above.

Parental effects on the child have also been demonstrated experimentally, for instance, the children of mothers who had been specially trained to be responsive in play subsequently were more compliant than children of other mothers (Parpal & Maccoby, 1985). In addition, maternal discipline strategies are affected by their socialization goals, for example, when in an experiment mothers were led to make their goal long-term compliance by their children, they used more reasoning than when only short-term compliance was their aim (Kuczynski, 1984). All this implies that effects arising from parents' conscious actions will influence the child.

Hoffman (1975b) presents a persuasive theoretical argument in favor of a preponderant effect of parents on children in the area of moral internalization. This argument rests on the fact of overwhelming parental power that enables parents to place far greater constraints on the child than the other way around. However, Hoffman also agrees that some factors in the child may influence parental discipline patterns. Some of these factors may be children's readiness to comply with certain discipline techniques rather than others, or their person-orientation, the latter probably being of congenital origin (cf. Bell, 1977). Moral internalization, under this view, is thus mediated by the disciplinary experiences that the child has had. Once Hoffman and Bell propound their arguments in detail, they are able to arrive at the common conclusion that, in disciplinary encounters, the parent dominates the child more than the child does the parent.

RECIPROCAL INFLUENCES AND TRANSACTIONAL EFFECTS

Common sense would dictate that reciprocal processes are constantly at work between parents and children. Empirical investigations of parent-infant dyads have, indeed, demonstrated reciprocal phasing and turn-taking (e.g., Brazelton, Koslowski, & Main, 1974; Schaffer, 1974b). However, the balance and actual interplay of parent and child influences in the socialization process are the most difficult aspect of this process to analyze and specify empirically. But some evidence, chiefly based on observations of parent-child interactions, exists. Patterson (1979), for instance, has shown how sons' aggressive behavior elicits aversive reactions on the part of their mothers, which then evoke greater aggressiveness in the boys, and so forth. In this way escalating "coercive cycles" are established between mothers and their aggressive sons.

In the observational project, discussed earlier, Lytton (1980, 1982) distinguished between immediate and medium- or long-term effects. The observational data indicated that in immediate interactions parents' influence outweighed that of the 2-year-old children in the area of com-

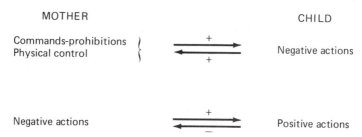

FIGURE 5.1. An escalating (*top*) and a homeostatic (*bottom*) feedback loop in mother-child relations (adapted from Lytton, 1980).

pliance, but the reverse held for attachment. This seems to agree with the everyday observation that parents make deliberate efforts to obtain the child's compliance, but tend to react to the child's attachment behavior. The direction of causal influence in the medium term (1 to 2 weeks) and in the long term for a number of child characteristics was also assessed. In the medium term, whenever a definite direction of effects could be identified, the preponderant influence ran from mother to child, though sometimes a secondary effect in the opposite direction was also noticeable. Such feedback loops—an escalating one and a balancing, or homeostatic one—are illustrated in Figure 5.1. In the latter case, mother's negative actions (e.g., criticism) increased the child's positive ones (e.g., compliance), and the child's positive actions served to reduce mother's negative ones over time. In no instance in any of these behavior systems did the son exert a unilateral influence on his mother, and this was true for long-term relationships over several years, too. The data and interview responses, however, also showed that the mother is influenced by the child's disposition and consciously accommodates her actions to suit the child's needs. Yet overall, the child has little power to mold the parent's enduring characteristics.

Sameroff (1975) has coined the term "transactional model" for conceptualizing parent-child reciprocal influences over time. Figure 5.2 illustrates how bidirectional processes between mother and child might operate, under this view, to produce emotional disturbance. The feedback loops, shown in Figure 5.1, are a rudimentary form of transactional influence, but measured only at two points in time. To demonstrate truly transactional effects, they have to be shown to function over a longer term and at more than two points in time. This has rarely been done. One example is Clarke-Stewart's (1973) study which indicated that from age 11 months to 14 months the primary direction of influence was from child to mother, that is, the child's attachment at 11 months tended to increase mother's attentiveness at 14 months; in turn, mother's attentiveness at 14 months tended to foster the child's attachment at 17 months. Transactional effects have also been noted in another study, when "difficultness" in 12-month-old boys led to mothers backing off from socialization pressures, which in turn

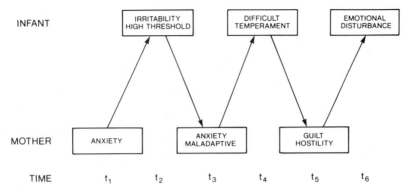

FIGURE 5.2. Hypothetical sequence of transactions in the etiology of emotional disturbance.

led to greater difficultness in these boys at 18 months (Maccoby & Jacklin, 1983).

These are relatively primitive models. More rigorous demonstrations of transactional effects may be possible with greater refinements of "causal modeling" techniques, which may come in the future. However, even with limited evidence, the transactional model represents, in our view, the most plausible theory for conceptualizing the influences that operate and interact in the socialization of the child.

The Family as a System: Mothers, Fathers, and Children

While at one time the study of parent-child relations was, in practice, the study of mother-child relations, father's role in socialization has become increasingly recognized and research has addressed various aspects of this role. Such research has been in keeping with, and prompted by, the spirit of an age that has seen the division of labor between men and women lose its rigidity.

Fathers have, it would appear, taken an increasing share in child rearing and child care ever since World War II. Though Kotelchuck (1972) reports only 27% of fathers took any regular part in caregiving for their 1-year-old children, Newson and Newson (1965, 1970), in England, concluded from *mothers'* interviews that over 50% of the fathers of 1-year-olds and 4-year-olds were participating highly in their infants' care, including bathing, diapering, and so forth. Lamb (1981), basing his conclusions on a number of studies, also sees a modern trend toward greater participation in child rearing by fathers. The participation rate in general increases with higher social status, reflecting greater equality and convergence of maternal and paternal roles at higher social class levels.

Mothers' and Fathers' Child-Rearing Characteristics

For young children a number of observation studies have provided us with reliable evidence on mothers' and fathers' roles in the socialization process. There are, no doubt, many similarities in how mothers and fathers behave, particularly towards their young infants. Often, for instance, spouses resemble each other as evidenced by correlations between them, that is, the spouses display similar degrees of, say, warmth or punishment (Lytton, 1980; Pedersen, 1980). Yet mothers differ from fathers in the mean level of many activities each engages in, and the salience that different activities occupy in the repertoire of each parent. Even with greater paternal participation, mothers still perform more of the physical care of their infants (Clarke-Stewart, 1978), and they hold them more for care giving, whereas fathers hold them more for play (Lamb, 1977). It has been a repeated finding that fathers, much more than mothers, engage in physically stimulating, rough-and-tumble play, composed of vigorous, abrupt, swiftly changing movements, sometimes accompanied by negative affect (Belsky, 1979; Clarke-Stewart, 1978; Lamb, 1977; Lytton, 1980). Mothers' games, on the other hand, center more on toys, or are traditional interchanges, such as "peek-a-boo"; above all, mothers are involved in far more verbal interchanges of all kinds with their children (Clarke-Stewart, 1978; Lytton, 1980; Pedersen, Anderson, & Cain, 1980).

Apart from play, mother interacts more with the young child, and intervenes more in his doings, often necessarily in a restraining way (Lytton, 1980; Pedersen, 1980). Lytton reports that with 2-year-old boys mothers also employ explanations, a cognitive method of control, much more than fathers do. Nowadays, mother no longer holds over the child the threat of father as the bogeyman and executioner. She is willing to take the major responsibility for the child's welfare and behavior, both when she is on her own with him and when father is present. However, father gives fewer directions to the child, relative to the time he is in the child's presence, and perhaps because of this, is obeyed more than mother. (This finding has been replicated with older children, cf. Hetherington, Cox, & Cox [1978].) Although father's interventions are important, he tends to assume a supportive role to mother in shaping the child's conduct (Lytton, 1980).

Overall, mother is not only the primary caregiver (even when she is working) and comforter, but also fills the role of primary agent of socialization. Therefore, when the child is young, she combines in her person what Talcott Parsons has termed the "instrumental" and the "expressive" roles, as Parsons himself has recognized. For older children we have to rely more on children's and parents' reports on mothers' and fathers' parenting styles (e.g., Hetherington et al., 1971; Lytton et al., 1986; Newson & Newson, 1978). There is general agreement on one fact: that mother is the more nurturant parent, and most studies report mothers as interacting more with their children than fathers do, both positively and in disciplinary matters.

Occasionally fathers, though they spell play and adventure for boys, are also seen as more demanding and severe. Fathers tend to play a more salient part in the rearing of boys than of girls, probably because shared interests and activities create a link between them (Kohn & Carroll, 1960; Newson & Newson, 1978).

A number of studies have segmented their observations into periods when only one parent (almost always the mother), and when two parents were with the child, and it has been found that the presence of the second parent changes the nature of the interactions, something that has been called a "second-order effect." Several studies agree that both parents interact less with their children when both of them are present than when each parent is alone with the child (Belsky, 1979a; Clarke-Stewart, 1978; Lamb, 1981; Lytton, 1980). This simply means that although overall interactions with the child will be increased, they are distributed among a greater number of persons than in the two-person setting. When mothers and fathers communicate with each other, they give less focused attention to the child (e.g., talking with or smiling at the child), but other interactions (e.g., holding, feeding liquids, rocking) are not decreased (Pedersen, Yarrow, Anderson, & Cain, 1979). Triadic situations are therefore important opportunities for the child to develop interactive skills.

When father is present, he takes a part in guiding the child's behavior and particularly sustains mother in dealing with children's misdemeanors. His presence adds authority to mother's voice in that she tends to issue fewer commands and is obeyed more than when she is on her own with the child, and thus his being there has a beneficial effect on the family climate (Lytton, 1980).

WHAT ARE MOTHERS' AND FATHERS' SPECIFIC INFLUENCES ON THE CHILD?

Each of the different types of experience that mother and father provide for the child is important in its own way. We have evidence (Clarke-Stewart, 1973, 1978; Lytton, 1980) that mother's emphasis on verbal interchanges has a formative influence on the child's verbal competence, which is basic to her whole cognitive development. Further we may speculate that the young child will derive a sense of the ways of her family and of society from mother's endeavors and explicit rationales in guiding her behavior.

Fathers may add a spatial dimension to children's experience by frequent and intense physical play interactions with them. In addition, they may influence cognitive development by acting in more task-oriented and informative ways, which they do particularly with sons (Bronstein, 1984).

Rough and vigorous physical play may be part of the generally active and assertive style of male interaction, a style which is culturally favored, but may also be connected to the stronger male musculature. Thus we have two distinctive interaction styles by mother and father, that may have biological ramifications and certainly are supported by cultural expectations, and each of which contributes to the child's development in different, important, and complementary ways.

However, research has not shown that fathers' "masculinity" (as measured by tests of typically masculine preferences) leads to greater masculine identification by sons. A strong sense of masculine identity in sons is fostered more by fathers who are nurturant and whom sons find a rewarding role-model to emulate (Mussen, Boutourline-Young, Gaddini, & Morante, 1963; Mussen & Distler, 1960; Mussen & Rutherford, 1963). Femininity in girls is similarly supported by a nurturant relationship with *both* parents, and by a mother who is an effective and competent role model (e.g., Mussen & Rutherford, 1963).

THE FAMILY AS A SYSTEM

Marital Relations and Child Development

By including father in the study of the child's early experiences, we transform the mother-child dyad into a family system comprised of both marital and parent-child relations. Marital relations, parenting practices, and child's development, under this model, enter into a variety of mutual relationships in which each may influence each (Belsky, 1981). The quality of marital relations, it has been repeatedly found, influences parental involvement with the child, for example, warmth and shared pleasure between the spouses and emotional support by the father help maternal adaptation to pregnancy and increase mother-child contact (Belsky, 1979b; Feiring & Lewis, 1978; Shereshefsky & Yarrow, 1973). Good relations between the spouses are linked both to sensitive parenting and to competence in the child (Goldberg & Easterbrooks, 1984), and they are also conducive to paternal participation in child rearing (Belsky, 1979b). One spouse's attitude in the home may also have repercussions on the other spouse's interactions with the child, for example, the wife's power assertion toward the child can be a reaction to the husband's power assertion towards her, and vice versa, as Hoffman (1963) found.

That parental disharmony and conflict are linked to poor outcome in the child, and particularly to conduct problems in boys who seem to be more affected by such discord than are girls, has long been known and was mentioned earlier in this chapter. Such deleterious effects in the child may well be mediated by a deterioration of the quality of parenting in such homes.

The negative effects of harsh or emotionally unstable parents have been demonstrated earlier, but there is consolation to be derived from the fact that if a stable and positive parent is available, the child may be able to establish compensatory good relationships with at least one parent, something which is likely to buffer the child against the worst ill effects of poor parenting (Hetherington, Cox, & Cox, 1982; Lytton, 1980; Rutter, 1979).

Although this claim may seem to contradict the adverse effect of inconsistent standards of discipline between parents found in earlier studies, it should be remembered that we here have in mind a responsive parent who still upholds reasonable standards, whereas the earlier studies contrasted a harsh, punitive father with a negligent, uncaring—and therefore indulgent—mother.

Siblings

Siblings willl be mentioned only briefly here, although they do, of course, form an important part of the family system and affect each other, as well as the relations between parents and each child. The arrival of a second child has dramatic effects on the firstborn. It results in considerable disturbance and unhappiness for a 2-year-old, and hence generates stress in the mother-child relationship. As the first year goes by, however, firstborns' difficulties decline and their affection for the newborn increases, as they adapt themselves to her presence and find new interest in playing with her (Dunn & Kendrick, 1982b).

It is especially when the mother is engaged in taking care of the new baby that relationships between her and the firstborn deteriorate and confrontations escalate. Mothers often try to compensate for a hostile older child by being especially friendly to the baby, but this may backfire by generating greater hostility in the firstborn (Dunn, 1983).

However, sibling interactions are more frequently friendly than hostile, as has been documented in studies of 20-month-old infants with siblings, 2 or 3 years older than they (Abramovitch, Corter, & Lando, 1979; Abramovitch, Corter, & Pepler, 1980). Young siblings interact a great deal with each other and imitation, above all by the younger of the older sibling, plays an important part in the relationship. Another outstanding feature of the relationship is its strong affective tone—both positive and negative. Its positive tone shows itself in friendly, cooperative, or prosocial behavior, its negative tone in "agonistic" acts, such as physical aggression, struggles over objects, and insults. The older siblings, because of their greater capabilities, initiate both more prosocial and more agonistic behavior. But even 2-year-olds can and do comfort older, and take care of younger siblings (Dunn, 1983). With these earliest interchanges children widen their social world beyond the compass of the parent-child relationship, and prepare for the larger world outside.

PARENTS' SHIFTING ROLES

We have already noted the trend toward greater participation by fathers in child rearing, a result both of more mothers taking paid employment and of a more egalitarian philosophy infiltrating the family. However, though husbands, when wives are employed, take on more child-care work, they tend to assume only marginally more household chores and leave primary responsibility for these to their wives (Bahr, 1974).

Are the different parenting styles that research has shown mothers and fathers exhibit, basic to their gender identities and dispositions, or are they simply by-products of the primary and secondary caregiver niches that they occupy? Can fathers be nurturers? There is some evidence that hormones play a part in preparing the female rat for caring for her young (Rosenblatt, 1969), but such effects need not necessarily apply to humans. Although, to our knowledge, there is no direct evidence on hormonal effects for humans, it has been shown that in girls there is a marked increase in preference for baby pictures over adult pictures after menarche, compared with younger girls and boys (Fullard & Reiling, 1976; Goldberg, Blumberg, & Kriger, 1982). Since in Goldberg et al.'s study the change in preference for infant pictures at menarche was not explained by varying child-care experience, interest in motherhood or sex-role self-image, biological processes seem the most likely explanation. Others, however, (e.g., Frodi & Lamb, 1978) attribute adolescent girls' greater responsiveness to babies to social rather than physiological factors.

When father takes over the primary caregiver role, do mother and father exchange their respective parenting roles completely? The sparse evidence that exists on nontraditional families suggests that they do not. Field (1978) reports that primary caregiver fathers still played more games with their infants and held them less than did primary caregiver mothers, and Lamb, Frodi, Hwang, Frodi, & Steinberg (1982) show that primary care-giver mothers were still more nurturant than primary caregiver fathers.

It seems, then, that some stereotypical maternal and paternal roles may be stereotypical precisely because they are reinforced by biological givens, though others may be consequences of parents' respective traditional functions. Further evidence on situations where traditional roles have been reversed will shed more light on the question of which is which. However, there are problems with the interpretation of such research: Role reversals are usually only transient arrangements, such as those reported in Lamb et al. (1982); moreover, role reversal willl be adopted more easily by men and women whose predispositions incline them in this direction (see below). Clearly, men *can* be as responsive to babies as women are, but in practice typically they are not. (For a review of biologically adapted qualities that mothers and fathers bring to parenting see Rossi, 1984).

We should not delude ourselves that greater participation in child rearing by fathers is due entirely to the inexorable march of progress in the 20th century. John Locke, in "Some Thoughts Concerning Education," published nearly 300 years ago, addressed advice on child rearing to fathers, because he thought they were more suited to this task—at least for older children. Mothers, he believed, only spoil children by "cockering and tenderness." But the fathers he addressed were leisured English gentry.

ANDROGYNOUS PARENTS

The term "androgynous" has emerged in recent times to describe individuals who possess what are conventionally considered as the desirable characteristics of both men and women, that is, persons who are both assertive and sensitive, both instrumental and expressive. It has further been claimed that androgynous persons are more likely to be "authoritative" parents, combining responsiveness with demandingness (Spence & Helmreich, 1978), and that their children would therefore be predicted to be more assertive, socially responsible, and competent than the children of sex-typed parents.

Investigations of androgynous and sex-typed parents (classified as such on the basis of self-reports) have shown that androgynous fathers do differ from masculine fathers in their parenting behavior. Androgynous fathers are more involved in child care and play (Russell, 1978) and they resemble androgynous mothers rather than masculine fathers in their child-rearing practices, that is, they are more responsive and nurturant, and less firm and punitive than masculine fathers. In accordance with their professed values, feminine mothers are responsive, and masculine fathers are firm (Baumrind, 1982). Androgynous women did not differ importantly from other women in either investigation.

However, Baumrind found that androgynous persons were not more likely to be authoritative parents, but instead were "child-centered" in their approach. Children of androgynous mothers or fathers were invariably less socially and cognitively competent than children of sex-typed parents, something that can be explained by the fact that children from child-centered homes tend to be generally less competent than children from firm or traditional homes.

Since Baumrind's (1982) study is the only one known to us that has tested the effects of androgynous parents on children's competence directly, it would be premature to draw sweeping conclusions from it. However, it does suggest tentative caution in evaluating claims for the benefits of androgyny.

Influences on Parents' Child-Rearing Practices

A variety of factors influence the child-rearing practices that parents adopt, for example, their personal characteristics, the norms of the social class or religious group to which they belong, and the values of the larger culture of which they are a part.

PARENTAL CHARACTERISTICS

Parents' characteristics that antedate the child's arrival affect their parenting practices. Parents' conservatism or authoritarianism, as assessed by questionnaire scales, is related to the use of power assertion, at least in lower class fathers (Hoffman, 1963), as well as to restrictiveness and orderliness training (Thomas, 1975). Mother's tendencies, assessed prenatally, have been found to be related to her general adaptation to pregnancy, and to later responsiveness to the child and good family functioning. Among these characteristics were: positive attitude to pregnancy, social adaptation, nurturance and ego strength, as well as absence of anxiety and depression (Heinicke, et al., 1983; Shereshefsky & Yarrow, 1973). Thus, a woman who has positive expectations and attitudes about motherhood, will be more responsive to and acceptant of her child and this, in turn, will be associated with better cognitive and social development of the child (e.g., Kaplan, Eichler, & Winickoff, 1980). The fact that she will thus feel rewarded for her effective mothering is likely to inspire her to persevere further with these adaptive practices, and thus a "transactional" process is set in motion. All these studies essentially found good personal adjustment in the mother to predict good outcomes in the child, but we must not forget that it is quite possible for such desirable qualities to be transmitted not only by the mother's handling of the child, but also genetically. None of these studies was designed to test this alternate explanation.

Parents' belief systems also affect their relations with their children. Parents' attributions for their children's behavior, for instance, change as the children develop. With age parents view their children's misconduct as increasingly intentional and caused by their dispositions. Such attributions, in turn, intensify the animosity with which the parents react to their children's behavior (Dix & Grusec, 1983).

The parent's and the child's sex, in interaction with each other, influence parental treatment of the child. Martin (1975) summarizes a number of studies (based on parents' and children's reports) which suggest that though mothers are generally seen as warmer, the opposite-sex parent is perceived as more benevolent, less strict, and more autonomy-granting than the same-sex parent.

CONTEXTUAL FACTORS IN CHILD REARING

Social-structural or contextual factors, particularly social class membership, exert an important influence on socialization practices. Social class is influential, because it is a carrier variable—it sums up a cluster of stable conditions, occupations, goals, and psychological attributes of parents. Many of the variables that characterize a social class, such as housing, material resources, and education, are salient influences on child-rearing attitudes and practices.

Bronfenbrenner (1958) summed up earlier work in the area, mainly based on interviews and ratings, by concluding that by the 1950s middle-class parents tended to use more "love-oriented," psychological discipline and were more responsive to the inner states of the child, whereas lower class parents tended to use more coercive, power-oriented discipline and were more concerned with the child's external behavior.

More recent studies that have used direct observation of mother-child interaction, have generally confirmed Bronfenbrenner's generalizations. (Some of these studies defined class by mother's education level, but for convenience we will here refer only to social class classifications.) Middle-class mothers and fathers, they found, make greater use of suggestions and explanations to the child, are more responsive to the child's needs, and more often provide positive, rather than negative feedback. Lower class parents, on the other hand, tend more towards coercion or power assertion (including physical punishment) and impose more restrictions on the child's freedom (Chamberlin, 1974; Lytton, 1980; Minton, Kagan, & Levine, 1971; Zussman, 1978). Reciprocal accommodation is also more characteristic of middle-class families in that greater compliance by the child is echoed by greater compliance by the parents with the child's wishes (Lytton, 1980). Middle-class mothers and fathers generally show a greater degree of involvement with their children's activities; in particular, they enter into more verbal communication with them and provide a more cognitively stimulating environment (Greenberg & Formanek, 1974; Lytton, 1980; Tulkin & Kagan, 1972). The expression of physical affection and contact, where this behavior was kept distinct from the influence techniques of praise and approval, on the other hand, shows no difference between the classes (Bayley & Schaefer, 1960; Lytton, 1980; Tulkin & Kagan, 1972). Affection, we are glad to note, is not the prerogative of the middle class.

The influence of social class may well be explained, in part, by the concrete conditions of life which it entails. Living space is an example, in that living in large families in a confined space means that aggression has to be controlled more tightly and hence discipline becomes more authoritarian. It has been found, for instance, that child-rearing attitudes become more permissive as the number of rooms in the house increases (Becker, 1964).

The differing control methods and styles of interactions adopted by different social classes may, however, also be due to their differing value systems and to the cumulative social experiences to which they have been exposed. It has been suggested that middle-class parents value curiosity, consideration for others, independence, and self-control in their children because they want to prepare them for positions, similar to their own, that require them to make decisions and take responsibility. Lower class parents, on the other hand, stress obedience to external authority because this is adaptive in the existing social structure in which they feel controlled by events, without being able to control them (Hess, 1970; Kohn, 1977). The more closely fathers are supervised at work, the more likely they are, in fact, to use physical punishment with their children (Kohn & Schooler, 1973, cited in Radke-Yarrow et al., 1983).

However, the more directive approach may also be a consequence of the fact that these parents have less time at their disposal for the niceties of life, since they tend to be overwhelmingly preoccupied with procuring its essentials. In any case, the gap between the social classes in North America (leaving aside ethnic contrasts) seems to have been narrowing, and there is considerable overlap between them, probably because of increasing equality in standards of living and education (Lytton, 1980; Zigler, Lamb, & Child, 1982).

Another factor that seems to play a role in determining parenting styles is religious group membership. Chamberlin (1974) found that in his middle-class American sample, 63% of authoritarian, but only 26% of more child-oriented mothers, were Catholic. Part of this differentiation was due to education, but even with education controlled, the association between religion and disciplinary practice was still marginally significant.

CULTURAL INFLUENCES

We cannot here do full justice to the topic of cross-cultural differences in child rearing. Yet it hardly needs saying that socialization practices are to a large extent culture-bound. Minturn and Lambert (1964) concluded from their study of six different cultures, spread around the globe, what we have already noted from social class comparisons and from developments across time, namely that child-rearing practices are determined more by a family's living pattern and economic activity than by psychological factors in the mother or her preconceived theories of child rearing. A study by Barry, Child, and Bacon (1959) provides an illustration: They found from an examination of ethnographic records of a large number of societies that societies with a high accumulation of food resources stressed compliance as a child-rearing value, whereas those with a low accumulation of food resources, and for whom hunting was therefore a preeminent need, showed predominant pressure toward assertion. Although these findings are suggestive, it must be remembered that the reliability of ethnographic accounts of vastly different societies is unknown.

We must not fall prey to the "ethnocentric fallacy," as Maccoby and Martin (1983) point out. What we consider optimal child rearing—firm control, with clearly explained reasons, room for the child's autonomous decision-making where appropriate, embedded in a climate of affection and sensitive responsiveness—may be optimal only where society regards self-regulation as the ideal mode of functioning of the individual. These practices promote self-regulation, but in societies where external social constraints take the place of self-regulation, such behaviors may not be ideal. Research evidence exists that practices frowned upon by North American "child experts" may be effective in different cultural settings. An example is Greenglass' (1972) study of the communication styles of immigrant Italian mothers and native-born Canadian mothers, and their relation to their children's resistance to temptation. Immigrant Italian mothers, as compared with native-born Canadian mothers, were more controlling and restrictive, and used justifications less. Resistance to temptation, however, was greater for the Italian than for the Canadian mothers' sons, when research findings in English-speaking communities generally would suggest that *less* control and *greater* use of reasoning would lead to stronger resistance to temptation. Greater reliance on external social constraints may, however, be a function of educational level and religion, as much as of ethnicity.

Comparisons of child-rearing practices between Germany and America, between England and America, and between English- and French-Canadian parents (Devereux, Bronfenbrenner & Suci, 1962; Devereux, Bronfenbrenner, & Rodgers, 1969; Lambert, Yackley, & Hein, 1971) have on the whole shown that the similarities outweigh the differences within Western culture. We would expect that the degree of external constraint imposed and expected in different countries *should* make a systematic difference to patterns of child rearing. Such effects may, however, become apparent only with strongly contrasted cultures.

Child Abuse

When child rearing goes wrong it easily turns into child abuse. The immediate antecedents of physical child abuse frequently involve attempts by parents to discipline their child (Gill, 1970). Reid (1986) argues that the probability of a child being physically injured by his or her parents is a function of the number of discipline confrontations and the degree to which such confrontations can be solved quickly without resort to physical punishment by the parent. It is appropriate, then, to discuss the issue in a chapter which deals with socialization practices.

Definitions of physical child abuse vary: The most helpful are those that include the notion of an intentional act on the part of a caretaker which results in physical injury to the child and which violates community standards of acceptable behavior toward children (Parke & Collmer, 1975). The reader should, however, be aware that much of the research literature defines child abuse to include psychological abuse, that is, emotional deprivation, or rejection, or even simply inappropriate parenting practices, judged "abusive" by social service agencies.

The first definition above recognizes that certain child-rearing practices that are considered totally acceptable in one culture may be viewed as abusive in another. For example, severe initiation rites are perceived as abusive in our own society. But a failure to subject adolescents to them in other societies could be seen as an instance of neglect. On the other hand, our own practices of making children sleep alone at night, straightening their teeth, or allowing them to "cry themselves out" may seem abusive to others (Korbin, 1980).

We must be careful, then, to view any apparently harmful act from the perspective of the culture in which it occurs. However, there may still be marked differences between cultures in the extent to which abuse occurs, that is, in the extent to which adults in that culture deviate from accepted practices and norms in a way considered to be harmful to the child. Korbin (1980) argues that our own society may be particularly prone to abuse, firstly because we make high demands for maturity at an early age in infancy, and secondly because our children are often raised in isolated nuclear or single-parent households where support from more experienced child rearers is not available and where unrealistically high expectations of the child therefore cannot be corrected.

THE CAUSES OF ABUSE

Abuse of the child has been seen variously as a function of personality or other defect in the parent, as the outcome of negative characteristics of the child, or as a response to stress and socioeconomic deprivation. We consider each of these approaches briefly.

Characteristics of Abusive Parents

Recently Wolfe (1985) has summarized the results of a number of investigations of the psychological characteristics of abusive parents, noting that the only aspects of personality functioning which seem to be associated with abusive parenting are general disenchantment with the parental role and stress-related symptoms. These characteristics, of course, may not be the precipitators of, but rather reactions to, incidents of child abuse. Abusive mothers *do* tend to have unrealistic expectations for mature behavior on the part of their children (Azar, Robinson, Hekimian, & Twentyman 1984), and may therefore tend to greater punitiveness because their high expectations are frequently unmet. They also are more likely to ascribe malevolent intention to the bad behavior of their children (Bauer & Twentyman, 1985), a condition presumably more likely to elicit anger and punishment.

It is frequently contended that abusive parents were themselves abused as children (e.g., Spinetta & Rigler, 1972). Although the evidence for this contention is primarily clinical in nature, the hypothesis makes enough sense from what we know about normal socialization processes that it merits serious consideration. Rohner (1975), on the basis of cross-cultural studies, argues that the roots of child abuse lie in the experience of parental rejection and that it is early emotional deprivation that leads parents to have unrealistic expectations that their children will fulfill their dependency needs (Spinetta & Rigler, 1972; Steele & Pollock, 1968). This hypothesis has led to the notion of "role reversal," the idea that abusive parents expect to be cared for by their children, rather than to care for them, and that they become angry when that care is not forthcoming. Again, the idea is interesting but the data as yet scant.

Characteristics of Abused Children

There is a relationship between low birth weight and abuse, even when the effects of social class are controlled for (Klein & Stern, 1980). A number of factors may account for this relationship. Infants who are premature are unattractive and so it is more difficult for parents to form a strong attachment to them, which serves as a protection against excessive anger. They are demanding and irritable and their cries are particularly aversive (Frodi, 1981). Their development is slow and so they are even more likely to frustrate and disappoint when they do not meet the expectations of their caretakers.

Abused children tend to be insecurely attached (Egeland, Sroufe, & Erickson, 1983), are less likely to respond to friendly overtures by adults (George & Main, 1979), and display more aggression as well as deficits in cognitive functioning (Hoffman-Plotkin & Twentyman, 1984). It is easy to see, of course, that any of these characteristics could be both the outcome as well as the cause of abuse.

Child Abuse and Social Class

Although child abuse occurs in all social classes, low levels of material and social resources do place families particularly at risk for abuse (Garbarino & Crouter, 1978). In the lower classes there is greater social isolation and hence less help, support, and information for a struggling parent (Garbarino & Sherman, 1980). Unemployment also occurs more frequently among lower class parents, and Steinberg, Catalano, and Dooley (1981) have demonstrated that increases in abuse are preceded by periods of high job loss. Presumably lack of employment leads to stress because of changes in marital relationships, lowered self-esteem, and reduction of income, with such stress making it more difficult to deal adequately with the demands of child rearing.

The Social-Interactional Approach

Recently investigators have begun to examine the behavioral interactions of abusive parents and their children. To assess control strategies used by abusive mothers, Oldershaw, Walters, and Hall (1986) videotaped their interactions with their children in a simulated home environment. They observed that abusive mothers, relative to controls, were more likely to use power-assertive control strategies, that they displayed much less positive affect, and that they were more intrusive, issuing twice as many commands. In turn, abused children were more noncompliant than control children. However, the fact that abusive mothers issued many more initial commands for obedience and that they were also more likely to issue commands independent of whether the child had been compliant or noncompliant (e.g., instructing the child to eat his sandwich and immediately issuing the command again even though the child had complied in the interim), suggests that some of the mothers' intrusiveness was a function of their own parenting style rather than due to the child's behavior. Compliance also produced positive reinforcement from control mothers while it was equally likely to elicit punishment or reinforcement in the abusive mothers. Hardly surprising, then, is the greater noncompliance of the abused children. Oldershaw et al. conclude that abusive mothers are inadequate socializing agents.

Other work shows that both parent and child are contributors to this process. Trickett and Kuczynski (1986), for example, found that abusive parents reported using punitive strategies more and reasoning strategies less when dealing with child misbehavior than did control parents. In turn, the children were described by these parents as more noncompliant and performing more aggressive misdeeds. On the basis of observations of children and their parents in the home, Reid (1986) reports that the vast majority of interactions in abusive families (90%) were of short duration, and positive or neutral in nature. In the remaining 10%, however, abusive acts were more likely to occur perhaps because these interactions were of longer duration. Reid concludes that abusive mothers, then, have difficulty handling discipline and that, with a propensity to longer disciplinary episodes, they become more at risk for abuse. Thus abusive parents appear to be less competent in their parenting strategies, while their children are less well behaved—a reaction to ineffective strategies, the cause of them, or probably an interaction of the two (Reid, Taplin, & Lorber, 1981; Trickett & Kuczynski, 1986).

Overall, we must recognize both the parents' and the child's contribution to abuse, that is, we should view it as an interactive process that involves parental competence/noncompetence, as well as situational demands arising from the child. Moreover, it is also embedded in a wider social context, an example of which is the social isolation from which abusive families often suffer.

Summary

We have discussed how child rearing through the centuries has been influenced by economic and social conditions of living, as well as by philosophical and religious points of view. These are still the crucial influences on child rearing, although the rise of scientific and quasi-scientific research has had some impact on parents over the last 50 years. The research paradigms, methods, and findings themselves, however, have stood under the aegis of the times and have been shaped by, as much as they have shaped, the prevailing climate of opinion.

Several strands of empirical research have produced converging evidence as to the effects of various socialization practices, something that we can regard as the current view in Western society. Parents never rely on just one child-rearing technique alone, of course, but they differ in their emphasis on certain practices, thus forming "parenting patterns." The constellation that has found most favor and support in the literature is Baumrind's "authoritative" pattern, which maintains a delicate balance between setting reasonable standards and respect for the child's autonomy, between control and encouragement of individuality. Such a pattern has been shown, on the whole, to lead to social responsibility, independence, self-esteem, and cognitive competence in children. There is also consistent evidence that parents' warmth is conducive to the achievement of internalized moral controls and cognitive competence. On the other hand, extreme reliance on power assertion as a method of control is likely to have the opposite results. The child will also play an active part in her own socialization by taking her parents as models, and by attributing—and being helped to attribute—certain characteristics to herself. If these attributions are positive they are likely to have beneficial results. Various theories have been invoked to explain the socialization effects noted, but the multifarious data do not fit comfortably into any one theory.

Socialization practices are explained best by historical trends and current ideologies. They work within a system of beliefs and goals. Thus in Western society, which lays great stress on self-regulation, the authoritative parenting pattern, which can include forceful reasoning and expression of strong affect about the child's deeds or misdeeds, seems to work well for most parents. In other cultures, where external constraints are the order of the day, more autocratic parenting patterns may well be functional.

We are still left with many mutually contradictory results and findings showing "no relationships." We must remember that any given effect will arise from an amalgam of attitudes, practices, and circumstances, and will, moreover, depend on the child's biological disposition. Hence clear relationships between parents' practices overall, and children's behavior overall will be blurred.

The child's disposition will affect not only the outcome of the socialization process, but also the parents' practices themselves, so that parents' and child's interrelationships are best viewed as "transactional," with each partner continually influencing the behavior of the other. The child, in a sense, is the "producer of her own development."

Mothers and fathers differ in their interactions with their children; moreover, the family acts as a system and parents exert their influence both directly and indirectly, through their relations with their spouses. In two-parent families the mother usually is the primary caregiver and main agent of socialization, while father plays a supportive role in this and is the "play-mate," at least with younger children. As the child gets older, father's involvement and socializing role increase in importance, particularly for boys.

According to Belsky (1984), three domains of determinants affecting the quality of parenting can be identified: personal psychological resources of parents, characteristics of the child, and contextual sources of stress and support. Each of these domains will influence parental functioning both directly and indirectly. We have met each of them in our progress through this chapter and have also noted influences deriving from the wider culture of which the family forms a part and which shapes its values and belief systems.

6
Widening Social Networks and Their Influences

In the last chapter we discussed the interactions that the child experiences in the home and the ways in which these interactions with parents and siblings influence her and are influenced by her. In Chapter 4 we also briefly touched on the early social interactions of the infant and saw that even the infant is interested in simple complementary interactions with peers, such as giving and receiving a ball. In this chapter we are going to follow the child into the wider world of friends, peers, and school, a world whose influence will grow in importance with increasing age. As the infant becomes a toddler and a preschooler, while still living in the protective and nurturing shell of her family, she also usually joins a group of unfamiliar children, where her capabilities are challenged and her self-reliance is tested while the horizons of her play are expanded. She goes from an environment in which she has an assured and cherished place to an environment where she has to win a place on her own merits.

The history of scientific investigations of peer relations has recently been well described by Hartup (1983) and for the historical perspective we will draw largely on this account. Theorizing about, and research into, peer relations go back to European thinkers, such as Emile Durkheim, Sigmund Freud, and Jean Piaget, among others. Though their less systematic methods of investigation would not meet modern scientific standards, the themes that engaged the attention of these early investigators are essentially those that have occupied researchers up to the present day, including, for instance, the formation and maintenance of groups and their influence as socializing agents.

The late 1920s saw advances in methodology, which typically originated in the United States. Methods for observing children in groups were refined and, in particular, categories based on overt behavior were devised, sampling methods were developed and methods for assessing the reliability of measurement were established. Much of this advance was due to the painstaking efforts of Dorothy Thomas (1929) and Florence Goodenough. The latter, for instance, put these methods to good use in studying anger in nursery school children (Goodenough, 1931). A second advance came in the 1930s with the work of Lewin and his colleagues who invented experimental techniques for studying social climate and styles of leadership (e.g., Lewin, Lippitt, & White, 1936). Lewin's work, which stimulated many investigations by others, was inspired by his "field theory" which was discussed in Chapter 1; characteristically it was linked to political issues, such as democracy versus authoritarianism, issues that were of great concern to Lewin, himself a victim of Nazism. The third advance came with the advent of "sociometric" methods (Moreno, 1934). In various versions of this method children are asked either to name those classmates whom they like most (and sometimes those whom they like least—though this raises a nice ethical point), or to rank-order their classmates in terms of a given characteristic (e.g., tendency to fight); children may also be asked to name the person they would most like to work or play with. This methodology became widely used for assessing children's social acceptance or rejection and, by inference, their social competence.

The study of peer relations went into a decline in the 1940s, 1950s and 1960s, when this topic generated little interest, partly because of the predominance of Freudian theory with its emphasis on parental socialization. An exception was the outstanding work by Sherif and his colleagues (1961) who studied group formation and intergroup relations, and the pioneering ecological studies by Barker and Wright (1955).

It was only in the 1970s that there came a remarkable upsurge of interest in peer relations and, particularly, in their significance for the child's development. Many descriptive studies appeared, similar to those of the 1930s. Observation of naturally occurring behavior became fashionable once again, but methods of observation became more systematic and rigorous, as described in Chapter 2. Theories were evolved about the formation of friendship and its significance for the development of the child, and interactions among friends were examined in detail by direct observation. Further, isolated and rejected children became the subjects of scientific scrutiny, and strategies for training them in the social skills that they presumably lacked, were devised. It is these developments that we will discuss in greater detail in subsequent sections.

Peer Relations and Social Competence

GROWING AWAY FROM THE FAMILY

Let us first discuss how the world of children widens to include not only the family, but also peers, how such peer relations and friendships develop, and how they are related to family interactions.

Family Relations—Peer Relations

It is sometimes thought that the child-parent relationship involves mainly authority-dependence, whereas peer relationships are marked by equality and reciprocity, with the partners making a joint effort to maintain the relationship (cf. Youniss, 1980). In Youniss' and Piaget's view, since morality is founded on cooperation and equality, it is peer interactions that form "the backbone of mature morality," with parents' influence coming second. However, as we have seen in the last chapter, child-parent relationships, too, are frequently reciprocal and children often perceive themselves as acting willingly and in cooperation with their parents, perhaps especially when parents reinforce this self-perception of voluntary cooperation. When the young perceive that their goals coincide with those of their parents, the children are all the more likely to engage in activities and share in decision-making with their parents. Hence the socializing influences of parent and peer relations do not stand in absolute contrast to each other, as this theory claims. Peer and parent cultures can coincide, at least for some parents, and their difference is relative (Maccoby & Martin, 1983). Nevertheless, the developmental equivalence of age-mates gives a unique flavor to their interactions. Peer means "equal" and this equality exists by right and natural status. This is never the case with parents since they, in contrast to peers, control life's resources.

Beyond toddlerhood there occurs a gradual shift in the relative importance of peers and adults in the child's life and the child slowly gravitates more towards her peers. They assume greater salience, while adults lose their exclusive importance in her life. At the nursery school age the toddler's proximity- and affection-seeking of adults is replaced by distal attention-seeking, and bids for attention become increasingly directed towards peers rather than adults (Hartup, 1983; Heathers, 1955). Thus interactive skills become increasingly differentiated and sophisticated over the preschool years. The child also develops abilities and needs that make her more open to interactions with peers. She develops greater cognitive complexity, and acquires increasing ability to see the perspective of others and hence a greater capacity for truly reciprocal relationships, as well as for cooperative and competitive activities. Whether as consequence or cause of these developments, the proportion of social activities that the child engages in with adults decreases steadily over the childhood years, while contact with other children increases. By age 11, nearly 50% of children's social activity involves peers, as Barker and Wright (1955) found.

Functions of Peer Relations

Why do children seek each other out? In general, we might say they do so because they can share common interests and amusement with other children—shared joy is double joy—and because they can engage in more complex and venturesome play with others than when alone.

Peer interactions serve many functions in the development of the child. Through them the child defines her role and status in relation to others in her generation and learns both follower and leader roles within the context of equality, in other words, she finds her own identity. Interactions with her peers make her sensitive to what matters to others, that is, they bestow social perception. They facilitate complex forms of play and, more particularly, fantasy play. Further, peers provide direct instruction in physical and cognitive skills and by acquiring these skills the child earns the respect of persons beyond those who accept her unconditionally. Lastly, they provide emotional support in unfamiliar or threatening circumstances, when parents are not available for reassurance.

The family, the world of friends and of school, and their interconnections are all environmental influences that shape the child's development and that operate in addition to the biological ones we have described earlier. The family *and* peers provide protection and support, as well as challenge, but the family's role is primarily a protective and nurturing one, whereas challenge is mainly the role of peers. Families generally love and care for the child no matter what she does, whereas peers are not so accepting. By mingling and learning to live with her peers the child becomes a member of her own generation, of the society in which she will continue to live.

Origins and Development of Peer Relations

Where do peer relations begin? Many children experience the essentials of peer relations in the family through their relations with siblings. The same reciprocity that characterizes peer relations is also inherent in sibling relations, but this reciprocity often occurs earlier with siblings than with peers. Children quite early know "what it feels like" to be the other and practice such "affective role-taking" by at times deliberately provoking, and at other times comforting younger, or even older siblings (Dunn, 1983). Thus siblings, like peers, develop in the child an understanding of others' needs and wishes, of her own and others' roles, as well as of social rules. Infants who have had experience with older siblings are more socially responsive and interact more with peers, so it seems that such experience with siblings facilitates later peer interaction (Vandell & Mueller, 1980).

Outside the family circle the beginnings of peer relations also can be seen quite early. Infants as young as 12 months already recognize as "friends" children whom they have met on two or three occasions and treat them differently by, for example, touching them more. Children at 12 to 24 months, even though unacquainted, can play games with each other and demonstrate sociability and interactional competence. The rules that they follow and the signals they use we recognize as those they will continue to use throughout their life span. Thus they give as well as receive a toy in reciprocal play and they provide manual or facial signals for turn-taking (Goldman & Ross, 1978).

Beyond infancy there is a developmental progression in patterns of friendship which is closely associated with the ability to manipulate symbols and the emergence of pretend play. Partnerships among infants in a child-care center, Howes (1983) reports, were based on exchange of objects, but by age 3 to 4 friendships were founded primarily on verbal exchanges. The older preschoolers engaged in more complex and reciprocal play than the younger groups, and it was stable friendship pairs that most frequently showed advances in the complexity of social interactions.

How do children's interactions with their own age-group differ from those with other age-groups? Children often associate with other children of widely differing ages, but generally they prefer to play with their own age-mates or older children rather than younger ones (e.g., Roopnarine & Johnson, 1984). Children of the same age, playing together, are more likely to be aggressive and boisterous and to engage in reciprocal play than are children of different ages (Edwards & Lewis, 1979; Whiting & Whiting, 1975). Another example of children adjusting their behavior to the age and maturity level of their partners is the fact that even 4-year-olds use shorter and less complex utterances when they talk to 2-year-old playmates, whereas they talk with as great complexity to age-mates as to adults (Shatz & Gelman, 1973).

Playing with children of the same age is the vehicle for socializing the capacity for give-and-take in both friendly and aggressive interchanges. For the younger child in a dyad of mixed ages social interaction is a forum for seeking assistance, for observing the behavior (and misbehavior) of older partners and thus for developing follower roles. For the older child in the dyad it is the arena for assertiveness, for refining social skills, like helping, and thus for developing leadership roles. Both same-age and mixed-age interactions are desirable for the development of social competence, since this consists of skills with peers as well as superiors and subordinates (Hartup, 1983).

The developmental progression in peer interactions that we mentioned earlier is seen in more effective cooperative play at older ages. This comes about because older children are more skillful at communicating verbally, transcending earlier nonverbal communication. Effective and informative communication requires the ability to take the perspective of one's partner in order to recognize which information is essential to the listener. Younger children (5 to 7 years old) are not very effective in providing critical feedback information in reponse to queries from listeners in a problem-solving situation, nor do they realize when others' communication is inadequate (Asher, 1978). Although younger children do have some speaking and listening skills, the ability to take the listener's point of view is more in evidence in later childhood (Asher, 1978; Karabenick & Miller, 1977). Seeing things from another's perspective is intrinsic to cooperative activity and interchanges, and hence the development of this ability will also shift child-child interactions into a new gear and make them more mutually adaptive.

Thus the development of social interactions is affected by the growth of cognitive abilities. But this development also occurs in the context of social experiences; for instance, exposure to certain models, such as altruistic acts or antisocial acts, can be related to changes in peer interactions (Hartup, 1983). The size of the group with which the child is usually involved also exerts an influence: For toddlers the amount of social interaction increases when they are habitually with one friend, but not when they are in group settings (Vandell & Mueller, 1977). Thus, cognitive development and social opportunities act together in fostering more complex and rewarding peer relations over the years.

Friendships

Friendship goes beyond casual and intermittent interaction with peers. Mary may play with John, Catherine, and Belinda in a group, but only Joanne is her "friend"—someone with whom she will play more often and more intimately. Thus friendship is characterized by constant, usually positively toned interactions. Indeed, friendships are specific attachments that resemble attachment to mother, and separation from a friend has similar disturbing effects as separation from mother. The phenomenon of friendship appears quite early, since even preschool children tend to interact more with some children than with others, a differentiation that is moderately stable (Hartup, 1975).

How are friendships formed? Children become friends in stages. Important in the first stage of friendship formation is exchange of information on common interests and clarity of communication between the partners, something which goes hand in hand with the establishment of a common ground of activity. Later comes the exploration of similarity and differences between the partners, self-disclosure, and the necessary resolution of conflicts. Here, too, there is a developmental progression in that children improve in acquaintanceship abilities, such as information exchange and conflict resolution, between the ages of 3 and 9 (Gottman, 1983).

What are children's conceptions of friendship? When children are asked "What is a friend?" or "How does someone show you that they are your friend?", 6- to 7-year-old children talk of friends as playmates with whom to share goods and physical activities; 9- to 10-year-olds, on the other hand, stress mutual sympathy and support, help and loyalty as important in friends, and they explicitly mention reciprocity as an ingredient of friendship. They also see the relationship as a stable arrangement (Youniss & Volpe, 1978). Some of their answers to the above questions illustrate these conceptions (Youniss & Volpe, 1978):

Boy, age 6: Somebody that likes you. (Why is that a friend?) They play with him.
Boy, age 6: They always say yes when I want to borrow their eraser.
Girl, age 6: Lets me play soccer with him.
Boy, age 10: If you need help, like you're hurt, he'll help you or get help.
Boy, age 9: It means that he's like a person that is close to you most of the

time and helps you do different stuff.

Girl, age 9: Somebody who can keep your secrets together. Two people who are really good to each other.

Girl, age 12: They both agree on the same things. You like their personality. Because you have the same ideas, you can talk more freely.

The reasons children give for choosing a particular friend involve their positive personal attributes (e.g., brave, kind, or loyal), as well as similarities of tastes and interests. Children describe their friends in highly differentiated terms—they know their friends' characteristics well. Mutual friends from age 6 onward are quite accurate in stating the similarities that link them to their partners, but it is only at age 9 that children develop a reciprocal awareness of their partners' differences from themselves (Ladd & Emerson, 1984). On the other hand, children describe disliked peers in more general, undifferentiated terms, for example, "he's mean" (Hartup, 1975). Even conflict promotes more mature social development between friends than it does between nonfriends (Nelson & Aboud, 1985).

Sex differences and roles also play a part in friendship choices. It is well known that children at least up to early adolescence prefer the company of their own sex to that of the other. This may be due to the fact that children of the same sex share similar interests. Nursery school boys, for instance, tend to play with blocks and movable toys, whereas girls' interactions center more on dramatic play and table activities (Charlesworth & Hartup, 1967). Children may derive intrinsic gratification from playing with others holding the same interests, but, of course, pressures from adults and other children reinforce the tendency, too.

Friendships, thus, for children as for adults, are an enormous source of support and fulfill important functions—identified by children themselves—in their social development.

The Influence of Parents and of Parent-Child Relations

Parents influence their children's friendship choices in various ways, for instance, through their choice of neighborhood, school, and their own friends, or by providing models of social relationships by supplying a home base for their children to play in, and by actively arranging social contacts for them. But they can influence their children's friendships only up to a point and mainly indirectly, not by dictatorial fiat, as some parents find out from hard experience. The following comment by a mother of a 4-year-old is an illustration: "We were friends, so we forced the kids on each other and it backfired. After we stopped doing that and got them together only when they asked, they did fine" (Rubin & Sloman, 1984, p. 235).

Furthermore, there is a connection between the quality of parent-child and of peer relations. Secure attachment to parents in infancy leads to social competence and good social relations in preschool, as we wrote in Chapter 4. MacDonald and Parke (1984) observed 3- to 4-year-old children playing with their parents in the home and interacting with peers in a nursery school and also obtained teacher ratings of children's popularity. Positive experiences in the home—father's physical play and active engagement with the child, and mother's verbal interaction—predicted good peer relations in nursery school, especially for boys. But high directiveness by father had adverse consequences for the peer popularity of both boys and girls. We can conclude that when the child "feels good" at home she also will have the confidence in herself that will lead to good social skills at school.

Poor relationships in the family, on the other hand, represent risk factors that may impair later social competence. Such risk arises particularly from tense, unhappy relations and disorganization in the family in general (Roff, Sells, & Golden, 1972), and sometimes connected with these—from mother's mental illness (Sameroff & Seifer, 1982). Strained family relations may at times end in divorce, which also adversely affects peer relations, as will be discussed in Chapter 11.

Instability and strained relations in the home clearly disturb children's equanimity and relations with the outside world. However, some children seem to be immune: over and above the effects from such a family situation there is also a coherence and stability to personality development, manifest in the child's adaptation to her social world across time and across different settings, and this may, indeed, make her relatively invulnerable to such adverse influences (see our discussion of "secure attachment" and "good adjustment" in Chapter 4).

THE GROWTH OF SOCIAL COMPETENCE

We will now explore what makes up social skills, how they develop in play and in interactions with peers, and what their implications and consequences are.

Play

Play is children's work and it fulfills important functions for their learning and development. As the poet put it:

The child's toys and the old man's reasons
Are but the fruits of the two seasons. (William Blake)

But play is not unique to the young of *Homo sapiens*. It becomes increasingly important for animals' development as one moves up the chain of species, and particularly as one moves up the series from Old World monkeys through the Great Apes to man. As species developed that learned various life-sustaining skills in their early years rather than having them "wired-in" and as the span of immaturity of the young lengthened, selection for the ability to learn by means of play may have become a crucial factor in evolution (Bruner, Jolly, & Sylva, 1976).

Bruner has speculated that play was related to the development of tool use in evolution. Thus play minimizes the consequences of one's actions and it therefore helps the child—and young animal—to learn in a less risky environment free from pressures to complete an act efficiently and successfully. This environment creates the flexibility of experimentation which makes novel uses of objects possible and which, in bygone millenia, according to Bruner, may have facilitated the invention of tools. Furthermore, the turn-taking that, as we noted in an earlier chapter, marks the rules of infant play, is also mirrored in the turn-taking rules of the beginnings of language. Hence Bruner and his colleagues hypothesize that historically the evolution of play may well have been the precursor of the emergence of language and symbolic behavior (Bruner et al., 1976).

Play also serves a function in the socioemotional development of the child. Given the "nonseriousness" and relative freedom from negative consequences of play, children can within its context test the limits of permissible behavior vis-à-vis parents or peers with relative impunity and thus learn social rules.

Psychoanalytic writers have analyzed the emotional function of play from a clinical point of view. It has been found in clinical experience that through play children can deal with emotionally overwhelming experiences by recreating such an experience in their minds; they can thereby come to terms with reality and with their emotions about it (Erikson, 1950). Such notions are intuitively appealing and plausible, though it is difficult to establish empirical proof for them. Clinical instances can, however, often be found as illustrations of how playful activities help children master anxieties. For example, children often play at doctors and nurses, when they are about to go into the hospital, and one of us has observed a 9-year-old boy, in a therapeutic setting, drawing a man behind bars when his own father was in prison. Play links inner and outer reality, as Winnicott (1964) has said. Analysts, such as Anna Freud, Melanie Klein, and Donald Winnicott, have all used play as the preferred medium of psychoanalysis with children, not simply to let them reenact painful experiences and thus help them come to terms with them, but because play is "the gateway to the unconscious" (Winnicott, 1964). The effectiveness of this approach, however, is not altogether evident (cf. Levitt, 1971).

Play is the normal medium through which peer interactions take place for children. In a classic study Parten (1932) analyzed the play interactions of 2- to 4½-year-old nursery school children. She divided these interactions into categories, based on the degree of association with others. These categories become prominent in the following order: first, solitary activities (e.g., stacking rings on a peg), then parallel play, in which children play side by side, say, in a sandbox, without coordinating their roles, and finally, cooperative play, defined as play organized around a theme (e.g., dramatizing family activities) with different roles assigned to different children. In Parten's study the proportion of solitary activities underwent a relative decline over age and that of cooperative play increased, and the same age changes have been confirmed in a more recent study (Harper & Huie, 1985). However, nonsocial activities, particularly parallel play, do not drop out altogether over the preschool years. Such nonsocial play remains quite common throughout the preschool period, but the number of companions and with it the proportion of cooperative play increases (Clark, Wyon, & Richards, 1969; Parten, 1932). It is this type of play, of course, which offers the opportunity for social interaction and facilitates the child's growing social competence.

Parten's (1932) categorization of play was based on degree of sociableness and she stressed the increasingly social nature of play. But play also has a cognitive function and categorizing play jointly by its social and cognitive functions, as Rubin, Watson, and Jambor (1978) have done, opens up a different perspective on age trends. Their cognitive categories are: *functional* play, that is, simple actions with objects, *constructive* play (building more complex structures), and *dramatic* play. In their study, all nonsocial play combined, that is, solitary plus parallel play, did not decline, rather what changed was the cognitive maturity and the task involvement in nonsocial actions. Thus functional solitary involvement with objects, such as stringing beads, declined between 4 and 5 years, but both constructive and dramatic parallel play (which is also nonsocial) actually increased over age. We can therefore conclude that nonsocial behavior that is cognitively mature remains important for many years.

In recent years sociodramatic or pretend play in particular has received renewed attention in research, often by direct observation of children at play (for a review see Rubin, Fein, & Vandenberg, 1983). Most sociodramatic play requires the cooperation of peers as an essential ingredient. In pretend play, it is thought, children are at an optimal level of arousal and feel relaxed, and hence feel able to explore new roles. Through it, then, they are helped to see things from others' points of view and understand the needs of others, they practice interactive rules, and they also establish their own self-identity. While such play still has egocentric features in that it is dominated by the child's own perspective, children also are constantly struggling to overcome this (e.g., in changing play roles: "Now I'm not the baby anymore, now I'm the Daddy"). Hence the pretense helps to lessen egocentrism.

Dramatic pretend play increases over the preschool years to about age 6, and declines thereafter. At later ages pretend play is replaced by attention to reality, and in the play of friends and groups the here-and-now, as in organized games with rules, occupies center stage. Thus social play becomes more organized and literal over age. This development occurs, one may speculate, because over the elementary school years children become less centered on their own thoughts and feelings and increasingly attuned to reality. Games with rules may indeed increase children's capacity to deal with the realities of social relations (Rubin, Fein, & Vandenberg, 1983).

Popularity and Social Skills

Popularity

Children's popularity and its correlates have recently been the subject of numerous enquiries that have come to remarkably similar conclusions. One way of assessing popularity (see the beginning of this chapter for others) is to use a sociometric procedure in which children are asked whom among their classmates they like most (LM) and whom they like least (LL). Dodge (1983), for example, classified as popular those children whose social preference score (LM – LL) was very high, as rejected those whose social preference score was very low, and as neglected those whose social impact score (LM + LL) was low; almost all the others were categorized as average. This kind of categorization distinguishes between the unpopular-rejected and the unpopular-neglected children, a distinction that has also been made by others.

From Dodge's (1983) and several other investigations (cf. also Hartup, 1983) certain dimensions that make up social competence emerge. It comes as no surprise that, in general terms, friendly, prosocial, responsive behavior and positive interactions lead to acceptance, whereas aversive reactions and antisocial behavior will tend to provoke rejection.

In order to understand how children become popular or unpopular in a group, Dodge (1983) formed playgroups from previously unacquainted second-grade boys. Children who later turned out to be popular in these new groups, from the beginning responded positively to the initiations of others; however, popular children approached others less often but were approached more often than nonpopular children. Furthermore, they showed an understanding that relationships develop and problems are solved over time. They realized that going for a thing directly may not be the most effective way of attaining it. So at first they waited in the new group and slowly increased conversation over time. A further valuable social skill that contributes to popularity is the ability to perceive a social situation accurately and then to enter a group by contributing relevant conversation (Putallaz, 1983). An important point, too, is that popular boys tend to be nonaggressive in their interactions and to set norms of behavior in a new group (Coie & Kupersmidt, 1983).

On the other hand, Dodge (1983) showed that boys who became rejected or neglected later were those who engaged in inappropriate kinds of behavior. Rejected boys, unlike neglected boys, directed more physical aggression towards their peers than did average children; indeed, they were more aggressive than any other group. Rejected or neglected boys were not socially inactive at first: in the early sessions they approached others quite frequently, but they were often rebuffed. But several studies demonstrate that nonpopular children generally tend to show ineptness in their initial approaches to others, for example, they may introduce irrelevant conversation that disrupts the ongoing interactions of a group (see below). They also disagree with others more, or more awkwardly, than do popular children, who have been sensitized by previous socializing experiences. Thus, when a popular child disagrees she would typically cite a general rule as the basis for disagreement and then provide an acceptable alternative action, for example, "No, you ain't. You ain't supposed . . . you ain't supposed to use this first. You're supposed to pick one of these." An unpopular child, on the other hand, tells another child quite specifically what she could not do and would not suggest an alternative action, for example, after the partner had used the word "bank" on a previous turn in the game: "No. Can't say 'bank' again" (Putallaz & Gottman, 1981).

Boys who have the social status of "neglected" in their own classroom sometimes see an unfamiliar group as a new chance: Though they are still relatively the least active children in such a new group, they are more socially active and visible than they were in the familiar group. However, very soon social status in the new group becomes very similar to the classroom-based status (Berndt, 1983; Coie & Kupersmidt, 1983). So it seems that often it is a child's habitual behavior that will land him in the same position.

It is heartening to know that the selection of a specific friend is not necessarily related to the friend's overall popularity, but often to particular interactions and reciprocity between the two friends. Thus, some children may display social competence and achieve acceptance in some dyadic relationships, even if they are not universally popular (Masters & Furman, 1981).

Newcomers in Peer Groups

Entering an existing group is a delicate process that requires some sensitivity and skill. In fact, children in small groups often resist the entry of any newcomers, not only that of unpopular children, because they do not wish to have their ongoing interaction disturbed. Corsaro (1981) has documented this process by observing groups of 3- to 5-year-old children in nursery school:

Steven and Jonathan are playing on climbing bars. Graham, a younger child, attempts to enter this game, but at first he is rebuffed. He returns later, and enlists the aid of Antoinette, who is his age, and of the teaching assistant. The latter points out that bars are a public place and that anybody can play there. Jonathan then decides to let the newcomers play and the following conversation ensues:

Jonathan to Steven: We want to talk about it. So—let—let, Steve, why don't we cooperate and why don't you agree to be a nice policeman?
Steven to Jonathan: O–o–okay. (Steven stretches out "okay" and seems unhappy, but resigned to the agreement.)

Jonathan to Steven: Here, shake hands.

Steven to Jonathan: We have to get those robbers.

Antoinette to Graham: Come on. We—come on. Let's go, Graham.

Steven to Jonathan: We have to get the robbers who stole the jewels.
  (p. 223)

And so, after negotiations, the newcomers are accepted into the group.

The process of entering an existing group has been studied by Putallaz and Gottman (1981) with 7- to 8-year-old children. Newcomers in general, they found, tended to act tentatively or shyly—they "hovered"—and unpopular children generally waited longer before making a first bid and took more time over entry. In their entry bids the unpopular children attempted to call attention to themselves by making statements about themselves, their own feeling, and opinions. They also diverted the group from an ongoing activity by asking for information about, and drawing attention to, irrelevant things, as in the following example, where Terry is trying to enter Janet and Vera's play:

Janet: OK, I want this one again.

Terry: This is fun, ain't it?

Janet to Vera: Do you want this one again?

Vera: I want this one.

Terry: This is a nice room, ain't it?

Janet to Vera: You can have this one. Here.

Terry: This is a nice table, ain't it?

The strategy of a popular child, however, is different, as is illustrated by the following example in which Matt is trying to enter Sam's and Craig's organized game:

Sam: Animals.

Craig: What'd you get . . . B?

Matt: What'd you go and pick?

Sam: Take another turn.

Matt: Bear.

Sam: Gorilla. Thank you, Matt.

Matt: Let's see.

Sam: Move ahead . . .

Matt: Your turn.

Craig: Animals. Bear.

Matt: Hey. Mix these up.

Craig: I know. Okay, hold it. Yeah, do that. I got move ahead 3. Ooh! How lucky can you get. 1, 2, 3. Your turn, Matt. (p. 141)

Notice that the newcomer enters into the ongoing conversation by making relevant comments about the game the other two are playing, gets thanked and accepted. But we should note that even popular children were unsuccessful in their entry bids 30% of the time in this study. However, the kind of entry behavior in small groups that children display is indicative of their social interactions in general and predicts later social status (Putallaz, 1983).

Other Attributes Connected to Popularity

Deficits in social skills are not the only source of unpopularity. It is also associated, for instance, with lower intelligence, even from preschool age onward (Quay & Jarrett, 1984; Roff et al., 1972), as well as with low academic achievement in school-aged children (Berndt, 1983). The best proof that low achievement is, indeed, partly responsible for low social status is the fact that tutoring rejected children in school subjects is an even surer way of enhancing their social acceptance than is training in social skills (Coie & Krehbiehl, 1984). However, high achievement tends to be more strongly correlated with prestige than it is with popularity (Hartup, 1983). Athletic prowess, too, as we might expect, leads to popularity and to high social dominance status (Bukowski & Newcomb, 1984; Savin-Williams, 1979).

Physical attractiveness is also related to popularity. Attractive children in elementary school are more accepted by their peers, have higher self-concepts, and receive better teacher ratings for intelligence and achievements, even when objective achievement scores are similar to those of unattractive children. Teachers have been observed to respond more positively to attractive than to unattractive children (Algozzine, 1977).

Is the greater acceptance of attractive children due to their physical appearance or to more sociable behavior on their part? The answer is not certain: There are few behavioral differences between younger attractive and unattractive children, but by age 5 unattractive children have been found to act more aggressively and in a negative fashion (Langlois & Downs, 1979); their unpopularity may therefore be due to this behavior, though this itself may be a reaction to others' unwelcoming response to their unattractive features. In any case, attractiveness appears to bestow greater popularity on girls rather than on boys at elementary school age (Dion & Stein, 1978).

Another factor connected to popularity is maturity, though more clearly in boys than in girls. Early maturing boys display greater poise and self-confidence and have long been known to be more popular and more socially advanced than late maturers (Jones & Bayley, 1950). Early maturing girls similarly enjoy more popularity and prestige than late maturers, but this advantage accrues to them only in junior high school, not in sixth grade of elementary school, where a "well-developed" girl may stand out negatively, as too different from expectations and from her age-mates (Faust, 1960).

All good things go together and therefore it is not surprising that a causal analysis in a longitudinal study (Bukowski & Newcomb, 1984) has shown that a general factor of social prominence ("liked by everybody," "good at sports," "good-looking") marks out some children and that this is causally related to subsequent peer acceptance.

Popularity Within and Between Social Class and Race Groups

Is popularity in working-class groups based on different attributes than it is in middle-class groups? Gottman, Gonso, and Rasmussen (1975) report that in a middle-class elementary school children gained popularity by dispensing more positive verbal reinforcements (e.g., approval), whereas in a working-class school they gained it by dispensing more nonverbal reinforcements (e.g., giving an object or affection). This reflects the more verbal orientation of middle-class children. At the same time, although some minor differences between boys from lower and higher income families exist, there is a striking communality of values that characterizes popularity across all income groups: male adolescents in all income groups have been found to label accepted peers as bright, fair, able to take a joke, good company, athletic and honest; rejected peers were characterized as pesty, noisy, conceited, silly, and effeminate (Feinberg, Smith, & Schmidt, 1958). Yet, even within similar IQ groups, elementary-school-aged children tend to choose children from social classes higher than their own as their companions (Grossmann & Wrighter, 1948).

Race cleavages in friendship preferences have been reported frequently (cf. Hartup, 1983). In a study of peer preferences in integrated classrooms Singleton and Asher (1979) asked third- and sixth-grade children how much they would like to play, and how much they would like to work with each classmate. This form of question is different from friendship nominations, as children could name as an acceptable play or work companion someone whom they would not regard as a "best friend." Children gave quite positive ratings to children of a race different from their own as work/play companions, though own-race choices predominated. Racial cleavages became stronger over age, particularly among black children, but sex accounted for more variance in these ratings than did race. Own-race preferences were, however, much more in evidence in choices of "best friends" than in choices of work or play companions (Asher, Singleton, & Taylor, 1982).

Is Popularity Stable and Consistent?

One would expect that popularity, like other human attributes, would be determined jointly by children's personal characteristics and by situational-environmental factors. Although the latter have generally been neglected in studies of this topic, it has been found that open classrooms, which tend to use small-group instruction, contain fewer extremely popular or extremely unpopular children than closed classrooms, where class-oriented lessons are the rule, that is, there is a more even distribution of popularity

in classrooms where there is greater opportunity for frequent peer interactions to occur (Hallinan, 1981).

Nevertheless, widespread evidence indicates that social status is quite
stable across different groups. We already noted the similarity of social
status rankings in newly formed experimental groups with those in the
classrooms from which the children came (Coie & Kupersmidt, 1983).
Moreover, across time, too, sociability and social status have been found to
be quite stable from toddlerhood at least to age 10 (Bukowski & Newcomb, 1984; Rubin & Daniels-Beirness, 1983). Negative or rejected status
is particularly stable both in the early years and and even over a 5-year
span from grade 5 onwards (Coie & Dodge, 1983).

So overall popularity/unpopularity seems to reside more within the child
than in the situation, when these situations are relatively similar (e.g.,
different classroom or classroom-like groups) though the identity of the
most popular children will vary between, say, the football field and the
chess club. Popular status among one's fellows and the self-esteem that
usually accompanies it may largely come about through early experiences
in the family and with peers. Some genetic component, however, also
appears partly to determine this personal attribute, since identical twins
are more similar than fraternal twins in social status, as determined by a
combination of peer choices and teacher ratings (correlations of .77 for
identical, and .53 for fraternal twins [Roff et al., 1972]).

Isolated Children

It is common to regard children who play alone as being "at risk" for later
adaptation in life, but is this widespread view justified for all kinds of solitary play? Rubin (1982) has recently subjected this conventional assumption to a more detailed scrutiny. He studied the play behavior of preschoolers (4- to 5-years-old) and of kindergarteners (5½-years-old) and identified
extreme groups, firstly of isolates, whose *nonsocial* behavior was more
than one standard deviation above the age-group mean (15% of the sample), and secondly of sociable children, whose *social* behavior was more
than one standard deviation above the age-group mean (15% of the sample). The remaining 70% were labeled as "normal."

Children's play was categorized by cognitive content—functional, constructive, and dramatic, as defined above, as well as by social involvement.
The isolates in general engaged in less sociodramatic play and in fewer
games with rules than others. Since these forms of play are cognitively
more advanced, this points to immaturity in isolates, something which was
confirmed by their lower mental ages. Solitary-functional and solitary-
dramatic play were found to be associated with poorer social skills and less
advanced cognitive development, whereas solitary-constructive play was
not. The former also declined with age, whereas the latter increased with
age. Hence solitary play in the functional and dramatic categories appears

to be a more immature form of play, while solitary-constructive activities have no such adverse connotations. Indeed, constructive play, for example, artwork or block construction, is often naturally carried out alone or in noninteractive proximity to someone else. (Parallel-constructive play, which is still essentially nonsocial, was even positively related to various social and cognitive skills, and to popularity.)

Isolates had poorer social skills than others in that they were more likely to respond to questions about how to deal with social difficulties with peers by suggesting that they would seek adult intervention, and by suggesting confrontational tactics (e.g., hit or grab). But their peers rated them as neither more disliked nor more liked than others, probably because they were invisible rather than obnoxious to them.

Solitary-constructive play—favored by isolated kindergarteners—can be seen to be a harmless and even adaptive pursuit, and hence the author concludes that solitary activities are not necessarily a bad thing. Nevertheless, solitariness overall did have some developmental costs. Even at the age of 4, it was the children who interacted most with their peers who were more socially and cognitively advanced, more playful and creative, and who had higher mental ages than others (Rubin, 1982).

Whether these solitary children in preschool turn into friendless children in elementary school, we do not know. What we do know is that solitariness often engenders unhappiness: One study has shown that third- to sixth-graders who had no friends in school, as determined by a peer sociometric measure, were more likely to report feeling lonely than others (Asher, Hymel, & Renshaw, 1984). More than 10% of all children reported loneliness and this feeling increased with age. We should not delude ourselves that these "loners" were well-adjusted children who did their own thing—on the contrary, they were unhappy and felt adrift. However, such isolates are at much lesser risk than are rejected children of becoming delinquent in later life (see below).

It would therefore be helpful if one could increase the acceptance of very isolated and rejected children by some adult intervention. Such "social skills training" usually consists of coaching unpopular children by verbal instruction and modeling in how to pay attention and listen to others, or how to share materials and take turns with other children, and so forth, or it may consist in setting up an opportunity for them to interact with others. Social skills training of various kinds has often been found to be effective in increasing the sociometric status of unpopular children at elementary school (e.g. Asher & Renshaw, 1981; Bierman & Furman, 1984) and at preschool, where having isolated children play with partners younger than themselves was particularly successful (e.g., Furman, Rahe, & Hartup, 1979). In Bierman and Furman's investigation coaching in conversational skills seemed to increase skillful social interaction, but not peer acceptance. Peer acceptance of these children was enhanced only by their actually interacting with others in pursuing a common goal where they could demonstrate the ability to contribute some skills to the common enterprise, for example, making friendly interaction films. That training in academic skills may sometimes be even more effective in enhancing social status (cf. Coie & Krehbiel, 1984, discussed above) does not detract from the merits of training social skills directly.

PEER GROUPS AND THEIR SOCIALIZING INFLUENCE

We now come to the peer group as such, which plays such an important role in middle childhood and adolescence. We will discuss its formation, its nature, and the influence it exerts.

Groups and Their Formation

One of the important contexts in which children learn and practice different roles and become socialized as members of their society are the informal groups that they form: twosomes, threesomes, or larger groups. Children also use such groups as reference points, in addition to the family, to guide their behavior. But no groups as cohesive entities exist at kindergarten level; they only come into being gradually at later ages. By age 9 groups are more in the nature of an agglomeration of interlinked dyads whose composition changes frequently, and it is only at adolescence that groups are relatively homogeneous and attain a fair degree of stability.

How groups form and what a powerful force they represent has been shown best perhaps in a classic study, the "Robber's Cave" experiment (Sherif et al., 1961). Sherif and his colleagues brought together 25 previously unacquainted 10-year-old boys for a summer camp and divided them into two separate bands which at first did not know of each other's existence. In order to encourage individuals to coalesce into a community, and to promote the emergence of group structure, the experimenters arranged situations that made cooperative activities unavoidable (a "natural experiment" reminiscent of Rousseau's ideas). For example, one day dinner had not been prepared by camp staff, although the ingredients were all available, and the boys had to fend for themselves. They soon set to work and within each group a division of labor occurred. Different status levels for different boys emerged: some were leaders and others followers. Later each group adopted a name for itself—the Rattlers and the Eagles. Thus initial strangers turned into a cohesive group that was marked by common goals and activities and that acquired a name and a structure. (We will follow the subsequent events in this experiment in a later section.)

Group Structures

Hierarchical structures are evident in many species—witness the term "pecking order," derived from fowl. Dominance hierarchies have often been studied in monkeys and apes, as they represent one way of describing group structure and of explaining some primate social behavior, though they are not the only basis of group relations. Dominance has usually been defined by success in agonistic exchanges, not by amount of aggression. The dominant member of the troop, once the position has stabilized, may show the least aggression. It is as if aggression increases in proportion to the need to assert one's rank and hence the alpha male (among monkeys) may not need to behave aggressively if his primacy is accepted by all (Hinde, 1974). Ethologists subscribe to the idea that such dominance hierarchies in primates serve adaptive functions for the species as a whole, in that they help towards reducing aggression and resolving social conflict within the group, as discussed in Chapter 1. Hierarchical structures also create or allow a division of labor and maximize access to food and to reproductive opportunities for the successful or "fit." For those lower in the pecking order, we may suppose, the hierarchy will provide opportunities of contact with individuals from whom problem-solving skills can be learned, and from whom they may derive protection. In addition, for these individuals the reduction of intragroup conflict will be particularly welcome.

The study of dominance hierarchies has recently been extended to humans (Savin-Williams, 1979; Strayer, 1980). The benefit for the dominant children is clear: high status confers privileges, such as being able to choose group activities according to their interests, and it bestows self-esteem and thus becomes its own reward. The benefit for the subordinate is less clear, but it has been noted that adolescents want to belong and to be approved by the peer group and some are willing to submit in order to achieve this security (Savin-Williams, 1979).

Successful aggression, as noted above, is one kind of behavior that plays a role in establishing dominance hierarchies. A study of dominance relations among preschool children, for instance, showed that the hierarchy based on attack-submission was almost completely linear and transitive, that is, when A successfully attacked B, and B successfully attacked C, then A also successfully attacked C (Strayer and Strayer, 1976).

In human groups an individual who directs and coordinates the behavior of others and who effectively initiates group activities, is said to have *social power*. This is by no means synonymous with being the most aggressive individual; rather, social power is determined by different attributes at different ages. At preschool age it is partly based on the initiation of aggressive acts (Sluckin & Smith, 1977), but also on the ability to keep possessions and know how to use them (Strayer, 1980). In middle childhood children who display social skills by their adeptness at directing games and organizing activities emerge as leaders (Sherif, et al., 1961). In early adolescence leadership is vested in individuals who are popular, have athletic ability, or are early maturers (Savin-Williams, 1980b), whereas in later adolescence, brightness and creativity, as well as popularity, lead to social power (Savin-Williams, 1980a). In general, dominance in the form of physical aggression is not central to social power in children's social organization. Power depends more on abilities that accord with the group's norms or that meet the group's objectives, and since these objectives will vary across situations, social power is also heavily influenced by specific situational factors (Hartup, 1983).

Preschoolers, too, not only fight, but also play and associate together in a friendly fashion, and an analysis of such cohesive activities demonstrates that they define the group's social structure quite differently from the way conflict does (Abramovitch & Strayer, 1978; Strayer, 1980). Thus, for agonistic or conflictful interactions children could be arranged in a hierarchical order that increased linearly from low to high dominance (see above). But no such linear order was discerned for affiliative interactions, which were defined as proximal behaviors and physical contact (Strayer, 1980). Social preferences were distributed equally without regard to the social dominance hierarchy in two out of three groups studied, that is, in these groups there existed no correlation between social preference and dominance, as defined by the outcome of agonistic exchanges. This means that knowledge of a child's position on the social dominance ladder did not necessarily predict her role in sociable interactions and the affiliative peer structure. The group in which the dominance and affiliative structures did converge, consisted of the oldest children (5 to 6 years old). In this group it was possible to identify some children who were competent in both the dominance and the affiliative dimensions, and these were the older children who possessed social skills greater than those of peripheral and isolated children (Strayer, 1980).

The two sexes form social networks in characteristically different styles. This is particularly noticeable in adolescence. Girls from puberty on stress understanding and intimacy as an important aspect of friendship and in adolescence they tend to associate in pairs or threesomes that form exclusive and intense relationships with each other, whereas boys' activities center on larger groups (Hartup, 1983; Savin-Williams, 1980b).

At adolescence, too, notable sex differences in the nature of groups and in the way social status is achieved or expressed have been observed in camp (Savin-Williams, 1979, 1980b). Girls' groups tend to be more ephemeral than boys' groups. If a structure is discernible in girls' groups, it is likely to be less tight and stable than are male adolescent groupings. In both sexes the most frequent way by which status is expressed is by verbal ridicule, but dominant boys by and large also assert their status by physical contact, verbal-physical threat or verbal argument (boys, overall, are three times more likely than girls to engage in physical assertiveness and to argue). Girl leaders, on the other hand, express their status by more subtle signs, for example, by recognizing some camp-mates and shunning others, by ignoring requests or by offering unsolicited advice.

Groups in late childhood help boys to learn cooperation and thereby to embark on more extensive activities and adventures than each could on his own (the Robbers' Cave experiment organized this—see above). Girls, on the other hand, as we noted, tend to enjoy intense, intimate friendships more, and girls' groups, therefore, have different purposes: They aid girls in developing desired interpersonal skills and sensitivities, and girls value them also for the opportunity simply to be with friends and relax (Savin-Williams, 1980b).

Peers' Influences

Peers influence and socialize each other, both toward socially desirable and undesirable ends. The older they get the more deliberately they do so.

One of the basic processes by which children learn from their peers is *imitation*, a behavior whose contributions to socialization in the everyday world are manifold; just to name one example, imitation is one of the factors making for sex-appropriate play among children (Perry & Bussey, 1979—see Chapter 10 for a longer discussion). Observation in preschool and elementary school classes has shown that a great deal of imitation of both verbal and motor acts occurs in day-by-day interactions (Abramovitch & Grusec, 1978). Imitation seems to decrease from nursery school to age 10, perhaps because deferred rather than immediate imitation and other subtle forms of observational influence become more favored over age. As might be expected, dominant children in a group are imitated more, but they also imitate more than others. This interesting phenomenon suggests that imitating one's peers may be an important way of influencing them.

The influence of groups can be observed as early as age 2. Experience in playgroups changes the ways in which toddlers interact with their parents and seems to enhance their social skills: Toddlers who have been in playgroups become more active and more responsive when their parents initiate interactions, and the parents themselves issue fewer commands and prohibitions (Vandell, 1979).

How do peer reinforcements affect children's self-regulation and "moral" behavior? This question has been studied experimentally with nursery school children, using the "resistance to deviation" paradigm (Furman & Masters, 1980; Parke, 1974). In one condition a prohibition on playing with an attractive toy was endorsed by peers, in another condition the prohibition was not peer-endorsed. At a certain point a second child who had been given permission to play with the "prohibited" toy appeared on the scene as a tempter. The degree to which a given child interacted with peers in the group turned out to be an influential modulating factor for that child's resistance to deviation. Children differed in the degree to which they attempted to enforce the rule on the "tempter." When the rule had been endorsed by peers, high interactors attempted to enforce the rule on the second child more than low interactors did. However, when the rule did not carry peer endorsement, low interactors enforced the rule more frequently than did high interactors (see Figure 6.1). Thus the high peer

PEER INFLUENCE DURING PEER PRESSURE TEST PERIOD:

ENCOURAGEMENT OF DEVIANT BEHAVIOR

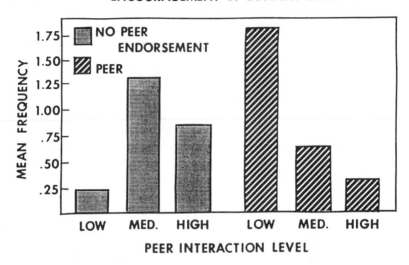

FIGURE 6.1. Encouragement of deviant behavior by the trained peer during the peer pressure test period. From "Rules, Roles, and Resistance to Deviation: Recent Advances in Punishment, Discipline, and Self-Control" by R.D. Parke, 1974, in A. Pick (Ed.), 1974, *Minnesota Symposia on Child Psychology, 8*, 111–143. Copyright 1974 by University of Minnesota Press. Reprinted by permission.

interactors seemed to attach value to the peer endorsement and acted accordingly, whereas the low interactors did not (Parke, 1974).

In a similar vein it has been found that unpopular children (as determined by sociometric choices) tend to deviate more than other children, both when peers and when teachers endorse a prohibition (Furman & Masters, 1980). Findings like these may be explained by a "social reference group" theory which proposes that the degree to which a person is influenced by a peer group is determined by both the attractiveness of that group and the status of the person within it. Hence high interactors, who are likely to have higher status in the group, as well as popular children, will be more ready to abide by and enforce peer-endorsed rules (Furman & Masters, 1980).

Cooperation and Competition

Whether children should be encouraged to cooperate or compete with each other, and what effects cooperation and competition have on performance and on children's lives in general is an important question for social science. It is reassuring to know that the number of positive, friendly interactions in general exceeds by about four to one the number of agonistic exchanges, as observed in a preschool setting (Walters, Pearce, & Dahms, 1957). Whether children play in a cooperative spirit or compete fiercely depends to a large extent on the setting in which they find themselves and on the rules of the game which, at least for young children, are often adult-imposed. Thus in an experimental peg-board game the behavior of 4-year-olds matched the conditions imposed by the experimenter: They helped each other when cooperation was rewarded by a prize for all, but acted individualistically and competitively when they had to compete for individual prizes (Nelson & Madsen, 1969).

Preference for competition or cooperation is to some extent affected by age. Cooperation emerges later than competition, since coordination requires advanced cognitive abilities, for example, delay of gratification, taking another's perspective, and the understanding of complex social dependencies. Competition under a winner-takes-all-condition, for instance, increased between ages 4 and 5, whereas cooperation under a shared rewards condition increased only between ages 6 and 8 in one investigation (McClintock, Moskowitz, & McClintock, 1977). No doubt, over age children learn to adopt strategies that are consonant with the goal structure of a given game or task.

When a verbal scale of attitudes to cooperation and competition was administered to over 2,000 students, ranging from second to 12th grade, consistent and highly significant sex differences were found, with girls showing increasing preference for cooperation, particularly from grade 8 on (Ahlgren & Johnson, 1979). This reveals an important sex difference in favor of females, since the girls' attitudes would generally be considered to be the more desirable ones.

That cooperative and competitive attitudes, and their associated emotions, often depend on the social setting and can be created and modified by engineering the situation toward certain ends, has been shown by the Robbers' Cave experiment, the story of which we will now continue (Sherif, et al., 1961—see above). When the two teams were pitted against each other, even in "friendly" competitive games, strong "in-group" and "out-group" feelings developed. As a result of competition, each group manifested greater solidarity and became more cohesive within itself, while at the same time displaying extreme hostility to the other group. Their mutual enmity expressed itself not only in verbal abuse, but also in actual physical aggression. Simple joint experiences, such as watching a movie together, only worsened the situation. The only means by which the counselors could establish greater amity between the two groups was to arrange a situation which necessitated a cooperative combined effort by both groups. When the water supply "broke down" one day the Eagles and the Rattlers joined forces in exploring what had caused the breakdown and in repairing it. In the process they abandoned their rivalry and developed more harmonious relations. Competition, it seems, is easier to establish than cooperation.

What matters in this question of cooperation or competition is, of course, not only the efficiency of work, but also the social climate and attitudes engendered. Such attitudes, it has been found, are more positive toward the self *and* toward fellow workers in cooperative situations, whereas in competitive conditions they are positive about the self at the expense of others (Bryant, 1977).

The Pull of Parental Versus Peer Influences

Are the culture and the influence of the peer group, particularly at adolescence, inimical to parental influence and to the values of society at large? At the beginning of this chapter we noted that the child's relations with parents and peers are not completely different in kind. But, as adolescence approaches, the child moves more into the orbit of her peers and certainly shares more activities with them. We have also discussed how peer opinion, when it endorses an adult-approved (by inference, a society-approved) prohibition, may be influential in fostering more mature moral behavior. However, what of the negative influences of peer pressures? And does the greater association with peers mean that the adolescent's value system changes and becomes opposed to that of her parents?

In a series of studies, summarized by Devereux (1970), Devereux, Bronfenbrenner, and their colleagues developed a Dilemmas Test which presented the 10- to 14-year old subjects with hypothetical situations that involved dilemmas of conduct, pitting adult-approved or autonomously held values against peer pressure toward deviance. One example was going to a movie with a group of friends who proposed that they should all lie about their age in order to ride on the bus at half-fare. The subjects were asked to what extent they would go along with this idea.

Of course not all children said that they would yield to such peer pressures. But the investigators concluded overall that frequent association with peers was a hazard for the development of socially approved standards in matters such as lying, stealing, cheating, trespassing, and so forth. Those who frequented peers' company the most, and particularly those who preferred gangs and large groups to going with best friends, declared themselves more ready to go along with the crowd in such deviant acts. Such children were also more likely to play in unsupervised groups and these groups were reported to engage in more misconduct. Each of these factors, these studies found, reduced guilt feelings and diminished the ability to resist peer temptation. The older the children were, within the given age range, the more responsive they became to peer pressure and the more their peer orientation increased (Devereux, 1970). These findings apply, by and large, to youth in America, England, and Germany, where parallel investigations were carried out. The cross-cultural aspects of this research will be discussed below.

Coleman (1961) earlier warned about the dangers of the adolescent peer culture in America, which he saw as being in conflict with adult goals and standards, and more recent research (e.g., Condry & Siman, 1974) also found that peer orientation in early adolescence, in contrast to adult orientation, was associated with socially undesirable behavior.

However, such a conflict between adult and peer values may not be general throughout adolescence and for all adolescents. Hence some of the factors that complicate the simple picture need closer examination.

Firstly, there are developmental age changes in attitudes toward parents and peers. These have been demonstrated in a mixed social class sample by an investigation that used Dilemma Tests similar to Devereux and Bronfenbrenner's (Berndt, 1979). Conformity to parents in neutral and prosocial situations (e.g., involving questions about what to wear and when to be helpful) gradually declines from third grade to senior high school. However, peer conformity for antisocial norms increases progressively from third to ninth grade, *but not beyond*. Indeed, peer conformity in neutral, prosocial, and antisocial behavior shows a curvilinear trend over age, and declines in senior high school after peaking at varying earlier ages (see Figure 6.2). Furthermore, the maximum degree of opposition

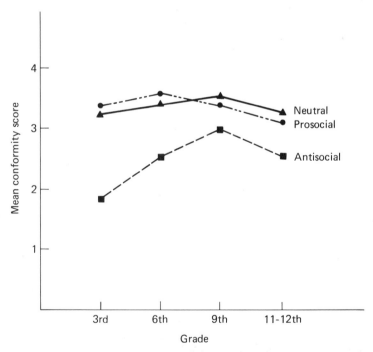

FIGURE 6.2. Mean scores for each grade on conformity to peers for different types of behaviors. (Higher scores indicate greater conformity, and the neutral point is 3.5.) From "Developmental Changes in Conformity to Peers and Parents" by T.J. Berndt, 1979, *Developmental Psychology, 15*, 608–616. Copyright 1979 by the American Psychological Association. Reprinted by permission.

between parent and peer orientation coincides with the peak age for succumbing to peers in antisocial situations. Thus it is clear from this careful research that, while children grow more independent vis-à-vis their parents over time, a period of conflict between parental and peer norms exists mainly at early adolescence (Berndt, 1979).

Secondly, there are some characteristics of youths and parents that will either intensify or help to bridge the parent-peer opposition. Thus, girls very consistently are less prone to succumb to a deviant peer culture than are boys (Devereux, 1970), and when they are peer-oriented they stress affiliative associations with their group, but engage in less socially undesirable behavior than do boys and also feel less rejected by their parents (Condry & Siman, 1974). Again, as with cooperation, we note the more socially responsible attitudes of females.

In the Devereux research program a group of autonomous children were identified, that is, those who were least influenced in their responses by an expectation that their answers would be exposed to either adults or peers. These children typically were also in the intermediate range between extreme conformity to adults or to peers. This and other research (e.g., Kandel & Lesser, 1972) suggests that such children who are independent from their parents, but also have positive and close relations with them, come from homes that give them moderate to high levels of support and nurturance and firm, but not oppressive levels of discipline and control; control for these children is relaxed but not abandoned, and it relies on democratic decision-making and on explanation of rules. It will also often be likely that children who have close relationships with their parents choose peers with a similar value system, so that they do not live in two separate, conflicting worlds.

The homes of gang-oriented children, on the other hand, are characterized by either high permissiveness or high punitiveness (Devereux, 1970). These children typically receive both less support and less control than adult-oriented children. The parents of peer-oriented children also show less concern and affection for them and by such passive neglect, rather than active maltreatment, push them into the peer culture, to which the children often conform out of necessity rather than choice (Condry & Siman, 1974). Youngsters living with both natural parents have also been found to be less susceptible to pressure from peers to engage in deviant behavior than youngsters living in single-parent homes or in stepfamilies. Thus, the integrity of the home is an important protector against pressures toward deviant behavior (Steinberg, 1987).

Teachers, too, influence their students' attitudes: Teachers in classes with more adult-oriented students are described by their pupils as more supportive and less punitive than teachers in classes with more peer-oriented students (Devereux, 1970). Of course, it may be factors in students that make for differential perception of teachers. A relevant finding comes from Rutter, Maugham, Mortimore, and Ouston (1979), who found in English secondary schools that "contra-school peer groups" tended to arise in schools where there was a heavy preponderance of less able children. Such groups may be formed from children who are indifferent to academic success because they see no hope of achieving it. But the schools' own climate and procedures also influenced students' attitudes and the relative frequency of behavior problems. (We will discuss this study again in a later section.)

The third factor that affects the parent/peer balance of influence is the issues involved. Thus, cheating and lying are regarded by most children as more serious core violations of moral behavior and generally elicit more adult-oriented replies than, for instance, Halloween pranks. As one 11-year-old boy said: "Mostly on things that don't matter very much, I try to do what the other kids are doing. If they all want to wear blue jeans, I wear them, too. But sometimes, when a whole gang of kids are playing together, things get sort of crazy, and then I try to think what my father would want me to do." (Devereux, 1970, p. 130). The educational plans of older adolescents are usually worked out in agreement with both parents and peers, and here parental influence is the stronger one (Kandel & Lesser, 1972); in other areas, particularly in the case of drug use, the influence of peers will, however, outweigh that of parents, and here the peer group does seem to act as a "cultural deviance model" (Kandel, 1973).

Some writers deny that conflict between the adult and the peer culture is endemic in adolescence or is at all severe (e.g., Douvan & Adelson, 1966). Kandel and Lesser (1972) report no such conflict in high school populations (14- to 18-year-olds) in the United States or in Denmark, except for the area of drug use (see above). In their study the extent of participation in the peer group was independent of adolescents' involvement with the family, not negatively related to it. They found, moreover, that adolescents who were in disagreement with their parents were also in disagreement with peers, and tended to be at odds with the world.

The reason why Kandel and Lesser found no perturbing peer-adult conflict may be simply that their sample consisted of older adolescents, an age by which peer-adult conflict has abated, as Berndt (1979) has shown. Researchers like Bronfenbrenner and Devereux, who stress the hazards and pervasiveness of adult-peer conflict, have looked at younger adolescents, an age when adult-peer conflict is, indeed, at its peak. If one recognizes that the two sets of findings apply to different age-groups, the apparent conflict between them vanishes; in fact, the two sets can be fitted together to generate the inverted U-shaped curve of adult-peer relations that Berndt has drawn (see Figure 6.2).

Piaget (1932) theorized that the reciprocity and equality inherent in peer relations is central to morality. Contrary to this contention, however, the evidence is convincing that strong and frequent peer associations that occur at the expense of adult associations are not conducive to good moral development. Golding in his novel "Lord of the Flies" created a cautionary tale about the disinhibiting effects of unsupervised, exclusive peer interactions on moral behavior. Nevertheless, peer experiences also have their value in that they provide certain cross-pressures, which after all also characterize adult life. Indeed, in the last resort, moral development consists in learning to find one's way between such cross-pressures and, particularly where the home has built sufficient ego-strength, such balancing of pressures may lead to autonomy of character (Devereux, 1970).

CROSS-CULTURAL PERSPECTIVES

As with parents' socialization practices, the nature and effects of the peer group are likely to be bound up with the demands of the culture in which it exists, and against which it sometimes reacts. In North America whence most of the evidence so far discussed originates, the development of an autonomous, self-regulating *individual* is highly prized, yet—paradoxically—the peer group is an influential magnet and radiating force in adolescence that often creates a "contra-culture." It may be that emphasis on individual rights has worked against a strong consensus on generally respected values in Western society. In other countries, for example, China, Japan, and Russia, greater stress is laid on achieving one's purpose in life through membership in a respected social order, with which it is natural and essential for the child to learn to identify and integrate.

What are the role and effect of the peer group in societies where collective, rather than individual, goals and achievements are stressed? Bronfenbrenner explored this question by means of the Dilemmas Test, discussed above, which he administered not only in the United States, but also in the Soviet Union, as well as in England and Germany (Bronfenbrenner, 1967, 1970; Devereux, 1970). In the later phases of this research the test was administered under three separate conditions. Under the *scientific* condition the 10- to 14-year-old students were told that the test was conducted for strictly scientific purposes and that their answers would not be revealed to anyone. Under the *adult* condition they were told that the results would be posted on charts that would be shown to parents and teachers. Under the *peer* condition the subjects were promised that the results would be shown only to their own peers. As differences among the Western countries were less clear, we will compare only the results for American and Soviet children.

The most outstanding finding was that in all three experimental conditions Soviet children were much less ready to engage in peer-endorsed deviant behavior than were their counterparts in any Western country. In all countries girls were more adult-conforming than were boys, and when told that parents would see their answers, students in all samples shifted their answers more towards adult-approved norms. However, the effects of the peer group were quite different in the Soviet Union, compared with the United States. When told that their answers would be seen by other children, American students were more inclined to go along with peer-condoned misconduct, whereas Soviet students showed the opposite tendency—they shifted towards greater adult-conformity. The peer group was evidently perceived by Soviet children as being in tune with society's standards in general.

In Soviet boarding schools the spirit of collective responsibility for the good of society is stressed even more than it is in day schools, and the reactions of 12-year-old children from these schools were in keeping with this atmosphere: They showed even more resistance to deviation than their age-mates in ordinary day schools (Bronfenbrenner, 1970).

Soviet children are expected by their teachers to take some personal action to correct any undesirable conduct by their classmates, and to call on the collective if this fails. In this way the peer group is used deliberately as a transmitter and reinforcer of Soviet society's values and children learn to identify with these—we know from research on socialization practices that children who enforce rules come to comply with them (Parke, 1974). Whereas in Western countries the peer group offers standards and values that are often at variance with those of adult society, in the Soviet Union peer pressures appear to extend and reinforce adult socialization pressures, even in early adolescence. Soviet youths are therefore faced with fewer diverging standards from different sources and are subject to more homogeneous influences (Bronfenbrenner, 1970). Whether this is good or bad depends on how important diversity and self-regulation of character are in one's philosophy of life. We should note that this picture applies to Soviet society of the 1960s and the general view is that this society itself has since then been changing toward somewhat greater emphasis on the value of individuality. However, no research appears to have been done in the Soviet Union on the peer group in recent years.

As we noted earlier, Kandel and Lesser (1972) did not find a marked conflict between adolescent and parental values at late adolescence either in the United States or in Denmark. Their survey reveals some cultural differences, however: Danish young people seem to feel more independent of their parents than do their American counterparts, but this independence coexists in the same individuals with a feeling of closeness to parents. Thus in this West European country parental and peer values appear to have been reconciled to a greater extent than in the United States, perhaps because Danish society has moved closer toward the goal of equality between parents and their children.

PEER RELATIONS AND BEHAVIOR DISORDERS

The quality of peer relations, like that of family relations, is associated with later adjustment. Rejected children are more likely to be aggressive and become delinquent, more likely to remain unaccepted by their peers, and more likely to experience mental health problems in adulthood (Roff &

Wirt, 1984). Rejected children, in other words, are at risk for later adjustment problems, but the risk status of isolated children is less clear (Asher & Dodge, 1986).

Roff and his colleagues (Roff et al., 1972) followed up several thousand boys from third grade to 10th grade and discovered different consequences arising from the quality of peer relations in different social classes. At the upper and middle socioeconomic status (SES) levels delinquency occurred most frequently in boys defined by the authors as rejected, but at the lowest SES level it occurred equally frequently among the most rejected and the best-liked boys. At all SES levels, therefore, poor peer relations are linked to delinquency, but at the lower SES level delinquency could also be an expression of the appropriate peer culture. Indeed, it is likely that those who have unsatisfactory peer relations in general form their own counter-gangs. This explains why strong and exclusive involvement with the peer culture—in delinquent gangs, for instance—seems to lead to socially undesirable behavior in some adolescents.

Thus delinquency may well arise from a concatenation of disturbed family relationships, troubled peer relations, and exposure to delinquent norms (Hartup, 1983; Roff et al., 1972). But bodily disturbances, such as frequent illness or headaches, in childhood also are indicators of later maladjustment. Hence troubled peer relations may simply be a part of general adjustment problems, although they will exacerbate existing difficulties, leading to later deviance by the combination and interactions of different processes.

Schools as Social Institutions

SCHOOLS AS SETTINGS FOR SOCIALIZATION

Family, playground, and school are the major settings of the child's life. Although these settings intersect and their populations often overlap, each of them affects the child's behavior in its own distinct way, since each has its own demands and expectations. As Rutter et al. (1979) remind us, the average child spends 15,000 hours of her life at school, and this fact alone makes the school an important aspect of the child's rearing environment.

The school has several purposes: For many centuries it has been "a place of learning," a name generally meant to denote its cognitive goals. But the learning has always included certain social and affective outcomes as well, such as the acquisition of social norms and rules, often called "character training" in the past. We usually want the school to include among its affective outcomes the fostering of children's social development, and therefore we expect it to help to create in children the ability to establish positive relations with others and cooperate with them, to resolve conflict by peaceful means, and ultimately to be able to make a productive contribution to society. Some may say that the school has been asked to do more than it can accomplish.

Theoretical emphases on individualized learning have encouraged, and the consistently diminishing class sizes of the last few decades have permitted, schools to modify traditional procedures and experiment with more flexible "open classrooms." The open classroom approach, often called "progressive" or "informal" teaching, generally refers to a style of instruction that involves flexibility of space, student choice of activity, varied learning materials, and more individual or small-group rather than large-group instruction (Horwitz, 1979). Traditional schooling, or "direct instruction," on the other hand, is defined by an academic and teacher-oriented focus, by large-group instruction, and by more controlled learning. Are the outcomes of the open classroom approach any different from those of traditional schooling, and in which ways do the two sets of outcomes differ?

Peterson (1979) has used the method of "meta-analysis" to summarize the findings of a great deal of research that has compared the two approaches. Such meta-analyses average the relative size of effects across all studies in the area under investigation (i.e., in this case, the effect of each teaching style on a given variable) in order to assess the size of the overall effect and to see whether it is significant. Such quantitative integrations of research have been criticized on various grounds. However, at least it can be said that such meta-analyses identify and quantify a number of aspects (including quality) of their component studies and thus produce a more objective summary than do narrative reviews, where the quality of studies and reviewers' biases remain unidentified and unknown.

The differences between the effects of the open classroom and those of the traditional approach, Peterson found, were very small for both cognitive and affective outcomes. As for cognitive outcomes, children in the traditional schools did slightly better on achievement tests, but slightly worse in creative thinking than those in the open classroom schools. On the other hand, the open approaches surpassed the traditional schools in some affective outcomes, for example, in creating positive attitudes to schools and in promoting independence and curiosity, but again, the effects were very small and nonsignificant.

This research may not have been more conclusive because the dichotomous distinction between open classroom and traditional instruction may be simplistic. It fails to take into account factors such as students' differing predispositions, or the extent to which a given teaching style was actually put into practice. Teachers are also adept at inventing unique combinations and at weaving together different components from both teaching styles, say, an individualized approach joined with teacher-controlled content of learning. Moreover, the advent of microcomputers has opened up the classroom to a much wider range of teaching behaviors than has been the case in the past. Research into some of the individual components of the open teaching style, in particular cooperative learning, has been more productive, and we will discuss this topic below.

THE SCHOOL AS A MORAL AND RESPONSIBLE SYSTEM

Educating students toward responsible behavior and civic participation—moral education—as we have said above, has long been considered part of the school's role. Schools may hope to accomplish this either by the "hidden curriculum," that is, as a by-product of academic instruction, the interpersonal relations that naturally occur and the implicit and explicit value system of the school, or on the other hand, they may institute special programs for this purpose. Some of these programs involve attempts to train children to think in morally more sophisticated or developmentally advanced ways. They have been based on discussions of moral dilemmas, derived from Lawrence Kohlberg's work, which will be discussed in greater detail in Chapter 9 (cf. Mosher, 1980). Students usually vary in the degree of progress they make in Kohlberg's system of moral stages as a result of such discussions—typically about a third of students advance by one stage of moral reasoning (Kohlberg, 1980). By the 1970s Kohlberg himself expressed dissatisfaction with the discussion approach. One reason for his disillusionment was the fact that teachers in a successful project, when followed up a year later, no longer carried on with the program. Kohlberg commented: "The operation was a research success but the educational patient died" (Kohlberg, 1980, p. 39). He also felt that attempts to instill principled morality in adolescents may be unrealistic, since even many adults do not reach this stage.

A crucial part of social education, he thought, was actual social participation, which, in effect, means that students should participate in running their own affairs at school. Together with others, Kohlberg therefore established a small alternative school, the "Cluster School," that contained students from different racial and SES backgrounds. Through the school's emphasis on self-governance, the students were forced to consider realistic school issues, and were not involved only in discussions of moral reasoning. The school achieved its goal to a limited extent: By making and enforcing their own rules, students—some of whom had experienced problems in other schools—were able to derive a sense of trust in others and to keep rules about stealing and attending class. They were less successful in keeping the school free from racial tension or in reducing the use of alcohol and drugs (Power & Reimer, 1978).

The London Secondary School Study

Ordinary public schools rely on ordinary teacher-student interactions, inside and outside the classroom, and on the school's rules and value system (the "hidden curriculum") to generate responsible behavior, as well as academic achievements. For evidence on what the processes and the outcomes are in such schools, we go to a study of 12 secondary schools in London, England (Rutter et al., 1979).

We will devote some attention to this study because: (1) it related academic and social-behavioral outcomes to school processes and school climate, (2) it was a large-scale study with a wide range of students, (3) it was soundly designed and executed, (4) it examined the school as a social organization, and (5) it assessed school processes by observations and other means. The obvious cross-cultural differences between England and North America in general school administrative arrangements, organization, and aims preclude any simplified generalization to the North American situation, but we will also draw on some parallel American studies for comparison. Goodlad (1984), for instance, showed that there is an astounding uniformity in regular classroom practices across all 38 U.S. schools that he examined: By far the most common pattern was for teachers to talk and lecture to the class as a whole and for students to listen. Rutter et al. (1979) make it clear that this pattern was replicated in London. Nevertheless, there were also differences in atmosphere and processes among both the English and the American schools (see below). It should be noted that Goodlad (1984) did not measure student outcomes and hence he could not relate school processes, or what went on in the schools, to student outcomes.

The 12 secondary schools of the London study covered an area of inner London that was predominantly working class, and 25% of the children came from immigrant families—most of them black. The teachers, therefore, clearly had to deal with many children who came from a deprived or disadvantaged background and all its attendant problems. The intake of children at age 11 covered the whole ability spectrum, but the schools received less than their fair share of bright children. The schools ranged in size from about 450 to 2,000 students and they differed in their emphasis on varying educational goals. As a group, they were quite typical of inner London schools. The data of the study were based on thousands of 11- to 15-year-old students in hundreds of first-, third-, and fifth-year classes.

Outcomes

The outcomes that the study measured were: (1) academic achievements, measured by success in public examinations, taken by about 60% of the children in the fifth year; (2) children's behavior, observed in classes and elsewhere—the categories noted reflected the common denominator of expectations in the schools and included, for instance, time of on-task behavior in class, truanting, fights, and disruptive behavior; (3) attendance, taken from school records; (4) delinquency, ascertained from police records.

There were considerable variations among schools in these outcomes, but the outcomes were highly intercorrelated, for example, disregarding one deviant school, academic success had a correlation of .79 with students' behavior, and other correlations among outcomes were similar. In other words, a school that had a high degree of examination success also tended to have well-behaved students and lower than average delinquency.

Outcomes tended to be better in schools with a relatively large intake of able children, but this did not just mean that able children were better students all around, rather the whole school was affected by a substantial core of bright children. When allowance was made for family background and children's personal characteristics at intake, however, large variations among schools still remained. In fact, intake balance, that is, the relative proportion of students of high and low ability, did not significantly influence the school's functioning itself, which was assessed directly (see below). Among the outcomes, officially noted delinquency was affected most and behavior in school least by the children's family background and ability level.

School size is a characteristic that has sometimes been related to students' quality of behavior and achievement. In the United States it has been found that smaller schools tend to present fewer behavior problems, probably because in smaller schools offenses are more visible, students have a greater commitment to the school, and they are more involved in its activities (McPartland & McDill, 1976). However, in London the differences in outcome were not due to physical factors, such as size of school, age of buildings, or space available. That size of school did not play a role in differentiating outcomes may be due to the fact that this sample of schools came from a relatively homogeneous urban area and did not include any very small schools.

School Processes

What did play a part in the London schools was the school processes. Measures that denoted "school process" were items that depended on decisions by teachers and administration and included such areas as homework, total teaching time, teachers' classroom style and availability to students, and so forth. One school process that was strongly and positively related to *all* outcomes was the school's "academic emphasis," assessed, among other things, by whether or not homework was given, by the amount of use of the library, and by total teaching time.

The teachers' class management was an important factor. In particular, children's classroom behavior was much better when the teacher spent little time on extraneous activities, such as setting up equipment, and most time on the lesson content. (Goodlad [1984] also found that less time spent on preparatory activities and more on lesson content was conducive to student satisfaction with the school.) For class-oriented lessons (and most of those observed were), learning outcomes were better in classes where teachers directed attention to the class as a whole and did not spend too much time on personal and interpersonal concerns of individuals. These findings are corroborated by those of Brophy and Evertson (1976), who studied U.S. elementary schools. Since these observations apply to lessons that were addressed to the whole class, the findings do not mean that properly organized small-group or individualized instruction will be unproductive.

The disturbing effect of directing attention away from the lesson content also applies to interventions directed at maintaining discipline: A high rate of interventions of this kind was associated with more disruptive student behavior. It may well be, of course, that the disruptive behavior evoked the frequent interventions, but it is of interest that schools that had a high proportion of behavior problems in their intake did not necessarily engage in frequent disciplinary interventions. Where these occurred frequently, they ultimately were counterproductive. Although the amount of formal punishment in a school appeared to make little difference to the quality of student behavior, a high degree of physical punishment was marginally associated with worse behavior, a relationship that echoes findings for parental punishment (see Chapter 5). Praise and approval by teachers also had predictable effects in that they were related to better behavior.

Students will be more ready to accept the school's values concerning achievements and behavior when they feel part of the school and sense that they "belong." Certain factors seemed to contribute to this feeling. For instance, children's behavior was better when pleasant conditions existed in a well-cared-for school, and when teachers made themselves readily available for consultation by students. Also, outcomes were better the more teachers and students shared common activities, for example, school outings. Both academic and behavioral outcomes improved in proportion to the number of students who were able to hold official positions in a school, such as being class representative. This result is no doubt due to the fact that in these schools a larger number of students shared responsibility for the good functioning of the institution, although it is clear that they did not participate in major decision-making.

Thirty-nine of the "school process" measures, described above, had significant correlations with one or another of the outcomes (e.g., achievements or behavior). These process items were summed to form an overall school process score that tended to be more strongly correlated with outcome than were individual process variables. This finding suggests that the various procedures in the school act toward the same end and express a value system that produces an overall school process effect. In other words, schools are characterized by what Rutter and his colleagues call an "ethos."

In the United States, too, it has been found that despite the regularities of practice, schools differ ". . . in the ways the humans in them, individually and collectively, cope with these regularities and relate to one another"

TABLE 6.1. Prediction of examination results by student, background, and school variables.

Order of entry into equation	% of variance explained	Significance
1 Ability group at age 11	14.45	<.001
2 Parental occupation	0.10	NS[a]
3 Balance at intake on ability and occupational, ethnic, and behavioral factors	10.31	<.001
4 School process score	1.06	<.001

Total variance explained = 25.92%
(multiple $r = 0.51$)

Note. From *Fifteen Thousand Hours: Secondary Schools and Their Effects on Children* by M. Rutter, B. Maughan, P. Mortimore, and J. Ouston, 1979, London: Open Books. Copyright 1979 by M. Rutter et al. Reprinted by permission.
[a] NS = not significant.

(Goodlad, 1984, p. 267). From a survey of recent U.S. research, Brophy has also identified teaching processes similar to the above as important ingredients in school effectiveness. He concluded that student achievement is more assured when an intellectual climate and academic emphasis pervade the school. The studies showed that students achieve more when teachers use effective management strategies so that academic learning time is maximized and students are taken through the curriculum briskly, but in small steps that allow high rates of success (Brophy, 1986).

In Which Direction Do Effects Run?

The question may legitimately be asked whether it was the children who made the schools what they were, or whether the schools created the characteristics of their particular children. Children in the first place always influence teachers by their dispositions and ability level, but then teachers' actions will also affect children and in this way cycles of reciprocal reinforcement and effects are created. Can one conclude therefore from a nonexperimental study that schools have a causal effect?

At least a tentative conclusion can be drawn by assessing how schools influence children's achievement and behavior after statistically controlling for nonschool factors, an analysis which the London study carried out. This demonstrated that schools differed among themselves in student behavior and academic success, even after accounting for the students' differing abilities and their parents' occupation at intake. Moreover, Table 6.1 shows that over and above the students' characteristics and background at age 11 (the first three groups of variables), school processes (the fourth variable) significantly predicted behavior and achievement. Further, school processes were more strongly associated with achievement at the end of secondary school than at the beginning. So the answer to our question—and the important message of this study—is that schools do have an independent effect on their students.

RELATIONS TO OTHERS

Having discussed the school's effect on children's social responsibility, we will now discuss another of its effects, that on children's relations with others. It is generally agreed, particularly in America, that the ability to maintain good relations with other people is an important social skill that the school should develop and certainly should not impede. We shall briefly note the effects of the school in three areas relevant to the development of social skills: cooperation, interracial relations, and the advent of microcomputers.

As we noted earlier, when children cooperate with each other in groups, children's attitudes to others are more positive than under competitive conditions. Indeed, a cooperative learning environment has a beneficial impact on many prosocial behaviors, such as helping, the expression of mutual concerns, empathy with others, as well as on attitudes toward school, learning and interracial relations (Slavin, 1979). Therefore, everything else being equal, cooperative learning environments would be preferable to competitive environments because of their social impact.

But what is the effect of cooperative learning on students' achievement? Many studies have investigated this question, and their overall results have been analyzed by Slavin (1983). A crucial point is that "cooperative" learning can be practiced in a variety of forms, depending on how the dimensions of task organization and reward are combined. One form consists of group study, following which students are individually assessed and the individuals' scores are summed to form group scores. The group is then given recognition for its score, for example, in class newsletters or by grades. In another form the group is rewarded for a group product, for example, a common worksheet. In another version still commonly practiced, students study in small groups, but are rewarded individually for their own performance. A variation of all these forms has the task organization arranged so that specific tasks are assigned to different individuals within the group (Slavin, 1983).

The upshot of these investigations is that cooperative learning increases students' achievement more than individual learning does when two ingredients are present: first, the group should be rewarded as a group, and second, individuals must realize that their effort is necessary for the group to succeed, as when individual scores are summed to form group scores, that is, there must be individual accountability. Studying in groups by itself, on the other hand, is neither more nor less effective than individual study; it is the reward structure that is responsible for the effects of group study (Slavin, 1983).

From this account one realizes that cooperative learning hardly ever occurs in pristine purity. Scores and grades are, perhaps inevitably, embedded in the school's ecology, as feedback about performance and as incentive, and thus competitive comparisons are never absent. Under cooperative learning conditions children cooperate within teams, but teams compete against one another. Hence in all these learning environments cooperation goes hand in hand with competition: Schools only reflect the larger society in this respect.

Let us now turn to interracial relations, a form of interpersonal relations that are of great concern to many thoughtful people. Many have assumed that by letting the young of different races learn and play together at school, racial conflict and prejudice would be reduced in society generally. Hence it was hoped that the desegregation of schools would improve interethnic understanding, and make for greater equalization of the achievement levels between minority ethnic groups and the white majority. However, in general, these hopes were not fulfilled. Studies overall do not show an improvement in achievement by blacks, nor was their self-esteem raised. In fact, prior to desegregation the self-esteem of blacks who lived in a black environment was higher than that of whites, and it decreased in desegregated classrooms, probably because blacks were driven to make unfavorable comparisons between their own performance and that of their white classmates (Gerard, 1983).

The assumption that desegregation by itself would work to reduce interracial tensions was, no doubt, unrealistic and based on poor psychological theory. Allport (cited in Minuchin & Shapiro, 1983) has pointed out that simple contact between different groups may lead to greater hostility and an intensification of stereotypes, unless the contact is of longer duration and includes actively shared goals and activities. The conditions that might help desegregation to work toward the expected ends, were in fact often not present in the schools (Gerard, 1983). But when goals were shared actively, for example, when children cooperated in learning tasks in biracial teams, the number of cross-racial friendship choices did increase. Thus the promotion of interethnic cooperation seems to be the best means of improving interracial relations (Slavin, 1979). It is also true that since desegregation the number of interracial contacts and opportunities for cooperative efforts have increased dramatically compared with the previous era, particularly in the southern United States.

Another aspect of the school that will have an impact on relations with others is the advent of microcomputers. The increasing frequency and pervasiveness of microcomputers in classrooms will affect the social organization and the social climate within them. Some fear that it will create a generation of introverted isolate 9-year-old computer buffs. Others think that it will give rise to a great deal of very intricate interactions around one computer screen and to greater and more genuine cooperation than we have ever seen. The actual outcome may depend greatly on the nature of the materials made available to children. Some of this software, for instance, is heavily dependent on competitive games between partners (cf. Lepper, 1985). In any case, the new technology is likely to antiquate the methods and concepts of cooperative or individualized learning used hitherto.

Schools clearly act as socializing agents and affect the social and personal development of the students within them. Recent concern has swung back once again from what schools do for their students' good adjustment and personal relations to what schools do in the way of transmission of culture and knowledge. However, this primary goal, too, is inextricably bound up with the school as a living, social organism (Rutter et al., 1979; Sarason & Klaber, 1985). Schools may not be the most crucial influence on children's lives: Coleman and his colleagues (1966) and Jencks and his associates (1972) have demonstrated that far more variance in achievements at school and later on can be explained by family than by school influences. Yet, as Rutter et al. have shown, school is an environment that clearly makes a very important impact on students and one that is amenable to change.

Summary

As children grow older, make friends with peers and later enter school, they become members of social networks beyond the family. Peer relations are founded on equality, but they are not fundamentally different from relations with parents who may also favor reciprocal accommodation, and rely on the child's willing cooperation. Through peer relations children define their own role and status in relation to others of their generation and with their help they are better able to explore the world.

With age children spend more and more time with their peer group and less with their family. Their growing cognitive capacity enables them to communicate better and to see things from another's perspective, and this makes for greater complexity of social interactions. By age 9, children mention mutual sympathy and reciprocal helping and sharing of interests as the eseential core of friendship, and up to early adolescence children's friendship choices go mainly to same-sex partners.

Play is the chief context of social interactions among children at younger ages and it is also a medium for learning about the world. By involving others and rehearsing social situations in play, children develop social competence.

Friendly, prosocial, and responsive behavior and positive interactions demonstrate social competence, and these qualities naturally lead to popularity among peers. Unpopular children, on the other hand, are characterized by aggressive behavior and inept approaches to others. But unpopularity is also associated with lower intelligence and achievements. In newly formed groups children often quickly assume the same social status that they had in their own classrooms. Thus popularity is a characteristic that shows some stability across situations of similar kinds, as well as over time.

Children who play regularly on their own are often a cause of worry to parents and teachers. Yet not all solitary play is unhealthy, for example, playing with blocks or doing artwork alone, or simply in parallel with others, need have no negative connotations for social competence. Constant solitariness has some psychological costs in that isolates tend to lack social skills. But it is rejected children who are mainly at risk for later adjustment difficulties.

Girls generally prefer to form twosomes or threesomes, but boys tend to congregate in larger numbers, although such groups are unstable up to adolescence. In these groups some children emerge as leaders, others as followers. However, "social power" is not synonymous with aggression; rather it depends on the possession of abilities that further the group's goals, such as the ability to direct games or organize activities.

Conflict between peer values and societal and parental values appears to be mainly a problem in early adolescence and less so later on. Intense and exclusive associations with peer groups, however, lead to the adoption of antisocial values. But children who come from homes that have given them solid emotional support and exercised reasonable discipline, can often thread their own independent course between adult and peer influences. Many youngsters, indeed, choose their friends so that these two sources of influence do not clash.

The influence of the peer group differs across cultures. Particularly in the Soviet Union, peers act as reinforcers and transmitters of general cultural values and are deliberately used as such by society, much more so than is the case in Western countries.

The school exerts an important influence on children through its goals and norms as a social organization. For instance, emphasis on cooperation, rather than competition, among students generates better attitudes toward others, including members of different ethnic groups, and can also produce efficient learning. Very frequently in classrooms cooperation goes hand in hand with competition.

There is evidence that academic achievements and good personal development and social responsibility are not incompatible goals. The kind of school "ethos" that makes for both good academic and good social-behavioral outcomes includes such factors as an academic climate, teachers taking a personal interest in their students and sharing activities with them, teachers refraining from frequent disciplinary interventions, and the school letting students assume responsibility for some of its activities.

Part III The Content of Development

7
Social Cognition

The study of social cognition deals with people's knowledge and thinking about psychological events—those that occur in others as well as in themselves—and with their conceptions of social relationships. With respect to knowledge of others, the focus has been on such events as others' thoughts, feelings, intentions, and motivations, as well as perceptions of their personalities. In the realm of knowledge of self, attention has centered on the development of the individual's notion of himself as distinct from others, on the growth of an image of the self—the self-concept—and on self-esteem. In the realm of social relationships, issues such as concepts of friendship, fairness, and authority, as well as conceptions of society and government, have been addressed. Thus a typical question asked by a researcher in the area of developmental social cognition has something to do with the way in which knowledge of others, of the self, or of relations between others, develops. When do young children realize that theirs is not the only way of viewing reality and that others may see the same events or problems quite differently? At what age can children recognize mirror images of themselves? How early can children understand that even if they are feeling happy others may feel sad? At what point do children understand that someone who carries out an act in order to get a reward or to avoid a punishment may not find that act intrinsically enjoyable? When do they become interested in the achievements of others as a way of evaluating their own? How do notions of what a friend is change as children grow older?

Although cognition is not a social activity, thinking about psychological processes very frequently has implications for social behavior. How we act toward others is in part, at least, a function of what we think is going on in their heads. If we think that someone is in distress then we may try to help them. If we think that someone intentionally tripped us, we will respond much differently than if we think the harm was accidental. How we act toward others is also a function of what we think about ourselves. If we have low self-esteem we probably will not act assertively and with confidence. This is why social cognition is an important area of study for social developmentalists and why it rates a chapter of its own in a book devoted to development in the social domain.

Social cognitive activities have been alluded to in the first few chapters of this book, and they will appear in the chapters that follow. For example, perceptions of the intentions of aggressors affect reactions to those aggressors (Chapter 8), reasoning about moral behavior bears some relationship to actual moral behavior (Chapter 9), and beliefs about one's sexual identity promote the adoption of sex-typed behavior (Chapter 10). This chapter provides a formal introduction to and explication of some of the central issues of concern to those studying social cognition. It will focus primarily on thinking and its antecedents, but only rarely on the behavioral consequences of that thinking. Essentially, we shall stay lost in thought, a limitation to be corrected in subsequent chapters.

Origins of Interest in Social Cognition

The antecedents of modern-day concerns in social cognition lie mainly (and obviously) in two areas: cognitive developmental psychology and social psychology.

THE CONTRIBUTION OF COGNITIVE DEVELOPMENTAL THEORY

The area of social cognition owes a large debt to Piaget, even though thinking about the social world was not his foremost interest. Piaget ventured away from a concern with developing knowledge of the physical world and logical thinking to the realm of social knowledge, however, when he addressed himself to the origins of morality: From Piaget (1932) we learn about children's changing perceptions of the origins and modifiability of social rules and about increasing emphasis on intention and decreasing emphasis on outcome in judging the morality of a deed. The work on morality was extended by Kohlberg (1969) who also theorized about the role of social cognition in the development of sex-typed behavior (Kohlberg, 1966). In all this work emphasis was placed on the importance of declining egocentrism in the development of role-taking skills and the child's increasing information-processing capacities as they relate to more accurate knowledge of other people's psychological activities.

In North America in the 1960s, interest in all matters cognitive intensified. The area of social developmental psychology was just as affected by this state of affairs as any other. Piaget's ideas about cognitive development became a springboard for the work of those who felt that knowledge about social thinking was a necessary prerequisite for the understanding of social behavior—an antidote to the behavioral emphasis of social learning theory—and social cognition became a favored area of investigation.

THE CONTRIBUTION OF SOCIAL PSYCHOLOGY

Concern with the self and its development is seen in the work of Baldwin (1897), Cooley (1902), and Mead (1925). All of them spoke to the importance of social interaction with others as the basis for the development of notions of self. Cooley, for example, saw the role of others as analogous to a social mirror, and coined the term "reflected" or "looking-glass" self. The self is composed of our imagination of our appearance to others, our imagination of their judgment of our appearance, and the resulting feeling about self (pride, mortification, etc.). These sorts of ideas were not easily pursued in the environment of behaviorism that flourished during the 1940s and 1950s, however, and social psychologists turned their attentions to less internal constructions as they tried to understand group functioning and interpersonal influence.

With the resurgence of interest in cognition, however, social psychologists returned to this earlier interest. Much social psychological research has focused in recent years on the study of social cognition, particularly the perception of self and others. The data clearly indicate that people make judgments and inferences about themselves and about others. They do so for a very good reason: to impose order on their world and their social interactions with others, to gain thereby a feeling of control over that world, and to guide their behavior in social contexts (Heider, 1958; Kelley, 1972). Once a basic set of relationships had been established about adult social cognition, the obvious next step was to inquire about the course of development of these relationships.

The cognitive developmental and social psychological approaches to social cognition are quite different. For the social psychologist interested in thinking about psychological processes, the emphasis is on the motivation for this activity, and on its effect on the individual's behavior. The emphasis has been different for the cognitive developmentalist interested in thinking about psychological processes, and has focused on the structures of mind that are responsible for age changes in the depth and organization of thinking and that make thinking increasingly accurate. The social psychologist wants to know *why* people make judgments about others, whereas the cognitive developmental psychologist wants to know *how* they do it.

Do We Think in the Same Way About the Physical and Social Worlds?

Why should the study of social and nonsocial cognition be carried out as apparently separate enterprises? Is there any reason to suppose that they involve separate principles of understanding? Piaget saw no reason to separate them, and slipped easily from discussion of the one to discussion of the other. Those limitations in cognitive capacity that affect the young child's ability to understand the nonsocial world have been designated by cognitive developmental theorists as also affecting understanding of the social world (e.g., Decarie, 1965). Thus, before object permanence is acquired at the end of the sensorimotor period, the child cannot realize that objects (both physical and social) have an existence apart from his actions on them. This total egocentrism of infancy comes to an end with the acquisition of mental representation and the knowledge that others exist independently and are objects to be known. Only when there is an awareness of others can there be an awareness of a distinctive self, also waiting to be known. When the preoperational child cannot focus on more than one dimension of a problem at a time and cannot, therefore, mentally reverse logical operations (e.g., cannot realize that a ball of clay reshaped into a long, thin, quantity of clay contains the same amount of clay), he is unable to take the perspective of others. He does not have the cognitive ability to see that there could be two sides to an issue, or that the same phenomenon could be viewed in different ways by two different people. Preschoolers are still rather egocentric. Reality is as *they* perceive it. Obviously they are not going to be very adept at role-taking, that is, knowing about the thoughts, feelings, and perceptions of others. With development comes the ability to decenter and mentally transform events. What is still not possible is logical reasoning about abstract ideas that have no basis in reality. Concrete operational children are tied to real examples of real problems. In the social domain this represents itself, for example, in the preadolescent's inability to think beyond immediate individuals to society at large.

Flavell (1985) has pointed out a number of parallels between social and nonsocial cognition which suggest the usefulness of treating them as facets of the same intellectual processes. First, both social and nonsocial thinking proceed from surface appearance to a concern with the construction of an inferred underlying reality. Young children fail conservation tasks because they respond to their immediate impressions rather than thinking about the processes which have produced a different appearance but have not produced different quantities. In the realm of person perception they pay attention to external characteristics before they attend to internal psychological ones. Second, in both domains of thinking children attend initially to the most salient characteristics of an event. Preoperational children fail the conservation of liquid problem because they do not relate height to width. They also have difficulty in noticing subtle social cues and pay attention only to what people are doing now, without considering what might have led up to their actions or what they might do in the immediate future. Third, the world comes to be seen as invariant in both domains. Objects exist over time, and people have underlying identities that persist in the presence of variations of mood and behavior. Flavell also notes that children learn how to think quantitatively about both social and nonsocial phenomena. They learn how to measure physical events in a precise fashion whereas, in the social realm, they acquire notions of fairness that include the idea that rewards and punishments should be allotted in accord with the deservedness of the recipient. Next, he notes, thinking becomes more abstract and hypothetical in both areas of inquiry.

One of the more interesting aspects of cognition is that it never is without errors, even in the mature adult. Even adults, for example, fail to understand the basic principles of probabilistic reasoning (Kahneman, Slovic, & Tversky, 1982). Their deductive reasoning is influenced by the content of what they are reasoning about (Johnson-Laird, 1983). In the social arena our adult inferences about others are also subject to bias and distortion. People make the "fundamental attribution error"—they are particularly prone to attribute the cause of someone's behavior to internal traits and dispositions rather than to external circumstances (Jones & Nisbett, 1971), whereas they are more likely to attribute their own behavior to situational circumstances. "You yelled at me because you are aggressive. I yelled at you because I was tired and frustrated."

The most pervasive problem for young children making inferences about others, however, is their egocentrism—their inability to see that there are other points of view than their own. Flavell, in fact, notes that egocentrism never goes away. All our lives, he suggests, we are "at risk" for egocentric thinking, for the simple reason that our own point of view is more available to us than is the point of view of other people. Moreover, it is difficult for us, even when we are trying to understand someone else's perspective, to forget about how the same thing appears to us. A mother tries to help her son work out geometric proofs, but has great difficulty in suppressing her irritation at his obtuseness about matters that are very clear to her. Although she momentarily realizes how hard it is for him, she keeps forgetting as she becomes immersed in her explanations. Flavell notes that we are even egocentric when we think about ourselves at another point in time and place: When we are depressed it is sometimes difficult to think that happiness was ever possible or that it will ever be possible again.

DIFFERENCES BETWEEN THINKING ABOUT THE PHYSICAL AND SOCIAL WORLDS

Clearly people are different from physcial objects—differences which have led some (e.g., Gelman & Spelke, 1981; Glick 1978; Hoffman, 1981) to suggest that the cognitive structures underlying thinking about them may be different. People can move under their own energy, they grow and reproduce, they know, perceive, feel, learn, and think. Knowledge of their behavior must be based less on logic and more on probability because they respond to internal forces as well as the external forces acting on them. The meaning of their behavior depends on the relationship they have to the observer. People are also constantly changing as they age, which obviously creates problems for the realization of consistency and permanence.

Although these differences would suggest that the development of social cognition should lag behind cognition about the physical world, Hoffman suggests that certain characteristics of social cognition make its development easier. Because social cognition often occurs in a social context there is opportunity for feedback—children are more likely to find out if they have made a mistake than when they are dealing with nonresponsive physical objects. The similarity between social cognizers and the object of their cognitions should also promote greater accuracy—although egocentrism gets in the way at times, decisions based on it and on normatively based attributions are more apt to be correct than incorrect. Hoffman also underlines the importance of emotion in the development of knowledge of others. Early empathic reactions to others make children sensitive to arousal in others, facilitating the recognition of social cues and motivating them to understand cognitively the psychological condition of the other.

The merit of the argument that separate processes underlie social and nonsocial thinking is not clear to us. Flavell (1985) maintains that it would be unwise to exaggerate the role of domain-specific cognitive processes, noting that ". . . the head that thinks about the social world is the self-same head that thinks about the nonsocial world" (p. 122). Social and non-social cognition are different enough to warrant separate consideration. That does not mean, however, that we should automatically assume that they work in qualitatively different ways.

The Development of Social Cognition

Our survey of social cognition will begin with a look at the development of knowledge of the psychological processes of others, followed by consideration of knowledge of the self. This order of presentation is arbitrary. Sense of self does not develop before sense of other, or vice versa: Priority depends on the aspect of knowledge being considered (Harter, 1983). The third aspect of social cognition—concepts of relations among individuals—will not be discussed in this chapter but rather in other chapters according to the relevance of the content.

KNOWLEDGE OF OTHERS

Researchers have looked at the development of knowledge of others in a variety of areas, including knowledge of others' visual perceptions, thoughts, feelings, intentions, motivations, and personality. We will consider each in turn.

Visual Percepts

Of all the areas of social cognition, that of knowledge of how others perceive visual objects no doubt has the fewest social implications. On the other hand, it is important to consider this literature because of the impact it has had on the field of social developmental psychology.

The classic demonstration in the area was provided by Piaget and Inhelder (1956) when they showed young children papier mâché models of three mountains and asked them to select from a set of pictures how the mountains would look to someone sitting at different locations in the room. The younger subjects could not solve the task, and frequently suggested that how the display looked from their own vantage point was how it would look from anyone else's. It was not until they were 9 to 10 years of age— at the end of the preoperational period—that the children performed accurately. Hence the conclusion that young children are egocentric and therefore incapable of activities requiring the ability to take the other's point of view. Much of the subsequent research activity in social cognition has been directed at qualifying this conclusion.

Although they fail Piaget and Inhelder's relatively difficult task, younger children are not totally devoid of the ability to understand how the visual world looks to others. One way of comprehending their abilities is to break down the perspective-taking task into its various components. Flavell and his colleagues, for example, have described two developmental levels, or stages of knowledge, concerning visual percepts (Flavell, 1974; Masangkay, McCluskey, McIntyre, Sims-Knight, Vaughn, & Flavell, 1974). At Level 1 the child has acquired the important insight that he and another person do not necessarily see the same object. At Level 2 the child knows that the same object looks different depending on the spatial location from which it is viewed. The challenge in this stage is to become increasingly accurate about exactly how the object looks.

Level 1 is fully achieved by the age of 3 years (Lempers, Flavell, & Flavell, 1977). When 18-month-olds are asked to show someone a picture they "share" it by holding it flat or by standing beside the person they are showing it to. At 24 months they turn the picture around and move it toward the other person so that only that other person can see it. By 30 months children can hide an object from another person by putting the object behind a screen (Flavell, Shipstead, & Croft, 1978). Thus the ability to provide objects for someone else's viewing develops before the ability to hide them.

Level 2 abilities take much longer to develop, depending on the complexity of the task. Most 3-year-olds can show an experimenter how something looks to another person by arranging an array of objects so that it looks the same to them as it does to that other person (Borke, 1975; Fishbein, Lewis, & Keiffer, 1972). They have trouble, however, telling whether a picture of the side view of a turtle looks right-side-up or upside down to the experimenter (Masangkay et al., 1974). They become better and better at spatial perspective-taking tasks through adolescence (Shantz, 1983).

Shantz notes that the tasks used to test visual perspective-taking ability are measuring not only differentiation between the self and others (the egocentric aspect) but they are also measuring the child's knowledge of spatial relationships. Learning about the latter is a cognitive challenge that seems independent of the former. Children do not make predominantly egocentric errors on various perspective-taking tasks (in the sense of suggesting they believe others see things as they do), something which is to be expected given that even preschoolers demonstrate an appreciation of the fact that others have a different point of view. They are simply not sufficiently advanced in problem-solving capacities such as the use of spatial rules and mental rotation strategies to be totally expert at identifying what is being seen at other vantage points, especially when the problem is complex. This argument is strengthened by the fact that performance on spatial perspective-taking tasks is affected by a variety of factors such as number of objects in an array and their symmetry of placement, the complexity of the objects themselves, what response the child is required to perform (to select a picture, reconstruct the scene, or turn an array), and where the child is placed relative to the individual whose perspective is being identified.

Thoughts

People are not mind readers, a fact which is just as well for the smooth functioning of social interactions. We probably would not want others to know everything we were thinking about them, nor would we want to know all that they were thinking about us. On the other hand, some knowledge or idea of others' thoughts is very helpful in guiding social behavior.

Just as in the area of visual perspective-taking, it is difficult to say *when* it is that children develop the skill of understanding the thoughts of other people, or at what point advances are more marked. The skill increases with age, but the age at which proficiency is achieved depends, again, on the task being used to measure it (Shantz, 1983). As with visual perspective-taking tasks the challenge is two-fold: overcoming egocentrism and developing sophisticated social inferential skills that allow the individual to accurately know the thoughts of others *as well as* knowing that they may have different thoughts. Some tasks are more challenging than others.

Cognitions about thoughts have been assessed in a number of ways. One approach has been to find out if children think other people know something about events to which, in fact, only the children themselves have had access. "Privileged information" tasks have been designed, among others, by Flavell, Botkin, Fry, Wright, and Jarvis (1968) and Chandler (1973). In one study using the privileged-information format, 2- to 6-year-old children saw a film in which the audio portion contained much information. Then their mothers saw the film, but with the sound turned off. When questioned about what their mother might know, the younger children assumed her knowledge was the same as theirs. Between the ages of 4 and 6 years their performance was much improved as they came to realize that she had been deprived of relevant information (Mossler, Marvin, & Greenberg, 1976). Children as young as 4 years of age are also able to modify their descriptions of games depending on whether their audience is a 2 year-old or an adult (Shatz & Gelman, 1973). On other tasks of perspective-taking performance is not so good so early. One of these is Selman's test of social perspective-taking.

Selman's Model

Robert Selman (Selman, 1976; Selman & Byrne, 1974) has devised a cognitive developmental model of the stages of growth in children's understanding of the social perspective of others. He argues that there are qualitative changes in this ability that have both a structural aspect, that is, a change in the way in which relationships between the perspectives of self and other are conceptualized, and a content aspect, that is, a change in how personality development, motivation, and other aspects of social relations are seen. In a procedure typical of the cognitive developmental area, Selman presents stories to subjects in which two individuals are in conflict and questions them about what might be happening to participants in the dilemma. A young girl, for example, likes to climb trees but she falls one day and is asked by her father not to climb trees anymore. This does not present a problem until her friend's kitten is caught up in a tree and she is the only one who can get it down. The issue, then, is how this dilemma might be perceived by the girl, her father, and her friend.

The answers of respondents are organized into stages of role-taking. At Stage 0 (about ages 4 to 6 years) children cannot distinguish between their own interpretation of an action and what they believe is the correct perspective. There is no role-taking because there is no need seen for it. The underlying psychological characteristics of others are not inferred, that is, children in this stage do not realize that others have different psychological perspectives. Everything is seen from the girl's point of view. Stage 1 (about ages 6 to 8 years) occurs when children see that they and others can have different interpretations of the same social situation. However, neither perspective can be related. One or the other is correct, but the child does not see that one person might attempt to consider the view of the other. Others are seen to choose actions for personal reasons. In response to the question, "Do you think Holly's [the girl's] father would get angry if he found out she climbed the tree" one child answers, "If he didn't know why she climbed the tree, he would be angry. But if Holly tells him why she did it, he would realize she has a good reason" (Selman, 1976, p. 304).

In Stage 2 (8 to 10 years) comes the realization that no perspective is absolutely valid. The self can see how events appear to the other, and the other can see things from the perspective of the self. These reflections, however, can occur only sequentially—two perspectives cannot be considered at the same time. Thus we have the following exchange:

Question: Do you think Holly would climb the tree?

Answer: Yes. She knows her father will understand why she did it.

Question: What do you think Holly's father would want Holly to do? In this situation would he want her to go up and get the kitten or not?

Answer: No.

Question: Why not?

Answer: Because he would be changing his order, and he wouldn't be a good father if he changed his mind. The father may think breaking a promise is worse, but he'd understand that Holly thinks saving the kitten's life is more important.

Question: Would all fathers think this way?

Answer: No, it all depends on what they think is more important. (Selman, 1976, p. 305)

In Stage 3 (ages 10 to 12) this limitation is overcome: Viewpoints can be considered simultaneously both by the participants in the conflict as well as by a third party. Social facts and interpersonal relationships have a shared nature. In the realm of friendship, for example, a friend moves from being someone who does favors for you and is nice to you (Stage 2) to being a member of a dyad that has permanence and continuity. In response to a question about whether or not a friend should engage in an illegal act to save someone's life we have this answer:

He'd really have to be the top friend to do it. Because I mean, you put yourself in your friend's place and you think, "Would he do it for me?" I guess it would depend on what kind of friends they have been. If they each have proven their friendship to each other, then maybe he would do it. It all depends on how strong a relationship it is, how long they've been friends. (Selman, 1976, p. 306)

Selman's last stage—Stage 4—is reached at 12 to 15 years. Now the level of the dyad is raised to the level of the general social system. Respondents can take the group perspective and see, for example, that dilemmas should be resolved in a way that satisfies society at large. People's thoughts and actions are seen as the result of their developing beliefs, values, and attitudes which allow understanding about their past behavior and prediction about their future behavior.

Notice the close parallels between Selman's stages of social perspective-taking and Piaget's stages of cognitive development. At Selman's Stage 0 children are totally egocentric. At Stage 1 they cannot mentally reverse operations by putting themselves in the other's position and relating it to their own, just as they cannot mentally see the same amount of water being poured back and forth between two differently shaped containers. By Stage 4 they are thinking in abstract terms, just as adolescents in Piaget's formal operational period are able to move beyond concrete examples of objects to their abstract representations.

If there are true stages of social cognitive understanding, which involve qualitatively different ways of viewing the same phenomenon, then these stages must satisfy certain criteria for a stage model. They must occur in invariant order in a given individual, and no stage should be skipped by the individual. This kind of information, of course, can be obtained only in a longitudinal study. Gurucharri and Selman (1982) evaluated role-taking ability in boys at three points in time, the first two assessments separated by 2 years and the second and third assessments separated by 3 years. Two dilemmas were given to all the boys, one about a choice between going to a movie with a new friend or helping an old friend with a problem and the other about a team captain's conflict between his responsbility as captain and his loyalty toward his peers. The interpersonal understanding scores of their 41 subjects are depicted in Figure 7.1. There was considerable upward movement over the 5-year period in the boys' scores. No subject stayed at the same level, and only eight of them did not advance at least one full stage level over the 5-year period. Only one subject declined. The data strongly indicate, then, that there is a stage-like progression in this particular measure of perspective-taking ability.

The Recursive Nature of Thought

Flavell (1985) argues that one of the most distinctive properties of thought is its potentially recursive nature. Thoughts can repeatedly operate on themselves, thereby producing complex and interrelated outcomes. The individual can think about the thoughts of others which can include their thoughts of the thoughts of the individual. We see the initial appearance of this kind of recursive thinking in Selman's Stage 2 of social perspective-taking where individuals are able to see not only their own view but also how their own view looks to others.

Flavell et al. (1968) asked when it is that children spontaneously engage in recursive thinking. They presented subjects with two cups, one of which had a nickel glued to the bottom and the other of which had two nickels glued to the bottom. Subjects were to fool another player by removing the money from one of the cups. The other player, who knew this would be done, had to guess which cup still had money and got to keep the money if he was correct. The subject's task was to explain why the other player would select a particular cup. These explanations became more complicated as children grew older, as they hypothesized that the other player would try to anticipate their own thinking which was designed to deceive. Recursive thinking does not, in fact, occur that frequently—by the age of 16 years fewer than 50% of subjects were verbalizing recursive explanations. One who did verbalize used the following line of reasoning:

. . . he might feel that we, that we know that he thinks that we're going to pick this cup so therefore I think we should pick the dime cup, because I think he thinks, he thinks that we're going to pick the nickel cup, but then he knows that we, that we'll assume that he knows that, so we should pick the opposite cup. (Flavell et al., 1968, p. 47)

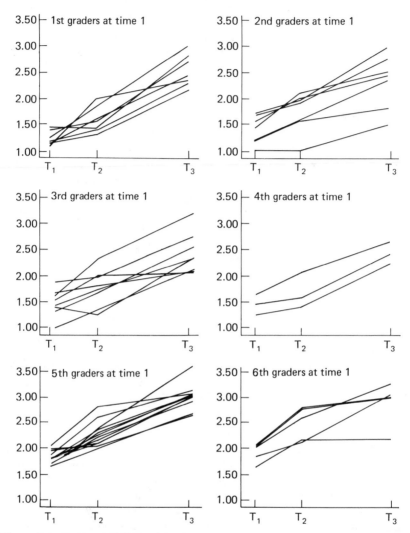

Figure 7.1. Each subject's overall quantitative interpersonal score (IUS) at each assessment by grade. From "The Development of Interpersonal Understanding During Childhood" by C. Gurucharri and R.L. Selman, 1982, *Child Development, 53*, 924–927. Reprinted by permission.

The spontaneous use of recursive thinking is also seen when children are asked to describe the personalities of their peers (Barenboim, 1977). Approximately 65% of 16-year-olds mentioned that their peers had thoughts about the thoughts of others.

At what point are children capable of *understanding* recursive thinking? This is the kind of question more frequently addressed by researchers interested in changing cognitive capacities. Miller, Kessel, & Flavell (1970) have documented improvements over time: Children up to the age of 11

FIGURE 7.2. One- and two-loop recursive thinking. From "A Test of Luria's Hypothesis Concerning the Development of Self-Regulation" by S.A. Miller et al., 1970, *Child Development, 41*, 613–623. Adapted by permission.

years are correct only about half the time in their ability to understand "one-loop" recursions, for example, "the boy is thinking that the girl is thinking of father." Correct understanding of "two-loop" recursions, for example, "the boy is thinking that the girl is thinking of the father thinking of the mother" are even rarer (about 35%). Representations of one-loop and two-loop recursive thinking appear in Figure 7.2—they are based on pictures that Miller et al. presented to their subjects. Two-loop recursive thinking does not strike us as something even mature adults would engage in very much, although they would no doubt be able to understand it.

Intentions

It is important to know whether or not a behavior has been intentionally produced. If someone accidentally treads on your toe your response will be very different than if you believe that he did so deliberately. Judgments of morality and responsibility depend on attributions of intentionality: Thus those who murder with intent merit greater punishment than those who kill accidentally. Because of the importance of intention in moral judgment, many investigators interested in moral development have asked at what age children begin to use considerations of intention when they are judging the goodness or badness of an act. These studies, however, will be considered in Chapter 9, for what we are concerned with in this chapter is not when information about intentionality is used but, rather, when it is that children are able to *understand* the concept of intentionality. Thus one may understand that something was done intentionally without *using* that information in assigning responsibility, just as one may understand recursive thinking without using it.

Children begin to distinguish between intentional and accidental events fairly early in life. The specific time at which this occurs, however, depends on the nature of the task presented to the child and the questions asked by the experimenter to elicit ideas about intentionality. King (1971), for example, asked young children to tell him what had happened and why in situations in which a boy tripped or ran into a tree versus ones in which the boy was pushed or tackled by another boy. Children at $4\frac{1}{2}$ years old did not distinguish in their responses between harm that occurred accidentally and that which occurred on purpose. The distinction appeared by the age of $5\frac{1}{2}$, and its accurate use was still increasing in subjects who were $8\frac{1}{2}$ years old. Berndt and Berndt (1975), on the other hand, specifically asked children if acts such as pushing a child who had a desired toy were done on purpose or not. With this more structured inquiry they found preschoolers were quite accurate at identifying intentional aggression but not as good at identifying accidental aggression (knocking over another child while running to get the desired toy). The latter ability improved with age, becoming nearly perfect by second grade if situations were described verbally and by fifth grade if they were presented visually.

Smith (1978) reports that adults and 6-year-olds are virtually identical in their judgments of intentionality. In Smith's study subjects saw an adult engage in an intentional or unintentional movement either when she was or was not looking and when the outcome was either desirable or not desirable, for example, knocking into a package of cookies while looking at a book, with the cookies ending up in a garbage pail. They were asked to say whether the adult had tried and wanted to obtain the outcome. Four-year-olds judged all acts as intentional, whereas 5-year-olds used only some of the evidence available to them, for example, they were inclined to judge acts as intentional if they eventuated in a positive outcome and unintentional if the outcome was negative. Smith also investigated the developing ability of young children to distinguish between voluntary acts such as walking and talking, involuntary acts such as sneezing and coughing, and "object-like" acts where an individual's movements are determined by external forces such as slipping on a rug and falling into a chair. In this case the 4-year-olds could tell that object-like acts are not intended, although they failed to differentiate voluntary and involuntary acts. By the age of 5, however, children were discriminating between the three sorts of events.

The ability to distinguish intentional from unintentional actions is pushed to an even earlier age in the work of Shultz (1980). Shultz reports that 3-year-olds knew that children who make mistakes when they are trying to say tongue twisters, or who pick up an incorrect item because they are wearing distorting glasses, do not mean to do these things. Even those who had not had personal experience with the tasks could still recognize lack of intentionality in a child who made errors. Thus we conclude once again that the ability to understand the psychological processes of others does not depend on the development of some unitary ability but is a function of the complexity of the situation and problem presented to the child.

Causes of Behavior

Knowing someone's intentions in performing an act aids in the assignment of responsibility for that act. Knowing what caused someone to perform the act is an additional aid in the assignment of responsibility. If people do things because they were forced to, they may be less responsible than if they appear to have been internally motivated. Inferring the causes of someone's behavior is also part of the larger task of imposing order on the world and trying to make events predictable. Thus answers to the question "Why did he do that?" enable us to blame or praise as well as to make informed guesses about future behavior.

Finding causes for people's behavior is the activity to which attribution theorists have paid particular attention. More than any other topic in developmental social cognition, this one owes its greatest debt to the theory and research of social psychologists. It is they who have spelled out the specific determinants of adult attributions and who have inspired, therefore, the obvious developmental question of how these determinants change over time. We begin, therefore, with a look at some of the basic tenets of attribution theory.

A number of models of the attribution process have been proposed (for example, Heider, 1958; Jones & Davis, 1965; Weiner, 1979). The one which has had the most substantial influence on developmental psychology is that of Kelley, (1967, 1973), probably because the phenomena it describes are most easily linked to the way in which the young child's cognitive capacities have been understood by developmental psychologists. Kelley begins with the straightforward notion that an effect is attributed to that possible cause with which, over time, it covaries. If two events happen in conjunction they are more likely to be seen as causally related than if they do not covary. He then goes on to distinguish two causes of behavior, internal (e.g., characteristics of the individual whose behavior is under scrutiny—his attitudes, values, etc.) and external (e.g., characteristics of the situation in which the individual is operating). In deciding whether the causes of behavior lie in the person or in the situation, people use three different types of information: distinctiveness (does the actor generally not behave that way to everyone), consensus (does everybody else behave the same way as the actor), and consistency (does the actor behave the same way all the time).

If a behavior is high in distinctiveness, consensus, and consistency it is attributed to causes external to the actor. If Fred is friendly only to Sara (high distinctiveness), if everyone is friendly to Sara (high consensus), and if Fred is always friendly to Sara (high consistency) then we must assume there is something about Sara that would elicit friendliness from anyone. On the other hand, if a behavior is low in distinctiveness, low in consensus, and high in consistency (Fred is friendly to everyone, not everyone is friendly to Sara, Fred is always friendly to Sara) then it will be attributed to internal causes. Fred is a friendly person. Events which do not occur consistently have to be attributed to transient circumstances.

By and large adults behave as Kelley says they should, with the following exceptions. They tend to see people as behaving for internal reasons, underemphasizing the role of situational factors (e.g., Snyder & Jones, 1974). This bias occurs because the behavior of actors is so salient (Jones & Nisbett, 1971), and also because observers may be unfamiliar with previous inconsistency in the actor's behavior (Mischel, 1968). Adults also tend not to use consensus information (Nisbett & Borgida, 1975), possibly because of a proneness to make their own assumptions about how others would behave rather than relying on the information they are given (Kassin, 1981).

The developmental question, of course, has to do with the age at which children begin to make causal inferences about behavior and when it is that they use consistency, distinctiveness, and consensus information. Because preoperational children can focus on only one element of a situation at a time, they should have difficulty in the kind of comparisons needed to utilize these cues. According to DiVitto and McArthur (1978) children as young as 5 and 6 years of age do use the covariation principle, although their attributions are somewhat limited. Distinctiveness and consistency cues are utilized, but only to make attributions about the actor's (as opposed to the target's) dispositions as causes of behavior. Consensus information is not used to make inferences about either the actor or the target. In concrete terms, first graders thought someone who consistently shared was kinder than someone who shared on only one occasion. Someone who shared with many others was seen to be kinder than someone who shared with only one person. More difficult, however, was the notion that someone with whom everybody shared was nicer than someone who was the target of very little sharing from others. By and large, 11-year-olds were able to use all three kinds of information in making attributions about both actors and targets.

The results of other studies have not been entirely consistent with Di-

Vitto and McArthur's. Both Shaklee (1976) and Ruble, Feldman, Higgins, and Karlovac (1979) note that 5-year-olds are capable of using consensus information. Ruble et al., for example, found that even 4-year-olds thought that actors who selected their favorite picture from among a collection of pictures liked the picture more if others disagreed with their choice than if they agreed. Ruble and Rholes (1983) suggest that the discrepant results of these studies may be due to the fact that Ruble et al. used videotaped stimuli, whereas DiVitto and McArthur used hypothetical stories—the former have been shown to facilitate the making of more mature judgments than the latter (Shultz & Butkowsky, 1977) presumably because videotaped stimuli make the acquisition of relevant information easier. They also suggest that differences in the response measures used in the two studies reduce their comparability. Once again, we note that the way in which social cognitive abilities are assessed determines the age at which children can demonstrate them.

The fact that children make mature judgments so early also gives rise to the issue of how their responses should be interpreted. Ruble and Rholes wonder if the data really indicate an emerging appreciation of the covariation principle, or whether subjects may simply be employing a rule that says more of a behavior (e.g., sharing) implies more of an attribute (e.g., kindness). Someone who always shares may be seen as kinder because he shares more, not because the behavior can be attributed to his inner state. Unfortunately, existing data do not allow us to untangle this confounding.

We have some idea of when children *can* use distinctiveness, consistency, and consensus cues. But when do they use them spontaneously? At what point do they actually look for consistencies in the behavior of others, use this information to make inferences about the characteristsic of others, and then behave in accord with the inferences that have been made? We do not know. As Ruble and Rholes observe, information provided by the experimenter in the laboratory situation is information which, in the naturalistic situation, children must seek out themselves by searching their memories for the needed data. The inability to focus on more than one episode of behavior at a time may make it difficult for young children to do so, even though they can apply the covariation principle (Flavell, 1977; Livesley & Bromley, 1973).

Multiply Determined Effects

Sometimes it is not a matter of choosing between two independent causes when making attributions about behavior, because some effects are multiply determined. Now the problem for the student of social cognition is one of determining how attributions are made when there are several possible causes operating. Someone who is generally argumentative will be more likely to get into trouble when provoked by a troublemaker than will someone who is more relaxed in such situations. In this case, however, the trouble is caused both by the disposition of the target person as well as by the provocations of the troublemaker. Kelley (1972, 1973) describes how adults use causal schemas that enable them to make quick attributional analyses in complex situations of this kind. The problem should be a difficult one for preoperational children because of the difficulty they have in considering two or more pieces of information simultaneously. The fact that causal schemas sometimes imply that two causes are negatively related makes the task an even more difficult one.

One schema used by adults is that of the *multiple sufficient cause*. It is a schema relevant to the situation in which there are two or more possible causes, each of which is sufficient to produce an effect. Sometimes employed in this situation is a *discounting principle* which says that when a plausible cause is present in a situation, then the role of another possible cause will be discounted. Usually an intrinsic cause will be discounted because the extrinsic cause is often more salient and more readily verifiable than the intrinsic cause. Studies suggest that children do not discount reliably until sometime between second and fourth grades. Thus, when told a story in which a child plays with a toy, either with or without some kind of external inducement to do so (the mother's command or her promise of a reward), fourth graders and adults ascribe greater desire for the toy to the child who played without inducement than to the child who played with it. The effect is even more pronounced when the extrinsic cause is a command rather than a reward. Kindergarteners do not discount, whereas second graders fall in between (Costanzo, Grumet, & Brehm, 1974; Karniol & Ross, 1976; Smith, 1975). In fact, not only do younger children fail to discount, they actually employ an additive principle in which they infer *greater* desire the more possible causes are present. This may be the case, however, because children who do not discount do not interpret rewards as bribes, still being at a point where associated adult sanctions play a role in evaluation of an act's goodness or badness. When the manipulative attempt of the actor is emphasized they then begin to discount (Karniol & Ross, 1979).

Children's use of the additive principle is significant because it indicates that they do have the capacity to make attributions even though those attributions are not like the attributions of adults. Ruble and Rholes suggest that, in addition to their failure to recognize manipulative attempts and to their respect for authority, young children's attributions are also limited by relatively small working memories. In situations where they do discount (e.g., Karniol & Ross, 1979) such behavior may be due to fewer demands placed on memory. Ease of task is also the explanation Ruble and Rholes offer for another puzzling demonstration of discounting, namely, Lepper, Greene, and Nisbett's (1973) observation that 3- and 4-year-old children lose interest in an intrinsically reinforcing activity when they are given material rewards for engaging in it. Ruble and Rholes point out that in the attribution paradigm subjects are asked to infer the toy preferences of a hypothetical child, whereas in Lepper et al.'s intrinsic motivation paradigm subjects simply choose whether or not to engage in an activity themselves. The latter is a much easier task, and it may therefore be easier for younger children to discount in that situation.

Another approach taken by adults when two or more plausible causes are present is to augment. Thus, if there is a plausible cause that could inhibit a behavior and a plausible cause that could facilitate it, then the role of the latter in producing the effect will be judged to be greater than if there had been no opposing force. Use of the *augmentation principle* has been well documented in adults and is seen to account for such phenomena as the sympathetic attitude held toward handicapped individuals (Scheier, Carver, Schultz, Glass, & Katz, 1978). It is not clear that young children use augmentation. Only by the age of 13 do subjects suggest that a boy must be more afraid of dogs if he is afraid of them even in the presence of his father as opposed to when he is alone (Shultz, Butkowsky, Pearce, & Shanfield, 1975). In a simpler situation, however, in which they used an animated film technique showing a triangle moving toward an object and overcoming an obstacle in the form of a square, Kassin and Lowe (1979) found that even 5-year-olds used the augmentation principle.

Kelley also proposed a *multiple necessary cause* schema to cover situations in which more than one causal event is necessary. Thus success at a difficult task takes both great effort and ability. The knowledge that more than one cause may be necessary to produce an event does not emerge until early adolescence (Erwin & Kuhn, 1979), although 9-year-olds are more willing to admit the possibility of multiple determination than are 5-year-olds. This finding parallels findings from the logical domain that not until adolescence can children recognize that two independent causes can simultaneously codetermine an outcome (Kuhn & Ho, 1977), an indication that logical operational constraints may limit reasoning ability in the social domain. We must, of course, allow for the possibility that simpler tasks could produce evidence of the use of this complex causal schema in younger children.

Do Children Make Causal Inferences Spontaneously?

Once again, the ability to make judgments about some aspect of the psychological functioning of others does not mean that these judgments occur spontaneously. It is certainly not clear that adults automatically make causal inferences about behavior even though they are able to do so in response to the questions of an experimenter (Bassili & Smith, 1986). The data, although not extensive, seem to suggest that spontaneous attempts to explain behavior observed in films and in acquaintances increase from middle childhood through early adolescence (Shantz, 1983).

Feelings

Now we turn to knowledge of other's feelings. This knowledge, coupled with the same or similar feeling in the observer, has been strongly implicated in the development of prosocial behavior, including sensitivity to others and to their need states.

Our discussion of feelings, then, will be twofold. It will deal with cognitions about the feelings of others and it will deal with emotional reactions to the feelings of others. The two events often occur together, although they can also occur separately. Thus Flavell (1985) speaks of three possible results when the individual is exposed to emotional arousal in others. The first he calls "noninferential empathy" where the expression of feelings triggers similar or related feelings in the observer but with no relevant social cognition. Noninferential empathy is seen very early. Flavell cites the observation that babies as young as 6 months are more likely to frown and cry when an adult is angry or sad than when the same adult is neutral or happy (Kreutzer & Charlesworth, 1973). It seems highly unlikely, however, that the baby has some mental representation of the adult's inner emotional state. The second possible outcome is "empathic inference"— an (appropriate) emotional response accompanied by some knowledge of the feeling state of the other. The third possiblity is "nonempathic inference"—knowledge of the other's feeling without any, or any relevant, feeling in the self. We can, for example, observe that another is in pain without feeling any emotion, or we might even feel happiness at his suffering. Nonempathic inference is frequently labelled affective perspective-taking, with the term "empathy" reserved for empathic inference. Flavell's distinction is useful, however, because it underlines the fact that empathic reactions can occur without accompanying cognitions, although this is more likely to be seen early in development.

Empathic and nonempathic inference have been assessed by providing children with pictures or slides depicting people in emotion-arousing situations, such as having a birthday party, losing a pet, or being lost themselves. Borke (1971, 1973) found that children as young as 4 years of age could correctly identify emotions in others by selecting the picture of an appropriate face. Happiness is most easily identified, with fear, sadness, and anger more accurately recognized between 4 and 7 years of age. In fact there are cultural differences in this ability, with Chinese middle-class children better than American children at identifying fear-provoking situations and more accurate at identifying sad situations than American children. To study the relation between empathic and nonempathic inference, Feshbach and Roe (1968) asked their 6- to 7-year-old subjects, "How do you feel?" and "How does the child in the story feel?" Not surprisingly, they found that children were likely to answer the second question correctly without necessarily reporting that they themselves were also experiencing the same emotion.

What does the child's ability to correctly identify an emotion in someone else really mean? Does it involve a genuine ability to take the other's point of view and behave in a nonegocentric fashion? Chandler and Greenspan (1972) argued that a correct response might more likely be due to the child's knowledge of how people generally feel in particular situations, their knowledge of how they themselves feel in similar situations, or a simple association between a specific situation and a specific emotion. The fact that children are better at identifying the emotions of people who are similar to them (Deutsch, 1975; Feshbach & Roe, 1968; Flapan, 1968; Rothenberg, 1970) could certainly be interpreted as an indication that knowledge of one's own reactions plays an important part in the identification of the reactions of others. Moreover, when children are shown pictures in which individuals display reactions that are inappropriate to the situation (e.g., a sad child at a birthday party, a boy who discovers his dog is missing and looks happy), they become worse with age at identifying the emotion (Iannotti, 1978; Kurdek & Rodgon, 1975). Such findings would also lead us to believe that children rely heavily on the situation and their knowledge of appropriate emotional responses to that situation in understanding the emotions being experienced by others. Being able to put one's self in the place of others appears to play a minor role in these studies.

The Development of Empathy

How do emotional reactions to happiness, sadness, anger, and so forth in others develop? Hoffman (1975a, 1982) has proposed a model that underlines how changes in both the cognitive and affective realms interact to promote this development in the domain of unpleasant emotions. According to the model, being able to experience emphathy depends on developmental changes in the cognitive differentiation of self and others. For children in the first year of life, self and other are fused and so distress in others is experienced as no different from emotion in the self. This is a rather primitive form of empathy, an unclear mixture of sensations from one's own body and the situation. It is what Flavell refers to as noninferential empathy. In a second stage, with the advent of rudimentary self-awareness, empathy is egocentric in the sense that children respond to others but do so with actions that may be more appropriate to the reduction of their own distress. Nevertheless, the beginnings of sympathetic distress—a feeling of concern for the other—can be seen at this point. We are now moving into the area of inferential empathy. By 2 or 3 years of age a third stage is entered. Elementary role-taking abilities have developed and altruistic attempts become more appropriate. Hoffman identifies a fourth stage of the cognitive sense of others which, he suggests, appears initially by later childhood and involves awareness of others as having experiences and identities beyond the immediate situation. Now empathy is distanced from the present and may reflect reactions to the general condition of others rather than to their immediate plight. Thus a rich man who has lost $50 should arouse less empathic distress than a poor man in the same plight.

Some of the most illuminating research on the development of reactions to distress in others has been carried out by Marian Radke-Yarrow, Carolyn Zahn-Waxler, and their colleagues. Their observations tie in very nicely with some of Hoffman's theoretical speculations. Because they have been most interested in relating empathic reactions in young children to these children's subsequent reactions (particularly altruistic reactions) we will reserve a detailed description of this work for Chapter 9. Let us just note here that the research—carried out with children between 10 and 30 months of age—does seem to indicate that very young children respond to distress in others by becoming distressed themselves. As they grow older they increasingly attempt to alleviate the distress of others by comforting them, attempting to elicit help from adults, and so on. If we make the highly likely inference that attempts to help others in distress reflect a cognitive awareness of their distress, then we may have an indication here of the progression from noninferential empathy to inferential empathy in reacting to distress in others. We know little, on the other hand, about the developmental path for reactions to positive emotions in others.

Personality

When we put together all our inferences about other people's intentions, thoughts, motivations, and feelings, along with their behavior, we sum it up in a description of what they are like. In this way we come to a conclusion about their personalities. What is to be gained by this activity of summing up? Once again, when people know something about a person's general characteristics or behavioral patterns then they have gained some more control over the world. It becomes easier for them to predict how others will respond to what they do, and to modify their own behavior so as to get others to behave in the ways they would like.

A number of investigators (e.g., Barenboim, 1977, 1981; Leahy, 1976; Livesley & Bromley, 1973; Peevers & Secord, 1973; Rosenbach, Crockett, & Wapner, 1973; Scarlett, Press, & Crockett, 1971) have looked at the development of children's descriptions of others. Usually, they have asked children to describe someone they know and whom they either like or dislike. (Rosenbach et al. asked children to describe someone they did not know.) Responses to this task have been impressively consistent and we can be fairly confident of the accuracy of the following observations. (Note, however, that if some investigators had used a different sort of task, the findings might not have been so consistent!) Young children, between the ages of 5 and 8 years, describe others in very concrete ways, referring to such things as their physical appearance, where they live, their family, and their possessions. Their descriptions are of peripheral and external events. Very often they are egocentric and self-referential (e.g., "She gives me nice presents. We play together.") Occasionally dispositional traits may be used in descriptions, but these are global, stereotyped, and evaluative (e.g., "He is mean"). This pattern of responding is especially striking given that it occurs even though children are specifically instructed not to describe the targets' physical characteristics such as how tall they are, or what sort of clothes they wear.

At about the age of 8 years, a quite dramatic and sudden shift takes place in the quality of descriptions of others. Children now begin to focus their descriptions more on traits and dispositions. They become more psychological in their approach. The dispositional statements are no longer global and stereotyped, but have become abstract and more precise in their meaning. External characteristics still appear, but now their function is the same as what we would expect in adult descriptions—they serve to underline or elaborate a more general point being made about internal characteristics. In this second phase of person description, however, there is still little integration. Traits are simply listed, and if contradictions appear they are not commented on or reconciled in any way. By adolescence descriptions have become quite sophisticated. They are organized, contradictions are discussed with attempts at explanation, and qualifications appear. The adolescent is sensitive to the complexities of personality.

Here are examples of the sorts of descriptions seen in these three stages, taken from Livesley and Bromley's (1973) study of the development of person perception in 320 English school children.

A girl, aged 7 years and 11 months, describes a woman she likes:

She is very nice because she gives my friends and me toffee. She lives by the main road. She has fair hair and she wears glasses. She is 47 years old. She has an anniversary today. She has been married since she was 21 years old. She sometimes gives us flowers. She has a very nice garden and house. We only go in the weekend and have a talk with her. (p. 214)

A boy, aged 10 years and 2 months, describes a girl he likes: "She is quite a kind girl . . . Her behavior is quite good most of the time but sometimes she is quite naughty and silly most of the time . . . " (p. 218).

And a boy, aged 15 years and 5 months, describes a man he dislikes:

He is very shy. He does not know how to answer snap questions. He does not talk very much. He always obeys his wife to the letter and never thinks for himself. He fusses over his wife but does not stay in all the time he is off work. There is a greater pull on him from his mother who is a hypochondriac. He very often visits her. (p. 222)

Theoretical Explanations

Now let us turn to the question of *why* children change in the way in which they describe the personality of others. The most obvious and most frequently cited explanation has to do with the young child's inability to reverse changes in objects and thus to integrate events that occur over time. Interestingly enough, it is at the age of 8 years—the point of demarcation between the preoperational and operational stages of cognitive functioning—that the most marked change in person description takes place, with a sudden change from external to internal attributions. It is at this point that children become less bound to concrete perceptual evidence and are able to decenter their thinking and integrate bits of information that have accumulated over time. The child can now look for underlying consistencies in behavior which enable him to put a label on the person exhibiting these separate examples of the same kind of behavior. Because his thinking is no longer static he can give up descriptions that are bound to specific situations in exchange for those requiring extrapolation from those situations. Indeed, there is evidence that children engage in behavioral comparisons (X runs faster than Y) with increasing frequency between the ages of 6 and 8 years, and that these then give way to an increased usage of psychological constructs (Barenboim, 1981).

Werner's organismic theory can also account for changes in person perception. According to Werner (1957) development proceeds from a state of relative globality and lack of differentiation to one of articulation and hierarchical organization and integration. Again, these notions fit in with the observed changes in person perception in which the number and complexity of constructs increases with age.

Quite a different sort of explanation from these two is proposed by Feldman (see Feldman & Ruble, 1981). Trained in the social psychological tradition, Feldman was inclined to look for external factors, rather than changes in cognitive ability, to explain the shift from external to dispositional description. Why do adults use trait labels when describing others? They do so in order to better understand and control their behavior. Perhaps, then, children fail to use trait labels because they have had less experience with the usefulness of being able to predict behavior and therefore do not perceive the importance of forming impressions of others. Without the motivation to achieve an in-depth understanding of someone else, children may take the easy way out by adopting a passive information-processing strategy which leads to a superficial description of the actor and his intentions.

To test this possibility Feldman showed 5- to 6-year-olds and 9- to 10-year-olds videotapes of children who were generous or stingy and physically coordinated or uncoordinated. She told half of her subjects that they would be playing games with the children in the videotape later on and that they would have to choose partners from among the videotape actors, whereas half were not given this information. Thus Feldman made it important for the first group of children to make inferences about the meaning of what they saw in the videotapes. When the children were subsequently asked to describe the children they had seen in the videotapes, those who were expecting to make a decision about future interactions made a greater proportion of abstract statements of an inferential nature

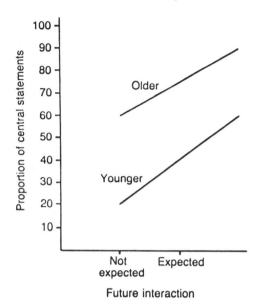

FIGURE 7.3. Proportion of central statements (abstract statements of an inferential nature, such as personality traits, motives, general habits) as a function of subject's age and expectation of interaction. From "The Development of Person Perception: Cognitive versus Social Factors" by N.S. Feldman and D.S. Ruble, 1981, in S.S. Brehm, S.M. Kassin, and F.X. Gibbons (Eds.), *Developmental Social Psychology* (pp. 191–206), New York: Oxford University Press. Reprinted by permission.

and also used more trait descriptions than did the children who were not expecting any future interaction. The latter tended to rely more on concrete descriptions of behavior. One child who was not expecting any future interaction said, "She was throwing balls into the bucket. She was throwing Frisbees at the target. She has dark hair. She went into another room." Another child, expecting interaction, reported, "She is good at games and she's probably nice. She tries very hard. I think she likes to play games."

A look at Figure 7.3, however, indicates that there were still age differences in the proportion of abstract, inferential statements made by the two groups of subjects. Regardless of expectations about future interactions, the younger children made fewer inferences than the older ones. Evidently, both changes in cognitive ability and changes in perceived need are playing a role in person perception.

THE SOURCES OF AGE-RELATED CHANGES IN SOCIAL COGNITION

Feldman's study brings us once more to the perennial issue of what are the sources of change in cognitive functioning. The Piagetian perspective places the emphasis on underlying cognitive operations or structures. To be sure, these are influenced by the child's experiences, but these experiences are viewed primarily in terms of their ability to facilitate or retard emerging structural changes. In our discussion of various aspects of social cognition it is clear that observed changes cannot all be accounted for by qualitative changes in cognitive functioning. Also to be considered are increasing efficiency in such cognitive functions as memory capacity. In addition, as children have more experience with different parts of complex tasks, these tasks become easier because their performance becomes routinized, and more mental resources can thereby be directed to other parts of the task (Case, 1978).

As well as considering changes internal to the child, we should not lose sight of the fact that events in the social environment are also playing a major part in the development of increasingly sophisticated social cognitive strategies and problem-solving. Alterations in parent socialization strategies, although possibly reflecting improving abilities to comprehend in the child, may also be producing those changes. Quite likely, as children grow older, parents tend to put more emphasis on intention in behavior and thus it is not surprising that children become better at differentiating between accidental and intentional outcomes. As children grow older concern for others may become a larger issue, and parenting strategies may include an increased emphasis on knowing about the thoughts, needs, and emotions of others.

A slightly different perspective on the role of environment is taken by Higgins and Parsons (1983) in their discussion of the characteristics of social-life phases as mediators of age-related changes in social cognition. They argue that many qualitative shifts in social development can be accounted for simply in terms of qualitative shifts in the child's social life. Entry to school, for example, brings with it a marked change in the social experience of the young child including activities and tasks participated in, position and roles, contacts and relationships, restrictions and privileges, and motives and concerns (see Chapter 6). As extracurricular activities increase, and as the form of education changes from public to high school, so too does the social life of the participant. With these changes come, inevitably, changes in how the social world is thought about. Small wonder that the preschooler appears to engage in little role-taking. He is the center of his own small world and his opportunities for role-taking are therefore very limited (although attendance at nursery school or day-care experience may broaden his horizons somewhat). When he reaches school, however, he takes on several new roles. He is still the son. But he is also now a student, as well as a member of a peer group, with the different demands that these positions place on him. He may also be a Boy Scout, a beginning student of the piano, and a T-ball player. With all these roles to juggle, the opportunity for understanding that there are different perspectives in life is greatly enhanced.

Higgins and Parsons provide some specific examples of how changes in social cognition may be accounted for by their social-life phases approach. We cite two of these. First, young children may not describe others in terms of personal traits because they have no need to do so. But as they are exposed to dramatically increasing numbers of different people when they reach school age they must resort to classifying them, a tendency increased by exposure to similar classification by authority figures. Second, Ruble et al. (1979) and Higgins and Bryant (1982) have observed a propensity in young children, when choosing a toy, to attribute its choice to the attractiveness of the object rather than to their own personal tastes. By the age of 9 years person attributions tend to outweigh attributions having to do with the quality of the object. Rather than reflecting a shift from focusing on concrete, observable features of the environment to more abstract, covert features, Higgins and Parsons suggest that the shift is a reflection of an increasing sense of personal responsibility and control over one's actions, which comes about with the dramatic increase from the preschool to the juvenile period in children's freedom to go places, do things, and be with people in the absence of constant adult supervision and direction. Of particular importance in this analysis is the emphasis on *dramatic* changes in environment as life settings shift abruptly. The transition from home to school is not gradual, but sudden. The changes it brings should, then, be sudden, not gradual. Rather than being attributed to a qualitative change in the way in which thinking is carried out, however, they are linked to external changes of a qualitative sort in the social world.

KNOWLEDGE OF SELF

Knowledge of self has, with a few exceptions, been considered quite independently of knowledge of others. Moreover, the way in which we come to know ourselves has received much less attention from researchers than has the way in which we come to know others. It has, however, been the object of a great deal of theorizing (see, for example, Harter, 1983). Most who have addressed the topic have concluded that there are two aspects to the self: self as subject and self as object. There is the knower (the "I")—an active agent that exists separately from other objects and people, and there is the perceived self (the "Me")—the object of the knower's attention (Harter, 1983). The latter has been considered in rather more detail than the former: Indeed, William James argued that there is no knower as such but, rather, a stream of consciousness, with the thoughts themselves being the thinker.

Knowledge of the self develops only in a social context. Children must learn that they are separate and different from others, both as knowers and as objects of knowledge. Once the realization of separateness occurs, the knower's task becomes one of deciding in what ways the self is similar and in what ways different from others. Much of this information is acquired from others, in their active evaluations and in the judgments which the child infers that they make, as well as in the comparison the child makes between himself and them.

This section of our chapter begins with a description of how the infant differentiates himself from other objects in the world and then comes to know himself as a physical entity. It then moves to a consideration of how the young child continues the process of differentiation, but with the focus now on the psychological rather than the physical dimension.

Development of Self During Infancy

Self as Subject

Ideas about the development of the self as knower, or subject, are mainly speculative. According to Freud, for example, the ego develops when the infant realizes that its mother does not automatically fulfill every need. Lewis and Brooks-Gunn (1979) suggest that the self as knower, or subject, develops through the contingent feedback provided by the external environment. The infant learns that his actions regularly produce reliable effects on the world. His hand opens and a rattle falls. He cries and mother comes. He emits a response and an adult imitates. Out of these experiences comes the realization of a separateness between self and others.

Self as Object

In studying knowledge of the self in infants, researchers have concerned themselves with only one dimension of that knowledge, namely visual recognition of that self, specifically, the face. The main reason for this has been the existence of some intriguing studies on visual self-recognition in primates, studies that have provided a model for infant studies. Intuitively, however, it does not seem farfetched to suggest the essence of self may somehow be contained in the general area of the face and, moreover, that knowledge of one's physical self may predate knowledge of one's psychological self.

Studies of self-recognition in animals were carried out by George Gallup (1977). Gallup was interested in how chimpanzees would react to their own mirror image and so he placed full-length mirrors in their cages. Initially the adult animals responded as though their reflection were another chimp, making threatening and conciliatory gestures. After 3 days, however, they started to use the mirrors to explore parts of their own bodies that they could not otherwise see. Then Gallup anaesthetized the animals and painted a bright red, odorless, nonirritating dye over one eye and on one ear. When they were returned to their cages and were once more exposed to mirrors the chimps immediately began active exploration of the marks— much more so than animals who had had no previous experience with mirrors. Gallup found that not all animals could recognize themselves in mirrors—monkeys, olive baboons, and gibbons failed to do so, regardless of age, even though they were capable of processing mirror images as evidenced by their ability to use a mirror to locate food out of their line of vision. Presumably only the more highly evolved of the great apes have a self-identity. If such a self-identity depends on experience with others, then animals reared in social isolation should not be able to recognize themselves in a mirror, possible because they have not had the opportunity to form the concept of a chimp face. This is exactly what Gallup found.

A number of investigators have seen in Gallup's technique a clever way of studying the emergence of self-identity in young children (e.g., Amsterdam, 1972; Bertenthal & Fischer, 1978; Lewis & Brooks-Gunn, 1979). In addition to using marks applied to the face (a dot of rouge placed surreptitiously by the mother on the baby's nose), they have used other tests as well. Babies have been dressed in vests to which rods have been attached with hats placed on top so that when the baby moved the hat moved; the hat, however, could only be seen in the mirror. They have lowered toys from the ceiling to slightly behind the baby's head so that the toy could only be seen in the mirror. In these latter two situations the assumption is that the infant has some knowledge of itself as an active, causal agent when it turns away from the mirror to see the real objects. Finally, older babies have been asked to label pictures and videotapes of themselves. This last task, of course, is different. It assesses recognition of one's physical features as opposed to recognition of one's self as an active agent. It also involves verbal ability.

By 15 months of age babies seem to have a strong sense of themselves as separate from others, and around this time are beginning to learn something about the nature of that self. Note that this visual knowledge of the physical self lags quite far behind knowledge of others. Indeed, as we have seen in our consideration of the attachment process, it is well before the end of the first year that infants can discriminate between different people in their environment.

Development of Self During Childhood

The mirror studies inform us about the emergence of a physical, external self. But what about the development of an internal, psychological one? Children must develop a self-concept, a summary statement of personal characteristics which is derived from past social experience and serves as a way of organizing that experience and as a guide to future behavior. Children must make cognitive generalizations about themselves, or develop what Markus (1980) terms "self-schemata." Kelly (1955) calls them "personal constructs" and differentiates between core constructs, which are central to one's identity, and peripheral constructs, which can be changed without any substantial modification of the core structure.

What, then, is the source of these constructs? Mead and other theorists of self emphasized the importance of the judgments others make of one in the development of the self-concept. According to them, children base their perceptions of themselves on how they believe others see them, an activity that requires the ability to take the perspective of others. Social comparison—comparing one's own abilities, proclivities, and actions with those of others—is another source of personal constructs or self-schemas. The importance of these two sources of information emerges in a study carried out by Bannister and Agnew (1976), who asked adults to think about how they first became aware of themselves as individuals when they were children. The adults recalled such events as being able to see someone who could not see them, as doing things their mother would not know about until they told her, and as being mocked by an adult for not being able to put together a radio that had been received for Christmas. Common to virtually all descriptions was the contrast between self and others that came through comparison with them or through a judgment by them. Without others, we reiterate, there can be no concept of self.

Developmental Characteristics of Self-Description

The same cognitive limitations and environmental conditions that affect the development of person perception also, not surprisingly, affect the development of self-perception. Several studies have shown that children's self-descriptions are initially based on external features such as activities, personal possessions, and physical features, and that with increasing age they become more internal by focusing more on traits and personality constructs. Again, the point of change seems to occur at about 8 years of age (Bannister & Agnew, 1976; Livesley & Bromley, 1973; Montemayor & Eisen, 1977). Also seen is a developmental shift from the all-or-none thinking of younger children to a more differentiated picture of the self. Harter (1982), for example, found that preschoolers denied that one can have two opposite emotions at once. If two feelings are experienced one must follow the other in time. By the age of 8 children recognize that two feelings of opposite valence can exist at the same time, but their targets must be different. Only by the age of 10 years do children recognize that one can have opposite feelings toward the same situation or person. We see a similar progression in Selman's stages of social-cognitive reasoning.

Although we have said that development of the self-concept depends on the making of distinctions between the self and others, it is also true that definitions of the self also include similarities between the self and some others. As children grow older, their self-concepts are extended to include the social roles they aspire to and the groups of which they are members (Maccoby, 1980). Indeed, as we age, the groups to which we belong and the roles we play increase in number. Our self-concept becomes more complex as we present different aspects of ourselves to different people. With some we are passive, with others aggressive, and with others still we present a demeanor of middle-of-the-road assertiveness.

Development of the Self-Concept: The Role of Social Comparison

By seeing how their behavior, values, and attitudes compare and contrast with those of others, children learn about themselves. In this comparison process they also engage in self-evaluative behavior. Thus they have more or less of something than do others and, to the extent that they put a value on that something, they may feel better or worse about themselves. An important question, then, is when children begin to engage in social comparison. Ruble (1983) points out that the point at which social comparison begins is a milestone in the self-socialization process, because the kinds of evaluations made of the self are bound to change dramatically once social comparison information is used. Indeed, once a self-concept has been established, that is, once children have defined their capacities and characteristics, then social comparison should be less important simply because comparison with others is more likely to be assimilated to schemas that are already formed.

Developmental changes in the use of social comparison information have been studied mainly in the domain of achievement. A number of investigators (Boggiano & Ruble, 1979; Ruble, Parsons, & Ross, 1976; Ruble, Boggiano, Feldman, & Loebl, 1980) have found that children do not utilize social comparison information until at least 7 years of age. Ruble et al. (1980), for example, asked children to play a ball game and manipulated their performance so that they were successful in hitting a target half the time—a result which made it difficult for the children to know how they had done in objective terms and enabled the experimenters to tell them they had done well or poorly in relation to other children. The experimenters then told the children they would play the game again, that they would be competing with other children, and that they would be able to win prizes if they did well and if they could make accurate estimates of how good their performance would be. The only way in which optimal outcomes could be achieved, then, was for the children to utilize information about the performance of others that the experimenters had made available to them. However, as we see in Table 7.1, it was only 9-year-olds whose predictions were affected by whether or not they had apparently succeeded or failed in comparison with others when they first played the game. Five- and 7-year-olds did not avail themselves of the information when making predictions about their future proficiency. This result was parallelled in the children's estimates of the certainty with which they thought they would beat others and in their estimates of their ability at the game. Ruble et al. report, as well, that the 9-year-olds made more references relevant to social comparison information in explaining their evaluations (e.g., "I must be pretty good because I beat all the others") than did the younger children.

Why do young children *not* use social comparison information? Apparently they are motivated to obtain information about the performance of others: Even 5-year-olds will push a button to find out how other children have done on a task (Ruble et al., 1976). Ruble (1983) proposes several possible reasons for children's failure to utilize information about the performance of others, all of which should sound familiar from our

TABLE 7.1. Mean predictions and certainty and ability ratings as a function of grade level and social-comparison condition.

	Condition		
Grade and dependent variable	Failure	Control	Success
Kindergarten			
Predictions	1.1	1.1	1.1
	(.74)	(.88)	(.88)
Certainty	2.9	2.8	3.0
	(.91)	(1.1)	(.85)
Ability	2.9	2.7	3.3
	(.88)	(.82)	(.48)
Second			
Predictions	0.5	1.0	0.7
	(.71)	(.67)	(.82)
Certainty	2.4	2.3	2.7
	(.63)	(.64)	(.50)
Ability	2.5	2.8	2.8
	(.71)	(.42)	(.63)
Fourth			
Predictions	0.4	1.1	1.7
	(.52)	(.32)	(.48)
Certainty	2.1	2.4	3.1
	(.55)	(.81)	(.37)
Ability	2.2	2.8	2.7
	(.63)	(.42)	(.48)

Note. The prediction measure ranges from 0 to 2, and the other measures range from 1 to 4. n = 10 per cell. Standard deviations are in parentheses. From "Developmental Analysis of the Role of Social Comparison in Self-Evaluation" by D.N. Ruble et al., 1980, *Developmental Psychology, 16,* 105–115. Reprinted by permission.

earlier discussions of why developmental changes in person perception take place. Young children think in concrete rather than abstract terms. Although they have information about the behavior of others, then, it may be difficult for them to realize the implications of this information for internal characteristics such as competence. Young children are less able to realize that behavior is stable, and hence they may not be able to use social comparison information to make judgments about future behavior. In fact, as Ruble points out, young children's skills are changing so rapidly that notions of stability may not be encouraged by the realities of their experience. Preschoolers *are* able to utilize social comparison information in making inferences about task difficulty for other children (Shaklee, 1976), and Ruble suggests that the lag for making inferences about the self may have two causes. First, it may reflect the young child's confusion of what it wants with what is real, a kind of egocentrism that decreases with age. Secondly, of course, it is easier for individuals to focus more on specific characteristics of the situation in which they are engaged and to avoid making generalizations about abilities and predispositions. With others the focus of attention is less likely to be on situational determinants. Finally, Ruble makes the quite plausible guess that increased use of social comparison information may also reflect an increased use by agents of socialization, as children grow older, of criteria involving comparison with the performance of others for the provision of positive reinforcement.

Development of the Self-Concept: The Role of Causal Attribution

People want to know why others do the things they do. It stands to reason that the same questioning attitude may exist with respect to things done by the self (Bem, 1972). Another mechanism that contributes to the formation of a self-concept, then, is the tendency for children to make attributions about their own behavior, either of an external or an internal nature. The process is illustrated by Smith, Gelfand, Hartmann, and Partlow (1979) who asked subjects to share some of their winnings from a game. In some cases the children were promised money if they complied, in some cases punishment if they did not comply, and in other cases no external pressure was applied. All children shared, but the reasons they gave for their generosity differed depending on the way the request had been made. As one would expect, children given external incentives in the form of reward or punishment attributed their sharing to that external coercion. Those who had not been so coerced were forced to see the cause of their sharing in some internal disposition. They shared "because they didn't want to be selfish" or "because they just liked to share." (The implications of this finding for socialization have been discussed in Chapter 5.)

Discussion of internal and external attribution in the context of self-knowledge brings us to a dimension of personality that has received substantial attention in the literature, namely, perceived locus of control. Some individuals have strong beliefs that they have power over their own lives, and that what happens to them is a result of their own actions. Others tend to see themselves as externally controlled, without power, manipulated by luck, fate, or other people (Rotter, 1954). One obvious candidate for differing self-perceptions of locus of control, then, is the tendency for children to make either external or internal attributions for their own actions. The child who is encouraged to do the former should be high in external control, the child encouraged to do the latter should be high in internal control. Parents no doubt play an important role in setting the conditions for these different attributions. Loeb (1975), for example, asked boys to build a tower out of blocks while their parents observed them. He found that parents who had boys with high internal locus of control allowed them to do the task largely by themselves, offering the occasional suggestion but never giving direct orders. Those of boys with high external locus of control behaved in the opposite way: They were more interfering and more inclined to tell their sons what to do. The study is correlational and more than one interpretation of the results is possible. But it makes good sense to suggest that intrusive parents promote external attributions in their children, whereas nonintrusive parents accomplish the opposite.

Development of the Self-Concept: The Role of Others

Loeb's study alerts us to the important role played by agents of socialization in the development of the self-concept. Cooley (1902) and Mead (1934) spoke of the "looking-glass self"—the concept of self arrived at through reflections of the way one is viewed by others. Parents react to their children's behavior with evaluative statements, expression of feelings, and reinforcement and punishment. That is their job. Such reactions also come from teachers, relatives, other adults, siblings, and peers. Out of all this input the child cannot help but receive messages about his abilities and penchants, as well as evaluations of those characteristics. It is the latter that contribute to individual differences in self-esteem, that is, whether the child has positive or negative feelings about himself.

By and large the evidence relevant to the role of others in the development of self-concept and self-esteem is indirect. We do know, however, that the labels adults attach to children have an effect on their subsequent behavior. Recall from Chapter 5 the study by Grusec & Redler (1980) in which children were gently induced to share their winnings from a game with needy children. After they had done so the experimenter commented on the behavior, suggesting that the children must have shared because they were kind and helpful people. The intervention was effective, leading the children to behave much more generously in a variety of situations than children who had not heard any comments, or who had simply been positively reinforced for their sharing ("that was a nice thing you did"). One explanation for the findings is that the experimenter's labeling had an effect on the child's self-concept, and that this mediated subsequent sharing. The fact that the labeling was effective for 8-year-olds but not for 5-year-olds strengthens this conclusion, because it should be only the 8-year-olds who would be able to use trait labels in organizing and directing their own behavior. Coopersmith (1967) reports that boys who are high in self-esteem have parents who show more approval, respect, appreciation, and affection than boys who are low in self-esteem. Presumably the self-concept of their sons, including its evaluative component, is a reflection of these parental behaviors.

If self-concept development is affected by the judgments of others it might be assumed that children who are particularly good at seeing the perspective of others should develop a more realistic self-concept. Leahy and Huard (1976) identified children's role-taking ability using a privileged information task. They then measured the discrepancy between their subject's "ideal self"—what they said they wished they were like, and their subject's "real self"—what they said they were like in reality. The children who were good at perspective-taking had a greater difference between their ideal and real selves, an indication that role-taking ability may be important in the development of understanding the difference between what one would like to be and what one really is.

Summary

This chapter focuses on children's thinking about the social world, and rarely on the behavioral consequences of that thinking. Our inquiries about social cognition have been influenced by cognitive developmental theory, which focuses on structures of mind responsible for age changes in the depth and organization of thinking about social events, and from social psychology, which focuses on the motivation for thinking about social matters. Although some have argued that different cognitive structures may underlie thinking about the social and physical worlds, there are marked similarities between the two domains which suggest they work in similar ways.

It has long been argued that children are egocentric, that is, they tend to attribute their own point of view to others. Piaget's classic demonstrations suggested that egocentrism, at least in the domain of visual perspective-taking, does not disappear until 9 to 10 years of age. Other demonstrations, however, indicate that children are much more sophisticated than originally was believed, and that tasks used to measure visual perspective-taking ability also differ in the problem-solving capacities they demand of subjects. Thus differences in the age at which visual perspective-taking ability appears to emerge may be in large part a function of the cognitive complexity of the task used to measure the ability. Measures of children's ability to understand the thoughts and intentions of others are also subject to the same concern: In these tasks children must not only know that others have different thoughts and intentions but they must also develop sophisticated inferential skills which allow them to know accurately what others are thinking and intending.

Attribution theorists have been particularly concerned with inferences people make about the causes of their own behavior and that of others. Developmental progressions can be traced in children's use of different principles for making attributions: Young children, for example, use an additive principle when inferring causation in which they assume greater desire to engage in an act when more possible causes are present. As they grow older, however, they begin to discount, that is, when a plausible cause for behavior is present then the importance of another possible cause will be denied. Again, different patterns in assignment of causality depend on the task used.

Very young children display noninferential empathy in which emotion in others triggers similar or related feelings in them, but without relevant social cognition. Later children are able to understand the feelings of others, either with or without experiencing these feelings. Descriptions of others are initially concrete and external, then focus on traits and dispositions, and finally become integrated. Explanations for these changes include changes in the structures underlying thinking, and increased need to categorize individuals in terms of central characteristics.

Knowledge of the self develops in a social context. Initially the infant must differentiate himself from other objects in the world. We do know that by about the age of 15 months babies can recognize themselves in mirrors. During early childhood the self-concept emerges, based on comparison of the self with others, on attributions—either external or internal —made about the causes of the self's own behavior, and on the evaluative judgments of others. As with descriptions of others, self-descriptions are initially based on external features and become more focused on internal traits and dispositions at about the age of 8 years.

8
The Development of Self-Control and the Problem of Aggression

Young children are impulsive, have difficulty carrying out long sequences of actions and working toward distant goals, find it hard to resist temptation, cannot alway control their emotions, and experience stress if they have to wait for exciting events. Often they cannot curb aggressive tendencies. When they are hungry they demand food, and when they are fatigued they cry. Temper tantrums are a common response to frustration.

Some individuals have particular difficulty in overcoming these early proclivities and learning to accommodate to the demands of society. Their behavior provides an exaggerated picture of the problems faced by any young child who is not yet proficient in the use of self-control behaviors necessary to cope with the demands of existence. To demonstrate what can happen when children have not acquired some of the basic lessons of self-control we borrow an example from the work of Redl and Wineman (1951). In the late 1940s they developed a residential treatment program for young boys whose parents or foster parents could no longer cope with their children's aggressive behavior. The following is a fairly typical instance of the difficulties therapists at Pioneer House faced:

After the group came home from school, Joe came into the office saying he wanted to talk with me about cigarettes. As soon as we sat down, he began in high crescendo and with various aggressive tactics to demand 10 cigarettes a day. I refused, reminding him of our deal calling for five cigarettes and how we had clarified that we would not increase the number of cigarettes beyond what he had originally claimed he "had to have" to avoid stealing or getting them illegally. Here he burst into tears and called me a string of anal obscene names, claiming I had promised him more. Without waiting for me to reply, he worked himself up to a veritable frenzy. "Yeah, you say you will give us whatever we want. Shit, bastards, fucker." I reminded him again that this was not what we had said. He could have five cigarettes because that was what he said he needed to begin with. He reacted by hurling threats at me about what he would do if I didn't give in. He would smoke behind my back. He would insult our cook so that she would leave. He would destroy my desk with tools from the workshop at night when I was asleep. I said, "You're very upset and angry. Maybe you're not used to being given a good deal. I understand how that can be. But we can't go any further on the number of cigarettes. Here, if you want your five, take them." Finally, after sitting there for a while, glaring at me, he got up and, slamming the door, went into the living room. There he sulked for 10 minutes, and then came back in, much more under control, and asked for his cigarettes, which I gave him. (Entry: 1/10/47, David Wineman; 1951, p. 224)

The important question for developmental psychologists is how individuals become capable of controlling and regulating their own behavior. Adults engage in self-denial and tolerate frustration; they resist temptation, delay gratification, and engage in self-punishment (e.g., by feeling guilty or depriving themselves of some form of pleasure) when they do not live up to their own expectations. How do they develop these abilities? What happened to Joe that he was so unable to cope with everyday frustrations that he had to be institutionalized?

The first part of this chapter will deal with issues of self-control and self-regulation—specifically with those processes involved in its emergence. Investigators interested in the problem have focused on a number of different behaviors that are manifestations of self-control and self-regulation. These include the ability to resist temptation, a phenomenon already considered in our discussion of socialization processes in Chapter 5. Psychologists also have studied the behavior of individuals who behave impulsively—who seem to have little control over their own actions and who are easily diverted from ongoing activities. Another aspect of self-control has been of particular interest to Walter Mischel and his associates who have considered the young child's ability to delay gratification, that is, to give up immediate rewards for the sake of larger, delayed rewards. Bandura and his colleagues have focused on the development of the ability to set standards of achievement for behavior and to engage in self-reward and self-punishment depending on whether or not those standards have been met. Finally, interest in children's emotional reactions to frustration has a long history, particularly as those reactions may lead to aggressive and hostile behavior on the part of the frustrated child.

Because aggression is a particularly serious form of lack of self-control the second half of the chapter will be devoted to its discussion. This discussion will include, however, all forms of aggression, and not just that which arises as a function of frustration or the blocking of goals.

Self-Control and Self-Regulatory Processes

SELF-CONTROL VERSUS SELF-REGULATION

Not infrequently, these terms are used interchangeably. Often, however, distinctions are made between them, although not always the same ones. We shall adopt Harter's (1983) usage: She describes self-regulation as the process whereby an individual maintains, in the absence of external direction or surveillance, a course of behavior designed to obtain a particular goal. Self-control, on the other hand, is used to describe the ability to inhibit a behavior, or to change the likelihood of its occurrence, when achievement of a goal is blocked. Most of our discussion will, in fact, center around self-control, since this is the area in which most research has been concentrated.

INTERNALIZATION OF VALUES AND LEARNING OF SKILLS

There are two processes involved in the development of self-control and self-regulation. First of all, the child must internalize a norm which stresses the value of self-control. Delay of gratification, impulse control, resistance to temptation, the setting of high standards of achievement, and nonaggressive reactions to frustration must come to be valued activities in and of themselves. Second, the skills which enable the child to adhere to internalized standards of behavior must be acquired. One may have come to value certain behaviors and still have difficulty displaying them. Thus physical fitness may be considered a desirable state of affairs in and of itself. The internalization of this value does not, however, make it all that easy to resist chocolate cake, jog, or stop smoking. "Will power" is not enough. But there *are* techniques to be learned that can make the execution of self-control and self-regulation much easier.

Internalization of Values

The internalization of values has been considered at length in Chapter 5. Reward, punishment, modeling the use of inductive reasoning, and a warm relationship with the socializing agent are all important for promoting acceptance of societal standards dealing with self-control.

A study by Bandura and Mischel (1965) demonstrates the major role of modeling and reasoning in the development of delay of gratification. They presented 9- and 10-year-old children with one of two models who, when given a choice between a less attractive reward they could have immediately or a more attractive reward for which they had to wait, consistently elected either the delayed or the immediate reward. The model who displayed delay of gratification chose wooden over plastic chess figures, for example, noting that they were of better quality and would last longer. The model who chose immediate gratification argued that chess figures are chess figures, that she could get some use out of them right away, and that you should make the most of each moment of life or it will pass you by. The models were effective: The first one influenced children to delay gratification and the second to choose immediate gratification. We know from the work of Bandura and his associates (e.g., Bandura, Grusec, & Menlove, 1967; Bandura & Kupers, 1964) that children will imitate models who deny themselves rewards unless they have achieved high levels of performance. It also has been demonstrated that models who adopt high standards of reward for themselves but encourage children to set more lenient standards for their own behavior influence children to accept lower standards than do those who both model and encourage high standards (Mischel & Liebert, 1966).

Rather than focus on the internalization of values related to self-control, however, thereby duplicating material already presented, we will devote our discussion of self-control and self-regulation to considering the skills that are necessary to implement them.

THE ACQUISITION OF SELF-CONTROL SKILLS

What skills must children learn in order to put into effect those values they have acquired through the process of internalization? How do they come to respond less quickly to their own demands and to behave in accord with the dictates of those around them?

Early Approaches

The question was first tackled by Freud. As we saw in Chapter 1, he proposed that development of the reality principle and secondary process thinking are necessary for the capacity to engage in self-control.

A rather different approach to the issue was taken by Skinner (1948) in his novel *Walden Two*. Skinner described several ways in which the children of Walden Two were taught to control their impulsive behavior. For example, those who had arrived home tired and hungry after a long walk were expecting supper. Instead of being given their meal, however, they were made to stand for 5 minutes in front of steaming bowls of soup. The children had been taught to accept such experiences as problems to be solved and that complaining would not work. One of the solutions they used was to distract themselves from the unpleasantness by joking and singing. Later, even this social device was not allowed. In this way they learned to cope with the frustration, showing little evidence of upset.

Neither Freud nor Skinner had much in the way of data to support their theory. For evidence we must turn to the Russian psychologist, A.R. Luria. Luria (1961, 1969) focused on the relationship between language and behavior, suggesting that children's behavior is initially regulated by the speech of others and subsequently by the child's own speech, with that control first exerted by overt and then by covert speech. In addition to this development in the *source* of control, Luria maintained that the *form* of control also changes as the child matures. At first the child responds only to the physical energy of speech sounds. Then speech exerts semantic control, with the child actually responding to its meaning. To use the Pavlovian terminology, the locus of control switches from the first to the second signal system.

Luria reached these conclusions after watching 3- to 5-year-old children who had been instructed to press a bulb when a green light came on and not to press it when a red light came on. He observed that the function of speech in controlling bulb-pressing changed over time. The youngest children performed best when they were silent. Slightly older children were helped by saying "squeeze" when the green light came on: They were hindered, however, by saying "don't squeeze" when they saw the red light, presumably because only the physical energy of the verbal command affected their behavior. Eventually children's behavior came to be controlled by the meaning of the self-instruction, so that overt verbalization subsequently could be replaced by covert verbalization.

Unfortunately, Luria's findings have not been replicated (e.g., Miller, Shelton, & Flavell, 1970). It is clear, however, that children do become better at inhibiting behavior as they grow older (Miller et al., 1970). Evidence that speech may initially exert physical rather than semantic control over behavior emerges from a study by Saltz, Campbell, and Skotko (1983) who report that 3- to 4-year-olds are less able to inhibit behavior when a command to do so is presented in a loud voice rather than a soft voice. Moreover, Luria's work has had a major impact on the formulations of researchers like Donald Meichenbaum who have been concerned with the role of verbal self-regulation in self-control. This work will be discussed below.

The Developmental Precursors of Self-Control

Beginning at birth, there are a number of changes that seem to relate directly to the ultimate development of self-control and self-regulation. Kopp (1982) is one of the few people who has addressed himself to these early precursors. She describes a series of phases through which the young child passes, with each phase involving a qualitative change in functioning that underlies a higher level of controlled behavior. Kopp avoids the more usual use of the term "stage" because she believes that there are gradual transitions between levels, rather than sharp boundaries. The phases of control are described in Table 8.1, along with the age at which they appear, their features, and, where relevant, their cognitive requirements. Note that self-control and self-regulation do not appear until 24 and 36 months of age, respectively. Nor is the progression complete, of course, by 36 months. What Table 8.1 does is to orient us to plausible early foundations on which self-control and self-regulation are based.

In the first phase—neurophysiological modulation—physiological mechanisms protect the young infant from stimulation that is too strong. For example, many stimuli are not processed simply because the central nervous system is incompletely developed. In addition, young infants have the means to protect themselves from excessive stimulation—as one illustration they soothe themselves by engaging in nonnutritive sucking so as to

TABLE 8.1. Views of early forms of self-initiated regulation.

Topic	Features	Developmental trends	Mediators
Control and system organization	Modulation of state of arousal, activation of early behaviors	Developmental agenda for late prenatal period to 3 months	Neurophysiological maturation, parent interactions and routines (feeding, sleeping, etc.)
Compliance	Responsivity to warning signals	Emergence 9–12 months	Bias toward social behavior, quality of mother-child relationship
Impulse control	Growth of ego, balance between action and verbalization	Emergence in the second year of life	Maturational factors (e.g., growth of language), availability of means for tension reduction, care-giver sensitivity to child's needs and attributes
Self-regulation	Interiorization of social conduct, motor inhibition	Reaction in the second year to adult commands, autoregulation to the child's own overt speech at 3–4 years, to covert speech (semantic meaning) at 6 years	Communicative and social interactions, growth of language and the directive function of speech
Self-regulation	Adoption of contingency rules that guide behavior irrespective of situational pressures	Preschool period onward	Cognitive processes (e.g., attentional strategies, plans, diversionary tactics); social class factors

Note. From "Antecedents of Self-Regulation: A Developmental Analysis" by C.B. Kopp, 1982, *Developmental Psychology, 18,* 199–204. Reprinted by permission.

reduce their own arousal levels and body movements. There are wide individual differences in how easily soothing takes place but we do not know as yet whether or not infants who are easily soothed develop into children who can easily exert control over their own behavior and who can regulate their actions with facility. The chief developmental burden is placed on maturation during this phase, although caretakers can assist in such ways as encouraging the development of routines.

The next phase, according to Kopp's analysis, is that of sensorimotor modulation. At this point infants can engage in voluntary motor behavior and can change that behavior in response to changes in the environment. They are able, for example, to reach out for a toy or to a person. Their behaviors reflect individual differences related to such temperamental predispositions as tempo and activity level (see Chapter 4). Responsive caretakers may also encourage the baby to engage in interactions with the environment. The baby learns to differentiate its own actions from those of others during this phase, an important landmark in the development of self, as we saw in Chapter 7.

Around the first year of life the phase of (external) control emerges. Now the child can comply with commands from the caretaker. The notion of intentionality in behavior becomes meaningful, behavior can be goal-directed, and children are consciously aware. They begin to walk and so new vistas are created, along with an increased awareness of body function. The self becomes increasingly differentiated from the rest of the world. As their memory improves children are able to recognize what their caretaker wants, and to inhibit their own behavior. Now the caretaker begins to assume a more important role in the development of these precursors of self-control, as the child is directed and encouraged in desired directions.

In the phase of self-control children are able to comply, to delay an act on request, and to behave as caretakers wish in the absence of external monitoring. These abilities are possible only because representational thought has developed, with the child able to use symbols to stand for objects and to recall images of absent objects and sustain those memories. By this time children have an understanding of their own continuing identity and can thus associate their own behavior with the demands of caretakers. Because of these abilities, or skills, it is now possible for the child, when motivated, to engage in self-control. Self-regulation, according to Kopp, is different merely in degree, not in kind, from self-control. It involves greater flexibility in adapting to changes.

What of the role of language in the development of self-control? According to Luria, as we have seen, speech cannot be used for self-regulation until the child is about 4 years of age. Kopp reports that children who develop language early are no different in amount of self-control from those whose language production skills develop later. She thus believes that Luria was correct in suggesting that early language does not influence self-control in any important way.

MECHANISMS OF SELF-CONTROL

Now we turn to the various mechanisms which help the young child to control his behavior. These include verbal self-regulation, the formulation of plans, and the employment of effective attentional strategies. Our discussion will center around their role in helping children to resist temptation and to delay gratification—the two forms of self-control that have received most attention from researchers.

Verbal Regulation

Mischel and Mischel (1977) interviewed children about the strategies they used to control their impulsiveness. Their interviews indicate that children know very well how important talking to themselves is in promoting control of their own behavior. Here is what one young girl told these investigators.

To control myself not to get so angry and mad and not hit so much I can just say (before I get into a fight), "Now, Joanie, do you want to get hurt? No! Do you want to get hit? No! Do you want to get into trouble? No!" So then, I don't hit as much 'cause I don't want to get hurt and everyone else is stronger than me. (p. 52)

Another subject, an 11-year-old, has mastered the progression from overt to covert verbalization:

If I had to teach a plan to someone who grew up in the jungle—like a plan to work on a project at 10 A.M. tomorrow—I'd tell him what to say to himself to make it easier at the start for him. Like if I do this *plan* [emphasized word] on time I'll get a reward and the teacher will like me and I'll be proud. But for myself, I know all that already so I don't have to say to myself—besides it would take too long to say and my mind doesn't have the time for all that, so I just remember that stuff about why I should do it real quick without saying—it's like a method I know already in math; once you have the method you don't have to say every little step. (p. 53)

The work of Meichenbaum has shed considerable light on the importance of people's speech to themselves, and the content of this speech, to their behavior. He has been particularly impressed with the way in which overt speech guides behavior, especially early in the course of mastery of a voluntary act. The beginning tennis player says, "Keep your eye on the ball," an overt self-verbalization that ceases when the task is mastered. Indeed, overt self-verbalization interferes with performance of a task that has been much practiced (Meichenbaum & Goodman, 1969).

Meichenbaum's early work was done with impulsive children—those who did poorly on the Matching Familiar Figures Test (Kagan, 1966). In this test children must choose from a selection of six similar items one that is identical to a standard picture. School-age children tend to respond to the task either slowly and with few errors ("reflective" children) or quickly and with many errors ("impulsive" children). Meichenbaum and his colleagues tried to train the impulsive children to become more reflective by modifying their self-verbalizations. They reasoned that inappropriate self-verbalizations were contributing at least in part to the problem in impulse control when they observed that the private speech of impulsive children tended to be immature, containing such things as word play and animal noises, whereas that of reflective children was more self-regulatory and more responsive to the demands of the situation in which the child found himself (Meichenbaum, 1971).

In their initial study (Meichenbaum & Goodman, 1971), impulsive children watched an adult complete a pencil and paper motor task in a nonimpulsive way while engaging in verbal behavior that included listing the requirements of the task, self-guidance, and self-reinforcement (e.g., "I have to go slowly. . . . Draw the line down, down, good. Good, I'm doing fine so far"). This was not enough, by itself, to influence the children's behavior for the better. As well, the children had to perform the task while being instructed by the adult, and finally engage in self-instruction at first overtly and then covertly. As a result of this training, performance on visual-motor tasks was much improved. The training procedure has been used effectively in other situations demanding self-control, including the modification of disruptive behavior in hyperactive children (Douglas, Parry, Martin, & Carson, 1976), and the production of improved cognitive functioning and prosocial behavior in aggressive boys (Camp, 1980).

What makes training in verbal self-regulation effective? McKinney (1973, cited by Meichenbaum, 1977) suggests that it accomplishes four things. It increases the distinctiveness of stimulus attributes of the situation, directs the child's attention to the relevant dimensions of the problem, assists the child in formulating a series of hypotheses about how to proceed with the task, and enables the child to maintain relevant information in short-term memory.

It is not, by the way, at all clear that self-instruction is always necessary in training self-control. Casey and Burton (1982), for example, discovered that under certain conditions self-instruction was no better than instruction by an experimenter. In their case they were trying to train children to be honest—not to add answers to a test paper when the children were grading it themselves. It may be that the nature of the task being taught is crucial in determining the necessity of control by self-verbalization.

Some Developmental Considerations

Although self-instructional training has a role in the guidance of at least some forms of self-control, the specific form the training must take changes as the child grows older (Carter, Patterson, & Quasebarth, 1979; Hartig & Kanfer, 1973; Toner & Smith, 1977; Miller, Weinstein, & Karniol, 1978). Thus preschoolers are better able to resist temptation and to delay gratification if they talk to themselves, and the content of the talk is irrelevant, unless it focuses directly on tempting objects. Saying, "I must not turn around and look at the toys," reciting "hickory-dickory-dock, the mouse ran up the clock," and counting are equally effective in increasing the ability of preschool children to resist distraction or the temptation to select an immediately available but less desirable prize. To speak directly about the attractive characteristics of a tempting object (e.g., to say, "The marshmallow is yummy"), however, is not helpful in promoting self-control. It appears, then, that self-instruction works for preschoolers because the effort required in doing so distracts them from temptation. When it focuses attention directly on the source of distraction, however, it become detrimental.

The story is different for older children. They also are adversely affected by focusing on the rewarding qualities of the tempting object. Often, however, they are quite able to resist temptation even without the aid of verbalization, possibly because they are generating their own self-instructions. Verbalizations that do facilitate self-control now have to be ones that are relevant to the temptation situation. If we assume that older children find it less effortful to talk to themselves than do younger children, then it makes sense that verbalization no longer serves the function of distraction. (Recall Luria's argument that the semantic content of speech becomes more important with age.) Relevant verbalizations may be useful because they help to focus attention on the task to be accomplished. This is an idea we now explore.

The Role of Attention

Most research in the area of attentional processes and self-control has been done by Walter Mischel and his colleagues. Where, they wondered, or in what way, should attention be focused in order to make self-denial more tolerable? They were particularly interested in children's ability to delay gratification, specifically, in how they come to defer immediate rewards for the sake of larger delayed rewards. As we have already seen, the kinds of things children say to themselves are important. But the things they think about during the delay period, the directions in which they turn their attention, are also important. Mischel (1974) notes that his concern with attention is not a new one. William James maintained that the essential characteristic of will, that is, of controlling one's own behavior and resisting immediate temptation, is to attend to the difficult situation. Freud noted that the very young infant's first attempts to deal with the problem of having to delay gratification involve the imagining of the desired object. If Freud and James were correct then the best way to learn self-control is to think about the delayed outcome. People on diets should think of the slimmer figure awaiting them.

In Mischel's studies children, usually preschoolers, are asked to indicate their preference for one of two rewards such as marshmallows and pretzels. They are then told that the reward they did not select, the less preferred reward, is one that they can have right away. They must wait, however, for the preferred reward: The experimenter will leave the room and they can have it only when he returns. Should they decide that they wish the less preferred reward they may summon the experimenter back to the room by pressing a buzzer at any time and this reward will then be theirs, but not the preferred one.

Some interesting facts about delay emerge from Mischel's studies. Being left alone *with* rewards produces less self-control than being left alone without them. Being told to think about "fun things" facilitates self-control relative to thinking about the rewards, and the ability to delay is greater when children see pictures of the rewards rather than the real things (Mischel & Ebbesen, 1970; Mischel, Ebbesen, & Zeiss, 1972; Mischel & Moore, 1973). These results suggest that distraction from thinking about temptation may be the key to delaying gratification. Remember that the children of "Walden Two" dealt with *their* delay problem by joking and singing. Mischel and Ebbesen noted similar behavior in their study on the part of the preschoolers who would sing, talk to themselves, and even fall asleep. Mischel reasoned that rewards have both informational and motivational properties, with the former reminding the child of the pleasant things that can ultimately be obtained and the latter serving merely to frustrate the child and make it more difficult to delay. Pictures have an informational function, while the actual physical presence of the rewards had too great a motivational impact.

It is clear, then, that the formulations of James and Freud have to be refined. Simply paying attention to the temptations one is trying to resist is not the answer. What matters is *how* one pays attention. Rather than focusing on the exciting qualities of the delayed reward, a situation that may produce frustration, one should focus on qualities of the reward that are less arousing. Now we are able to understand, of course, why it is that self-verbalizations that focus on the attractive qualities of tempting rewards are detrimental in producing resistance to temptation. There are conditions under which looking at and being instructed to think about rewards *can* be helpful—these occur when children have to work in order to get them (Patterson & Carter, 1979). Perhaps children who have to work think of the rewards in terms of how to obtain them rather than in terms of actually having them. If so, they thereby pay attention to achieving rather than consuming the goal.

Developmental Issues in the Deployment of Attention

The ability of children to effectively employ attention in a situation that demands self-control will depend, of course, on the development of a number of cognitive processes. They must be able to keep their attention diverted from the source of the temptation, remember what they are trying to do, engage in fantasy about distracting activities, imagine the outcome of their efforts, and perceive an end to goals that extend over time (Grusec & Mills, 1982). These processes are made possible by the development of representational thought: The ability to use thoughts and words to represent objects and events, and the capacity to think not only about the immediately perceivable but about events that are removed in space and time are required before effective self-control is possible.

When we discussed the role of verbal self-regulation in the facilitation of self-control we noted that older children may be using spontaneous self-instruction, but that younger children require training to do so. We now ask the same question about the deployment of attention in self-control. Mischel has demonstrated that preschoolers do not automatically engage in the appropriate attentional strategies that would better enable them to delay gratification. When do children know enough to do it by themselves? According to Yates and Mischel (1979) knowledge about and the use of attentional strategies develops about the same time as spontaneous verbal self-instruction. Children under the age of 7 years, when given the choice between looking at real objects or at symbolically presented ones while they waited, preferred the real objects—a counterproductive preference. Not only did the children have a preference for viewing the real objects but they also spent more time actually looking at them. Thus they made the process of delay much more difficult for themselves. Yates and Mischel then told the children to look at what they thought would most help them to delay: The children, erroneously, viewed real and symbolic objects about equal amounts of time.

Another strategy the children could have used would have been to look at objects that were irrelevant to their goal of delaying gratification. Again, however, children up to the age of about 7 years showed no inclination to view irrelevant more than relevant objects, even when instructed to choose the most helpful strategy. Knowledge of self-control strategies begins at about the age of 8 years and becomes increasingly sophisticated (Mischel & Mischel, 1977).

The Role of Expectation in the Acquisition of Self-Control Skills

As children grow better at self-instruction, the formulation of plans, and the employment of effective attentional strategies, they grow better at self-control. Self-control, then, is a form of achievement and, as with other achievement situations, efforts at self-control can result either in success or failure. The way in which individuals react to this success or failure affects their expectations about future effort—or their sense of self-efficacy—in self-control. This, in turn, influences the motivation to initiate and maintain future effort. Having the motivation to initiate and maintain the effort it takes to use self-control skills, then, is a major component of the ability to be self-controlled (Grusec & Mills, 1982; Karoly, 1982). No matter how capable children are of controlling themselves, they will not try very hard to do so if they believe their efforts will result in failure. Feelings of efficacy, then, should be as important in the domain of self-control as they are in other domains. An individual who reacts to frustration with aggression may believe this is the only response of which he is capable. Thus opportunities to practice and improve abilities may be lost.

The importance of expectation has been pointed out by Bugenthal,

Whalen, and Henker (1977). They identified two attributional styles in hyperactive boys, one in which the boys generally attributed success to luck and one in which they attributed it to effort. They then compared the effectiveness of two different training programs for self-control, one based on self-instruction and the other on a program in which social reinforcement was administered by the trainers. Children who were accustomed to making attributions of success to effort responded better to the self-instruction program than they did to the social reinforcement program, whereas the reverse was true for those who attributed success to luck. We see, then, that individuals who think they can control their own behavior are more responsive to attempts to get them to do just that, whereas those who feel externally controlled react better to external control. Bugenthal et al. also found that the children who were on medication did better after a social reinforcement intervention than they did after participation in the self-instruction program. If one assumes that children on medication do not perceive themselves as playing a role in the control of hyperactivity, then it makes good sense that they would not be very responsive to suggestions that they engage in self-instruction as a means of modifying their impulsive behavior. Harter (1983) suggests that verbal self-regulation of behavior may be effective because it is accompanied by the knowledge that one can have an effect on one's own behavior and that one is responsible for one's ensuing successes and failures. Such a procedure teaches the user that he is in control, or responsible.

SELF-CONTROL AS A PERSONALITY TRAIT

To this point we have been concerned with the situational and developmental determinants of self-control. Still to be addressed is the question of whether or not self-control can be considered a personality variable, a trait which guides behavior across situations and over time. Are some individuals more self-controlled than others? Do some people tolerate frustration, resist temptation, and delay gratification more easily than others? Jeanne and Jack Block have argued that they do. The Blocks have used the term "ego control" to refer to the kinds of activities we have been discussing in this chapter. They have been influenced in their thinking by both psychoanalytic theory and Kurt Lewin's field theory. In psychoanalytic theory, as already noted, ego control finds its origins in the structures that are hypothesized to develop when the young child must deal with the dictates of reality. Thus the reality principle demands that satisfaction be postponed and that discomfort be temporarily suffered in order ultimately to achieve gratification. Ego control also emerges as a concept in Lewin's description of the psychological system. He speaks in terms of needs separated from each other by boundaries that have different permeabilities in different individuals. When the boundaries are very permeable tension spills from one psychological system into the other. When they are impermeable the systems are isolated or compartmentalized. Overcontrolled individuals, then, are those with impermeable boundaries; they are the individuals who habitually delay gratification, inhibit their emotions, and control their impulses. Undercontrollers, who have highly permeable boundaries, are just the opposite.

Longitudinal studies (Block, 1971; Block & Block, 1980) have demonstrated the existence of a trait or enduring characteristic of ego control. Using a variety of methodologies and assessment techniques including observation, self-report, and responses to standardized tests, these investigators have provided impressive evidence for consistency in ego control, that is, in ability to delay gratification, control impulses, and to inhibit impulsivity, over time. This consistency holds for males and females, with assessments having been made at the ages of 3, 4, 5, and 7 years.

In addition to identifying a trait of ego control, Block (1971) has investigated its antecedents. Genetic and constitutional factors may be important. As well, however, clear relationships between the presence or absence of ego-control and parent socialization practices have been found. Overcontrolled adults come from families that emphasize structure, order, and conservative values. Undercontrolled adults come from conflict-ridden homes where parents have discrepant values. Parents neglect their teaching roles, place fewer demands for achievement on the child, and make fewer demands for responsible behavior.

Aggression

Anger in response to frustration poses a problem in self-control. A not infrequent response to that anger is aggression. But not all aggression is a product of frustration. Some aggression can be instrumental in nature, motivated not by anger but by the desire to obtain a goal such as power, status, or the acquisition of attractive resources. An attempt to capture this distinction is evident in efforts people have made to differentiate hostile aggression—aggression whose primary goal is the inflicting of injury, and instrumental aggression—aggression whose goal is not to injure but to achieve some other end, such as obtaining an object or gaining territory (see Feshbach, 1970). Others (e.g., Rule & Nesdale, 1976), concerned that aggression that appears hostile may sometimes actually have instrumental components, such as gaining respect from others, have distinguished between angry and nonangry aggression. Whatever the labels one chooses to use, it is clear that there are varieties of aggression. We turn now to a consideration of these varieties, as well as to a more detailed consideration of the behavior, which has been specifically the focus of much theorizing and research. The issue of sex differences in aggression is left to Chapter 10.

DEFINING AGGRESSION

What is aggression? As is true of most social behaviors, the range of possible definitions is great, and knowledge of how investigators have struggled to arrive at a satisfactory definition is informative.

One of the more popular definitions of aggression was provided by Dollard, Doob, Miller, Mowrer, and Sears (1939) in an influential monograph entitled *Frustration and Aggression.* They defined aggression as behavior whose goal was injury of the person toward whom it was directed. Note that a behavior could not be aggressive unless the actor had intended that it cause harm. But it was this notion of intention that created problems, because it meant that aggression involved more than just an observable act or collection of acts. The definition requires that inferences be made about events preceding the act. Yet these inferences are frequently based on the act itself, and so this definitional approach raises questions about the meaningfulness of assigning intention independent status (Bandura & Walters, 1963). Often it also is difficult to make a reliable decision about someone's intentions when they are not publicly observable. If a child on the playground is engaged in a vigorous game and hits a playmate, was the action intentional, or was it an accidental by-product of his activity?

Another approach to the definition of aggression involves consideration, not of the antecedents of the behavior, but of its outcome. To Buss (1961), for example, aggression involves the delivery of a noxious stimulus in an interpersonal context. But now we are faced with the difficulty that in many situations the delivery of noxious stimuli would not be considered aggressive by anyone. Dentists hurt their patients and parents discipline their children, most frequently in an attempt to help. Also, this approach to definition fails to take into account the situation where an injury is accidental.

Probably the most useful approach to the definitional problem is one that realizes that constructs like aggression (as well as dependency, attachment, morality, altruism, and so on) cannot be considered solely in terms of their objective, observable properties. They involve social judgements by observers. Bandura (1979) argues that an adequate understanding of what aggression is will be possible only when we understand why people label some behaviors as aggressive and others as not. A host of factors determine these judgements, including not only the perceived intention of the actor but the form, intensity, and consequences of the response, the role and status of both the actor and the recipient of the injury, and the values of the labeler. For Bandura, then, aggression is an injurious behavior that is socially defined as aggressive depending on a number of factors that reside both in the judge of the behavior as well as the performer of the behavior.

THE "PROBLEM" OF AGGRESSION

One thinks of aggression as a disturbing characteristic of human nature. The child's aggressive tendencies must be redirected in socially acceptable directions. Self-control must be learned and hostile behavior suppressed. In some of his theoretical formulations Freud saw aggression as the consequence of an instinct for destruction both of the self and of others (Freud, 1959). Indeed, in the second half of the 20th century we are all too aware that our frequent belligerent response to international conflict has come dangerously close to spelling an end for the human race. But if aggression has no redeeming merits why, then, does it exist?

It is this kind of question to which ethological and sociobiological theories provide a ready answer. Aggression among members of the same species is ubiquitous because it is functional for personal and social adaptation. It serves to transmit the genes of the successful aggressor to the next generation. For males aggressive behavior facilitates mate selection so that the most "fit" have easiest access to females for reproductive purposes. As well, aggression helps to distribute population optimally and establish social structures to diminish the need for continued conflict, which in the end would be counterproductive. For females aggression becomes an important mechanism for protecting offspring, particularly while they are still dependent. Nor should one forget that aggression works quite well as a way of inhibiting the undesirable behavior of others.

Just because aggression is functional, however, does not mean that it is inevitable. Nor does it mean that it is not amenable to intervention and modification through socialization experiences. Cairns (1986) notes that complex social behaviors like aggression need to be especially amenable to change not only through the course of individual development but through evolutionary mechanisms as well. It would be disastrous if species could not experience rapid evolutionary change in social behavior and organization when changes in the environment required them. Indeed, attempts to selectively breed for social behaviors are habitually successful (Fuller & Thompson, 1978). Genetic effects on aggressive behavior, achieved through breeding, are rapid and robust, appearing in full force usually by three generations and often after a single generation. The same social patterns that appear to be so responsive to genetic manipulation are also exceedingly responsive to the effects of experience. Thus aggression is highly sensitive both to phylogenetic as well as to ontogenetic pressures (Cairns, MacCombie, & Hood, 1983).

HISTORICAL AND THEORETICAL APPROACHES TO THE STUDY OF AGGRESSION

Different theoretical approaches to the understanding of aggression have directed its study very closely. A consideration of these approaches, then, provides at the same time a historical survey of research in the field. In none of these approaches, by the way, is the conceptualization of aggression at all developmental in nature. The theories were designed to explain aggression with little or no thought given to changes over time.

Psychoanalytic Theory

Originally Freud postulated two groups of instincts: sexual and a mixture of self-preservative actions, cognitive functions, and moral restrictions. These were not adequate, however, to explain satisfactorily such human characteristics as sadism, masochism, and self-destructive acts. In *Beyond the Pleasure Principle*, Freud therefore proposed two new instincts, Eros and Thanatos, the former including all life-enhancing and constructive drives and the latter all tendencies toward aggression and self-destruction. The aim of the death instinct, or Thanatos, which Freud linked to biological processes, was the cessation of stimulation. But life-preserving forces block the primary self-direction of destructive forces and lead them to be manifested outwardly, in the form of aggression toward others. Aggression then, which was viewed as a drive, was thought of as the death wish turned toward others. (Such a conceptualization currently has little support even among psychoanalytic theorists.)

The Frustration-Aggression Hypothesis

In his earlier thinking Freud had treated aggression not as an instinct, but as a response to frustration and pain (Freud, 1925). It was this earlier formulation on which the influential frustration-aggression hypothesis was modeled (Dollard et al., 1939). In their monograph these researchers offered the first systematic treatment by experimental psychologists of the phenomenon of aggression, with a combination of psychoanalytic and learning theory principles as their guide. According to Dollard et al. aggression is always a consequence of frustration and frustration always leads to aggression.

This strong statement of the hypothesis, however, was the object of criticism. It was pointed out that other events than frustration, such as the intrusion of a stranger into the group, could produce aggression (Durbin & Bowlby, 1939). We know, of course, that simply exposing children to aggressive models increases the probability that they will display aggressive behavior. It was also noted that aggression was only one possible response to frustration, with other reactions such as regression and increased attempts at problem-solving also possible. Thus Barker, Dembo, and Lewin (1941) demonstrated that when preschoolers were frustrated by having a barrier placed between themselves and attractive toys some responded with pushing, hitting, and kicking, but others regressed—they cried, whimpered, and gave up trying to get at the toys. It was these sorts of criticisms that were responsible for a revision of the hypothesis (Miller, 1941; Sears, 1941). The frustration-aggression hypothesis now held that aggression was but one possible response to frustration, albeit the dominant one—a dominance established at an early age. Other responses could be strengthened or weakened as a result of learning experiences.

Displacement and Catharsis

The frustration-aggression hypothesis assumed that aggression elicited by frustration must be reduced, from which two important ideas emerged. One was the notion of displacement, the idea that if aggression could not be directed at the source of frustration because of fear of punishment, then it would be directed at a similar but less threatening object. Here we have an explanation for why the worker who has been angered by his employer returns home at night to aggress against his spouse, child, or dog, with the object of aggression depending on the extent of his fear of retaliation or guilt and the extent of similarity to the employer.

The second notion was that of catharsis, the idea that all acts of aggression, regardless of their relationship to the source of frustration, reduce aggressive motivation. The catharsis hypothesis assumes that reduction of aggression occurs regardless of whether aggression is witnessed by or performed by the individual himself. The first form of the hypothesis leads to the belief that people who watch boxing matches or aggressive television programming will be consequently drained of their aggression: This is a position we shall examine closely when we consider the effects of television violence on viewer aggression later in this chapter. It should come as no surprise, however, that there is virtually no evidence that such activity reduces aggression. Indeed, just the opposite may be the case.

Tests of the second form of the catharsis hypothesis, that direct aggression reduces subsequent aggression, have produced more mixed results. Aggressive play does not reduce subsequent aggression in young children, but increases it (e.g., Feshbach, 1956; Turner & Goldsmith, 1976). On the other hand, adults given the opportunity to aggress against someone who has insulted them behave less aggressively later on (by, for example, administering fewer electric shocks for mistakes made on a learning task) than adults who have not had the opportunity to aggress (Konecni, 1975; Konecni & Ebbesen, 1976). Berkowitz (1973) has suggested, however, that this kind of result need not be taken as evidence for catharsis but could be explained by the arousal of guilt after initial retaliation that then mitigates against further aggression. Alternatively, reduced aggression after inital retaliation may result from the possibility that retaliation distracts the actor from rumination about the original frustration (Bandura, 1973). In any case, one need not resort to explanations that involve the assumption of an aggressive drive.

Social Learning Theory

In *Adolescent Aggression* (1959), Bandura and Walters had treated the problem of juvenile delinquency from the mixed perspective of Hullian learning and psychoanalytic theory. They were impressed, however, with the major role played by reinforcement contingencies alone in the genesis of teenage aggression. Parents of antisocial boys, for example, punished their children for aggression directed toward themselves but actively encouraged aggressive behavior when it was aimed at peers. In addition, these parents frequently employed erratic and harsh discipline, thereby providing models for antisocial acts. As Bandura and Walters moved more and more toward a social learning position less influenced by psychoanalytic theory, and as their research moved from an interview and correlational format to the study of social behavior in the experimental laboratory, their interest continued to focus on aggression. Moreover, they became particularly interested in the role of modeling in the promulgation of aggressive, antisocial behavior.

Studies carried out in a laboratory setting demonstrated quite convincingly that children who watch an adult assault a large, plastic clown will behave more aggressively toward the doll themselves (Bandura, Ross, & Ross, 1961). Aggression that is rewarded is more likely to be copied by preschoolers than that which is punished (Bandura, Ross, & Ross, 1963b). Aggression is imitated whether it is exhibited by human beings or cartoon characters, and whether it is displayed in a film, television, or live format (Bandura, Ross, & Ross, 1963c.) When adults express disapproval of exhibitions of aggressive behavior then the probability of imitation is decreased (Grusec, 1973; Hicks, 1968). Children will even imitate aggressive behavior when they themselves are its victim: Thus children who were taught a task and punished for their mistakes employed this same teaching strategy when they subsequently taught the task to a peer (Gelfand, Hartmann, Lamb, Smith, Mahan, & Paul, 1974).

As we saw in Chapter 1, the artificiality of these studies led to some concern about how widely the conclusions could be applied. Nevertheless, the findings were highly suggestive. Correlational findings of relationships between parents' use of punishment as a discipline technique and increased aggressive behavior in their offspring indicated that similar mechanisms of modeling could well be operating in real life. The catharsis hypothesis, in its vicarious form, had been laid to rest.

The Ethological Approach

In contrast to the learning position, and more in line with the Freudian, the ethologists argued that a repertoire of aggressive patterns of behavior emerges as a function of maturation. Lorenz (1965) describes aggression as an instinctual system whose energy comes from within the organism. This energy builds up and must be discharged by external stimuli in the environment that release it. The three-spined stickleback, for example, exhibits a stereotyped pattern of aggressive behavior when presented with a particular stimulus—a red belly (see Chapter 3). How much aggression is displayed depends on how much aggressive energy has been stored and on the strength of appropriate releasing stimuli. Although much of the ethological work focuses on animal aggression, the belief is that frustrations, insults, and threats are releasing stimuli for aggression in human beings.

In Lorenz's account aggression serves to keep the population level low enough so that it can be supported by the resources available in the environment. It results in the selection of the best animals for reproduction. Finally, it serves to protect the young so as to guarantee their survival. We have already noted these functions when discussing the utility of aggression. It bears repeating, however, that despite the adaptive significance and importance of aggression in the evolutionary scheme of things, it must not be forgotten that human cognitive capacities are such that they allow other mechanisms for coping with problems of resource availability, selection for reproduction, and defense of the young. Moreover, the human capacity for thought, planning, and communication, as well as deviation, distortion, and denial, indicates that it is a very narrow view which reduced aggression to a fixed reaction to eliciting stimuli. Nor is there any good neurophysiological evidence for the notion that aggressive energy accumulates until it is discharged.

For these reasons the ethological view of aggression has not been well received by developmental psychologists. Nevertheless, the approach has become more influential in recent years, particularly as investigators have tried to decipher the function served by aggression in peer groups. This work has already been discussed in Chapter 6.

BIOLOGICAL DETERMINANTS OF AGGRESSION

The rest of this chapter mostly deals with environmental influences on aggression. Investigators have devoted considerable effort, however, to understanding the biological determinants of aggression, particularly in animals, and so a complete discussion ought to provide at least an overview of the role played by hormones, physical characteristics, neurological factors, and genes in the expression of aggression. These characteristics do not affect aggression in a direct way. Rather, they operate by affecting such outcomes as the individual's size, activity level, and responsiveness to stimulation. It is the latter characteristics, then, that mediate between biology and hostile behavior, making the latter more or less likely to occur or to be modified by experience.

Hormonal Effects on Aggression

The effects of hormones on aggression has been the subject of several recent reviews (Cairns, 1979b; Parke & Slaby, 1983; Tieger, 1980) and we will draw on these in our discussion. Hormones appear to operate in two different ways. They organize behavior, that is, their presence or absence early in development has an unalterable effect on later aggression, and they activate behavior, that is, they have an effect on contemporaneous aggression.

Organizing Function

The administration of male hormones either perinatally or neonatally to female mice and rats increases their later aggression. The administration of female hormones perinatally or neonatally to males decreases later aggression. Similarly, the absence of male hormones, through early castration, reduces later aggression. It is not clear that the effects of injected hormones, however, mirror the effects of naturally occurring hormones, a fact which makes interpretation of the data problematic (Tieger, 1980).

Studies by Ehrhardt and her colleagues (e.g., Money & Ehrhardt, 1972; Ehrhardt & Baker, 1974) suggest that hormones are not implicated in the development of aggression in humans, as we noted in Chapter 3. Recall they found that females who had received excessive amounts of androgen prenatally showed greater physical energy and were more "tomboyish" in their behavior in childhood and adolescence than normal controls, but did not differ in amount of aggression. More recently, however, Reinisch (1981) reported that boys and girls who had been exposed to synthetic progestins during gestation appeared more physically aggressive, as assessed by the Leifer-Roberts Index, a self-report measure that predicts well to actual behavior. Her subjects were between 6 and 18 years at the time of measurement. Whether the increase in aggression reflects greater initiation of aggression or is restricted to retaliatory reactions to aggression in others is not clear (Parke & Slaby, 1983).

Activating Function

There is a relationship between the level of male hormone and the amount of contemporaneous aggressive behavior in rats and rhesus monkeys. However, female hormones also increase dominance and aggression in female chimpanzees (Birch & Clark, 1950; Michael, 1968), a finding that suggests that the situation is not all that simple. With human beings the findings are mixed. A number of studies have reported a relationship between testosterone and antisocial behavior, but others have not (Parke & Slaby, 1983). There does seem to be a relationship between testosterone level and some kinds of aggression: In 16-year-old Swedish boys, for example, plasma testosterone level was a predictor of self-reports of physical and verbal aggression, especially to provocation and threat. In addition, it was related to impatience and irritability (Olweus, Mattsson, Schalling, & Low, 1980). A relationship between testosterone level and aggressive reponse to provocation is also reported by Mattsson, Schalling, Olweus, and Low (1982, cited by Parke & Slaby, 1983) in young institutionalized male offenders.

Clearly, conclusions must be carefully drawn. Hormones may influence some forms of aggressive behavior, but not necessarily all. The ways in which they influence behavior may be diverse. For example, Tieger (1980) notes that one effect of the introduction of androgen into an organism is that it produces increased body weight, greater hair growth, and masculinized appearance of the genitalia. It is these characteristics that may be responsible for heightened aggression. It must be noted, as well, that the relationship between hormones and behavior is bidirectional. Thus aggression can cause increases in testosterone level as well as testosterone causing increases in aggression.

Physical Characteristics and Aggression

Physical size and strength are obviously going to be correlated with success at aggression and, therefore, with continued aggression. Boys who mature early in adolescence are more dominant and assertive than boys who mature late (Mussen & Jones, 1957): One assumes that the early maturers are more likely to be successful when they aggress, and that they then come to rely on aggression as a useful way of controlling others.

Another feature related to aggression is physical appearance. Research indicates that people tend to attribute greater aggressiveness to physically unattractive than to physically attractive children, even when those children are very young. Langlois and Downs (1979) found that there were no differences in the aggressiveness of attractive and unattractive 3-year-olds, but that differences *had* emerged by the age of 5. The point is that unattractive children are exposed to the expectations of others and that they soon conform to those expectations.

Neurological Conditions and Aggression

Destruction or electrical stimulation of the hippocampus appears to produce aggression, probably because hippocampal damage leads to heightened sensitivity of sensory systems. Nor are the effects automatic, but depend on such factors as the animal's position in the dominance hierarchy and prior social experience. Cats raised in isolation, for example, are less discriminating in their object of attack than are cats without the experience of social isolation (Cairns, 1979b).

Increases in aggressiveness and assertiveness are not an inevitable consequence of brain damage in human beings. Outbursts of rage are inclined to occur in some individuals suffering from certain types of psychomotor epilepsy, however, and these outbursts are set off by quite trivial events (Cairns, 1979b).

Genetic Variation and Aggression

We have already examined the evidence for the heritability of personality characteristics such as aggressiveness, assertiveness, and activity level in Chapter 3. The role of genetic variation in the development of aggression is significant, at least in animals, albeit not strong. But the mechanism through which genetics reveals itself is a complex one and the role of experience a strong modifier.

THE BEGINNINGS OF AGGRESSION

The Nature of Early Peer Conflict

When does aggression first appear, and what are its characteristics? People have been interested in social conflict among peers for a long time, documenting its occurrence at least as early as the second year of life. Conflicts in the very young, however, most often seem to center around issues of space and resources and were often viewed by researchers as having neither aggressive nor hostile qualities, indeed, as being "socially blind" (Parke & Slaby, 1983). Lately it has been argued that a closer inspection of early conflict shows it to involve, in fact, the same kinds of socially significant events that one sees in later aggressive interchanges (Hay & Ross, 1982). Thus the content of toddler quarrels is similar to that of the quarrels of older children: Not only are toddlers concerned about space and resources, but they also have disputes over social issues such as peer violation of social norms or peer actions that are too intrusive. Verbalizations are appropriate to the situation and the opponent ("mine" when the child wishes to claim ownership, "no" to protest an apponent's actions). Conflict occurs over objects even when duplicates are available, an indication that possession of an object by another child increases its attractiveness to a young observer and is therefore more likely to elicit aggression as a way of getting it.

Aggression and Prosocial Behavior

In addition to observing its occurrence in the very young child, another way to learn about aggression's early characteristics is to think about its relationship to other behaviors. Consider, for example, the correlation between hostile behavior and prosocial behavior. Examination of this relationship has been a favorite pastime, for the obvious reason that those characteristics which one would expect to inhibit aggression—concern for others and an apparent ability to understand their needs and feelings—are just the characteristics that should facilitate prosocial actions. Yet the data are definitely mixed. Sometimes the relationship is positive, sometimes negative, and sometimes nonexistent (Cummings, Hollenbeck, Iannotti, Radke-Yarrow, & Zahn-Waxler, 1986).

Cummings et al. have concluded from the variety of findings that when aggression is infrequent, more assertive than hostile, and most frequently situationally determined that it will coexist with an ability to help others. They suggest that children who are well adjusted can benefit from some amount of interpersonal aggression because it teaches them about conflict resolution as well as helping them to understand the effects of their own harmful behavior on others. In this way sensitivity to the feelings of others is developed. Aggression that is more hostile and chronic, however, does not favor the learning of empathy and concern because these reactions are overridden by anger and upset.

By and large incompatibility between aggression and prosocial behavior is more likely to be observed in older than in younger children, with the changing relationship also more likely to be seen in boys than in girls (Cummings et al., 1986; Feshbach & Feshbach, 1986). At younger ages, then, aggression may be more a reflection of social outgoingness, activity, and maturity. Why older boys cannot be both hostile and caring is unclear, although Cummings et al. offer the following speculations. They note that levels of aggression are higher in boys than in girls on average, and that boys may experience greater hostility as a result. As well, our society is more inclined to reward girls than boys for altruism. The combination of hostility and minimal reinforcement for altruism could produce a negative self-image which is associated with lessened concern for others.

Aggression and Assertiveness

Another set of relationships, which may help to characterize the nature of early aggression, is that between aggression and assertion. Psychoanalytic ego psychologists have argued that assertion and aggression emerge from a common source, aggressive drive energy (Hartmann, Kris, & Lowenstein, 1949). Thus the young child's insistence on his own rights and determination to express his own competence could be an important component of aggression. If this were the case we should see positive relationships between aggression and assertion, particularly in the young. Such positive relationships do appear in a study reported by Feshbach and Feshbach (1986). They measured assertion (giving suggestions, opinions, and information) and aggression in kindergarten and third-grade children using teacher ratings, children's self-reports, and observations of the children planning and constructing a miniature playground. They did not find aggression and assertion to be related when self-reports were the dependent variable; children do discriminate between what they perceive to be their own aggressive and assertive behaviors. On the basis of teacher ratings and observations, however, a quite different conclusion can be drawn. These measures were positively and significantly correlated for the younger boys and girls and for the older girls. Thus early aggression does appear to have positive elements associated with it in the form of efforts at self-assertion and autonomy, as well as being a marker of social outgoingness, activity, and maturity. Presumably increasing maturity enables the boy to distinguish more prosocial patterns of assertion from more hostile patterns of aggression. Such a distinction may be more difficult for older girls whose assertiveness is less likely to be tolerated (Freundl, 1977) and who may therefore have more trouble learning to distinguish between two behaviors that are both regarded negatively.

AGGRESSION AS A PERSONALITY TRAIT

Is aggressive behavior stable? Does early aggression predict later aggression? The classic study of this problem was a longitudinal assessment by Kagan and Moss (1962) who found considerable stability of aggression between early childhood and adulthood for boys but not for girls. The explanation usually provided for this difference is that the environment of boys is more encouraging of aggression and therefore supports its continued expression, whereas for girls, this is not the case.

We have already noted that aggression has some biological basis. Behavioral problems, including aggression, are associated with a difficult temperament early in life (Thomas, Chess, & Birch, 1968). Olweus (1980) reports that the temperament of boys, defined as a combination of high activity level and intensity of reaction, is a good predictor of peer ratings of aggression in adolescence. There is good reason, then, to believe that constitutional factors may provide a basis for behavior stability.

A number of other investigators report stability of aggression both in boys and in girls. Olweus (1979) reviewed 16 studies of children—primarily boys—who ranged in age from 2 years to 18 years at the time of first testing and who were reassessed anywhere from 6 months to 21 years later. Degree of stability was a positive linear function of the time between assessments and the subject's age at the beginning of the study. Overall, the degree of stability was substantial, not much lower than that found with intelligence. In a later paper Olweus (1982, cited by Parke & Slaby, 1983) considered six studies of the stability of aggression in comparable samples of boys and girls up to 19 years of age with an average age of 7 years and follow-up intervals ranging from 6 months to 10 years. The average correlation between measures of aggression at the two points in time was .497 for males and .439 for females. Recently, Huesmann, Eron, Lefkowitz, and Walder (1984) have reported the results of a longitudinal study of 600 subjects from the ages of 8 to 30 years. They estimated the stability of aggression over these years to be about .50 for boys and .35 for girls. Huesmann et al. also demonstrated that early aggressiveness is a good predictor of severe antisocial aggressiveness in the young adult, manifesting itself in criminal behavior, physical aggression, and child abuse for both males and females and spouse abuse and delinquent driving behavior for males.

The answer to the continuity question, then, is that aggression does appear to be reasonably stable for both boys and girls, at least through adolescence. The work of Kagan and Moss would suggest that the picture changes somewhat for females, however, when they enter adulthood—an observation supported by the lower correlation for girls obtained by Huesmann et al. Contributing to stability where it exists may be inborn temperamental factors and continued similarity of environmental circumstances, as well as the tendency of individuals to select from their environment those situations and events that serve to maintain a prevailing disposition. The fact that stability does decrease over time, of course, underlines the fact that environmental events also are contributing to some change over time.

EMOTIONAL AND COGNITIVE MEDIATORS OF AGGRESSION

Most studies of aggression have focused on relationships between environmental events and hostile responses to those events, regardless of whether the research has been inspired by psychoanalytic, social learning, or ethological approaches. Lately, in keeping with the general shift in the field, affective and cognitive events as mediators between stimulus events and reactions have captured the attention of students of aggression. If makes sense that children who do not have good problem-solving skills, for example, or who cannot take the perspective of others, will have difficulty dealing with aggression-arousing situations. In the first half of this chapter the importance of self-instruction and attentional processes in the development of self-control, including the ability to inhibit aggressive tendencies, was considered. We turn now to a consideration of cognitive and affective factors as they relate specifically to aggression.

Empathy and Perspective-Taking Skills

Shantz (1983) is surprised at the prevalent belief that advanced social-cognitive skills should be positively related to the frequency of prosocial behavior and negatively related to the frequency of antisocial behavior. Why, she wonders, should this position be held so strongly when social information and understanding can serve both positive and negative goals. Although it is true that social knowledge and skills probably can help in the effective expression of hostility against a target, there are also good reasons for expecting a strong negative relationship between social cognitive understanding and aggression. Knowledge of another's needs ought to aid in the avoidance of conflict, the reduction of misunderstandings, and the facilitation of cooperation. Observation of the injurious effects of aggression on another, if it leads to empathic distress in the perpetrator, ought to inhibit the inflicting of pain and distress in the future.

By and large, the evidence does suggest a negative relationship between empathy and role-taking ability on the one hand, and aggression on the other. Chandler (1973) and Chandler, Greenspan, and Barenboim (1974) report that delinquent and emotionally disturbed, aggressive boys were deficient in their role-taking skills and that training in role-taking skills led to decreases in their deviance. Feshbach and Feshbach (1986) note the robustness of the relationship between empathy and aggression, especially for boys. Kurdek (1978), however, reports a *positive* correlation between disruptive behavior in the classroom and perspective-taking skills.

A Social Information-Processing Model of Aggression

A different approach to the analysis of aggression from a cognitive standpoint is taken by Kenneth Dodge. Dodge (1985, 1986) notes that there are a number of steps children go through in settings which could elicit aggression, and that processing and interpretation of information at each of these steps will determine the nature of their responding. If performance at some point in the progression is unskilled either because of deficits in cognitive ability or biases in interpretation then the outcome will be socially maladaptive behavior.

Initially the appropriate cues must be the object of attention. If bias is operating at this point (information suggesting an aggressive act might have been accidental is ignored, for example) or the child has cognitive deficits (e.g., younger children are more inclined to attend to specific behaviors and concrete features of the environment, whereas older children take into account traits and habits), then deviant behavior could result. The second step in Dodge's model requires the child to interpret social cues. Was the peer acting benignly or was he intentionally trying to cause harm? At this point cognitive deficits and attributional biases can get the observer into trouble. Aggressive children, for example, are much more likely to attribute hostility to the provocative act of a peer than are nonaggressive children, and are therefore more likely to respond with retaliatory aggression (Dodge, 1980; Dodge & Tomlin, 1983). Because aggressive and nonaggressive children do not differ in frequency of aggression when their attributions are the same, it seems that it is, indeed, attributional differences that mediate aggressive behavior.

Next comes the generation of possible responses to the actor's behavior. Should I hit back? Should I go to an adult for help? Should I give up? Aggressive boys, asked to generate possible responses to aggressive provocation, initially give competent ones, but their subsequent responses are less so compared with those of nonaggressive boys (Richard & Dodge, 1982). Now the child must select one of the responses generated, evaluating its possible consequences: Aggressive boys are less able to recognize the inadequacy of certain potential responses than are nonaggressive boys (Dodge, 1985). The obvious last step requires the ability to carry out the response adequately. It does not help to decide to respond to aggression with a verbal thrust and clever repartee if this is beyond the individual's capabilities.

Although Dodge's model is presented from the perspective of the observer it does have implications for the actor and, indeed, emphasizes the reciprocal nature of aggressive interchanges. Note that when confronted with an ambiguous situation aggressive children are more inclined to attribute intentionality to the peer and to behave aggressively. But now the peer is a recipient of (to him) apparently unjustified hostility. He dislikes the aggressive child and responds in an unfriendly fashion. Such behavior merely reinforces the aggressive child's tendency to see hostility in ambiguous situations. In this way the model predicts that there will be a positive relationship between the amount of aggression a child directs toward peers and the frequency with which peers direct aggression to the child. The prediction is not an obvious one, since it might be assumed that aggressive boys are bullies who dominate their nonaggressive peers. But it appears to be an accurate one. In a study of the development of social interactions of 7-year-old boys in play groups over a 2-week period, Dodge (1986) reports a significant correlation ($r = .41$) between the frequency with which boys in the groups initiated aggression and the frequency with which they were targets of aggression.

THE SOCIALIZATION OF AGGRESSION

In this final section we focus on two specific aspects of the socialization of aggression: its development in family interactions and as a result of exposure to televised violence. We have chosen these two areas for a reason. The former has been the object of some very elegant research that sheds light on the nature of reciprocal family interchanges. The latter has received attention from a great many researchers and the results of their work has important political and social implications—as such it should be viewed with particular care.

Coercive Interactions in the Family

We have already discussed, in Chapter 5, some of the work of Gerald Patterson. For many years Patterson (e.g., 1980, 1982, 1984, 1986) has studied parent-child and sibling interaction in the families of aggressive boys. He observes that in these families there is a high incidence of aggressive or coercive behavior on the part both of parents (threats, scolding, hitting) and of children (yelling, hitting, defiance). Both mothers and fathers are much more likely to initiate conflict, that is, to launch unprovoked attacks, with their aggressive children than are the parents of normal controls. Moreover, aggressive children are more likely to counterattack than normal children. As well as occurring more frequently in aggressive families, aggressive exchanges continue for a longer time than in normal families and also tend to escalate in intensity.

What is it that causes this escalation of conflict? According to Patterson small increases in the intensity of one person's attack are matched by the other person to try to get the other person to comply. When this happens both members of the dyad are reinforced, one by compliance and the other by the cessation of aversive behavior. Suppose, for example, that requests for the mother's attention by a child are ignored. The child becomes more demanding by yelling, and possibly even cursing. Eventually the mother yields and begins to pay attention. The child, who in this case is labeled the coercive member of the dyad, is reinforced by the mother's attention. The mother is reinforced by cessation of the child's aversive behavior.

Characteristics of both the child and the parent in aggressive families mean that the pattern of escalation is more likely to be observed there than in less troubled families. Parents in aggressive families tend to be inconsistent in their use of punishment, which simply teaches children to be more persistent in their responding because they have learned that eventually the parent will give in to their wishes. In addition, parents in aggressive families are more likely to label neutral events as antisocial than prosocial (Patterson, 1986), so that they may have more occasions to perceive as warranting negative reaction. On the child's side, Patterson finds that aggressive children are less responsive to social stimuli, including social reinforcement and social punishment (threats, scolding). The source of this reduced responsiveness may be constitutional as well as the result of indiscriminate use of positive and aversive feedback by parents in aggressive families. Thus these parents are more likely to punish prosocial behavior as well as to reward deviant behavior and so reward and punishment lose their meaning.

The great virtue of Patterson's work is that it so nicely demonstrates the interactive nature of parent and child in the development of aggression. Moreover, Patterson has provided observational data which allow one to see moment-by-moment changes in that interaction and to identify specific events which serve to mold it. We see elements in Patterson's explanation that are familiar from previous discussions—the role of (negative) reinforcement, constitutional and learned differences in responsivity to social stimuli—in the context of observations where we can see their effects at work. Certainly other variables are also functioning in the situations Patterson describes. Aggressive parents provide models of aggressive behavior (although Patterson tends to put more emphasis on the ineffective pairing of punishment as a causal factor in the generation of aggression). Patterson's aggressive, or power assertive, parents no doubt arouse hostility and reactance in their child, which reduce the chances of compliance. They probably also provide an environment not particularly conducive to the development of empathic concern for others. No doubt both parents and children in aggressive families make the kinds of maladaptive attributions of which Dodge speaks, and which serve to promote further hostility.

The Issue of Television Violence

Certain topics in psychology arouse greater emotional reaction than others, thereby becoming the target of more heated debate. Later, for example, we shall see how the question of sex differences in psychological functioning has led to discrepancies in findings, interpretation, and emphasis that can often be seen to result from biases in personal belief systems. We are not suggesting that deliberate distortion is occurring, but we are maintaining that the beliefs and attitudes of researchers cannot help but influence their approach to data collection and organization, a point already made in Chapter 1. For the present we turn to another politically tinged issue, the question of whether or not television violence has an adverse effect on those who watch it, converting peaceful viewers into aggressive and hostile ones. Since the advent of television in our society, this question has become a major research issue.

Despite hundreds of published articles and surveys in the area, using virtually every methodological approach described in Chapter 2, the answer even to the apparently simple question of whether (let alone how) violence on television produces aggression in its viewers is unclear. Parke and Slaby (1983) write:

. . . the accumulated evidence nevertheless establishes a reliable link between children's experience of viewing televised violence and their passive acceptance of aggression performed by others. . . . television clearly deserves its new-found status as a major contributor to the development of children's aggression. (p. 593)

Other reviewers disagree with this position. Freedman (1984), for example, concludes that:

. . . the available literature does not support the hypothesis that viewing violence on television causes an increase in subsequent aggression in the real world. It remains a plausible hypothesis, but one for which there is, as yet, little supporting evidence. (p. 244)

Is it possible to reconcile these opposing viewpoints? Our own biases and predilections will determine what parts of the relevant literature we choose to emphasize and whether we assign studies with ambiguous results to the category of support or nonsupport of the hypothesis. We hope the reader may gain some understanding, however, of how different sets of individuals might come to quite different conclusions based on consideration of the same data.

Television's Role in the Development of Aggression: The Research

We begin with two facts, namely, that children watch a great deal of television (well over 3 hours a day, according to Parke & Slaby) and that a disproportionate amount of the material seen on television is aggressive in content. According to Gerbner, Gross, Morgan, and Signorielli (1980), for example, violent acts occur on American television at the average rate of five every hour during prime-time viewing and 18 every hour during the day on weekends. The conditions for the modeling of aggressive behavior, or at least for becoming more accepting of aggression in the real world, are obviously there.

We begin our assessment of the literature with the results of a meta-analysis by Andison (1977). He considered 67 studies relevant to the question of whether or not exposure to television violence increases aggressive behavior. Of these 67 studies 76% indicated that it did, 5% indicated that it reduced aggression, and 19% found no effect. The findings were generally more positive for laboratory experiments than for field experiments and surveys (87% for the former and 70% for the latter). Parke and Slaby attribute this difference to the greater sensitivity of laboratory studies, which eliminate many of the confounding variables present in less controlled studies. Freedman (1984, 1986) rejects the findings of laboratory studies to date as relevant to the issue for several reasons. Measures used generally have been only analogues of aggression (e.g., punching an inflated plastic doll). The work arguably has suffered from strong experimenter demands whereby a researcher shows a violent program to a child and then follows it with a test, a procedure which suggests that aggressive behavior is acceptable and even desirable. Only a small sample of violent programs appearing on television have been sampled—and not a mixture of violent and nonviolent fare which is a more typical pattern of exposure in real life. Although the early finding by Bandura, Ross, and Ross (1963c) that children would imitate the aggressive behavior of a model who pummeled and abused a Bobo doll are impressive, there is, as we observed in Chapter 2, no real answer to the question of whether or not this and other similar effects (e.g., Bandura, 1965; Bandura & Huston, 1961; Berkowitz & Geen, 1966; Berkowitz & Rawlings, 1963; Grusec, 1972, 1973; Hicks, 1968; Rosekrans, 1967) are simply a function of the peculiar characteristics of the experimental laboratory.

In addition to this confusion about the relative merits of laboratory experiments, it must be acknowledged that a large number of studies other than laboratory experiments designed to show the negative effects of violent television are not without their difficulties. Although the field experiments have overcome some (but not all) of the problems of artificiality, close scrutiny reveals problems of interpretation. We shall present in some detail the results of two of the most frequently cited studies in order to demonstrate the point.

Leyens, Camino, Parke, and Berkowitz (1975) assigned groups of boys living in institutional cottages to a condition in which they viewed violent films or neutral films for several days. By and large the boys in the former condition became more aggressive (as assessed by yelling, stamping feet, poking others during film viewing, as well as interpersonal, verbal and physical aggression following viewing) than those in the latter. However, the effects did not always generalize to all measure of aggression; they were generally short-lived, and sometimes appeared to hold only for boys who were high in aggression to begin with (although lack of reported statistical comparisons makes this difficult to verify). Moreover, the fact that all boys in a given group lived together meant that aggression in one boy necessarily involved aggression in another—an interdependence that makes interpretation of the results difficult.

Friedrich and Stein (1973), in a study already described in Chapter 2, had nursery school children view either violent, neutral, or prosocial television shows. Neither violent nor prosocial programming produced any change on measures of aggression on the playground. When children were divided into those who had been initially high or low in aggression, however, small differences emerged. Highly aggressive children decreased in aggression and children low in aggression increased in aggression, but the decline of the former was less if they had been in the aggressive viewing condition. When three males in the neutral condition were eliminated from the analysis, however, in order to equate groups on initial aggression, these effects did not reach an acceptable level of statistical significance.

Results of this kind make it easy to interpret the data as indicating a relationship between violence on television and aggressive behavior—after all, findings are in the right direction although not always achieving statistical significance—or as indicating the case is simply not proved. Add to this ambiguous picture the results of a study in which the outcome was in the opposite direction (Feshbach & Singer, 1971) and the picture becomes even more confused. (Recall from Chapter 2, however, that although Feshbach and Singer found that aggression decreased in boys who watched television with aggressive content, their procedure suffered from the fact that some participants in the control group, as a result of their strong complaints, were allowed to watch some aggressive programming. The study, therefore, has its own set of problem.) None of these studies, then, provides strong support for the hypothesis that violence on television produces antisocial behavior in its viewers.

Now we turn to the correlational studies, which also have drawbacks. A large number of studies (summarized by Parke & Slaby) find a significant relationship between amount of viewing of violent programming and level of aggression, although the effect is sometimes obtained only for boys. The correlations are never large, usually in the neighborhood of .20, and the question still remains about the direction of causality. Using cross-lagged panel analysis Eron, Huesmann, Lefkowitz, and Walder (1972) found that for boys (but not for girls) there was the suggestion of a causal relationship between early viewing of televised violence and, 10 years later, ratings by peers of aggressive behavior. Singer and Singer (1981), who also used cross-lagged panel analysis but over much shorter periods of time, found mixed relations between the viewing of violence and aggression in preschoolers. Nor does a recent study by Huesmann, Lagerspetz, and Eron (1984) provide overwhelming evidence for a causal relationship. In their study of American children in grades one to five, they found, using regression analyses, that the relationship between viewing of violence and aggression was bidirectional for girls, with television violence appearing to promote aggressiveness, and aggressiveness appearing to promote an interest in watching violent programming. For boys the relation ran in only one direction, but that was from aggressiveness to violent viewing.

What are we to conclude on the basis of this information? The data are variable and rarely overwhelming, and seem to us to suggest a marginal implication of the viewing of television violence in the development of aggression. Many children can watch the depiction of aggressive and antisocial behavior on television without being adversely affected by it. Such a conclusion is strengthened by the success of Huesmann, Eron, Klein, Brice, and Fischer (1983) in modifying the aggressive behavior of young children who watched a great deal of television violence by changing their attitudes to this form of conflict resolution. The important thing to note is that the amount of television violence they subsequently watched did not change relative to that of the control group. Now, however, there was no longer, for them, a correlation between television viewing and aggression. They had, in some sense, become inoculated against the effects of what they were seeing. Similarly, we would expect that many children are inoculated against the effects of antisocial television content by certain socialization experiences, including alternate models of conflict resolution, exposure to the effects of their behavior on others, discussion with parents, and so on.

Developmental Changes in Responsivity to Television Violence

Is there an age at which children are more susceptible to the effects of television violence? We do know that young children, to about 8 years of age, are unable to remember the motives of aggressive characters and do not evaluate the aggression of characters in terms of their motivation (Collins, Berndt, & Hess, 1974). Although the modeling of aggression is affected by whether or not it is seen to be justified (Collins & Zimmermann, 1975), this is not the case with younger observers. In addition, harmful consequences following aggression suppress imitation of aggression. But when scenes depicting aggression and its harmful consequences are separated by short commercial messages (the usual condition under which television is viewed), 8-year-olds are just as aggressive as if there had been no harmful consequence presented. They do not seem to be able to remember the connection (Collins, 1973). Such outcomes would indicate that younger children are less inclined to respond to the events surrounding aggressive behavior and thus are less susceptible to those events that might lead to inhibition of imitation.

The Desensitizing Effects of Television Violence

In addition to increasing the viewer's own aggression it has been suggested that television violence makes observers more willing to tolerate violence in others. The second problem has not been addressed in such great detail as the first. Nevertheless, it does appear that young children are less likely to intervene when they observe an aggressive exchange in others, or to seek adult help when they have just observed a violent film (Drabman & Thomas, 1974; Thomas & Drabman, 1975). One of the lessons television may teach is that violence is a fact of life and hence must be accepted. Perhaps this is even more important than any effect it might have on aggressive behavior, particularly if more people are prone to accept the message of acceptability than are to be affected in their behavior.

Summary

Two processes are involved in the development of self-control and self-regulation—the internalization of norms stressing the value of the behavior and the learning of skills that enable adherence to the norms. This chapter focuses on the latter.

There are a number of phases through which young children pass that are related to self-control and self-regulation. Babies, for example, use nonnutritive sucking as a way of soothing themselves. Later, children can begin to comply with commands from others and to inhibit their own behavior. When representational thought develops self-control becomes possible because children can conform in the absence of external monitoring.

Luria's work on verbal self-regulation of behavior had a marked impact on the thinking of Meichenbaum who has demonstrated that impulsive children can become more reflective in their behavior by being trained to instruct themselves to work carefully and slowly. Several studies indicate that verbal self-regulation works for young children because it distracts them from temptation, whereas for older children it helps to focus attention on the task to be accomplished. Attention, however, must be focused not on the exciting qualities of a reward but on its less frustrating characteristics. Children have acquired knowledge of various self-control strategies by 8 years of age and become increasingly sophisticated thereafter. Another variable that has been shown to affect self-control is the individual's expectation that he will be successful at the behavior.

There appears to be a stable trait of ego control. Constitutional as well as socialization factors are important in its development.

The most useful approach to the definition of aggression is one which takes into account both behavior and judgment of the observer. Aggression serves a variety of functions including protection of offspring, optimal distribution of population, and the reduction of need for further aggression. It is, however, highly responsive to genetic and experiential modification.

The frustration-aggression hypothesis initially stated that aggression is always a consequence of frustration and frustration always leads to aggression. Revision of the formulation suggested that aggression was but one possible response to frustration, albeit the dominant one. Displacement and catharsis were two ideas to emerge from the hypothesis, the latter having two forms: that the observation of aggression drains the viewer of aggressive impulses and that direct aggression reduces subsequent aggression. There is virtually no evidence for the first form of the hypothesis.

Hormones, physical characteristics, neurological factors, and genes play some role in the expression of aggression by affecting such characteristics as body size, activity level, and responsiveness to stimulation. Aggression appears in the very young. Mild aggression and prosocial behavior, as well as aggression and assertiveness, appear to be positively correlated, particularly in preschoolers. Moreover, aggression appears to be a stable aspect of personality over time.

Cognitive factors, including role-taking ability and information-processing capacity, have been shown to be important determinants of aggressive behavior. In addition, socialization experiences such as initiation of conflict and inconsistent use of punishment by parents promotes its occurrence. Aggressive children are less responsive to social stimuli so that they are less amenable to socialization attempts. Although much has been written about the effects of television violence on aggression in young children, the data are mixed and subject to a variety of possible interpretations.

9
Morality and Altruism

The Nature of Morality

The social interactions of human beings are guided by elaborate sets of rules and regulations. These criteria for conduct help to make life predictable: They order the behavior of participants so that social exchanges can be carried out safely and efficiently. Among the rules governing social behavior are a subset that are regarded as more important, and their violation as more serious, than others. It is this subset that comprises a moral code and is considered to be fundamental to human functioning. Moral codes contain rules for behavior that seem self-evident, rather than determined by arbitrary social agreement. They comprise strongly held values that appear to need no justification for their existence. They are not statements of fact, nor are they subject to empirical test. They pertain to what ought to be, not what is.

Many moral beliefs find formal expression in legal systems and religious directives. The Ten Commandments, for example, and the Golden Rule express certain moral values and principles as do laws against killing, physical assault, and theft. Some of the issues with which moral systems concern themselves include physical and psychological harm to others, turstworthiness, duty and obligation, and recognition of private property. Thus, as a general rule, we refrain from attacking or killing others, we argue that honesty is the best policy, and we keep promises. If we do kill or behave in a dishonest or untrustworthy fashion, we often deny it, redefine our act, or justify our behavior in terms of a higher moral principle. Moreover, if we are truly moral, we are so not out of fear of punishment for our failure to follow moral rules but because the behavior advocated by these rules seems to us to be inherently correct. For this reason, then, legal sanctions should be unnecessary in a totally moral world. Even in the absence of formal laws or informal regulations, and of formal or informal sanctions, violations of moral prohibitions are disruptive to human social interaction. Adherence to moral prohibitions is universally applauded.

For centuries moral philosophers have struggled with the problem of defining the nature of morality, of describing the essence of vice and virtue, good and bad, right and wrong. They have tried to understand why people do not take the path of least resistance, what is the distinction between moral and legal issues and matters of etiquette and good taste, and how one can differentiate between moral, political, religious, and aesthetic values.

One approach to defining morality, popular among psychologists, has been simply to avoid the issue by denying that there is anything special about moral acts as opposed to any other class of behavior. Thus morality is defined as whatever society says it is. In one example of this approach Eysenck (1976) defines conscience, the reservoir of moral values, as a "conditioned reflex," an avoidance of punished behavior motivated by the reduction of anxiety. In a similar vein Berkowitz (1964) defines moral values as "evaluations of action believed by members of a given society to be 'right'." The problem with this relativistic approach is its implicit acceptance of the morality or immorality of any behavior, regardless of its content. Most of us would argue that although slavery may have been acceptable in various societies at various points in history, it was never moral, and that loyal Nazis who slaughtered Jews were behaving immorally by failing to disobey the orders of their superiors. Indeed, morality involves consideration for the needs of others, balanced against the needs of the self. In this sense it is influenced by society because it concerns itself with the successful interaction between individuals in society who are obligated, if society is to survive, to be participants in a social network and to undertake the responsibilities of being part of that network.

For moral philosophers, and increasingly frequently for psychologists concerned with moral development, discussions of the nature of morality generally revolve around the issues of justice, fairness, and equity. It is this principle, that all individuals must be treated justly (although not necessarily identically), that provides the guide for moral conduct. It is important to remember that the principle does not dictate, nor often even make obvious, those specific behaviors that are derived from it. Laurence Kohlberg (1970), a major figure in the psychological study of moral development, makes this point when he argues that justice is not a rule but a principle, and that a principle is a guide for choosing desirable behavior. The principle of justice may lead us to make exceptions to codes of conduct on moral grounds: Cheating, lying, and stealing may be moral if they, in fact, contribute to justice. Robin Hood is a folk hero because he stole from the rich to give to the poor. Theft in order to save a life may be justified because the right to life predominates over the right to property: To put property before life would therefore produce greater injustice than to put life before property. In summary, then, there are exceptions to rules but not exceptions to principles.

Morality and Altruism

So far our discussion has focused on proscribed behaviors, that is, on acts such as aggression, theft, and deception that are prohibited by society. Sometimes morality demands that individuals engage in prescribed behavior when they have behaved immorally, in an active attempt to restore the equity they have upset. A person who lied to another, for example, might try to restore the balance of justice by making restitution in the form of confession, apology, or the restoring of loss that might have been suffered by the victim as a result of the lie. There are, in addition, a large number of prescribed acts that have been assumed by virtually all psychologists (for exceptions, see Haan, 1982; Krebs, 1982) to belong to the class of moral imperatives, and these are acts of altruism. As with morality the definition of altruism has been subject to much debate. Perhaps the most popular is that it is an act designed to benefit another (such as helping, sharing, giving, showing concern, comforting, and defending) that is not motivated by self-gain (hence internalized), and that may be of some cost to the altruist.

Careful consideration of this definition, however, should make clear that it can violate the principle of justice or equity, which governs moral acts. For altruism goes beyond the maintenance of equity and, in fact, creates inequity. It means that the recipient who has received some benefit can now be in a more advantageous position than the donor, indeed, an even more advantageous state if the altruistic act has involved self-sacrifice. Hence the recipient is in a state of obligation that must be repaid if equity is to be restored.

Sociobiologists have dealt with this problem by developing the concept of reciprocal altruism (Trivers, 1971), as we noted in Chapter 1. They argue that all altruistic acts should lead to some return benefit to the altruist that is larger than the initial cost suffered by the altruist. One major form of this benefit is the reciprocation of altruism at a future time. It is argued (e.g., Trivers, 1983) that those who fail to reciprocate in this system do not survive to reproduce because they are deprived of future altruism by disillusioned altruists. Subtle cheating, whereby altruism may not be returned in equal or greater quantity, is more difficult to detect because of the complexities of long-term social interaction. In order to minimize this subtle cheating, however, a protective mechanism has evolved which involves a sense of fairness coupled with moralistic aggressiveness when cheating tendencies are discovered. Feelings of guilt also motivate a cheater to make reparation for an earlier failure to reciprocate altruism and thereby avoid the penalty that would otherwise ensue.

Although the notion of reciprocal altruism sheds light on why sacrifices might be made for others, it does not enable one to understand why behavior for which there is no hope of reciprocation might occur—a salient feature of our original definition of altruism. If help is given to others simply because it will be repaid in the future, then this is not true altruism as it has been understood by researchers in the area. Nor does the concept of reciprocal altruism take into account the fact that altruism may be experienced as a mixed blessing by the recipient because it can elicit feelings of failure, inferiority, and dependency (Fisher, Nadler, & Whitcher-Alagna, 1982). The fact remains, then, that morality and altruism are different from each other. Moreover, a review of the relevant research literature does suggest that morality and altruism develop differently and that people do make a distinction between them on several different dimensions.

First of all, even very young children appear to distinguish between morality and altruism. Thus Smetana (1981) interviewed preschoolers about their attitudes to a variety of misdemeanors and found that they believed such behaviors as hitting, throwing water at another child, and shoving—all proscribed acts—would be wrong even if there were no specific rule in their school about not doing them. Refusing to share a toy—an instance of lack of altruism—was, on the other hand, not considered to be wrong if a school did not have a rule requiring it. In a similar vein, Weston and Turiel (1980) asked 4- to 11-year-olds their relative opinions of two schools, one of which had a rule saying other people could be hit and the other of which had a rule permitting refusal to share one's snack. The latter school was rated more favorably than the former. This set of findings supports the view that children as young as $2\frac{1}{2}$ years of age discriminate between the commission of transgression and the omission of altruism, considering the rules for altruism to be more malleable than those for morality or proscribed acts.

Looking at a somewhat different aspect of children's thinking, Eisenberg (1982) reports that children's reasoning about altruism is more advanced and somewhat different from their reasoning about prohibition-oriented behavior. Preschoolers use a great deal of reasoning having to do with the needs and feelings of others when dealing with altruism (Eisenberg-Berg, 1979; Eisenberg-Berg & Hand, 1979; Eisenberg-Berg & Neal, 1979), whereas this kind of rationale does not emerge until adolescence (as we shall see later in this chapter) when proscribed behavior is the focus of judgment. Also, children in the earliest stage of thinking about prohibited acts cite avoidance of punishment as a reason for conformity with these prohibitions. Such a punitive orientation, with its marked concern for authority, is virtually absent in the initial stage of thinking about altruism (e.g., Bar-Tal, Raviv, & Leiser, 1980; Dreman & Greenbaum, 1973; Eisenberg-Berg & Neal, 1979; Ugurel-Semin, 1952). Again it is evident that young children view morality and altruism differently.

A second line of evidence for the position that morality and altruism are distinct comes from studies of mother's child-rearing practices. Studies of the discipline techniques mothers use when dealing with the commission of misdemeanors and the failure to behave prosocially indicate that they, too, consider these classes of misdeed to be discriminably different. Mothers report, for example, that they use punishment when their children engage in prohibited acts such as lying, aggression, and failure to comply with parental requests, but not when they fail to be altruistic. In the latter case they tend to rely more on empathically oriented reasoning, which focuses on the feelings of others—reasoning they use to a much lesser extent when dealing with prohibited behavior (Grusec & Dix, 1986; Grusec, Dix, & Mills, 1982). In addition, they are more upset by the commission of prohibited acts than they are by failures to be prosocial even when the perceived seriousness of these two classes of misdeed is held constant. Thus they appear to be firm in their attempts to obtain morality and to allow more freedom of choice in the case of altruism. No doubt the distinction they make helps to account for the differences in children's reasoning noted by Eisenberg, Smetana, and by Weston and Turiel. The presence or absence of a punitive orientation in parent discipline may result in its parallel presence or absence in children's judgments about prohibited and prescribed behavior. Also, the use of punishment for the commission of misdeeds may underline the fact that they are wrong regardless of whether or not formal rules exist, whereas reasoning for failures to be altruistic emphasizes the element of choice an individual has in whether or not to aid another. Thus altruism is nice, but not mandatory.

A final source of evidence for the distinction between morality and altruism is in the work of Mussen, Harris, Rutherford, and Keasey (1970). They asked children to identify those of their fellow students who would do such things as follow rules when the teacher was not around, never copy another person's answers on a test or steal, would stick up for a child who was being teased, and who would bawl someone out for hurting another child. The responses to these items, when factor analyzed, yielded two dimensions which the investigators labeled honesty (the items involving obedience, not cheating, and not stealing) and altruism (the items involving defending and comforting). The findings of Mussen et al., then, indicate that behaviors we consider moral correlate with each other, as do those we consider to be altruistic, but that children who are highly moral are not necessarily highly altruistic, nor are those who are high in altruism necessarily those who are high in morality. Mussen et al. also found that the maternal child-rearing practices associated with high morality and high altruism were different. For boys honesty correlated wth maternal control, lack of nurturance, and lack of overprotection, whereas altruism correlated with maternal non-punitiveness, use of praise, and encouragement of achievement. For girls honesty was correlated with maternal nonpunitiveness, nurturance, and encouragement of independence and a sense of responsibility, whereas altruism was correlated with maternal induction, permissiveness, consideration, and encouragement of high standards.

These three sets of data support our contention that morality and altruism are distinct aspects of human functioning and that relationships that hold for one of them should not be assumed to hold for the other. Indeed, it would not be unreasonable to suggest that the course of development for morality is different from that for altruism. There are, however, areas of overlap between the two. First, role-taking ability—knowledge of what other people are thinking and feeling—is considered to play an important part in the development of both morality and altruism, as will be evident throughout the course of this chapter. Second, there are many similarities between altruism and reparation after transgression, that is, the attempt to restore the balance of justice after it has been upset by a moral deviation, with the only difference lying in the identity of the transgressor. The similarity between the two is clear in the following anecdote. One of us recently observed two boys, aged about 2 and 3 years, standing in a motel lobby with their mother. The 3-year-old had been annoying the 2-year-old who turned to his mother and began to cry. The mother slapped the older boy and said, "Don't do that!" At this point the 3-year-old put his arms around his brother and kissed him gently on the back of the neck. The younger boy immediately stopped crying. Had the 2-year-old been crying because someone else had been annoying him the act would have been one of altruism. Because the actor was the transgressor, however, the act was one of reparation for deviation. It would not be surprising if the two were confused in a young child's thinking. In fact, such confusion is evident in the observation that very young children sometimes seem concerned that they may have been the cause of someone's distress even when this is clearly not the case. Thus a young child who encountered her mother crying hugged her and said, "Did I make you sad?" even though she had in no way been responsible for her mother's unhappiness (Zahn-Waxler & Radke-Yarrow, 1982).

Morality, however, seems central to the maintenance of human social functioning, whereas altruism is less straightforward. Although altruism can add substantially to the quality of human life, it can also be destructive if it requires too much self-sacrifice for the donor or too much resentment or feeling of obligation on the part of the recipient. This distinction suggests that courses of action and sources of conflict may be more clear-cut, salient, and self-evident in the case of morality than in the case of altruism. As a result it should be a less complex task to socialize a child to be moral than to be altruistic. Indeed, the complexities surrounding altruism are captured in an analysis of its determinants by Peterson (1982). She points out that the potential altruist must learn that "I should help or give to *deserving* individuals who are in X level of *need*, and are *dependent* on *me* for help, when I can *ascertain and perform* the necessary behavior and when the *cost* or *risk* to me does not exceed Y *amount* of my currently available resources." Such extreme complexity does not surround the behavior of the moral individual who does not have to make decisions about deservedness, need, dependency, ability, or cost. In this chapter we shall look at the development and correlates of morality and altruism with these distinctions, as well as areas of overlap, in mind.

Altruism and Prosocial Behavior

As we have noted, an altruistic act is one done for its own sake and not because of hope of reward or fear of punishment from some external source. The child who shares his toy with a friend in hope that the friend will share her ice cream in return is not an altruist. His behavior is self-serving. It is often not easy, however, to identify an altruist's motive. Does a business which makes a generous charitable donation do so out of genuine concern for the needy or to enhance its corporate image? This problem of interpretation has led psychologists to coin the term "prosocial behavior," which is used to refer to any act that benefits another, regardless of the actor's motive. Use of the term is an admission that researchers are often unable to identify the intention or motive for generous acts. This does not mean, however, that the problem of intention is not a central one in the understanding of either altruism or morality.

Morality and Social Convention

Eliot Turiel and his coworkers have demonstrated that in a variety of situations children and adults distinguish between moral transgressions—events such as hurting and stealing, which have an intrinsic effect on the welfare and rights of others, and violations of social conventions—events such as forms of address, styles of attire, and modes of eating designed to ensure fluid social interaction and maintain social order. Adults have been found to respond to children's moral transgressions by providing rationales for appropriate behavior and reflecting on the feelings of victims, whereas they react to violations of social conventions with commands, threats of sanction, and statements about disorder: Their responses seem to reflect the arbitrariness of social conventions and the intrinsic harm of moral transgressions. Similarly, preschoolers react to moral transgressions by focusing on the act's consequences such as emotional arousal, injury, and loss, or by seeking to involve adults. They display no reaction to violations of social conventions, although older children do with statements of rule, ridicule, disorder, and deviation (Nucci & Nucci, 1982a, 1982b; Nucci & Turiel, 1978). Similar relationships have been found in the Virgin Islands (Nucci, Turiel, & Encarnacion, cited by Nucci & Nucci, 1982b), a suggestion that the distinction is not peculiar to our own culture. Also, moral transgressions are rated as more serious than violations of social conventions, as deserving more punishment, and as being wrong even in the absence of a school rule forbidding them (Smetana, 1981; Weston & Turiel, 1980).

In a similar vein, Much and Shweder (1978), who studied the excuses young children made when they were accused of wrongdoing, found that moral violations were denied, redefined ("I didn't take the toy, I borrowed it"), or justified in terms of someone's prior transgression ("He hit me first"), that is, moral rules were treated as unalterable, intrinsically valid, and beyond negotiation. Violations of social conventions, in contrast, met with references to circumstances and consequences ("I didn't feel like it"; "The teacher wasn't around").

Given this pattern of findings Turiel (1978) has argued that young children in the course of interacting in and learning about the social world very quickly distinguish between the domains of morality and social convention. Their formulations about morality originate from perceptions of the intrinsic consequences of an event on the welfare and rights of others and are structured by underlying concepts of justice, whereas they see social conventions as arbitrary, with alternative actions just as capable of serving the same function of social organization. To infer from studies of the development of knowledge about and adherence to social conventions that we have learned something about the development of morality, argues Turiel, is like studying children's understanding of mathematical problems to gain insight into their understanding of morality. Yet this is what many investigators have done. Turiel suggests that one explanation for apparently contradictory research findings can be found in the realization that one study was concerned with social conventions and the other with moral rules. We shall see examples of this throughout the chapter.

Some acts do not fall neatly into the morality-social convention distinction. Altruism, of course, is one. Eating with one's hands or using crude language may represent violations of social conventions for some people, whereas others may find them personally offensive and psychologically harmful. The work of Turiel and others, however, alerts one to the fact that not all socially sanctioned behaviors are equivalent, that there is a difference between the Ten Commandments, a city's bylaws, and the dictates of an expert on social etiquette. One does well to keep these distinctions in mind when studying development in the moral and prosocial domains.

A History of Research on Morality and Prosocial Behavior

Psychoanalytic views on the development of conscience or the superego guided early research on the development of morality. Thus identification was seen as the major mechanism through which moral values were acquired. Children came to behave morally either to avoid feelings of guilt for transgression inflicted by the conscience or because they had internalized the values they perceived their same-sex parent to hold. Altruism, as we have defined it, has little place in the psychoanalytic formulation except, perhaps, as a reaction formation against greed (e.g., Ekstein, 1978). In the 1950s and 1960s studies of socialization, guided mostly by social learning theory, focused on establishing which child-rearing approaches were most likely to foster the development of resistance to temptation, guilt, confession, reparation after deviation, and internalization of moral values. Initially these were correlational studies assessing the relationship between parent practices and children's behavior and moral internalization. Later, however, researchers moved into the laboratory where they could study under more controlled conditions the roles of reward, punishment, and reasoning in the development of resistance to temptation and behavioral reactions to transgression. Many of these studies have been reviewed in Chapter 5.

One well-known and frequently quoted study, which stands outside this mainstream of research, is the Character Education Inquiry (Hartshorne & May, 1928–1930). This study is most frequently cited for its conclusion that morality is situation-specific, with there being little relationship between various indices of moral development. What has caused many psychologists to question this conclusion is the fact that Hartshorne and May were interrelating measures of morality and social convention (Turiel, 1978), that reanalysis of their data yielded a general factor of morality accounting for between 35 and 40% of the variance (Burton, 1963), and that combining assessments of honesty and altruism so that the final index is a reliable measure yields high correlations between each index and children's reputations for honesty and altruism (Rushton, Jackson, & Paunonen, 1981).

In contrast to the concern of social learning theorists with moral behavior, cognitive developmentalists addressed the issue of moral thought. Baldwin (1897) argued that children learn to distinguish between themselves and others by imitation and by the experience of effort which is part of their own actions but not the actions of others, and that it is the increasing understanding of self and others that forms the basis for morality. Expanding on Baldwin's ideas, Piaget pointed out that the young child's egocentrism must be overcome before a real understanding of others, and hence morality, can be achieved. Being able to take the role of others was also a theme in the writings of George Herbert Mead. Laurence Kohlberg, influenced by both Piaget and Mead, has developed an extremely influential theory about the development of moral reasoning, which has guided the bulk of research in the area from the 1970s to the present.

Interest in prosocial behavior is of much more recent vintage. Although there was a substantial concern in the 1920s and 1930s with children's responses to the distress of others (e.g., Bridges, 1931; Murphy, 1937; Stern, 1924; the work of Hartshorne & May, 1928–1930) it was only in the 1970s that research on prosocial behavior began again, which it did in a most intensive fashion. The work was initially in response to the burgeoning interest of social psychologists whose discovery of altruism is generally attributed to the murder, in 1964, of a young New York woman in full view of dozens of people, none of whom tried to help her in any way. The interest was no doubt maintained by the social and political turmoil of the 1960s, which led to questioning of social injustices and the role of individuals in correcting these injustices even when they had not been the perpetrators. In keeping with the times, most early studies of prosocial behavior in children were conducted in the experimental laboratory and guided by social learning theory. More recently researchers have turned to observational studies and have begun to look at the origins and development of concern for others, paying closer attention to its cognitive and affective components.

The Development of Morality

How do we become moral creatures whose behavior is guided by principles of justice, fairness, and equity? There have been two major approaches to this question, one emphasizing that moral principles are transmitted from one generation to the next through the process of socialization, and the other emphasizing that they are acquired as developing organisms become more capable of logical thought and of making sense of social interactions. Thus morality has been said to come either from the transmission of values or from their construction by individuals as experience and cognitive capacity increase. In the final analysis these should probably not be considered mutually exclusive mechanisms in the acquisition of morality.

In Chapters 5 and 6 we discussed the ways in which children are socialized to accept the values of society. Having dealt previously with socialization theory and research we will now turn to a consideration of moral thought and construction.

THE DEVELOPMENT OF MORAL THINKING

For cognitive developmentalists a moral act is one based on a conscious prior judgment of rightness or wrongness. Thought is primary since a given act can be a manifestation of any number of underlying cognitions, only a few of which are moral. In this approach the issue of intention is faced squarely, although that of behavior is not.

The Piagetian Approach

Piaget's *The Moral Judgment of the Child* was published in 1932. In many ways, with its emphasis on the child's construction of morality, it was a reaction to the writings of the sociologist Emil Durkheim who put forth a view of moral development very much within the socialization camp. Piaget's theory was based on his studies of the beliefs of Genevan children about the rules for playing marbles as well as their answers to questions about stories depicting people who either accidentally or intentionally committed misdemeanors of either a mild or serious nature.

Initially, according to Piaget, children are in the stage of heteronomous morality (also known as the stage of moral realism). They believe rules

must be obeyed because they are sacred and unalterable, and they judge
the propriety of an act on the basis of the magnitude of its consequences,
the extent to which it conforms to established rules, and whether or not it
elicits punishment. Thus an act is automatically bad if it is followed by
negative consequences, even if they are accidental; this is Piaget's notion
of "immanent justice." In the developmentally more advanced stage of
autonomous morality (also known as the stage of morality of cooperation
and reciprocity) children come to see that rules are maintained through
reciprocal social agreement and that they are therefore subject to modification. As well, rightness and wrongness are judged now in terms of
the actor's intentions rather than amount of damage done. A boy who
accidentally breaks one cup while stealing jam is worse than one who
accidentally breaks 15 cups while helping his mother. Although the negative consequences were more substantial in the latter case, and would
therefore have led to judgments of greater naughtiness in younger children, intentions come to weigh importantly in judgments of older children.
Punishment is no longer seen as impersonally ordained, and duty and
obligation, rather than being viewed as obedience to authority, now involve consideration for the welfare of others and the ability to put one's
self in their place.

According to Piaget these changes in moral thinking reflect more sophisticated cognitive abilities. Beliefs in immanent justice decrease because
children no longer confuse natural consequences with arbitrary ones.
Because they are less egocentric they can put themselves in the place of
others, understanding that intentions are important and that one's actions
have an effect on others. Some of these changes in thinking reflect the
child's shift from intense interaction with parents to interactions with
peers. Parents encourage immature thought because they promote a relationship of authority figure and subordinate, whereas relationships with
peers are ones of equality. Parents also tend to punish misdeeds by responding to amount of damage done rather than to the actor's intention.
As a result of the shift to peers in their social relations children must strive
to understand the point of view of others, or take their role, in an attempt
to work out mutually satisfying ways of maintaining social interactions. No
doubt parents were more authoritarian in Piaget's day, and it is quite possible that parents who adopt more egalitarian approaches to child rearing
would facilitate moral development. Piaget would not have disagreed with
this position.

The Problem of Intention

The issue of young children's apparent inability to identify intention has
occupied a number of investigators who have argued that Piaget underestimated their ability in this area. Austin, Ruble, and Trabasso (1977),
for example, point out that in Piaget's stories information about severity of

consequences always came last and, because of their limited memory capacities, children may have forgotten the information about intention. Indeed, when information about intention was moved to the last position in stories children began to use it in their judgments. Confounded in Piaget's stories is intention and amount of damage done. This has led researchers to argue that children focus their attention on large amounts of damage and ignore, as a result, information about intention. When amount of damage is held constant, even 5-year-olds judge an actor who did something intentionally as more culpable (Imamoglu, 1975; Rule, Nesdale, & McAra, 1974). Thus, although limited cognitive capacities affect children's use of information about intention in their moral judgment, they do understand the concept and do use it if they are not distracted by other information. Shultz (1980) reports that children as young as 3 years of age can differentiate reflexive knee jerks and voluntary leg movements, identifying the latter as intentional and the former as not. Even very young children, then, seem to have a grasp of the intentional-unintentional dichotomy as we, indeed, argued in Chapter 7.

Kohlberg's Approach

Beginning with the ideas of James Baldwin, G. H. Mead, and Piaget, Kohlberg (1969, 1971, 1976) has outlined six stages in the development of moral thinking. These stages modify and extend those of Piaget through adolescence into adulthood and draw on people's ideas about moral issues concerning life, law, morality and conscience, authority, punishment, and formal obligation. By presenting individuals with stories involving moral conflicts or dilemmas, and asking them to make judgments about why a particular way of solving the dilemma is better, Kohlberg was able to describe developmental changes in how moral issues are viewed.

The most frequently quoted of Kohlberg's dilemmas deals with Heinz, whose wife is dying of cancer. A druggist has discovered a drug that may save her life, but he is charging an exorbitantly high price for it. Heinz cannot afford to buy the drug and so he borrows half the necessary money, explaining to the druggist that his wife is dying and offering to pay the remaining money later. The druggist refuses to give him the drug and Heinz, in desperation, steals it. Another dilemma involves a poor man, Valjean, who stole food and medicine for his family. Sent to prison, he escapes and goes to live in another part of the country under a new name. He saves money, builds a factory, and is exceedingly generous to his workers. After the passage of 20 years he is recognized by a tailor as the escaped convict who is still being sought by the police. In yet another conflict a boy is told by his father he can go to camp if he works hard and saves his money. The boy does so, but the father reneges on his promise and demands the money for himself. The boy is tempted to disobey his father's demand.

In all cases subjects are asked what the person in conflict should do and then justify the chosen course of action. The actual choice of action is unimportant: It is the rationale for the choice that is of interest. Justifications are assigned to one of three levels of moral functioning. There are two stages at each level, the second stage being a more advanced and organized form of the general level of the perspective. These levels and their associated stages have the following characteristics:

Preconventional morality (level 1): Rules are obeyed to avoid punishment or gain personal reward. In *Stage 1* obedience is seen as important for its own sake, authorities to have superior power, and conformity as required to avoid punishment. In *Stage 2* right action consists of serving one's own interests and letting others do likewise. Reciprocity is of prime importance, a "you scratch my back and I'll scratch yours" approach.

Conventional morality (level 2): At this level it is valuable to maintain the expectations of others (family, group, or nation). One must be loyal to the expectations of others and to the social order, and identify with them. In *Stage 3* good behavior is defined as what pleases others or is approved of by them, and one's intentions now become important. In *Stage 4* right behavior means doing one's duty, respecting authority, and maintaining the social order for its own sake.

Postconventional morality (level 3): Here good behavior is defined as adherence to moral principles that are valid independent of the individual's identification with the group. At *Stage 5* right action involves individual rights and standards agreed upon by society. Laws can be changed by mutual agreement, values are relative (except for those of life and liberty), and obligations should be honored. In *Stage 6* right is defined in accord with self-chosen ethical principles of justice, reciprocity, and equality of human rights, and respect for the dignity of human beings.

One way of characterizing the differences between levels is that in preconventional morality rules and social expectations are external to the self. In conventional morality the self has identified with or internalized the rules and expectations of others. And in postconventional morality the self is differentiated from the rules and expectations of others and values are defined in terms of self-chosen principles.

Kohlberg reports (e.g., Kohlberg, 1976) that level 1 is typical of children to about the age of 9, some adolescents, and adult criminal offenders. Level 2 characterizes the thinking of adolescents and most adults in our own as well as other societies, whereas level 3 is typical of a minority of adults. These changes over time can be seen in the answers at different ages to the question "Why shouldn't someone steal from a store?" At the age of 10 one child's answer was "It's not good to steal from the store. It's against the law. Someone could see you and call the police." The same person when aged 17 responded to the same question with "It's a matter of law. It's one of our rules that we're trying to help protect everyone, protect property. . . . If we didn't have these laws . . . our whole society would get out of kilter." And at the age of 24 he responded, "It's violating another person's rights, in this case to property."

Because Kohlberg's is a stage theory it requires that certain conditions be met, namely that each stage involve a qualitatively different way of thinking about the same problem, that the stages occur in an invariant sequence, that responses at a given stage share an underlying organization that can be determined even when tasks are dissimilar, and that each stage is increasingly differentiated and integrated (Kohlberg, 1969). Early attempts to validate the stage model have not always been completely successful (e.g., Kohlberg & Kramer, 1969). Recently, Colby, Kohlberg, Gibbs, and Lieberman (1983), using a new scoring system, analyzed the responses of 53 boys from whom data had been obtained between 1956 and 1976. The results of this longitudinal study provide strong support for the basic assumptions of the model. Thus subjects proceeded through the stages in the hypothesized sequence without skipping any stage. And there was consistency in the stage scores assigned for different dilemmas, with the majority of subjects receiving all scores at two adjacent stages.

Absent from this new analysis, however, is Stage 6, both because none of the interviews seemed to be intuitively at that stage in the sample considered and because the dilemmas used did not differentiate well between Stages 5 and 6. Indeed, most of Kohlberg's information about Stage 6 seems to have come from interviews with philosophers as well as from his own introspections (Damon, 1983).

The Relation Between Cognitive Development, Perspective-Taking Ability, Moral Development, and Moral Behavior

Kohlberg views the development of moral thinking as part of a sequence that also includes the development of logical thinking and of the ability to take the perspective of others. He argues that logical thinking has priority—advanced moral reasoning is not possible without advanced logical reasoning so that, for example, an individual who has not attained the highest stages of formal operational thinking cannot think at the postconventional level of morality. This is because only at the formal operational stage can individuals think abstractly and consider relations between systems—the ability necessary to see human beings as operating in different social systems and hence to see morality as something beyond conventional systems of social organization. Although it is possible to be at a higher logical stage than the parallel moral stage (not having mastered those additional tasks necessary for that moral stage), the reverse, then, is not possible. In between logical and moral thinking in this horizontal sequence is thinking about the thoughts and feelings of others—taking their role or perspective. Recall from our discussion in Chapter 7 that, according to Selman (1976), children progress from an inability to see that their own view of events and that of others can differ at all, to a final sophisticated realization that social systems are made up of conventional perspectives shared by all members and considered by them in social communication and understanding. Parallel social role-taking and moral judgment stages are depicted in Table 9.1. Development in social role-taking precedes and is necessary for development in the parallel stage of moral reasoning, whereas logical development precedes and is necessary for parallel role-taking development. Role-taking is less difficult than moral reasoning because it does not involve the additional tasks of judging fairness and what is right and wrong.

The final step in the horizontal sequence is moral behavior. One cannot behave in a highly moral way without having achieved a high stage of moral reasoning, although it is certainly possible to reason at a level higher than one's level of conduct. The validity of the theory therefore, in Kohlberg's eyes, does not depend on its ability to predict behavior; this is determined by a variety of factors other than stage of moral reasoning. Its validity depends (as noted earlier) on the proposed stages occurring in an invariant sequence with each succeeding stage being a more adequate way of reasoning about moral dilemmas than the preceding one.

Kohlberg argues, then, that moral reasoning is related to logical reasoning. Higher stages, among other things, represent more logical and therefore better ways of viewing moral dilemmas. As well as occurring in invariant order, the same stages should also occur universally, appearing in all cultures because all cultures provide the conditions that necessitate moral integration, namely, social interaction, role-taking, and social conflict. Accordingly, Snarey (1985) has reviewed cross-cultural studies addressed to the issue of moral reasoning and its development. These studies have been conducted in a wide range of societies including India, Israel, Turkey, Iran, Taiwan, Zambia, Guatemala, and New Zealand. They have involved Western European populations, Non-European cultures influenced by the West, and tribal folk populations (e.g., Kalskagamuit Eskimos, rural Kenyan Kipsigis). In all Snarey found 45 studies—38 of them cross-sectional and seven longitudinal. The longitudinal studies are particularly important because they alone are able to demonstrate the orderliness of stage development within a given individual. Snarey found that Kohlberg's assumptions were generally supported. Stages occurred in invariant order, with skipping of stages and regression from a higher to a lower stage rarely observed. One disturbing aspect of the data was the relative absence of postconventional thinking in many groups. This Snarey attributes to an incompleteness in Kohlberg's description of postconventional reasoning, with certain mature forms of reasoning occurring in other cultures that do not appear in our own. For example, in New Guinea, blame for Heinz's dilemma is sometimes placed on the community—a reflection of collectivist moral principles missing in our own society.

TABLE 9.1. Parallel structured relations between social role-taking and moral judgment.

	Stages	
Social role-taking stage		Moral judgment stage

Stage 0—egocentric viewpoint (Age range 3–6)
Child has a sense of differentiation of self and other but fails to distinguish between the social perspective (thoughts, feelings) of other and self. Child can label other's overt feelings but does not see the cause and effect relation of reasons to social actions.

Stage 0—premoral stage
Judgments of right and wrong are based on good or bad consequences and not on intentions. Moral choices derive from the subject's wishes that good things happen to self. Child's reasons for his choices simply assert the choices, rather than attempting to justify them.

Stage 1—social-informational role-taking (Age range 6–8)
Child is aware that other has a social perspective based on other's own reasoning, which may or may not be similar to child's. However, child tends to focus on one perspective rather than coordinating viewpoints.

Stage 1—punishment and obedience orientation
Child focuses on one perspective, that of the authority or the powerful. However, child understands that good actions are based on good intentions. Beginning sense of fairness as equality of acts.

Stage 2—self-reflective role-taking (Age range 8–10)
Child is conscious that each individual is aware of the other's perspective and that this awareness influences self and other's view of each other. Putting self in other's place is a way of judging his intentions, purposes, and actions. Child can form a coordinated chain of perspectives, but cannot yet abstract from this process to the level of simultaneous mutuality.

Stage 2—instrumental orientation
Moral reciprocity is conceived as the equal exchange of the intent of two persons in relation to one another. If someone has a mean intention toward self, it is right for self to act in kind. Right defined as what is valued by self.

Stage 3—mutual role-taking (Age range 10–12)
Child realizes that both self and other can view each other mutually and simultaneously as subjects. Child can step outside the two-person dyad and view the interaction from a third-person perspective.

Stage 3—orientation to maintaining mutual expectations
Right is defined as the Golden Rule: Do unto others as you would have others do unto you. Child considers all points of view and reflects on each person's motives in an effort to reach agreement among all participants.

Stage 4—social and conventional system role-taking (Age range 12–15 +)
Person realizes mutual perspective-taking does not always lead to complete understanding. Social conventions are seen as necessary because they are understood by all members of the group (the generalized other) regardless of their position, role, or experience.

Stage 4—orientation to society's perspective
Right is defined in terms of the perspective of the generalized other or the majority. Person considers consequences of actions for the group or society. Orientation to maintenance of social morality and social order.

Note. Age ranges for all stages represent only an average approximation based on studies to date. From "Social-Cognitive Behavior" by R.L. Selman, 1976, in T. Lickona (Ed.), *Moral Development and Behavior* (p. 309), New York: Holt, Rinehart & Winston. Copyright 1976 by T. Lickona. Reprinted by permission.

The Role of Experience

In Kohlberg's system environment plays a role in moral development, accounting for some variability by providing differential opportunities for role-taking. These role-taking opportunities arise through social relationships with parents and peers as well as through participation in the political, economic, and legal institutions of society. To be effective they must provide opportunities for leadership, communication, responsibility, and decision-making. In cultures in which there is less complexity in social roles and interactions one would not expect higher stages of moral reasoning to be reached. In keeping with this position Nisan and Kohlberg (1982) report that development was slower in Turkey in a traditional village than in a modern city where opportunities for role-taking were presumably greater. Parikh (1980) reports that, as with American subjects (Olejnik, 1980), there is among upper-middle-class East Indians a relationship between parent's use of reasoning and encouragement of their children's expression of views and the level of their children's moral judgment. Here environment is demonstrated to play a parallel role in two relatively diverse cultural settings.

Evaluation of the Theory

No theory that is clearly stated and compelling can escape criticism, and Kohlberg's is no exception. His moral dilemmas often involve situations that are foreign to children and more likely to be faced in adulthood. By not providing them with familiar material he may have underestimated children's moral capacities. Several investigators have criticized the theory as being biased against women (e.g., Gilligan, 1977, 1982; Haan, 1977; Holstein, 1976). Gilligan contends that Kohlberg's system is insensitive to typically feminine concerns for welfare, caring, and responsibility and that these concerns are assigned to lower stages of thought. Because Kohlberg's stages were established initially from data provided by male subjects only, and because protagonists in the stories are always male (although one of the stories in Colby et al. does involve a female protagonist), she argues that the typically feminine morality of responsibility has been missed out in favor of the more masculine morality of rights, with the latter focusing on traditional male values such as rationality, detachment, and impersonality. The widely shared belief has been that women tend to fixate at Stage 3 with its orientation to the approval and feelings of others, whereas men progress to Stage 4, which emphasizes the maintenance of social order. Some of the strength is taken from this argument, however, in a review by Walker (1984) of 77 published papers providing data pertinent to the issue of sex differences in moral reasoning. Walker concludes that there is no consistent evidence for their existence. Thus the belief that women are less morally advanced than men, or that they are treated improperly in the Kohlbergian scheme, appears unjustified.

This does not mean that there may not be sex differences in preferences for various orientations in the making of moral judgments. Gibbs, Arnold, and Burkhart (1984) have found that whereas males and females do not differ in levels of moral judgment attained, females at Stage 3 do use more empathic role-taking rationales than do males at Stage 3. These investigators report another difference in the Stage 3 reasoning of males and females: No male, but 21% of the females in their study, used intrapersonal approval or disapproval as a reason for choosing a particular course of action. This greater use of reasons related to conscience (or self-reward and self-punishment) by females is, of course, quite contrary to Freud's contention that females have weaker superegos than males.

An additional area of criticism has to do with Kohlberg's argument that logical thinking has priority in the development of moral reasoning. Here the evidence is mixed, with some investigators finding the predicted relationships and others not (e.g., Faust & Arbuthnot, 1978; Haan, Weiss, & Johnson, 1982; Krebs & Gilmore, 1982; Walker, 1980, 1982). Haan et al. argue that social interaction, not logical competence, is at the core of morality and that the kind of thinking required in moral negotiations is practical and intuitive, rather than abstract and logically formal.

Another form of the argument that cognitive competence and moral thinking are not intimately linked is put forth by social learning theorists. They argue that much, if not all, of moral thinking is determined by the models of reasoning to which individuals are exposed, as well as differential reinforcement and punishment they receive contingent on the quality of their moral verbalization. Young children may use authority-oriented reasoning because they are more likely to be exposed to threats of punishment for misbehavior. However, they may be quite capable, for example, of *comprehending* empathically oriented reasoning (Eisenberg's work on stages of prosocial reasoning, cited earlier in this chapter, suggests this ability exists quite early) but not use it in their reasoning because they are not exposed to models who use it. Indeed, there are some striking parallels between conceptualizations of the socialization process and stages of moral thinking. Socialization has been successful when children conform not because of external contingencies (cf. level 1 of moral judgment) but because they have identified with agents of socialization and internalized their values (cf. level 2), or because they attribute their behavior to self-chosen rather than externally imposed courses of action (cf. level 3). Are we seeing in Kohlberg's stages, then, a reflection of the success of socialization techniques as children grow older?

Turiel's work on morality and social convention supports the contention that there are multiple structures in the child's social thinking rather than the one basic structure Kohlberg hypothesizes as underlying social development. Kohlberg suggests that only at Stage 5—in early adulthood—do individuals reject convention as arbitrary while endorsing beliefs that are based on moral principles of justice. But Turiel and others have found that

even very young children can differentiate between moral and conventional concerns, an indication that Kohlberg has misjudged early capacities.
Thus Kohlberg has failed to appreciate the moral abilities of the young and
that moral capacity may not, therefore, be so closely related to cognitive
capacity as he maintains. We see a similar qualification of the unidi-
mensional approach of both Kohlberg and Piaget in the work of William
Damon.

Damon and the Child's Social World

Damon (1977, 1980) argues that rather than looking for the roots of moral
thinking in children's judgments about abstract dilemmas, one is more likely to find them in such things as the rules by which they govern their daily
activities. By investigating the social world of the child in its own terms, of
course, Damon borrows from Piaget. Damon has also shifted attention
from conceptions of wrongdoing, disobedience, culpability, and punishment—the more usual subject of study—to a direct focus on ideas of
justice. In childhood, Damon contends, justice is more commonly practiced in the realms of sharing and distribution of resources, that is, in the
positive domain, and so, in order to study moral development, he has
presented children between the ages of 4 and 12 years with hypothetical
situations in which they are asked to decide how goods should be fairly
distributed. In one scenario, for example, a group of four children make
bracelets for an adult who offers 10 candy bars in exchange for their effort.
The children have different characteristics, with one making the most and
the prettiest bracelets, one being bigger than the others, and one being
younger and unable to work as well or as quickly as the others. The task,
then, is to decide on the fairest way of sharing the candy bars.

In keeping with the cognitive developmental approach, Damon has
charted stages in children's thinking about fairness and justice. For very
young children positive justice is seen as equivalent to their own desires,
that is, they appear to have no sense of justice. They then move into a stage
where they display a rudimentary notion of merit (e.g., "The biggest
should get the most"), then on to a stage where strict equality is the rule.
After this, however, children begin to believe that some people are more
deserving than others and that justice involves taking into account notions
of merit and fair exchange. Next comes a stage where children can coordi-
nate varying claims to justice. Equal acts should be rewarded equally and
resources should be administered on the basis of merit and fair exchange.
As well, however, differential rewarding may be necessary to maintain the
equality of persons, that is, extra resources may have to be given to those
with special needs to compensate for inequalities that existed prior to the
distribution of resources in the hypothetical situation. Thus hungry people
may need extra food. This Damon labels as the benevolent mode of sharing. Finally, considerations of equality and reciprocity are coordinated. It

is recognized that all participants should be given their due, although this does not mean that they should be treated equally.

Notable in Damon's studies of moral reasoning are the relatively sophisticated ideas of justice evidenced by quite young children, as well as the absence of the early orientation to authority so emphasized by both Piaget and Kohlberg. Beliefs were, according to Damon, deeply held and certainly not external to the child's value system. Young children were not wedded to social rules imposed by adults and appeared to be quite capable of developing conceptions of morality out of their earliest associations with other people.

Damon discounts Kohlberg's contention that moral thinking is an aspect of logical ability. He maintains that morality, as well as other aspects of social knowledge such as beliefs about friendship, the relationship between obedience and authority, and social rules, customs, and conventions, each have their own distinct developmental characteristics. He argues, however, that they all share general organizing principles which contribute to some degree of relationship among them. These principles do include two important cognitive skills, the ability to classify or group events and the ability to know how change in one dimension makes up, or compensates, for change in another dimension (e.g., as seen in Piaget's conservation tasks). In the area of positive justice children's classification of persons, values, personal attributes, and claims to justice help to determine allocations of reward. Compensatory abilities are revealed in the child's achievemet of balance and equity when attempting to distribute outcomes in a just way.

SOME MORE THOUGHTS ON THE RELATIONSHIP BETWEEN MORAL THOUGHT AND MORAL CONDUCT

By most people's definitions an act is truly moral only insofar as the intentions behind it are not self-serving. Thus most individuals would agree that honesty motivated by fear of parental punishment or a long prison sentence does not qualify as an example of moral conduct. The point has been well made by cognitive developmental theorists. It is disturbing to note, however, that acts which are repugnant to many may be perpetrated with the most moral of intentions. Haan (1982), in fact, argues that all people (including Adolf Eichmann) consider themselves to be moral creatures, and she quotes the words of Protagoras that "all men properly say they are righteous whether or not they really are. Or else if they do not lay claim to righteousness they must be insane." Not infrequently self-deception, distortion, and redefinition are necessary to support this view of one's self as moral and to provide justification for one's own acts. But the need to see our own behavior and that of others as just may well be necessary for peace of mind and a sense of security. If we do not act morally toward others why should they act morally toward us? The most appropriate behavioral manifestations of our moral principles, however, do evolve on both an individual and a social level.

Despite the difficulty in deciding what is truly moral conduct, there is enough cultural consensus to have enabled investigators to consider the relationships between moral thought and behavior. If behavior emerges out of thought, then, there should be a fairly strong relationship between the two. For many cognitive-developmental theorists, however, the argument for such a relationship is not so compelling, and they see moral judgment, for example, as independent of moral conduct or even as justification for conduct after the fact. The complexity of the link, if it does exist, has been acknowledged even by some of the foremost proponents of the cognitive developmental position. Kohlberg, as we have noted, outrightly rejects the existence of a relation between his stages of moral judgment and conduct as necessary to demonstrate the validity of his theory. Damon shares this position. He has found, in fact, that stages of distributive justice relate inconsistently to children's actual attempts to share resources and points out that self-interest no doubt intervenes between thought and behavior. Thus it is one thing to reason abstractly about how individuals should distribute resources and quite another to engage in acts that might interfere with one's own enjoyment of those resources.

Undeterred by such arguments many researchers have proceeded to look for a link between moral thought and conduct. In view of the problems we have just described it is perhaps remarkable that they have had a degree of success. In a review of the relevant literature Blasi (1980) concludes that the opinion that moral reasoning and moral behavior are independent dimensions "is revealed to be a well-advertised myth." The picture is not impressively consistent. Blasi notes that nine of 11 studies that have compared the moral reasoning of deliquents and nondelinquents have shown the former to be more immature in their reasoning. Of 11 studies assessing the relationship between honesty and moral judgment, however, six have demonstrated a positive correlation, two no correlation, and three a negative correlation. Quite clearly, even if one accepts the view that moral thought precedes and helps to determine moral action, a number of other variables intervene to modify that action. These variables include the selfish desire to preserve one's own resources, the extent to which one is capable of exhibiting self-control, and the ability to redefine what is just and fair.

MORALITY: CONSTRUCTED AND TRANSMITTED

Morality, as we have outlined, is viewed either as constructed by the child out of his experience in social interaction or as the result of the transmission of cultural values by agents of socialization. Here are some further observations relevant to the issue. As we saw in Chapter 5, parents actively attempt to instill moral behavior, and it is difficult to believe that their efforts have no effect. As parents reason in the course of socialization they do convey moral principles. Olejnik (1980) reports that individuals at more advanced levels of moral judgment describe their parents as having used reasoning when they disciplined, whereas those at less advanced levels describe their parents as power assertive. There is, then, a relationship between moral judgment level and the socialization technique used by parents, with the possibility that it is the socialization technique which produces both sophistication of thought and internalization of standards of behavior. Moral judgment, as well as moral behavior, may be the result of transmission of information and values from parents to children.

As well, children manufacture some of their ideas about justice out of personal experience with injustice as well as the observation of injustice to others. Even young children have ideas about what is just and fair and immutable. Children state that stealing is wrong, even in places where there is no rule to that effect (Turiel, 1978), and it seems unlikely that anyone has given them this specific piece of information. How moral beliefs are constructed, however, is unclear. Kohlberg and Piaget maintain that peer interactions that pose cognitive conflict are most effective in facilitating moral change, but others (e.g., Youniss, 1980) emphasize the importance of cooperation and communication with peers. Nor should the role of parent teaching be ignored in this regard. It is highly likely that children themselves generalize from their experience with parent discipline and reasoning, deriving for themselves conceptions of morality that are based on, but expanded from, the material with which they are confronted. A study by Leon (1984) is instructive in this regard. Leon was interested in the similarities between mothers and their young sons in their usage of information about intention and damage to determine the amount of punishment deserved for a misdeed. He divided his mothers into three groups: those who took both damage and intention into account in their judgments, those who ignored damage when the misdeed was accidental but not when it was performed with malicious intent, and those who punished on the basis of damage alone. The judgments of their sons turned out to match very closely the judgments of the mothers. Leon points out that although this finding is certainly supportive of a social learning theory position which argues that children match the moral arguments of their parents, it does indicate that something other than observational learning is going on. Children cannot simply imitate mothers who are making complicated judgments about interactions of intent and damage because they must first figure out what the mother's rule is and then formulate their own. The area of generalization from parent instruction is one that has been uncharted by socialization theorists.

The Development of Prosocial Behavior

The roots of morality, as we have noted, can be seen very early in the course of development. Although sophisticated moral judgment may be the domain of adolescents and adults, even preschoolers appear to have an intuitive grasp of what is just and fair. This is a major message of much recent work in the area of morality. In the last few years researchers have been pushing back the origins of prosocial development in a similar manner.

For a long time the preschooler was characterized as helpless, demanding, dependent on others, and quite self-centered. This is not to say that many observers had not, in fact, noted the prosocial capacities of the young child. Stern (1942), Piaget (1932), Murphy (1937), and Lewin (1942), for example, all speak of the young child's sensitivity to the needs of others. But somehow these observations were lost in the prevailing theoretical zeitgeist which strongly emphasized the egocentric nature of the first few years of life. Concern for others was thought to be delayed until the period of concrete operational functioning when, for the first time, individuals were sufficiently grown out of their egocentrism to be able to understand another's point of view and to see that the needs of others might be different from their own. We have already seen in Chapter 7 that role-taking and empathic abilities, assumed to be essential ingredients for prosocial development, do emerge much earlier in the course of development.

THE ROOTS OF ALTRUISM

Sharing and Helping

As long ago as 1787, Tiedemann noted that very young children both show and give objects to others (Rheingold, Hay, & West, 1976). More recent evidence for this tendency has been provided by Rheingold et al. In a series of laboratory studies they demonstrated that 18-month-old children frequently bring the attention of both parents and strangers to objects by pointing at them as well as actually sharing them. Field observations by these investigators indicated that such behavior occurs as early as 12 months of age. In fact, Rheingold et al. note that parents had been recipients of their children's gifts for so long they hardly noticed the behavior and usually were unable to identify the time at which it had first appeared. What, one may ask, do children intend by these early attempts at prosocial action? Rheingold et al. argue that their behavior is not egocentric, that children who share are not doing so to get attention, help, or praise. The act occurs without parental prompting or encouragement and seems to be quite independent of external circumstance, a genuine contribution to social interaction. Although this early giving may not involve great amounts of self-sacrifice, it still seems to indicate a rudimentary awareness of the needs of others.

Rheingold has also documented the early appearance of helping (Rheingold, 1982). She observed children between the ages of 18 and 30 months with their parents, as well as with strangers, having instructed the adults to carry out a variety of household chores including setting a table, organizing scattered magazines and playing cards, folding laundry, sweeping, and making up a bed. More than half the younger children and all the older children helped with the majority of tasks. They appeared to enjoy themselves, to know what they were trying to achieve (i.e., they were not just playing), and they were better at helping the older they were. Parents' incidental reports of their children's behavior confirmed this picture—2-year-olds help with the dusting and sweeping and they put clothes into the dryer. These are not acts parents actively work to encourage, for many reported that they tried to do chores when their children were asleep to avoid the interference caused by less than totally efficient help-giving. Why do children help? Rheingold suggests that young children are interested in people and their activities, that they enjoy imitating them, sometimes in creative ways, that they take pleasure in companionship and exercising skills, and that helping is also maintained by adult recognition of their efforts. This picture is supported by the fact that children were most likely to help when they were near parents who were performing a task in a clear way, who were describing what they were doing, and who were even suggesting their children might help. Helping did not occur when work was done away from the children's view or was left incomplete. Did these children actually have a conscious intent to help thus qualifying their behavior as altruistic? As with sharing, early helping does not show signs of being totally egocentric but gives the appearance of being part of a desire to interact in and contribute to a social situation.

Comforting and Defending

Not only do young children seem capable of appreciating the needs and interests of others as evidenced by their eagerness to share and help, but they also respond in prosocial ways to the emotional distress of those around them. These reactions have been studied in children aged 10 to 29 months by Marian Radke-Yarrow, Carolyn Zahn-Waxler, and their colleagues (e.g., Zahn-Waxler, Radke-Yarrow, & King, 1979) who present a convincing case for their being instances of true altruism. By training mothers to observe their children's behavior these investigators were able to chart children's responses to both naturally occurring and simulated distress. In all, three cohorts of children were studied for 9 months each, with the first cohort 10 months old at the beginning of the study, the second 15 months, and the third 20 months. The reactions of these three cohorts are described in Table 9.2.

As the reader can see, early responses consist primarily of looking at the distressed person, crying, whimpering, laughing, and smiling. These decrease with time and are replaced by increased seeking of the caretaker (most frequent in Cohort B), increased imitation, and marked attempts at altruistic or prosocial intervention. The content of these prosocial interventions also becomes more sophisticated with time. A younger child, at 69 weeks, offered her bottle to a tired mother, then lay down beside her, patted her, and drank from the bottle. An older child, at 104 weeks, responded to the cries of a young sibling by saying, "Sister is crying, let's go to her. Let me hold her. You'd better nurse her, mommy; does she have a burp?" Prosocial interactions were not always appropriate as with the child who offered her bottle to a tired mother, or as with another child who soothed a mother who was crying because she was peeling onions. But they clearly contained the elements of genuine concern for others.

Earlier in this chapter we noted the close link between altruism and attempts at reparation after harm-doing. Table 9.2 includes only children's reactions to distress in others that they witnessed as bystanders. In Table 9.3 we see their reactions to distress in others that they themselves had caused. The similarity to Table 9.2 is impressive, with distress cries the predominant response in the youngest children, followed by positive affect. As with reactions to distress in which they were merely bystanders, these responses decreased and were replaced by increasing prosocial intervention or, more specifically, reparation for deviation. Older children wipe up messes they have made, apologize, and promise to be better behaved in the future. The major difference between reactions to distress as a bystander and as a causal agent lies in the greater incidence of aggression in the latter case. Once initiated, the inflicting of distress may continue.

Not only are the beginnings of concern for others seen at an early age, but they also appear to provide the prototype for later altruism. When the children studied by Radke-Yarrow and Zahn-Waxler were observed again at the age of 7 years, two-thirds of them showed patterns of prosocial responding that were qualitatively similar to those displayed at the age of 2 years. A girl who was caring and solicitous when young—comforting her upset mother—behaved in an analogous way at 7 by giving her sandals to a barefooted friend who had to walk on hot pavement. A boy who, when young, protected a friend by pushing his assailant into a swimming pool later pushed someone who had stepped into a grocery line in front of his grandmother.

As with sharing and helping we may ask about the causes of early comforting and defending. Whereas the adoption of specific value systems and adherence to learned norms involving notions of reciprocity, responsibility, or deservedness have been posited to underlie the acquisition of altruism, Zahn-Waxler et al. point out that this could hardly be the case for very young children. One obvious source for their behavior is in the model provided by the caring acts of others. Children see adults comforting and protecting others and are also the recipients of such acts themselves. The many instances mothers reported of patting, kissing hurts, caressing, and providing bandages, food, and toys attest to this important antecedent. The fact that mothers who were identified as providing empathic caregiving had more altruistic children suggests that these mothers were modeling, and their children were imitating, sensitive reactions to need. Mothers who

TABLE 9.2. Children's reactions to distress in others. Average percentage of distress incidents to which the child responded.

	Ages (in weeks)					
	38–61	62–85	62–85	86–109	86–109	110–134
	Cohort A T-1, %	Cohort A T-2, %	Cohort B T-1, %	Cohort B T-2, %	Cohort C T-1, %	Cohort C T-2, %
A. Natural distresses observed by child						
No response	10	11	7	7	11	10
Orients to emotion	26	33	21	16	8	5
Distress cries	28	14	16	12	5	10
Seeks caregiver	2	10	26	25	11	18
Positive affect	7	5	9	5	5	4
Aggression	4	10	12	11	8	13
Imitation	4	14	16	19	14	12
Prosocial intervention[a]	11	11	16	30	39	32
B. Simulated distresses observed by child						
No response	15	10	11	14	21	23
Orients to emotion	19	33	9	11	6	4
Distress cries	5	4	9	3	4	2
Seeks caregiver	19	30	48	29	22	26
Positive affect	29	24	19	9	7	6
Aggression	4	6	6	10	9	2
Imitation	12	13	22	22	26	12
Prosocial intervention[a]	4	5	19	30	33	33

Note. From "The Development of Altruism: Alternative Strategies" by C. Zahn-Waxler and M. Radke-Yarrow, 1982, in N. Eisenberg (Ed.), *The Development of Prosocial Behavior* (pp. 109–137), New York: Academic Press. Reprinted by permission.

[a] In comparisons of prosocial behaviors of children of the same age but of different lengths of participation in the study (i.e., Cohort A_{Time2} with B_{Time1} and B_{Time2} and C_{Time1}) there were no significant differences between groups.

used explanations accompanied by strong affect when their children deviated were also likely to have altruistic offspring.

Another source of comforting and defending lies in the child's capacity to empathize with distress in others, that is, to experience vicariously their emotional state (see Chapter 7 for a discussion of its development). This ability has played a prominent role in many conceptualizations of the altruistic process. Awareness of the distress of others, it is argued, leads to a state of empathic arousal that is distressing. Thus helping and comforting are carried out in order to reduce empathic distress. Knowledge of the development of empathic capacities, therefore, should shed light on our understanding of early altruism. Certainly the work of Radke-Yarrow and Zahn-Waxler reflects a developing awareness of the feelings and needs of others in very young children.

TABLE 9.3. Children's reactions to distress they have caused. Average percentage of distress incidents to which the child responded.

	Ages (in weeks)					
	38–61	62–85	62–85	86–109	86–109	110–134
	Cohort A T-1, %	Cohort A T-2, %	Cohort B T-1, %	Cohort B T-2, %	Cohort C T-1, %	Cohort C T-2, %
No response	15	9	12	6	6	5
Orients to emotion	12	15	7	8	3	2
Distress cries	55	40	26	27	22	19
Seeks caregiver						
Positive affect	20	19	17	19	13	13
Aggression	17	22	34	29	22	44
Imitation	10	14	10	8	24	24
Prosocial						
intervention	2	6	16	25	31	24

Note. From "The Development of Altruism: Alternative Strategies" by C. Zahn-Waxler and M. Radke-Yarrow, 1982, in N. Eisenberg (Ed.), *The Development of Prosocial Behavior* (pp. 109–137), New York: Academic Press. Reprinted by permission.

The Relationship Between Empathy and Altruism

The widely hypothesized relationship between empathy and altruism has prompted many investigators to attempt to document its existence. The number of studies generated has not been as great as the number aimed at finding a relationship between moral judgment and moral behavior, but the results are equally confused. Two reviews of the relevant research (Radke-Yarrow, Zahn-Waxler, & Chapman, 1983; Underwood & Moore, 1982) concluded that there was as yet no compelling support for the hypothesis that altruism and empathy are correlated. The findings are a mixture of positive, negative, and no relationship between the two variables. Eisenberg and Miller (1987) suggest that empathy and altruism *are* related, but the relationship depends on how empathy is measured. Moreover, on the basis of meta-analytic studies, the relationship appears to be weaker for children than for adults. Eisenberg and Miller propose this is because affect and behavior become more integrated with age. Thus young children may lack the ability to help constructively or they may have difficulty understanding the meaning of their own vicarious arousal.

One problem with trying to relate empathy and altruism has been in the way in which empathy is measured. Many studies have used the test devised by Feshbach and Roe (1968) in which children are shown series of slides depicting happy, sad, fearful, and angry events happening to others and asked how these pictures make them feel. If they report feelings that match those of the character in the story then this is assumed to be evidence of empathic responding. We have already discussed some of the limitations of the Feshbach and Roe instrument in Chapter 7. Among other things it assumes that empathy is a unitary trait and that individuals who are high in the ability to empathize with distress and need in others should be able to experience *all* emotions vicariously. A reasonable alternative, however, may be that some individuals are especially adept at empathizing with negative emotions—sadness, fear, and anger as opposed to happiness and pride—and that it is this particular ability that promotes altruism. In accord with this view Sawin (1979) has reported that negative empathy relates to helping for first graders (but not third graders), whereas positive empathy does not. Feshbach (1982), in a study of third and fourth graders, did find that negative but not positive empathy and altruism were related, but only among boys. For girls both positive and negative empathy correlated with prosocial behavior. In fact, Eisenberg and Miller found it was other measures of empathy, such as self-reports of empathy in simulated distress situations and physiological indices, which were more likely to predict altruism. Unfortunately, most of the studies using these measures have been conducted with adults.

Another difficulty with studies in the area centers around the measures of prosocial behavior that have been used. They are a fairly mixed group. Thus we know something about empathy and altruism in more than one narrowly defined situation. But it is not clear that researchers have always been dealing with altruistic acts, engaged in without hope of personal gain. Some may have been motivated by hope of social approval or of reciprocation, or may have been a response to demand characteristics imposed by an experimental situation. Also, if we consider that some acts of altruism may be motivated by the enjoyment of social interaction or by the desire to exercise helping skills, then we should really not expect to find a correlation between empathy and altruism when considering them.

In addition to these problems of measurement and selection of variables is the possibility that too much empathic arousal could well be detrimental to the display of concern for others inasmuch as it interferes with effective help-giving. Radke-Yarrow et al. (1979), for example, describe one pattern of reaction to distress that occurred in some children in which unhappiness in others produced obvious upset in the observer, but where the response to this upset was simply to block out or avoid the distress cues. As well, it should be remembered that no amount of empathic arousal is likely to produce much altruism unless the skills for reducing distress have been acquired. If effective aid to others has not been modeled or taught in some way, then it is unlikely that unhappiness in others can do much beyond producing anguish and primitive shows of concern.

Other motives, besides the reduction of sympathetic distress, can motivate altruism. We have already referred to some, such as a desire for mastery and the enjoyment of social interaction. As children grow older, however, the variety of socialization experiences that they undergo may promote additional sources of motivation. Although these experiences may build on and refine empathic ability by sensitizing children to the feelings of others, they also may lead to the internalization of a norm of social responsibility or develop a self-concept which includes the characteristics of concern and kindness that must be lived up to. Thus the role of empathy could be minor in many individuals who are nevertheless very altruistic people.

Altruism and Perspective-Taking

It may be that a social-cognitive variable more consistently necessary to the display of altruism is that of social-cognitive and affective perspective-taking, that is, knowledge of the thoughts, feelings, and needs of others. This basic ability is necessary if only to identify that others are in need as well as to determine actions that might satisfy their need. While a variety of motivational devices could propel an individual into a state of altruistic action, there must be some knowledge of demand for and appropriateness of a given action. The data support this contention. Studies attempting to relate children's ability to identify another person's thoughts, intentions, motives, or social behavior (social-cognitive perspective-taking) and altruism, or to relate their ability to identify another person's feelings, reactions, or concern (affective perspective-taking) and altruism have not consistently found statistically significant positive relationships. But, unlike studies of empathy and altruism, negative relationships are not in evidence. Moreover, using meta-analytic procedures, Underwood and Moore (1982) concluded that there is indeed evidence for a reliable relationship between social-cognitive and affective perspective-taking and altruism.

The importance of role-taking ability is also demonstrated in two studies in which investigators actually attempted to train children to understand the perspective of others. Staub (1971) had kindergarten children act out situations in which one child needed help and another provided it, playing both roles. As a result of the training girls were more likely to respond to sounds of distress coming from an adjacent room, whereas boys were more likely to share candy with a boy whose parents were unable to buy a birthday present for him. In a second training study (Iannotti, 1978) boys were read a series of stories. Some were asked to imagine themselves in the position of a particular character and asked about his reactions, whereas others were asked to imagine the point of view and reactions of more than one character. Boys in the control group were asked questions about the story's content. Iannotti found that his training increased both social perspective-taking ability and altruism, with altruism being even greater in the perspective-switching than the perspective-taking condition. This increase was evidenced, however, only in 6-year-olds and not in 9-year-olds, who may already have had quite well-developed role-taking abilities.

MOOD AND SHARING

Affect plays an important role in the expression of altruism in many ways. Its source may lie in empathic arousal, in guilt over failure to live up to one's self-image, or in the pleasure of social interaction, display of mastery, and identification with respected others. Another source is the momentary mood state of the altruist, an affective variable that has received considerable attention. A number of studies, using adults as subjects, have demonstrated that people will help others more after they have experienced either an unpleasant or a pleasant event compared with a neutral one (Isen, 1970; Kidd & Berkowitz, 1976; Konecni, 1972). The findings for children, however, are somewhat different. Although positive experiences also promote altruism, negative ones have no effect or even depress it.

In the studies with children moods have been manipulated by giving children experiences with success or failure or by instructing them to think about happy or sad events. They have then been given the opportunity to share money or tokens anonymously with others. Thus, in a typical experiment, Moore, Underwood, and Rosenhan (1973) had 7- and 8-year-olds think about things that made them happy or sad or, in a neutral condition, to count slowly. They were then given the chance, when unobserved, to share money with other children whom they neither knew nor would ever see. Children in the sad condition shared less than those in the neutral control group, whereas those in the happy condition shared most of all. Similar patterns of findings have been reported by Barnett and Bryan (1974); Isen, Horn, and Rosenhan (1973); Rosenhan, Underwood, and Moore (1974); Rushton and Littlefield (1979); and Underwood, Froming, and Moore (1977). Also, in a very different sort of situation, Strayer (1980), observing preschoolers in a nursery school, found that those who displayed happy emotions were more likely to respond empathically to others (by sharing their emotional experiences, providing positive reinforcement, and comforting) than those who more frequently displayed sad emotions. The effect, then, is not confined to one very specific situation. Finally, in a successful attempt to trace the expected developmental change in the effects of negative mood, Cialdini and Kenrick (1976) found that negative affect somewhat depressed the donation of prize coupons among younger children but increased it significantly for those 15 years of age and more.

Additional light has been shed on the relationship between mood and donation in the work of Barnett, King, and Howard (1979). They asked children to describe happy, sad, or neutral events that had happened to themselves—the usual manipulation—or to another child. Sad thoughts about the self had the usual effect of depressing donation, whereas sad thoughts about another increased donation substantially, even beyond that of children who thought about happy experiences. In a later study, Barnett, Howard, Melton, and Dino (1980) found that thinking sad thoughts about others enhanced altruism (in this case, making activity booklets for sick children while waiting for an adult to return), but only in the case of children who were highly empathic. These two studies demonstrate that it is not any kind of unpleasant affect that suppresses altruism in children, but only that which causes them to focus on themselves. Such a self-orientation may produce an insensitivity or inattentiveness to the needs of others. Thinking about the misfortunes of others produces a different kind of negative affect, namely, empathic arousal, which can motivate concern for others.

Why do people become more generous and helpful when they are in a good mood, and why do only adolescents and adults always behave more prosocially when in a bad mood? Several suggestions have been offered. Being in a good mood increases the attractiveness of others (Clore, 1975) and may therefore incline one to be more helpful. Isen, Shalker, Clark, and Karp (1978) found that adults in a good mood were able to recall positive events better than negative or neutral ones. A happy individual could be more helpful, then, if pleasant memories of previous helping sprang to mind. As for the facilitating effects of negative mood in older individuals, it may be that once norms of social responsibility are internalized, altruism is gratifying and its performance leads to feelings of virtue that help to offset the unpleasantness of a bad mood. In a similar vein, Cialdini, Kenrick, and Baumann (1982) elaborate a "negative state relief" model in which they suggest that the act of being altruistic is reinforcing and can therefore be used to make the self feel good. It takes a period of socialization, however, for altruism to acquire this ability. Thus social reinforcement, reduction of empathic arousal, and reciprocity for helping when repeatedly paired with altruistic acts finally instill altruism with secondarily reinforcing qualities.

REASONING ABOUT PROSOCIAL BEHAVIOR

As with moral behavior, a way of assessing whether or not prosocial acts are truly altruistic is to discover the reasons or motivations underlying them. Researchers interested in altruism have done this by modeling their procedures after those used by Piaget and Kohlberg. Baldwin and Baldwin (1970), for example, asked children to judge the relative kindness of acts varying in such attributes as their intentionality and the presence or absence of a request from an authority figure. They found that as children grow older they judge an act as kind only if it is intentional and by choice, involves self-sacrifice, and is not in response to a social obligation such as returning a favor. For young children acts are more likely to be seen as good if they are followed by reward rather than by punishment (Jensen & Hughston, 1971; Leahy, 1979), a characteristic reminiscent of Piaget's notion of immanent justice. Moreover, with increasing age, acts done to help someone in need are seen as more meritorious than are those done to repay a favor (Peterson, 1980).

Eisenberg (Eisenberg-Berg, 1979; Eisenberg, 1982), modeling her approach after Kohlberg's, has devised a series of dilemmas involving situations where individuals have to choose between satisfying their own needs and those of others. These situations are different from Kohlberg's in that external prohibition—law, formal obligation, punishment, and authority—plays no role, and different from Damon's in that principles of equality and merit are not central. One of Eisenberg's stories, written for a female subject, is the following:

One day a girl named Mary was going to a friend's birthday party. On her way she saw a girl who had fallen down and hurt her leg. The girl asked Mary to go to her house and get her parents so the parents could come and take her to the doctor. But if Mary did run and get the child's parents she would be late for the birthday party and miss the ice cream, cake, and all the games. What should Mary do? Why?

Eisenberg administered this and similar stories to children ranging in age from 7 to 17 years and was able to identify stages of prosocial judgment, with lower stages characterizing the judgments of younger children and higher stages the judgments of older children. There are five stages in all, which Eisenberg describes in the following terms:

Stage 1—Hedonistic, pragmatic orientation: Correct behavior is that which satisfies the actor's own needs.

Stage 2—"Needs of others" orientation: Concern is with the physical, material, and psychological needs of others, but is expressed simply, for example, "He's hungry."

Stage 3—Approval and interpersonal orientation and/or stereotyped orientation: Concern now is with stereotyped images of good and bad people and behavior and with the approval of others, for example, "It's nice to help."

Stage 4a—Empathic orientation: Here there is evidence of sympathetic responding and an awareness of the consequences of one's actions for others.

Stage 4b—Transitional stage: At this point justifications for behavior involve internalized norms, values, duties, or responsibilities, or refer to the need to protect the rights and dignity of others. They are, however, weakly stated (e.g., "It's just something I've learned and feel").

Stage 5—Strongly internalized stage: In the final stage the ideas of Stage 4b are strongly expressed.

Several things should be noted about this sequence of judgments. First of all, Kohlberg's Stage 1 reasoning is virtually absent (as we noted at the beginning of this chapter). Eisenberg also finds that prosocial reasoning is more advanced than Kohlberg's prohibition-oriented reasoning and that even preschoolers make needs-oriented, empathic judgments. This is a reflection, we would suggest, of adults' greater usage of empathic reasoning in the prosocial domain. The salience of empathic reasoning in prosocial conflicts is further evidenced by its existence as a separate category rather than its being grouped with interpersonal and approval-oriented reasoning as Kohlberg does in his Stage 3. Unlike prohibition-oriented reasoning, where individuals generally give up lower-stage reasoning as they advance to higher levels, Eisenberg finds that older children use a variety of stages of prosocial reasoning. Thus not only do they verbalize advanced notions of empathic concern and internalized values, but they also employ justifications more typical of younger children, particularly when they are rationalizing decisions not to help a needy other. Nevertheless, in a longitudinal study of children between 4 and 8 years old, Eisenberg, Lennon, and Roth (1983) established that hedonic reasoning decreases steadily with age and that there is a simultaneous increase with age in needs-oriented reasoning.

Eisenberg has also addressed the question of whether or not prosocial reasoning and altruistic behavior are related. Mature prosocial reasoning and willingness to help an experimenter with a dull task are related for adolescent boys but not adolescent girls (Eisenberg-Berg, 1979). Among preschoolers spontaneous sharing correlates with maturity of prosocial reasoning, whereas spontaneous helping does not (Eisenberg-Berg & Hand, 1979). Similar inconsistent results have been noted for relationships between prosocial behavior and prohibition-oriented reasoning (Blasi, 1980). Given the variety of variables that intervene between reasoning and behavior, the weakness of these relationships is hardly surprising.

CONSISTENCY AND CONTINUITY OF ALTRUISTIC BEHAVIOR

By the generally accepted definition, altruism includes any behavior intended to benefit others and is done without hope of personal gain. The question remains, however, whether altruistic acts co-occur. Is there an altruistic individual—one who is always helpful, generous, and supportive? Another form the question takes is whether specific altruistic behaviors are consistent across time and place or whether they depend on specific characteristics of situations in which individuals find themselves.

If one considers the material discussed in the last half of this chapter it should be evident that not all altruistic acts are reflections of the same underlying trait. We have argued that the developmental antecedents of helping, sharing, comforting, and defending are different, with empathic arousal, the desire to exercise helping skills, social reinforcement, and pleasure in companionship differentially implicated in each behavior. To the extent that empathic abilities, desire for mastery, exposure to social reinforcement, and sociability vary in a given individual, one would not expect the prosocial acts they underlie to be consistently evident in that individual.

Indeed, the data hardly present a picture of a generalized disposition for altruism. Thus Eisenberg-Berg and Hand (1979) did not find sharing and helping to be related in preschoolers, nor did Green and Schneider (1974) find them to be related in 5- to 14-year-olds. Weissbrod (1976) reports no relationship between sharing and emergency helping—responding to cries of distress from an adjacent room—among 6-year-olds. Krebs and Sturrup (1974) note a weak correlation of .21 between offering help and support and Dlugokinski and Firestone (1974) report moderate correlations, ranging from .19 to .38, among donation, peer ratings of consideration, understanding of kindness, and espousal of other-centered values.

On the other hand, Rubin and Schneider (1973) found sharing candy and helping a peer were correlated ($r = .40$) and Elliott and Vasta (1970) report sharing of candies and pennies—two very similar behaviors—to be significantly related ($r = .65$). When they combined several measures of sharing with and helping peers to form composite scores, Strayer, Wareing, and Rushton (1979) found that the two classes of behavior were highly related ($r = .62$). They did not, however, find that prosocial behaviors directed to peers correlated with those directed to adults. Grusec (1985) reports for 4-year-olds substantial correlations among measures of naturally occurring altruism: The correlations for helping, sharing, showing concern, and protecting ranged from .45 to .61. For 7-year-olds correlations were much less significant. Though many more studies have assessed the relationships between various indices of altruism (see Radke-Yarrow, Zahn-Waxler, & Chapman, 1983, for a review), the picture does not change. It is neither overwhelmingly positive nor negative. There is some, but not great, consistency within individuals in prosocial behavior.

What about consistency in specific prosocial behaviors across time and situation? Here there are fewer studies to consider. Block and Block (described in Mussen & Eisenberg-Berg, 1977) found that teachers' ratings of generosity, helpfulness, and empthy in 4-year-olds were significantly related to their generosity 1 year later. Baumrind (in Mussen and Eisenberg-Berg, 1977) reports a correlation of .60 for boys and .37 for girls between social responsibility exhibited in nursery school and 5 to 6 years later. We have already noted that consistent patterns of prosocial responding appeared between the ages of 2 and 7 in two-thirds of the children studied by Radke-Yarrow, Zahn-Waxler, and their colleagues. Bar-Tal and Raviv (1979) report high correlations between measures of willingness to volunteer to help younger children over a 2-year period. On the whole the results for continuity of behavior across time and place are somewhat more impressive than those for consistency between various behavioral indices of altruism.

Correlates of Different Altruistic Acts

Another, and more instructive, way of approaching the question of consistency is to consider the various correlates of different altruistic acts. If the pattern of relationships varies from act to act this is evidence, of course, that the acts are not simply manifestations of the same underlying disposition. There are enough data to enable this kind of comparison for at least two classes of altruism, generosity and helping. Note that generosity involves self-sacrifice, the giving up of material possessions that have some personal value. Helping, on the other hand, does not involve the sacrifice of material resources. Although it may demand time and effort it is far from always the case that the loss of these commodities is unpleasant. For example, aiding another may result in enjoyable social interaction, be a reasonably entertaining way of passing one's leisure time, or may even satisfy a desire to control the actions of others.

Because generosity requires self-sacrifice it should be related more to maturity of social and moral functioning than would helping with its possibly more self-gratifying outcomes. And this is, indeed, the case. As noted earlier, generosity relates to level of prosocial judgment, whereas helping does not (Eisenberg-Berg & Hand, 1979). Frequency of helping, but not sharing, is related to attempts to take other children's possessions (Eisenberg, Pasternack, Cameron, & Tryon, 1984), and helping—but not comforting or sharing—is related to antisocial behaviors (Bryant & Crockenberg, 1980).

Helping seems to be an activity in which children are more willing to engage than is sharing. Spontaneous helping occurs more frequently than spontaneous sharing both in the home and in the preschool (Bar-Tal, Raviv, & Goldberg, 1982; Grusec, 1985). Preschoolers always respond to requests for help, but respond to requests for sharing only 80% of the time (Eisenberg et al., 1983). Eisenberg-Berg and Hand noted that helping was frequently used by preschoolers as a means of initiating social interactions, whereas sharing was not. Interaction with nurturant and permissive adults increases emergency helping but decreases generosity (Grusec, 1971; Staub, 1970; Weissbrod, 1976). Presumably, being in a permissive situation with a kindly adult makes children feel freer to follow their natural inclination to respond to the need of others for help and to keep pennies and gift certificates for themselves. Age trends appear to reflect, as well, differential willingness to engage in these two activities. Generosity increases with age (Radke-Yarrow, Zahn-Waxler, & Chapman, 1983), whereas there is a curvilinear relationship with age for emergency helping (Staub, 1970). Among kindergarten children, who have minimal knowledge of how to intervene successfully, amount of helping is low. It peaks for more skilled second graders and then decreases for sixth graders who are reluctant to do something which might, for some reason, arouse adult disapproval. In essence, then, generosity appears to reflect the consequences of socialization and mature social functioning, whereas helping may be more a manifestation of a desire for and enjoyment of social interaction.

To this point we have focused our discussion on helping and sharing that are spontaneous in nature. Much prosocial behavior, however, is in response to requests for aid from others. Requested and spontaneous altruism appear to be unrelated, with the former probably more a reflection of conformity than of concern for others (Grusec, 1985). Neither sharing nor helping in response to another's request are related to prosocial reasoning (Eisenberg-Berg & Hand, 1979). Children who comply with requests for help are relatively dependent, submissive, and bland in the affect they show to others, whereas children who engage in much spontaneous behavior are relatively socially responsive (Eisenberg, Cameron, Tryon, & Dodez, 1981).

Given these differences between prosocial acts, it seems the more challenging question is how to explain that amount of consistency in behavior that *does* exist. To the degree that all altruistic acts depend on the ability to understand another person's point of view, it may be this ability is the mediating variable accounting for moderate correlations among prosocial acts in a given individual. In addition, some socialization techniques may be more likely to produce generalized altruism. We know, for example, that attributing prosocial characteristics to 7 and 8-year-olds contingent on their sharing produces concomitant increases in a variety of helping acts. The effects of social reinforcement, on the other hand, are limited to the act they follow (Grusec & Redler, 1980). Parents who use reasoning that involves reference to a wide range of altruistic acts, then, may produce more consistently prosocial offspring than those who confine their reactions to specific situations. We have discussed the reasons for this in Chapter 5.

Summary

Moral principles are those concerned with issues of justice, fairness, and equity. They provide guides for acceptable behavior. Altruism—behavior designed to help another at no benefit (and even possibly cost) to the altruist—is distinguished from morality because it leads to a situation of inequity, that is, the altruist loses resources while the recipient of his help gains them. Evidence suggests that children view these two classes of behavior differently, that parents socialize them differently, and that they are, in fact, not related in the same individual. Psychologists have also made a distinction between morality and social conventions. The latter guide social interactions and maintain social order, but they are arbitrary, unlike moral transgressions, which involve intrinsic harm to the welfare and rights of others.

Much of the study of morality has been guided by Kohlberg's formulations. He has been concerned with thinking about moral dilemmas, arguing that actual choices of behavior are less instructive than are the reasons people provide for their choices. He maintains that there are stages of development, with each stage representing a qualitatively different way of thinking about moral issues. The stages also occur in an invariant sequence, different reasons associated with each stage have a similar underlying organization, and each stage is increasingly differentiated and integrated. By and large the data, including a large number of cross-cultural studies, support Kohlberg's contentions. Kohlberg also maintains that moral thinking is part of a horizontal sequence that begins with the development of logical thinking, moves to the ability to take the perspective of others, and ends with moral thinking. Evidence for this progression is not so clear-cut. Differential opportunities for role-taking experience also affect the stage of moral reasoning that is reached.

Damon has provided a somwhat different view of the development of morality by focusing on the rules children use for sharing and distributing resources. He also finds stages of development, moving from complete self-interest to recognition that all participants should be given what is their due according both to their contribution and their need. Both Kohlberg and Damon acknowledge that the link between level of moral thought and moral behavior is a complex one, with motivational variables entering decisions about whether or not to translate thought into behavior.

The approaches of Kohlberg and Damon, who maintain that morality is constructed by the child out of his experience, stand in contrast to those of socialization theorists who maintain that moral values are transmitted by socializing agents. It would appear that both the principles transmitted by others, as well as the child's generalizations from those principles and from his other experiences, determine the way in which he both thinks about moral issues and behaves.

Altruism develops very early, with evidence that children between the ages of 1 and 2 years are capable of sharing, helping, comforting, and defending those in need at least at a rudimentary level. Underlying these behaviors may be a variety of motives including pleasure in companionship, the desire to exercise increasing skills, and empathic arousal. Altruism occurring at later ages, of course, also may be guided by adoption of specific value systems including the learning of norms of reciprocity, responsibility, and deservedness. Although it has been argued by many that the ability to empathize with the needs of others is a prime determinant of altruism, much research suggests that the relationship between empathy and altruism is not a strong one. Because so many other motivators may be operating in the production of altruism the weakness of the relationship should not be surprising. What does seem to relate more strongly to altruism is the ability to take the perspective of others. With this ability the potential altruist is able to identify the needs of others as well as to know how those needs might be satisfied.

Assessments of children's reasoning about dilemmas involving the needs of others have been made. As with reasoning about moral dilemmas there does appear to be stage-like development, although children also utilize a variety of stages of thinking at the same time. Although the relationships among different kinds of altruistic behavior are not strong, there does seem to be consistency over time and across situations for given altruistic acts.

10
Sex Differences and Sex Roles

The topic of sex differences has fascinated humankind for many centuries. Its discussion arouses deep emotions, as people's concepts and feelings about themselves are deeply involved in any consideration of the relative roles and characteristics of the two sexes. In research in this area, perhaps more than in many others, emotions are never far from the surface and it would therefore be an idealistic illusion to pretend that this research can be completely objective. As noted in Chapter 1, our current belief systems will influence the conceptual framework that we impose on data that generally offer a certain latitude to interpretation. How the cumulative import of evidence may lend itself to legitimately differing interpretations and how these will vary according to one's prior notions, has been discussed in Chapter 8 in connection with the debate on TV and violence. Ideology has introduced an element of subjectivity into the interpretation of research on sex differences that has varied in degree. At one end of the spectrum we find differing interpretations of somewhat ambiguous data, at the other end lie the—conscious or unconscious—suppression and distortion of clear evidence. We will discuss researcher bias later in connection with an investigation that has brought into the open this often hidden phenomenon. While we have our point of view, which we will explain below, we have looked at the evidence with care and have tried to keep our biases in check in interpreting and reporting it.

As part of acquiring an identity people develop characteristics that tend to be associated with their sex, but they also adopt some characteristics that are considered typical of the opposite sex; every individual thus creates an amalgam of sex-typed attributes that is specific to him- or herself. The fact that this process is also part of social development gives the topic a place in this book. After presenting some of the background of the study of sex roles and differences we will discuss various areas of behavior and personality characteristics where sex differences have been examined in empirical studies. We will then examine sex typing, that is, the process whereby attributes and behavior are categorized by sex, and how this may come about. Finally we will consider environmental, biological, and interactive explanations for the origins of sex differences.

In some writings those human characteristics that are biologically based and directly related to reproductive function have been called "sex characteristics," whereas psychological features or attributes linked by society to the biological state of male or female have been called "gender characteristics" (e.g., Deaux, 1985). It is doubtful, however, whether this distinction is viable since the very question of whether a given characteristic is mainly biologically based or mainly a result of the psychological expectations of the environment is still hotly debated. Hence the distinction is often difficult to maintain, and provides no conceptual advantage. We have therefore chosen not to try and make it, but to refer in general to "sex characteristics" or "sex typing." We will use the term "sex role" to refer to behavior that is culturally accepted as appropriate for each sex.

History and a Point of View

The strength of the fascination with the nature of the differences between men and women can be understood, when one realizes that the division into two sexes in animals and humans is the most obtrusive and the most affect-laden dimorphic split known to humans. Interest in these differences has been expressed in literature dating back at least to Plato and Aristotle. Freud, as we saw in Chapter 1, was especially concerned with sex differences in the area of morality, although his ideas on the subject have not stood up to the test of empirical research.

Empirical research on sex differences and their explanations has been conducted for decades. Margaret Mead carried out anthropological studies in Samoa and New Guinea in the 1920s and her conclusions regarding sex roles, reported in books such as *Coming of Age in Samoa* (1928), became well known and influential in subsequent decades. Under the influence of Franz Boas' theory of cultural determinism, she set out with the idea that any social institution or role, including sex role, can be explained first and foremost by cultural factors and this is, indeed, what she found in these studies. Her main conclusion was that biological sex and temperament are essentially independent of each other (Mead, 1935). She reported, for instance, that among the Tchambuli people the temperamental qualities traditionally associated with each sex in Western countries were, in fact, reversed: aggressive-dominant behavior was considered appropriate for females and sensitive-artistic temperament for males.

However, more recent investigations of Samoan and New Guinean societies have cast doubts on Mead's accounts (Fortune, 1939; Freeman, 1983), calling them an "anthropological myth." Fortune reported that he found warfare well developed among the Arapesh (whom Mead had reported to be entirely peaceable); moreover, it was the men who were the warriors. Freeman obtained information from some Samoan men and women who remembered being Mead's adolescent informants. It appears that she was frequently duped by them—partly because of her lack of command of the language—into believing in a blissful state of primitive innocence marking adolescent sexual relations, something that conformed to her romantic notion and preconceptions. Hence her reports about the qualities associated with each sex in these societies must also be regarded with some scepticism.

Many empirical studies of the 1950s and 1960s, carried out in the United States, yielded information about sex differences (e.g., Sears, et al., 1965) or examined the development of sex-linked characteristics (e.g., Hetherington, 1972). Investigators of that time conceptualized sex-linked characteristics as spread along the bipolar axis, masculine-feminine, and, in accord with the value system of the times, "sex-appropriate" behavior was considered a desirable goal for each sex. With the advent of the Women's Liberation Movement and greater female consciousness came a change in the value system, which meant that sex-inappropriate behavior, or a combination of the most positively viewed "masculine" and "feminine" behaviors (e.g., decisiveness coupled with gentleness), was seen to be desirable. The resulting personality was called "androgynous," and its antecedents and correlates have been the subject of research under the new perspective (e.g., Deaux, 1984; Russell, 1978). In addition, whereas clinical interventions designed to induce changes in sex-typed behavior were first directed at enhancing masculine or feminine behavior, as appropriate, later they often become more concerned with bringing about androgynous behavior (e.g., Johnston, Ettema, & Davidson, 1980).

A Viewpoint

James Thurber once asked "Is sex necessary?" Strictly speaking it is not, since reproduction can be asexual. Sexual reproduction, however, has evolved in most animal species with resulting costs, as well as benefits. The cost of sexual reproduction has to be measured by the enormous amount of energy and time that members of the species devote to the search and selection of mates and by the breakup of valuable combinations of genes that happens in meiosis, when only half of each parent's genes are transmitted to the new zygote. On the other hand, sexual reproduction pays off because it produces highly variable offspring, including rare individuals who show superior fitness in a specific environmental context (Daly & Wilson, 1983). It has also brought about various psychological adaptations, necessary or helpful to the function of sexual reproduction, and it has generated expectations in the culture that are consonant with these adaptations and that exert their own independent influence on people, for example, the expectation of assertiveness for males.

As we noted earlier, the question of the origins of sex differences has often been cast in the form of an antithesis: biological *or* environmental, nature *or* nurture. This, of course, is too simplistic an approach: Most phenomena in the area of sex roles and sex differences are not easily encompassed by a single explanation. Multiple explanations for them are usually more to the point, explanations which are complementary and not mutually exclusive since they operate at different levels. Thus the explanation of sex differences in behavior by sex-differentiated upbringing, peer pressures, or stereotypes often may be appropriate, since such influences are undeniably involved, but they do not address the question of the biological function of the behavior in question. Explanations in terms of psychological needs, socialization, or economic variables do not exclude explanations at the level of reproductive strategies and biological function; rather, the two sets of explanations are complementary.

It is to the broader implications of the differences in reproductive strategies between males and females that we will now turn. Females generally invest more in each offspring and hence have a lower reproductive potential. Females' greater parental investment can be seen even at conception, since the ovum—much larger than the sperm—provides nutrients for the future organism. Males show greater variability in reproductive success: some father far more young than any female, but others die barren, as shown in fruit flies (Daly & Wilson, 1983). Furthermore there is reproductive competition among males who fight and die for the chance to inseminate females—woundings and deaths among male rhesus monkeys climb dramatically during the mating season (Daly & Wilson, 1983). Men, too, engage in fights over women, as illustrated in many an opera and newspaper story, although the frequency of such fights and their ultimate course vary in accordance with cultural expectations and societal inhibitions.

There are consequences that arise from these different amounts of investment. A male is willing to spend a little time on *any* mating opportunity and often courts indiscriminately; a female, on the other hand, must be more selective, as mismating may cost her much in wasted nurture and in lost reproductive potential. Natural selection, at least in the past, has assured that behavior is appropriate for reproductive success, and hence optimal strategies of males and females have differed. But differing reproductive strategies may have implications in other areas, too. Where certain psychological attributes and behavior have been instrumental in ensuring reproductive success, these have come under the influence of natural selection, with a given attribute being differentially favored for the sex whose reproductive strategy it benefited (Daly & Wilson, 1983). At the same time such biologically favored differences have called forth certain reactions and expectations in society that have become independent of their origin (stereotypcial) and have themselves entrenched and reinforced the differences. We must also realize that although it was essential for reproductive success to be strengthened in the Pleistocene to ensure the survival of the human species, reproductive success in many modern societies, far from being a central goal, is actually antithetical to social progress, and hence such selection pressures may no longer apply.

We will now review the areas in which investigators have looked for the existence of sex differences, although under the microscope of empirical investigation, not all have been found to be well established.

Areas of Sex Differences

RESEARCH INTEGRATION

Before proceeding to the following sections to examine the research on sex differences in different domains of psychological functioning, we must discuss the question of how we will digest and come to terms with the voluminous literature in this field.

For research up to 1974 concerning sex differences in most of the behavioral areas, which we will discuss below, Maccoby and Jacklin's (1974) monumental study has assembled a very reliable and comprehensive data base. Maccoby and Jacklin have drawn up a summary table for each area that they explore, for example, verbal ability or impulsivity (e.g., see Table 10.2 later in this chapter). For each table they categorize the studies they survey into those showing a difference favoring boys, those favoring girls, and those showing no difference, and compare the numbers in each category. This has been called the "box score" approach; it ignores the quality of individual studies and is a rather simple method. Nevertheless, Maccoby and Jacklin's work is a valuable data base that we will draw on, but we will also incorporate evidence from later studies, above all from quantitative integrations of research in a given area. The procedures and rationale of such meta-analyses have been explained in Chapter 6.

Although we will use Maccoby and Jacklin's (1974) data base, we do not always concur with their conclusions. We will make our own interpretations, based on the total evidence from earlier and later studies, particularly meta-analytic ones, which are more numerous in this area than in others covered in this book. It should be noted that quantitative meta-analyses restrain the reviewer from giving free rein to his/her preconceptions in interpreting the evidence. Differing explanations for the origins of these sex differences will be discussed in a separate section later on.

DIVISION OF LABOR

Division of the work required to maintain the family and the group is perhaps the most ubiquitous of sex differences and will be the first area discussed. Though its existence has often been noted—and deplored—in Western industrialized societies, it is in fact less pervasive and systematic there than in primitive ones. In a survey of subsistence activities in over 220 primitive societies, it was found that hunting was done by men in all, and grinding of grain was done exclusively or mainly by women in all but 11 societies (D'Andrade, 1966; see Table 10.1). Such division of labor in societies that depend for their livelihood on physical activities is, no doubt, a derivative of male and female physical attributes and of the assignment of parental care to women: Males tend to perform activities that require strenuous effort and mobility, whereas female activities tend to be physically easier and restricted to an area near home. But this division of labor is also generalized from activities based directly on physical sex-linked characteristics to activities that are only indirectly based on these characteristics, for example, men fight (an activity directly related to physical sex-linked characteristics) and it was they who exclusively manufactured weapons in these societies. In this way socially expected sex roles evolved.

Among mammals females alone have the capacity not only to bear offspring, but also to suckle them, and hence responsibility for basic parental care is usually theirs, with rare exceptions such as the New World monkey species of marmosets with whom fathers carry out this care. In birds, on the other hand, males can provide basic nutrition and care as readily as females and they therefore display a greater tendency to biparental care.

Thus the division of labor between the sexes can be explained at the level of biological necessities or conveniences, but society takes over from these and then develops role expectations, which offer another level of explanation. That such roles can be changed to some extent is shown by the very recent trend towards greater equalization of child care and household responsibilities among human mothers and fathers, as noted in Chapter 5.

What happens when a whole community tries to break away from traditional, rigid sex roles and establish equality between the sexes not only in political power, but also in occupational roles? This is a natural experiment that the Israeli kibbutz movement, inspired by egalitarian zeal, started to carry out in the 1920s and 1930s (Gerson, 1978; Spiro, 1979). Child care was entrusted to professional children's nurses, and children lived in Children's Houses (except for a couple of hours in the evening spent with their parents), so that mothers would be freed from their traditional child-care duties and would be free to work, like men, anywhere. The kibbutz pioneers essentially tried to abolish the family.

However, this has not lasted. There still is complete political equality and opportunity for both sexes in the kibbutz and the highest positions of personal respect are also accorded to men and women, regardless of sex. Yet the second generation of women, who had been reared in a philosophy of sex equality, has more recently adopted more traditionally female values again. In particular, these women have wanted to become more closely involved with parenting and with their families, although they also hold jobs outside the home. It is not that the desire for sexual equality has diminished. But, Spiro concludes, the maternal role (downgraded in earlier times) has been revalued, and women feel confident in this. "Instead of seeking 'status identity' with men in a system of sex-role uniformity, (the new generation of women) seek 'status equivalence' in a system of sex-role differentiation" (Spiro, 1979, p. 106).

TABLE 10.1. Cross-cultural data from 224 societies on subsistence activities and division of labor by sex.

Activity	Number of societies in which activity is performed by				
	Men always	Men usually	Either sex	Women usually	Women always
Pursuit of sea mammals	34	1	0	0	0
Hunting	166	13	0	0	0
Trapping small animals	128	13	4	1	2
Herding	38	8	4	0	5
Fishing	98	34	19	3	4
Clearing land for agriculture	73	22	17	5	13
Dairy operations	17	4	3	1	13
Preparing and planting soil	31	23	33	20	37
Erecting and dismantling shelter	14	2	5	6	22
Tending fowl and small animals	21	4	8	1	39
Tending and harvesting crops	10	15	35	39	44
Gathering shellfish	9	4	8	7	25
Making and tending fires	18	6	25	22	62
Bearing burdens	12	6	35	20	57
Preparing drinks and narcotics	20	1	13	8	57
Gathering fruits, berries, nuts	12	3	15	13	63
Gathering fuel	22	1	10	19	89
Preservation of meat and fish	8	2	10	14	74
Gathering herbs, roots, seeds	8	1	11	7	74
Cooking	5	1	9	28	158
Carrying water	7	0	5	7	119
Grinding grain	2	4	5	13	114

Note. Reprinted from "Sex Differences and Cultural Institutions" by R.G. D'Andrade in The Development of Sex Differences, edited by Eleanor E. Maccoby, with the permission of the publishers, Stanford University Press. Copyright 1966 by the Board of Trustees of the Leland Stanford Junior University.

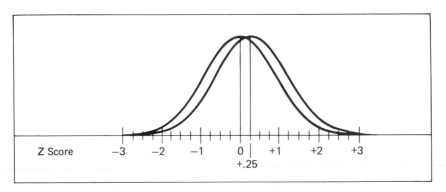

FIGURE 10.1. Two normal distributions with means .25 standard derivations apart, that is, with an effect size of .25. This is approximately the magnitude of the gender difference in verbal ability. From "How Large Are Cognitive Gender Differences?" by J.S. Hyde, 1981, *American Psychologist, 36*, 892–901. Reprinted by permission.

It may be that the division of labor is not entirely a matter that is, or can be, arbitrarily imposed by the culture.

COGNITIVE ABILITIES AND ACHIEVEMENT

Verbal Abilities

That girls are superior in verbal abilities—in vocabulary, fluency, anagrams, or reading—is one of the more solidly established facts in the area of sex differences. However, the relative rates of verbal development of boys and girls seem to converge and then draw apart again at different stages of childhood. In infancy and toddlerhood there is some evidence—though tenuous—that girls are ahead in vocalization and vocabulary. During the elementary school years verbal tests show very little difference between the sexes, but from adolescence onward girls draw ahead. This female superiority is not shown in every study, but it is clear in the vast majority of them, including some with very large samples, and in all countries where such studies have been done (Maccoby & Jacklin, 1974). It is not true that the lower reading level of boys overall and the larger proportion of retarded readers among boys is a phenomenon that is confined to America where most studies have been carried out, since, for example, it also occurs in England (cf. Rutter, Tizard, & Whitmore, 1970).

We should discuss here the practical importance and meaningfulness of documented sex differences, such as the one in verbal ability. It is true that whenever a difference in the mean level of performance of males and females has been established, the distribution of scores of the two sexes overlap to a large extent, as can be seen in Figure 10.1. The magnitude of the difference illustrated in Figure 10.1 is roughly that of the sex difference in verbal ability, namely, .25 of a standard deviation. Hyde (1981), who estimated this effect size in her meta-analysis of Maccoby and Jacklin's sample of studies from adolescence on, considered it to be small and unimportant. However, as Rosenthal and Rubin (1982) have pointed out, even when mean differences are small, differences in the proportions of males and females at the extremes of the distribution or above and below the median may be substantial and have practical significance. Thus, the effect size of .25 of a standard deviation implies that 60% of females versus 40% of males will be above the common median in verbal ability—not a negligible factor.

Mathematical and Spatial Abilities

Male superiority in mathematical and spatial tasks is as well established as female superiority in verbal ability. That boys perform better than girls at mathematics has been shown in studies of large samples from seventh grade on. Benbow and Stanley (1980, 1983) conducted a search for precocious mathematicians among seventh and eighth graders. In 1983 the top 3% of students in mathematics *or* in verbal ability were eligible to enter the talent search and there was an equal number of boys and girls among the 39,000 top flight students who were given the Scholastic Aptitude Test's (SAT) quantitative and verbal scales. The smallest difference in mean scores between males and females on the SAT quantitative scales was 30 points in favor of males. At higher levels of performance the difference was more dramatic: at scores of over 700 (obtained by about 1 in 10,000 students) the male : female ratio was 13 : 1. The girls were matched with the boys on intellectual ability, age, grade, and voluntary participation. The tests took place before mathematics courses became optional in schools and, therefore, before the number of mathematics courses chosen could differentiate between the sexes. Nor were there any differences between boys and girls in stated interest in mathematics or in special mathematics programs taken earlier. All these factors are sometimes advanced as reasons for females' poorer performance in mathematics, but they did not explain the differences in this study.

The *average* level of mathematical ability, too, is higher in boys than in girls, at least from early adolescence on, and this superiority persists when the groups are equated for the number of mathematics courses they have taken (Maccoby & Jacklin, 1974). Hyde (1981) calculated in her meta-analysis that the overall effect size for the difference in mathematical ability is .43 of a standard deviation—rather more than it was for verbal ability. Differing motivational processes for males and females may partly explain male superior quantitative abilities (see "Achievement Motivation" below).

There is also good evidence that boys show greater variability in mathematical ability, that is, there are relatively more boys than girls at both extreme ends of the distribution (Maccoby & Jacklin, 1974). The effects of this at the extreme high end has been demonstrated vividly by the Benbow and Stanley studies. A similar, but less pronounced trend towards greater variability for boys has also been shown in verbal ability, but there its effect is mainly noticeable at the low end, for example, by the preponderance of boys in special-help classes for reading (Maccoby & Jacklin, 1974).

Spatial tasks are of different kinds: They may involve mental translation from two-dimensional to three-dimensional space, as in counting blocks depicted on paper, or they may require mental rotation, for example, of gears on cogwheels, shown in pictures, or the judging of verticality independently of a misleading frame (Rod-and-Frame Test), or they may involve disembedding smaller figures from larger, more complex ones (Embedded Figures Test). Boys' greater spatial ability in mental rotation and judging verticality has been demonstrated repeatedly in studies with large samples and good measures not only at adolescence, but also in middle childhood, and has been reconfirmed by meta-analytic studies (Hyde, 1981; Linn & Petersen, 1986). No sex difference, however, has been found in the kind of spatial visualization involved in the Embedded Figures Test (Linn & Petersen, 1986). Hyde (1981) found the median effect size for spatial abilities in favor of boys to be .48, or nearly half a standard deviation. We will discuss possible causes of male superiority in this area in a later section.

It is of interest to note that more recent studies of mathematical and spatial abilities in males and females have shown smaller differences than did earlier ones (Rosenthal & Rubin, 1982). This "catching up" by females may be due to greater emphasis on female achievements in recent times, and it is also possible that sex selection for college (the samples were mainly college students) differed between the earlier and the later cohorts. In any case, the explanation for the catch-up must be a cultural, not a genetic or biological one.

Analytical Abilities

Analytical reasoning ability, of course, enters into mathematical problem-solving, but "breaking set" and "restructuring" can also be tested separately, for example, by expecting subjects to use familiar objects and tools in a novel way to solve a physical problem. Luchins' Water Jar Problems are another example of a test requiring the subject to "break set." In these tasks the subject first has to solve problems like the following: "You are to bring back exactly 6 quarts of water from the river, when you have only a four-quart and a nine-quart jar to measure with." After several similar problems have been given, a task that has an easy, straightforward solution is presented to test whether the subject can break the previously established "set" and see the simple solution quickly. Males have been found to be better at this than females in 86% of studies (Maccoby & Jacklin, 1974). Maccoby and Jacklin state that anagrams, in which females are superior, require a similar restructuring of the stimulus, so males may be better at breaking set in spatial situations and females in verbal tasks. Block (1976), however, points out that insight problems, such as the Water Jar Tasks, require the discovery or discernment of a new strategy, whereas anagrams require the more or less systematic application of a recurring process. For the former it is necessary that the subject spontaneously sees that a novel way of looking at things will facilitate the solution—a different kind of task from resorting words in as many different ways as possible. It is the former task that represents a more analytical "breaking of set," Block suggests, and it is in this that males seem superior.

Fifty-three studies of sex differences on formal operational reasoning in the Piagetian sense have been summarized by a meta-analysis and this, too, confirmed male superiority in reasoning, particularly in proportional reasoning, measured by tasks such as setting the equilibrium on a balance or predicting the projection of shadows (Meehan, 1984).

Achievement and Achievement Motivation

It is often maintained that women are less interested in achievement for its own sake and less motivated by an internal desire to excel at a task. If this assertion were correct its truth should manifest itself in the first place by girls obtaining lower grades than boys at school: However, the opposite is, in fact, the case throughout the school years, except for mathematical achievement (Maccoby & Jacklin, 1974). Nor is there truth in the assertion that achievement-related motives in general sway women less than men. Spence and Helmreich (1983) have identified three separate factors in achievement tendencies: work (i.e., desire to work hard and do a good job), mastery (meeting internal standards of excellence), and competition (wish to beat others). Women students have been found to score higher than men in work, whereas men score higher on mastery and competition. Thus, differences may exist, not in achievement motivation overall, but in the kind of motives that inspire men and women. Although these measures are derived from a questionnaire, the "work" and "mastery" motives do predict achievements in real-life settings.

There may also be differences in the patterns of motivation that characterize boys and girls. In a study cited by Dweck (1986) the brightest girls showed greater debilitation after failure, that is, lower motivation and performance, than other girls or any boys. The brightest boys, in contrast, were the only group for whom failure resulted in facilitation, that is, better performance. Dweck proposes that girls' lower mathematical achievement may be partly attributable to such differing motivational patterns, since both sex differences in mathematics and sex differences in motivation are greatest among the brightest students. Overall, girls not only show more debilitation in the face of failure, but they also have a lower preference for novel or challenging tasks and they attribute failure more frequently to lack of ability. New units and courses in mathematics after grade school tend to involve new skills and new concepts, often more difficult than the concepts the child has mastered in the past. In the verbal area, on the other hand, no such new levels of qualitatively different tasks are encountered. The fact that bright girls would have less confidence that they could master such new concepts would help to explain their generally lower achievements in the quantitative area (Dweck, 1986).

Since children are more inclined to engage in activities that are traditionally considered appropriate for their sex (see below), the sex-appropriateness of an activity may well be related to achievement in it and therefore the lower school achievements of boys in language and related subjects have sometimes been attributed to the fact that learning from books is often classified as a feminine activity (Huston, 1983). (The reader should note that for simplicity's sake we will from now on use the term "sex-appropriate" without qualification, but we always mean by it that an activity is simply traditionally considered to be sex-appropriate.)

Whatever the validity of this explanation for differences in school achievements, in adulthood it does appear that the highest achievements in science, the professions, and the arts are won by men. It is probably accurate to state that women's achievements stay closer to the mean than men's, that is, women are less represented at the extreme high, as well as at the extreme low end of achievement (Hoffman, 1972). A number of well-known facts about women's role in society are sufficient to explain this disparity. Thus, household tasks have traditionally fallen to women and women often have found it difficult to combine these with single-minded pursuit of excellence. In the past women also rarely held jobs, and very high achievements and productivity, for instance in the realm of music by men like Bach, were frequently a response to the demands of the job and the need to keep a family. Women's greater affiliative tendencies may also make conflicts between affiliation and achievement more likely in women and hence adversely affect their performance. However, there is also another side to the coin. As Hoffman (1972) puts it: "A loss in intellectual excellence due to excessive affiliative needs, then, might seem a small price to pay if the alternative is a single-minded striving for mastery." (p. 150)

SOCIAL BEHAVIOR

What sex differences have been shown to exist in social behavior?

Play and Activity

The fact that boys and girls play in separate groups and often in different ways and with different toys, is one of the best known and one of the earliest sex differences noted in social behavior. Starting in preschool boys tend to be more active physically than girls. In nursery school they spend more time outdoors and use about $1\frac{1}{2}$ times as much space as girls do. Boys engage more in large motor play in the sand, on the tractor, or on climbing structures, whereas girls spend more time indoors at craft tables and in kitchens (Harper & Sanders, 1975). Maccoby and Jacklin's (1974) summary also shows that, from age $2\frac{1}{2}$ to 11, in all studies that showed any difference in activity level between the sexes, boys were the more physically active group, and they also tended to be more exploratory and curious than girls. In subhuman primates young males also have been observed to display more rough-and-tumble play (Harlow, 1962). Girls are active, too, of course, but in more physically constrained and sedentary ways (Maccoby & Jacklin, 1874; Tauber, 1979a). They also like to spend more time in well-structured activities than in unstructured ones (Huston, Carpenter, Atwater, & Johnson, 1986).

A preference for sex-typed toys can be seen in boys as early as age 2, even before they have realized the traditional sex-appropriateness of the toys (Blakemore, LaRue, & Olejnik, 1979). Boys' preference for sex-typed play is more pronounced than that of girls in the perschool years (Maccoby & Jacklin, 1985; Perry, White, & Perry, 1984), and between the ages of 4 and 8 boys' preference for masculine activities increases monotonically. With girls matters are more complex and there is no clear increase by age in sex-typed preferences during the elementary school years (Kohlberg & Zigler, 1967). In view of males' greater spatial ability, noted above, it is of interest that participation in masculine types of play activities has been found to predict spatial ability in both sexes, in other words, girls in general may be missing out on something here (Connor & Serbin, 1977).

Boys and girls tend to prefer interacting and playing with members of their own sex rather than with those of the other sex and this tendency has been observed from age 2 onward at least up to grade 6 (Strayer & Pilon, 1985; Luria & Herzog, 1985). In an examination of this process of sex segregation in nursery school Maccoby and Jacklin (1985) found that it was girls who were the first to initiate segregation and the authors thought that girls actively avoid boys because of the latters' domineering behavior (we will discuss evidence for this below). By age 5 they found that three-quarters of the children were playing in same-sex groups, although there was no teacher pressure for same-sex play. It is the girls and boys themselves who establish the segregation spontaneously, probably because they find the manner of playing and interests of same-sex children more compatible with their own. Interestingly, girls whose fathers played most with them at home tended to prefer girls' groups more than did other girls, perhaps as a compensatory mechanism. Girls' participation in same-sex groups was associated with good development of prosocial characteristics, but this was not the case for boys' participation in their same-sex groups. It seems that all-girl groups have a considerably greater socializing influence—for the good—than all-boy groups.

Given all these pressures for sex segregation, how does the atypical child fare who defies convention and crosses the boundary lines? One study has observed closely how a successful fifth-grade tomboy operates. Her acceptance by boys and her access to their segregated activities was based on specific athletic, fighting, and verbal skills that are appropriate to boys' groups. She would, for instance, say "I'll beat you up!"—and proceed to do so. She had a "buddies" kind of relationship with boys and avoided "going with" any particular boy in order to eschew any sexual overtones. At the same time she maintained access to the world of girls by being friends with the most popular girl in the class and by guarding girls' groups against male invasions by her muscular threats (Thorne, 1985).

Higher activity level in boys also tends to be accompanied by greater impulsivity, that is, insufficient control of impulse, inability to delay gratification, and risk-taking (Block, 1983). The undercontrol of impulse is shown in more acting-out behavior which, at a more extreme level, turns into behavior problems, something much more common in boys than in girls (Eme, 1979). An investigation that observed children inobtrusively at spots in a zoo that invited risk-taking has also demonstrated that boys are more prone to show curiosity and associated risk-taking behavior in such a setting (Ginsburg & Miller, 1982).

Thus there is abundant evidence that boys and girls differ from early on in their play choices, in activity level, and impulsivity.

Fears Versus Self-Confidence

Cultural stereotypes generally portray females to be more anxious than males. However, observational studies of timidity often show no difference between the sexes, though when there is one, it is women who display greater fearfulness (Maccoby & Jacklin, 1974). Teacher ratings and self-reports do consistently rate girls and women as more anxious, but this may be due to the fact that boys and men are simply less willing to admit to anxiety, since this is thought to be a feminine trait (Maccoby & Jacklin, 1974.

Contrary to popular opinion, females overall think as highly of themselves as males do (i.e., have as much self-esteem), but the two sexes probably differ in the domains in which they claim to be performing well and to have high competence. Males tend to ascribe to themselves a sense of power to control events, or to describe themselves in terms of efficacy or "agency." Females, on the other hand, emphasize their superiority in interpersonal relations, and describe themselves as socially sensitive, nurturing, and considerate of others, that is, they portray themselves more in terms of "communion" (Maccoby & Jacklin, 1974).

Social Orientation and Sensitivity

Claims, such as the above, that females display greater interpersonal interests and awareness are, of course, in accord with general preconceptions. But empirical studies, we think, overall have also borne out these notions. Maccoby and Jacklin disagree and suggest that any differences that may exist between the two sexes in this area are more of kind than of degree. Boys, for instance, tend to congregate in larger groups, whereas girls are more prone to associate in pairs or small groups (1974, p. 349— see also Chapter 6, this book). However, this difference, and its implication that girls are more inclined to intimacy, is interesting in itself. Moreover, Maccoby's earlier data (Maccoby, 1966) also suggest that females show greater social orientation in some respects. Thus, girls seek proximity with friends and value friendship more, in other words they are more affiliative than boys (cf. also L.W. Hoffman, 1977). Girls and women also show more interest in social activities, and their tastes in books and TV shows are directed more to the gentler aspects of interpersonal relations rather than to sports activities, violence, or science. Girls' greater tendency to cooperation (see Chapter 6) also indicates greater emphasis on interpersonal relations.

Whether girls, as part of this interpersonal cluster, are given to be more "dependent" on others is a moot question. If dependency is defined as seeking proximity of parents and resisting separation from them (nowadays reconceptualized as "attachment"), then young girls, indeed, do not display this kind of behavior more than boys do, as Maccoby and Jacklin's (1974) summary table demonstrates. (This is part of the reason why Maccoby and Jacklin relegate the notion of a sex difference in sociability to the realm of unfounded myth.) However, there is some evidence that girls are more prone to seek help (another definition of dependency); for instance, toddler-age girls ask for help three times as often as boys (Fagot, 1978).

It is well established that females show greater sensitivity in decoding social cues and, in particular, nonverbal cues of emotion, expressed in the face, by the body or by sounds. Hall (1978), in a meta-analysis of studies in this area, found that overall the female mean exceeded the male mean in decoding ability by about .40 of a standard deviation. This social sensitivity may be traced to cultural expectations, namely, that girls should relate well to others and attend to interpersonal matters. But it also would make evolutionary sense if sensitivity were "wired in," since mothers are more likely to be caregivers and a mother's sensitivity would enable her better to detect signals of distress in the young and thus improve her offspring's survival chances.

Another form of social sensitivity is empathy, that is, the ability to experience another person's emotional state vicariously. Recent surveys, one a qualitative review (M. Hoffman, 1977b) and another a quantitative meta-analysis (Eisenberg & Lennon, 1983), of studies covering ages from infancy to adulthood, have found that girls and women surpass boys and men in this ability. Such greater empathy by females has been observed in verbal responses, and somewhat less in facial responses, to a picture or story describing harrowing experiences, as well as in self-reports of distress, for instance, when someone else receives a shock. Even female infants utter sympathetic cries in response to other infants' distress cries more readily than do male infants. However, since physiological measures have in general not shown any sex differences and self-reports may be influenced by stereotypical beliefs, it may be thought that the reported sex difference in empathy is illusory. Nevertheless, the evidence still points to greater female empathy in observed verbal, and to some extent in facial, responses. Empathy, as M. Hoffman (1977b) suggests, may be part of a general prosocial affective orientation of concern for others.

Nurturance

In Chapter 5 we already noted that girls tend to be more responsive to babies than boys, a difference that emerges strongly after puberty. We also showed that human fathers can be, and often are, nurturant, although in most species females care for the offspring. Nurturant behavior also characterizes virgin females among nonhuman primates, for examples, among free-ranging vervet monkeys near the Zambezi River juvenile females have often been observed carrying, holding, or grooming infant monkeys. Juvenile males, on the other hand, were never seen to show protective or caring behavior to newborn infants, nor were older males (Lancaster, 1976).

A qualitative review (Berman, 1980) of studies of women's and men's responsiveness to the young clearly shows that in the overwhelming majority of cases females are more responsive to infants and children than males are, both in preference and in behavioral measures. In only one study (Parke & O'Leary, 1975) have fathers been shown to be more nurturant in that, when visiting newly delivered mothers in hospital, they hold the baby more than mothers do; clearly, these are special circumstances where mother may well be holding back. Berman chooses to stress the various modulating factors that affect the degree of responsiveness, for example, age or whether or not women have infants themselves (those who do are more responsive); sometimes, too, the sex difference is significant only for some measures, and not for others. Still, the overall message from the literature clearly is that females are more responsive to infants than males. It should be remembered, however, that the findings demonstrate what the two sexes *do*, not what they are capable of.

Aggression

That males are more aggressive than females is not only generally accepted but also well documented. Males are the more aggressive sex in most, though not all, species (Cairns, 1979b). Males among subhuman primates display considerably greater aggression than females, except in two species (tamarins and plata monkeys), and this is true also for chimpanzees, humans' closest relatives (Maccoby & Jacklin, 1980).

Among humans there is consistent evidence for greater aggression by males. A recent meta-analysis of studies of sex differences in aggression (Hyde, 1984), that included recent as well as earlier research, found that the overall difference amounted to one-half of a standard deviation, that is, it is as large as the largest of the differences in cognitive abilities, namely, spatial ability. Boys are more aggressive than girls from early ages on and a meta-analysis of studies of children below 6 years of age shows the overall difference to be highly significant (Maccoby & Jacklin, 1980). This is true of physical aggression and to a lesser extent of more indirect forms of aggression, such as verbal taunts which, indeed, often are a preliminary to physical attacks. Aggressive acts are a property of an interacting pair or group, not simply of an individual, as Cairns (1979b) points out, and it is boy-boy pairings that are particularly prone to give rise to such agonistic interchanges (Maccoby & Jacklin, 1980).

The overall greater aggressiveness of boys could arise either from boys on average having a higher propensity to aggressive behavior than girls, or from boys being overrepresented in the extreme group of highly aggressive children. A naturalistic observation study of elementary-school-aged children in school playgrounds has found that both these conditions do, in fact, hold for physical aggression (Williams, Joy, Kimball, & Zabrack, 1985). That there are more boys at the high end of the aggression spectrum is also implied by the fact that far more boys than girls show conduct problems, as is apparent from many clinical studies (cf. Eme, 1979).

Boys' greater aggressiveness will be affected in part by some of their other characteristics or experiences, as Tieger (1980) rightly points out. Boys' higher activity level, for instance, will lead them into more agonistic interchanges, and so may the generally higher rates of interaction in same-sex male pairs. It is also true that boys' aggressiveness is reduced when they are assigned child-care duties, as is more frequently the case with girls (Maccoby & Jacklin, 1980). But such factors can only be part of the explanation. Greater male aggression has been found consistently in different cultural subgroups, as well as cross-culturally in different Western societies and in nonindustrial societies, for example, in Ethiopia (Omark, Omark, & Edelman, 1975). There is therefore evidence for its universality, although the above-mentioned contributing factors will also apply in different cultures.

Dominance

With young boys dominance is achieved by success in agonistic encounters (see Chapter 6), but at later ages dominance is not synonymous with the exercise of brute force. Rather, a person dominates another person or a group when he or she has influence on the other's or the group's behavior, or directs and organizes their activities. The literature up to 1974, cited in Maccoby and Jacklin's summary table, overall indicates that in almost all

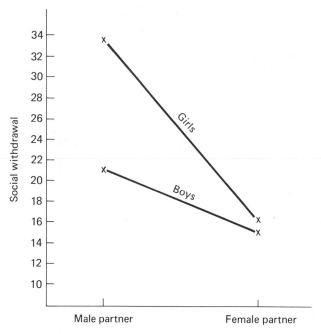

FIGURE 10.2. Mean scores: social withdrawal (fuss/cry plus stay in proximity to mothers), by sex of subject and sex of partner. From "Social Behavior at 33 Months in Same-Sex and Mixed-Sex Dyads," by C.N. Jacklin and E.E. Maccoby, 1978, *Child Development*, *49*, 557–569. Reprinted by permission.

studies which reported a sex difference, using observation, report, self-report, or personality scales, males turn out to be the dominant sex. This is so in the younger age-groups, as well as in the samples over 18, though qualifications must be made for adult groups (see below). A male dominance effect has been observed as early as 33 months of age (Jacklin & Maccoby, 1978): When unacquainted pairs of children were brought together in a playroom and girls were paired with boys, girls tended to stand passively watching their partners. When boys said "no" or "don't" they withdrew to stand near their mothers, or cried, but neither girls nor boys withdrew when they played with girl partners (see Figure 10.2). Since boys hardly engaged in any aggressive acts, apart from "grabbing" toys (and girls did this, too), it is not clear to which signals emanating from boys the girls responded—it may have been tone of voice or nonverbal gesture. In any case, it would appear that girls felt less able to control the situation when they interacted with boys.

One cross-cultural study (Whiting & Pope, 1974, cited by Maccoby and Jacklin, 1974), however, showed that in most cultures young girls are more likely than boys to try to control others in a prosocial direction, in that they offer more responsible suggestions, such as not to go near the fire. Girls in middle childhood also seem to be the equals of boys in Machiavellian manipulations, for example, in persuading others by devious means to eat bitter crackers (Maccoby & Jacklin, 1974).

When adult groups are formed, in the past men have tended to be the dominant individuals initially, as is shown for instance, by the fact that men have been chosen as jury foremen disproportionately to their numbers (Maccoby & Jacklin, 1974). One may conjecture, however, that women's changing status and their movement into more highly regarded work roles will bring about a change in this area, too. The emergence of several female heads of government around the globe is an illustration of this change of climate.

Compliance and Susceptibility to Influence

Do females more easily yield to the influence of others than males? Girls appear to be more compliant with adult requests than boys are (Maccoby & Jacklin, 1974). The question of whether men and women in adulthood differ in how easily they are influenced has been examined by meta-analytic studies (Becker, 1986; Eagly & Carli, 1981). The overall results of the investigations summarized indicated that women were more persuasible than men and that they also conformed more than men when they were in a state of uncertainty and group pressure towards conformity was exerted, (e.g., when a majority announced an incorrect judgment of the length of some lines). The authors investigated the hypothesis that the sex difference may be due to the possibly greater masculine content of the areas in which the subjects were exposed to influence attempts, thereby giving an advantage to men because of their greater familiarity with these matters. This hypothesis was not borne out, however.

RESEARCHER BIAS?

Of greatest importance for research in general, and for research into sex differences in particular, is the fact that Eagly and Carli (1981) discovered that *male* authors reported a larger difference in the degree to which women and men can be influenced than *female* authors did. Although the studies taken as a whole showed a significant difference, this was due to the preponderance of male authors. The studies conducted by women, examined separately, did not produce a significant mean sex difference, although the tendency was still in the same direction (of women being more easily influenced). Eagly and Carli also reanalyzed by sex of author Hall's (1978) study of sex differences in decoding nonverbal communication, which we discussed earlier. They found that male authors, though ascribing greater decoding accuracy to women, reported a smaller sex difference than female authors did, a finding that parallels the analysis of studies of susceptibility to influence.

In summary, male authors have found men to be relatively independent, less subject to group pressures, and more accurate in decoding nonverbal information than female authors have. By contrast, female authors have found women to be somewhat less readily influenced and more accurate in decoding nonverbal communications than male authors have! In other words, both men and women researchers portray their own sex more favorably than do researchers of the opposite sex.

In examining possible causes of this sex-of-researcher effect, Eagly and Carli found that male or female researchers did not slant the content of the tasks given to subjects towards the interests of their own sex. They thought that a possible reason for the effect might lie in the possibility that researchers designed research settings so that members of their own sex were more comfortable in them and hence also more self-confident and less persuasible. Errors in analysis, too, unfortunately occur all too frequently, and they are likely to go in the direction of one's predilections. The experimental research on the "self-fulfilling prophecy" has also shown that effects may emanate from the preconceptions of experimenters. Eagly and Carli (1981) could not ascertain the sex of the experimenters, that is, the persons who were in contact with the subjects in the various studies, and hence they could not scrutinize experimenter effects in their review. Obviously, many complications enter into the research enterprise and into the process of reaching conclusions, complications of which we are not fully aware, but of which we should take account. (See also the discussion on television and violence in Chapter 8.)

We have now discussed the main areas of behavior in which the existence of sex differences has been explored by empirical studies. Some differences that are popularly believed to mark the two sexes have been found to exist only in moderated form or in subareas, for example, in achievement motivation, as we noted. In other areas there is no good evidence for consistent sex differences at all, although they are popularly believed to exist; this is the case for instance, for dependence in young children (manifested by proximity- and comfort-seeking), self-esteem, and altruism, as discussed in Chapter 7.

Origins and Explanations of Sex Differences

In discussing various manifestations of sex differences the question where such differences in behavior originate obtrudes constantly, and it is time that we turned our attention to it. One knows of course that differences in the reproductive system and genital organs are embedded in the genes and are directly affected by different hormones; but does this apply to psychological characteristics and behavior that is not part of the reproductive system, for example, aggression or verbal ability? The view that sex differences in behavior may be due mainly, or even entirely, to what society expects of each sex, that is, to the *role* in which society has cast men and women is often opposed to the view that these differences are caused directly by biological factors. But explanations in terms of these two sources of influence, the cultural and the biological, need not be mutually exclusive, as we stated in the Introduction. We have already discussed such dual explanations for the evolution of a sex-based division of labor. However, we do want to know what evidence exists for the action of each influence and how they might intermesh and build on one another. In this section we will therefore examine cultural-environmental and biological explanations; we will consider how stereotypical concepts about the sexes—sex typing—develop, and finally we will reiterate and elaborate a viewpoint that takes both facets of influence into account.

ENVIRONMENTAL ASPECTS

Differential Socialization in the Family

"As the twig is bent, so the tree will grow." With this horticultural analogy in mind, it is usually thought that the parents, along with their general influence, also largely bend the young twig into the male or female direction. The general thesis is that parents, like everybody, are affected by sex stereotypes current in society and therefore their child-rearing practices will encourage and reinforce sterotypical behavior differentially in boys and girls, and thereby produce in their children a reflection of the stereotypical images that had originally guided them—a kind of self-fulfilling prophecy. Parents, of course, feel and think differently about boys and girls, and in some ways treat them differently from the beginning, as when they follow the convention of different colors of clothes for the two sexes. A preference for male offspring has also been reported for most countries (L.W. Hoffman, 1977), with a consequential greater investment of resources in male children.

Parents' beliefs about what is right for a boy or girl and their hopes for their own sons and daughters typically run along stereotypical lines. Thus in one study, parents desired occupational and career success for their sons more than for their daughters, whereas they hoped that the latter would grow up to be unselfish, loving, attractive, and well-mannered (L.W. Hoffman, 1977). But the goal that parents cherished most was identical for both sexes, namely, that the children should be happily married. Parents' attitudes about sex stereotypes, the degree to which they hold them, and the expectancies they have of their children are, however, generally poor predictors of these children's actual sex-stereotyped behavior and play interests at preschool and early elementary-school age (Lott, 1978; Meyer, 1980; Schau, Kahn, Diepold, & Cherry, 1980). Parents' belief systems by themselves, therefore, are not a good explanation for the emergence of sex-stereotypical behavior in their offspring.

Is it true that parents can shape at will typical masculine or feminine behavior in their child by their *practices*? An extreme case of parents' child-rearing direction influencing the child's sex-role has been reported by Money and Ehrhardt (1972). In this case a male identical twin lost his penis in a circumcision accident at 7 months and, on medical advice, it was then decided that the best course of action was to reassign the child's sex as feminine. The child underwent castration, plastic surgery and hormone replacement therapy, and was treated completely as a girl. The little girl in contrast to her twin brother, it seems, adopted the female characteristics that her mother fostered very readily. Her mother reported to the hospital: "She seems to be daintier. Maybe it's because I encourage it. . . . One thing that really amazes me is that she is so feminine. I've never seen a little girl so neat and tidy as she can be when she wants to be . . . She is very proud of herself, when she puts on a new dress or I set her hair. . . ." However, while the mother's assiduous socializing efforts appear to have borne fruit, one must also realize that this child lacked male hormonal influence from early on and therefore differed from her identical twin brother in a crucial biological way and not only in the direction of socialization. This is also an isolated, clinical report with all the usual limitations of such reports.

However, what scientific evidence exists for parents' differential socialization of boys and girls and in which behavioral areas has it been documented? For research up to 1974 Maccoby and Jacklin (1974) have assembled a very substantial data base. But this section of their book has evoked considerable criticism, particularly on account of their overall conclusion that their survey "has revealed a remarkable degree of uniformity in the socialization of the two sexes." (p. 348). The authors themselves were aware of some of the limitations of their evidential base, for example, that very little evidence was available about fathers, who stress differences between the sexes more than mothers do (e.g., Langlois & Downs, 1980). Further criticism, particularly by Block (e.g., 1978), was directed at the fact that the vast majority of the studies of differential socialization, available and summarized by Maccoby and Jacklin, were on children 5 years old or younger, and socialization differences may well become more pronounced at a later age. The Newsons (1978), for instance, in their longitudinal study of a large sample of English families noted differential socialization practices for the first time at age 7 and not earlier. There is thus some justification for these criticisms. However, at a later age parental practices may also reflect more the child's developed characteristics and their continuing experiences with the child. (We will further discuss this point below.)

Where quantitative integrations of research are available, these have been cited in earlier sections of this chapter, but no such integration in the domain of differential socialization of boys and girls has been carried out as yet. We will therefore make use of Maccoby and Jacklin's (1974) data base, but incorporate evidence from later studies that fill the gaps noted above and make our own interpretations, based on the evidence from the earlier and later studies together. Inevitably, our preconceptions will influence the interpretation of somewhat conflicting evidence, and others might put a differing emphasis on it.

In discussing the various areas in which parents' possibly differential behavior toward boys and girls has been examined, we will go from areas in which evidence for differences has been notably absent to areas in which the documentation of socialization differences is clearest and most unequivocal, with evidence for the existence of differences increasing in certainty as we proceed.

Amount of Interaction

In the first year of life parental interactions with infants consist of but a few simple behavior patterns, such as smiling, touching or talking, and these patterns are very similar for both sexes (Field, 1978). The sheer amount of time that parents spend interacting with boys does not seem to differ from that spent with girls, at least in the early years. This is the upshot of the evidence assembled by Maccoby and Jacklin (1974) and the fact has been reconfirmed by Fagot (1978) and Smith and Daglish (1977). However, there seems to be a tendency for fathers to interact more with sons (and mothers with daughters, to some extent) when the opportunity exists, both at preschool age (Cherry & Lewis, 1976; Weinraub & Frankel, 1977) and at elementary-school age (Margolin & Patterson, 1975). Perhaps this interaction between sex of parent and sex of child occurs because each parent feels more responsible for the upbringing and the development of the child of his or her sex.

For verbal interaction, the weight of the evidence presented by Maccoby and Jacklin (1974) leans toward the conclusion that after the first year of life parents do talk more to girls than to boys, although there is some variability among studies and subgroups (e.g., among social class groups). Mothers also use longer utterances to girls (Cherry & Lewis, 1976). Whether this is the cause of, or a reaction to, girls' greater verbal facility is unclear.

Tolerance of Aggression

Aggressive behavior is generally disapproved of by parents. Although observations in the home could only include aggressive behavior towards parents or siblings, the overall conclusion from such observations must be that parents are no more tolerant of boys' than of girls' aggressive behavior in the home, certainly up to age 7 (Fagot, 1978; Goshen-Gottstein, 1981; Maccoby & Jacklin, 1974). Table 10.2 provides a summary. However, within this general similarity of treatment, mothers may react differently from fathers to sons versus daughters. When parents in one study were

TABLE 10.2. Tolerance of aggression (or competitiveness).

Study	Age (n)	Difference	Comment
Tasch, 1952	0–17 years (85)	Boys	Father expects more aggressiveness; worried if unaggressive. Father worries over disobedience (father interview)
Stayton et al., 1971	9–12 months (25)	None	Frequency of discipline-oriented physical interventions by mother (home observation)
Goshen-Gottstein, 1981	5–42 months (22)	None	Twins, triplets at home. Mother's positive and negative reinforcement of aggression against adults, siblings, or objects
Fagot, 1978	20–24 months (24)	None	Response to aggressive behavior observed at home
Minton et al., 1971	27 months (90)	Girls	Less often reprimanded for aggression toward mother (home observation)
Block, 1972	3 years (90)	Boys	Mother and father believe competitive games are beneficial (questionnaire)
		Girls	Father allows anger toward himself (questionnaire)
Baumrind & Black, 1967	3–4 years (95)	Boys	Mother tolerates verbal protest, believes in less control of parent-directed verbal and/or physical aggression (interview)
Lapidus, 1972	3–4 years (30)	Boys	Mother makes self-deprecatory statements during game
Rothbart & Maccoby, 1966	3–4 years (98 mothers, 32 fathers)	None	Mother lets child win, encourages cooperation (observation)
		None	Mother's and father's reaction to other-directed aggression (written response to tape of child's voice)
Sears et al., 1953	3–5 years (40)	Boys	Mother permits aggression toward herself
		Girls	Father permits aggression toward himself
		None	Mother's responsiveness to aggression (interview)

Study	Age (N)	Direction	Measure
Serbin et al., 1973	3–5 years (225 pupils, 15 teachers)	Girls	Lower likelihood of teacher response to child's aggressive or destructive ($p < .08$) behavior; fewer loud reprimands for disruptive act
J. Gordon & Smith, 1965	3–4 years, 6–7 years (48)	None	Permissiveness for aggression (mother interview)
Newson & Newson, 1968	4 years (700)	None	Mother does not intervene in children's quarrels; encourages, permits aggression toward parents (English sample)
Sears et al., 1965, and personal communication	4–5 years (40)	None	Permissiveness of aggression toward parents; demands aggression toward peers (parent interview and observation)
Sears et al., 1957	5 years (379)	Boys	Mother more permissive of aggression toward parents and peers; mother's encouragement to fight back if attacked (interview)
		None	Punishment for aggression
Lambert et al., 1971	6 years (73)	Girls	Parental acceptance of show of anger (parent response to taped hypothetical situations, English-Canadian and French-Canadian samples)
		None	Parental acceptance of insolence
		Boys	Mother's acceptance of insolence (French-Canadian sample only)
		Girls	Father's acceptance of insolence (French-Canadian sample only)
		None	Parent's reaction to argument between child and baby, and between child and baby after child is hurt
		Boys	Mother sides more with child in argument between child and guest (French-Canadian sample only)
		Girls	Father sides more with child in argument between child and guest
Levitin & Chananie, 1972	6–7 years (40 teachers)	None	Teacher approval of aggressive behavior in hypothetical boy or girl (questionnaire)
Newson & Newson, 1976	7 years (700)	None	Reactions to peer quarrels include physical attacks. Mothers' interview responses

Note. Adapted and printed from *The Psychology of Sex Differences* by Eleanor Emmons Maccoby and Carol Nagy Jacklin with the permission of the publishers, Stanford University Press. Copyright 1974 by the Board of Trustees of the Leland Stanford Junior University.

asked to react to a voice identified either as a "boy's" or a "girl's" voice, they showed themselves to be more accepting of insolence from an opposite-sex child than from a same-sex child (Rothbart & Maccoby, 1966), again perhaps because each parent has greater concern for the proper upbringing of a child of their own sex.

For knowledge of how parents react to children's aggression outside the home, one has to rely on parental reports, but there again parents do not appear to make any difference between the sexes (e.g., Newson & Newson, 1970, 1978). At least in the middle classes, with whom most research has been done, parents in general tend to encourage their children to solve interpersonal problems in rational and nonconfrontational ways and discourage resort to violence. At the same time parents usually want their children to "stand up for themselves," when attacked. Working-class parents may be more inclined to encourage retaliation in kind to a physical attack than middle-class parents ("If anybody hits you, clout 'em back!"); Newson and Newson (1978) found such a social class difference in their English sample (mothers' reports), but found no difference being made between sons and daughters.

One of the authors once knew a working-class father who not only spurred his son on from the sidelines to keep battling away in a fight with an age-mate, but also gave the school's principal, who tried to intervene and stop the fight, a black eye, thus also setting his son the desired example. But, we should stress, this is merely an anecdote of an isolated incident!

Positive Feedback About Behavior

The findings assembled by Maccoby and Jacklin on praise and positive feedback (which include teachers', as well as parents' actions) indicate that most studies find no difference in positive feedback directed to the two sexes, and later-published studies of parent influences in the early years (e.g., Fagot, 1978; Smith & Daglish, 1977) do not change the tenor of these conclusions. Where sex-related differences are found, those in favor of one sex are counterbalanced by others going in the opposite direction. We will discuss teachers' socialization effects in a later section.

Encouragement of Achievement

When encouragement of achievement is defined as mother's pressure on the child to perform competently on a task, no overall differences between the sexes emerge, although the evidence is scanty (Maccoby & Jacklin, 1974). Yet Rothbart (1971) and Rothbart and Rothbart (1976) found, contrary to the general stereotype, that at 5 years of age first-born girls were subject to greater achievement pressure than first-born boys. Part of this achievement pressure manifested itself by mothers being quicker to offer help to girls than boys, that is, they reinforced help-seeking. The authors label this quick help-giving "anxious intrusion" and they argue that this tactic reinforces dependency in girls. But they do not suggest that it would have the same effect on first-borns of both sexes, although they too were the recipients of more "anxious intrusion" than were later born children.

Young adolescents report that fathers are somewhat more involved with their school mathematics work and mothers with their school language work, irrespective of the child's sex. However, neither parent encourages mathematical achievement more in boys and verbal achievement more in girls in adolescence, and hence differential parental encouragement does not explain the known sex differences in these areas (Raymond & Benbow, 1986).

Parents emphasize career orientation as more important for their sons, as we noted above, and, in line with this greater emphasis, expect them to go to college more. But parents do not seem to differentiate between the sexes in the actual interest they evince in, and the encouragement they provide for, their children's high school achievements in general (Raymond & Benbow, 1986).

Warmth

The upshot of many studies using observation in the home or a laboratory playroom is that parents treat their sons and daughters with equal affection and nurturance throughout the early years up to about 6 or 7 (Maccoby & Jacklin, 1974). This is shown, for instance, by similar patterns of smiling and touching in the first year (Field, 1978). However, daughters as early as 1 year old may receive more physical affection from their fathers than sons do, as demonstrated in a laboratory situation by Snow, Jacklin, and Maccoby (1983). At later ages girls generally report experiencing greater warmth from their parents than boys (Maccoby and Jacklin included 15 comparisons between ages 9 and 18 in their review). Block (1978) obtained reports from parents of 12-year-olds in six countries and later retrospective accounts from these children when they were 21-year-old students, and these reports agreed that parent-daughter relationships were marked by greater warmth and physical closeness than parent-son relationships. Whether such different findings for different ages are due to actual developmental changes or to the fact that reports are more likely to be subject to the operation of cultural stereotypes is difficult to say. There is also a hint (e.g., from the fact that both parents believe girls to be more trustworthy) that with adolescents parents may react to perceived, or actual, differences in their children. If older girls thus do experience greater physical closeness and warmth in their relationships with parents, for whatever reasons, this may well have a positive influence on their own nurturant behavior later.

Reward for Dependency

Although it is generally supposed that parents accept manifestations of dependency more readily from girls than from boys, there is no good evidence overall for such a generalization for the early years. Most of the studies on this topic indicate that parents do not react differently to young boys' than to young girls' proximity- or comfort-seeking (Maccoby & Jacklin, 1974). Nor do boys and girls at this age differ in these behaviors, as we discussed above. Of those studies that indicate a difference in parental responsiveness to sons and daughters (including studies published since 1974), about half suggest that parents are more responsive to boys' acts of dependency, and half to girls'. Interestingly, two studies of twin families have reported, contrary to expectations, that mothers encouraged dependency and provided nurturance more for boys than for girls (Cohen, Dibble, & Grawe, 1977, who used questionnaires, and Goshen-Gottstein, 1981, who employed direct observation). On the other hand, as discussed above, mothers have been reported to give more contingent reinforcement to daughters' than to sons' help-seeking—a form of dependency that even young girls show more than boys (Rothbart & Rothbart, 1976; cf. Fagot, 1978).

There is also some evidence that reactions to dependency bids depend on the sex of the parent as well as on the sex of the child. Thus, when parents reacted to taped voices of a "boy" and a "girl," mothers showed greater permissiveness for boys' acts of comfort-seeking, and fathers for those of girls (Rothbart & Maccoby, 1966). (The greater affection demonstrated by fathers to daughters in the Snow et al. [1983] study is a comparable phenomenon.)

Although the evidence for parents' reward of dependency is mixed, it comes mainly from the early years. We also should note that whereas authors looking for sex differences usually refer to their criterion variable as "dependent behavior" or "dependency," comfort- and proximity-seeking in 1- to 2-year-olds has recently come under the umbrella of attachment theory. So far as we know, no sex-related differences in mother's responsiveness to this behavior have been reported in the attachment literature. Girls' dependence may, however, be encouraged at later ages and in more subtle ways, namely by their being closed off from independence and venturesomeness, a topic which we will discuss in the next section.

Independence Granting

Children can be given varying degrees of freedom with respect to their activities and the area where they are allowed to play—this is one kind of independence. For this type of independence the evidence on the whole suggests parents make few differentiations by sex in the preschool years. Indeed, some mothers and fathers are particularly concerned about the scrapes some venturesome little boys might get themselves into and therefore impose considerable restrictions on their movements and activities (Maccoby & Jacklin, 1974). However, the picture changes in middle childhood. At that time, it is clear, boys are allowed to roam over a wider area, are given more freedom how to spend their time, and are kept less under adult surveillance than girls (L.W. Hoffman, 1977; Newson & Newson, 1978). Indeed, greater restrictions on girls from later childhood on probably occur the world over because of the danger of sexual molestation. The Newsons called this the "chaperonage factor" and found, unsurprisingly, that chaperonage was greater for girls generally and also increased with a rise in social class. They comment: ". . . the chaperonage factor exerts an important influence upon the daily life experience of girls as compared with boys even by the tender age of seven, ensuring that girls lead a more sheltered and protected existence. This in itself is of interest: but the implications are of greater consequence, since children who are kept under closer and more continuous surveillance must inevitably *come under consistently greater pressure towards conformity with adult standards and values.*" (p. 109). In this way, then, girls are granted less autonomy than boys, with all that this implies. Moreover, differential treatment in this area, as well as in the fostering of dependence, increases with age.

However, there is another way in which parents can promote independence, namely by giving children room, as they get older, to differentiate themselves from their parents and make their own decisions. There is little evidence regarding this type of autonomy, but the little there is suggests that mothers encourage girls as much as boys in taking responsibility for themselves, whereas fathers emphasize this more in boys (Block, 1978).

Punishment

We now come to areas where there is wide agreement that parents treat sons and daughters differently. The evidence is overwhelming that boys get the hard end of the stick, both literally and metaphorically, more often than girls. Moreover, this observation applies over a wide age range. Often the more severe punishment may occur because boys are more prone to get into mischief. Minton et al. (1971), for instance, identified an escalating sequence in disciplinary encounters: The first step was a simple command, and girls often stopped what they were doing at this. If the child continued with his or her misdemeanor, mother would escalate the intensity of her prohibition and finally end up spanking the child—most usually a boy. In more recent studies fathers, in particular, have been found to use physical punishment and verbal prohibitions more with boys than girls (Block, 1978; Smith & Daglish, 1977). Thus fathers are "harder" on boys. Snow et al. (1983) observed in their study that boys also were more likely to touch tempting and disaster-prone objects in the room and hence would elicit prohibitions more frequently. But when allowance was made for the child's behavior, no sex difference in father's prohibitions remained. Already at the early age of 12 months, therefore, sex differences in the child's behavior elicit differential behavior by father.

Encouragement of Sex-Typed Activities

Here there is general agreement that parents actively encourage, and approve of, sex-typed activities (e.g., block play for boys and doll play for girls) in both sexes. This differential reinforcement has been observed in experimental situations and in the home, as well as noted in reports (Maccoby & Jacklin, 1974). One way in which this differential reinforcement is assessed is to devise experiments in which sex of child is actually manipulated to isolate the influence of parents' stereotypical views of the two sexes from the child's effect on the parents through his or her behavioral tendencies. For example, Frisch (1977) and Smith and Lloyd (1978) labeled the same infant either as a boy or as a girl for different adults. Although there was no difference in behavior between the male and female infants they used in their studies, adults offered dolls more often to infants labeled "girls," and hammers and mechanical toys more often to infants labeled "boys," and they also elicited more motor behavior in "boys" in some studies. This finding implies that adults' behavior may be governed more by their own stereotypes than by the child's propensities, but this applies only in a situation where the adults have no knowledge of the child other than the sex label and are not influenced by the child's individual characteristics.

We have discussed positive responses in general, but it is of course important to know to which specific behavior in either sex parents respond positively. Home and laboratory observations of young children have shown that parents praise block play and elicit gross motor play and active behavior more in boys, and praise doll play more in girls (Fagot, 1978; Langlois & Downs, 1980; Tauber, 1979b). Snow et al. (1983) examined father's toy offerings to 1-year-olds in a laboratory situation: Fathers were less likely to give dolls to boys than to girls, but gave trucks, shovel, or vacuum cleaner as frequently to boys as to girls. Thus in this investigation, as in others with older children, fathers were more concerned about boys' sex-inappropriate play than about girls'. What was interesting in this study was that when boys were given a doll they played less with it, and when given a vacuum cleaner they played more with that than girls did. This finding seems to indicate that boys show greater interest in mechanical toys, and that not only do fathers differ in sex-typed offers, but 1-year-old boys and girls also already differ in preferences for toys conventionally associated with each sex, when the opportunity for playing with them is equalized.

Father's disapproval and fear of boys being "sissies" is, in fact, the most pronounced aspect of differential treatment of boys and girls, and fathers are often much more emotionally involved than mothers in ensuring "masculinity" in their sons and shielding them from "femininity." The obverse of this coin is that they also play a role in the development of femininity in their daughters and often show great awareness of this aspect of their daughters' behavior (Maccoby & Jacklin, 1974). Mothers, on the other hand, seem to emphasize differences between their sons and daughters less, perhaps because they are more familiar with them as individuals through their day-to-day contact with them.

Maternal Employment

When a mother is employed outside the home, this changes the sex roles that her children see enacted around them and thereby narrows the differences in these roles. Employed mothers and their husbands report greater similarity in the tasks they perform at home than do nonemployed wives and husbands, as in the former case household chores are shared more equally (Gold & Andres, 1978b). There is a consistent finding from several studies that children whose mothers are employed have less fixed stereotypes about sex-appropriate social behavior (they see women as more competent and men as warmer) and about parental task division than do children of nonemployed women (Gold & Andres, 1978a, b; Hoffman, 1979; Marantz & Mansfield, 1977). Although such sex stereotypes are more relaxed for both sons and daughters of employed mothers, sex-typical preferences and social behavior tend to be affected only in daughters: They are more career- and achievement-oriented, have higher self-esteem, and admire their mothers more. In an equality-minded society these can be seen as beneficial effects flowing from mothers' employment. There is also another side to the coin: Fathers with employed wives in working-class families are held in less regard by their young sons than when wives are not employed. There may be some factual basis to this as such fathers are less ample providers, making it necessary for their wives to work (Gold & Andres, 1978a).

Appraisal

What conclusions can we draw from this literature? Do parents deliberately socialize boys and girls in different directions? Clearly they do when it comes to what are considered to be sex-appropriate activities, for example, playing with certain toys, and they also differentiate in the matter of punishment in that they are harder on boys—something that is partly elicited by boys' often more troublesome behavior. Some differences emerge from middle childhood on; parents grant boys more independence and are warmer to, and more protective of, girls. But then qualifications enter into the argument: "independence" only in the sense of allowing greater freedom of movement, and "warmth" in the sense of physical contact.

The supposition that boys receive more encouragement and pressure for achievement, and particularly school achievement, has received very little support. Since there seems to be no difference either in the amount of praise that boys and girls receive either overall or for school achievement, there is no evidence that parents enhance boys' self-esteem but undermine that of girls. Further, parents do not tolerate aggression in boys any more than in girls, and therefore the greater aggressiveness of boys cannot be explained by parents' differential reinforcement of it.

Two further generalizations impose themselves: parents' practices for the two sexes in some areas diverge more from school age on than before, and fathers in general make greater and more deliberate differences than mothers do.

The main question, however, is whether parents make the differences that we have noted because in rearing their children they are influenced by sex stereotypes and want to recreate these, or because they react to their children's differing natures? The experimental manipulations we mentioned earlier in which parents react differently to the same infant labeled alternatively as "boy" or "girl," suggest that parents' actions often are triggered by the stereotypical beliefs they hold. However, it is possible that when adults are not familiar with children, and only know their sex label, this may elicit more stereotyped offerings of toys. Thus the label may influence adults' behavior more than actual sex does when they are familiar with a child's distinctive characteristics.

Indeed, it is a reasonable assumption that parents reinforce stereotypes because they work with biological givens and react to children as they find them. In Chapter 5 we have cited evidence that indicates that early personality and temperamental differences in children affect parents' reactions, which in turn will influence children's development. Studies such as Snow et al.'s (1983) also suggest that existing differences between boys and girls, for instance in their play preferences, and parental sex stereotypes coact at a very early age. Hence it seems very likely that biological factors in the child, either of genetic origin or stemming from the biological environment, together with parents' prior expectations and values, will affect parents' actions and will set up transactional cycles of mutual influences, shaping both future actions by parents and the future development of the child.

Differential Socialization by School, Peers, and the Media

Some socialization of sex-typed behavior clearly takes place in the family, but children's behavior will also be shaped towards sex-appropriateness by the socializing influences of the playground and the school. We have already discussed some of these latter influences in Chapter 6. Earlier critics of the school were concerned that the school might act as a feminizing environment for boys. Its stress on conformity to rules and its long hours of compulsory physical inactivity were considered to be, and indeed are, more consonant with girls' than with boys' natural inclinations. Children, too, classify school and school-related objects or activities as feminine (Minuchin & Shapiro, 1983). More recently investigators have asked how it is that girls who thrive in this climate and who get good grades at school, fall behind males in later life.

Is school a feminizing environment? It has been claimed that teachers evaluate "masculine," active, and independent behavior negatively and consider it disruptive, but value "feminine" characteristics, such as task orientation and obedience. It has, indeed, been found that teachers approve of task-oriented behavior and disapprove of aggressive behavior, regardless of whether it is performed by boys or girls (Etaugh & Harlow, 1975; Smith & Green, 1975). Indeed, boys may receive more disapproval. Serbin et al. (1973) report that boys in preschools were, true to stereotype, more disruptive than girls, but they also received a higher *rate* of teacher response to disruptive behavior, calculated as a proportion of this behavior. Perhaps any kind of attention by the teacher, even of a negative kind, reinforces boys' aggressiveness? It has been found in a study of English nursery schools that when the teacher intervened in conflicts the aggressive act was more likely to be unsuccessful than when she did not intervene, and thus teacher intervention, far from reinforcing aggression, discouraged it (Smith & Green, 1975). Teacher attention, therefore, does not appear to be responsible for the higher aggressiveness of boys.

Other observational studies in preschool and elementary schools have confirmed that boys receive more disapproval, scolding, and negative comments than girls do (Cherry, 1975; Yarrow et al., 1971). Partly this will, no doubt, be a function of boys' generally more active, aggressive, and disruptive behavior. Teachers in elementary schools, it appears, also approve of dependency more than of aggression and they approve of dependency even more in boys than in girls (Etaugh & Hughes, 1975).

When it comes to play activities that could be potentially constructive or disruptive, teachers seem to favor the more sedentary over the gross-motor, more muscular activities. Thus Fagot and Patterson (1969) found that when play activities in preschool were classified as "masculine" or "feminine" according to the preferences that boys and girls actually showed, teachers reinforced "feminine" play (e.g., dolls' house, painting) by both sexes more than they did "masculine" play (e.g., blocks, trucks). However, teachers do not generally disapprove of boys or girls who engage in moderate cross-sex play (Fagot, 1977a).

To sum up: Teachers seem to reinforce "feminine" sex-typed behavior, but not "masculine," for both sexes, and sometimes, as in the case of play with blocks, their actions go beyond what the classroom situation demands. On the other hand, it is teachers' responsibility to encourage task orientation and to discourage aggressive behavior. Hence, what they often actually do is to respond to behavior in terms of whether it is appropriate to classroom activities.

Another important question is whether teachers encourage intellectual endeavor and achievement more in one sex than the other. Although there is evidence that teachers' reactions to boys' learning activities often differ in kind from that to girls, it is more difficult to know which sex derives the greater advantage. Serbin et al. (1973) found, as did Cherry (1975), that teachers, in addition to reacting more negatively to boys, also had more positive interactions with them than with girls: This took the form of responding to bids for attention, as well as of instruction and praise. Other researchers, however (e.g., Miller & Dyer, 1975), have found that girls receive more reinforcement for learning activities and have more instructional contact with teachers than boys do. Girls, in the Serbin study, were rewarded simply for standing close to teachers, who then showed affection to them. On the other hand, teachers encourage self-reliance and independent achievement more in boys than in girls, as some evidence shows (Brophy, 1985).

Serbin et al., (1973) interpret the greater amount of instructional help for boys as providing them with models of, and consequently with encouragement for, problem-solving. (It will be remembered, Rothbart and Rothbart [1976] interpreted similar help-giving to girls by mothers as "anxious intrusion" and inimical to independent problem-solving: One wonders whether there is a double standard in research on sex differences.) It is quite plausible, as Serbin and her colleagues suggest, that preschool boys receive more instructional help in some classes because they need more direction in acquiring skills, since they are more immature, more impulsive, and less coordinated than girls. Overall, however, it seems unlikely that teachers favor intellectual achievement more in one sex than the other (cf. Minuchin & Shapiro, 1983). However, teachers probably play some part in reinforcing traditional sex stereotypes, but observational studies in classrooms suggest that their responses are determined more by the situation and children's behavior than by their own preconceptions (Brophy, 1985).

One may ask whether the teacher behaviors that we have discussed are a function of the fact that most teachers studied have been female. However, studies that have compared female with male teachers' reactions in elementary schools have not revealed as great a difference between them as one might have imagined. Both male and female teachers in elementary schools react to dependency, aggressive, and disruptive behavior in similar ways, as described above (Etaugh & Harlow, 1975; Etaugh & Hughes, 1975). One investigation in preschools found that male teachers showed more physical affection and joined children's play more readily than female teachers did. This may be a result of the self-selection of more nurturant men as preschool teachers. It also appeared that the amount of experience teachers had was a more influential factor in their reactions than whether they were male or female (Fagot, 1977b). Thus teachers' professional role is more crucial in determining their behavior than is their sex.

Peers, however, are a more potent force than teachers in socializing children in sex-typed ways. Despite the absence of teacher reinforcement of masculine-type play, the boys in the Fagot and Patterson study fully maintained their sex-customary preferences over the year, a finding that could be attributed to the positive reinforcement (e.g., reciprocation in play) they received from their peers (Fagot & Patterson, 1969; Lamb & Roopnarine, 1979). However, 2-year-old boys' sex-typical play behavior has been found to be very resistant to negative reinforcement by both peers and teachers (Fagot, 1985). Thus, reinforcement is not everything and this behavior seems to be deeply ingrained in boys.

Television is perhaps the most powerful influence of all in socializing—and, indeed, oversocializing—children in sex-typed thinking and behavior. In most programs adult males and females are very often shown in sex-stereotyped professional and domestic roles, and sex-sterotyped personal-social behavior is the rule. Impressionable young viewers are easily induced by such potent visual images to form sex-stereotyped notions, as well as to imitate the actors. Recent shifts in the social climate regarding sex roles do not seem to have affected the media as much as society in general (Huston, 1983).

Theories of Sex Typing

How does the whole complex of sex-related differences—something called "sex typing"—develop in a social environment? We will now turn to a discussion of theories that attempt to explain this development. Sex typing refers to a broad range of phenomena. It refers to the acquisition of sex-typed or sex-appropriate preferences and behavior and it also includes the development of sex stereotypes, that is, perceptions or self-perceptions of personality dispositions or behavior as characteristically masculine or feminine. Sex stereotypes, preferences, and behavior have been found to be modestly intercorrelated, and this demonstrates that some relationship exists among these different dimensions of sex typing (Huston, 1983).

The term "sex typing" itself implies that the process is a social one that is guided by environmental forces. The two principal theories that have attempted to explain the development of sex typing are social learning theory and cognitive developmental theory. Social learning theory focuses on sex differences in behavior, although, in Bandura's elaboration of it, any explanation of behavior must also take cognitive events into account. Social learning theory explains the acquisition of sex differences in behavior by the same mechanisms (viz., reinforcement and modeling) that apply to all kinds of social behavior. (See Chapter 1 for a detailed discussion.) It suggests children adopt sex-appropriate behavior because throughout their lives they are reinforced for watching same-sex models and for imitating their behavior.

For cognitive-developmental theory, by contrast, the acquisition of concepts of sex stereotypes is paramount, with differences in behavior arising as a consequence of these concepts (e.g., Kohlberg, 1966). The theory asserts that children watch and imitate same-sex models preferentially because they see them as similar to themselves and because sex-appropriate acts are consonant with their self-concept and sexual self-identity. However, the two theories should not be seen as mutually exclusive—they both assign an important role to modeling, for instance, but, according to Kohlberg, modeling can be effective only when sex-role categorization has taken place. The steps in this development will be explored below.

A cognitive view of sex stereotyping is also espoused by theorists who perceive sex stereotyping as an information-processing strategy. Viewed from the vantage point of this theory, sex stereotypes, like all concepts, serve as schemas that organize and structure information. There is, indeed, evidence that stereotyping aids memorization (Koblinsky, Cruse, & Sugawara, 1978). Thus sex stereotyping is a normal cognitive process that, because it categorizes and pigeonholes a variety of behaviors and attitudes, makes for economy and efficiency in thought processes. In this way sex stereotypes can be seen as helpful aids in thinking and are not necessarily incorrect or illogical simply because they involve typological thinking (Martin & Halverson, 1981). Since this last theory does not deal with the acquisition of sex-typed behavior we will not discuss it further.

Development of Sex Typing and Sex-Typed Behavior

Let us now turn to the empirical literature on the development of sex typing and sex-typed behavior to see how far it confirms the theories that we have outlined. Kohlberg (1966) cites Gesell who found that the vast majority of 3-year-olds can correctly answer the question "Are you a little boy or a little girl?" Slaby and Frey (1975) also report that 91% of 2- to 5-year-olds answered this question correctly and nearly 100% knew the sex of a boy and a girl doll shown to them. So it seems that sex-role identity is established by about 3 years of age.

However, this is simple categorization and recognition of identity. Further steps consist of understanding first that sex is stable and then that it does not change either by wishing or by transformation of external characteristics. Slaby and Frey (1975), indeed, confirmed the sequence: First children identify a doll's sex and their own sex correctly (gender identity), then they understand that a person's sex stays the same over the years (gender stability), and only later do they come to realize that sex stays the same, even if they wished otherwise and even when outward appearances, such as clothing or activities, would seem to indicate the opposite (gender consistency). Table 10.3 indicates that nearly all children follow this sequence in order and only very few acquire the concept of consistency before that of stability. This sequence (identity-stability-consistency) is identical to the developmental progression first put forward by Kohlberg (1966); however, it is quite another matter whether a knowledge of the concepts of sex identity, stability, and consistency is a prerequisite for the acquisition of sex-appropriate behavior, as the cognitive view claims.

Interestingly, the clues that children use to decide in the first place on the sex of a doll or figure presented to them are superficial, external ones. McConaghy (1979) presented 4- to 10-year-old Swedish boys and girls with jigsaw figures of a boy and a girl with genitals in place. Some of the children who had recognized that sex was permanent (i.e., had acquired the concept of stability), nevertheless were willing to turn a boy into a girl when he was given long hair and a dress, despite the genitals. Indeed, the understanding that genitals define sex, that is, that they are a necessary

TABLE 10.3. Scale of gender constancy, based on three question sets.

Type	Question set			% of children (total = 100)			Age (in months)	
	Gender identity	Gender stability	Gender consistency	Boys	Girls	Combined	Mean	Range
Stage								
1	–	–	–	9	16	13	34	26–39
2	+	–	–	26	16	20	47	35–62
3	+	+	–	17	31	25	53	36–68
4	+	+	+	48	34	40	55	41–67
Nonstage								
A	+	–	+	0	3	2	35	
B	–	+	–	0	0	0		
C	–	+	+	0	0	0		
D	–	–	+	0	0	0		

Note. From "Development of Gender Constancy and Selective Attention to Same-Sex Models" by R.G. Slaby and K.S. Frey, 1975, *Child Development, 46,* 849–856. Reprinted by permission.

condition of the definition of each sex, always followed the acquisition of sex stability, so this recognition is part of the notion that sex is resistant to external transformation.

The idea that certain kinds of play are "appropriate" for boys, and others are generally associated with girls also comes early, and children show that they possess this concept by age 3 (Blakemore et al., 1979). It is generally known that the rigidity of sex stereotyping reaches its peak in the early school years and that peer pressure against opposite-sex typed behavior is very strong at that age. As knowledge of what is and what is not sex-appropriate increases over age, insistence on sex-stereotyped behavior then, in fact, becomes less rigid over the elementary-school years. Greater flexibility of thought about sex boundaries probably is a corollary of the advance in general cognitive growth that occurs in middle childhood (Kohlberg, 1966; Serbin & Sprafkin, 1986).

How does sex-typed behavior then develop according to the two theories? As Kohlberg (1966) points out, not only cognitive developmental theory, but social learning theory, too, though it does not emphasize cognitive stereotypes, must assume that children have acquired concepts of sex-typed actions, since children have to know what is sex-appropriate before they can imitate such actions preferentially. Thus social learning theory and cognitive developmental theory both hypothesize that sex-appropriate behavior originates in the following sequence: (1) children observe behavior, (2) based on this observation they acquire notions of sex stereotypes, and (3) they imitate and adopt sex-appropriate behavior preferentially. The two theories differ, however, in the reasons they give for the adoption of sex-appropriate behavior, as we illustrated.

Do children, indeed, acquire sex-appropriate behavior in this sequence? How important is the role of imitation in this acquisition? It might be thought that parents are the most readily available and most important sex-role models for their children. However, they send some mixed messages: mothers, not fathers, more often drive children around in the family automobile, although it is father who will tend to potter about the car. Which parent do boys emulate in their fascination with car play, and which parent do girls emulate in being less enamored of this? Boys are not more masculine when their fathers express strong masculinity, and girls are not more feminine because of their mothers' pronounced femininity (Mussen & Rutherford, 1963). Nor do children necessarily imitate the same-sex parent. Whom children choose to imitate depends much more on the parents' relative dominance or perceived power (Bandura, Ross, & Ross, 1963a). That stereotypes—derived from somewhere in the child's environment—overshadow even the most obvious of parental models is illustrated by the story, recounted by Maccoby and Jacklin (1974), of a little girl who insisted that girls will be nurses and only boys will be doctors, in the face of the fact that her own mother was a doctor! For all these reasons identification with parents has not played a role in recent models of sex-role development (Huston, 1983).

Nevertheless, there is good evidence that children do tend to imitate the behavior of same-sex models. This occurs before 6 years of age, although it is not as prevalent as is often thought at that age; it is in somewhat older children that the tendency to imitate same-sex behavior seems to emerge more strongly. The important influence on these older children's imitation or preference is not the same-sex model per se, but whether the child is convinced that the behavior is sex-appropriate. Thus in one study certain shapes of polygons were alleged by the experimenter to be preferred by boys or girls, respectively. Six- and 7-year-old boys and girls selected by preference those items that had been labeled as sex-appropriate for them (White, 1978). This suggests a strong influence emanating from the climate of social opinion, as expressed by the experimenter-imposed label. Girls also have been shown to imitate modeled feminine behavior more than boys do, regardless of the sex of the model displaying this sex-typed behavior, and boys exhibited a similar trend for the imitation of masculine behavior. These results clearly indicate that sex-appropriateness, not sex of model, is the more important factor for imitation (Barkley, Ullman, Lori, & Brecht, 1977).

However, the main question is whether children as young as 2 or 3 imitate sex-typical behavior for the simple reason that this has been designated as appropriate for each sex. In other words, does such behavior result from children's attempts to match their behavior to sex-role stereotypes, or do they prefer these types of actions for other reasons? Indeed, do sex stereotypes precede sex-typed behavior? In an interesting recent study, Perry, White, and Perry (1984) tested this hypothesis in 2-, 3-, 4-, and 5-year-olds. They first elicited the children's toy preferences by giving them a choice of toys to play with, and then assessed their knowledge of stereotypes, as expressed about pictures of sex-typed and neutral toys. The results indicated that boys' development of sex-typed preferences *preceded* their acquisition of sex-role stereotypes by about 1 year. The data on girls did not confirm or refute the hypothesized sequence. This finding for girls may be connected to girls' relatively weaker sex typing, already shown in other research. The authors write: ". . . if anything, boys' sex-typed preferences may contribute to their acquisition of broader masculine stereotypes rather than be a consequence of them" (p. 2119).

This finding is not an isolated one, as other researchers have also found that in 2- to 3-year-olds sex-typed toy and activity preferences occur without any awareness of the traditional sex typing of the toys (Blakemore et al., 1979; Bussey, 1985, Weinraub et al., 1984). Cognition, in the form of knowledge of sex stereotypes, is therefore not necessary in the development of sex-typed preferences and cognitive-developmental theory is not supported by these findings. Preferences and behavior come first, knowledge of stereotypes comes afterward. It should be stressed that this conclusion applies to young children and that knowledge of sex stereotypes does play a role in selective imitation processes in elementary-school-aged children, where, indeed, imitation "is alive and well" (Perry & Bussey, 1979).

Social learning theory, on the other hand, would be supported by these findings on young children, if one adopts the explanation that the sex-typed preferences arose because parents from early on gave their infants and toddlers sex-appropriate toys and encouraged and rewarded them for such activities. In other words, it is external reinforcement that led to sex-appropriate behavior. However, biological factors, such as differences in the brain or in hormonal preparation, may also play a role in propelling children towards some activities rather than others. The evidence from androgenized girls, although it is not conclusive, supports such reasoning (see Chapter 3). The next section will discuss such biological factors.

BIOLOGICAL ASPECTS

Having discussed aspects of the child's environment and experience that influence sex differences, we will now turn to evidence that shows that some of these differences can also be rooted in biological factors.

Cerebral Asymmetry

There is evidence that the brain structure and the cerebral organization of males and females differ. A study of the brains of 4-year-old children who had died found, for instance, that the right hemisphere was at a more advanced state of maturation (myelinization) in boys and the left hemisphere in girls (Levy, 1980). Such maturation is related to the readiness of each hemisphere to execute its specific functions. For 95% of the human population it is language functions that are localized in the left, and spatial functions that are localized in the right hemisphere. In the 5% of the population in whom these functions are reversed, the cognitive sex differences also are reversed (Levy, 1980).

It might be argued that the earlier maturation of the left and right hemispheres in girls and boys, respectively, is due to their differing experiences—more language experiences for girls and more explorations in open space and experiences with three-dimensional objects for boys. However, as we just noted, in some left-handers language functions are localized in the right and spatial functions in the left hemisphere, that is, the specializations of the hemispheres are reversed. There is some evidence, although it is only suggestive since it is based on small numbers, that in such cases (with the specializations of the hemispheres reversed) girls do better on a spatial task and boys do better at a language-like task (Reid, 1980, cited in Levy, 1980). It is difficult to imagine that the culture could reinforce verbal functions in girls with left hemisphere language, but spatial functions in girls with right hemisphere language. Hence the greater maturation of the left hemisphere in girls and of the right hemisphere in boys is likely to be of biological origin.

In studies on the effects of brain lesions it also has been discovered that spatial functions in males depend almost exclusively on the right hemisphere, whereas in females they can be localized in either hemisphere. Such evidence leads to the conclusion that females are less lateralized in their hemispheric functions than males are and that the way in which the two hemispheres integrate information differs in the two sexes (Levy, 1980). We should also remember, however, that within-sex variation in cerebral and cognitive organization very likely is much larger than between-sex variation and that there is a considerable overlap of distributions.

Hormones

The fetus is exposed to sex hormones (androgens or testosterone for males, estrogen for females) that have an *organizing* function both for internal and external sex organs and for behavior in postnatal life. The most potent organizing hormone is androgen. The mechanisms of sexual differentiation are similar in all mammals. A neuter sex does not exist; rather, in the absence of androgen or when there are no gonads at all, development turns by default in the female direction. Not only the reproductive system, but also the brain, as we have noted, is organized as male or female, and there is a species-specific critical period in fetal or early postnatal life when hormonal mechanisms bring about this organization. Later, in the mature organism, circulating sex hormones have an *activating* function for sexual and certain other kinds of behavior (Daly & Wilson, 1983). A great deal of research attention has been paid to the relation of hormones to aggression and spatial ability.

The effects of hormones on aggression have been discussed in Chapter 8. Overall, the experimental work with animals clearly shows that androgens have both an organizing and an activating function with respect to aggression. As Maccoby and Jacklin state, ". . . human research to date is consistent with the existence of such effects in humans. Thus it remains a reasonable hypothesis that some such processes do occur in humans" (1980, p. 974). They also may partly explain the sex difference in aggression.

Spatial Ability

The role that hormones play in sex differences in spatial ability is much less clear than for aggression. Sex differences in spatial ability exist before puberty and do not become any greater afterward, so it appears that pubertal hormonal changes are not responsible for these sex differences. But hormonal differences mark the sexes throughout life and exposure to hormones is responsible for differential brain organization prenatally or shortly after birth (Linn & Petersen, 1986). It has also been shown recently that females who were exposed to heightened levels of adrenal androgen prenatally (adreno-genital syndrome) performed better on spatial tasks than did females not so affected (Resnick, Berenbaum, Gottesman, & Bouchard, 1986). Hormonal mechanisms therefore also seem to affect spatial ability. It is likely that any biological factors that may affect spatial ability arise early in development and interact with sex-role expectations to produce the noted performance differences (Linn & Petersen, 1986).

Hormones may be the mediating mechanism through which biological-genetic factors operate. At one time it was thought that the sex difference in spatial ability could be accounted for by a recessive gene, located in the X-chromosome which, because of its location, was more frequently expressed in males than in females (Vandenberg & Kuse, 1979). At first this hypothesis seemed to be supported by evidence from family genetic studies and the correlation patterns of spatial ability that these showed between mothers/fathers and sons/daughters. However, subsequent evidence has been inconsistent and therefore the verdict on the theory must be "not proven." That spatial ability in general is under genetic influence, however, is a well-documented fact (Vandenberg & Kuse, 1979).

There is good evidence that biological factors of one kind or another play an important role in some human sex differences. Since it is inextricably involved in the metabolic processes of every cell, the gene is relevant to every developmental process in an organism. Biological factors, however, will interact with the differential experiences of the two sexes to produce observed performance differences. Moreover, environmental influences also affect biological functions, for example, nutrition, physical activity, or psychological stimuli are known to raise or lower hormone levels in humans. Hence we must recognize that environmental events will modify the effects of biological predispositions.

ANDROGYNY

As we noted earlier, sex stereotypes are schematizations, and are not necessarily inaccurate. Although schematizations are often built on a kernel of truth, by simplifying they often exaggerate. Thus, instead of stating that "males, on average, tend to be somewhat superior to females in math reasoning," the extreme stereotype would state that "females are no good at math." This is both illogical overgeneralization and inaccurate stereotyping of a group.

Typically the more extreme stereotypes are applied to people with whom one has only slight familiarity and does not recognize characteristics that mark them out as individuals. An example of this tendency is the fact that college students rate the typical woman or man as more extreme on sex-role stereotypes than they rate themselves (Rosenkrantz, Vogel, Bee,

Broverman, & Broverman, 1968). One suspects that individuals are more aware of, and acknowledge more readily, a mixture of typical and atypical qualities in themselves than they do in others.

Research since the 1970s has shown a shift toward more egalitarian attitudes and a movement away from endorsement of traditional roles for men and women. Traditional attitudes are more likely to be held by older, less educated, lower income persons and by more assiduous church-goers (Deaux, 1985). On the other hand, more recently the feminist claim that sex differences need not and should not exist has given way to an acceptance of the existence of certain behavioral divergences between the sexes, and some feminists (e.g., Betty Friedan) have emphasized that women should not uncritically endorse masculine values and goals and strive to emulate these, but should rather proclaim the equal worth and importance of feminine values.

To measure the degree to which individuals do or do not conform to sex stereotypes, masculinity and femininity scales have been developed, the most widely known of which are Bem's Sex Role Inventory (BSRI; cf. Bem, 1979), and the Personal Attributes Questionnaire (PAQ; Spence, Helmreich, & Stapp, 1975). The PAQ was intended to be limited to socially desirable attitudes. Its items were selected by having adults rate adjectives as applying to an ideal and a typical man and woman. The masculinity and femininity scales consist of adjectives that were considered desirable attributes for both sexes and for which the rating of one sex was significantly higher than that of the other. The adjectives on the masculinity scale, for instance, include "independent," "active," and "competitive," and those on the femininity scale include "able to devote self to others," "gentle," and "helpful." Rather than considering these scales as measuring broadly all the characteristics associated with males and females, it may be more justifiable to view them, without linkage to sex labels, as measures of dominance and self-assertion or "agency," on the one hand, and of nurturance and warmth, or "communion," on the other. The main assumption underlying the construction of these scales is that masculinity and femininity are not opposite poles of one continuum, but that they are independent dimensions. Indeed, correlations between the scales have been found to be low and even positive for adults as well as for children (Hall & Halberstadt, 1980; Huston, 1983).

Perhaps the most important aspect of this research is that it has militated against the earlier notion that proper sex typing is necessary for good psychological development and has, to the contrary, put forward the concept of "androgyny" as desirable. (We discussed androgyny briefly in relation to childrearing in Chapter 5.) Spence and her colleagues call "androgynous" those who are high on both scales of the PAQ and who therefore possess the desirable attributes of both males and females, and they define those with low scores on both scales as "undifferentiated." Androgyny for Bem (1979), however, is not a combination of desirable masculine and feminine traits, but means attaching less importance and efficacy to sex-based differentiations.

Some of the new shine of androgyny has by now worn off and critics have chipped away at its image. Thus androgyny researchers have been accused of themselves maintaining the traditional masculine/feminine distinction by using it for the definition of androgyny (Deaux, 1984). In a review of studies in the androgyny tradition Taylor and Hall (1982) found that masculinity, as measured by such scales as the PAQ and the BSRI, was more predictive of psychological health than was femininity. However, those who had high scores on both masculinity and femininity scales were more likely to have good mental health than any other group, that is, androgyny was closely linked to optimal psychological functioning. In this case the mental health tests were independent of the sex-role measures and androgyny was apparently shown to be a "good thing." However, some circularity is often present in research into the attributes of androgynous individuals since, as conceptualized by Spence and her coworkers (see above), androgyny reduces to social desirability and is synonymous with psychological health, maturity, and lack of need for conformity (Huston, 1983). However, the theory performs the useful service of emphasizing that certain attributes will be of value, irrespective of whether they are seen as typically masculine or feminine.

A Synthesis

We will now attempt a synthesis of the varying explanations of existing sex differences that we have discussed earlier and in this way take up and expand the viewpoint that we offered at the beginning of the chapter.

As discussed above, natural selection ensures that behavior is appropriate for reproductive success and optimal male and female strategies differ in achieving this. Variations in activities and personal attributes between the sexes may also, at one level, be considered from the point of view of their adaptation to reproductive success. Thus it is probable that the rough-and-tumble play of male young monkeys is not just a functionless side effect of sexual differentiation, but is a useful experience for preparing infant monkeys for the competitiveness and aggression they will need later for securing a mate. Similarly, females' interest in the young is relevant to developing maternal skills, which naturally are of importance in successful rearing.

Biological factors are important not only through their direct influences, but also on account of the indirect effects they elicit from the environment. People treat boys and girls differently because of anatomical differences, and because of differences in their reproductive functions and roles. Nothing occurs in the absence of environmental influence. But genes, too, affect all developmental processes, as we noted earlier. The development of the organism over time is a product of the coaction of preexisting structure and of the environment in which the structure lives. Even though environmental influences are more clearly and strongly related to behavioral sex differences in some areas of functioning (e.g., in choice of toys and play activities) and less so in others (e.g., in aggression), this does not justify denying the influence of environmental factors on the latter.

Moreover, the environment does not only act as a mediator of biological factors, but also sets up expectations and stereotypes that come to act independently of biological necessities. Such cultural factors play an enormous role in the development of different behavior in the two sexes. Some societies strengthen original differences by segregating males from females in early life, by training young males in warfare by war games, and by subjecting males and females to sex-specific initiation rites. Other societies attempt to reduce sex differences by teaching young males to inhibit aggression and to replace it by nonviolent means of resolving conflicts. Western society is ambivalent about these matters. Although it has traditionally emphasized sex differences, more recent enlightened opinion has advocated their reduction and the deliberate inculcation in each sex of the virtues of the opposite one.

Summary

Scientific enquiry has been concerned with the extent of the psychological differences that mark the two sexes, but even more so with their origins and explanations. Quite a number of quantitative integrations of research in this area exist so that general trends in the field as a whole are becoming evident. It has been found, for instance, that the more recent studies have reported smaller differences between the sexes than did earlier ones.

When we write about existing and documented sex differences it must be remembered that this merely means that the average in a given attribute is higher for one sex than for the other; however, there is always a large degree of overlap in the distribution of scores, and the largest mean difference reported in meta-analyses is only about half a standard deviation.

In the area of cognitive abilities it is well established that females on average surpass males in verbal competence, particularly from adolescence on. Males, on the other hand, have been found to be superior in visuo-spatial performance from middle childhood, and in mathematical reasoning from adolescence on, even when the two sex groups have been equated for the number of mathematics courses taken. There is little evidence that achievement motivation per se differs between the sexes, but men and women show such motivation in different ways and more strongly in fields that are of particular interest to each sex.

In the area of social behavior there is good evidence that women show greater social orientation, for example, greater sensitivity in decoding non-verbal cues and greater empathy in responses to others, and also that they manifest greater responsiveness and nurturance to the young. On the other hand, males have been found to be the more physically aggressive sex the world over. Whether women are more open to influence and more compliant than men is a moot question, and there is no evidence for any overall differences in self-esteem or in altruistic behavior.

Do parents' differential socialization practices for boys and girls explain existing sex differences? Parents do, we found, encourage sex-appropriate play and activities in boys and girls, and fathers emphasize this aspect more than mothers do. Parents are also more conscious of boys' misdemeanors and mete out more punishment to them. Parents' actions are influenced by their preconceptions, but some of the differences in treatment will occur in response to their children's individualities (partly of biological origin). However, their socialization practices do not by themselves account for differences in cognitive abilities, nor do parents tolerate or reinforce aggression in boys any more than in girls.

The early development of sex-typed activities cannot be explained by postulating that young children preferentially imitate certain behavior simply because it is considered sex-appropriate: sex-typed preferences and behavior have repeatedly been observed in young children before they show any awareness of traditional sex stereotypes. No doubt, the reinforcing pressures exerted by the socializing environment of parents and peers partly account for the early acquisition of sex-typed activities. Further, the action of biological forces must not be forgotten.

The reproductive strategies of the sexes differ and some psychological attributes could have arisen because they favored the reproductive success of either males or females. The organization of the brain has been shown to differ between males and females and there is some evidence that hormones play a part in sex differences in aggression and spatial ability.

Biological factors will have direct effects on sex differences, but they also act indirectly, for example, by eliciting differential treatment of boys and girls by parents and peers, and also by setting up certain social expectations and stereotypes that will then themselves reinforce sex differences.

Part IV   Some Social Issues

11
Divorce and Its Aftermath

Social developmental research often addresses itself to pressing social problems, the results of which have implications for social policy and planning. In the last section of this book we will discuss some of this research. Practical policy decisions will never be based on research findings alone, but will always have to take into account the social and political context in which they are made. However, it is important that such practical decisions, whenever possible, not be made in the absence of findings from replicated, sound research that are applicable to the population in question and have been carefully interpreted.

In this chapter we will examine what effect divorce, and the change in family structure this brings about, has on children. In the next chapter we will consider what research can reveal about the consequences that the permanent separation from mother or a temporary separation from her might, or might not, have on the child's development. There are many social policy issues to which we might have addressed ourselves. We have selected two that are representative in the difficulties they present for researchers, have received substantial attention from developmental psychologists, and speak to issues that currently are important in a rapidly changing world.

The Effects of Divorce

Discussions of the effect of divorce on children frequently begin with a citing of statistics. Family dissolution is becoming an everyday phenomenon, particularly in North America. It is predicted that about 50% of all marriages currently contracted in the United States will end in divorce, and approximately 2 million American children go through the experience of divorce annually. Glick (1979) estimates that by 1990 close to 50% of children will spend at least part of their lives not living continuously with both biological parents because of divorce. In Canada, about 60,000 divorces occur annually, with 48% involving dependent children. This means that every year about 50,000 Canadian children are directly affected by divorce. Nor do the statistics take into account separations and desertions that are not represented in the formal statistical data. In Europe the number of divorces has increased dramatically in the least two decades. In some countries, such as Sweden, Denmark, Hungary, Finland, West Germany, Great Britain, and France, there are more than 300 divorces per 1,000 marriages in a given year, whereas in other countries such as Spain, Italy, Greece, and the Netherlands the rate is still relatively low—135 for every 1,000 marriages (Boh, 1986). Nevertheless, changing religious views as well as changing economic and social conditions indicate that the rate will continue to rise.

In fact, family dissolution is not a new phenomenon. What has altered is the cause of that dissolution. What was once brought about by the death of a parent is now caused by the breakdown of marriage. Although parental death is a stressful event for a child, it appears to be less stressful than divorce (Rutter, 1981) for reasons we will discuss in the next chapter. Briefly, what characterizes divorce, and does not characterize separation caused by a parent's death, is the implication of active abandonment of the child by his parent.

Divorce statistics are often offered so as to impress the reader with shocking evidence of the breakdown of society's traditional forms of organization. A more useful way to use them, however, is to see them as evidence of major changes taking place in society and in the lives of many children. Divorce is a fact of life. It is an event that the average child has a good chance of experiencing. For the psychologist, then, the issue becomes one of assessing the impact of this not uncommon happening on the child's development and of seeing how negative effects can be minimized or even of how the experience can make a positive contribution to development.

AN ECOLOGICAL PERSPECTIVE ON DIVORCE

Divorce is complex, involving cultural, social, legal, economic, and psychological considerations. Bronfenbrenner's ecological analysis of development (Bronfenbrenner, 1977) provides a useful framework, then, for understanding it. Recall from Chapter 1 his argument that development must be conceptualized not only in terms of temporal and physical events that occur in the child's immediate environment but in terms of events in the wider social world as well. By viewing divorce at various levels—from the immediate one to that of society at large—it is possible to gain an overview of its nature and consequences. For such a perspective we turn to Kurdek (1981), who has provided an ecological analysis of divorce and its effects on children.

At the level of the macrosystem, that is, of society's beliefs and ideologies, Kurdek makes several observations. He notes that the form and function of the family has changed in the last few years. Emphasis is now on individualism and personal satisfaction and the family serves primarily a psychological rather than economic, religious, or educational need (the latter having been taken over by the state). When psychological needs are not being met it therefore becomes easier for married partners to change the situation by dissolving the marriage. Women's increasing economic independence makes it more possible for them to contemplate divorce, as well as improving their adjustment to it. A new concern for the rights of children means that the child's best interests take precedence over the needs of parents in conflict and that attention can therefore focus on what is best for the child in the divorce situation, including the right to legal representation in matters of custody.

Kurdek moves to the next level, the exosystem, which includes those social factors that impinge on the setting in which the child is located, even though they do not directly affect him. He notes that uncontrollable changes in the child's environment such as a new residence, straitened economic circumstances, and reduced availability of one parent (and even two, if the mother must now go to work) may take their toll on the child's adjustment.

The next level is that of the microsystem, representing intrafamilial relationships both before and after divorce. Here we see the results of parental emotional turmoil on the child, of the removal of a buffer parent who can mediate a problematic relationship between the child and the other parent, as well as of increasingly close ties between the child and the custodial parent as the child takes over some of the role of the missing partner. These issues will receive greater attention in the course of this chapter. Finally, the ontogenetic system—representing the various competencies the child has for dealing with stress—determines in a very immediate domain how that child will react to the divorce process. Here age and sex have been variables of particular interest. Their effects will be discussed below.

DIVORCE OR NOT DIVORCE: THE EFFECTS OF MARITAL DISCORD

Some would argue that an unhappy marriage should not be dissolved because of the adverse effect such dissolution can have on the children. As will be illustrated in Chapter 12, much has been made of the possibility that separation from a parent—most usually the mother—will have negative effects on a child's development because of the feelings of insecurity and anxiety engendered by the separation (e.g., Bowlby, 1973). In fact, most children of divorce reside with their mother, so that arguments about mother separation lose their force. On the other hand, given what we know about the strong ties that children can develop toward their fathers, the fact of separation from *either* parent is a cause for some concern.

A recent review of the relevant evidence (Emery, 1982) indicates that interparental conflict may be the better explanation for child problems associated with divorce than the fact of divorce itself. Emery offers several reasons for this conclusion. First, as we have already noted, children seem to suffer more when their homes are broken by divorce or parental separation than when the break is due to death of a parent, an indication that variables beyond separation are at work. Second, children from broken homes that were relatively free of conflict are less likely to have problems than those from unbroken homes that were conflict-ridden (Hetherington, Cox, & Cox, 1979). Third, children's reactions to divorce and discord have many features in common, for example, they frequently include lack of self-control. Fourth, children whose parents continue to be in conflict after the divorce have more problems than do those whose parents are in less conflict (Kelly & Wallerstein, 1976). Finally, at least two studies (Block, Block, & Gjerde, 1986; Lambert, Essen, & Head, 1977) suggest that many problems seen in children from broken homes were present before the divorce. In sum, although the separation inherent in divorce may have a harmful effect on a child's development, marital discord is also detrimental to the course of development. Staying together for the sake of the children has little to recommend it.

The Contribution of Marital Discord

What are the results of marital discord, results which reveal themselves after divorce and which may mistakenly be attributed to the fact of divorce itself? Emery suggests several. The research indicates that marital turmoil is strongly related to lack of self-control; the evidence for overcontrol as an outcome is more inconsistent (Hetherington, Cox, & Cox, 1978). Marital discord seems to be more strongly related to maladaptive behavior in boys than in girls, although girls may have problems that are less likely to be labeled as troublesome, such as becoming anxious, withdrawn, or very well behaved (Block, Block, & Morrison, 1981). A particularly warm relationship with at least one parent can help to attenuate the effects of discord—when this is missing discord takes its toll (Hess & Camara, 1979; Hetherington et al., 1979). Another variable whose effects are exacerbated when there is marital discord is parental psychopathology (Rutter, 1971).

Emery proposes several mechanisms through which marital discord might produce these effects. Modeling is one: The conflict generated by warring parents provides an example of the undercontrolled behavior to which boys in particular are prone. Marital disagreement may well lead to inconsistency in discipline of the child, with resultant troubled behavior; such a hypothesis explains sex differences in undercontrol since research shows that sons are disciplined about equally by both parents, whereas daughters are disciplined more by their mothers (Margolin & Patterson, 1975). It is boys, therefore, who will suffer most from the inconsistency. Evidence that inconsistency is, in fact, a product of marital turmoil and a predictor of later problems in children is provided by Block et al. (1981).

These researchers found that parental disagreement about child rearing in intact families was related both to subsequent divorce and to future undercontrol in the behavior of boys and overcontrol in the behavior of girls. Nor, of course, should we lose sight of the distinct possibility that children with problems help to produce marital discord: The problems exhibited by children of divorce may, partially at least, be those that helped to produce the divorce in the first place.

A STRUCTURAL VERSUS FAMILY PROCESS APPROACH

If conflict between parents is a more important determinant of how well the child develops than is parental marital status, then it follows that comparing children from divorced and intact families would not be the most productive approach to research in the area. Yet studies of the effects of divorce have traditionally concentrated simply on the differences between children from divorced and nondivorced families, focusing on the effects of change in structure of the child's living arrangements. This approach provides little information about quality of the child's family life before the divorce, nor does it take into account changes that occur after divorce and the impact these might have on the child. Thus some divorced parents remain in conflict, whereas others (once initial anger has subsided) develop new and constructive relationships with each other. The qualitative aspects of these new relationships need to be examined.

A better way to conduct research on the effects of divorce, then, is to see marital dissolution as a disruptive, often traumatic, event that changes family relationships but does not end them. This approach involves the study of family process variables rather than family structure. It encourages researchers to look at the family situation both prior to the divorce as well as at various points in time after the divorce has taken place.

Hess and Camara (1979) conducted one of the first studies orienting psychologists to this point of view. Concerned with the deficiencies of the structural model, they viewed divorce as a potential source of interruption in normal development. They began with a clinical evaluation of the impact of divorce on the child. First, it threatens primary bonds between the child and the parent who is leaving the family residence, thereby creating the risk of depression, anxiety, anger, and withdrawal in the child. Second, the situation creates conflicts of loyalty for the child who must become guarded and discreet lest he reveal information to one of his parents that might be hurtful to the other. Demands for sensitivity and awareness of the feelings and needs of others may be raised to an impossible level. Finally, divorce requires children to change their perceptions of social reality and to alter their concepts of the nature of the family and the roles of members of that family. All these stresses require time and energy from the child that would otherwise be devoted to school performance and peer interaction. Events that help to neutralize these sources of stress include coopera-

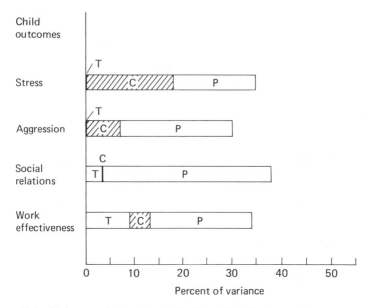

FIGURE 11.1. Unique and shared contribution of family type and process variables to child outcomes. P = unique combination of process variables. T = unique combination of family type. C = contribution common to both type and process variables. From "Post-Divorce Family Relationships as Mediating Factors in the Consequences of Divorce for Children" by R.D. Hess and K.A. Camara, 1979, *Journal of Social Issues*, *35*, 79–96. Reprinted by permission.

tion and collaboration between the parents in order to preserve the two parent-child bonds, a close relationship between parent and child so as to enhance their roles as agents of socialization and nurturance, and maintained contact with the parent who does not have custody. Usually this is the father who, of course, has an important and unique role to play in the child's development.

Using this clinical framework, Hess and Camara studied children aged 9 to 11 years from 16 divorced and 16 intact families. For the former group parent separation had occurred 2 to 3 years before the collection of data and mothers had custody in all cases. Using information from interviews of the children, their parents, and their teachers, Hess and Camara found that children from divorced families showed greater stress and less productive work styles than those from intact families. They also tended to be more aggressive. However, Hess and Camara observed that variation in parent behavior was greater *within* each group than it was between the divorced and intact groups. When the family types were combined level of parental harmony and relationship between the mother and child and father and child were at least as highly related to stress, aggression, and school achievement as was the fact of divorce. The researchers were able to demonstrate that statistically, in fact, process variables were making a unique and substantial contribution to child outcomes independent of family status, rather than merely being an indicator of the interaction occurring in families involved in divorce. This outcome is depicted in Figure 11.1. Finally, variations among families in postdivorce relationships were also important predictors of the child's adjustment. Parental harmony was less important than the quality of relationship between the child and his non-custodial father.

VARIABLES AFFECTING A CHILD'S RESPONSE TO PARENT SEPARATION

Now we turn to a more detailed consideration of those variables that affect adjustment to separation and divorce.

The Effects of Sex

One of the strongest and most consistent findings emerging from the research is that boys react less well to divorce than girls. In considering the findings it must be remembered that children, in the greatest proportion of cases, live with their mothers after the separation. Until recently, sole custody has been awarded to mothers in most divorce cases. It becomes impossible to untangle the effects of separation from a father figure, then, from all other variables that could affect outcome. This can be accomplished only when there are enough cases of father custody to allow comparisons between boys and girls living in either a father-absent or a mother-absent family. With this caveat in mind we turn to some of the research.

One of the most frequently cited studies of divorce, which deals among other things with the effects of sex on adjustment to parent separation, is the California Children of Divorce Project (Wallerstein & Kelly, 1980). The project followed 60 families who had separated in the early 1970s and who eventually divorced. Five years after separation Wallerstein and Kelly still had contact with 58 of the original families. Participants were parents and their children who availed themselves of a 6-week divorce counseling service, which focused primarily on the child's reaction to separation and divorce. These were families, then, who were having enough difficulty that they sought professional help, albeit of a minimal kind. Virtually all children were in the custody of their mothers, but the extent and quality of interaction with their fathers varied greatly. There was no control group, and methods of data analysis are not clearly presented. Nevertheless, using the results of open-ended interviews, Wallerstein and Kelly present a wealth of provocative case material, and many of their conclusions later received support from more rigorously conducted investigations.

At the 18-month followup Wallerstein and Kelly observed a widening gap between the sexes, particularly among younger children, in how they had reacted to parental separation. Nearly twice as many girls as boys had improved in their adjustment and functioning from the initial assessment. Young girls were judged better able to establish good relationships with adults and peers, and they were more empathic, psychologically sensitive, independent, and better able to enjoy play and make use of fantasy. Interviewers judged that young boys were more opposed to the divorce (although girls were reported to be angrier with their mothers about it), that they felt more stressed, longed more intensely for their father, and were more preoccupied with fantasies about reconciliation. Girls had more friends and were more inclined to use them for support. At the end of 5 years these differences had disappeared (one supposes either because, with the passage of time, boys had eventually adjusted or because the young children were now closer to adolescence and better able to cope).

Another longitudinal study of divorce was carried out in Virginia by Mavis Hetherington and her associates (Hetherington, 1981; Hetherington, Cox, & Cox, 1978; Hetherington, Cox, & Cox, 1979). They studied 48 white, middle-class parents and their preschool children and a matched control group of nuclear families. Interviews with parents, structured diary records, laboratory and home observations of parent-child interactions, observations of teacher-child and peer-child interactions, ratings of children by parents and teachers, and results of personality tests formed the data base. Data were collected 2 months, 1 year, and 2 years following the divorce. Hetherington et al. also observed sex differences in children's reactions to divorce. They found that disturbances in social and emotional development in young girls had, by and large, disappeared in the 2-year followup. Boys did show improvements in functioning but, relative to girls and to children from intact families, still exhibited more sustained noncompliance and aggressive behavior when interacting with their mothers. They were also reported to be more antisocial and impulsive, less self-controlled, less able to delay immediate gratification, and more rebellious both at home and in school.

The adverse reaction of boys to living in a single-parent family, that is, with their mother alone, has been documented by many other researchers. Hammond (1979) found that boys in single-mother households were more distractable, acted out more, and were less satisfied with parent attention than were boys and girls from intact families or girls from single-mother families. In another study (Hodges and Bloom, 1984) boys were found to be more depressed initially after separation than girls, more disruptive both initially and 6 months after separation, and more agitated both initially and at the 6-month follow-up. Differences occurred regardless of age, which ranged, in this case, from very young to 18 years of age. By 18 months after separation sex differences had disappeared.

Are there long-term effects of single parenting on boys and girls? Relevant to this question are a number of older studies that have focused on the effects of father absence, regardless of reason, on the sex-role and moral development of boys and girls. Up to the middle-school years boys from mother-headed families appear to be more dependent, less masculine, more feminine in self-concepts, and less aggressive than boys from intact families. They also show greater verbal than physical aggression. In adolescence these differences disappear, or "compensatory masculinity" in the form of excessively assertive behavior appears (e.g., Biller & Bahm, 1971; McCord, McCord, & Thurber, 1962; Santrock, 1970). As well, boys from mother-headed families have less well-internalized standards of moral judgment (Hoffman, 1970b). Studies of the effects of father absence on girls, which are fewer in number, have not found similar differences between the behavior of girls in mother-headed and girls in intact families (Bach, 1946; Santrock, 1970).

Although the evidence is strong, then, for a differential effect of divorce on boys and girls, there is also some indication that divorce may have harmful effects on girls that reveal themselves later in the course of development. Women who have been separated from their fathers when they were young are more likely to have unsatisfactory sexual relationships (Fisher, 1973; Jacobson & Ryder, 1969). In a study of lower and middle-class adolescent girls from divorced and widowed families, Hetherington (1972) found unusual patterns of relating to males. When separation was the result of paternal death girls were sexually anxious, shy, and uncomfortable around males relative to those from intact families. When they were observed at a recreation center dance they tended to remain with other girls, placed themselves near the back of the group of girls (boys usually congregated at one end of the hall and girls at the other), and many spent a good part of the evening hiding in the ladies' room. The daughters of divorcees, on the other hand, were sexually precocious and inappropriately assertive with males. They spent more time standing near the boys at the dance, more frequently asked them to dance, and more frequently touched them. When they were interviewed in the laboratory daughters of divorcees responded no differently to a female interviewer than did those of widows or girls from intact families. But they sat closer to a male interviewer, were more open in their body position, and made greater eye contact with him. At the opposite extreme were the daughters of widows who smiled very little, maintained little eye contact, and sat rigidly with their bodies oriented away from the male interviewer. In a follow-up study the daughters of divorcees had married younger and were more likely to be pregnant at the time of the wedding. A word of caution is in order, however. Hetherington's girls were from somewhat special families who had no males (brothers or stepfathers) in the household, so care should be exercised in drawing conclusions from the study about long-term effects of divorce.

Another factor to be considered before concluding that boys suffer more from divorce than girls is that boys and girls may adjust *differently* to divorce (e.g., Block et al., 1986; Emery, 1982). Girls' adjustment may involve overcontrolled behavior such as withdrawal, anxiety, and excessively "good" behavior. Because these are much easier forms of behavior for parents and teachers to tolerate they tend not to be labeled as problematic, although they certainly do have their own impact on psychological functioning.

Causes of Sex Differences

Keeping these reservations in mind, then, what might account for the differential reaction of boys and girls to divorce? Boys receive less support and nurturance and are viewed in a more negative way by mothers, teachers, and peers in the period immediately after divorce than are girls (Hetherington et al., 1978; Santrock, 1975). Thus they are deprived of the social support they particularly need at this time. Divorced mothers of boys report feeling more stress and depression than do divorced mothers of girls (Colletta, 1978; Hetherington et al., 1978) and so may reflect this in their treatment of sons. As well as receiving more nurturance and being viewed more positively by their mothers, it has been suggested that a special bond develops between girls and their mothers in single-parent homes that does not develop in the intact family (Clingempeel, Brand, & Ievoli, 1984)—a bond that gives a further advantage to girls in helping them to cope with the disruption in their lives.

Another reason boys do poorly is that father absence results in loss of a role model for them. The father is often a more effective authority figure than the mother, as well as a model for control over aggression—both characteristics of special importance for boys who have more difficulty than girls in the domain of self-control. As well, boys are more likely than girls to receive ineffective discipline from their mothers, a situation that improves dramatically during the second year after divorce and appears to be reflected in subsequent improved behavior in boys (Hetherington, 1979).

Boys may be further stressed by the problems that frequently arise when the noncustodial parent tries to maintain contact with them. If we assume that the relationship between a boy and his father is, on average, closer than that between a girl and her father, then problems in this area ought to affect them more. And, indeed, there are problems! Wallerstein and Kelly provide numerous examples of fathers who failed to visit their children at the appointed time, whose visits were made difficult by acrimony between the mother and her former spouse, who forgot their children's birthdays, and who gradually came to see less and less of their offspring. Although girls had similar experiences to relate to the interviewers, it does not require much extrapolation from the data to assume that, with a better relationship with their mothers, they were better able to cope with disappointments caused by disruptions in paternal visits.

One might conclude, on the basis of these observations, that boys would be better off in the custody of their fathers. Indeed, there is evidence that this could be the case. In a comparison of 6 to 11-year-olds living in single-father, single-mother, and two-parent families, Santrock and Warshak (1979) found that children living with the parent of the opposite sex were more antisocial, less warm, more demanding, and more dependent than those living with the parent of the same sex.

The story is not complete, however. In a recent report, Block et al. (1986) have suggested that some of the problems manifested by boys may, in fact, have occurred long *before* the marriage breakup. They took advantage of the fact that some children in their longitudinal study of personality and cognitive development would inevitably experience the divorce of their parents. In fact, approximately 40% of the families did divorce or separate. They had, then, a record of behavior of boys and girls in a variety of areas before separation occurred, and before anyone had any idea that it might occur. Block et al. report that prior to divorce children exhibited the same kinds of patterns of behavior that are usually associated with children after divorce. Boys from families that eventually divorced were more aggressive, impulsive, and full of misguided energy relative to boys from families that did not experience divorce. The behavior was consistently displayed from preschool years to adolescence. For girls the picture was very different and, in fact, not easy to characterize. At the age of 4 years girls began to reflect the stress presumably induced by the problems of their parents. But, relative to boys, they were less affected by family problems.

Block et al.'s findings are very important in indicating that the behavioral problems exhibited by boys when their parents separate are not solely a function of maternal custody. Boys seem to be more severely affected by parental conflict than girls. Block et al. point out, of course, that fathers may have been psychologically absent in conflicted families long before the separation. They also suggest that the emotional bond between fathers and sons is stronger than that between fathers and daughters and that this may mean parental disagreements promote more conflicts of loyalty for boys than for girls. We noted two other possible explanations earlier: Sons are more likely than daughters to be disciplined by both parents and thus the inconsistent discipline accompanying marital discord may be more devastating for boys. As well, the aggressive model provided by warring parents will be more readily imitated by boys than by girls.

Once again, then, we see that a process approach to understanding the effects of divorce is more profitable than a structural approach. Marital conflict is a major factor in the creation and evolution of problems in children. This is not to say, however, that parent separation itself may not have additional consequences for the developmental process.

The Effects of Age

When are children most likely to be harmed by separation and divorce? Is there an age when the event can be dealt with more easily? Clearly children at different ages have different social and cognitive competencies, find themselves in different settings, and are attempting to solve different developmental tasks. They therefore must respond differently to stress. According to Wallerstein and Kelly divorce takes its toll at all ages. What differs is the way in which children at different ages react to it. We will describe their observations in some detail because they are rich in content. They *are* limited, however, by the unclear nature of the data analysis and by the absence of other studies to either confirm or disconfirm them.

Wallerstein and Kelly observed that preschool children were most likely to react to divorce by regressing in the area of their most recent achievement, such as toilet training or going to nursery school. Routine separation produced fear, and sleeping disturbances developed. Children became concerned with abandonment and starvation. They were irritable and demanding. Some became more aggressive, whereas others inhibited their aggression. Some blamed themselves for the marriage breakup. Obviously these changes in behavior must have been a source of further stress for the mother who was already having to deal with serious problems of her own, and who therefore had less energy to deal with the new problems of her child.

Children between 5 and 8 years of age grieved openly. They cried and sobbed and, unlike younger children, were unable to fantasize that one day their situation would be put right. They were preoccupied with feelings of rejection and fears of replacement. Boys in particular yearned for the missing father and expressed anger at their mother for driving their father away. Children at this age did not usually feel responsible for the divorce, but they did long for reunion of the parents. They also felt seriously divided in loyalties to their parents and were unable to make a choice, even when urged to do so by the mother. School performance declined.

Nine- to 12-year-olds responded in their own distinctive fashion. They were angry, particularly with the parent they saw as causing the divorce. Twenty-five of the 131 children in the sample formed strong and often long-lasting alignments with one parent against the other—most frequently it was with the mother against the father. They grieved, were anxious, felt lonely, and had a sense of their own lack of power. Approximately half the children in the sample showed deterioration in school performance.

Adolescents, already experiencing their own age-related difficulties as they strove toward disengagement from their parents, acquired additional problems with the separation. They became anxious as they realized that their parents were vulnerable. They became preoccupied with the fate of their own futures and with a fear of their own sexual and marital failure. Unlike their 9- to 12-year-old siblings they were either conflicted in issues of loyalty or they rejected both parents.

Not all children in the Wallerstein and Kelly sample reacted in these negative ways to the separation of their parents. Some of the 5- to 8-year-olds, for example, appeared untroubled by family events and managed to continue apparently undisrupted lives. Troubles experienced by their parents sometimes brought out positive characteristics in the children. In the 9- to 12-year group, for example, Wallerstein and Kelly observed several children who were able to be helpful to their parents and whose maturity and compassion seemed to be enhanced by their situation. Adolescents frequently concerned themselves with how to avoid making the same mistake as their parents. As they felt pressed to assign responsibility for the marital failure, these boys and girls began to look for standards to guide their own behavior and achieved impressive levels of performance in the domain of morality. They became concerned with the importance of candor among people and of kindness. One girl vowed not to lie because she did not want to be caught in the web of dishonesty her parents had created for each other by virtue of their extramarital affairs.

Although not all children responded badly, then, it is still informative to consider the nature of the disturbance when it did occur. Children's reactions to the strain of family disruption are colored by changing cognitive abilities, increasingly accurate perceptions of the causes of behavior in others, decreased ability to fantasize, and by the changing importance of attachment to the parent as a source of security and help in coping with life.

Although older children experience their own kind of grief in response to parent separation, many researchers have suggested they are less harmed by the event. We have seen that mothers can fail to offer the structure of routines, the authoritative control, and the nurturance that are particularly important for younger children. Older children can make do without this external framework better than younger children (Hetherington, 1979). The increased demands for maturity made by divorced mothers are more easily responded to by older than younger children (Hetherington, 1979), and they may even benefit from the mother's greater reliance on them (Clarke-Stewart, Friedman, & Koch, 1985). Wallerstein and Kelly also note that the ability of older children to assign responsibility for the divorce where it belongs (i.e., not to themselves), and to use social support systems outside the home helps them to recover more quickly.

Other Variables Mediating the Effects of Divorce

We have already referred to other variables that affect the child's response to divorce. First, the extent of conflict between the parents, both before, during, and after the divorce, plays a marked role in the child's adjustment. Particularly important is the nature of agreement between parents about the discipline process, as well as agreement and harmony about visitation arrangements (Hess & Camara, 1979; Hetherington et al., 1978; Wallerstein & Kelly, 1980). Inconsistent discipline promotes behavior problems, and conflict over form and nature of access sets the stage for the kind of distress we noted above. Additionally, a continued positive relationship with her former husband appears to be an important social support system for the divorced mother and is predictive of better adjustment on her child's part (Hetherington et al., 1978). A second important variable is the quality of the relationship between both the custodial parent and the child as well as the noncustodial parent and child (Hess & Camara, 1979; Schoettle & Cantwell, 1980; Wallerstein & Kelly, 1980) including, particularly for the custodial parent, the nature of disciplinary interactions. We have seen that it is in the first year after divorce that mothers tend to become depressed, self-involved, less supportive, and ineffective in their disciplinary interventions (Hetherington et al., 1978). Thus children at this time are particularly exposed to inconsistent discipline.

Also implicated in successful adjustment is the level of functioning of the parents before and after the divorce (Wallerstein & Kelly, 1980). When parents separate, the economic circumstances of the custodial mother and her child frequently deteriorate, in part because a large proportion of ex-husbands do not contribute to child support (Hetherington, 1979). Hetherington notes that if mothers are forced to begin work at the time of divorce young children suffer not only the loss of the noncustodial parent but a disruption in the relationship with the mother. Thus they experience the double loss of both mother and father, with an accompanying potential for increase in behavior disorders. Mothers are under added stress because they now are dealing not only with their own emotional problems but with the added burden of a job. Life-style becomes chaotic with erratic meals, fluctuating bedtimes, and school tardiness. If the family must move there is a further disruption in the life of the child. Old friends who might provide support are removed and quality of life may deteriorate if the new neighborhood is less advantaged than the old.

The last variable is the amount of information the child has about the divorce and its causes. The situation is an obviously difficult one for children to comprehend but they are, in fact, often neglected at exactly the time when they are most in need of information and help (Bonkowski, Boomhower, & Bequette, 1985; Kurdek & Siesky, 1979). Over three-quarters of the children in the California Children of Divorce study, for example, received insufficient explanations for the divorce, and it was these children who most frequently experienced fear and regression. Those who had been given minimal explanations and to whom marital conflict had not been obvious were among the most troubled 5 years after the separation. Although teachers might be a great help in aiding the child to come to terms with his new situation, many parents were too embarrassed and uncomfortable to tell teachers about the separation (Wallerstein, 1980). Obviously parents who are unable to communicate well with their children about the separation will also have difficulties with them in other areas. It seems highly likely, nevertheless, that a clear understanding of what is happening must be of some help to the child who is trying to cope with altered life circumstances.

Conclusion

Having considered those events that can help to lessen the negative impact of parent separation, we now ask if it is possible for a child to witness the disruption of family life as he has known it without experiencing any pain. The answer must be that even if all else is well—parent conflict is minimized, discipline is consistent, relationships between members of the family are good, the economic condition of the new family unit is stable, information is available, and so on—the potential loss of an attachment figure remains an unalterable fact. Here, of course, the nature of custody and amount and quality of contact with both parents becomes important—issues we will discuss in the next section of this chapter. But even the stress of separation may have a strengthening effect on the child's development. We have noted instances where children mature earlier, become more thoughtful and questioning, and provide needed emotional support for others. Given that the evidence so strongly indicates that marital conflict itself is a major cause of harm to the child, divorce cannot be seen as inevitably harmful. It will be a normal event in the lives of a large number of children, and it has the potential for good as well as harm.

A NOTE ON CUSTODY ARRANGEMENTS

Beliefs about where children whose parents have divorced are most appropriately placed have changed over the years. Throughout the 19th century fathers tended to be given custody both because children were seen to be the father's natural property and because their labor was deemed essential to him. By the end of the century mothers were the preferred parent for custody as society began to believe that they were best equipped to provide love and nurturance for their offspring and, no doubt, because fathers no longer needed their labor in an industrial society. In the early 1970s Goldstein, Freud, and Solnit (1973) argued that custody decisions should be made quickly and not changed, so as to protect the child from disruption and uncertainty. Although they did not make a special case for the mother, it was still she who was seen as better equipped for the parent role. Of late we have seen strong efforts on the part of some fathers to gain custody, efforts to which the courts have responded in the belief that biology has not given mothers exclusive claim to parenting skills and that favoring the mother is a form of sex discrimination. Although most custody arrangements are decided informally between parents, without resort to the courts, informal arrangements seem to have mirrored those arrangements dictated by the legal system.

In all these models of custody the assumption is that one parent must assume responsibility for the child of a marriage that has ended. But this need not be the case. There are societies in which the parent-child bond cannot be reversed, regardless of what has happened to the formal relationship between mother and father (Mead, 1970; Stack, 1976). In the last few years joint custody, where both parents have power over decisions relating to all aspects of the child's welfare, has assumed increasing popularity. Indeed, since 1980 in the State of California, judges have been required to give preference to a joint custody settlement and to justify the making of any other kind of award.

Although there is still little in the way of research allowing for a direct evaluation of the advantages and disadvantages of joint custody, it is worth inquring whether this arrangement might be a reasonable solution to some of the problems that can arise after separation. We borrow from observations made by Clingempeel and Reppucci (1982) for our discussion.

A salient feature of joint custody is that parents have more frequent interactions with each other and that their ability to cooperate therefore becomes essential. Particularly if children are moving back and forth between residences, extensive consultation is necessary to make the process go smoothly. Indeed, the opportunities for conflict between parents are intensified as they try to work out when, where, and how their children will live. Obviously, if the degree of conflict between them is already high at the time of divorce, the chances that joint custody will work are slim. Aside from this obvious problem, are there other difficulties this arrangement presents? Critics of joint custody have argued that it may lead to a continued wish for the reunion of parents, working against the ultimate goal, which must be acceptance of the permanence of separation. Goldstein et al. (1973) argued that joint custody is undesirable because children are incapable of maintaining close relationships with two parents nor can they cope with repeated separations. One must acknowledge, however, that there is ample evidence children are capable of forming multiple attachments, and that the separation involved in repeatedly moving between two parents is substantially different from that involved in institutionalization or even in the daily separation that day-care entails.

The advantages of a joint custody arrangement are discussed by Clingempeel and Reppucci. It appears to be a way of overcoming the problem that children seem to do better in the company of the same-sex parent. Thus brothers and sisters who, presumably, do not wish to be separated, would have the benefits of exposure to both a male and female parent figure. The sharing of child-rearing responsibilities means that children will have greater cognitive and social stimulation than if their lives are confined to one household. In a joint custody arrangement one parent can continue to act as a buffer against an inadequate parent, just as happens in nuclear families. Finally, joint custody may help to reduce the stress created by unsatisfactory visiting arrangements for the noncustodial parent. Although her sample was small, Grief (1979) found that separation for both fathers and children in joint custody and mother custody families was more difficult in the latter than the former.

Joint custody arrangements asume that both parents want their children with them, and it assumes that both can work together in the interests of their children with minimal conflict. When these conditions are met joint custody becomes an interesting alternative to the usual view of a winner and a loser in the child custody battle. The extent to which it facilitates adjustment to divorce must remain unclear, however, until there is more research.

Remarriage and Reconstituted Families

Divorce is not a permanent state. The average length of time between separation and remarriage is 3 years (Glick, 1984). As Furstenberg (1980) notes, being in a single-parent family is "a waystation rather than a destination." In Canada 75% of single parents remarry. In the United States 80% of those who divorce remarry and over 60% of these remarriages involve children under 18 years of age. Herndon (1982) predicts that by 1990 the predominant family form will be the stepfamily.

Typically, stepfamilies consist of a natural mother, a stepfather, the mother's children, and children born of the new union. However, stepmothers, natural fathers, and children are not uncommon, not only because the number of custodial fathers is increasing but because noncustodial fathers may in fact be assuming greater amounts of responsibility for child rearing. These new arrangements should, theoretically, be an improvement over the single-parent situation. Sharing of tasks between married adults, increased social and emotional support systems, and (in the case of single mothers) improvements in the economic situation ought to ease the burdens of sole responsibility for children. But the picture is not so rosy. The divorce rate for second marriages is 10% higher than that for first marriages (Glick, 1984). Moreover, there appears to be a higher divorce rate for second marriages involving children from a previous marriage than for second marriages where there are either no children or where the children were born in the second marriage (Cherlin, 1978).

PROBLEMS IN RECONSTITUTED FAMILIES

What accounts for this disappointing situation? Cherlin (1978) attributes it to the absence of social regulations governing the conduct of reconstituted families. There are, for example, no guidelines regulating the interaction between former spouses and between the former and current partner, there is no commonly accepted terminology for members of the kinship network, there is a problem in controlling the possibility of incest among stepfamily members, and there is no clear way of dealing with overlapping and competing interests of parents. In the absence of such guidelines the potential for conflict is greatly increased. What should be done, for example, if a new spouse thinks his partner is spending too much time with her old spouse? Are long telephone conversations or dinner together appropriate? What should children call their stepparent? If it is "Dad" should he be referred to by this term in the presence of the biological father? We do not have rules for these situations.

A number of specific problems are faced by members of reconstituted families (Walker & Messinger, 1979). In our society there is supposed to be a bond of love between parents and their children. As we have seen in Chapter 4, however, this bond takes time to develop and depends on extended interactions that begin from the time of birth. When new parents enter the family it is hardly surprising that attachment does not immediately take place—either of parent to child or child to parent. Yet we are uncomfortable with a family unit that does not include this emotional relationship, and we see it as an indication of trouble as well as a cause for guilt and disappointment, instead of as a natural occurrence. Discipline presents another problem, made even more difficult by the fact that effective discipline requires a warm relationship between parent and child (see Chapter 5). Natural parents are unsure of how much disciplining they wish their new spouses to do, feeling conflict between the wish for help in this task and protectiveness toward their children. In addition, children may feel resentful at being told what to do by someone who is not their biological parent. Children and stepparents experience guilt and loyalty conflicts. For the children it is a matter of having to choose between a natural parent and a stepparent. For the stepparent it is guilt about having left children from a previous family. Finally, financial conflicts create difficulties for reconstituted families. Even in the absence of economic deprivation these conflicts are salient (Visher & Visher, 1978). Stepfathers must often provide for two families, with accompanying resentment caused by the allocation of resources outside the family unit. Robinson (1984) reports that the relative amounts of money spent on natural and stepchildren are often perceived as a measure of love and devotion by both spouse and children.

A Structural Versus Family Process Approach

With all these potential problems, just what are the effects of their parents' remarriage on children? In a review of the relevant research Ganong and Coleman (1984) found little consistent evidence that remarriage of the parent is, in fact, harmful to children, with some studies finding negative, some positive, and some no effects. There was no evidence, overall, that children in reconstituted families exhibit more problem behavior, more negative attitudes to themselves or others, or that their school performance, personality characteristics, or social development are adversely affected. Most of the studies reviewed, however, failed to consider variables relevant to an understanding of the differential effects of stepfamily structures on children. As in the case of divorce one needs to look at processes operating in families, rather than just the structure of those families. And, as in the case of divorce, these process variables are important.

The best predictor of children's adjustment to their parent's remarriage is the amount of conflict in the new family perceived to exist by its members (Raschke & Raschke, 1979). The quality of the relationship between stepchild and stepparent is also very important in the happiness and satisfaction experienced by the family, as well as in various social and cognitive outcomes experienced by the child. The quality of other family relations, including those between husband and wife and between child and natural parent, is not a predictor of the child's well-being (Crosbie-Burnett, 1984; Furstenberg, 1980; Furstenberg & Nord, 1985; Perkins & Kahan, 1979; Pink & Wampler, 1985).

Who Does Best in the Reconstituted Family?

Some children respond better to the introduction of a stepparent than others. If we can identify them then we can better understand the effects of remarriage. Oldershaw (1987) has proposed an interesting way of doing this. She reminds us that certain children are more negatively affected by living in a single-parent family than are others and she hypothesizes that those who are harmed by the arrangement will respond best to the new situation of a reconstituted family. On the other hand, those who are doing well in a single-parent family should react less well to the change in their circumstances brought about by remarriage of the single parent. Oldershaw's discussion is limited to the case of stepfather families because we know more about this particular structure and about its precursors than we know about stepmother families and their precursors.

As we have seen, boys fare less well than girls in the single-parent family, both because they have lost a male role model and because mothers find them more difficult to discipline. Boys should prosper from the introduction of a stepfather who provides the missing role model. Girls, on the other hand, function well in the mother-headed family, often developing a special bond with their parent. Introduction of a new parent with its accompanying threat to the bond disrupts a relatively satisfactory arrangement. We also know that older children do better than younger children in the single-parent family. They can respond well to the greater demands for self-reliance and independence placed on them by their mothers, and are less affected by her failures to impose structure and control on their lives. If the mother's remarriage removes some of their autonomy then they should be unhappier than younger children who should thrive on reimposed structure and control.

Oldershaw has reviewed the literature on stepparenting as it relates to her hypothesis. Young boys are reported to form intense and strong relationships with stepfathers, which appear to result in greater independence and self-control both at home and at school (Hetherington, Cox, & Cox,

1982; Wallerstein & Kelly, 1980). Santrock, Warshak, Lindbergh, and Meadows (1982), using behavioral observations of single-parent, nuclear, and stepparent families, established that boys show more warmth toward stepfathers than do girls, whereas girls show greater anger toward their mothers than do boys. On the basis of behavioral measures and self-report, Clingempeel, Brand, and Ievoli (1984) and Clingempeel and Segal (1986) report that girls exhibit less positive and more negative behavior toward stepparents than do boys, showing less affection and more detachment. These differences in behavior are not accompanied by differences in the behavior of stepparents toward their stepchildren.

As for the effects of age, Oldershaw also finds support for her hypothesis. Younger children, that is, those below about 9 years of age, have been reported to be more likely to accept a stepfather than older children and to be more willing to readjust and accommodate to the new situation (Robinson, 1984). Lutz (1983) found that adolescents of the same age who had been members of a reconstituted family for less than 2 years perceived a greater level of stress than did those who had been members for longer than 2 years. Although this finding was attributed to the possibility that perceived stress dissipates with time, Oldershaw notes that adolescents who experienced greater stress (i.e., had been living with a stepparent for less than 2 years) had also experienced remarriage of their parent at a later age than those who experienced less stress. In a study by Steinberg (1987), children from both single-parent and stepparent families were more susceptible to peer pressure to engage in deviant behavior (as measured by a series of hypothetical dilemmas) than were children from intact families. Oldershaw observes, however, that younger children from stepparent families clearly showed *lower* susceptibility scores than children from single-parent families, whereas the reverse was true for the older children. These scores are presented in Table 11.1. In keeping with her hypothesis, then, it was the older children who suffered most from the remarriage of their mother, possibly because they were the ones who lost most.

What these observations show is how important it is to consider the state of the child before and after remarriage before making predictions about adjustment. If parental remarriage means an improvement in children's situations relative to their previous experience then they will respond well. If it means a less satisfying situation then they will not.

Summary

The high incidence of divorce in all parts of the Western world reflects a change in the structure of society. Divorce, rather than being viewed as a catastrophic event in the child's life, should be viewed as an aspect of life for many children.

Bronfenbrenner's ecological analysis of development helps to structure

TABLE 11.1 Susceptibility to antisocial peer
pressure (mean scores) as a function of family
structure and grade level.

	Family structure	
Grade	Intact	Stepfamily
Total	$n = 491$	$n = 109$
	55.15	55.61
	(10.20)	(11.10)
5th	$n = 113$	$n = 21$
	50.12	47.43
	(8.03)	(5.92)
6th	$n = 119$	$n = 34$
	52.88	51.97
	(9.87)	(8.00)
8th	$n = 121$	$n = 33$
	59.30	62.30
	(10.64)	(10.82)
9th	$n = 138$	$n = 21$
	57.58	64.38
	(9.47)	(9.74)

Note. Standard deviations are in parentheses. From
"Single Parents, Stepparents, and the Susceptibility
of Adolescents to Antisocial Peer Pressure" by L.
Steinberg, 1987, *Child Development, 58*, 269–275.
Reprinted by permission.

our understanding of variables relating to the effects of divorce on children. Social, economic, and political changes in society make divorce more
acceptable. Divorce leads to a change in the child's environment such as a
new neighborhood or reduced access to one or both parents. Parental
adjustment problems and changes in the relationship between the child and
his parents take their toll on adjustment. Finally, characteristics of children
themselves, such as age and sex, must be considered.

The research evidence suggests that it is not the effects of divorce itself
that have negative effects on children's behavior, but the conflict between
parents that predates and accompanies divorce. Marital conflict, for example, is correlated with inconsistent discipline which leads to problems in
self-control. Such variables as parental harmony and relationship between
the child and his parents are better predictors of adjustment than whether
or not the parents are divorced.

One of the most consistent findings is that boys are more negatively
affected by divorce than are girls. They take longer to recover from its
initial effects and they show greater problems with self-control and compliance. Their problems may be a function of absence of a father figure
and the particular difficulties mothers have in coping with boys since, in
the great majority of cases, mothers have custody of their children.

There is some suggestion that girls may suffer adverse effects later in the course of development and that they may react with overcontrolled behavior, which is perceived to be less of a problem. Recent evidence also suggests that boys have problems prior to the divorce, an indication that they are more adversely affected by marital discord than girls and that they may contribute to marital discord.

Children at various developmental stages react differently to divorce. For example, preschoolers who have problems characteristically regress, whereas adolescents become preoccupied with their own future and the vulnerability of their parents. Older children, however, seem to suffer less because they can find social support systems outside the family and because they often respond well to increased demands for autonomy made by their mothers. In some cases, children are strengthened by the experience of divorce.

An alternative to the notion that one of the divorced parents must assume sole responsibility for the welfare of the children is the arrangement of joint custody, whereby both parents have power over decisions relating to the child. Joint custody might work well when conflict between parents is minimal and when both parents want the child. At the moment there is not enough research to tell.

The majority of divorced parents remarry. Living in a reconstituted family, however, presents its own problems. According to Cherlin this occurs because our society has no regulations governing the behavior of stepfamilies, and so the conditions for conflict are exaggerated. Problems revolve around discipline and money. The less the perceived conflict in the family and the better the relationship between child and stepparent the better will be the child's adjustment. The children who may do best in the reconstituted family are those who were doing poorly in the single-parent family.

12
Threats to Secure Attachment

Secure attachment to a mother (or father) figure has been considered a cornerstone of the child's development, something we discussed in Chapter 4. The previous chapter has considered the effects of divorce, which often involves the severance of ties with fathers. The present chapter will examine what light research can throw on the consequences that the permanent, or temporary, separation from *mother* might, or might not, have on the child's cognitive and social development.

Disruption of Attachment Bonds

One of the social problems that has sparked research and theoretical and practical discussion is what happens in the absence of a secure attachment bond between a young child and a mother figure. This situation has usually been called "maternal deprivation." Several distinct meanings have often been ascribed to this term. The central meaning of the term is being reared in an institution and the lack of an identifiable, enduring attachment figure that this usually entails. The term has also been used to refer to the distortion or inadequate quality of interaction that may occur in an intact family. A third meaning is the simple break in relations brought about by the departure from home of child or mother, whether this ushers in a shorter or longer period of separation. Ill effects may, indeed, arise from any of these or from a combination of them. In discussing the last two aspects, we will subordinate them to the focal concern of this section, namely, the development of children reared in institutions.

CHILDREN REARED IN INSTITUTIONS

In the past, investigations under the rubric "maternal deprivation" have been mainly concerned with children who suffered long-term separation from their families by being removed from home and, in particular, being placed in an institution. This condition implies a more or less permanent disruption of attachment bonds, or lack of opportunity to form them, and is "depriving" in this sense. Since any adverse effects seen in these children may arise from other factors, as we will see, both "maternal deprivation" and "disruption of attachment bonds" may be somewhat misleading terms, if they are taken to imply a judgment as to the cause of the effects.

History

Concern with the effects of institutional rearing emerged in the 1940s with the publication of the classic studies by Bowlby (1946), Spitz (1946), and Goldfarb (1943, 1945). Bowlby's interest in the topic of "maternal deprivation" and its converse, the nature of the child's attachment to a mother figure, was aroused by his study of 44 "juvenile thieves" whom he contrasted with other children, also referred to a child guidance clinic, but for nondelinquent problems. His most striking finding was that 17 of the 44 delinquents, and 12 out of 14 children who were unable to form any relationship or to express affection ("affectionless" character), had suffered prolonged separation from their mothers before age 5, as against two of the 44 comparison children. Spitz (1946) described the behavior of infants who in their first year of life lived in an institution where care was inadequate and inconsistent, and found that they at first cried continually, and later lapsed into a state of depression, lying or sitting with expressionless eyes and frozen, immobile faces. He concluded that if favorable mother-infant relations were reestablished within 3 months, the outlook was good, but not so if the separation lasted more than 5 months. Goldfarb (1943) studied adolescents who had spent their first 3 years in an institution that was deficient in all manner of stimulation and normal contact, and thus he demonstrated the consequences of the extreme in severity of deprivation. He noted that in adolescence the institution group was inferior to a comparison group of foster-home children in intellectual ability, particularly language function, that they were more distractible and aggressive, and that 13 of 15 institutionalized children were incapable of forming deep or lasting ties with others.

Observe that all these studies involved long-lasting separation. Short-term separation of young children from mother or home—say, of less than 1 month—has been shown to occasion considerable distress in the child, and this distress increases with the length of the separation, but no lasting ill effects have been demonstrated (Rutter, 1981).

From a review of these and other studies of institutionalized children Bowlby (1951) formed his theory of "maternal deprivation" and concluded that the prolonged deprivation of young children of maternal care may have grave and often irreversible consequences for their later development, and, in particular, that it may commonly produce an "affectionless character," that is, psychopathy. This theory had a considerable impact both on theoretical views on the genesis of some behavior disorders and on practical policies in social work and in hospitals.

Bowlby's theory may easily be misconstrued and overgeneralized. Therefore it is important to note what he did *not* claim: (1) that the child must form an attachment to her biological mother, or even to a female—it could be a mother substitute or the father—although, in the majority of cases, it will be the mother; (2) that *some* care by supplementary mother figures, for example, relatives or day-care workers, is bound to be harmful—though he postulated that the child will form a principal attachment to one person; (3) that provided the child was cared for by her mother, inadequate mothering was of no consequence.

Studies of monkeys confirmed the existence of ill effects arising from long-term separation of the young from their care givers: the well-known studies by Harlow and his colleagues showed that when rhesus monkeys were reared in total isolation for 6 months they suffered from severe social and sexual malfunctioning as adults (Harlow, 1958; Harlow, Harlow, & Suomi, 1971). In a more recent study, however, species differences were noted: Only rhesus monkeys were observed to show all the deviant behaviors that, according to Harlow, followed isolation rearing, whereas pigtailed and crab-eating macaques exhibited only some of them. Genetic differences between these species were thought to be responsible for these variations (Sackett, Ruppenthal, Fahrenbruch, Holm, & Greenough, 1981).

More Recent Studies

Were the conclusions drawn by theorists concerned with maternal deprivation exaggerated? More recent studies have, in fact, reconfirmed earlier findings that children who spent their early years in institutional care show behavior problems at school, and delinquency and social maladaptation in adulthood (Rutter, 1981; Rutter & Quinton, 1984). Let us first look at the findings of some of these studies.

It is very likely that the lack of stimulation and lack of play opportunities found in the bleaker institutions of the 1940s may themselves give rise or contribute to retardation (cf. Dennis, 1960). In recent decades, however, great improvement has taken place in child-care institutions (or "residential nurseries," as they are called in England), both in their physical facilities and in their child-care practices. They are no longer the grim places of despair, devoid of all stimulating objects or persons, described by Spitz (1946) or Goldfarb (1943). One of the best designed of recent research programs is that by Tizard and her colleagues (e.g., Tizard & Rees, 1975; Tizard & Hodges, 1978). The residential nurseries in which Tizard and her colleagues carried out their research were of relatively high quality. Units of six children lived together in living rooms furnished in homelike style, the supply of toys and books was plentiful, and the staff-child ratio was generous. There was also no dearth of conversation between staff and children, although the quality of talk by staff varied in spontaneity and information value. However, close personal relationships between staff and children were discouraged. Moreover, what is probably of greatest

TABLE 12.1. WPPSI and WISC IQs of children tested at age 8.

		WPPSI IQ at $4\frac{1}{2}$ years		Full-scale IQ at 8 years	
Group	N	Mean	SD	Mean	SD
Adopted between 2 and 4 years	20	116.1	11.6	115.0	12.0
Restored between 2 and 4 years	9	98.2	10.4	103.4	16.6
Adopted after $4\frac{1}{2}$ years	5	104.8	12.2	100.6	17.6
In institution throughout	7	105.1	10.4	98.6	9.9
Fostered after $4\frac{1}{2}$ years	3	102.7	8.5	94.7	2.3
Restored after $4\frac{1}{2}$ years	4	98.8	9.7	93.0	18.8
London comparison	29	111.9	11.7	110.4	13.8

Note. WPPSI = Wechsler Preschool and Primary Scale of Intelligence. WISC = Wechsler Intelligence Scale for Children. SD = standard deviation. From "The Effect of Early Institutional Rearing on the Development of 8-Year-Old Children" by B. Tizard and J. Hodges, 1978, *Journal of Child Psychology and Psychiatry, 19*, 99–118. Reprinted by permission.

consequence, is the fact that by age $4\frac{1}{2}$ a child, on average, had had 50 caretakers look after her (Tizard, Cooperman, Joseph, & Tizard, 1972; Tizard & Hodges, 1978).

Tizard and Rees (1975) assessed the development of a group of $4\frac{1}{2}$-year-old children who had spent their first years in institutions and some of whom had been adopted or restored to their natural mothers. They compared these children's behavior and intelligence with those of a comparison group of home-reared working-class children from the same geographical area. At age 4, IQs were all within the normal range, but those who had been adopted before that age had a higher mean IQ than those who remained in the institution. (Since the IQ of these two groups had been similar at 2, this difference was not likely to be due to selective placement by IQ.) At age 4 it was thought encouraging that the institutional children, whether adopted or not, had no more serious behavior problems than did the comparison children. It was expected that the children who had left the institution would continue along normal paths of development. However, as is frequently found, the 4-year-old children in institutions formed few selective attachments or deep relationships to their caregivers, but showed more clinging and following behavior than did home-reared children (Tizard & Rees, 1975). Overall, the authors thought that the ill effects of early institutional rearing were minimal and had been greatly exaggerated.

Tizard and Hodges' (1978) results are of importance because they followed up the same children at age 8, by which time some more children had been adopted or restored to their mothers. At 8, the IQs of all groups were in the normal range (90+) and had not changed much over the previous 4 years (see Table 12.1). The level of IQ was significantly related to a simple report by the mother or housemother (in the institution) as to whether or not the child was attached to her, and thus it appears that emotional factors were closely intertwined with intellectual progress. That the

TABLE 12.2. Items on children's behavior questionnaire on which adopted and restored children differed from classmate comparisons (teachers' reports).

Somewhat or very true	% adopted children so described	% restored children so described	% London controls so described
Very restless	69[a]	77[a]	22
Squirmy, fidgety child	69[b]	62[a]	22
Often damages or destroys property	22	46[a]	20
Frequently fights or is quarrelsome	48[a]	46[a]	29
Not much liked by other children	44[a]	54[a]	30
Tends to be on own	52	69[a]	33
Irritable, touchy	57[a]	54[a]	22
Frequently sucks thumb or finger	26[a]	23[a]	4
Is often disobedient	48[b]	77[b]	15
Cannot settle to anything for long	48[b]	69[b]	26
Often tells lies	39[a]	69[b]	22
Resentful or aggressive when corrected	61[b]	62[b]	19
Seeks attention from strange adults	52[b]	69[b]	7
Seeks attention from teacher	45[b]	69[b]	15

Note. From "The Effect of Early Institutional Rearing on the Development of 8-Year-Old Children" by B. Tizard and J. Hodges, 1978, *Journal of Child Psychology and Psychiatry*, *19*, 99–118. Reprinted by permission.
[a] $p < .05.$ [b] $p < .01.$

restored children had the lowest IQs may be connected to the fact that fewer biological mothers thought their restored children were attached to them than did adoptive mothers. The mean reading scores of the different groups of children followed the same order as their IQs, with those of the restored group being lowest and those of the adopted group being highest.

By age 8, moreover, problems had emerged in the behavioral area. All institutional children, whether adopted, restored to their natural families, or still in the institution, had far more problems, as reported by teachers on Rutter's maladjustment screening questionnaire (Rutter, 1967), than did the comparison group. The problems that distinguished the children who had been in an institution from the comparison group were mainly conduct problems, for example, disobedience, inability to settle down to a task for long, and attention-seeking from adults and teachers (see Table 12.2). The number of problems was also negatively related to IQ and to whether or not a child was said to be attached to her mother. The restored children exhibited more conduct problems than the adopted children and this may be explained by the mutual lack of attachment between them and their mothers. All these children, who had spent their earliest years in institutions, therefore demonstrated a progressive development from indiscriminate friendliness and lack of attachments at 4 to behavior problems in middle childhood. These results ran counter to the researchers' prior views and to their findings on 4-year-olds, and the more recent findings forced them to conclude that early experiences did affect children's later development (Tizard & Hodges, 1978). We will discuss below possible mechanisms for these effects.

Although these children were only 8 years old, we now have other evidence on the adjustment and parenting effectiveness of adults who had been cared for in institutions in their early years. One study retrospectively inquired into the childhood of mothers of repeatedly institutionalized children, that is, it was a "retrospective" study (Quinton & Rutter, 1984). This inquiry revealed that the mothers of the "in care" group had themselves been separated from their parents for longer periods significantly more often than the matched comparison mothers. There were only three families in the "in care" group in which neither mother nor father had suffered at least two childhood adversities—the latter defined to include, apart from separation, parental marital discord and harsh discipline. Thus, from a retrospective point of view, almost all cases of parenting breakdown could be linked to adversities in the parents' childhood and hence intergenerational continuity was almost complete.

A second study was a "prospective" study that started with girls who had spent a substantial portion of their childhood years in an institution, followed them up in adult life when they were mothers, and compared them with women who as children had lived in the same general area of London (Dowdney, Skuse, Rutter, Quinton, & Mrazek, 1985; Rutter & Quinton, 1984). These mothers were interviewed and some of them were observed interacting with their children. Poor psychosocial functioning, as measured by personality disorder, criminality, marital problems, and so forth, was much more pronounced in ex-institutional women than in matched controls, and the outcome was especially poor for those who had experienced disrupted parenting (including parental discord) before age 2. As Table 12.3 shows, 35% of the ex-institutional women themselves experienced transient or permanent difficulties in parenting their own children, whereas none in the comparison group had manifested such a parenting breakdown. The reason for the children being taken into care was not abusive treatment or neglect, but simply that the mothers could not cope. The ex-institutional mothers evinced lower sensitivity to their children's needs, they expressed more negative affect outside disciplinary confrontations, they ignored their children's requests and communications more, and made more frequent attempts to control their children. As a corollary of their mothers' poorer interactions with them, the children initiated more dependency bids than did the comparison children.

This study, therefore, also demonstrated that children raised in institutions later suffer from social-emotional and parenting difficulties to a greater extent than other individuals, and also that parenting difficulties often show some continuity across generations. (Other aspects of the study will be discussed below under "reversibility.")

Thus, it has been found both in earlier studies and in careful investigations of more recent date, that institutional care in the early years seems to

TABLE 12.3. Pregnancy and parenting histories.

	Ex-care women (n = 81) %	Comparison group (n = 42) %	Statistical significance		
			χ^2	df	p
Ever pregnant	72	42	8.50	1	<.01
Pregnant by 19	42	5	16.75	1	<.001
Had surviving child	60	36	5.85	1	<.02
Of those with children	(n = 49) %	(n = 15) %			
without male partner	22	0	Exact test, p = .039		
any children ever in care/fostered	18	0	Exact test, p = .075		
any temporary or permanent parenting breakdown	35	0	Exact test, p = .02		
living with father of all children	61	100	6.52	1	<.02

Note. df = degrees of freedom. From "The Nature and Qualities of Parenting Provided by Women Raised in Institutions" by L. Dowdney et al., 1985, Journal of Child Psychology and Psychiatry, 26, 599–625. Reprinted by permission.

be related to later behavior and personality difficulties. But this bare fact does not take account of some of the factors that may modify the outcome, or explain the mechanisms whereby these effects come about, or address the question to what extent the adverse outcomes can be reversed by later experiences. It is to these issues that we will now turn.

FACTORS MODIFYING THE EFFECTS OF INSTITUTIONAL REARING

As a result of numerous investigations it has become clear that the outcomes of institutional rearing are by no means uniform and that various factors, such as those we are about to discuss, will intensify or mitigate them.

Reasons for Separation

Bowlby's thesis claimed that it was the disruption of the attachment bond to mother, caused by prolonged separation, that was at the root of the child's difficulties. If this is the case, *any* kind of longer separation from the mother in the early years should produce the sort of effects that we have seen follow institutional rearing. To test this thesis Bowlby and his colleagues (Bowlby, Ainsworth, Boston, & Rosenbluth, 1956) carried out a study on children who had spent months or years before age 4 in a tuberculosis (TB) sanatorium in the country, far away from their homes, because of the supposedly curative properties for TB of salubrious country air. These children were assessed when they were aged 6 to 13 and had returned home, and were compared with classmate controls. No difference in IQ between sanatorium children and controls was found, few sanatorium children were delinquent, and only a few minor symptoms of social maladjustment (e.g., withdrawing into daydreams, lacking concentration) were noted more frequently in them than in the controls. These findings led Bowlby to retract more far-reaching earlier claims and to conclude that ". . . statements implying that children who experience institutionalization and similar forms of severe . . . deprivation in early life *commonly* develop psychopathic or affectionless characters are incorrect" (Bowlby et al., 1956, p. 242).

One other important reason for separation from mother, apart from disrupted relations or neglect in the home, is death. The consequences of separation due to death differ markedly from those due to institutionalization for other reasons. Parental death (of mother or father) has been associated with only a very slight rise in delinquency rate (Rutter, 1981), and even this may be due to other causes, for example, previous prolonged physical illness of the parent. Children do, of course, have to live through their grief and there may be adjustment difficulties, but such difficulties after a child loses a parent through death differ from those after divorce or breakup of the home (cf. Chapter 11). In particular, the tendency to relatively severe personality disturbances and behavior problems noted in institutionalized children are absent in children bereaved through death (Rutter, 1981).

Thus, the outcomes for children's intellectual and personality development differ considerably, depending on the reason for separation and disruption of the bond with the family. Separation in itself is clearly not a single causative factor.

It must not be thought that it is only a break in the relationship with mother that will affect children. Disruption of the relationship with father because of death (mentioned above) or because of a breakup of the family will also have effects, for example, a "broken home" has often been cited as a major factor in delinquency (Rutter & Madge, 1976) and a "broken home" usually means loss of a daily relationship with father. The effects of father's absence have been discussed in greater detail in Chapter 11.

Previous Relationship with Mother

There has been much speculation, but few hard data, on the effects the quality of the child's earlier relationship with her mother has on her reaction to being separated from her. Data on hospital admission show that short-term distress is lessened when the child has had a good relationship with her mother previously (Rutter, 1981), perhaps because the quality of the relationship has given the child an inner security that carries over into the period of separation. Studies on rhesus monkeys have indicated that it is the infant monkeys with more tense relationships with their mothers who suffer most from long-term separation (Hinde & Spencer-Booth, 1970). This may well be so with human infants, too, but some confirmation from research with humans is necessary before this is accepted as fact.

Opportunity to Develop Attachments After Separation

It seems plausible to suppose that the quality of relationships with stable, caring persons *after* separation is a factor in the outcome for the child. In fact, the opportunity to have a continuing relationship and to form an attachment with a single person has been shown to mitigate the effects of separation. Pringle and Bossio (1960) made a study of children who had been removed from home before the age of 5 and had spent more than half their lives in an institution, where they were still living. On the basis of personality and adjustment tests and observation these investigators divided children into a "severely maladjusted" group and a (rather small) "notably stable" group. They found that *all* the stable children had either maintained regular contact with their parents or formed a dependable, lasting relationship with a mother substitute in the Children's Home, whereas none in the maladjusted group had been able to build up such a relationship. In a similar vein, beneficial effects on children were noted when elderly "foster grandparents" gave special nurturance to institutional children daily over a number of years (Saltz, 1973).

Perhaps the most notable fact about the arrangements in the institutions studied by Tizard and her colleagues was the absence of such stable relationships, and this may, indeed, have led to the adverse outcomes there. We must note, moreover, that simply ending the separation from mother by restoring the child to her was not the answer to the problem, as often the child did not feel attached to the mother, nor the mother to the child and previous difficulties between them resurfaced. It was precisely the fact of *not* being attached to mother (something that happened more frequently with restored children than with adopted children) that was linked to multiple problems.

Quality of Care

We mentioned earlier that the policy of the institutions studied by Tizard and her collaborators was aimed at providing a family-like climate and normally stimulating environment. However, there were variations in the organization of the residential nurseries and in the quality of communication between staff and children (Tizard et al., 1972). Thus some staff explained happenings or told stories to the children, addressed them spontaneously and warmly, whereas other staff confined their communications to instructions or to a "That's nice." Overall, the mean language scores of 2- to 5-year-old children were average and no "institutional retardation" was observed. But language comprehension was significantly related to the quality of staff talk, to the frequency with which caregivers answered children, and to an "organizational score" for the institution, which comprised staff autonomy, staff experience, the length of time the same staff member cared for a group of children, and the staff/child ratio (Tizard et al., 1972). It is clear that the quality of communication and the organizational structure of the institution can ameliorate adverse cognitive outcomes in the children.

Age of Child and Duration of Deprivation

Does the age at which the child suffers a break in relationships make a difference? It is generally agreed that when the break occurs before the age of 6 months, no lasting damaging effects occur. Since the attachment bond to the caregiver (mother) develops most strongly between about 6 and 15 months (see Chapter 4), and since organisms are most vulnerable to damage during the time of most rapid development (Rutter, 1981), it is reasonable to assume that disruption or distortion of relationships with mother at this age will have the most serious consequences. Some evidence does, indeed, point in this direction: Children who were removed from home before the age of 1 or 2 seemed to be more retarded and severely maladjusted (Pringle & Bossio, 1960) and suffered more detrimental effects in adulthood than other institutionalized children (Rutter & Quinton, 1984). On the other hand, Tizard and Hodges (1978) report that even late-adopted children were still able to form stable attachments to their adoptive mothers, although they too manifested behavior problems.

As for the duration of institutionalization, although the data are weak, the evidence suggests that the longer the deprivation of stimulation and emotional attachment persists, the more adverse the effects (Rutter, 1981; Tizard & Hodges, 1978).

Sex and Temperament of the Child

The literature has little to say about sex differences in response to early and prolonged institutional care. However, as Chapter 11 showed in detail, boys are more vulnerable to stresses arising from discord and instability in the family and therefore this might well also apply to stresses inherent in removal from home (Rutter, 1981).

We know that "difficult temperament" may lead to later behavior problems and this evolution, noted in intact families, is thought to come about mainly when parents' attitudes and skills do not mesh with the child's temperamental qualities (Thomas & Chess, 1977; Rutter, 1971; cf. Chapter 4). On the basis of this evidence we may hazard the guess that poor prior temperamental attributes (e.g., tenseness or poor adaptability) will also heighten the ill effects on the child of separation from home and prolonged institutional care, but, surprisingly, little direct evidence is available on this important question (Rutter, 1981).

CAUSES OF ADVERSE EFFECTS

Bowlby (1951) and others hypothesized that the crucial factor underlying the adverse effects associated with institutional rearing was the disruption of the attachment bond to the mother and deprivation of maternal love and care. Let us now consider this and other rival hypotheses concerning the origins of the adverse effects in institutional children in the light of further evidence.

Deprivation of Stimulation or Deprivation of Maternal Care?

Some of the severe intellectual retardation noted in early studies (e.g., Spitz, 1946; Goldfarb, 1943) may well have been due to deprivation of any kind of sensory stimulation, and some short-term intervention studies (e.g., Schaffer, 1965) have shown that providing deliberate social and verbal stimulation diminishes or eliminates developmental retardation. However, even in high quality institutions the intelligence and achievements of the children staying in the institutions were markedly lower than those of a home-reared comparison group or than those adopted before age 4 (Tizard & Hodges, 1978—see above). Despite well-intentioned policies this may have resulted from some lack in meaningful, well-adapted verbal communication in these institutions (cf. Tizard et al., 1972), and the process may be similar to that which leads to lower intellectual competence in children from large families (Rutter, 1981). So a large part of intellectual retardation is likely to be due to lack of stimulation and this can be remedied by the provision of a more adequate environment, as the early adoptees' higher IQ level shows. On the other hand, it would be foolish to deny that social and cognitive aspects of development are linked and interdependent: For instance, the institutional children in the above studies also showed lower task involvement at school than did the comparison group, and both IQ and reading level were related to whether or not a child was attached to a mother or mother substitute. There is evidence, therefore, that the emotional security derived from the existence of some stable relationship in children's lives also plays a part in ensuring adequate intellectual functioning.

Disruption of Attachment Bonds or Disturbed Family Relationships?

Do the greater risks of behavior problems and delinquency in institution-reared children come about because the separation from home has disrupted stable attachment bonds to mother? Some of the modifying factors we reviewed above, plus other evidence, argue against accepting this as the main mechanism. Firstly, separation through death, where relationships up to that time were presumably fairly normal and harmonious, does not have the same ill effects as separation following divorce or breakup of the home, where prior relationships are likely to have been marked by family discord, stress, and instability (see above).

Secondly, Bowlby's sanatorium study—where children did not come from a disrupted home—did not discover the adverse effects that had been expected (see above). Thirdly, it has been demonstrated that most of the behavioral disturbance noted in children living in institutions was already present before removal from home (Lambert, Essen, & Head, 1977). (Similarly, as noted in Chapter 11, boys from subsequently divorcing families, displayed marked undercontrol of impulse and aggression even before the divorce [Block et al., 1986]). The fourth and last strand of evidence derives from children who have been returned to their own families and whose attachment bonds could therefore, in theory, be reinstated. However, in Tizard and Hodges' (1978) study discussed above, these children had the highest number of behavior problems and the lowest IQs, and they and their mothers were less often attached to each other than any other group; in other words, the restored children were living in the least favorable environment and fared worst. Bohman and Sigvardsson (1979) found a very similar situation applying to their restored children. Indeed, as the sad tale of these children demonstrates, it is quite possible for a child to suffer deprivation of emotional needs without physical separation from mother and family, and this condition may be worse than actual separation.

All this suggests that the adverse characteristics of institutionalized children, and particularly the conduct problems of boys, are not simply due to separation and the consequent disruption of an existing secure attachment bond. They are more likely to stem from discord and instability in the home and the accompanying distortion in relationships within the family, which very likely contributed to the removal from home. The effect of such distorted relationships, we assume, is to prevent children from forming secure and reciprocated attachment bonds (as opposed to showing intense attachment behavior). The thread that links together children who are removed from homes wracked by discord and instability and children who spend their earliest years in institutions before any attachment bond has been formed, seems to be the lack of opportunity to form such a secure and reciprocated attachment bond to one or a few persons. Children who have undergone such experiences are at risk for developing behavior problems or, in extreme cases, affectionless psychopathy. Thus early experiences seem to play a critical role in some aspects of later development, although separation per se may not be the decisive circumstance. Rather, the crucial factor may well be the conflict and instability in the home with its consequent lack of secure attachment.

In addition to these environmental adversities, however, the likelihood that genetic factors also play a part in the genesis of behavior problems must not be forgotten. No evidence linking emotional instability in parents directly to children's behavior problems has so far appeared (Rutter, 1981). But there is evidence from adoption studies (Hutchings & Mednick, 1977) and from separation studies (Rutter, 1971) that when the biological parents show a life-long personality disorder, including criminality, *and* adverse environmental factors are present, such as marital discord or criminality in the adoptive parents, children are more prone to develop behavior problems or delinquency than when no parental deviance is evident. In other words, genetic potentialities operate in interaction with environmental adversities: Genetic factors make the child more susceptible to delinquency-producing factors in the environment, but environmental factors determine whether genetically based problems become manifest.

Reversibility of Adverse Effects

Whether the effects of disrupted parenting in early life are reversible has always been one of the most hotly debated points in the controversy surrounding Bowlby's theory. While Bowlby's pessimism in this regard was at first countered by more optimistic reports of recovery (cf. Clarke & Clarke, 1976), more recent investigations give cause for renewed concern. The Rutter and Quinton (1984) followup in adulthood of women who had spent their early years in institutions (see above) clearly gives no ground for optimism regarding complete recovery in *personality and social func-*

TABLE 12.4. Women's social functioning, own childhood deviance, and problems of spouse for ex-institutional women.

	Good functioning			
	No childhood deviance of women[a]		Childhood deviance of women[b]	
	n	%	n	%
No spouse	11	9	14	7
Deviant spouse	10	30	12	0
Nondeviant spouse	9	67	9	22

Note. From "Long-Term Follow-Up of Women Institutionalized in Childhood: Factors Promoting Good Functioning in Adult Life" by M. Rutter and D. Quinton, 1984, *British Journal of Developmental Psychology, 2*, 191–204. Reprinted by permission.
[a] $\chi^2 = 7.46$, $df = 2$, $p < .025$. [b] $\chi^2 = 3.301$, $df = 2$, not significant.

tioning, and the results of Tizard and Hodges' (1978) followup at an earlier age lead to the same conclusion. The latter study, on the other hand, as well as earlier ones (cf. Clarke & Clarke, 1976), indicates that given a complete change of environment (adoption), *intellectual functioning*, on average, can be expected to reach normal levels.

Of course, not every child living in an institution will display behavior problems or will bear life-long scars. Rutter and Quinton (1984) identified certain protective factors that made for better outcomes in adulthood. The *absence* of behavior difficulties in childhood and the absence of deviance (e.g., criminal record, psychiatric disorder) in the parents were two such factors: they reduced the chances of later personality disorder in the ex-institutional adults, thus illustrating the possible influence of genetic background in conjunction with early experiences. Marriage to a nondeviant spouse was another factor that facilitated good social functioning (see Table 12.4). This could have been an artifact, in that girls who were relatively well adjusted in childhood could have chosen better functioning spouses; however, investigation showed that such a tendency was not present in this sample. In other words, such a marriage had an independent ameliorating effect. Positive experiences at school—another environmental influence—also made for better psychosocial functioning, independently of other factors. Thus there are some buffering factors that can channel the social developmental of individuals who spent their early years in institutions toward benign outcomes.

In view of the seeming risks of institutional rearing, young children (below, say, 7 years) who are in need of care because of neglect or ill use in their own families, are in North American practice almost always placed in foster homes. The hope is that by providing stable care in a family environment the ill effects of discontinuous care can be avoided. Thus, it may be thought that the dangers of institutionalization are no longer of current concern.

Research on the effects of foster care on the children has been less well documented and less rigorous than that on institutional care (see Kadushin, 1978, for a summary). Moreover, the same children will often have experienced both forms of substitute care. In cognitive functioning fostered children seem to be the equals of home-reared children from similar social backgrounds, something which, as we noted, is also the case for institutionalized children. Negative behavioral and emotional outcomes have been found mainly for children who were committed to foster care at a very young age (cf. Kadushin, 1978), although some studies have found no greater emotional problems in fostered children overall than in other children from similar social strata, and such problems have therefore been attributed to "inner city-living" (Swire & Kavaler, 1977, cited in Kadushin, 1978). So behavior problems may be somewhat less prevalent among fostered than among institution-reared children. In any case, where behavior and emotional problems are found, they are likely to have characterized these children before foster care, as has been found to be the case for institutionalized children (see above).

However, the evidence for the assumption that foster care gives rise to less adverse outcomes than does institutional rearing is sparse: "With regard to dependent and neglected children, there is a widespread presumption that the living environment provided by a foster family home or group home is better than that provided by a residential institution . . . the empirical evidence for that position of incomplete." (Koshel, 1973, cited in Kadushin, 1978). Nevertheless, it seems plausible that being reared in foster homes or in small group homes is more benign and more pleasant for the children concerned than being reared in large institutions, provided the child is not drifting from foster home to foster home.

All in all, it does appear that the early years have a special importance for bond formation, and that through it they have an influence on later social development, which is not easily or completely erased by later experiences. In addition, genetic factors may compound or, on the other hand, offer protection against, the effects of adverse early experience.

Day Care

So far we have discussed mainly the effects of residential care, that is, of a more or less long-lasting separation of a young child from her mother. Does a daily repeated separation, followed by a daily reunion, which out-of-home care involves, have similar effects for the child's intellectual, emotional, or social development?

This is an important question in view of the increasing role that various forms of nonmaternal care play in modern Western and Eastern societies. In recent decades there has been a substantial influx of married women, not to speak of single mothers, into the labor force. In 1981, 48% of preschool-aged children in the United States had mothers who were employed. Fifteen years earlier the percentage was less than half as large (Clarke-Stewart, 1984). In Canada the figures are very similar, with nearly half the married women with preschool-aged children being employed in 1981 (Pence, 1985). Of course, working women make different kinds of arrangements for the care of their children. Infants, in particular, are much more likely to be cared for by a babysitter in the family's own home, or by a relative or other person in another home (a "day-care home" or "family day home"), rather than in group day care, that is, day-care centers.

"Group day care" caters for a group of children, the number of children in the room varying from about 8 to 20, depending on age, whereas in a "family day home" a mother looks after some unrelated children together with her own. Here the maximum number of children will usually be six, including the mother's own, if the home is licensed by a state or local authority. Frequently, however, parents make informal arrangements with unlicensed family day homes, although these are illegal in most countries. In the United States, 54% of infants aged 0 to 2 years, needing non-maternal care, are cared for in day-care homes, and only 27% in infant day care centers. Among 3- to 5-year-olds, however, the proportions are reversed, with 57% of children being in group day care and 32% being cared for in day-care homes (Rodes & Moore, 1975). It may come as a surprise that licensed facilities—centers and family day homes—provide only 17% of all out-of-home care for children of all ages in the United States, all others needing nonmaternal care being in unlicensed family day homes or with babysitters (Ruopp & Travers, 1982).

Although custodial care of the child, when the mother is at work, is an important raison d'être for day care, there has been a growing tendency to consider the educational and enriching role that day care can play as an even more compelling reason for its existence, and it has in fact been used as a form of intervention, intended to bestow cognitive and social benefits on disadvantaged children. One of the foremost programs along these lines is the Abecedarian program in North Carolina (cf. Ramey, Dorval, & Baker-Ward, 1983; Ramey & Farran, 1983).

HISTORY

Concerns about the effects of day care spring from a generalization of Bowlby's theory of "maternal deprivation" which, as we saw in the previous section, was originally proposed to define and explain the effects of more permanent separation. The concerns that some people have felt are of two kinds. Firstly, it is argued that the daily separation from mother will, like permanent separation, render the child's attachment bonds to her mother insecure. Since a one-to-one relationship generally is impossible in a group day-care center, the child will, as a result, have no opportunity to form a strong attachment bond to a single caregiver, with supposed dire consequences for the child's future social and emotional development. Secondly, it is feared that the intellectual stimulation that the child will receive when she has to share the attentions of one or two adults with a large number of other children, will be diluted compared with the stimulation she can obtain when she shares the attentions of her mother with only a few siblings.

These concerns have spawned a voluminous research literature of relatively recent date, since day care has come into widespread use among middle-class families—and hence has aroused psychological questioning—only in the last two decades. The first published study on the effects of day care on the child's attachment to her mother dates from 1970 (Caldwell, Wright, Honig, & Tannenbaum, 1970). The literature has been well reviewed by Belsky and Steinberg (1978) and again by Belsky (1985).

The research design of studies comparing children in various kinds of day care with children at home in general does not meet the strictest standards of scientific rigor, since the family's needs make it in practice impossible to assign children at random to day care or home care. Therefore groups of day-care and home-care children may differ on important variables prior to day care, something that only a few studies have attempted to control for. Nevertheless, the findings of the existing day-care literature are probably not as worthless as may at first appear. Firstly, some studies *did* control for family background (see below). Secondly, we have reason for placing some reliance on the results of the literature in general simply because these results are surprisingly consistent across a large number of studies. The investigations on which we will draw were carried out not only in high-quality university-affiliated day-care centers, but also in ordinary centers, varying in quality and in the socioeconomic strata that they serve.

Is Security of Attachment Affected by Day Care?

The prime concern about day care from the beginning, as we noted above, has been that the young child may not be able to form any lasting secure bond to mother or a mother figure in this situation. Since, as we noted in Chapter 4, security of attachment in essence means good adjustment, this would indeed be a serious consequence. One study by a student of Ainsworth (Blehar, 1974) is often quoted in support of the thesis that day care weakens the child's attachment to her mother. Blehar studied four groups of children: (1) 30-month-old children in day-care centers, (2) 40-month-old day-care children, (3) 30-month-old home-care children, and (4) 40-month-old home-care children. She compared these groups in Ainsworth's "strange situation," and found that day-care children of both ages avoided the mother after separation more than did home-care children, something which she interpreted as a sign of disturbance in the day-care children. However, the meaning of this finding must be in doubt, since she also found that groups 1 and 4 (a day-care and a home-care group) clustered

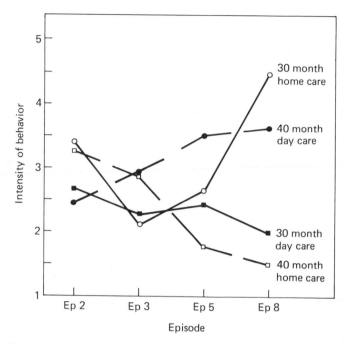

FIGURE 12.1 Proximity-seeking of mother. Episodes in "strange situation." Episode 8 is reunion with mother. From "Anxious Attachment and Defensive Reactions Associated With Day Care" by M.C. Blehar, 1974, *Child Development*, *45*, 683–692. Reprinted by permission.

together in many separation-related behaviors, and groups 2 and 3 formed another distinct cluster. This applied, for instance, to proximity-seeking, coded separately from proximity-avoidance (see Figure 12.1). The fact that two clusters, each composed of a day- and a home-care group, emerged, which displayed contrasting separation behaviors, suggests that these behaviors were pre-existing attributes of the children and not a result of day care.

The Ainsworth group (cf. Chapter 4) typically interpret the absence of proximity-seeking as "anxious avoidance," but this is a matter of theoretical orientation. Others have also found that day-care children seek mother's proximity less (see Figure 12.2), but they may interpret this as reflecting greater maturity and independence in these children (e.g., Clarke-Stewart, 1984). Most investigators have found very few differences in attachment behavior between day-care and home-care children (Kagan et al., 1978; Moskowitz, Schwartz, & Corsini, 1977; Ragozin, 1980; other studies cited by Belsky, 1985). The developmental course of crying on separation from mother has, in fact, been found to be very similar for day-care and home-care children, as discussed in Chapter 4.

Blehar's (1974) study, which also has been criticized for some method-

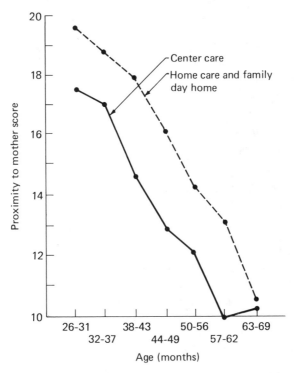

FIGURE 12.2. Children's physical proximity to mother in two laboratory assessments. From "Daycare: A New Context for Research and Development" by A. Clarke-Stewart, 1984, in M. Perlmutter (Ed.), *Minnesota Symposia on Child Psychology, Vol. 17* (pp. 61–100), Hillsdale, NJ: Erlbaum. Reprinted by permission.

ological deficiencies, upon scrutiny does not bear the interpretation that hazardous emotional consequences flow from day care and, taking all the studies together, it would seem this fear has been greatly exaggerated, at least for children above 3. Of course, the daily separation from mother may place some stress on many children, and Ragozin (1980), for instance, noted a fair amount of crying by children when mothers came to fetch them in the evening, but this often turns out to be a transient distress reaction that marks the early separation experiences on admission to day care, but which abates later on (Belsky, 1985). That attachment to mother is still strong and secure in day-care children has been confirmed by the repeated finding that mother, rather than the day-care worker, is the preferred attachment figure in natural contexts, and a source of secure attachment in the "strange situation" (Kagan et al., 1978; Krentz, 1983; Ragozin, 1980). We concluded in the previous section that the ill effects of institutional rearing were likely to be due to prior discord and consequent distorted relationships in the home or to the complete absence of any continuing bond to a stable caregiver in the institution, plus possible genetic factors. Obviously, these circumstances are not an integral part of the day-care situation as such, although they may occur in some families using day care. Hence the conclusions about institutional rearing cannot be extrapolated to the repeated separations and reunions and the shared caregiving that day care implies.

SOCIAL DEVELOPMENT

Does day care affect children's social development and adjustment and their interactions with others? Quite a number of investigations have shown differences between day-care and home-care children in this regard. Day-care children, particularly if they have been in group day care since infancy, interact more with peers rather than adults, are inclined to be more assertive and aggressive both verbally and physically, and are more given to running about; they are also less conforming to adult standards and less cooperative (Schwarz, Strickland, & Krolick, 1974; Robertson, 1982). Moore (1964) discovered similar effects in Scandinavian children. That the experiences of day care may be the causative factor here is suggested by the fact that children who have been in day care longer have been found to be more aggressive than those who have attended for a shorter time (Haskins, 1985). Some of these findings, based on teacher ratings, may be explained by teachers confusing greater motor activity with aggressiveness; nevertheless, no study has yet found home-care children to be more aggressive than day-care children (Haskins, 1985).

A comprehensive and well-designed study of day care has been carried out in Bermuda where 90% of children are in some form of out-of-home care by age 2. After controlling for the children's prior family background (e.g., mother's education and ethnicity) it was found that children who began group care in infancy were rated as more maladjusted (hyperactive, aggressive, or anxious) at age 3 or older than those who were cared for by sitters or in family day homes for the early years and who began center care at later ages (McCartney, Scarr, Phillips, Grajek, & Schwarz, 1982).

Naturally there are some discordant studies in which no rearing-group differences emerged in children's friendliness, compliance, or cooperation with adults, although these are fewer in number (Ramey et al., 1983; Gunnarson, 1978—a Swedish investigation).

Overall it seems that day-care experience does affect social behavior: In particular, day-care children engage in more social interaction with their peers, both of a positive and a negative kind. Some of the effects may, indeed, be undesirable, but they are not universal. They are accentuated when children from an early age have been congregating with large groups of other children, where they have had to learn to fend for themselves. To some extent these effects may be a function of the characteristics and practices of specific programs. (We will discuss the effects of differing quality of programs below.) But since such effects have been noted in Scandinavia and Bermuda, as well as in America, they cannot simply be a phenomenon engendered by the American practice of age-segregated peer groups.

Cognitive Development

Since children from large families tend to score lower on ability and achievement tests, even when social class is controlled (e.g., Breland, 1974), it might be thought that a congregation of even larger numbers of same-aged children and less contact with adults, typical of the usual day-care center, might trigger a deterioration in intellectual abilities. The opposite expectation would arise for some day-care programs from the fact that day care has sometimes been deliberately used as an educational and enriching intervention for disadvantaged children. Have these predictions been borne but for different types of day-care programs?

We will discuss these cognitive outcomes only briefly here. The pessimistic prediction for ordinary day care has, on the whole, not been borne out since, overall, little difference in cognitive ability has been found between day-care and home-care children (cf. Belsky, 1985). It seems that most ordinary day-care centers provide a sufficiently stimulating intellectual diet to ensure adequate cognitive development in their charges. The experimental enrichment programs, on the other hand, appear to live up to the optimistic prognosis set out for them: They seem to advance the intellectual ability of disadvantaged children to a higher level than might otherwise be expected (e.g., Ramey et al., 1983). This is true at least so far as the followups have taken us (up to age 5), but research on intervention programs in general warns us that it would be risky to prognosticate beyond this.

Effects on the Family

We have so far looked at the effects of day care on the child's development, which has been the concern of most day-care research. But one should examine out-of-home care also from a broader ecological perspective, to see whether day care—by now as established an institution in most Western and Eastern societies as schools—has more wide-ranging effects on the family, as well as on broader social systems such as employment practices and the work force. Here we will consider how mothers are affected by their children's enrollment in day care.

Ramey and his colleagues report encouraging results in this regard. Mothers of children who were enrolled in their experimental day-care program interacted more with their children and their mutual play activities lasted twice as long as those of the control group whose children were not in day care. It is of interest to note that this may have come about because of the children's impact on their mothers, since these children vocalized more and fussed less, thus making mutual play more enjoyable for the mothers (Ramey et al., 1983).

Furthermore, when these children from disadvantaged backgrounds who had been in the experimental program since infancy were 5 years old, their mothers had achieved higher education levels and held more skilled jobs than the control group mothers did, and their child-rearing attitudes resembled more those of middle-class mothers (Ramey et al., 1983; Ramey & Farran, 1983). It seems that contact with the experimental program influenced the mothers' educational attitudes and aspirations. A study of day care in Pennsylvania reported that as mothers' satisfaction with substitute care increased, so did their marital and employment satisfaction, showing that day care can have quite far-reaching effects (Peters, 1973, cited in Belsky & Steinberg, 1978).

Another report, however, suggests that children's enrollment in day care may not always have beneficial effects on mothers' attitudes and practices. Mothers of children attending a cognitively oriented day-care program in Canada showed steadily rising scores on Caldwell's Inventory of Home Stimulation between 11 and 18 months, but thereafter their scores decreased until by 44 months they were below their initial level. A parallel up and down movement was observed for questions regarding mother's interest in the child's education and her positive attitude to the child. This picture suggests that the ultimate effect of day care may have been to allow these mothers to feel less responsible for their children's welfare (Fowler & Khan, 1975, cited Belsky & Steinberg, 1978).

Since these findings are few in number and rather tentative, it is probably unwise to speculate too much about the reasons for the inconsistencies. We should not draw too definite conclusions from the reports, but rather take them as an indication that the effects of day care *can* reach beyond the child.

GROUP DAY CARE VERSUS DAY-CARE HOMES

Children, and particularly younger children, often receive nonmaternal care from relatives, friends, or in family day homes, rather than in group day care, as we noted above. Informal care by babysitters is difficult to study, as it is largely inaccessible to researchers and only one study known to us has systematically included such care in its investigation (Clarke-Stewart, 1984). However, family day homes have been subjected to scrutiny by several research projects, and various aspects of their functioning and effects have been compared with those of group day care.

One of these projects is the New York City Infant Day Care Study (Golden et al., 1978) whose subjects were children between 6 and 36 months of age, mainly from lower class families. The study found that the physical facilities, that is, the amount of equipment, the variety of play materials, and the space available, as well as nutrition and the quality of health care, were superior in day-care centers compared with licensed family day homes. On the other hand, the family day homes excelled on social factors: The child/adult ratio was better and, no doubt because of this, adults and children engaged in more social interaction and children received more individual attention. But no *qualitative* difference was evident in the cognitive and language stimulation or the positive affective contact (e.g., affection and comforting) that the caregivers provided. Despite this similar quality of stimulation in the two modes of rearing, the IQ scores of the children in family day homes declined, whereas the children in day-care centers maintained their intellectual performance between 18 and 36 months. This difference was thought to have come about only between the ages of 2 and 3, and it was attributed to the fact that the teacher in charge of 2- to 3-year-olds in day-care centers had to be a licensed nursery school teacher, who may have provided the children with academic learning experiences. In aspects of psychological development other than IQ, for example, social competence and emotional functioning, the children in the two rearing groups did not differ. It must be stressed that the caregiver/child ratio was extremely favorable in both forms of care (less than 1:3 for both groups combined), something which gave the centers an unusual advantage.

In this study there were few differences in children's experiences or development in the two modes of care during the first 2 years of life. The Bermuda project (McCartney et al., 1982), however, found that children who had experienced group care as infants were more maladjusted than children whose first years were spent with sitters or in family day homes. There is curently renewed concern about infant day care. As Gamble and Zigler (1986) state: ". . . the existing evidence is such that blanket statements about the benign effects of infant day care on social competence, especially in males, may be premature" (p. 39). The authors of the New York Infant Day Care Study and others, in fact, feel that family day homes should be the method of choice for care for the under-2-year-olds, because of the more personal atmosphere and the greater attention from caregivers, as well as lower cost.

Parameters of Quality

What constitutes "quality" in day-care settings, that is, which aspects of day-care organization and children's day-to-day experiences in day care are associated with good outcomes in the children?

Organizational Structure

The National Day Care Study, carried out in the United States in the late 1970s, examined broad characteristics of day-care centers, for example, physical facilities, training of caregivers, the number of children cared for together in a group (group size), and the adult/child ratio, to see whether or not they influence the outcome variables: caregiver and child behavior and children's cognitive test performance (Ruopp & Travers, 1982; Ruopp, Travers, Glantz, & Coelen, 1979). The study examined 67 day-care sites in three large cities spread across the United States and observed, interviewed, or tested about 200 caregivers and about 1,400 children. The project therefore has some important comments to make about certain structural aspects of day-care organization and its conclusions are of interest to policymakers, as well as to teachers and psychologists.

Two main factors significantly influenced the outcomes: the absolute group size and caregivers' training in child development and early childhood education. In smaller groups (e.g., 12 rather than 24 children) children were more cooperative and responsive, engaged in more spontaneous conversation and creative activities, and were less likely to wander about aimlessly or run wild; in addition, their standardized test performance was better. Training in child development increased caregivers' initiations of social interaction with the children—for example, praising, comforting, responding, instructing—and made for larger gains on tests by the children.

In *infant* centers (studied as part of the larger project) a high adult/child ratio (fewer children per caregiver) was as important as group size and was associated with less distress in the infants. But the caregiver/child ratio in *preschool* day care made only a marginal, not a strong, difference to the outcomes. High ratios in larger groups did not offset the disadvantage of grouping large numbers of children together. A higher ratio made management of the children easier, that is, it meant less commanding and correcting. A higher ratio also gave caregivers more time for interacting with other adults, cleaning up, and so forth, but it did not necessarily lead to more time spent with individual children.

It would be misleading to conclude from this that adult/child ratio is of no importance. Some other studies, cited by Belsky (1985), have reported that when the adult/child ratio is very favorable—for example, 1:3 or better, and this we assume will often automatically mean small groups—more spontaneous talk by children and more conversations and positive interactions between caregivers and children result. However, the National Day Care Study findings draw our attention to the fact that it is the class composition that matters, with group size being more important than the nominal adult/child ratio, since the latter can be manipulated to cover many different kinds of arrangements.

Another aspect of the organizational structure of day-care centers that can affect child outcomes is the stability of care. Children prefer stable caregivers, who have looked after them over a longer period and with whom they have established a relationship, over others and are seldom distressed when they are left with such stable caregivers in day care (Cummings, 1980). These observations demonstrate that stability of care is important for the emotional functioning of children in day care, as it is for institutionalized children, as noted earlier.

The majority of children in Clarke-Stewart's research (1984) changed from some form of home care (including babysitters and family day homes) to center care during the period of the project. Clarke-Stewart was able to use this fact to tease out the determinants of cognitive ability by examining the predictors of *gains* in cognitive ability in children who moved from home to center care, thus overcoming some of the difficulties inherent in her sample. She combined maternal characteristics with center characteristics as predictor variables and found that the following measures significantly predicted cognitive gains in the children: The number of older children in the day-care class, stability of caregiver, greater maternal knowledge about child rearing, and fewer hours of maternal employment. The interesting points of these findings are that association with *older* children was important, and so was the time that mother had available for her child, both factors that are likely to have meant better verbal stimulation for the child.

Daily Experiences

Which are the day-to-day experiences that promote children's development and welfare in day care? The Bermuda study (McCartney et al., 1982), in looking at this question, first controlled for family background (e.g., mother's education), then for age at entry and time in group care, and lastly for the overall quality of care, assessed by an inventory. The researchers then observed and coded the amount of linguistic stimulation that the children received and various other aspects of day-care center life. The results showed that children's language development was, indeed, significantly affected by their daily experiences, over and above the other factors that had been controlled. Children scored higher on tests of language competence in centers where adults talked more to them. Other factors that seemed to facilitate their language development were a low noise level, a structured program that gave them little free-play time, little visual distraction surrounding the center, and the presence of many visitors. When the center's overall quality was good, children also tended to be friendly, sociable, considerate to others, and to manifest little dependent behavior.

Since we have just noted that children's linguistic development is enhanced by exposure to adult language, it is of interest to see what differences there are between home and day care in the language that children use and hear. We will therefore describe a study devoted to this topic, which provides some food for thought. Tizard and her colleagues (Tizard, Hughes, Carmichael, & Pinkerton, 1983a, b) in England observed 4-year-old girls at home and in nursery schools, where the emphasis is educational rather than custodial. Although the children were of mixed social background, the main interest of the study lies in the observed speech of the working-class children, as their verbal "deficits" have often been studied and sometimes been found to be a myth (cf. Labov, 1970). The authors discovered that working-class children use a much more restricted range of complex language and express fewer interests at school than they do at home. At school very few extended discussions took place, as teachers went rapidly from child to child. These fleeting contacts precluded discussions in depth. Teachers asked far more questions than mothers did and the teachers were responsible for sustaining the conversation. These centered around present play activities and rarely went beyond the present context. Although teachers often used more complex language than mothers did, because the teachers talked much less to the children, the latter were less exposed to complex language at school than at home. That the working-class girls were nevertheless not deficient in verbal skills was shown by their conversation at home, where their speech was marked by complex language usage, such as talk about future plans and past events, or "if-then" sentences. The authors, therefore, attributed the children's restricted language use at school to inhibitions and lack of self-confidence in the presence of the teacher, an authority figure.

The longest conversation between a teacher and a child that Tizard and her colleagues recorded went as follows:

Teacher: That's beautiful (looking at child's drawing). What's this? (points at figure).
Child: A dog.
Teacher: A dog?
Child: But he hasn't got no legs.
Teacher: Just didn't want any legs, did he? What's that bit there?
Child: I dunno.
Teacher: Will you write your name on it?
(Child does not reply, teacher writes child's name on drawing.)

The same child, while she was making a pool of water in the earth in her garden at home, carried on a conversation that contained a "why" and other questions. When the water leaked into the ground she said: "Oh well, we better put stones in then. Better get a little chunk of dirt so it won't go down. That one won't do, this is better. There. That'll save it. Now it won't go away, will it?"

Other research has uncovered similar differences between mother-child interactions at home and caregiver-child interactions in day-care homes (Long, Garduque, & Peters, 1983; Stith & Davis, 1984). In light of these findings it is puzzling why so many studies have been able to report a cognitive advantage for lower class children exposed to day care.

CONCLUSIONS

There is considerable variation in the quality of day care, as we have seen. The evidence suggests that the organizational structure of day care affects children's day-to-day experiences and these in turn affect their development. Thus, it seems that when groups of preschoolers are not too large and when caregivers have had training in how to deal with young children, caregivers tend to be more involved with the children, to be more emotionally responsive, and to use language in more stimulating ways. The children then are likely to be more capable, more cooperative, and better adjusted. These conditions for optimal development are remarkably consistent with those found to hold for family rearing, too, as Belsky (1985) points out.

Taking all kinds of day care together, it appears that day care does not put children's cognitive development at risk, but we should exercise caution in accepting the claims for cognitive benefits that specially designed day-care programs may bestow on disadvantaged children, until we know that these benefits are long lasting.

There is good agreement that day care does not disrupt children's emotional bonds to their parents. However, perhaps where conditions are not optimal, it may instigate some undesirable social behaviors. There is some evidence that being reared amid the larger groups usual in day-care centers may be more stressful for younger children, under 2 or 3 years of age, and that this may then result in some maladaptive behaviors (McCartney et al., 1982). Therefore, children under 3 may be better off if they are reared in a protective environment by a caring and understanding person in the company of only a few other children, as Rutter (1982) and the authors of the New York City Day Care Study suggest.

Not all the answers about the effects of day care are in yet, by any means, and hence we cannot be certain that day care carries no risks, although so far very few risks have been uncovered. However, even if shared caregiving is harmless, a stable and enduring relationship with a caring parent figure is of importance for the child's development and welfare.

Summary

The two sections of this chapter discuss the effects on the young child of two distinct kinds of separation from mother or a mother figure: The first deals with more or less permanent separation that institutionalized rearing implies; the second deals with the daily separation and reunion that day care entails.

Studies of institutionalized children in the 1940s gave rise to Bowlby's "maternal deprivation theory," which proposed that the prolonged deprivation of young children of care by a single mother or mother figure prevented the formation of secure attachment bonds and may have grave consequences for their later psychological development and, in particular, may lead to delinquency. Some later studies questioned whether institutionalized rearing inevitably results in maladjustment. However, more recent investigations have reconfirmed that even good institutional rearing at an early age is associated with behavior problems in childhood and with personality and parenting difficulties in adulthood, though some protective factors may ameliorate the situation. The evidence for the supposed superiority in outcomes of foster care, compared with institutional rearing, is not yet very clear.

Later studies also showed that the cause of the adverse outcomes does not lie in separation from mother as such: Separation through death or by a prolonged stay in a TB sanatorium, for instance, is not associated with the same kind of maladjustment as is institutionalization for other reasons. Rather, the adverse effects on behavior and personality can be traced to discord and instability in the family, which usually precede removal from home and preclude the formation of secure attachment bonds to one or a few persons, as does institutional rearing from birth. In addition, genetic factors may also be implicated. Thus, there is good evidence that experiences during the early years have a special importance for the establishment of a healthy personality.

Conclusions regarding the effects of discord and instability in the home and of the institutional rearing that may possibly result therefrom can, however, not be generalized to daily out-of-home care (day care), which has become an increasingly widespread practice in recent decades. The latter represents a form of multiple shared caregiving, and earlier fears about its effects have so far, on the whole, not been borne out.

Day care does not preclude the establishment of secure attachment bonds, nor does it seem to put cognitive development at risk. However, day care may produce some undesirable social-behavioral effects, particularly when a child enters group care in infancy. It is likely that the good development of very young children is ensured better by rearing in the intimate atmosphere of a family home in the company of but a few other children, provided the child receives stimulation and individual attention from a caring and understanding adult.

References

Abramovitch, R., Corter, C., & Lando, B. (1979). Sibling interaction in the home. *Child Development, 50*, 997–1003.

Abramovitch, R., Corter, C., & Pepler, D.J. (1980). Observations of mixed-sex sibling dyads. *Child Development, 51*, 1268–1271.

Abramovitch, R., & Grusec, J.E. (1978). Peer imitation in a natural setting. *Child Development, 49*, 60–65.

Abramovitch, R., & Strayer, F. (1978). Preschool social organization: Agonistic, spacing, and attentional behaviors. In L. Krames, P. Pliner, & T. Alloway (Eds.), *Advances in the study of communication and affect: Aggression dominance and individual spacing*, (Vol. 4, pp. 67–127). New York: Plenum Press.

Adamson, L.B. & Bakeman, K. (1985). Affect and attention: Infants observed with mothers and peers. *Child Development, 56*, 582–593.

Ahlgren, A., & Johnson, D.W. (1979). Sex differences in cooperative and competitive attitudes from second through 12th grade. *Developmental Psychology, 15*, 45–49.

Ainsworth, M.D.S. (1972). Attachment and dependency: A comparison. In J.L. Gewirtz (Ed.), *Attachment and dependency*. New York: John Wiley & Sons.

Ainsworth, M.D.S. (1973). The development of infant-mother attachment. In B. Caldwell & H. Ricciuti (Eds.), *Review of child development research*, (Vol. 3, pp. 1–94). Chicago: University of Chicago Press.

Ainsworth, M.D.S., Bell, S.M., & Stayton, D.J. (1974). Infant-mother attachment and social development: "Socialization" as a product of reciprocal responsiveness to signals. In M.P.M. Richards (Ed.). *The integration of a child into a social world* (pp. 99–135). London: Cambridge University Press.

Ainsworth, M.D.S., Blehar, M.C., Waters, E., & Wall, S. (1978). *Patterns of attachment: A psychological study of the strange situation*. Hillsdale, NJ: Lawrence Erlbaum Associates.

Algozzine, O. (1977). Perceived attractiveness and classroom interaction. *Journal of Experimental Education, 46*, 63–66.

Allport, G.W. (1937). *Personality: A psychosocial interpretation*. New York: Holt, Rinehart and Winston.

Altmann, J. (1980). *Baboon mothers and their infants*. Cambridge: Harvard University Press.

Amsterdam, B.K. (1972). Mirror self-image reactions before age two. *Developmental Psychology, 5*, 297–305.

Anderson, K.E., Lytton, H., & Romney, D.M. (1986). Mothers' interactions with normal and conduct-disordered boys: Who affects whom? *Developmental Psychology, 22*, 604–609.

Andison, F.S. (1977). T.V. violence and viewer aggression: A cumulation of study results 1956–1976. *Public Opinion Quarterly, 41*, 314–331.

Anisfeld, E., & Lipper, E. (1983). Early contact, social support and mother-infant bonding. *Pediatrics, 72*, 79–83.

Arend, R., Gove, F., & Sroufe, L.A. (1979). Continuity of individual adaptation from infancy to kindergarten: A predictive study of ego-resiliency and curiosity in preschoolers. *Child Development, 50*, 950–959.

Aries, P. (1962). *Centuries of childhood: A social history of family life.* (R. Baldick, Trans.), New York: Alfred A. Knopf.

Aronfreed, J. (1961). The nature, variety, and social patterning of moral responses to transgression. *Journal of Abnormal and Social Psychology, 63*, 223–240.

Aronfreed, J., & Reber, A. (1965). Internalized behavioral suppression and the timing of social punishment. *Journal of Personality and Social Psychology, 1*, 3–16.

Asher, S.R. (1978). Children's peer relations. In M.E. Lamb (Ed.), *Social and personality development* (pp. 91–113). New York: Holt, Rinehart and Winston.

Asher, S.R., & Dodge, K.A. (1986). Identifying children who are rejected by their peers. *Developmental Psychology, 22*, 444–449.

Asher, S.R., & Renshaw, P.D. (1981). Children without friends: Social knowledge and social skill training. In S.R. Asher & J.M. Gottman (Eds.), *The development of children's friendships* (pp. 273–296). Cambridge: Cambridge University Press.

Asher, S.R., Hymel, S., & Renshaw, P.D. (1984). Loneliness in children. *Child Development, 55*, 1456–1464.

Asher, S.R., Singleton, L.C., & Taylor, A.R. (1982). *Acceptance vs. friendship: A longitudinal study of racial integration.* Paper presented at the meeting of the American Educational Research Association, New York.

Austin, V.D., Ruble, D.N., & Trabasso, T. (1977). Recall and order effects as factors in children's moral judgments. *Child Development, 48*, 470–474.

Azar, S.T., Robinson, D.R., Hekimian, E., & Twentyman, C.T. (1984). Unrealistic expectations and problem-solving ability in maltreating and comparison mothers. *Journal of Consulting and Clinical Psychology, 52*, 687–691.

Azrin, N.H., & Lindsley, O.R. (1956). The reinforcement of cooperation between children. *Journal of Abnormal and Social Psychology, 52*, 100–102.

Bach, G.R. (1946). Father-fantasies and father-typing in father-separated families. *Child Development, 17*, 63–80.

Bahr, S. (1974). Effects on power and division of labor in the family. In L.W. Hoffman & F.I. Ney (Eds.), *Working mothers: An evaluative review of the consequences for wife, husband and child* (pp. 67–185). San Francisco: Jossey-Bass.

Bakeman, R., & Brown, J.V. (1980). Early interaction: Consequences for social and mental development at 3 years. *Child Development, 51*, 437–447.

Baldwin, A.L. (1948). Socialization and the parent-child relationship. *Child Development, 19*, 127–136.

Baldwin, A.L. (1949). The effect of home environment on nursery school behavior. *Child Development, 20*, 49–61.

Baldwin, A.L., & Baldwin, C. (1970). Children's judgments of kindness. *Child Development, 41*, 29–47.

Baldwin, A.L., Kalhorn, J., & Breese, F.H. (1945). Patterns of parent behavior. *Psychological Monographs*, *58*, (3, Whole No. 268).

Baldwin, A.L., Kalhorn, J., & Breese, F.H. (1949). The appraisal of parent behavior. *Psychological Monographs*, *63*, (4, Whole No. 299).

Baldwin, J.M. (1897). *Social and ethical interpretations in mental development: A study in social psychology*. New York: MacMillan.

Ban, P.L., & Lewis, M. (1974). Mothers and fathers, girls and boys: Attachment behavior in the one-year-old. *Merrill-Palmer Quarterly*, *20*, 195–204.

Bandura, A. (1965). Influence of a model's reinforcement contengencies on the acquisition of imitative responses. *Journal of Personality and Social Psychology*, *1*, 589–595.

Bandura, A. (1969). A social-learning theory of identificatory processes. In D.A. Goslin (Ed.) *Handbook of socialization theory and research* (pp. 213–262). Chicago: Rand McNally.

Bandura, A. (1973). Aggression: A social learning analysis. New York: Holt, Rinehart and Winston.

Bandura, A. (1974). Behavior theory and the models of man. *American Psychologist*, *29*, 859–869.

Bandura, A. (1977a). *Social learning theory*. Englewood Cliffs, NJ: Prentice-Hall.

Bandura, A. (1977b). Self-efficacy: Toward a unifying theory of behavioral change. *Psychological Review*, *84*, 191–215.

Bandura, A. (1979). Psychological mechanisms of aggression. In M. von Cranach, K. Foppa, W. Lepenies, & D. Ploog (Eds.), *Human ethology: Claims and limits of a new discipline* (pp. 316–356). Cambridge: Cambridge University Press.

Bandura, A. (1981). Self-referent thought: A developmental analysis of self-efficacy. In J.H. Flavell & L.D. Ross (Eds.), *Social cognitive development: Frontiers and possible futures* (pp. 200–239). Cambridge: Cambridge University Press.

Bandura, A., Grusec, J.E., & Menlove, F.L. (1967). Some social determinants of self-monitoring reinforcement systems. *Journal of Personality and Social Psychology*, *5*, 449–455.

Bandura, A., & Huston, A.C. (1961). Identification as a process of incidental learning. *Journal of Abnormal and Social Psychology*, *63*, 311–318.

Bandura, A., & Kupers, C.J. (1964). Transmission of patterns of self-reward through modeling. *Journal of Abnormal and Social Psychology*, *69*, 1–9.

Bandura, A., & McDonald, F. (1963). The influence of social reinforcement and the behavior of models in shaping children's moral judgment. *Journal of Abnormal and Social Psychology, 67*, 274–281.

Bandura, A., & Mischel, W. (1965). Modification of self-imposed delay of reward through exposure to live and symbolic models. *Journal of Personality and Social Psychology*, *2*, 698–705.

Bandura, A., Ross, D., & Ross, S.A. (1961). Transmission of aggression through imitation of aggressive models. *Journal of Abnormal and Social Psychology*, *63*, 575–582.

Bandura, A., Ross, D., & Ross, S.A. (1963a). A comparative test of the status envy, social power, and secondary reinforcement theories of identificatory learning. *Journal of Abnormal and Social Psychology*, *67*, 527–534.

Bandura, A., Ross, D., & Ross, S.A., (1963b). Vicarious reinforcement and imitative learning. *Journal of Abnormal and Social Psychology*, *67*, 601–607.

Bandura, A., Ross, D., & Ross, S.A., (1963c). Imitation of film-mediated aggressive models. *Journal of Abnormal and Social Psychology*, *66*, 3–11.

Bandura, A., & Walters, R.H. (1959). *Adolescent aggression*. New York: Ronald Press.

Bandura, A., & Walters, R.H. (1963). *Social learning and personality development*. New York: Holt, Rinehart and Winston.

Bannister, D., & Agnew, J. (1976). The child's construing of self. In A.W. Landfield (Ed.), *Nebraska symposium on motivation* (Vol. 24, pp. 99–125). Lincoln: University of Nebraska Press.

Barenboim, C. (1977). Developmental changes in the interpersonal cognitive system from middle childhood to adolescence. *Child Development*, *48*, 1467–1474.

Barenhoim, C. (1981). The development of person perception in childhood and adolescence: From behavioral comparisons to psychological constructs to psychological comparisons. *Child Development*, *52*, 129–144.

Barker, R.G., Dembo, T., & Lewin, K. (1941). Frustration and regression: An experiment with young children. *University of Iowa Studies in Child Welfare*, *18*, (386).

Barker, R.G., & Wright, H.F. (1955). *Midwest and its children*. New York: Harper & Row.

Barkley, R.A., Ullman, D.G., Lori, O., & Brecht, J.M. (1977). The effects of sex typing and sex appropriateness of modeled behavior on children's imitation. *Child Development*, *48*, 721–725.

Barnett, M.A., & Bryan, J.H. (1974). Effects of competition with outcome feedback on children's helping behavior. *Developmental Psychology*, *10*, 838–842.

Barnett, M.A., King, L.M., & Howard, J.A. (1979). Inducing affect about self or other: Effects on generosity in children. *Developmental Psychology*, *15*, 164–167.

Barnett, M.A., Howard, J.A., Melton, E.M., & Dino, G.A. (1982). Effect of inducing sadness about self or other on helping behavior in high- and low-empathic children. *Child Development*, *53*, 920–923.

Barrera, M.E., Rosenbaum, P.L., & Cunningham, C.E. (1986). Early home intervention with low-birth-weight infants and their parents. *Child Development*, *57*, 20–33.

Barry, H.A., Child, I.L., & Bacon, M.K. (1959). Relation of child training to subsistence economy. *American Anthropology*, *61*, 51–63.

Bar-Tal, D., & Raviv, A. (1979). Consistency of helping-behavior measures. *Child Development*, *50*, 1235–1238.

Bar-Tal, D., Raviv, A., & Goldberg, M. (1982). Helping behavior among preschool children: An observational study. *Child Development*, *53*, 396–402.

Bar-Tal, D., Raviv, A., & Leiser, T. (1980). The development of altruistic behavior: Empirical evidence. *Developmental Psychology*, *16*, 516–524.

Bassili, J.N., & Smith, M.C. (1986). On the spontaneity of trait attribution: Converging evidence for the role of cognitive strategy. *Journal of Personality and Social Psychology*, *50*, 239–245.

Bates, J.E. (1980). The concept of difficult temperament. *Merrill-Palmer Quarterly*, *26*, 299–319.

Bates, J.E., & Bayles, K. (1984). Objective and subjective components in mothers' perceptions of their children from age 6 months to 3 years. *Merrill-Palmer Quarterly*, *30*, 111–130.

Bates, J.E., Maslin, C.A., & Frankel, K.A. (1985). Attachment security, mother-child interaction, and temperament as predictors of behavior-problem ratings at age three years. In I. Bretherton & E. Waters (Eds.). Growing points of attachment theory and research. *Monographs of the Society for Research in Child Development, 50*, (1–2, Serial No. 209).

Bauer, W.D., & Twentyman, C.T. (1985). Abusing, neglectful and comparison mothers' responses to child-related and non child-related stressors. *Journal of Consulting and Clinical Psychology, 53*, 335–343.

Baumrind, D. (1971). Current patterns of parental authority. *Developmental Psychology Monographs, 4*, (No. 1, Pt. 2).

Baumrind, D. (1973). The development of instrumental competence through socialization. In A. Pick (Ed.), *Minnesota Symposia on Child Psychology* (Vol. 7, pp. 3–46). Minneapolis: University of Minnesota Press.

Baumrind, D. (1980). New directions in socialization research. *Psychological Bulletin, 35*, 639–652.

Baumrind, D. (1982). Are androgynous individuals more effective persons and parents? *Child Development, 53*, 44–75.

Baumrind, D. (1983). Rejoinder to Lewis' reinterpretation of parental firm control effects: Are authoritative families really harmonious? *Psychological Bulletin, 94*, 132–142.

Bayley, N., & Schaefer, E.S. (1960). Relationships between socioeconomic variables and the behavior of mother toward young children. *Journal of Genetic Psychology, 96*, 61–77.

Becker, B.J. (1986). Influence again: An examination of reviews and studies of gender differences in social influence. In J.S. Hyde & M.C. Linn (Eds.), *The psychology of gender: Advances through meta-analysis* (pp. 178–209). Baltimore: The Johns Hopkins Press.

Becker, W.C. (1964). Consequences of different kinds of parental discipline. In M.L. Hoffman & L.W. Hoffman (Eds.), *Review of Child Development Research* (Vol. 1, pp. 169–208). New York: Russell Sage Foundation.

Becker, W.C., Peterson, D.R., Luria, Z., Shoemaker, D.J., & Hellmer, L.A. (1962). Relations of factors derived from parent interview ratings to behavior problems of five-year-olds. *Child Development, 33*, 509–535.

Beckwith, L., & Cohen, S.E. (1980). Interactions of preterm infants with their caregivers and test performance at age 2. In T.M. Field, S. Goldberg, D. Stern, & A.M. Sostek (Eds.), *High-risk infants and children: Adult and peer interactions* (pp. 155–178). New York: Academic Press.

Beckwith, L., & Cohen, S.E. (1984). Home environment and cognitive competence in preterm children during the first 5 years. In A.W. Gottfried (Ed.), *Home environment and early cognitive development: Longitudinal research* (pp. 235–271). New York: Harcourt, Brace & Jovanovich.

Bell, R.Q. (1968). A reinterpretation of the direction of effects in studies of socialization. *Psychological Review, 75*, 81–85.

Bell, R.Q. (1977). Socialization findings re-examined. In R.Q. Bell & R.V. Harper (Eds.), *Child effects on adults* (pp. 53–84). Hillsdale, NJ: Lawrence Erlbaum Associates.

Bell, R.Q., & Chapman, M. (1986). Child effects in studies using experimental or brief longitudinal approaches to socialization. *Developmental Psychology, 22*, 595–603.

Bell, R.Q., & Waldrop, M.F. (1982). Temperament and minor physical anomalies. In Ciba Foundation Symposium 89. *Temperamental differences in infants and young children* (pp. 206–220). London: Pitman.

Beller, E.K. (1955). Dependence and independence in young children. *Journal of Genetic Psychology, 87*, 25–35.

Belsky, J. (1979a). Mother-father-infant interactions: A naturalistic observational study. *Developmental Psychology, 15*, 601–607.

Belsky, J. (1979b). *The interrelation of parenting, spousal interaction and infant competence: A suggestive analysis.* Paper presented at the Biennial Meeting of the Society for Research in Child Development, San Francisco, CA.

Belsky, J. (1981). Early human experience: A family perspective. *Developmental Psychology, 17*, 3–33.

Belsky, J. (1984). The determinants of parenting: A process model. *Child Development, 55*, 83–96.

Belsky, J. (1985). Day care: Developmental effects and the problem of quality care. *Journal of the Canadian Association for Young Children, 9*, 53–74.

Belsky, J., & Steinberg, L.D. (1978). The effects of day care: A critical review. *Child Development, 49*, 929–949.

Bem, D.J. (1972). Self-perception theory. In L. Berkowitz (Ed.), *Advances in experimental social psychology* (Vol. 6, pp. 2–62). New York: Academic Press.

Bem, D.J., & Allen, A. (1974). On predicting some of the people some of the time: The search for cross-situational consistencies in behavior. *Psychological Review, 81*, 506–520.

Bem, S.L. (1979). Theory and measurement of androgyny: A reply to the Pedhazur-Tetenbaum and Locksley-Colten critiques. *Journal of Personality and Social Psychology, 37*, 1047–1054.

Benbow, C.P., & Stanley, J.C. (1980). Sex differences in mathematical ability: Fact or artifact? *Science, 210*, 1262–1264.

Benbow, C.P., & Stanley, J.C. (1983). Sex differences in mathematical reasoning: More facts. *Science, 222*, 1029–1031.

Berkowitz, L. (1964). *Development of motives and values in a child.* New York: Basic Books.

Berkowitz, L. (1973). The case for bottling up rage. *Psychology Today, 7*, 24–31.

Berkowitz, L., & Geen, R.G. (1966). Film violence and the cue properties of available targets. *Journal of Personality and Social Psychology, 3*, 525–530.

Berkowitz, L., & Rawlings, E. (1963). Effects of film violence on inhibitions against subsequent aggression. *Journal of Abnormal and Social Psychology, 66*, 405–412.

Berman, P.W. (1980). Are women more responsive than men to the young? A review of developmental and situational variables. *Psychological Bulletin, 88*, 668–695.

Berndt, T.J. (1979). Developmental changes in conformity to peers and parents. *Developmental Psychology, 15*, 608–616.

Berndt, T.J. (1983). Correlates and causes of sociometric status in childhood: A commentary on six current studies of popular, rejected and neglected children. *Merrill-Palmer Quarterly, 29*, 439–448.

Berndt, T.J., & Berndt, E.G. (1975). Children's use of motives and intentionality in person perception and moral judgment. *Child Development, 46*, 904–912.

Bertalanffy, L. von. (1968). *General system theory.* New York: Braziller.

Bertenthal, B.I., & Fischer, K.W. (1978). Development of self-recognition in the infant. *Developmental Psychology*, *14*, 44–50.

Bierman, K.L., & Furman, W. (1984). The effects of social skills training and peer involvement on the social adjustment of preadolescents. *Child Development*, *55*, 151–162.

Bijou, S.W., & Baer, D.M. (1960). The laboratory-experimental study of child behavior. In P.H. Mussen (Ed.), *Handbook of research methods in child development* (pp. 140–197). New York: John Wiley & Sons.

Bijou, S.W., & Baer, D.M. (1961). *Child development: A systematic and empirical theory* (Vol. 1). New York: Appleton-Century-Crofts.

Biller, H.B., & Bahm, R.M. (1971). Father-absence, perceived maternal behavior, and masculinity of self-concept among junior high school boys. *Developmental Psychology*, *4*, 178–181.

Birch, H.G., & Clark, G. (1950). Hormonal modification of social behavior. IV. The mechanism of estrogen-induced dominance in chimpanzees. *Journal of Comparative and Physiological Psychology*, *43*, 181–193.

Blakemore, J.E.O., LaRue, A.A., & Olejnik, A.B. (1979). Sex-appropriate toy preference and the ability to conceptualize toys as sex-role related. *Developmental Psychology*, *15*, 339–340.

Blasi, A. (1980). Bridging moral cognition and moral action: A critical review of the literature. *Psychological Bulletin*, *88*, 1–45.

Blehar, M.C. (1974). Anxious attachment and defensive reactions associated with day care. *Child Development*, *45*, 683–692.

Block, J.H. (1971). *Lives through time*. Berkeley: Bancroft Books.

Block, J.H. (1976). Issues, problems, and pitfalls in assessing sex differences: A critical review of "The psychology of sex differences." *Merrill-Palmer Quarterly*, *22*, 283–308.

Block, J.H. (1978). Another look at sex differentiation in the socialization behaviors of mothers and fathers. In J.A. Sherman, & F.L. Denmark (Eds.), *The psychology of women: Future directions in research* (pp. 29–87). New York: Psychological Dimensions.

Block, J.H. (1983). Differential premises arising from differential socialization of the sexes: Some conjectures. *Child Development*, *54*, 1335–1354.

Block, J.H., & Block, J. (1980). The role of ego-control and ego-resiliency in the organization of behavior. In W.A. Collins (Ed.), *Minnesota Symposium on Child Psychology* (Vol. 13, pp. 39–101). Hillsdale, NJ: Lawrence Erlbaum Associates.

Block, J.H., Block, J., & Gjerde, P.F. (1986). The personality of children prior to divorce: A prospective study. *Child Development*, *57*, 827–840.

Block, J.H., Block, J., & Morrison, A. (1981). Parental agreement-disagreement on child-rearing orientations and gender-related personality correlates in children. *Child Development*, *52*, 965–974.

Blum, G.S., & Miller, D.R. (1952). Exploring the psychoanalytic theory of the "oral character." *Journal of Personality*, *20*, 287–304.

Blurton Jones, N. (1972). Comparative aspects of mother-child contact. In N. Blurton Jones (Ed.), *Ethological studies of child behavior* (pp. 97–127). Cambridge: Cambridge University Press.

Boggiano, A.K. & Ruble, D.N. (1979). Competence and the over-justification effect: A developmental study. *Journal of Personality and Social Psychology*, *37*, 1462–1468.

Boh, K. (1986). *Changes of work and family patterns from a European perspective.* Paper presented at CFR Seminar, Jerusalem, Israel.

Bohman, M., & Sigvardsson, S. (1979). Long-term effects of early institutional care: A prospective longitudinal study. *Journal of Child Psychology and Psychiatry, 20,* 111–117.

Bonkowski, S.E., Boomhower, S.J., & Bequette, S.Q. (1985). What you don't know *can* hurt you: Unexpressed fears and feelings of children from divorcing families. *Journal of Divorce, 9,* 33–45.

Borke, H. (1971). Interpersonal perception of young children: Egocentrism or empathy? *Developmental Psychology, 5,* 263–269.

Borke, H. (1973). The development of empathy in Chinese and American children between three and six years of age: A cross-cultural study. *Developmental Psychology, 9,* 102–108.

Borke, H. (1975). Piaget's mountains revisited: Changes in the egocentric landscape. *Developmental Psychology, 11,* 240–243.

Bowers, K.S. (1973). Situationism in psychology: An analysis and a critique. *Psychological Review, 80,* 307–336.

Bowlby, J. (1946). *Forty-four juvenile thieves, their characters and home life.* London: Bailliere, Tyndall & Cox.

Bowlby, J. (1951). Maternal care and mental health. *Geneva: World Health Organization: Monograph Series* (Serial No. 2).

Bowlby, J. (1958). The nature of the child's tie to his mother. *International Journal of Psychoanalysis, 39,* 350–373.

Bowlby, J. (1971). *Attachment and loss: Attachment* (Vol. 1). London: Pelican Books.

Bowlby, J. (1973). *Attachment and loss: Separation* (Vol. 2). London: Hogarth.

Bowlby, J., Ainsworth, M., Boston, M., & Rosenbluth, D. (1956). The effects of mother-child separation: A follow-up study. *British Journal of Medical Psychology, 29,* 211.

Brackbill, Y. (1958). Extinction of the smiling response in infants as a function of reinforcement schedule. *Child Development, 29,* 115–124.

Brackbill, Y. (1979). Obstetrical medication and infant behavior. In J.D. Osofsky (Ed.), *Handbook of infant development* (pp. 76–125). New York: John Wiley & Sons.

Brazelton, T.B., Koslowski, B., & Main, M. (1974). The origin of reciprocity: The early mother-infant interaction. M. Lewis & L.A. Rosenblum (Eds.) *The effect of the infant on its caregiver.* New York: John Wiley & Sons.

Bregman, E.O. (1934). An attempt to modify the emotional attitudes of infants by the conditioned response technique. *Journal of Genetic Psychology, 45,* 169–198.

Breitmayer, B.J., & Ramey, C.T. (1986). Biological nonoptimality and quality of postnatal environment as codeterminants of intellectual development. *Child Development, 57,* 1151–1165.

Breland, H.M. (1974). Birth order, family configuration and verbal achievement. *Child Development, 45,* 1011–1019.

Breland, K., & Breland, M. (1961). The misbehavior of organisms. *American Psychologist, 16,* 681–684.

Bretherton, I., & Ainsworth, M.D.S. (1974). Responses of one-year-olds to a stranger in a strange situation. In M. Lewis & L.A. Rosenblum (Eds.), *The origins of fear* (pp. 131–164). New York: John Wiley & Sons.

Bridges, K.M.B. (1931). *The social and emotional development of the preschool child*. London: Routledge & Kegan Paul.

Broman, S.H., Nichols, P.L., & Kennedy, W.A. (1975). *Preschool IQ: Prenatal and early development correlates*. Hillsdale, NJ: Lawrence Erlbaum Associates.

Bronfenbrenner, U. (1958). Socialization and social class through time and space. In E.E. Maccoby, T.M. Newcomb, & E.L. Hartley (Eds.), *Readings in social psychology* (pp. 400–425). New York: Holt, Rinehart and Winston.

Bronfenbrenner, U. (1961). The changing American child—A speculative analysis. *Journal of Social Issues*, *17*, 6–18.

Bronfenbrenner, U. (1963). Developmental theory in transition. In H.W. Stevenson (Ed.), *Child Psychology. The 62nd Yearbook of the National Society for the Study of Education* (pp. 517–542). Chicago: National Society for the Study of Education.

Bronfenbrenner, U. (1967). Response to pressure from peers versus adults among Soviet and American school children. *International Journal of Psychology*, *2*, 199–207.

Bronfenbrenner, U. (1970). *Two worlds of childhood*. New York: Russell Sage.

Bronfenbrenner, U. (1977). Toward an experimental ecology of human development. *American Psychologist*, *32*, 513–531.

Bronstein, P. (1984). Differences in mothers' and fathers' behaviors toward children: A cross-cultural comparison. *Developmental Psychology*, *20*, 995–1003.

Brooks, J., & Lewis, M. (1976). Infants' responses to strangers: Midget, adult and child. *Child Development*, *47*, 323–332.

Brophy, J. (1985). Interactions of male and female students with male and female teachers. In L.C. Wilkinson & C.B. Marrett (Eds.), *Gender influences in classroom interaction* (pp. 115–142). New York: Academic Press.

Brophy, J. (1986). Teacher influences on student achievement. *American Psychologist*, *41*, 1069–1077.

Brophy, J.E., & Evertson, C.M. (1976). *Learning from teaching: A developmental perspective*. Boston: Allyn & Bacon.

Broughton, J.M. (1981). The genetic psychology of James Mark Baldwin. *American Psychologist*, *36*, 396–407.

Bruner, J. (1972). The nature and uses of immaturity. *American Psychologist*, *27*, 1–22.

Bruner, J.S. (1977). Early social interaction and language acquisition. In H.R. Schaffer (Ed.), *Studies in mother-infant interaction* (pp. 271–289). London: Academic Press.

Bruner, J.S., Jolly, A., & Sylva, K. (Eds.). (1976). *Play: Its role in development and evolution*. Harmondsworth, Middlesex: Penguin Books.

Bruner, J.S., & Sherwood, V. (1976). Peekaboo and the learning of rule structures. In J.S. Bruner, A. Jolly, & K. Sylva (Eds.), *Play: Its role in development and evolution* (pp. 277–285). London: Penguin Books.

Bryant, B.K. (1977). The effects of the interpersonal context of evaluation on self- and other-enhancement behavior. *Child Development*, *48*, 885–892.

Bryant, B.K., & Crockenberg, S.B. (1980). Correlates and dimensions of prosocial behavior: A study of female siblings with their mothers. *Child Development*, *51*, 529–544.

Bryant, P.E., & Trabasso, T. (1971). Transitive inferences and memory in young children. *Nature*, *232*, 456–458.

Bryden, M.P. (1979). Evidence of sex-related differences in cerebral organization. In M.A. Wittig & A.C. Petersen (Eds.), *Sex-related differences in cognitive functioning* (pp. 121–143). New York: Academic Press.

Buck, R. (1981). The evolution and development of emotion expression and communication. In S.S. Brehm, S.M. Kassin, & X.F. Gibbons (Eds.), *Developmental social psychology* (pp. 127–151). New York: Oxford Univesity Press.

Bugenthal, D., Whalen, C., & Henker, B. (1977). Causal attributions of hyperactive children and motivational assumptions of two behavior-change approaches: Evidence for an interactionist position. *Child Development, 48*, 874–884.

Bukowski, W.M., & Newcomb, A.F. (1984). Stability and determinants of sociometric status and friendship choice: A longitudinal perspective. *Developmental Psychology, 20*, 941–952.

Burns, A., & Goodnow, J.J. (1979). *Children and families in Australia: Contemporary issues and problems*. Sydney: Allen & Unwin.

Burton, R.V. (1963). Generality of honesty reconsidered. *Psychological Review, 70*, 481–499.

Buss, A.H. (1961). *The psychology of aggression*. New York: John Wiley & Sons.

Buss, A.H., & Plomin, R. (1975). *A temperament theory of personality development*. New York: John Wiley, & Sons.

Buss, A.K. (1975). The emerging field of the sociology of psychological knowledge. *American Psychologist, 30*, 988–1002.

Bussey, K. (1985). *Influence of peers and cognitions on same-sex modeling*. Paper presented at Biennial Meeting of Society for Research in Child Development, Toronto.

Bynner, J.M., & Romney, D.M. (1985). LISREL for beginners. *Canadian Psychology, 26*, 43–49.

Cairns, R.B. (Ed.), (1979a). *The analysis of social interactions: Methods, issues, and illustrations*. Hillsdale, NJ: Lawrence Erlbaum Associates.

Cairns, R.B. (1979b). *Social development: The origins and plasticity of interchanges*. San Francisco: W.H. Freeman.

Cairns, R.B. (1980). Developmental theory before Piaget: The remarkable contributions of James Mark Baldwin. (Review of *Mental development in the child and the race* and of *Social and ethical interpretations in mental development* by J.M. Baldwin). *Contemporary Psychology, 25*, 438–440.

Cairns, R.B. (1986). An evolutionary and developmental perspective on aggressive patterns. In C. Zahn-Waxler, E.M. Cummings, & R. Iannoti (Eds.), *Altruism and aggression* (pp. 58–87). New York: Cambridge University Press.

Cairns, R.B., & Green, J.A. (1979). How to assess personality and social patterns: Observations or ratings? In R.B. Cairns (Ed.), *The analysis of social interactions: Methods, issues, and illustrations* (pp. 209–226). Hillsdale, NJ: Lawrence Erlbaum Associates.

Cairns, R.B., MacCombie, D.M., & Hood, K.E. (1983). A developmental-genetic analysis of aggressive behavior in mice. *Journal of Comparative Psychology, 97*, 69–89.

Caldwell, B.M., Wright, C.M., Honig, A.S., & Tannenhaum, J. (1970). Infant care and attachment. *American Journal of Orthopsychiatry, 40*, 397–412.

Camp, B.W. (1980). Two psychoeducational treatment programs for young aggressive boys. In C.K. Whalen, & E. Henker (Eds.), *Hyperactive children: The social ecology of identification and treatment*. New York: Academic Press.

Campbell, S.B.G. (1979). Mother-infant interaction as a function of maternal ratings of temperament. *Child Psychiatry and Human Development, 10*, 67–76.

Campos, J.J., Barrett, K.C., Lamb, M.E., Goldsmith, H.H., & Stenberg, C. (1983). Socioemotional development. In M.M. Haith & J.J. Campos (Eds.), *Handbook of Child Psychology. Vol. II: Infancy and developmental psychobiology* (pp. 783–916). New York: John Wiley & Sons.

Campos, J.J., & Stenberg, C.R. (1981). Perception, appraisal and emotion: The onset of social referencing. In M.E. Lamb & L.R. Sherrod (Eds.), *Infant social cognition: Empirical and theoretical considerations* (pp. 273–314). Hillsdale. NJ: Lawrence Erlbaum Associates.

Carey, W.B. (1972). Measuring infant temperament. *Journal of Pediatrics, 81*, 414.

Carey, W.B., Lipton, W.L., & Myers, R.A. (1974). Temperament in adopted and foster babies. *Child Welfare, 53*, 352–359.

Carlson, D.B., & Labarba, R.C. (1979). Maternal emotionality during pregnancy and reproductive outcome: A review of the literature. *International Journal of Behavioural Development, 2*, 343–376.

Carr, S., Dabbs, J., & Carr, T. (1975). Mother-infant attachment: The importance of the mother's visual field. *Child Development, 46*, 331–338.

Carter, D.B., Patterson, C.J., & Quasebarth, S.J. (1979). Development of children's use of plans for self-control. *Cognitive Therapy and Research, 4*, 407–413.

Case, R.S. (1978). Intellectual development from birth to adulthood. A neo-Piagetian interpretation. In R.W. Siegler (Ed.), *Children's thinking: What develops?* (pp. 37–71). Hillsdale, NJ: Lawrence Erlbaum Associates.

Casey, W.M., & Burton, R.V. (1982). Training children to be consistently honest through verbal self-instructions. *Child Development, 53*, 911–919.

Chamberlin, R.W. (1974). Authoritarian and accommodative child-rearing styles: Their relationships with the behavior patterns of 2-year-old children and with other variables. *Behavioral Pediatrics, 84*, 287–293.

Chandler, M.J. (1973). Egocentrism and antisocial behavior. The assessment and training of social perspective taking skills. *Developmental Psychology, 9*, 326–332.

Chandler, M.J., & Greenspan, S. (1972). Ersatz egocentrism: A reply to H. Borke. *Developmental Psychology, 7*, 104–106.

Chandler, M.J., Greenspan, S., & Barenboim, C. (1974). Assessment and training of role-taking and referential communication skills in institutionalized emotionally disturbed children. *Developmental Psychology, 10*, 546–553.

Chandler, T.A., Wolf, F.M., Cook, B., & Dugovics, D.A. (1980). Parental correlates of locus of control in 5th-graders: An attempt at experimentation in the home. *Merrill-Palmer Quarterly, 26*, 185–195.

Chapman, M., & Zahn-Waxler, C. (1982). Young children's compliance and non-compliance to parental discipline in a natural setting. *International Journal of Behavioural Development, 5*, 81–94.

Charlesworth, R., & Hartup, W.W. (1967). Positive social reinforcement in the nursery school peer group. *Child Development, 38*, 993–1002.

Cherlin, A. (1978). Remarriage as an incomplete institution. *American Journal of Sociology, 84*, 634–650.

Cherry, L. (1975). The preschool teacher-child dyad: Sex differences in verbal interaction. *Child Development, 46*, 532–535.

Cherry, L., & Lewis, M. (1976). Mothers and two-year-olds: A study of sex-differentiated aspects of verbal interaction. *Developmental Psychology*, *12*, 278–282.

Cheyne, J.A., & Walters, R.H. (1969). Intensity of punishment, timing of punishment, and cognitive structure as determinants of response inhibition. *Journal of Experimental Child Psychology*, *7*, 231–244.

Children's Bureau, United States Department of Health, Education, and Welfare (1914 and later). *Infant Care*. Washington, DC.

Cialdini, R.B., & Kenrick, D.T. (1976). Altruism as hedonism. A social development perspective on the relationship of negative mood state and helping. *Journal of Personality and Social Psychology*, *34*, 907–914.

Cialdini, R.B., Kenrick, D.T., & Baumann, D.J. (1982). Effects of mood on prosocial behavior in children and adults. In N. Eisenberg (Ed.), *The development of prosocial behavior* (pp. 339–359). New York: Academic Press.

Clark, A.H., Wyon, S.M., & Richards, M.P.M. (1969). Free play in nursery school children. *Journal of Child Psychology and Psychiatry*, *10*, 205–216.

Clarke, A.M., & Clarke, A.D.B. (Eds.). (1976). *Early experience: Myth and evidence*. London: Open Books.

Clarke-Stewart, A.K. (1973). Interactions between mothers and their young children: Characteristics and consequences. *Monographs of the Society for Research in Child Development*, *38*, (6–7, Serial No. 153).

Clarke-Stewart, A.K. (1978). And daddy makes three: The father's impact on mother and young child. *Child Development*, *49*, 466–478.

Clarke-Stewart, A.K. (1984). Daycare: A new context for research and development. In M. Perlmutter (Ed.), *Minnesota Symposia on Child Psychology* (Vol. 17, pp. 61–100). Hillsdale, New Jersey: Lawrence Erlbaum Associates.

Clarke-Stewart, A.K., & Apfel, N. (1978). Evaluating parental effects on child development. In L.S. Shulman (Ed.), *Review of Research in Education*, *6*, 49–119.

Clarke-Stewart, A.K., Friedman, S., & Koch, J. (1985). *Child development: A topical approach*. New York: John Wiley & Sons.

Clausen, J.A. (Ed.), (1968). *Socialization and society*. Boston: Little, Brown & Co.

Clingempeel, W.G., Brand, E., & Ievoli, R. (1984). Stepparent-stepchild relationships in stepmother and stepfather families: A multimethod study. *Family Relations*, *33*, 465–473.

Clingempeel, W.G., & Reppucci, N.D. (1982). Joint custody after divorce: Major issues and goals for research. *Psychological Bulletin*, *91*, 102–127.

Clingempeel, W.G., & Segal, S. (1986). Psychological adjustment of children in stepmother and stepfather families. *Child Development*, *57*, 474–484.

Cloninger, C.R., & Reich, T. (1983). Genetic heterogeneity in alcoholism and sociopathy. In S.S. Kety, L.P. Rowland, R.L. Sidman, & S.W. Matthysse (Eds.), *Genetics of neurological and psychiatric disorders* (pp. 145–166). New York: Raven Press.

Clore, G.L. (1975). *Interpersonal attraction: An overview*. Morristown, NJ: General Learning Press.

Cohen, D.J., Dibble, E., & Grawe, J.M. (1977). Parental style: Mothers' and fathers' perceptions of their relations with twin children. *Archives of General Psychiatry*, *34*, 445–451.

Coie, J.D., & Krehbiehl, G. (1984). Effects of academic tutoring on the social status of low-achieving, socially rejected children. *Child Development*, *55*, 1465–1478.

Coie, J.D., & Dodge, K.A. (1983). Continuities and changes in children's social status: A five-year longitudinal study. *Merrill-Palmer Quarterly*, *29*, 261–282.

Coie, J.D., & Kupersmidt, J.B.A. (1983). Behavioral analysis of emerging social status in boys' groups. *Child Development*, *54*, 1400–1416.

Coie, J.D., & Krehbiehl, G. (1984). Effects of academic tutoring on the social status of low-achieving, socially rejected children. *Child Development*, *55*, 1465–478.

Colby, A., Kohlberg, L., Gibbs, J., & Lieberman, M. (1983). A longitudinal study of moral judgment. *Monographs of the Society for Research in Child Development*, *48* (1–2, Serial No. 200).

Coleman, J.S. (1961). *The adolescent society*. New York: The Free Press.

Coleman, J.S., Campbell, E.Q., Hobson, C.J., McPartland, J., Mood M., Weinfeld, F.D., & York, R.L. (1966). *Equality of educational opportunity*. Washington, DC: U.S. Government Printing Office.

Colletta, N.D. (1978). Divorced mothers at two income levels: Strees, support and child-rearing practices. Unpublished thesis, Cornell University, New York.

Collins, W.A. (1973). Effect of temporal separation between motivation, aggression, and consequences: A developmental study. *Developmental Psychology*, *8*, 215–221.

Collins, W.A., Berndt, T.V., & Hess, V.L. (1974). Observational learning of motives and consequences for television aggression: A developmental study. *Child Development*, *65*, 799–802.

Collins, W.A., & Zimmermann, S.A. (1975). Convergent and divergent social cues: Effects of televised aggression on children. *Communication Research*, *2*, 331–346.

Collis, G.M., & Schaffer, H.R. (1975). Synchronization of visual attention in mother-infant pairs. *Journal of Child Psychology and Psychiatry*, *16*, 315–320.

Condry, J., & Siman, M.L. (1974). Characteristics of peer- and adult-oriented children. *Journal of Marriage and the Family*, *36*, 543–554.

Connor, J.M., & Serbin, L.A. (1977). Behaviorally-based masculine and feminine-activity-preference scales for preschoolers: Correlation with other classroom behaviors and cognitive tests. *Child Development*, *48*, 1411–1416.

Cook, T.D., & Campbell, D.T. (1979). *Quasi-experimentataion: Design and analysis issues for field settings*. Chicago: Rand McNally.

Cooley, C.H. (1902). *Human nature and the social order*. New York: Charles Scribners.

Coopersmith, S. (1967). *The antecedents of self-esteem*. San Francisco: W.H. Freeman.

Corah, N.L., Anthony, E.J., Painter, P., Stern, J.A., & Thurston, D.L. (1965). Effects of perinatal anoxia after seven years. *Psychological Monographs*, *79*, 3 (Whole No. 596).

Corbett, J. (1977). Mental retardation—psychiatric aspects. In M. Rutter & L. Hersov (Eds.), *Child psychiatry: modern approaches*, Oxford: Blackwell Scientific Publications.

Corsaro, W.A. (1981). Friendship in the nursery school: Social organization in a peer environment. In S.R. Asher & J.M. Gottman (Eds.), *The development of children's friendships* (pp. 207–241). Cambridge: Cambridge University Press.

Costanzo, P., Grumet, J., & Brehm, S. (1974). The effects of choice and source of constraint on children's attribution of preference. *Journal of Experimental Social Psychology*, *10*, 352–364.

Crano, W. (1977). What do infant mental tests test? A cross-lagged panel analysis of selected data from the Berkeley Growth Study *Child Development*, *48*, 144–151.

Crockenberg, S. (1981). Infant irritability, mother responsiveness and social-support influences on the security of infant-mother attachment. *Child Development*, *52*, 857–865.

Crosbie-Burnett, M. (1984). The centrality of the step relationship: A challenge to family theory and practice. *Family Relations*, *33*, 459–463.

Cummings, E.M. (1980). Caregiver stability and day care. *Developmental Psychology*, *16*, 31–37.

Cummings, E.M., Hollenbeck, B., Iannotti, R., Radke-Yarrow, M., & Zahn-Waxler, C. (1986). Early organization of altruism and aggression: Developmental patterns and individual differences. In C. Zahn-Waxler, E.M. Cummings, & R. Iannotti (Eds.), *Altruism and aggression* (pp. 165–188). New York: Cambridge University Press.

Daly, M., & Wilson, M. (1983). *Sex, evolution and behavior*. Boston: PWS Publishers.

Damon, W. (1977). *The social world of the child*. San Francisco: Jossey-Bass.

Damon, W. (1980). Patterns of change in children's social reasoning: A two-year longitudinal study, *Child Development*, *51*, 1010–1017.

Damon, W. (1983). *Social and personality development*. New York: W.W. Norton & Co.

D'Andrade, R.G. (1966). Sex differences and cultural institutions. In E.E. Maccoby (Ed.), *The development of sex differences* (pp. 173–203). Stanford: Stanford University Press.

Daniels, D., Dunn, J., Furstenberg, F.F., & Plomin, R. (1985). Environmental differences within the family and adjustment differences within pairs of adolescent siblings. *Child Development*, *56*, 764–774.

Daniels, D., & Plomin, R. (1985). Origins of individual differences in infant shyness. *Developmental Psychology*, *21*, 118–121.

Darwin, C. (1872). *The expression of emotion in man and animals*. London: John Murray.

Darwin, C. (1877). A biographical sketch of an infant. *Mind*, *2*, 285–294.

Davidson, E.G. (1976). *Gene activity in early development*. New York: Academic Press.

Davis, H.V., Sears, R.R., Miller, H.C., & Brodbeck, A.J. (1948). Effects of cup, bottle, and breast feeding on oral activities of newborn infants. *Pediatrics*, *3*, 549–558.

Dawkins, R. (1976). *The selfish gene*. Oxford: Oxford University Press.

Deaux, K. (1984). From individual differences to social categories: Analysis of a decade's research on gender. *American Psychologist*, *39*, 105–116.

Deaux, K. (1985). Sex and gender. *Annual Review of Psychology*, *36*, 49–81.

Decarie, T.G. (1965). *Intelligence and affectivity in early childhood*. New York: International Universities Press.

de Chateau, P. (1980). Early postpartum contact and later attitudes. *International Journal of Behavioural Development*, *3*, 273–286.

de Chateau, P., & Wiberg, B. (1977). Long-term effect on mother-infant behavior of extra contact during the first hour postpartum. I. First observations at 36 hours. *Acta Pediatrica Scandinavica*, *66*, 137–144.

Dennis, W. (1960). Causes of retardation among institutional children: Iran. *Journal of Genetic Psychology*, *96*, 47–59.

Deutsch, F. (1975). The effects of sex of subject and story character on preschoolers' perceptions of affective responses and interpersonal behavior in story sequences: A question of similarity of person. *Developmental Psychology*, *11*, 112–113.

Devereux, E.C. (1970). The role of peer-group experience in moral development. In J.P. Hill (Ed.), *Minnesota Symposia on Child Psychology* (Vol. 4, pp. 94–140). Minneapolis: University of Minnesota Press.

Devereux, E.C., Bronfenbrenner, U., & Rodgers, R.R. (1969). Child-rearing in England and the United States: A cross-national comparison. *Journal of Marriage and the Family*, *32*, 257–270.

Devereux, E.C., Jr., Bronfenbrenner, U., & Suci, G.J. (1962). Patterns of parent behavior in the United States of America and the Federal Republic of Germany: A cross-national comparison. *International Social Science Journal*, *14*, 488–506.

Dion, K.K., & Stein, S. (1978). Physical attractiveness and interpersonal influence. *Journal of Experimental Social Psychology*, *14*, 97–108.

DiVitto, B., & McArthur, L.Z. (1978). Developmental differences in the use of distinctiveness, consensus, and consistency information for making causal attributions. *Developmental Psychology*, *14*, 474–482.

Dix, T.H., & Grusec, J.E. (1983a). Parent attribution processes in child socialization. In I. Sigel (Ed.), *Parental belief systems: Their psychological consequences for children* (pp. 201–233). Hillsdale, NJ: Lawrence Erlbaum Associates.

Dix, T.H., & Grusec, J.E. (1983b). Parental influence techniques: An attributional analaysis. *Child Development*, *54*, 645–652.

Dlugokinski, E.L., & Firestone, I.J. (1974). Other centeredness and susceptibility to charitable appeals: Effects of perceived discipline. *Developmental Psychology*, *10*, 21–28.

Dodge, K.A. (1980). Social cognition and children's aggressive behavior. *Child Development*, *51*, 162–170.

Dodge, K.A. (1983). Behavioral antecedents of peer social status. *Child Development*, *54*, 1386–1399.

Dodge, K.A. (1985). A social informational processing model of social competence in children. In M. Perlmutter (Ed.), *Minnesota Symposium on Child Psychology* (pp. 77–125). Hillsdale, NJ: Lawrence Erlbaum Associates.

Dodge, K.A. (1986). Social information-processing variables in the development of aggression and altruism in children. In C. Zahn-Waxler, E.M. Cummings, & R. Iannotti (Eds.), *Altruism and aggression*. New York: Cambridge University Press.

Dodge, K.A., & Tomlin, A. (1983). *The role of cue-utilization in attributional biases among aggressive children*. Unpublished manuscript, Indiana University.

Dollard, J., Doob, L.W., Miller, N.E., Mowrer, O.H., & Sears, R.R. (1939). *Frustration and aggression*. New Haven: Yale University Press.

Dollard, J., & Miller, N.E. (1950). *Personality and psychotherapy: An analysis in terms of learning, thinking, and culture*. New York: McGraw-Hill.

Douglas, V., Parry, P., Martin, P., & Carson, C. (1976). Assessment of a cognitive training program for hyperactive children. *Journal of Abnormal Child Psychology*, *4*, 389–410.

Douvan, E., & Adelson, J. (1966). *The adolescent experience*. New York: John

Wiley & Sons.

Dowdney, L., Skuse, D., Rutter, M., Quinton, D., & Mrazek, D. (1985). The nature and qualities of parenting provided by women raised in institutions. *Journal of Child Psychology and Psychiatry*, *26*, 599–625.

Drabman, R.S., & Thomas, M.H. (1974). Does media violence increase children's toleration of real-life aggression? *Developmental Psychology*, *10*, 418–421.

Dreman, S.B., & Greenbaum, C.W. (1973). Altruism or reciprocity: Sharing behavior in Israeli kindergarten children. *Child Development*, *44*, 61–68.

Drillien, C.M. (1964). *The growth and development of the prematurely born infant.* Baltimore: Williams and Wilkins.

Dunn, J. (1983). Sibling relationships in early childhood. *Child Development*, *54*, 787–811.

Dunn, J., & Kendrick, C. (1980). Studying temperament and parent-child interaction: Comparison of interview and direct observation. *Developmental Medicine and Child Neurology*, *22*, 484–496.

Dunn, J., & Kendrick, C. (1982a). Temperamental differences, family relationships and young children's response to change within the family. In Ciba Foundation Symposium 89. *Temperamental differences in infants and young children* (pp. 87–105). London: Pitman.

Dunn, J., & Kendrick, C. (1982b). *Siblings: Love, envy and understanding.* Cambridge: Harvard University Press.

Durbin, E.F.M., & Bowlby, J. (1939). Personal aggressiveness and war. In E.F.M. Durbin, & G. Catlin (Eds.), *War and democracy.* London: Kegan, Paul, Trench, Trubner.

Dweck, C.S. (1986). Motivational processes affecting learning. *American Psychologist*, *41*, 1040–1048.

Dworkin, R.H. (1977). *Genetic and environmental influences on person-situation interactions.* Paper presented at the meeting of Behavior Genetics Association, Louisville, KY.

Dworkin, R.H., Burke, B.W., Maher, B.A., & Gottesman, I.I. (1977) Genetic influences on the organization and development of personality. *Developmental Psychology*, *13*, 512–521.

Eagly, A.H., & Carli, L.L. (1981). Sex of researchers and sex-typed communications as determinants of sex differences in influenceability: A meta-analysis of social influence studies. *Psychological Bulletin*, *90*, 1–20.

Eaves, L.J., & Eysenck, H.J. (1975). The nature of extraversion: A genetical analysis. *Journal of Personality and Social Psychology*, *32*, 102–112.

Edwards, C.P., & Lewis, M. (1979). Young children's concepts of social relations: Social functions and social objects. In M. Lewis & L.A. Rosenblum (Eds.), *The child and its family* (pp. 245–266). New York: Plenum Press.

Egeland, B., & Farber, E.A. (1984): Infant-mother attachment: factors related to its development and changes over time. *Child Development*, *55*, 753–771.

Egeland, B., & Sroufe, L.A. (1981). Attachment and maltreatment. *Child Development*, *52*, 44–52.

Egeland, B., Sroufe, A., & Erickson, M. (1983). The developmental consequences of different patterns of maltreatment. *Child Abuse and Neglect*, *7*, 459–469.

Ehrhardt, A. (1973). Maternalism in fetal hormonal and related syndromes. In J. Zubin & J. Money (Eds.), *Contemporary sexual behavior: Critical issues in the 1970s* (pp. 99–115). Baltimore, MD: Johns Hopkins University Press.

Ehrhardt, A.A., & Baker, S.W. (1974). Fetal androgens, human central nervous system differentiation and behavior sex differences. In R. Richart, R. Friedman, & R. VandeWiele (Eds.), *Sex differences in behavior*. New York: John Wiley & Sons.

Eisenberg, N. (1982). The development of reasoning regarding prosocial behavior. In N. Eisenberg (Ed.), *The development of prosocial behavior* (pp. 219–249). New York: Academic Press.

Eisenberg, N., Cameron, E., Tryon, K., & Dodez, R. (1981). Socialization of prosocial behavior in the preschool classroom. *Developmental Psychology, 17*, 773–782.

Eisenberg, N., & Lennon, R. (1983). Sex differences in empathy and related capacities. *Psychological Bulletin, 94*, 100–131.

Eisenberg, N., Lennon, R., & Roth, K. (1983). Prosocial development: A longitudinal study. *Developmental Psychology, 19*, 846–855.

Eisenberg, N., & Miller, P.A. (1987). The relation of empathy to prosocial and related behaviors. *Psychological Bulletin, 101*, 91–119.

Eisenberg, N., Pasternack, J.F., Cameron, E., & Tryon, K. (1984). The relation of quantity and mode of prosocial behavior to moral cognitions and social style. *Child Development, 55*, 1479–1485.

Eisenberg-Berg, N. (1979). Development of children's prosocial moral judgment. *Developmental Psychology, 15*, 128–137.

Eisenberg-Berg, N., & Hand, M. (1979). The relationship of preschoolers' reasoning about prosocial moral conflicts to prosocial behavior. *Child Development, 50*, 356–363.

Eisenberg-Berg, N., & Neal, C. (1979). Children's moral reasoning about their own spontaneous prosocial behavior. *Developmental Psychology, 15*, 228–229.

Ekman, P. (1972). Universal and cultural differences in facial expression of emotion. *Nebraska Symposium on Motivation, 1971* (pp. 207–283). Lincoln: University of Nebraska Press.

Ekman, P., & Oster, H. (1979). Facial expressions of emotion. *Annual Review of Psychology, 30*, 527–554.

Ekstein, R. (1978). Psychoanalysis, sympathy, and altruism. In L. Wispe (Ed.), *Altruism, sympathy, and helping: Psychological and sociological principles* (pp. 165–175). New York: Academic Press.

Elliot, R., & Vasta, R. (1970). The modeling of sharing: Effects associated with vicarious reinforcement, symbolization, age, and generalization. *Journal of Experimental Child Psychology, 10*, 8–15.

Emde, R.N., Gaensbauer, T., & Harmon, R. (1976). Emotional expression in infancy: A biobehavioral study. *Psychological Issues Monograph, 10* (Serial No. 37).

Eme, R.F. (1979). Sex differences in childhood psychopathology: A review. *Psychological Bulletin, 86*, 574–595.

Emery, R.E. (1982). Interparental conflict and the children of discord and divorce. *Psychological Bulletin, 92*, 310–330.

Emmerich, W. (1977). Structure and development of personal-social behaviors in economically disadvantaged preschool children. *Genetics Psychology Monograph, 95*, 191–245.

Endler, N.S., & Magnusson, D. (1976). Toward an interactional psychology of personality. *Psychological Bulletin, 83*, 956–974.

Erikson, E.H. (1950). *Childhood and society*. New York: W.W. Norton & Co.

Eron, L.D., Banta, T.J., Walder, L.O., & Laulicht, J.H. (1961). Comparison of data obtained from mothers and fathers on child rearing practices. *Child Development*, *32*, 457–472.

Eron, L.D., Huesmann, L.R., Lefkowitz, M.M., & Walder, L.O. (1972). Does television violence cause aggression? *American Psychologist*, *27*, 253–263.

Eron, L.D., Walder, L.L., Huesmann, L.R., & Lefkowitz, M.M. (1974). The convergence of laboratory and field studies of the development of aggression. In J. De Wit and W.W. Hartup (Eds.), *Determinants and origins of aggressive behavior* (pp. 347–380). The Hague: Mouton.

Erwin, J., & Kuhn, D. (1979). Development of children's understanding of the multiple determination underlying human behavior. *Developmental Psychology*, *15*, 352–353.

Etaugh, C., & Harlow, H. (1975). Behaviors of male and female teachers as related to behaviors and attitudes of elementary school children. *Journal of Genetic Psychology*, *127*, 163–170.

Etaugh, C., & Hughes, V. (1975). Teachers' evaluations of sex-typed behaviors in children: The role of teacher and sex and school setting. *Developmental Psychology*, *11*, 394–395.

Eysenck, H.J. (1976). The biology of morality. In T. Lickona (Ed.), *Moral development and behavior* (pp. 108–123). Holt, Rinehart, & Winston.

Fagot, B.I. (1977a). Consequences of moderate cross-gender behavior in preschool children. *Child Development*, *48*, 902–907.

Fagot, B.I. (1977b). *Preschool sex stereotyping: Effect of sex of teacher vs. training of teacher*. Paper presented at the Biennial Meeting of the Society for Research in Child Development, New Orleans, LA.

Fagot, B.I. (1978). The influence of sex of child on parental reactions to toddler children. *Child Development*, *49*, 459–465.

Fagot, B.I. (1985). Beyond the reinforcement principle: Another step toward understanding sex role development. *Developmental Psychology*, *21*, 1097–1104.

Fagot, B.I., & Patterson, G.R. (1969). An in vivo analysis of reinforcing contingencies for sex-role behaviors in the preschool child. *Developmental Psychology*, *1*, 563–568.

Faust, D., & Arbuthnot, J. (1978). Relationship between moral and Piagetian reasoning and the effectiveness of moral education. *Developmental Psychology*, *14*, 435–436.

Faust, M.S. (1960). Developmental maturity as a determinant of prestige in adolescent girls. *Child Development*, *31*, 173–184.

Feinberg, M.R., Smith, M., & Schmidt, R. (1958). An analysis of expressions used by adolescents of varying economic levels to describe accepted and rejected peers. *Journal of Genetic Psychology*, *93*, 133–148.

Feinman, S., & Lewis, M. (1983). Social referencing at ten months: A second-order effect on infants' responses. *Child Development*, *54*, 878–887.

Feiring, C., & Lewis, M. (1978). The child as a member of the family system. *Behavioral Science*, *23*, 225–233.

Feldman, N.S., & Ruble, D.N. (1981). The development of person perception: Cognitive versus social factors. In S.S. Brehm, S.M. Kassin, & F.X. Gibbons (Eds.), *Developmental social psychology* (pp. 191–206). New York: Oxford University Press.

Feldman, S.S., & Nash, S.C. (1979). Changes in responsiveness to babies during adolescence. *Child Development*, *50*, 942–949.

Feshbach, N.D. (1974). The relationship of child-rearing factors to children's aggression, empathy and related positive and negative social behaviors. In J. De Wit & W.W. Hartup (Eds.), *Determinants and origins of aggressive behavior* (pp. 427–436). The Hague: Mouton.

Feshbach, N.D. (1982). Sex differences in empathy and social behavior in childen. In N. Eisenberg (Ed.), *The development of prosocial behavior* (pp. 315–338). New York: Academic Press.

Feshbach, N.D., & Roe, K. (1968). Empathy in six- and seven-year-olds. *Child Development, 39*, 133–145.

Feshbach, S. (1956). The catharsis hypothesis and some consequences of interaction with aggressive and neutral play objects. *Journal of Personality, 24*, 449–462.

Feshbach, S. (1970). Aggression. In P.H. Mussen (Ed.), *Carmichael's manual of child psychology* (3rd ed., Vol. 2, pp. 159–259). New York: John Wiley & Sons.

Feshbach, S., & Feshbach, N.D. (1986). Aggression and altruism: A personality perspective. In C. Zahn-Waxler, E.M. Cummings, & R. Iannotti (Eds.), *Altruism and aggression* (pp. 189–217). New York: Cambridge University Press.

Feshbach, S., & Singer, R.D. (1971). *Television and aggression: An experimental field study*. San Francisco: Jossey-Bass.

Field, T. (1978). Interaction behaviors of primary versus secondary caretaker fathers. *Developmental Psychology, 14*, 183–184.

Field, T.M. (1980). Interactions of preterm and term infants with their lower- and middle-class teen age and adult mothers. In T.M. Field, S. Goldberg, D. Stern, & A.M. Sostek (Eds.), *High-risk infants and children: Adult and peer interactions* (pp. 113–132). New York: Academic Press.

Field, T.M., Dempsey, J.R., & Shuman, H.H. (1981). Developmental follow-up of pre- and postterm infants. In S.L. Friedman & M. Sigman (Eds.), *Preterm birth and psychological development*. New York: Academic Press.

Fishbein, H.D., Lewis, S., & Keiffer, K. (1972). Children's understanding of spatial relations: Coordination of perspectives. *Developmental Psychology, 7*, 21–33.

Fisher, J.F., Nadler, A., & Whitcher-Alagna, S. (1982). Recipient reactions to aid. *Psychological Bulletin, 91*, 27–54.

Fisher, S.F. (1973). *The female organism: Psychology, physiology, fantasy*. New York: Basic Books.

Flapan, D. (1968). *Children's understanding of social interaction*. New York: Teachers College Press.

Flavell, J.H. (1963). *The developmental psychology of Jean Piaget*. Princeton, NJ: Van Nostrand & Co.

Flavell, J.H. (1974). The development of inferences about others. In T. Mischel (Ed.), *Understanding other persons*. Totowa, NJ: Rowman & Littlefield.

Flavell, J.H. (1977). *Cognitive development*. Englewood Cliffs, NJ: Prentice-Hall.

Flavell, J.H. (1985). *Cognitive development*. Englewood Cliffs, NJ: Prentice-Hall.

Flavell, J.H., Botkin, P.T., Fry, C.L., Jr., Wright, J.W., & Jarvis, P.E. (1968). *The development of roletaking and communication skills in children*. New York: John Wiley & Sons.

Flavell, J.H., Shipstead, S.G., & Croft, K. (1978). Young children's knowledge about visual perception: Hiding objects from others. *Child Development, 49*, 1208–1211.

Fortune, W.W. (1939). Arapesh warfare. *American Anthropologist, 41*, 22–41.

Fouts, G., & Atlas, P. (1979). Stranger distress: Mother and stranger as reinforcers. *Infant Behavior and Development, 2*, 309–318.

Freedman, D.G. (1974). *Human infancy: An evolutionary perspective.* Hillsdale, NJ: Lawrence Erlbaum Associates.

Freedman, J.L. (1984). Effects of television violence on aggressiveness. *Psychological Bulletin, 96*, 227–246.

Freedman, J.L. (1986). Television violence and aggression: A rejoinder. *Psychological Bulletin, 100*, 372–378.

Freedman, L.S., Werthmann, M.W., Jr., & Waxler, M. (1983). *Physiologic jaundice as a predictor of sensory, neurological and affective function in low risk preterm infants.* Paper presented at the Biennial Meeting of the Society for Research in Child Development, Detroit.

Freeman, D. (1983). *Margaret Mead and Samoa: The making and unmaking of an anthropological myth.* Cambridge: Harvard University Press.

Freud, A., & Dann, S. (1951). An experiment in group upbringing. *Psychoanalytic Study of the Child, 6*, 127–168.

Freud, S. (1925). *Collected papers.* London: Hogarth Press.

Freud, S. (1927). *Beyond the pleasure principle.* New York: Boni and Liveright.

Freud, S. (1930). *Three contributions to the theory of sex.* New York: Nervous and Mental Disease Publishing Co. (original work published 1905).

Freud, S. (1933/1937). *New introductory lectures on psychoanalysis.* London: Hogarth Press and Institute of Psychoanalysis.

Freud, S. (1959). Formulations regarding the two principles in mental functioning. In *Collected papers* (Vol. 4). New York: Basic Books.

Freundl, P.C. (1977). When is aggression assertive? Unpublished doctoral dissertation, University of California, Los Angeles.

Friedrich, L.K., & Stein, A.H. (1973). Aggressive and prosocial television programs and the natural behavior of preschool children. *Monographs of the Society for Research in Child Development, 38* (Serial No. 151).

Frisch, H.L. (1977). Sex stereotypes in adult-infant play. *Child Development, 48*, 1671–1675.

Frodi, A.M. (1981). Contributions of infant characteristics to child abuse. *American Journal of Mental Deficiency, 85*, 341–349.

Frodi, A.M., & Lamb, M.E. (1978). Sex differences in responsiveness to infants: A developmental study of psychophysiological and behavioral responses. *Child Development, 49*, 1182–1188.

Fullard, W., & Reiling, A.M. (1976). An investigation of Lorenz's "babyness." *Child Development, 47*, 1191–1193.

Fuller, J.L., & Thompson, W.R. (1978). *Foundations of behavior genetics* (2nd ed.). St. Louis, Missouri: C.V. Mosby & Co.

Furman, W., & Masters, J.C. (1980). Peer interactions, sociometric status, and resistance to deviation in young children. *Developmental Psychology, 16*, 229–236.

Furman, W., Rahe, D.F., & Hartup, W.W. (1979). Rehabilitation of socially withdrawn preschool children through mixed-age and same-age socialization. *Child Development, 50*, 915–922.

Furstenberg, F.F. (1980). Reflections on remarriage. *Journal of Family Issues, 1*, 443–453.

Furstenberg, F.F., & Nord, C.W. (1985). Parenting apart: Patterns of childrearing after marital disruption. *Journal of Marriage and the Family*, *47*, 893–904.

Gaensbauer, T.J., Schultz, L., & Connell, J.P. (1983). Emotion and attachment: Interrelationships in a structured laboratory paradigm. *Developmental Psychology*, *19*, 815–831.

Gallup, G.G. (1977). Self-recognition in primates: A comparative approach to the bidirectional properties of consciousness. *American Psychologist*, *32*, 329–338.

Gamble, T.J., & Zigler, E. (1986). Effects on infant day care: Another look at the evidence. *American Journal of Orthopsychiatry*, *56*, 26–42.

Ganong, L.H., & Coleman, M. (1984). The effects of remarriage on children: A review of the empirical literature. *Family Relations*, *33*, 389–406.

Garbarino, J. (1976). A preliminary study of some ecological correlates of child abuse: The impact of socioeconomic stress on mothers. *Child Development*, *47*, 178–185.

Garbarino, J., & Crouter,A. (1978). Defining the community context for parent-child relations: The correlates of child maltreatment. *Child Development*, *49*, 604–616.

Garbarino, J., & Sherman, D. (1980). High-risk neighborhoods and high-risk families: The human ecology of child maltreatment. *Child Development*, *51*, 188–198.

Garcia, J., & Koelling, R.A. (1966). The relation of cue to consequence in avoidance learning. *Psychonomic Science*, *4*, 123–124.

Gardner, W., & Thompson, R.A. (1983). *A cluster-analytic evaluation of the strange-situation classification system*. Paper presented at the Biennial Meeting of the Society for Research in Child Development, Detroit.

Gelfand, D.M., Hartmann, D.P., Lamb, A.K., Smith, C.L., Mahan, M.A., & Paul, S.C. (1974). The effects of adult models and described alternatives on children's choice of behavior management techniques. *Child Development*, *45*, 585–593.

Gelman, R., & Spelke, E. (1981). The development of thoughts about animate and inanimate objects: Implications for research on social cognition. In J.H. Flavell & L. Ross (Eds.), *Social cognitive development: Frontiers and possible futures* (pp. 43–63). New York: Cambridge University Press.

George, C., & Main, M. (1979). Social interactions of young abused children: Approach, avoidance, and aggression. *Child Development*, *50*, 306–318.

Gerard, H.B. (1983). School desegregation: The social science role. *American Psychologist*, *38*, 869–877

Gerbner, G., Gross, L., Morgan, M., & Signorielli, N. (1980). The mainstreaming of America. *Journal of Communication*, *30*, 12–29.

Gergen, K.J. (1973). Social psychology as history. *Journal of Personality and Social Psychology*, *26*, 309–320.

Gerson, M. (1978). *Family, women, and socialization in the Kibbutz*. Lexington, MA: Lexington Books.

Gewirtz, J.L. (1954). Three determinants of attention-seeking in young children. *Monographs of the Society for Research in Child Development*, *19* (2, Serial No. 59).

Gewirtz, J.L. (1965). The course of infant smiling in four child-rearing environments in Israel. In B.M. Foss (Ed.), *Determinants of infant behavior*. (Vol. 3, pp. 205–248). New York: John Wiley & Sons.

Gewirtz, J.L. (1972). Attachment, dependence, and a distinction in terms of stimulus control. In J.L. Gewirtz (Ed.), *Attachment and dependency*. New York: John Wiley & Sons.

Gibbs, J.C., Arnold, K.D., & Burkhart, J.E. (1984). Sex differences in the expression of moral judgment. *Child Development, 55*, 1040–1043.

Gill, D.G. (1970). *Violence against children*. Cambridge, Ma: Harvard University Press.

Gilligan, C. (1977). In a different voice: Women's conceptions of self and of morality. *Harvard Educational Review, 47*, 481–517.

Gilligan, C. (1982). *In a different voice: Psychological theory and women's development*. Cambridge, MA: Harvard University Press.

Ginsburg, H.J., & Miller, S.M. (1982). Sex differences in children's risk-taking behavior. *Child Development, 53*, 426–428.

Glick, J. (1978). Cognition and social cognition: An introduction. In J. Glick & A.K. Clarke-Stewart (Eds.), *The development of social understanding* (pp. 1–9). New York: Gardner Press.

Glick, P.C. (1979). Children of divorced parents in demographic perspective. *Journal of Social Issues, 35*, 170–182.

Glick, P.C. (1984). Marriage, divorce, and living arrangements: Prospective changes. *Journal of Family Issues, 5*, 7–26.

Glueck, S., & Glueck, E.T. (1950). *Unraveling juvenile delinquency*. Cambridge, MA: Harvard University Press.

Gold, D., & Andres, D. (1978a). Relations between maternal employment and development of nursery school children. *Canadian Journal of Behavioural Sciences 10*, 116–129.

Gold, D., & Andres, D. (1978b). Developmental comparisons between 10-year-old children with employed and non-employed mothers. *Child Development, 49*, 75–84.

Goldberg, S. (1983). Parent-infant bonding: Another look. *Child Development, 54*, 1355–1382.

Goldberg, S., Blumberg, S.L., & Kriger, A. (1982). Menarche and interest in infants: Biological and social influences. *Child Development, 53*, 1544–1550.

Goldberg, S., Brachfeld, S., & DiVitto, B. (1980). Feeding, fussing and play: Parent-infant interaction in the first year as a function of prematurity and perinatal medical problems. In T.M. Field, S. Goldberg, D. Stern, & A.M. Sostek (Eds.), *High-risk infants and children: Adult and peer interactions* (pp. 133–153). New York: Academic Press.

Goldberg, W.A., & Easterbrooks, M.A. (1984). Role of mental quality in toddler development. *Developmental Psychology, 20*, 504–514.

Golden, M., Rosenbluth, L., Grossi, M., Policare, H., Freeman, H., & Brownlee, E. (1978). *The New York City Infant Day Care Study*. New York: Medical and Health Research Association of New York City.

Goldfarb, W. (1943). Effects of early institutional care on adolescent personality. *Journal of Experimental Education, 12*, 106.

Goldfarb, W. (1945). Psychological privation in infancy and subsequent adjustment. *American Journal of Orthopsychiatry, 15*, 247.

Goldman, B.D., & Ross, H.S. (1978). Social skills in action: An analysis of early peer games. In J. Glick & K.A. Clark-Stewart (Eds.), *The development of social understanding* (pp. 177–212). New York: Gardner Press.

Goldsmith, H.H. (1983). Genetic influences on personality from infancy to adulthood. *Child Development, 54*, 331–355.

Goldsmith, H.H., & Campos, J.J. (1982). Toward a theory of infant temperament. In R.N. Emde & H.J. Harmon (Eds.), *The development of attachment and affiliative systems* (pp. 161–193). New York: Plenum Press.

Goldsmith, H.H., & Gottesman, I.I. (1981). Origins of variation in behavioral style: A longitudinal study of temperament in young twins. *Child Development, 52*, 91–103.

Goldstein, J., Freud, A., & Solnit, A. (1973). *Beyond the best interests of the child.* New York: Free Press.

Goodenough, F.L. (1931). *Anger in young children.* Minneapolis: University of Minnesota Press.

Goodlad, J.L. (1984). *A place called school.* New York: McGraw-Hill.

Goodnow, J.J. (1984). Parents' ideas about parenting and development: A review of issues and recent work. In M.E. Lamb, A.L. Brown, & B. Rogoff (Eds.), *Advances in developmental psychology*, (Vol. 3, pp. 193–242). Hillsdale, NJ: Lawrence Erlbaum Associates.

Goshen-Gottstein, E.R. (1981). Differential maternal socialization of opposite-sexed twins, triplets and quadruplets. *Child Development, 52*, 1255–1264.

Goslin, D.A. (Ed.) (1969). *Handbook of socialization theory and research.* Chicago: Rand McNally.

Gottesman, I.I. (1966). Genetic variance in adaptive personality traits. *Journal of Child Psychology and Psychiatry, 7*, 199–208.

Gottesman, I.I. (1974). Developmental genetics and ontogenetic psychology: Overdue detente and propositions from a matchmaker. In A.D. Pick (Ed.), *Minnesota Symposium on Child Psychology* (Vol. 8, pp. 55–80). Minneapolis: University of Minnesota Press.

Gottman, J.M. (1983). How children become friends. *Monographs of the Society for Research in Child Development, 48* (3, Serial No. 201).

Gottman, J., Gonso, J., & Rasmussen, B. (1975). Social interaction, social competence, and friendship in children. *Child Development, 45*, 709–718.

Goy, R.W., & Kemnitz, J.W. (1983). Early, persistent, and delayed effects of virilizing substances delivered transplacentally to female rhesus fetuses. In G. Zbinden et al. (Eds.), *Application of behavioral pharmacology in toxicology* (pp. 303–314). New York: Raven Press.

Graham, P., Rutter, M., & George, S. (1973). Temperamental characteristics as predictors of behavior disorders in children. *American Journal of Orthopsychiatry, 43*, 328–339.

Green, F.P., & Schneider, F.W. (1974). Age diffrences in the behavior of boys on three measures of altruism. *Child Development, 45*, 248–251.

Greenberg, M., Crnik, K., Ragozin, A., & Robinson, N. (1983). *Social interaction in preterm and full term mother-infant pairs across the first year of life.* Paper presented at the Biennial Meeting of the Society for Research in Child Development, Detroit.

Greenberg, S., & Formanek, R. (1974). Social class differences in spontaneous verbal interaction. *Child Study Journal, 4*, 143–153.

Greenglass, E. (1972). A cross-cultural study of the relationship between resistance to temptation and maternal communication. *Genetic Psychology Monographs, 86*, 119–139.

Grief, J.B. (1979). Fathers, children and joint custody. *American Journal of Orthopsychiatry*, *49*, 311–319.

Grinder, R.E. (1962). Parental child-rearing practices, conscience, and resistance to temptation of sixth grade children. *Child Development*, *33*, 803–820.

Grossmann, K., & Grossman, K.E (1983). *Cultural and temperamental aspects of infant attachment behavior patterns*. Paper presented at the Meeting of the Society for Research in Child Development, Detroit.

Grossmann, K., Grossmann, K.E., Spangler, G., Suess, G., & Unzner, L. (1985). Maternal sensitivity and newborns' orientation responses as related to quality of attachment in Northern Germany. In I. Bretherton & E. Waters (Eds.), *Growing points of attachment theory and research*. *Monograph of the Society for Research in Child Development*, *50* (1–2, Serial No. 209).

Grossmann, K., Thane, K., & Grossmann, K.E. (1981). Maternal tactual contact of the newborn after various postpartum conditions of mother-infant contact. *Developmental Psychology*, *17*, 158–169.

Grossmann, B., & Wrighter, J. (1948). The relationship between selection-rejection and intelligence, social status, and personality among 6th-grade children. *Sociometry*, *11*, 346–355.

Groves, P.M., & Rebec, G.V. (1976). Biochemistry and behavior: Some central actions of amphetamine and antipsychotic drugs. *Annual Review of Psychology*, *27*, 91–128.

Grusec, J.E. (1971). Power and the internalization of self-denial. *Child Development*, *42*, 93–105.

Grusec, J.E. (1972). Demand characteristics of the modeling experiment: Altruism as a function of age and aggression. *Journal of Personality and Social Psychology*, *22*, 139–148.

Grusec, J.E. (1973). Effects of co-observer evaluations on imitation: A developmental study. *Developmental Psychology*, *8*, 141.

Grusec, J.E. (1982). The socialization of altruism. In N. Eisenberg (Ed.), *The development of prosocial behavior* (pp. 139–166). New York: Academic Press.

Grusec, J.E. (1985). Socializing concern for others in the home. Unpublished manuscript, University of Toronto.

Grusec, J.E., & Abramovitch, R. (1982). Imitation of peers and adults in a natural setting: A functional analysis. *Child Development*, *53*, 636–642.

Grusec, J.E., & Dix, T. (1986). The socialization of altruism. In C. Zahn-Waxler, E.M. Cummings, & R. Iannotti (Eds.), *Altruism and aggression* (pp. 218–237). Cambridge: Cambridge University Press.

Grusec, J.E., Dix, T., & Mills, R. (1982). The effects of type, severity, and victim of children's transgressions on maternal discipline. *Canadian Journal of Behavioural Science*, *14*, 276–289.

Grusec, J.E., & Kuczynski, L. (1980). Direction of effect in socialization: A comparison of the parent's versus the child's behavior as determinants of disciplinary techniques. *Developmental Psychology*, *16*, 1–9.

Grusec, J.E., Kuczynski, L., Rushton, J.P., & Simutis, Z.M. (1978). Modeling, direct instruction, and attributions: Effects on altruism. *Developmental Psychology*, *14*, 51–57.

Grusec, J.E., Kuczynski, L., Rushton, J.P., & Simutis, Z.M. (1979). Learning resistance to temptation through observation. *Developmental Psychology*, *15*, 233–240.

Grusec, J.E., & Mills, R. (1982). The acquisition of self-control. In J. Worell (Ed.), *Psychological development in the elementary years* (pp. 151–183). New York: Academic Press.

Grusec, J.E., & Redler, E. (1980). Attribution, reinforcement, and altruism: A developmental analysis. *Developmental Psychology, 16*, 525–534.

Gunnarson, L. (1978). *Children in day care and family care in Sweden: A follow-up.* Bulletin No. 21, Department of Educational Research, University of Gothenburg.

Gurucharri, C., & Selman, R.L. (1982). The development of interpersonal understanding during childhood. *Child Development, 53*, 924–927.

Haan, N. (1977). *Coping and defending: Processes of self-environment organization.* New York: Academic Press.

Haan, N. (1982). Can research on morality be scientific? *American Psychologist, 37*, 1096–1104.

Haan, N., Weiss, R., & Johnson, V. (1982). The role of logic in moral reasoning and development. *Developmental Psychology, 18*, 245–256.

Hall, J.A. (1978). Gender effects in decoding nonverbal cues. *Psychological Bulletin, 85*, 845–857.

Hall, J.A., & Halberstadt, A.G. (1980). Masculinity and femininity in children: Development of the Children's Personal Attributes Questionnaire. *Developmental Psychology, 16*, 270–280.

Hallinan, M.T. (1981). Recent advances in sociometry. In S.R. Asher & J.M. Gottman (Eds.) *The development of children's friendships* (pp. 91–115). New York: Cambridge University Press.

Halverson, C.F., Jr., & Waldrop, M.F. (1970). Maternal behavior toward own and other preschool children: The problem of "ownness." *Child Development, 41*, 839–845.

Halverson, C.F., & Waldrop, M.F. (1976). Relations between preschool activity and aspects of intellectual and social behavior at age 7½. *Developmental Psychology, 12*, 107–112.

Hamilton, W.D. (1963). The evolution of altruistic behavior. *American Naturalist, 97*, 354–356.

Hamilton, W.D. (1964). The genetical theory of social behavior. *Journal of Theoretical Biology, 7*, 1–59.

Hammond, J. (1979). Children of divorce: A study of self-concept, academic achievement, and attitudes. *Elementary School Journal, 12*, 55–62.

Harlow, H.F. (1958). The nature of love. *American Psychologist, 13*, 673–685.

Harlow, H.F. (1962). The heterosexual affectional system in monkeys. *American Psychologist, 17*, 1–9.

Harlow, H.F., Harlow, M.K., & Suomi, S.J. (1971). From thought to therapy. *Science, 59*, 538–549.

Harper, L.V., & Huie, K.S. (1985). The effects of prior group experience, age and familiarity on the quality and organization of preschoolers' social relationships. *Child Development, 56*, 704–717.

Harper, L.V., & Sanders, K.M. (1975). Preschool children's use of space: Sex differences in outdoor play. *Developmental Psychology, 11*, 119.

Harris, B. (1979). Whatever happened to Little Albert? *American Psychologist, 34*, 151–160.

Harter, S. (1982). Children's understanding of multiple emotions: A cognitive-developmental approach. In W.F. Overton (Ed.), *The relationship between social and cognitive development* (pp. 147–194). Hillsdale, NJ: Lawrence Erlbaum Associates.

Harter, S. (1983). Developmental perspectives on the self-system. In E.M. Hetherington (Ed.), *Carmichael's manual of child psychology* (4th ed., Vol. 4, pp. 275–385). New York: John Wiley & Sons.

Hartig, M., & Kanfer, F. (1973). The role of verbal self-instructions in children's resistance to temptation. *Journal of Personality and Social Psychology, 25,* 259–267.

Hartmann, H., Kris, E., & Lowenstein, R. (1949). Notes on the theory of aggression. In A. Freud (Ed.), *The psychoanalytic study of the child* (Vol. 3). New York: International Universities Press.

Hartshorne, H., & May, M.A. (1928). *Studies in the nature of character. Vol. I: Studies in deceit.* New York: MacMillan.

Hartshorne, H., & May, M.A. (1929). *Studies in the nature of character. Vol. II: Studies in self-control.* New York: MacMillan.

Hartshorne, H., & May, M.A. (1930). *Studies in the nature of character. Vol. III: Studies in the organization of character.* New York: MacMillan.

Hartup, W.W. (1975). The origins of friendship. In M. Lewis & L.A. Rosenblum (Eds.), *Friendship and peer relations* (pp. 11–26). New York: John Wiley & Sons.

Hartup, W.W. (1983). Peer relations. In E.M. Hetherington (Ed.), *Handbook of child psychology: Vol. IV. Socialization, personality, and social development* (pp. 103–196). New York: John Wiley & Sons.

Haskins, R. (1985). Public school aggression among children with varying day-care experience. *Child Development, 56,* 689–703.

Hatfield, J.S., Rau, L.F., & Alpert, R. (1967). Mother-child interaction and the socialization process. *Child Development, 38,* 36–434.

Hay, D.F., & Ross, H.S. (1982). The social nature of early conflict. *Child Development, 53,* 105–113.

Heathers, G. (195). Emotional dependence and independence in nursery school play. *Journal of Genetic Psychology, 87,* 37–57.

Hebb, D.O. (1946). On the nature of fear. *Psychological Review, 53,* 259–276.

Heider, F. (1958). *The psychology of interpersonal relations.* New York: John Wiley & Sons.

Heinicke, C.M., Diskin, S., Ramsey-Klee, D.M., & Given, K. (1983). Pre-birth parent characteristics and family development in the first year of life. *Child Development, 54,* 194–208.

Helson, R. (1966). Personality of women with imaginative and artistic interests: The role of masculinity, originality, and other characteristics in their creativity. *Journal of Personality, 34,* 1–25.

Herndon, A. (1982). Do we know enough about the predominant family form of the 21st century? *Wake Forest,* 36–37.

Hess, R.D. (1970). Social class and ethnic influences on socialization. In P.H. Mussen, (Ed.), *Carmichael's Manual of Child Psychology* (Vol. 2, pp. 457–558). New York: John Wiley & Sons.

Hess, R.D., & Camara, K.A. (1979). Post-divorce family relationships as mediating factors in the consequences of divorce for children. *Journal of Social Issues, 35,* 79–96.

Hess, R., Kashigawi, K., Azuma, H., Price, G.G., & Dickson, W. (1980). Maternal expectations for early mastery of developmental tasks and cognitive and social competence of preschool children in Japan and the United States. *International Journal of Psychology, 15*, 259–272.

Hetherington, E.M. (1972). Effects of father absence on personality development in adolescent daughters. *Developmental Psychology, 7*, 313–326.

Hetherington, E.M. (1979). Divorce: A child's perspective. *American Psychologist, 34*, 851–858.

Hetherington, E.M. (1981). Children and divorce. In R. Henderson (Ed.), *Parent-child interaction: Theory, research, and prospects*. New York: Academic Press.

Hetherington, E.M., Cox, M., & Cox, R. (1978). The aftermath of divorce. In J.H. Stevens, Jr., & M. Matthews (Eds.), *Mother-child, father-child relations* (pp. 149–176). Washington, NAEYC.

Hetherington, E.M., Cox, M., & Cox, R. (1979). The development of children in mother-headed families. In D. Reiss & H.A. Hoffman (Eds.), *The American Family: Dying or developing* (pp. 117–145). New York: Plenum Press.

Hetherington, E.M., Cox, M., & Cox, R. (1982). Effects of divorce on parents and children. In M. Lamb (Ed.), *Nontraditional families* (pp. 233–288). Hillside, NJ: Lawrence Erlbaum Associates.

Hetherington, E.M., Stouwie, R.J., & Ridberg, E. (1971). Patterns of family interaction and child-rearing attitudes related to three dimensions of juvenile delinquency. *Journal of Abnormal Psychology, 78*, 160–176.

Hicks, D.J. (1968). Effects of co-observer's sanctions and adult presence on imitative aggression. *Child Development, 39*, 303–309.

Higgins, E.T., & Bryant, S.L. (1982). Consensus information and the "fundamental attribution error": The role of development and in-group versus out-group knowledge. *Journal of Personality and Social Psychology, 43*, 889–900.

Higgins, E.T., & Parsons, J.E. (1983). Stages as subcultures: Social-cognitive development and the social life of the child. In E.T. Higgins, W.W. Hartup, & D.N. Ruble (Eds.), *Social cognition and social development: A sociocultural perspective* (pp. 15–62). New York: Cambridge University Press.

Hinde, R.A. (1974). *Biological bases of human social behavior*. New York: McGraw-Hill.

Hinde, R.A. (1983). *Biological bases of the mother-child relationship*. Invited address to the Biennial Meeting of the Society for Research in Child Development, Detroit.

Hinde, R.A., Easton, D., Meller, R., & Tamplin, A. (1983). Nature and determinants of preschoolers' differential behaviour to adults and peers. *British Journal of Developmental Psychology, 1*, 3–19.

Hinde, R.A., & Spencer-Booth, Y. (1970). Individual differences in the responses of rhesus monkeys to a period of separation from their mothers. *Journal of Child Psychology and Psychiatry, 11*, 159–176.

Hobbes, T. (1651/1885). *Leviathan*. London: George Routledge & Sons.

Hodges, W.F., & Bloom, B.L. (1984). Parent's report of children's adjustment to marital separation: A longitudinal study. *Journal of Divorce, 8*, 33–50.

Hoffman, L.W. (1972). Early childhood experiences and women's achievement motives. *Journal of Social Issues, 28*, 129–155.

Hoffman, L.W. (1977). Changes in family roles, socialization and sex differences. *American Psychologist, 32*, 644–657.

Hoffman, L.W. (1979). Maternal employment: *American Psychologist, 34,* 859–865.

Hoffman, M.L. (1963). Personality, family structure, and social class as antecedents of parental power assertion. *Child Development, 34,* 869–884.

Hoffman, M.L. (1970a). Conscience, personality, and socialization techniques. *Human Development, 13,* 90–126.

Hoffman, M.L. (1970b). Moral development. In P.H. Mussen (Ed.), *Carmichael's Manual of Child Psychology* (3rd ed., Vol. 2, pp. 261–360). New York: John Wiley & Sons.

Hoffman, M.L. (1971). Identification and conscience development. *Child Development, 42,* 1071–1082.

Hoffman, M.L. (1975a). Developmental synthesis of affect and cognition and its implication for altruistic motivation. *Developmental Psychology, 11,* 607–622.

Hoffman, M.L. (1975b). Altruistic behavior and the parent-child relationship. *Journal of Personality and Social Psychology, 31,* 937–943.

Hoffman, M.L. (1975c). Moral internalization, parental power, and the nature of parent-child interaction. *Developmental Psychology, 11,* 228–239.

Hoffman, M.L. (1977a). Personality and social development. *Annual Review of Psychology, 28,* 295–321.

Hoffman, M.L. (1977b). Sex differences in empathy and related behaviors. *Psychological Bulletin, 84,* 712–722.

Hoffman, M.L. (1981). Pespectives on the difference between understanding people and understanding things. The role of affect. In J.H. Flavell & L. Ross (Eds.), *Social cognitive development: Frontiers and possible futures* (pp. 67–81). New York: Cambridge University Press.

Hoffman, M.L. (1982). Development of prosocial motivation: Empathy and guilt. In N. Eisenberg (Ed.), *Development of prosocial behavior* (pp. 281–313). New York: Academic Press.

Hoffman, M.L., & Saltzstein, H.D. (1967). Parent discipline and the child's moral development. *Journal of Personality and Social Psychology, 5,* 45–57.

Hoffman-Plotkin, D., & Twentyman, C.T. (1984). A multimodal assessment of behavioral and cognitive deficits in abused and neglected preschoolers. *Child Development, 55,* 794–802.

Holstein, C.B. (1976). Irreversible, stepwise sequence in the development of moral judgment: A longitudinal study of males and females. *Child Development, 47,* 51–61.

Horwitz, R.A. (1979). Psychological effects of the "Open Classroom." *Review of Educational Research, 49,* 71–86.

Howes, C. (1983). Patterns of friendship. *Child Development, 54,* 1041–1053.

Hubert, N., Wachs, T.D., Peters-Martin, P., & Gandour, M. (1982). The study of early temperament: Measurement and conceptual issues. *Child Development, 53,* 571–600.

Huesmann, L.R., Eron, L.D., Klein, R., Brice, P., & Fischer,P. (1983). Mitigating the imitation of aggressive behaviors by changing children's attitudes about media violence. *Journal of Personality and Social Psychology, 44,* 899–910.

Huesmann, L.R., Eron, L.D., Lefkowitz, M.M., & Walder, L.O. (1984). Stability of aggression over time and generations. *Developmental Psychology, 20,* 1120–1134.

Huesmann, L.R., Lagerspetz, K., & Eron, L.D. (1984). Intervening variables in the T.V. violence relation: Evidence from two countries. *Developmental Psychology, 20*, 746–775.

Hunt, J. McV. (1961). *Intelligence and experience*. New York: Ronald Press.

Huston, A.C. (1983). Sex-typing. In E.M. Hetherington (Ed.), *Handbook of child psychology, Vol. IV. Socialization, personality and social development* (pp. 387–467). New York: John Wiley & Sons.

Huston, A.C., Carpenter, C.J., Atwater, J.B., & Johnson, L.M. (1986). Gender, adult structuring of activities, and social behavior in middle childhood. *Child Development, 57*, 1200–1209.

Hutchings, B., & Mednick, S.A. (1977). Criminality in adoptees and their adoptive and biological parents: A pilot study. In S.A. Mednick & K.O. Christiansen (Eds.), *Biosocial bases of criminal behavior*, (pp. 127–141). New York: Gardner Press.

Hyde, J.S. (1981). How large are cognitive gender differences? *American Psychologist, 36*, 892–901.

Hyde, J.S. (1984). How large are gender differences in aggression? A developmental meta-analysis. *Developmental Psychology, 20*, 722–736.

Iannotti, R.J. (1978). Effect of role-taking experiences on role-taking, empathy, altruism, and aggression. *Developmental Psychology, 14*, 119–124.

Imamoglu, E.M. (1975). Children's awareness and usage of intention cues. *Child Development, 46*, 39–45.

Isaacs, S. (1932). *The nursery years* (enlarged ed.). London: Routledge & Kegan Paul.

Isen, A.M. (1970). Success, failure, attention, and reaction to others: The warm glow of success. *Journal of Personality and Social Psychology, 15*, 294–301.

Isen, A.M., Horn, N., & Rosenhan, D.L. (1973). Effects of success and failure on children's generosity. *Journal of Personality and Social Psychology, 27*, 239–247.

Isen, A.M., Shalker, T.E., Clark, M., & Karp, L. (1978). Affect, accessibility of material in memory, and behavior: A cognitive loop? *Journal of Personality and Social Psychology, 36*, 1–12.

Israel, A.C., & Brown, M.S. (1979). Effects of directiveness of instructions and surveillance on the production and persistence of children's donations. *Journal of Experimental Child Psychology, 27*, 250–261.

Izard, C.E. (1979). *Maximally discriminative facial movement scoring system*. Unpublished manuscript, University of Delaware.

Jacklin, C.N., & Maccoby, E.E. (1978). Social behavior at 33 months in same-sex and mixed-sex dyads. *Child Development, 49*, 557–569.

Jacobson, G., & Ryder, R.E. (1969). Parental loss and some characteristics of the early marriage relationship. *American Journal of Orthopsychiatry, 39*, 779–787.

Jarvik, L.F., Klodin, V., & Matsuyama, S.S. (1973). Human aggression and the extra Y chromosome—fact or fantasy? *American Psychologist, 28*, 674–682.

Jencks, C.S., Smith, M., Acland, H., Bane, M.J., Cohen, D., Gintis, H. Heyns, B., & Michelson, S. (1972). *Inequality: A reassessment of the effects of family and schooling in America*. New York: Basic Books.

Jensen, L., & Hughston, K. (1971). The effect of training children to make moral judgments that are independent of sanctions. *Developmental Psychology, 5*, 367.

Joffe, J.M. (1969). *Prenatal determinants of behavior*. Oxford: Pergamon Press.

Joffe, L.S. (1981). *The quality of mother-infant attachment and its relationship to compliance with maternal commands and prohibitions*. Paper presented at the

Biennial Meeting of the Society for Research in Child Development, Boston.

Johannesson, I. (1974). Aggressive behavior among school children related to maternal practices in early childhood. In J. Dewit & W.H. Hartup (Eds.), *Determinants and origins of aggressive behavior* (pp. 413–426). The Hague: Mouton.

Johnson-Laird, P.N. (1983). *Mental models*. Cambridge, Massachusetts: Harvard University Press.

Johnston, J., Ettema, J., & Davidson, T. (1980). *An evaluation of freestyle: A television series to reduce sex-role stereotypes*. Report from Center for Research on Utilization of Scientific Knowledge. Institute for Social Research, University of Michigan, Ann Arbor.

Jones, E.E., & Davis, K.E. (1965). From acts to dispositions: The attribution process in person perception. In L. Berkowitz (Ed.), *Advances in experimental social psychology* (Vol. 2, pp. 220–286). New York: Academic Press.

Jones, E.E., & Nisbett, R.E. (1971). *The actor and the observer: Divergent perceptions of the causes of behavior*. Morristown, NJ: General Learning Press.

Jones, H.E. (1955). Perceived differences among twins. *Eugenics Quarterly, 5*, 98–102.

Jones, M.C., & Bayley, N. (1950). Physical maturing among boys as related to behavior. *Journal of Educational Psychology, 41*, 129–148.

Jöreskog, K.G., & Sorbom, P. (1978). *LISREL IV Users Guide*, 93 pages. Chicago: National Educational Research.

Joslyn, W.D. (1973). Androgen-induced social dominance in infant female rhesus monkeys. *Journal of Child Psychology and Psychiatry, 14*, 137–145.

Josselyn, I.M. (1948). *Psychosocial development of children*. New York: Family Service Association of America.

Kadushin, A. (1978). Children in foster families and institutions. In H.S. Maas (Ed.), *Social services research: Review of studies* (pp. 90–148). Washington, DC: National Association of Social Workers.

Kagan, J. (1966). Reflection-impulsivity: The generality and dynamics of conceptual tempo. *Journal of Abnormal Psychology, 71*, 17–24.

Kagan, J. (1974). Discrepancy, temperament and infant distress. In M. Lewis & L.A. Rosenblum (Eds.), *The origins of fear* (pp. 229–248). New York: John Wiley & Sons.

Kagan, J. (1981). *The second year: The emergence of self-awareness*. Cambridge, Massachusetts: Harvard University Press.

Kagan, J. (1982a). The construct of difficult temperament: A reply to Thomas, Chess and Korn. *Merrill-Palmer Quarterly, 28*, 21–24.

Kagan, J. (1982b). *Review of research in infancy*. New York: Grant Foundation Publication.

Kagan, J., Kearsley, R.B., & Zelazo, P.R. (1978). *Infancy: Its place in human development*. Cambridge, Massachusetts: Harvard University Press.

Kagan, J., & Moss, H.A. (1962). *Birth to maturity: A study of psychological development*. New York: John Wiley & Sons.

Kagan, J., Reznick, G.S., Clarke, C., Snidman, N., & Garcia-Coll, C. (1984). Behavioral inhibition to the unfamiliar. *Child Development, 55*, 2212–2225.

Kahneman, D., Slovic, P., & Tversky, A. (1982). *Judgment under uncertainty: Heuristics and biases*. New York: Cambridge University Press.

Kandel, D. (1973). Adolescent marihuana use: Role of parents and peers. *Science, 181*, 1067–1070.

Kandel, D.B., & Lesser, G.S. (1972). *Youth in two worlds*. San Francisco: Jossey-Bass.

Kantrow, R.W. (1937). An investigation of conditioned feeding responses and concomitant adaptive behavior in young infants. *University of Iowa Studies in Child Welfare, 13* (No. 3).

Kaplan, F.K., Eichler, L.S., & Winickoff, S.A. (1980). *Pregnancy, birth and parenthood*. San Francisco: Jossey-Bass.

Karabenick, J.D., & Miller, S.A. (1977). The effects of age, sex, and listener feedback on grade school children's referential communication. *Child Development, 48*, 678–683.

Karniol, R., & Ross, M. (1976). The development of causal attributions in social perception. *Journal of Personality and Social Psychology, 34*, 455–464.

Karniol, R., & Ross, M. (1976). Children's use of a causal attribution schema and the inference of manipulative intentions. *Child Development, 50*, 463–468.

Karoly, P. (1982). Self-management problems in children. In E.J. Mash & L. Terdal (Eds.), *Behavioral assessment of childhood disorders*. New York: Guilford Press.

Kassin, S.M. (1981). From laychild to "layman": Developmental causal attribution. In S.S. Brehm, S.M. Kassin, & F.X. Gibbons (Eds.), *Developmental social psychology* (pp. 169–190). New York: Oxford Univeristy Press.

Kassin, S.M., & Lowe, C.A. (1979). On the development of the augmentation principle: A perceptual approach. *Child Development, 50*, 728–734.

Kelley, H.H. (1967). Attribution theory in social psychology. In D. Levine (Ed.), *Nebraska Symposium on Motivation* (Vol. 15, pp. 192–240). Lincoln: University of Nebraska Press.

Kelley, H.H. (1972). Attribution in social interaction. In E.E. Jones, D.E. Kanouse, H.H. Kelley, R.E. Nisbett, S. Valins, & B. Weiner (Eds.), *Attribution: Perceiving the causes of behavior*. Morristown, NJ: General Learning Press.

Kelley, H.H. (1973). The processes of causal attribution. American Psychologist, *28*, 107–128.

Kelly, G.A. (1955). *A theory of personality: The psychology of personal constructs*. New York: W.W. Norton.

Kelly, J.B., & Wallerstein, J.S. (1976). The effects of parental divorce: Experience of the child in early latency. *American Journal of Orthopsychiatry, 46*, 20–32.

Kelly, P. (1976). The relation of infant's temperament and mother's psychopathology to interactions in early infancy. In K.F. Riegel & J.A. Meacham (Eds.), *The developing individual in a changing world*. (Vol. II, pp. 664–675). Chicago: Aldine Publishing Co.

Kessen, W. (1979). The American child and other cultural inventions. *American Psychologist, 34*, 815–820.

Kett, J.F. (1971). Adolescence and youth in nineteenth-century America. *Journal of Interdisciplinary History, 2*, 283–298.

Kidd, R.F., & Berkowitz, L. (1976). Dissonance, self-concept, and helpfulness. *Journal of Personality and Social Psychology, 33*, 613–622.

King, M. (1971). The development of some intention concepts in young children. *Child Development, 42*, 1145–1152.

Klaus, M., Jerauld, R., Kreger, N., McAlpine, W., Steffa, M., & Kennell, J. (1972). Maternal attachment: Importance of the first postpartum days. *New England Journal of Medicine, 286*, 460–463.

Klaus, M., & Kennell, J. (1982). *Parent-infant bonding*. St. Louis: C.V. Mosby

Klein, M., & Stern, L. (1980). Low birth-weight and the battered child syndrome. In G.J. Williams & J. Money (Eds.), *Traumatic abuse and neglect of children at home* (pp. 200–207). Baltimore: Johns Hopkins University Press.

Klinnert, M.D., Emde, R.N., & Butterfield, L. (1983). *Social referencing: The infant's use of emotional signals from a friendly adult.* Paper presented at the Biennial Meeting of the Society for Research in Child Development, Detroit.

Koblinsky, S.G., Cruse, D.F., & Sugawara, A.I. (1978). Sex role stereotypes and children's memory for story content. *Child Development, 49,* 452–458.

Kohlberg, L. (1966). A cognitive-developmental analysis of children's sex-role concepts and attitudes. In E.E. Maccoby (Ed.), *The development of sex differences* (pp. 82–173). Stanford: Stanford University Press.

Kohlberg, L. (1969). Stage and sequence: The cognitive-developmental approach to socialization. In D.A. Goslin (Ed.), *Handbook of socialization theory and research* (pp. 347–480). Chicago: Rand McNally.

Kohlberg, L. (1970). Education for justice: A modern statement of the Platonic view. In N.F. Sizer & T.R. Sizer (Eds.), *Moral education: Five lectures.* Cambridge, MA: Harvard University Press.

Kohlberg, L. (1971). Stages of moral development as a basis for moral education. In C.M. Beck, B.S. Crittenden, & E.V. Sullivan (Eds.), *Moral education: Interdisciplinary approaches* (pp. 23–92). Toronto: University of Toronto Press.

Kohlberg, L. (1976). Moral stages and moralization: The cognitive-developmental approach. In T. Lickona (Ed.), *Moral development and behavior* (pp. 31–53). New York: Holt, Rinehart, & Winston.

Kohlberg, L. (1980). High school democracy and educating for a just society. In R. Mosher (Ed.), *Moral education: A first generation of research and development* (pp. 20–51). New York: Praeger.

Kohlberg, L., & Kramer, R.B. (1969). Continuities and discontinuities in childhood and adult moral development. *Human Development, 12,* 93–120.

Kohlberg, L., & Zigler, E. (1967). The impact of cognitive maturity on the development of sex-role attitudes in the years 4 to 8. *Genetic Psychology Monographs, 75,* 89–165.

Kohn, M.L. (1977). *Class and conformity, a study in values* (2nd ed.). Chicago: University of Chicago Press.

Kohn, M.L., & Carroll, E.E. (1960). Social class and the allocation of parental responsibilities. *Sociometry, 23,* 372–392.

Kohn, M.L., & Schooler, C. (1973). Occupational experience and psychological functioning: An assessment of reciprocal effects. *American Sociological Review, 38,* 91–118.

Konecni, V.J. (1972). Some effects of guilt on compliance: A field replication. *Journal of Personality and Social Psychology, 23,* 30–32.

Konecni, V.J. (1975). Annoyance, type and duration of postannoyance activity, and aggression: The "cathartic effect." *Journal of Experimental Psychology: General, 104,* 76–102.

Konecni, V.J., & Ebbesen, E.B. (1976). Disinhibition versus the cathartic effect: Artifact and substance. *Journal of Personality and Social Psychology, 34,* 352–365.

Konner, M. (1979). Biological bases of social development. In M.W. Kent & J.E. Rolf (Eds.), *Primary prevention of psychopathology: Vol. 3: Social competence in children* (pp. 97–119). Hanover, NH: University Press of New England.

Konner, M. (1982). Biological aspects of the mother-infant bond. In R.N. Emde & R.J. Harmon (Eds.), *The development of attachment and affiliative systems*. New York: Plenum Press.

Kopp, C.B. (1982). Antecedents of self-regulation: A developmental perspective. *Developmental Psychology, 18*, 199–204.

Kopp, C. (1983). Risk factors in development. In J. Campos & M. Haith (Eds.), *Handbook of Child Psychology* (Vol. 2, pp. 1081–1182). New York: John Wiley & Sons.

Korbin, J.E. (1980). The cultural context of child abuse and neglect. *Child Abuse and Neglect, 4*, 3–13.

Kotelchuck, M. (1972). *The nature of the child's tie to his father*. Unpublished doctoral dissertation, Harvard University.

Kotelchuck, M. (1976). The infant's relationship to the father: Experimental evidence. In M. Lamb (Ed.), *The role of the father in child development* (pp. 329–344). New York: John Wiley & Sons.

Krebs, D. (1982). Altruism—a rational approach. In N. Eisenberg (Ed.), *The development of prosocial behavior* (pp. 53–76). New York: Academic Press.

Krebs, D., & Gilmore, J. (1982). The relationship among the first stages of cognitive development, role-taking abilities, and moral development. *Child Development, 53*, 877–886.

Krebs, D., & Sturrup, B. (1974). Role-taking ability and altruistic behavior in elementary school children. *Personality and Social Psychology Bulletin, 1*, 407–409.

Krentz, M.S. (1983). *Differences between mother-child and caregiver-child attachments of infants in family day care*. Paper presented at Biennial Meeting of the Society for Research in Child Development, Detroit.

Kreutzer, M.A., & Charlesworth, W.R. (1973). *Infants' reactions to different expressions of emotion*. Paper presented at the meeting of the Society for Research in Child Development, Philadelphia.

Kroger, R.O. (1982). Explorations in ethogeny with special reference to the rules of address. *American Psychologist, 37*, 810–820.

Kuczynski, L. (1984). Socialization goals and mother-child interaction: Strategies for long-term and short-term compliance. *Developmental Psychology, 20*, 1061–1073.

Kuhn, D., & Ho, V. (1977). The development of schemes for recognizing additive and alternative effects in a "natural experiment" context. *Developmental Psychology, 13*, 515–516.

Kurdek, L. (1978). Relationship between cognitive perspective-taking and teachers' rating of children's classroom behavior in grades one through four. *Journal of Genetic Psychology, 132*, 21–27.

Kurdek, L.A. (1981). An integrative perspective on children's divorce adjustment. *American Psychologist, 36*, 856–866.

Kurdek, L.A., & Rodgon, M. (1975). Perceptual, cognitive, and affective perspective-taking in kindergarten through sixth-grade children. *Developmental Psychology, 11*, 643–650.

Kurdek, L.A., & Siesky, A.E. (1979). An interview study of parents' perceptions of their children's reactions and adjustments to divorce. *Journal of Divorce, 3*, 5–17.

Labov, W. (1970). The logic of nonstandard English. In F. Williams (Ed.), *Language and poverty: Perspectives on a theme* (pp. 153–189). Chicago: Markham.

Ladd, G.W., & Emerson, E.S. (1984). Shared knowledge in children's friendships. *Developmental Psychology, 20,* 932–940.

Lamb, M.E. (1976). Twelve-month-olds and their parents: Interactions in a laboratory playroom. *Developmental Psychology, 12,* 237–244.

Lamb, M.E. (1977). Father-infant and mother-infant interaction in the first year of life. *Child Development, 48,* 167–181.

Lamb, M.E. (1978a). Influence of the child on marital quality and family interaction during the prenatal, perinatal and infancy periods. In R.M. Lerner & G.B. Spanier (Eds.), *Child influences on marital and family interaction: A life-span perspective* (pp. 137–163). New York: Academic Press.

Lamb, M.E. (1978b). Qualitative aspects of mother- and father-infant attachment. *Infant Behavior and Developmlent, 1,* 265–275.

Lamb, M.E. (1981). Fathers and child development: An integrative overview. In M.E. Lamb (Ed.), *The role of the father in child development* (pp. 1–70). New York: John Wiley & Sons.

Lamb, M.E. (1983). Early mother-neonate contact and the mother-child relationship. *Journal of Child Psychology and Psychiatry, 24,* 487–494.

Lamb, M.E., Frodi, A.M., Hwang, C.P., Frodi, M., & Steinberg, J. (1982). Mother- and father-infant interaction involving play and holding in traditional and non-traditional Swedish families. *Developmental Psychology, 18,* 215–221.

Lamb, M.E., & Roopnarine, J.L. (1979). Peer influences on sex-role development in preschoolers. *Child Development, 50,* 1219–1222.

Lamb, M.E., Thompson, R.A., Gardner, W.P., Charnov, E.L., & Estes, D. (1984). Security of infantile attachment as assessed in the "strange situation": Its study and biological interpretation. *The Behavioral and Brain Sciences, 7,* 127–171.

Lambert, L., Essen, J., & Head, J. (1977). Variations in behavior ratings of children who have been in care. *Journal of Child Psychology and Psychiatry, 18,* 335–346.

Lambert, W.E., Yackley, A., & Hein, R.N. (1971). Child training values of English Canadian and French Canadian parents. *Canadian Journal of Behavioural Science, 3,* 217–236.

Lancaster, J.B. (1976). Play-mothering: The relations between juvenile females and young infants among free-ranging vervet monkeys. In J.S. Bruner, A. Jolly, & K. Sylva (Eds.), *Play: Its role in development and evolution* (pp. 368–382). London: Penguin Books.

Langlois, J.H., & Downs, A.C. (1979). Peer relations as a function of physical attractiveness: The eye of the beholder or behavioral reality? *Child Development, 50,* 409–418.

Langlois, J.H., & Downs, A.C. (1980). Mothers, fathers, and peers as socialization agents of sex-typed play behavior in young children. *Child Development, 51,* 1237–1247.

Leahy, R.L. (1976). Developmental trends in qualified inferences and descriptions of self and others. *Developmental Psychology, 12,* 546–547.

Leahy, R.L. (1979). Development of conceptions of prosocial behavior: Information affecting rewards given for altruism and kindess. *Developmental Psychology, 15,* 34–37.

Leahy, R.L., & Huard, C. (1976). Role taking and self-image disparity in children. *Developmental Psychology, 12,* 504–508.

Lee, C.L., & Bates, J.E. (1985). Mother-child interaction at age two years and perceived difficult temperament. *Child Development, 56,* 1314–1325.

Lempers, J.D., Flavell, E.R., & Flavell, J.H. (1977). The development in very young children of tacit knowledge concerning visual perception. *Genetic Psychology Monographs, 95,* 3–53.

Leon, M. (1984). Rules mothers and sons use to integrate intent and damage information in their moral judgments. *Child Development, 55,* 2106–2113.

Lepper, M.R. (1973). Dissonance, self-perception, and honesty in children. *Journal of Personality and Social Psychology, 25,* 65–74.

Lepper, M.R. (1981). Intrinsic and extrinsic motivation in children: Detrimental effects of superfluous controls. In W.A. Collins (Ed.), *Minneapolis Symposia on Child Psychology* (Vol. 14, pp. 155–214). Minneapolis: University of Minnesota Press.

Lepper, M.R. (1985). Microcomputers in education: Motivational and social issues. *American Psychologist, 40,* 1–18.

Lepper, M.R., Greene, D., & Nisbett, R.E. (1973). Undermining children's intrinsic interest with extrinsic rewards: A test of the "overjustification" hypothesis. *Journal of Personality and Social Psychology, 28,* 129–137.

Lerner, R.M., & Busch-Rossnagel, N. (Eds.), (1981). *Individuals as producers of their development.* New York: Academic Press.

Levitt, E.E. (1971). Research on psychotherapy with children. In A.E. Bergin & S.L. Garfield (Eds.), *Handbook of psychotherapy and behavior change: An empirical analysis* (pp. 474–494). New York: John Wiley & Sons.

Levy, J. (1980). Cerebral assymetry and the psychology of man. In M.C. Wittrock (Ed.), *The brain and psychology* (pp. 245–321). New York: Academic Press.

Lewin, K. (1942). Changes in social sensitivity in child and adult. *Childhood Education, 19,* 53–57.

Lewin, K., Lippitt, R., & White, R.K. (1938). Patterns of aggressive behavior in experimentally created "social climates." *Journal of Social Psychology, 10,* 271–299.

Lewis, C.C. (1981). The effects of parental firm control: A reinterpretation of findings. *Psychological Bulletin, 90,* 547–563.

Lewis, M., & Brooks, J. (1974). Self, other and fear: Infants' reactions to people. In M. Lewis & L.A. Rosenblum (Eds.), *The origins of fear* (pp. 195–228). New York: John Wiley & Sons.

Lewis, M., & Brooks-Gunn, J. (1979). *Social cognition and the acquisition of self.* New York: Plenum Press.

Lewis, M., Weinraub, M., & Ban, P.L. (1973). *Mothers and fathers, girls and boys: Attachment behavior in the first two years of life.* Paper presented at the Biennial Meeting of the Society for Research in Child Development, Philadelphia.

Leyens, J.P., Camino, L., Parke, R.D., & Berkowitz, L. (1975). Effects of movie violence on aggression in a field setting as a function of group dominance and cohesion. *Journal of Personality and Social Psychology, 32,* 346–360.

Linn, M.C., & Petersen, A.C. (1986). A meta-analysis of gender differences in spatial ability: Implications for mathematics and science achievement. In J.S. Hyde & M.C. Linn (Eds.), *The psychology of gender: Advances through meta-analysis* (pp. 67–101). Baltimore: The Johns Hopkins Press.

Livesley, W.J., & Bromley, D.B. (1973). *Person perception in childhood and adolescence.* London: John Wiley & Sons.

Lobitz, W.C., & Johnson, S.M. (1975). Parental manipulation of the behavior of normal and deviant children. *Child Development, 46,* 719–726.

Locke, J. (1693/1884). *Some thoughts concerning education.* London: C.J. Clay & Sons.

Loeb, R.C. (1975). Concomitants of boys' locus of control examined in parent-child interactions. *Developmental Psychology, 11,* 353–358.

Loeb, R.C., Horst, L., & Horton, P.J. (1980). Family interaction patterns associated with self-esteem in preadolescent girls and boys. *Merrill-Palmer Quarterly, 26,* 205–217.

Loeber, R., & Dishion, T. (1983). Early predictors of male delinquency: A review. *Psychological Bulletin, 94,* 68–99.

Loehlin, J.C. (1986). Heredity, environment and the Thurstone Temperament Schedule. *Behavior Genetics, 16,* 61–73.

Loehlin, J.C., Horn, J.M., & Willerman, L. (1981). Personality resemblance in adoptive families. *Behavior Genetics, 11,* 309–330.

Loehlin, J.C., & Nichols, R.C. (1976). *Heredity, environment and personality.* Austin, Texas.: University of Texas Press.

Londerville, S., & Main, M. (1981). Security of attachment, compliance and maternal training methods in the second year of life. *Developmental Psychology, 17,* 289–299.

Long, F., Garduque, L., & Peters, D. (1983). *Continuity between home and family day care.* Paper presented at Biennial Meeting of the Society for Research in Child Development, Detroit.

Lorenz, K. (1966). *On aggression.* New York: Harcourt, Brace & World.

Lorenz, K.Z. (1935). Der Kumpan in der Umvelt des Vogels. *Journal of Ornithology, 83,* 137–213; 289–413.

Lott, B. (1978). Behavioral concordance with sex-role ideology related to play areas, creativity, and parental sex typing of children. *Journal of Personality and Social Psychology, 36,* 1087–1100.

Luria, A. (1961). *The role of speech in the regulation of normal and abnormal behaviors.* New York: Liveright.

Luria, A. (1969). Speech and formation of mental processes. In M. Cole & I. Maltzman (Eds.), *A handbook of contemporary Soviet psychology.* New York: Basic Books.

Luria, Z., & Herzog, E. (1985). *Gender segregation across and within settings.* Paper presented at the Biennial Meeting of the Society for Research in Child Development, Toronto.

Lutz, P. (1983). The stepfamily: An adolescent perspective. *Family Relations, 32,* 367–375.

Lytton, H. (1971). Observation studies of parent-child interaction: A methodological review. *Child Development, 42,* 651–684.

Lytton, H. (1980). *Parent-child interaction: The socialization process observed in twin and singleton families.* New York: Plenum Press.

Lytton, H. (1982). Two-way influence processes between parents and child—when, where and how? *Canadian Journal of Behavioural Science, 14,* 259–275.

Lytton, H., Watts, D., & Dunn, B.E. (1986). Stability and predictability of cognitive and social characteristics from age 2 to age 9. *Genetic, Social and General Psychology Monographs, 112,* 363–398.

Lytton, H., Watts D., & Dunn, B.E. (1988). The stability of genetic determination from age 2 to age 9: A longitudinal study. *Social Biology*, in press.

Maccoby, E.E. (Ed.) (1966). *The development of sex differences*. Stanford: Stanford University Press.

Maccoby, E.E. (1980). *Social development: Psychological growth and the parent-child relationship*. San Diego, California: Harcourt, Brace & Jovanovich.

Maccoby, E.E. (1984). Socialization and developmental change. *Child Development*, *55*, 317–328.

Maccoby, E.E., & Jacklin, C.N. (1974). *The psychology of sex differences*. Stanford, CA: Stanford University Press.

Maccoby, E.E., & Jacklin, C.N. (1980). Sex differences in aggression: A rejoinder and a reprise. *Child Development*, *51*, 964–980.

Maccoby, E.E., & Jacklin, C.N. (1983). The "person" characteristics of children and the family as environment. In D. Magnusson & V.L. Allen (Eds.), *Human development: An interactional perspective* (pp. 75–92). New York: Academic Press.

Maccoby, E.E., & Jacklin, C.N. (1985). *Gender segregation in nursery school: Predictors and outcomes*. Paper presented at the Biennial Meeting of the Society for Research in Child Development, Toronto.

Maccoby, E.E., & Martin, J.A. (1983). Socialization in the context of the family: Parent-child interaction. In E.M. Hetherington (Ed.), *Handbook of child psychology: Vol. 4. Socialization, personality and social development* (pp. 1–102). New York: John Wiley & Sons.

MacDonald, R., & Parke, R.D. (1984). Bridging the gap: Parent-child play interaction and peer interactive competence. *Child Development*, *55*, 1265–1277.

Main, M., & Weston, D. (1981). The quality of the toddler's relationship to mother and father: Related to conflict behavior and the readiness to establish new relationships. *Child Development*, *52*, 932–940.

Main, M., & Weston, R.D. (1982). Avoidance of the attachment figure in infancy: Descriptions and interpretations. In C.M. Parkes & J. Stevenson-Hinde (Eds.), *The place of attachment in human behavior*. New York: Basic Books.

Marantz, S.A., & Mansfield, A.F. (1977). Maternal employment and the development of sex-role stereotyping in 5- to 11-year-old girls. *Child Development*, *48*, 668–673.

Margolin, G., & Patterson, G.R. (1975). Differential consequences provided by mothers and fathers for their sons and daughters. *Developmental Psychology*, *11*, 537–538.

Markus, H. (1980). The self in thought and memory. In D.M. Wegner & R.R. Vallacher (Eds.), *The self in social psychology* (pp. 102–138). New York: Oxford University Press.

Martin, B. (1975). Parent-child relations. In F.D. Horowitz (Ed.), *Review of Child Development Research* (Vol. 4, pp. 463–540). Chicago: University of Chicago Press.

Martin, C.L., & Halverson, C.F. (1981). A schematic processing model of sex typing and stereotyping. *Child Development*, *52*, 1119–1134.

Maruyama, G., & McGarvey, B. (1980). Evaluating casual models: An application of maximum-likelihood analysis of structural equations. *Psychological Bulletin*, *87*, 502–512.

Masangkay, Z.S., McCluskey, K.A. McIntyre, C.W., Sims-Knight, J., Vaughn,

B.E., & Flavell, J.H. (1974). The early development of inferences about the visual percepts of others. *Child Development, 45*, 357–366.

Masters, J.C., & Furman, W. (1981). Popularity, individual friendship selection, and specific peer interaction among children. *Developmental Psychology, 17*, 344–350.

Matas, L., Arend, R., & Sroufe, L.A. (1978). Continuity of adaptation in the second year: The relationship between quality of attachment and later competence. *Child Development, 49*, 547–556.

Matheny, A.P. (1980). Bayley's Infant Behavior Record: Behavioral components and twin analyses. *Child Development, 51*, 1157–1167.

Matheny, A.P., & Dolan, A.B. (1980). A twin study of personality and temperament during middle childhood. *Journal of Research in Personality, 14*, 224–234.

Matheny, A.P. Jr., Riese, M.L., & Wilson, R.S. (1985). Rudiments of infant temperament: Newborn to 9 months. *Developmental Psychology, 21*, 486–494.

Mayr, E. (1982). *The growth of biological thought: Diversity, evolution and inheritance.* Cambridge: Harvard University Press.

McCall, R.B. (1977). Challenges to a science of developmental psychology. *Child Development, 48*, 333–344.

McCall, R.B., Eichorn, D., & Hogarty, P. (1977). Transitions in early mental development. *Monographs of the Society for Research in Child Development, 42* (3, Serial No. 171).

McCall, R.B., Appelbaum, M.I., & Hogarty, P.S. (1973). Developmental changes in mental performance. *Monographs of the Society for Research in Child Development, 38* (3, Serial No. 150).

McCartney, K., Scarr, S., Phillips, D., Grajek, S., & Schwarz, J.C. (1982). Environmental differences among day care centers and their effects on children's development. In E.F. Zigler & E.W. Gordon (Eds.), *Day care: Scientific and social policy issues* (pp. 126–173). Boston, MA: Auburn House.

McClintock, C.G., Moskowitz, J.M., & McClintock, E. (1977). Variations in preferences for individualistic, competitive, and cooperative outcomes as a function of age, game class, and task in nursery school children. *Child Development, 48*, 1080–1085.

McConaghy, M.J. (1979). Gender permanence and the genital basis of gender: Stages in the development of constancy of gender identity. *Child Development, 50*, 1223–1226.

McCord, A., McCord, J., & Howard, A. (1961). Familial correlates of aggression in nondelinquent male children. *Journal of Abnormal and Social Psychology, 62*, 79–93.

McCord, J. (1979). Some child-rearing antecedents of criminal behavior in adult men. *Journal of Personality and Social Psychology, 37*, 1477–1486.

McCord, J., McCord, W., & Thurber, E. (1962). Some effects of paternal absence on male children. *Journal of Abnormal and Social Psychology, 64*, 361–369.

McCord, W., McCord, J., & Zola, I.K. (1959). *Origins of crime.* New York: Columbia University Press.

McNeal, E.T., & Cimbolic, P. (1986). Antidepressants and biochemical theories of depression. *Psychological Bulletin, 99*, 361–374.

McPartland, J.M., & McDill, E.L. (1976). Research on crime in schools. In J.M. McPartland & E.L. McDill (Eds.), *Violence in schools* (pp. 3–33). Lexington, MA: Lexington Books.

Mead, G.H. (1925). The genesis of the self and social control. *International Journal of Ethics* (XXXV, No. 3), 251–273.

Mead, G.H. (1934). *Mind, self, and society*. Chicago: University of Chicago Press.

Mead, M. (1928). *Coming of age in Samoa*. New York: William Marrow.

Mead, M. (1935). *Sex and temperament*. New York: William Morrow.

Mead, M. (1970). Anomalies in American postdivorce relationships. In P. Bohannon (Ed.), *Divorce and after: An analysis of the emotional and social problems of divorce* (pp. 97–112). New York: Doubleday.

Mednick, S.A., Moffitt, T.E., Pollock, V., Talovic, S., Cabrielli, W.F. Jr., & Van Dusen, K.T. (1983). The inheritance of human deviance. In D. Magnusson & V.L. Allen (Eds.), *Human development: An interactional perspective*. (pp. 221–242). New York: Academic Press.

Meehan, A.M. (1984). A meta-analysis of sex differences in formal operational thought. *Child Development, 55*, 1110–1124.

Meichenbaum, D. (1971). The nature and modification of impulsive children. Paper presented at the Biennial Meeting of the Society for Research in Child Development, Minneapolis.

Meichenbaum, D. (1977). *Cognitive-behavior modification: An intergrative approach*. New York: Plenum Press.

Meichenbaum, D., & Goodman, J. (1969). The developmental control of operant motor responding by verbal operants. *Journal of Experimental Child Psychology, 7*, 553–565.

Meichenbaum, D., & Goodman, J. (1971). Training impulsive children to talk to themselves: A means of developing self-control. *Journal of Abnormal Psychology, 77*, 115–126.

Merrill Bishop, B. (1951). Mother-child interaction and the social behavior of children. *Psychological Monographs, 65* (11, Whole No. 328).

Meyer, B. (1980). The development of girls' sex-role attitudes. *Child Development, 51*, 508–514.

Michael, R.P. (1968). Gonadal hormones and the control of primate behavior. In R.P. Michael (Ed.), *Endocrinology and human behavior*. Oxford: Oxford Unviersity Press.

Miller, D.T., Weinstein, S.M., & Karniol, R. (1978). Effects of age and self-verbalization on children's ability to delay gratification. *Developmental Psychology, 14*, 569–570.

Miller, L.B., & Dyer, J.L. (1975). Four preschool programs: Their dimension and effects. *Monographs of the Society for Research in Child Development, 40* (5–6, Serial No. 162).

Miller, N.E. (1941). The frustration-aggression hypothesis. *Psychological Review, 48*, 337–342.

Miller, P.H., Kessel, F.S., & Flavell, J.H. (1970). Thinking about people thinking about people thinking about . . . A study of social cognitive development. *Child Development, 41*, 613–623.

Miller, S.A., Shelton, J., & Flavell, J.H. (1970). A test of Luria's hypothesis concerning the development of self-regulation. *Child Development, 41*, 651–665.

Minton, C., Kagan, J., & Levine, J.A. (1971). Maternal control and obedience in the two-year-old. *Child Development, 42*, 1873–1894.

Minturn, L., & Lambert, W.W. (1964). *Mothers of six cultures: Antecedents of child rearing*. New York: John Wiley & Sons.

Minuchin, P.P., & Shapiro, E.K. (1983). The school as a context for social development. In E.M. Hetherington (Ed.), *Handbook of Child Psychology, Vol. IV, Socialization, personality and social development* (pp. 197–274). New York: John Wiley & Sons.

Mischel, W. (1968). *Personality and assessment*. New York: John Wiley and Sons.

Mischel, W. (1973). Toward a cognitive social learning reconceptualization of personality. *Psychological Review, 80*, 252–283.

Mischel, W. (1974). Processes in delay of gratification. In L. Berkowitz (Ed.), *Advances in experimental social psychology* (Vol. 7, pp. 249–292). New York: Academic Press.

Mischel, W., & Ebbesen, E.B. (1970). Attention in delay of gratification. *Journal of Personality and Social Psychology, 16*, 329–337.

Mischel, W., Ebbesen, E.B., & Zeiss, A. (1972). Cognitive and attentional mechanisms in delay of gratification. *Journal of Personality and Social Psychology, 21*, 204–218.

Mischel, W., & Liebert, R.M. (1966). Effects of discrepancies between observed and imposed reward criteria on their acquisition and transmission. *Journal of Personality and Social Psychology, 3*, 45–53.

Mischel, M., & Mischel, H.N. (1977). Self-control and the self. In T. Mischel (Ed.), *The self: Psychological and philosophical issues* (pp. 31–64). Totowa, NJ: Rowan & Littlefield.

Mischel, W., & Moore, B. (1973). Effects of attention to symbolically presented rewards upon self-control. *Journal of Personality and Social Psychology, 28*, 172–179.

Miyake, K. (1983). *Relation of temperamental disposition to classification of attachment*. Paper presented at the Biennial Meeting of the Society for Research in Child Development, Detroit.

Money, J., & Ehrhardt, A.A. (1968). Prenatal hormonal exposure: Possible effects on behavior in man. In R.P. Michael (Ed.) *Endocrinology and human behavior* (pp. 32–48). Oxford: Oxford University Press.

Money, J., & Ehrhardt, A.A. (1972). *Man and woman, boy and girl*. Baltimore: The Johns Hopkins Press.

Montemayor, R., & Eisen, M. (1977). The development of self-conceptions from childhood to adolescence. *Developmental Psychology, 13*, 314–319.

Moore, B.S., Underwood, B., & Rosenhan, D.L. (1973). Affect and altruism. *Developmental Psychology, 8*, 99–104.

Moore, T. (1964). Children of full-time and part-time mothers. *International Journal of Social Psychiatry, 2*, 1–10.

Moreno, J.L. (1934). *Who shall survive?* Washington, DC: Nervous and Mental Disease Publishing Company.

Mosher, R. (Ed.) (1980). *Moral education: A first generation of research and development*. New York: Praeger.

Moskowitz, D.S., Schwartz, J.C., & Corsini, D.A. (1977). Initiating day care at three years of age: Effects on attachment. *Child Development, 48*, 1271–1276.

Mossler, D.G., Marvin, R.S., & Greenberg, M.T. (1976). Conceptual perspective-taking in 2- to 6-year-old children. *Developmental Psychology, 12*, 85–86.

Mowrer, O.H. (1960). *Learning theory and the symbolic processes*. New York: John Wiley & Sons.

Much, N., & Shweder, R. (1978). Speaking of rules: The analysis of culture in breach. In W. Damon (Ed.), *New directions for child development: Vol. 2. Moral development.* San Francisco: Jossey-Bass.

Mueller, E., & Lucas, T. (1975). A developmental analysis of peer interaction among toddlers. In M. Lewis & L.A. Rosenblum (Eds.), *Friendship and peer relations* (pp. 223–257). New York: John Wiley & Sons.

Mueller, R. (1976). A chapter in the history of the relationship between psychology and sociology in America: James Mark Baldwin. *Journal of the History of the Behavioural Sciences, 12,* 240–253.

Murphy, L.B. (1937). *Social behavior and child personality.* New York: Columbia University Press.

Mussen, P.H. (1967). Early socialization: Learning and identification. In T.M. Newcomb (Ed.), *New directions in psychology, III* (pp. 51–110). New York: Holt, Rinehart & Winston.

Mussen, P.H., Boutourline-Young, H., Gaddini, R., & Morante, L. (1963). The influence of father-son relationships on adolescent personality and attitudes. *Journal of Child Psychology and Psychiatry, 4,* 3–16.

Mussen, P.H., & Distler, L. (1960). Child rearing antecedents of masculine identification in kindergarten boys. *Child Development, 31,* 89–100.

Mussen, P.H., & Eisenberg-Berg, N. (1977). *Roots of caring, sharing, and helping.* San Francisco: W.H. Freeman.

Mussen, P.H., Harris, S., Rutherford, E., & Keasey, C.M. (1970). Honesty and altruism among preadolescents. *Developmental Psychology, 3,* 169–194.

Mussen, P.H., & Jones, M.C. (1957). Self-conceptions, motivations, and interpersonal attitudes of late and early maturing boys. *Child Development, 28,* 243–256.

Mussen, P.H., & Rutherford, E. (1963). Parent-child relations and parental personality in relation to young children's sex-role preferences. *Child Development, 34,* 589–607.

Nash, J. (1978). *Developmental Psychology* (2nd ed.) Englewood Cliffs, NJ: Prentice-Hall.

Nelson, K. (1973). Structure and strategy in learning to talk. *Monographs of the Society for Research in Child Development, 38* (Serial No. 149).

Nelson, J., & Aboud, F.E. (1985). The resolution of social conflict between friends. *Child Development, 56,* 1009–1017.

Nelson, L., & Madsen, M.C. (1969). Cooperation and competition in four-year-olds as a function of reward. *Developmental Psychology, 1,* 340–344.

Newson, J., & Newson, E. (1965). *Patterns of infant care in an urban community.* London: Penguin.

Newson, J., & Newson, E. (1970). *Four years old in an urban community.* London: Penguin.

Newson, J., & Newson, E. (1974). Cultural aspects of childrearing in the English-speaking world. In M.P.M. Richards (Ed.), *The integration of a child into a social world* (pp. 53–82). London: Cambridge University Press.

Newson, J., & Newson, E. (1978). *Seven years old in the home environment.* London: Penguin.

Nichols, R.C. (1979). Heredity and environment: Major findings from twin studies of ability, personality and interests. *Monographs of the International Association for the Advancement of Ethnology and Eugenics,* No. 6.

Nisan, M., & Kohlberg, L. (1982). Universality and variation in moral judgment: A longitudinal and cross-sectional study in Turkey. *Child Development, 53,* 865–876.

Nisbett, R.E., & Borgida, E. (1975). Attribution and the psychology of prediction. *Journal of Personality and Social Psychology, 32,* 932–943.

Nucci, L.P., & Nucci, M.S. (1982a). Children's social interactions in the context of moral and conventional transgressions. *Child Development, 53,* 403–412.

Nucci, L.P., & Nucci, M.S. (1982b). Children's responses to moral and social conventional transgressions in free-play settings. *Child Development, 53,* 1337–1342.

Nucci, L.P., & Turiel, E. (1978). Social interactions and the development of social concepts in preschool children. *Child Development, 49,* 400–407.

Oldershaw, L. (1987). *The transition from single-parent to stepparent families: How children react.* Unpublished paper, University of Toronto.

Oldershaw, L., Walters, G.C., & Hall, D.K. (1986). Control strategies and non-compliance in abusive mother-child dyads: An observational study. *Child Development, 57,* 722–732.

Oleinick, M., Bahn, A., Eisenberg, L., & Lilienfeld, A. (1966). Early socialization experiences and intrafamilial environment. *Archives of General Psychiatry, 15,* 344–353.

Olejnik, A.B. (1980). Adults' moral reasoning with children. *Child Development, 51,* 1285–1288.

Olweus, D. (1979). Stability and aggressive reaction patterns in males: A review. *Psychological Bulletin, 86,* 852–875.

Olweus, D. (1980). Familial and temperamental determinants of aggressive behavior in adolescent boys: A causal analysis. *Developmental Psychology, 16,* 644–666.

Olweus, D., Mattsson, A., Schalling, D., & Low, H. (1980). Testosterone, aggression, physical and personality dimensions of normal adolescent males. *Psychosomatic Medicine, 42,* 253–269.

Omark, D.R., Omark, M., & Edelman, M. (1975). Formation of dominance hierarchies in young children. In T.R. Williams (Ed.), *Psychological anthropology* (pp. 289–315). The Hague: Mouton.

Ottinger, D., & Simmons, J. (1964). Behavior of human neonates and prenatal maternal anxiety. *Psychological Reports, 14,* 391–394.

Parikh, B. (1980). Development of moral judgment and its relation to family environmental factors in Indian and American families. *Child Development, 51,* 1030–1039.

Paris, S.G., & Cairns, R.B. (1972). An experimental and ethological analysis of social reinforcement with retarded children. *Child Development, 43,* 717–729.

Parke, R.D. (1969). Effectiveness of punishment as an interaction of intensity, timing, agent nurturance, and cognitive structuring. *Child Development, 40,* 213–235.

Parke, R.D. (1974). Rules, roles and resistance to deviation: Recent advances in punishment, discipline and self-control. In A. Pick (Ed.), *Minnesota Symposia on Child Psychology* (Vol. 8, pp. 111–143). Minneapolis, University of Minnesota Press.

Parke, R.D. (1979). Interactional designs. In R. Cairns (Ed.), *The analysis of social interactions* (pp. 15–35). Hillsdale, NJ: Lawrence Erlbaum Associates.

Parke, R.D., & Collmer, C.W. (1975). Child abuse: An interdisciplinary analysis.

In E.M. Hetherington (Ed.), *Review of child development research* (Vol. 5). Chicago: University of Chicago Press.

Parke, R.D., & O'Leary, S. (1975). Father-mother-infant interaction in the newborn period: Some findings, some observations, some unresolved issues. In K. Riegel & J. Meacham (Eds.), *The developing individual in a changing world.* (Vol. 2). The Hague: Mouton.

Parke, R.D., & Slaby, R.G. (1983). The development of aggression. In E.M. Hetherington (Ed.), *Handbook of child psychology* (4th ed., Vol. 4, pp. 547–641). New York: John Wiley & Sons.

Parpal, M., & Maccoby, E.E. (1985). Maternal responsiveness and subsequent child compliance. *Child Development, 56,* 1326–1334.

Parsons, J.E. (1982). Biology, experience and sex-dimorphic behaviors. In W.R. Grove & G.R. Carpenter (Eds.), *The fundamental connection between nature and nurture* (pp. 137–170). Lexington, MA: Lexington Books.

Parten, M.B. (1932). Social participation among preschool children. *Journal of Abnormal and Social Psychology, 27,* 243–269.

Pasamanick, B., & Knobloch, H. (1966). Retrospective studies of the epidemiology of reproductive casuality: Old and new. *Merrill-Palmer Quarterly, 12,* 7–26.

Pastor, D.L. (1981). The quality of mother-infant attachment and its relationship to toddlers' initial sociability with peers. *Developmental Psychology, 17,* 326–335.

Patterson, C.J., & Carter, D.B. (1979). Attentional determinants of children's self-control in waiting and working situations. *Child Development, 50,* 272–275.

Patterson, G.R. (1974). A basis for identifying stimuli which control behaviors in natural settings. *Child Development, 45,* 900–911.

Patterson, G.R. (1979). A performance theory for coercive family interaction. In R. Cairns (Ed.), *The analysis of social interactions* (pp. 119–161). Hillsdale, NJ: Lawrence Erlbaum Associates.

Patterson, G.R. (1980). Mothers: The unacknowledged victims. *Monographs of the Society for Research in Child Development, 45* (5, Serial No. 186).

Patterson, G.R. (1982). *Coercive family processes.* Eugene, OR: Castilia Press.

Patterson, G.R. (1984). Microsocial process: A view from the boundary. In J.C. Masters & K. Yarkin-Levin (Eds.), *Boundary areas in social and developmental psychology* (pp. 43–66). Orlando: Academic Press.

Patterson, G.R. (1986). Maternal rejection: Determinant or product of deviant child behavior? In W.W. Hartup & Z. Rubin (Eds.), *Relationships and development* (pp. 73–94). Hillsdale, NJ: Lawrence Erlbaum Associates.

Patterson, G.R., & Cobb, J.A. (1971). A dyadic analysis of "aggressive" behaviors. In J.P. Hill (Ed.), *Minnesota Symposium on Child Psychology,* (Vol. 5, pp. 72–129). Minneapolis: University of Minnesota Press.

Patterson, G.R., & Reid, J.B. (1970). Reciprocity and coercion: Two facets of social systems. In C. Neuringer & J.L. Michael (Eds.), *Behavior modification in clinical psychology* (pp. 133–177). New York: Appleton-Century Crofts.

Pedersen, F.A. (Ed.), (1980). *The father-infant relationship.* New York: Praeger.

Pedersen, F.A., Anderson, B.J., & Cain, R.L. (1980). Parent-infant and husband-wife interactions observed at age 5 months. In F.A. Pedersen (Ed.), *The father-infant relationship* (pp. 71–86). New York: Praeger.

Pedersen, F.A., Yarrow, L.J., Anderson, B.J., & Cain, R.L. (1979). Conceptualization of father influences in the infancy period. M. Lewis & L. Rosenblum

(Eds.), *The child and its family* (pp. 45–66). New York: Plenum Press.

Peevers, B.H., & Secord, P.R. (1973). Developmental changes in attribution of descriptive concepts to persons. *Journal of Personality and Social Psychology, 27*, 120–128.

Pence, A.R. (1985). Day care in Canada and the restructured relationships of family, government and labor force. *Journal of the Canadian Association for Young Children, 9*, 27–41.

Perkins, T.F., & Kahan, J.P. (1979). An empirical comparison of natural-father and stepfather family systems. *Family Process, 18*, 175–184.

Perry, D.G., & Bussey, K. (1979). The social learning theory of sex differences: Imitation is alive and well. *Journal of Personality and Social Psychology, 37*, 1699–1712.

Perry, D.G., & Perry, L.C. (1983). Social learning, causal attribution and moral internalization. In J. Bisanz, G.L. Bisanz, & B.D. Kail (Eds.), *Learning in children: Progress in cognitive development research*, (pp. 105–136). New York: Springer-Verlag.

Perry, D.G., White, A.J., & Perry, L.C. (1984). Does early sex typing result from children's attempts to match their behavior to sex role stereotypes? *Child Development, 55*, 2114–2121.

Petersen, A.C. (1979). Hormones and cognitive functioning in normal development. In M.A. Wittig & A.C. Petersen (Eds.), *Sex-related differences in cognitive functioning* (pp. 189–214). New York: Academic Press.

Peterson, L. (1980). Developmental changes in verbal and behavioral sensitivity to cues of social norms of altruism. *Child Development, 51*, 830–838.

Peterson, L. (1982). An alternative perspective to norm-based explanations of modeling and children's generosity: A reply to Lipscomb, Larrieu, McAllister, and Bregman. *Merrill-Palmer Quarterly, 28*, 283–290.

Peterson, P.L. (1979). Direct instruction reconsidered. In P.L. Peterson & H.J. Walberg (Eds.), *Research on teaching* (pp. 57–69). Berkeley, CA: McCutchan.

Phoenix, G.H., Goy, R.W., & Resko, J.A. (1969). Psychosexual differentiation as a function of androgenic stimulation. In N. Diamond (Ed.), *Reproduction and sexual behavior*. Bloomington, IN: Indiana University Press.

Piaget, J. (1932). *The moral judgment of the child*. London: Routledge & Kegan Paul.

Piaget, J., & Inhelder, B. (1956). *The child's conception of space*. London: Routledge & Kegan Paul.

Pink, J.E.T., & Wampler, K.S. (1985). Problem areas in stepfamilies: Cohesion, adaptability, and the stepfather-adolescent relationship. *Family Relations, 34*, 327–335.

Plomin, R. (1982). Childhood temperament. In B. Lahey & A. Kazdin (Eds.), *Advances in clinical child psychology* (Vol. 6). New York: Plenum Press.

Plomin, R., DeFries, J.C., & McClearn, G.E. (1980). *Behavioral genetics: A primer*. San Francisco: W.H. Freeman.

Plomin, R., & Foch, T.T. (1980). A twin study of objectively assessed personality in childhood. *Journal of Personality and Social Psychology, 39*, 680–688.

Plomin, R., & Rowe, D. (1979). Genetic and environmental etiology of social behavior in infancy. *Developmental Psychology, 15*, 62–72.

Portenier, L. (1939). Twinning as a factor influencing personality. *Journal of Educational Psychology, 30*, 542–547.

Power, D., & Reimer, J. (1978). Moral atmosphere: An educational bridge between moral judgment and action. In W. Damon (Ed.), *New directions for child development: Vol. 2. Moral Development* (pp. 115–116). San Francisco: Jossey-Bass.

Power, T.G., & Chapieski, M.L. (1986). Childrearing and impulse control in toddlers: A naturalistic investigation. *Developmental Psychology, 22,* 271–275.

Pringle, M.L.K., & Bossio, V. (1960). Early prolonged separations and emotional adjustment. *Journal of Child Psychology and Psychiatry, 1,* 37–48.

Pulkkinen, L. (1982). Self-control and continuity from childhood to adolescence. In P.B. Baltes & O.G. Brim (Eds.), *Life-span development and behavior* (Vol. 4, pp. 63–105). New York: Academic Press.

Putallaz, M. (1983). Predicting children's sociometric status from their behavior. *Child Development, 54,* 1417–1426.

Putallaz, M., & Gottman, J.M. (1981). Social skills and group acceptance. In S.R. Asher & J.M. Gottman (Eds.), *The development of children's friendships* (pp. 116–149). Cambridge: Cambridge University Press.

Quay, L.C., & Jarrett, O.S. (1984). Predictors of social acceptance in preschool children. *Developmental Psychology, 20,* 793–796.

Quinton, D., & Rutter, M. (1984). Parents with children in care. II. Intergenerational continuities. *Journal of Child Psychology and Psychiatry, 25,* 231–250.

Radke-Yarrow, M.R., Campbell, J.D., & Burton, R.V. (1968). *Child rearing: An inquiry into research and methods.* San Francisco: Jossey-Bass.

Radke-Yarrow, M.R., Scott, P.M., & Zahn-Waxler, C. (1973). Learning concern for others. *Developmental Psychology, 8,* 240–260.

Radke-Yarrow, M.R., & Zahn-Waxler, C.Z. (1979). Observing interaction: A confrontation with methodology. In R.B. Cairns (Ed.), *The analysis of social interactions: Methods, issues, and illustrations* (pp. 37–65). Hillsdale, NJ: Lawrence Erlbaum Associates.

Radke-Yarrow, M., Zahn-Waxler, C., & Chapman, M. (1983). Children's prosocial dispositions and behavior. In E.M. Hetherington (Ed.), *Handbook of child psychology, Vol. 4: Socialization, personality and social development* (pp. 469–546). New York: John Wiley & Sons.

Radke-Yarrow, M., Zahn-Waxler, C., & Scott, P.M. (1971). Child effects on adult behavior. *Developmental Psychology, 5,* 300–311.

Ragozin, A. (1978). A laboratory assessment of attachment behavior in day-care children. In H. Beex (Ed.), *Social issues in developmental psychology* (pp. 218–232). New York: Harper & Row.

Ragozin, A.S. (1980). Attachment behavior of day-care children: Naturalistic and laboratory observations. *Child Development, 51,* 409–415.

Ramey, C.T., Dorval, B., & Baker-Ward, L. (1983). Group day care and socially disadvantaged families: Effects on the child and the family. In S. Kilmer (Ed.), *Advances in early education and day care* (Vol. 3, pp. 69–106). Greenwich, CT: JAI Press.

Ramey, C.T., & Farran, D. (1983). *Intervening with high-risk families via infant day care.* Paper presented at Biennial Meeting of the Society for Research in Child Development, Detroit.

Rapaport, D. (1959). The structure of psychoanalytic theory: A systematizing attempt. In S. Koch (Ed.), *Psychology: A study of a science: Vol. III. Formulations of the person and the social context* (pp. 55–183). New York: McGraw-Hill.

Raschke, H.J., & Raschke, V.J. (1979). Family conflict and children's self-concepts: A comparison of intact and single-parent families. *Journal of Marriage and the Family*, *41*, 367–374.

Raymond, C.L., & Benbow, C.P. (1986). Gender differences in mathematics: A function of parental support and student sex typing? *Developmental Psychology*, *22*, 808–819.

Redl, F., & Wineman, D. (1951). *Children who hate*. Glencoe, Illinois: The Free Press.

Reid, J.B. (1986). Social-interactional patterns in families of abused and non-abused children. In M. Zahn-Waxler, E.M. Cummings, & R. Iannotti (Eds.), *Altruism and aggression: Biological and social origins* (pp. 238–255). New York: Cambridge University Press.

Reid, J.B., Taplin, P.S., & Lorber, R. (1981). A social interactional approach to the treatment of abusive families. In R.B. Stuart (Ed.), *Violent behavior: Social learning approaches to prediction, management and treatment*. New York: Bruner-Mazel.

Reinisch, J.M. (1981). Prenatal exposure to synthetic progestins increases potential for aggression in humans. *Science*, *211*, 1171–1173.

Resnick, S.M., Berenbaum, S.A., Gottesman, I.I., & Bouchard, T.J. (1986). Early hormonal influences on cognitive functioning in congenital adrenal hyperplasia. *Developmental Psychology*, *22*, 191–198.

Rheingold, H.L. (1956). The modification of social responsiveness in institutional babies. *Monographs of the Society for Research in Child Development*, *21* (Serial No. 2).

Rheingold, H.L. (1969). The social and socializing infant. In D.A. Goslin (Ed.), *Handbook of socialization theory and research* (pp. 779–790). Chicago: Rand McNally.

Rheingold, H.L. (1982). Little children's participation in the work of adults, a nascent prosocial behavior. *Child Development*, *53*, 114–125.

Rheingold, H.L., & Eckerman, C.O. (1970). The infant separates himself from his mother. *Science*, *168*, 78–83.

Rheingold, H.L., & Eckerman, C.O. (1973). Fear of the stranger: A critical examination. In H. Reese (Ed.), *Advances in child development and behavior* (Vol. 8, pp. 185–222). New York: Academic Press.

Rheingold, H.L., Gewirtz, J.L., & Ross, H.W. (1959). Social conditioning of vocalizations in the infant. *Journal of Comparative and Physiological Psychology*, *52*, 68–73.

Rheingold, H.L., Hay, D.F., & West, M.J. (1976). Sharing in the second year of life. *Child Development*, *47*, 1148–1158.

Ribble, M. (1943). *The rights of infants*. New York: Columbia University Press.

Richard, B.A., & Dodge, K.A. (1982). Social maladjustment and problem solving in school-aged children. *Journal of Consulting and Clinical Psychology*, *50*, 226–233.

Richards, M.P.M. (Ed.). (1974). *The integration of a child into a social world*. London: Cambridge University Press.

Riegel, K.F. (1972). Influence of economic and political ideologies on the development of developmental psychology. *Psychological Bulletin*, *78*, 129–141.

Ringler, N.M., Kennell, J.H., Jarvella, R., Navojosky, B.J., & Klaus, M.H. (1975). Mother-to-child speech at 2 years—effects of early postnatal contact. *Behavioral Pediatrics*, *86*, 141–144.

Robertson, A. (1982). Day care and children's responsiveness to adults. In E.F. Zigler & E.W. Gordon (Eds.), *Day care: Scientific and social policy issues* (pp. 152–173). Boston, MA: Auburn House.

Robinson, B.E. (1984). The contemporary American stepfather. *Family Relations, 33*, 381–388.

Rodes, T., 7 Moore, J. (1975). *National child care consumer study*. Washington, DC: Administration for Children, Youth, and Families.

Roff, J.D., & Wirt, R.D. (1984). Childhood social adjustment, adolescent status, and young adult mental health. *American Journal of Orthopsychiatry, 54*, 595–602.

Roff, M., Sells, S.B., & Golden, M.M. (1972). *Social adjustment and personality development in children*. Minneapolis: University of Minnesota Press.

Rogosa, D. (1980). A critique of cross-lagged correlation. *Psychological Bulletin, 88*, 245–258.

Rohner, R.P. (1975). *They love me, they love me not: A worldwide study of the effects of parental acceptance and rejection*. Human Relations Area File Press. Yale University.

Roopnarine, J.L., & Johnson, J.E. (1984). Socialization in a mixed-age experimental program. *Developmental Psychology, 20*, 828–832.

Rosekrans, M.A. (1967). Imitation in children as a function of perceived similarity to a social model and vicarious reinforcement. *Journal of Personality and Social Psychology, 7*, 307–315.

Rosen, B.C., & D'Andrade, R. (1959). The psychosocial origins of achievement motivation. *Sociometry, 22*, 185–217.

Rosenbach, D., Crockett, W.H., & Wapner, S. (1973). Developmental level, emotional involvement, and the resolution of inconsistency in impression formation. *Developmental Psychology, 8*, 120–130.

Rosenblatt, J.S. (1969). The development of maternal responsiveness in the rat. *American Journal of Orthopsychiatry, 30*, 36–56.

Rosenhan, D.L., Underwood, B., & Moore, B. (1974). Affect moderates self-gratification and altruism. *Journal of Personality and Social Psychology, 30*, 546–552.

Rosenkrantz, P.S., Vogel, S.R., Bee, H., Broverman, I.K., & Broverman, D.M. (1968). Sex-role stereotypes and self-concepts in college students. *Journal of Consulting and Clinical Psychology, 32*, 287–295.

Rosenthal, R., & Rubin, D.B. (1982). Further meta-analytic procedures for assessing cognitive gender differences. *Journal of Educational Psychology, 74*, 708–712.

Rossi, A. (1984). Gender and parenthood. *American Sociological Review, 49*, 1–19.

Rothbart, M.K. (1971). Birth-order and mother-child interaction in an achievement situation. *Journal of Personality and Social Psychology, 17*, 113–120.

Rothbart, M.K. (1981). Measurement of temperament in infancy. *Child Development, 52*, 569–578.

Rothbart, M.K., & Goldsmith, H.H. (1985). Three approaches to the study of infant temperament. *Development Review, 5*, 237–260.

Rothbart, M.K., & Maccoby, E.E. (1966). Parents' differential reactions to sons and daughters. *Journal of Personality and Social Psychology, 4*, 237–243.

Rothbart, M.K., & Rothbart, M. (1976). Birth order, sex of child, and maternal helpgiving. *Sex Roles, 2*, 39–46.

Rothenberg, B.B. (1970). Children's social sensitivity and the relationship to interpersonal competence, intrapersonal comfort, and intellectual level. *Developmental Psychology*, *2*, 335–350.

Rotter, J.B. (1954). *Social learning and clinical psychology*. New York: Prentice-Hall.

Rousseau, J.J. (1762/1974). *Emile, or on education*. London: J.M. Dent & Sons.

Rubin, K.H. (1982). Social and social-cognitive developmental characteristics of young isolate, normal, and sociable children. In K.H. Rubin & H.S. Ross (Eds.), *Peer relationships and social skills in childhood* (pp. 363–374). New York: Springer-Verlag.

Rubin, K.H., & Daniels-Beirness, T. (1983). Concurrent and predictive correlates of sociometric status in kindergarten and Grade 1 children. *Merrill-Palmer Quarterly*, *29*, 337–351.

Rubin, K.H., Fein, C.G., & Vandenberg, B. (1983). Play. In E.M. Hetherington (Ed.), *Handbook of child psychology: Vol. IV. Socialization, personality, and social development* (pp. 693–774). New York: John Wiley & Sons.

Rubin, K.H., & Schneider, F.W. (1973). The relationship between moral judgment, egocentrism, and altruistic behavior. *Child Development*, *44*, 661–665.

Rubin, K.H., Watson, K.S., & Jambor, T.W. (1978). Free-play behaviors in preschool and kindergarten children. *Child Development*, *49*, 534–536.

Rubin, Z., & Sloman, J. (1984). How parents influence their children's friendships. In M. Lewis (Ed.), *Beyond the dyad* (pp. 223–250). New York: Plenum Press.

Ruble, D.N. (1983). The development of comparison processes and their role in achievement-related self-socialization. In E.T. Higgins, W.W. Hartup, & D.N. Ruble (Eds.), *Social cognition and social development: A sociocultural perspective* (pp. 134–157). New York: Cambridge University Press.

Ruble, D.N., Boggiano, A.K., Feldman, N.S., & Loebl, J.H. (1980). Developmental analysis of the role of social comparison in self-evaluation. *Developmental Psychology*, *16*, 105–115.

Ruble, D.N., Feldman, N.S., Higgins, E.T., & Karlovac, M. (1979). Locus of causality and the use of information in the development of causal attributions. *Journal of Personality*, *47*, 595–614.

Ruble, D.N., Parsons, J.E., & Ross, J. (1976). Self-evaluative responses of children in an achievement setting. *Child Development*, *47*, 990–997.

Ruble, D.N., & Rholes, W.S. (1983). The development of children's perceptions and attributions about their social world. In J.H. Harvey, W. Ickes, & R.F. Kidd (Eds.), *New directions in attribution research* (Vol. 3). Hillsdale, NJ: Lawrence Erlbaum Associates.

Rule, B.G., & Nesdale, A.R. (1976). Emotional arousal and aggressive behavior. *Psychological Bulletin*, *83*, 851–863.

Rule, B.G., Nesdale, A.R., & McAra, M.J. (1974). Children's reactions to information about the intentions underlying an aggressive act. *Child Development*, *45*, 794–798.

Ruopp, R.R., & Travers, J. (1982). Janus faces day care: Perspectives on quality and cost. In E.F. Zigler & E.W. Gordon (Eds.), *Day care: Scientific and social policy issues* (pp. 72–101). Boston: Auburn House.

Ruopp, R., Travers, J., Glantz, F., & Coelen, C. (1979). *Children at the center: Summary findings and their implications*. Cambridge: Abt Books.

Rushton, J.P., Brainerd, C.J., & Pressley, M. (1983). Behavioral development and construct validity: The principle of aggregation. *Psychological Bulletin*, *94*, 18–38.

Rushton, J.P., Jackson, D.N., & Paunonen, S.V. (1981). Personal Nomothetic or idiographic? A response to Kenrick and Stringfield. *Psychological Review, 88*, 582–589.

Rushton, J.P., & Littlefield, C. (1979). The effects of age, amount of modeling and a success experience on seven- to eleven-year-old children's generosity. *Journal of Moral Education, 9*, 55–56.

Russell, G. (1978). The father role and its relation to masculinity, femininity, and androgyny. *Child Development, 49*, 1174–1181.

Rutter, M. (1967). A children's behaviour questionnaire for completion by teachers: Preliminary findings. *Journal of Child Psychology and Psychiatry, 8*, 1–11.

Rutter, M. (1971). Parent-child separation: Psychological effects on the children. *Journal of Child Psychology and Psychiatry, 12*, 233–260.

Rutter, M. (1979). Maternal deprivation, 1972–1978: New findings, new concepts, new approaches. *Child Development, 50*, 283–305.

Rutter, M. (1981). *Maternal deprivation reassessed.* Harmondsworth, England: Penguin.

Rutter, M. (1982). Social-emotional consequences of day care for preschool children. In E.F. Zigler & E.W. Gordon (Eds.), *Day care: Scientific and social policy issues* (pp. 3–32). Boston: Auburn House.

Rutter, M., & Giller, H. (1983). *Juvenile delinquency: Trends and prespectives.* Harmondsworth, Middlesex: Penguin Books.

Rutter, M., & Madge, N. (1976). *Cycles of disadvantage.* London: Heinemann.

Rutter, M., Maugham, B., Mortimore, P., & Ouston, J. (1979). *Fifteen thousand hours: Secondary school and their effect on children.* London: Open Books.

Rutter, M., & Quinton, D., (1984). Long-term follow-up of women institutionalized in childhood: Factors promoting good functioning in adult life. *British Journal of Developmental Psychology, 2*, 191–204.

Rutter, M., Quinton, D., & Yule, B. (1977). *Family pathology and disorder in children.* London: John Wiley & Sons.

Rutter, M. Tizard, J., & Whitmore, K. (1970). *Education, health and behaviour.* London: Longman.

Sackett, G.P. (1966). Monkeys reared in isolation with pictures as visual input: Evidence for an innate releasing mechanism. *Science, 154*, 1468–1473.

Sackett, G.P., Ruppenthal, G.C., Fahrenbruch, E.E., Holm, R.A., & Greenough, W.T. (1981). Social isolation rearing effects in monkeys vary with genotype. *Developmental Psychology, 17*, 313–318.

Saltz, E., Campbell, S., & Skotko, D. (1983). Verbal control of behavior: The effects of shouting. *Developmental Psychology, 19*, 461–464.

Saltz, R. (1973). Effects of part-time "mothering" on IQ and SQ of young institutionalized children. *Child Development, 44*, 166–170.

Sameroff, A.J. (1975). Early influences on development: Fact or fancy? *Merrill-Palmer Quarterly, 21*, 267–294.

Sameroff, A.J. (1983). Developmental systems: Contexts and evolution. In P. Mussen (Ed.), *Handbook of child psychology* (Vol. 1, pp. 237–294). New York: John Wiley & Sons.

Sameroff, A.J., & Chandler, M.J. (1975). Reproductive risk and the continuum of caretaking casualty. In F.D. Horowitz, E.M. Hetherington, S. Scarr-Salapatek, & G.M. Siegel (Eds.), *Review of Child Development Research* (Vol. 4, pp. 187–244). Chicago: University of Chicago Press.

Sameroff, A.J., & Seifer, R. (1983). Familial risk and child competence. *Child Development, 54*, 1254–1268.

Santrock, J.W. (1970). Paternal absence, sex-typing, and identification. *Developmental Psychology, 2*, 264–272.

Santrock, J.W. (1975). Father absence, perceived maternal behavior and moral development in boys. *Child Development, 46*, 753–757.

Santrock, J.W., & Warshak, R.A. (1979). Father custody and social development in boys and girls. *Social Issues, 35*, 112–125.

Santrock, J.W., Warshak, R., Lindbergh, C., & Meadows, L. (1982). Children's and parents' observed social behavior in stepfather families. *Child Development, 53*, 472–480.

Sarason, S.B., & Klaber, M. (1985). The school as a social situation. *Annual Review of Psychology, 36*, 115–140.

Savin-Williams, R.C. (1979). Dominance hierarchies in groups of early adolescents. *Child Development, 50*, 923–935.

Savin-Williams, R.C. (1980a). Dominance hierarchies in groups of middle to late adolescent males. *Journal of Youth and Adolescence, 9*, 75–85.

Savin-Williams, R.C. (1980b). Social interactions of adolescent females in natural groups. In H.C. Foot, A.J. Chapman, & J.R. Smith (Eds.), *Friendship and social relations in children* (pp. 343–364). New York: John Wiley & Sons.

Sawin, D.B. (1979). Assessing empathy in children: A search for an elusive construct. Paper presented at the Biannual Meeting of the Society for Research in Child Development, San Francisco.

Scarlett, H.H., Press, A.N., & Crockett, W.H. (1971). Children's descriptions of peers: A Wernerian developmental analysis. *Child Development, 42*, 439–453.

Scarr, S. (1968). Environmental bias in twin studies. *Eugenics Quarterly, 15*, 34–40.

Scarr, S. (1969). Social introversion-extraversion as a heritable response. *Child Development, 40*, 823–833.

Scarr, S., & Kidd, K.K. (1983). Developmental behavior genetics. In M.M. Haith & J.J. Campos (Eds.), *Handbook of Child Psychology*. New York: John Wiley & Sons (Vol. 2, pp. 345–434).

Scarr, S., & McCartney, K. (1983). How people make their own environments: A theory of genotype—environment effects. *Child Development, 54*, 424–435.

Scarr, S., & Salapatek, P. (1970). Patterns of fear development during infancy. *Merrill-Palmer Quarterly, 16*, 53–90.

Scarr, S., Webber, P.L., Weinberg, R.A., & Wittig, M.A. (1981). Personality re-resemblance among adolescents and their parents in biologically related and adoptive families. *Journal of Personality and Social Psychology, 40*, 885–898.

Schaefer, E.S. (1965). A configurational analysis of children's reports of parent behavior. *Journal of Consulting Psychology, 29*, 552–557.

Schaefer, E.S., & Bayley, N. (1963). Maternal behavior, child behavior, and their interrelations from infancy through adolescence. *Monographs of the Society for Research for Child Development, 28* (3, Serial No. 87).

Schaffer, H.R. (1965). Changes in developmental quotient under two conditions of maternal separation. *British Journal of Social and Clinical Psychology, 4*, 39–46.

Schaffer, H.R. (1966). The onset of fear of strangers and the incongruity hypothesis. *Journal of Child Psychology and Psychiatry, 7*, 95–106.

Schaffer, H.R. (1974a). Cognitive components of the infant's response to strangeness. In M. Lewis & L.A. Rosenblum (Eds.), *The origins of fear* (pp. 11–24). New York: John Wiley & Sons.

Schaffer, H.R. (1974b). Early social behavior and the study of reciprocity. *Bulletin, British Psychological Society, 27*, 209–216.

Schaffer, H.R. (1979). Acquiring the concept of the dialogue. M.H. Bornstein & W. Kessen (Eds.), *Psychological development from infancy: Image to intention* (pp. 279–306). Hillsdale, NJ: Lawrence Erlbaum Associates.

Schaffer, H.R., & Emerson, P.E. (1964a). The development of social attachments in infancy. *Monographs of the Society for Research in Child Development, 29*(3, Serial No. 94).

Schaffer, H.R., & Emerson, P.E. (1964b). Patterns of response to physical contact in early human development. *Journal of Child Psychology and Psychiatry, 5*, 1–13.

Schau, C.G., Kahn, L., Diepold, J.H., & Cherry, F. (1980). The relationships of parental expectations and preschool children's verbal sex typing to their sex-typed toy play behavior. *Child Development, 51*, 266–270.

Scheier, M.F., Carver, C.S., Schulz, R., Glass, D.C., & Katz, I. (1978). Sympathy, self-consciousness, and reactions to the stigmatized. *Journal of Applied Social Psychology, 8*, 270–282.

Schneider-Rosen, K., & Cicchetti, D. (1984). The relationship between affect and cognition in maltreated infants: Quality of attachment and the development of visual self-recognition. *Child Development, 55*, 648–658.

Schoettle, V.C., & Cantwell, D.P. (1980). Children of divorce. *Journal of the American Academy of Child Psychiatry, 19*, 453–475.

Schwarz, J.C., Strickland, R.G., & Krolick, G. (1974). Infant day care: Behavioral effects at preschool age. *Developmental Psychology, 10*, 502–506.

Scott, J.P. (1962). Critical periods in behavioral development. *Science, 138*, 949–958.

Sears, R.R. (1941). Nonaggression reactions to frustration. *Psychological Review, 48*, 343–346.

Sears, R.R. (1951). A theoretical framework for personality and social behavior. *American Psychologist, 6*, 476–483.

Sears, R.R. (1957). Identification as a form of behavioral development. In D.B. Harris (Ed.), *The concept of development* (pp. 149–161). Minneapolis: University of Minnesota Press.

Sears, R.R. (1961). The relation of early socialization experience to aggression in middle childhood. *Journal of Abnormal and Social Psychology, 63*, 466–492.

Sears, R.R. (1975). Your ancients revisited: A history of child development. In E.M. Hetherington (Ed.), *Review of child development research* (Vol. 5). New York: Russell Sage Foundation.

Sears, R.R., Maccoby, E.E., & Levin, H. (1957). *Patterns of child rearing*. Evanston, Illinois: Row-Peterson.

Sears, R.R., Rau, L., & Alpert, R. (1965). *Identification and child rearing*. Stanford, CA: Stanford University Press.

Seligman, M.E.P. (1975). *Helplessness: On depression, development, and death*. San Francisco: W.H. Freeman.

Selman, R.L. (1976). Social-cognitive understanding: A guide to educational and clinical practice. In T. Lickona (Ed.), *Moral development and behavior: Theory, research, and social issues* (pp. 299–316). New York: Holt, Rinehart, & Winston.

Selman, R.L., & Byrne, D.F. (1974). A structural-developmental analysis of levels of role taking in middle childhood. *Child Development, 45*, 803–806.

Serbin, L.A., O'Leary, K.D., Kent, R.N., & Tonick, I.J. (1973). A comparison of teacher response to the preacademic and problem behavior of boys and girls. *Child Development, 44*, 796–804.

Serbin, L.A., & Sprafkin, C. (1986). The salience of gender and the process of sex typing in three- to seven-year-old children. *Child Development, 57*, 1188–1199.

Shaffer, D.R. (1977). Social psychology from a social developmental perspective. In C. Hendrick (Ed.), *Perspectives on social psychology*. Hillsdale, NJ: Lawrence Erlbaum Associates.

Shaffer, D.R. (1979). *Social and personality development.* Monterey, CA: Brooks/ Cole Publishing.

Shaklee, H. (1976). Development in inferences of ability and task difficulty. *Child Development, 47*, 1051–1057.

Shantz, C. (1983). Social cognition. In P. Mussen (Ed.), *Handbook of Child Psychology*, (4th ed., Vol. 3, pp. 495–555). New York: John Wiley & Sons.

Shatz, M., & Gelman, R. (1973). The development of communication skills: Modification in the speech of young children as a function of listener. *Monographs of the Society for Research in Child Development, 38* (Serial No. 152).

Shereshefsky, P.M., & Yarrow, L.J. (1973). *Psychological aspects of a first pregnancy and early postnatal adaptation.* New York: Raven Press.

Sherif, M., Harvey, O., White, B.J., Hood, W.R., & Sherif, C. (1961). *Intergroup conflict and cooperation: The Robbers' Cave experiment.* Norman: University of Oklahoma Press.

Shields, J. (1976). Polygenic influences. In M. Rutter & L. Hersov (Eds.), *Child psychiatry: Modern approaches* (pp. 22–46). Oxford: Blackwell Scientific Publications.

Shirley, M.M. (1933). *The first two years: A study of twenty-five babies: Vol. 2. Intellectual development.* Minneapolis: University of Minnesota Press.

Shultz, T.R. (1980). Development of the concept of intention. In W.A. Collins (Ed.), *Minnesota symposia on child psychology* (Vol. 13, pp. 131–164). Hillsdale, NJ: Lawrence Erlbaum Associates.

Shultz, T.R., & Butkowsky, I. (1977). Young children's use of the scheme for multiple sufficient causes in the attribution of real and hypothetical behavior. *Child Development, 48*, 464–469.

Shultz, T.R., Butkowsky, I., Pearce, J.W., & Shanfield, H. (1975). Development of schemes for the attribution of multiple psychological causes. *Developmental Psychology, 11*, 502–510.

Siegelman, M. (1966). Loving and punishing parental behavior and introversion tendencies in sons. *Child Development, 37*, 985–992.

Singer, J.L., & Singer, D.G. (1981). *Television, imagination and aggression: A study of preschoolers' play.* Hillsdale, NJ: Lawrance Erlbaum Associates.

Singleton, L.C., & Asher, S.R. (1979). Racial integration and children's peer preferences: An investigation of developmental and cohort differences. *Child Development, 50*, 936–941.

Skinner, B.F. (1948). *Walden two.* New York: MacMillan.

Slaby, R.G., & Frey, K.S. (1975). Development of gender constancy and selective attention to same sex models. *Child Development, 46*, 849–856.

Slavin, R.E. (1969). Effects of biracial learning teams on cross-racial friendships. *Journal of Educational Psychology, 71*, 381–387.

Slavin, R.E. (1983). When does cooperative learning increase student achievement? *Psychological Bulletin, 94*, 429–445.

Sluckin, A.M., & Smith P.K. (1977). Two approaches to the concept of dominance in preschool children. *Child Development, 48*, 917–923.

Smetana, J.G. (1981). Preschool children's conceptions of moral and social rules. *Child Development, 52*, 1333–1336.

Smith, C., & Lloyd, B. (1978). Maternal behavior and perceived sex of infant: Revisited. *Child Development, 49*, 1263–1266.

Smith, C.L., Gelfand, D.M., Hartmann, D.P., & Partlow, M.E.Y. (1979). Children's causal attributions regarding help giving. *Child Development, 50*, 203–210.

Smith, M.C. (1975). Children's use of the multiple sufficient cause schema in social perception. *Journal of Personality and Social Psychology, 32*, 737–747.

Smith, M.C. (1978). Cognizing the behavior stream: The recognition of intentional action. *Child Development, 49*, 736–743.

Smith, M.E. (1932). The preschool child's use of criticism. *Child Development, 3*, 137–141.

Smith, P.B., & Pedersen, D.R. (1983). *Maternal sensitivity and patterns of attachment*. Paper presented at the Biennial Meeting of the Society for Research in Child Development, Detroit.

Smith, P.K., & Daglish, L. (1977). Sex differences in parent and infant behavior in the home. *Child Development, 48*, 1250–1254.

Smith, P.K., & Green, M. (1975). Aggressive behavior in English nurseries and play groups: Sex differences and response of adults. *Child Development, 46*, 211–214.

Smith, P.K., & Sloboda, J. (1986). Individual consistency in infant stranger encounters. *British Journal of Developmental Psychology, 4*, 83–92.

Snarey, J.R. (1985). Cross-cultural universality of social-moral development: A critical review of Kohlbergian research. *Psychological Bulletin, 97*, 202–231.

Snow, M.E., Jacklin, C.N., & Maccoby, E.E. (1983). Sex-of-child differences in father-child interaction at one year of age. *Child Development, 54*, 227–232.

Snyder, M.L., & Jones, E.E. (1974). Attitude attribution when behavior is constrained. *Journal of Experimental Social Psychology, 10*, 585–600.

Solomon, R.L., Turner, L.H., & Lessac, M.S. (1968). Some effects of delay of punishment on resistance to temptation in dogs. *Journal of Personality and Social Psychology, 8*, 233–238.

Sorce, J., Emde, R.N., Campos, J.J., & Klinnert, M. (1985). Maternal emotional signaling: Its effects on the visual cliff behavior of one-year-olds. *Developmental Psychology, 21*, 195–200.

Spence, J.T., & Helmreich, R.L. (1978). *Masculinity and femininity: Their psychological dimensions, correlates, and antecedents*. Austin: University of Texas Press.

Spence, J.T., & Helmreich, R.L. (1983). Achievement-related motives and behaviors. In J.T. Spence (Ed.), *Achievement and achievement motives: Psychological and sociological approaches* (pp. 7–74). San Francisco: W.H. Freeman.

Spence, J.T., Helmreich, R.L., & Stapp, J. (1975). Ratings of self and peers on sex-role attributes and their relation to self-esteem and conceptions of masculinity and femininity. *Journal of Personality and Social Psychology*, *32*, 29–39.

Spieker, S.J., & Booth, C.L. (1985). Family risk typologies and patterns of insecure attachment. Paper presented at Meeting of the Society for Research in Child Development, Toronto.

Spinetta, J.J., & Rigler, D. (1972). The child-abusing parent: A psychological review. *Psychological Bulletin*, *77*, 296–304.

Spiro, M.E. (1979). *Gender and culture: Kibbutz women revisited*. Durham, NC: Duke University Press.

Spitz, R.A. (1946). Hospitalism: A follow-up report. In *Psychoanalytic study of the child* (Vol. 2, p. 113). New York: International Universities Press.

Spock, B. (1946/1957), *Baby and child care*. New York: Pocket Books.

Sroufe, L.A. (1985). Attachment classification from the perspective of infant-caregiver relationships and infant temperament. *Child Development*, *56*, 1–14.

Sroufe, L.A., Fox, N.E., & Pancake, V.R. (1983). Attachment and dependency in developmental perspective. *Child Development*, *54*, 1615–1627.

Sroufe, L.A., & Wunsch, J.P. (1972). The development of laughter in the first year of life. *Child Development*, *43*, 1326–1344.

Staats, A.W. (1975). *Social behaviorism*. Homewood, II: Dorsey Press.

Stack, C.B. (1976). Who owns the child? Divorce and child custody decisions in middle-class families. *Social Problems*, *23*, 505–515.

Staub, E. (1970). A child in distress: The influence of age and number of witnesses on children's attempts to help. *Journal of Personality and Social Psychology*, *14*, 130–140.

Staub, E. (1971). The use of role playing and induction in children's learning of helping and sharing behavior. *Child Development*, *42*, 805–817.

Stayton, D.J., Hogan, R., & Ainsworth, M.D.S. (1971). Infant obedience and maternal behavior: the origins of socialization reconsidered. *Child Development*, *42*, 1057–1069.

Steele, B.F., & Pollock, C.B. (1968). A psychiatric study of parents who abuse infants and small children. In R.E. Helfer & C.H. Kempe (Eds.), *The battered child* (pp. 103–147). Chicago: University of Chicago Press.

Steinberg, L. (1987). Single parents, stepparents, and the susceptibility of adolescents to antisocial peer pressure. *Child Development*, *58*, 269–275.

Steinberg, L.D., Catalano, R., & Dooley, D. (1981). Economic antecedents of child abuse. *Child Development*, *52*, 975–985.

Stern, W. (1924). *Psychology of early childhood*. New York: Holt, Rinehart & Winston.

Stettner, L.J., & Loigman, G.A. (1983). *Emotion cues in baby faces as elicitors of functional reaction choices*. Paper presented at the Biennial Meeting of the Society for Research in Child Development, Detroit.

Stevenson, S.S. (1948). Paranatal factors affecting adjustment in childhood. *Pediatrics*, *2*, 154–162.

Stevenson, H.W., Weir, M.W., & Zigler, E.F. (1959). Discrimination learning in children as a function of motive-incentive conditions. *Psychological Reports*, *5*, 95–98.

Stewart, R.B. (1981). *Sibling attachment relationships*. Paper presented at the Biennial Meeting of the Society for Research in Child Development, Boston.

Stith, S.M., & Davis, A. (1984). Employed mothers and family day care substitute caregivers: A comparative analysis of infant care. *Child Development*, 55, 1340–1348.

Stott, D.H. (1969). The child's hazard in utero. In J.G. Howells (Ed.), *Modern perspectives in international child psychiatry* (pp. 19–60). Edinburgh: Oliver & Boyd.

Stratton, P. (1982). Biological preprogramming of infant behavior. *Journal of Child Psychology and Psychiatry*, 24, 301–309.

Strayer, F. (1980). Social ecology of the preschool peer group. In W.A. Collins (Eds.), *Minnesota Symposia on Child Psychology* (Vol. 13, pp. 165–196), Hillsdale, NJ: Lawrence Erlbaum Associates.

Strayer, F.F., & Pilon, D. (1985). *The origins of sexually based peer discriminations*. Paper presented at the Biennial Meeting of the Society for Research in Child Development, Toronto.

Strayer, F.F., & Strayer, J. (1976). An ethological analysis of social agonism and dominance relations among preschool children. *Child Development*, 47, 980–989.

Strayer, F.F., Wareing, S., & Rushton, J.P. (1979). Social constraints on naturally occurring preschool altruism. *Ethology and Sociobiology*, 1, 3–11.

Strayer, J. (1980). A naturalistic study of empathic behaviors and their relation to affective states and perspective-taking skills in preschool children. *Child Development*, 51, 815–822.

Super, C.M., & Harkness, S. (1982). The infant's niche in rural Kenya and metropolitan America. In L.L. Adler (Ed.), *Issues in cross-cultural research*. New York: Academic Press.

Suttie, I.D. (1935). *The origins of love and hate*. London: Kegan Paul.

Svejda, M.J., Campos, J.J., & Emde, R.N. (1980). Mother-infant "bonding": Failure to generalize. *Child Development*, 51, 775–779.

Taub, H.B., Goldstein, R.M., & Caputo, D.V. (1977). Indices of neonatal prematurity as discriminators of development in middle childhood. *Child Development*, 48, 797–805.

Tauber, M.A. (1979a). Parental socialization techniques and sex differences in children's play. *Child Development*, 50, 225–234.

Tauber, M.A. (1979b). Sex differences in parent-child interaction styles during a free-play session. *Child Development*, 50, 981–988.

Taylor, M.C., & Hall, J.A. (1982). Psychological androgyny: Theories, methods and conclusions. *Psychological Bulletin*, 92, 347–366.

Tennes, K. (1982). The role of hormones in mother-infant transactions, In R.N. Emde & R.J. Harmon (Eds.), *The development of attachment and affiliative systems*. New York: Plenum Press.

Thomas, A., Birch, H.G., Chess, S. Hertzig, C., & Korn, S. (1963). *Behavioral individuality in early childhood*. New York: New York University Press.

Thomas, A., & Chess, S. (1977). *Temperament and development*. New York: Brunner/Mazel.

Thomas, A., Chess, S., & Birch, H. (1968). *Temperament and behavior disorders in children*. New York: New York University Press.

Thomas, A., Chess, S., Birch, H., Hertzig, M., & Korn, S. (1963). *Behavioral individuality in early childhood*. New York: New York University Press.

Thomas, A., Chess, S., & Korn, S.J. (1982). The reality of difficult temperament.

Merrill-Palmer Quarterly, 28, 1–20.

Thomas, D. (1929). Introduction: The methodology of experimental sociology. *Child Development Monographs: Teachers College, Columbia University, 1*, 1–21.

Thomas, D.R. (1975). Conservatism, authoritarianism and child rearing practices. *British Journal of Social and Clinical Psychology, 14*, 97–98.

Thomas, M.H., & Drabman, R.S. (1975). Toleration of real-life aggression as a function of exposure to televised violence and age of subject. *Merrill-Palmer Quarterly, 21*, 227–232.

Thompson, R.A., & Lamb, M.P. (1984). Infants, mothers, families and strangers. In M. Lewis (Ed.), *Beyond the dyad* (pp. 195–222). New York: Plenum Press.

Thorne, B. (1985). *Crossing the gender divide: What tomboys can teach us about processes of sex segregation.* Paper presented at the Bienniel Meeting of the Society for Research in Child Development, Toronto.

Thurston, J.R., & Mussen, P.H. (1951). Infant feeding gratification and adult personality. *Journal of Personality, 19*, 449–458.

Tieger, T. (1980). On the biological basis of sex differences in aggression. *Child Development, 51*, 943–963.

Tinbergen, N. (1951). *The study of instinct.* Oxford: Oxford Univesity Press.

Tizard, B., Cooperman, O., Joseph, A., & Tizard, J. (1972). Environmental effects on language development: A study of young children in long-stay residential nurseries. *Child Development, 43*, 337–358.

Tizard, B., & Hodges, J. (1978). The effect of early institutional rearing on the development of eight-year-old children. *Journal of Child Psychology and Psychiatry, 19*, 99–118.

Tizard, B., Hughes, M., Carmichael, H., & Pinkerton, G. (1983a). Children's questions and adults' answers. *Journal of Child Psychology and Psychiatry, 24*, 269–281.

Tizard, B., Hughes, M., Carmichael, H., & Pinkerton, G. (1983b). Language and social class: Is verbal deprivation a myth? *Journal of Child Psychology and Psychiatry, 24*, 533–541.

Tizard, B., & Rees, J. (1975). The effect of early institutional rearing on the behavior problems and affectional relationships of four-year-old children. *Journal of Child Psychology and Psychiatry, 16*, 61–74.

Toner, I.J., & Smith, R.A. (1977). Age and overt verbalization in delay-maintenance behavior in children. *Journal of Experimental Child Psychology, 24*, 123–128.

Torgersen, A.M. (1981). Genetic aspects of temperamental development: A follow-up study of twins from infancy to six years of age. In L. Gedda, P. Parisi, & W.E. Nance (Eds.), *Twin Research 3: Part B: Intelligence, Personality and Development* (pp. 261–268). New York: Alan R. Liss.

Torgersen, A.M., & Kringlen, E. (1978). Genetic aspects of temperamental differences in twins. *Journal of American Academy of Child Psychiatry, 17*, 433–444.

Trickett, P.K., & Kuczynski, L. (1986). Children's misbehaviors and parental discipline strategies in abusive and nonabusive families. *Developmental Psychology, 22*, 115–123.

Trivers, R.L. (1971). The evolution of reciprocal altruism. *The Quarterly Reveiw of Biology, 46*, 35–57.

Trivers, R.L. (1974). Parent-offspring conflict. *American Zoologist, 14*, 249–264.

Trivers, R.L. (1983). The evolution of cooperation. In D.L. Bridgeman (Ed.), *The nature of prosocial development* (pp. 43–60). New York: Academic Press.

Truby King, F. (1937). *Feeding and care of baby* (rev. ed.). London: Oxford University Press.

Tryon, R.C. (1940). Genetic differences in maze learning in rats. *Yearbook of the National Society for the Study of Education, 39*, 111–119.

Tulkin, S.R., & Kagan, J. (1972). Mother-child interaction in the first year of life. *Child Development, 43*, 31–41.

Turiel, E. (1978). Social convention and the development of societal concepts. In W. Damon (Ed.), *New directions in child development*. Vol. 1, *Social cognition*, San Francisco: Jossey-Bass.

Turner, C.W., & Goldsmith, D. (1976). Effects of toy guns and airplanes on children's antisocial free play behavior. *Journal of Experimental Child Psychology, 21*, 303–315.

Ugurel-Semin, R. (1952). Moral behavior and moral judgment of children. *Journal of Abnormal and Social Psychology, 47*, 463–474.

Underwood, B., Froming, W.J., & Moore, B.S. (1977). Mood, attention, and altruism: A search for mediating variables. *Developmental Psychology, 13*, 541–542.

Underwood, B., & Moore, B. (1982). Perspective-taking and altruism. *Psychological Bulletin, 91*, 143–173.

Vandell, D.L. (1979). Effects of a playgroup experience on mother-son and father-son interaction. *Developmental Psychology, 15*, 379–385.

Vandell, D.L., & Mueller, E.C. (1977). *The effects of group size on toddlers' social interactions with peers*. Paper presented at meeting of the Society for Research in Child Development, New Orleans.

Vandell, D.L., & Mueller, E.C. (1980). Peer play and friendships during the first two years. In H.C. Foot, A.J. Chapman, & J.R. Smith (Eds.), *Friendships and social relations in children* (pp. 181–208). New York: John Wiley & Sons.

Van Praag, H.M. (1977). *Depression and schizophrenia: a contribution on their chemical pathologies*. New York: Spectrum.

Vandenberg, S.G. (1967). Hereditary factors in normal personality traits (as measured by inventories). *Recent Advances in Biological Psychiatry, 9*, 65–104.

Vandenberg, S.G., & Kuse, A.R. (1979). Spatial ability: A critical review of the sex-linked major gene hypothesis. In M.A. Wittig & A.C. Petersen (Eds.), *Sex-related differences in cognitive functioning* (pp. 67–95). New York: Academic Press.

Vaughn, B.E., Bradley, C.F., Joffe, L.S., Seifer, R., & Barglow, P. (1987). Maternal characteristics measured prenatally are predictive of ratings of temperamental "difficulty" on the Carey infant temperament questionnaire. *Developmental Psychology, 23*, 152–161.

Vaughn, B., Taraldson, B., Crichton, L., & Egeland, B. (1981). The assessment of infant temperament: A critique of the Carey infant temperament questionnaire. *Infant Behavior and Development, 4*, 1–18.

Visher, E.B., & Visher, J.S. (1978). Common problems of stepparents and their spouses. *American Journal of Orthopsychiatry, 48*, 256–262.

Waddington, C.H. (1957). *The strategy of the genes*. New York: Macmillan.

Walker, K.N., & Messinger, L. (1979). Remarriage after divorce: Dissolution and reconstruction of family boundaries. *Family Process, 18*, 185–192.

Walker, L.J. (1980). Cognitive and perspective-taking prerequisites for moral development. *Child Development, 51*, 131–139.

Walker, L.J. (1982). The sequentiality of Kohlberg's stages of moral development. *Child Development, 53*, 1330–1336.

Walker, L.J. (1984). Sex differences in the development of moral reasoning: A critical review. *Child Development, 55*, 677–691.

Wallerstein, J. (1980). The impact of divorce on children. *Psychiatric Clinics of North America, 3*, 455–468.

Wallerstein, J., & Kelly, J. (1980). *Surviving the breakup: How children and parents cope with divorce.* New York: Basic Books.

Walters, G.C., & Grusec, J.E. (1977). *Punishment.* San Francisco: W.H. Freeman.

Walters, J., Pearce, D., & Dahms, L. (1957). Affectional and aggressive behavior of preschool children. *Child Development, 28*, 15–26.

Waters, E. (1978). The reliability and stability of individual differences in infant-mother attachment. *Child Development, 49*, 483–494.

Waters, E., Wippman, J., & Sroufe, L.A. (1979). Attachment, positive affect and competence in the peer group: Two studies in construct validation. *Child Development, 50*, 821–829.

Watson, J.B. (1913). Psychology as a behaviorist views it. *Psychological Review, 20*, 158–177.

Watson, J.B. (1925). *Behaviorism.* New York: W.W. Norton.

Watson, J.B. (1928). *Psychological care of infant and child.* New York: W.W. Norton.

Watson, J.B., & Rayner, R. (1920). Conditioned emotional reactions. *Journal of Experimental Psychology, 3*, 1–14.

Weiner, B. (1979). A theory of motivation for some classroom experiences. *Journal of Educational Psychology, 71*, 3–25.

Weiner, B. (1980). A cognitive (attribution)-emotion-action model of motivated behavior: An analysis of judgments of help-giving. *Journal of Personality and Social Psychology, 39*, 186–200.

Weinraub, M., Clemens, L.P., Sockloff, A., Ethridge, T., Gracely, E., & Myers, B. (1984). The development of sex role stereotypes in the third year. *Child Development, 55*, 1493–1503.

Weinraub, M., Frankel, J. (1977). Sex differences in parent-infant interaction during free play, departure and separation. *Child Development, 48*, 1240–1249.

Weissbrod, C.S. (1976). Noncontingent warmth induction, cognitive style, and children's imitative donation and rescue effort behaviors. *Journal of Personality and Social Psychology, 34*, 274–281.

Wenar, J., & Coulter, J.B. (1962). A reliability study of developmental histories. *Child Development, 33*, 453–462.

Werner, E.E., Bierman, J.M., & French, F.E. (1971). *The children of Kauai: A longitudinal study from the prenatal period of age ten.* Honolulu: University of Hawaii Press.

Werner, E.E., & Smith, R.S. (1982). *Vulnerable but invincible: A longitudinal study of resilient children and youth.* New York: McGraw Hill.

Werner, H. (1957). The conception of development from a comparative and organismic point of view. In D. Harris (Ed.), *The concept of development* (pp. 149–161). Minneapolis: University of Minnesota Press.

Wesley, J. (1872). *Works*. London: Wesleyan Conference Office.

Weston, D., & Turiel, E. (1980). Act-rule relations: Children's concepts of social rules. *Development Psychology, 16*, 417–424.

White, D.G. (1978). Effects of sex-typed labels and their source on the imitative performance of young children. *Child Development, 49*, 1266–1269.

Whiting, B.B., & Whiting, J.J.M. (1975). *Children of six cultures*. Cambridge: Harvard University Press.

Williams, T.M., Joy, L.A., Kimball, M.M., & Zabrack, M.L. (1985). Are most boys more aggressive than most girls? *Cahiers de Psychologie Cognitive, 5*, 375.

Wilson, E.O. (1975). *Sociobiology*. Cambridge, Massachusetts: Harvard University Press.

Wilson, E.O. (1978). *On human nature*. Cambridge: Harvard University Press.

Winnicott, D. (1964). *The child, the family and the outside world*. London: Penguin.

Winterbottom, M. (1958). The relation of need for achievement in learning experiences in independence and mastery. In J. Atkinson (Ed.), *Motives in fantasy, action and society* (pp. 453–478). Princeton: Van Nostrand.

Witkin, H.A., Mednick, S.A., Schulsinger, F., Bakkestrom, E., Christiansen, K.O., Goodenough, D.R., Hirschhorn, K., Lundsteen, C., Owen, D.R., Philip, J., Rubin, D.B., & Stocking, M. (1976). Criminality in XYY and XXY men. *Science, 193*, 547–555.

Wolfe, D.A. (1985). Abusive parents: An empirical review and analysis. *Psychological Bulletin, 97*, 462–496.

Wolfenstein, M. (1955). Fun morality: an analysis of recent American child-rearing literature. In M. Mead & M. Wolfenstein, *Childhood in Contemporary Cultures* (pp. 168–178). Chicago: University of Chicago Press.

Yarrow, L.J. (1963). Research in dimensions of early maternal care. *Merrill-Palmer Quarterly, 9*, 101–114.

Yarrow, M.R. (1963). Problems of methods in parent-child research. *Child Development, 34*, 215–226.

Yarrow, M.R., Scott, P.M., & Waxler, C.Z. (1973). Learning concern for others. *Developmental Psychology, 8*, 240–260.

Yarrow, M.R., Waxler, C.Z., & Scott, P.M. (1971). Child effects on adult behavior. *Developmental Psychology, 5*, 300–311.

Yates, B.T., & Mischel, W. (1979). Young children's preferred attentional strategies for delaying gratification. *Journal of Personality and Social Psychology, 37*, 286–300.

Yogman, M.W., & Zeisel, S. (1983). *Dietary precursors of serotonin and newborn state behavior*. Paper presented at the Biennial Meeting of the Society for Research in Child Development, Detroit.

Young, J.Z. (1971). *An introduction to the study of man*. Oxford: Oxford University Press.

Young, J.Z. (1978). *Programs of the brain*. Oxford: Oxford University Press.

Youniss, J. (1980). *Parents and peers in social development: A Sullivan-Piaget perspective*. Chicago: University of Chicago Press.

Youniss, J., & Volpe, J. (1978). A relational analysis of children's friendships. In W. Damon (Ed.), *Social cognition*. (pp. 1–22). San Francisco: Jossey-Bass.

Zahn-Waxler, C. (1984). Review of E.T. Higgins, D.N. Ruble, & W.W. Hartup

(Eds.), *Social cognition and social development: A sociocultural perspective.* Cambridge, England: Cambridge University Press. In *Contemporary Psychology, 29,* 889–890.

Zahn-Waxler, C., & Radke-Yarrow, M. (1982). The development of altruism: Alternative strategies. In N. Eisenberg (Ed.), *The development of prosocial behavior* (pp. 109–137). New York: Academic Press.

Zahn-Waxler, C., Radke-Yarrow, M., & King, R.A. (1979). Child rearing and children's prosocial initiations toward victims of distress. *Child Development, 50,* 319–330.

Zarbatany, L., & Lamb, M.E. (1983). *Soial referencing as a function of information source: mothers vs. strangers.* Paper presented at the Biennial Meeting of the Society for Research in Child Development, Detroit.

Zigler, E.F., Lamb, M.E., & Child, I.L. (1982). *Socialization and personality development.* New York: Oxford University Press.

Zivin, G. (1983). *Affect development: Evolutionary influences on the course of affect socialization.* Paper presented at the Biennial Meeting of the Society for Research in Child Development, Detroit.

Zussman, J.U. (1978). Relationship of demographic factors to parental discipline techniques. *Development Psychological, 14,* 685–686.

Author Index

Subject Index